Great Events from History

Gay, Lesbian, Bisexual, Transgender Events

1848-2006

Great Events from History

Gay, Lesbian, Bisexual, Transgender Events

1848-2006

Volume 2
1983-2006
Appendixes
Indexes

Editorial Board

Lillian Faderman, California State University, Fresno
Horacio Roque Ramírez, University of California, Santa Barbara
Yolanda Retter, University of California, Los Angeles
Stuart Timmons, AUTHOR, *The Trouble with Harry Hay*
Eric C. Wat, AUTHOR, *The Making of a Gay Asian Community*

SALEM PRESS
Pasadena, California   Hackensack, New Jersey

Editor in Chief: Kenneth T. Burles
Editorial Director: Christina J. Moose   *Research Supervisor:* Jeffry Jensen
Acquisitions Editor: Mark Rehn   *Cover and Page Design:* James Hutson
Project Editor: Desiree Dreeuws   *Photo Editor:* Cynthia Breslin Beres
Production Editor: Andrea E. Miller   *Editorial Assistant:* Dana Garey

Cover photos (pictured clockwise, from top left): AIDS ribbon (AP/Wide World Photos); Stand Up & Represent (AP/Wide World Photos); Lesbian Rights NOW (Hulton Archives/Getty Images); rainbow flag (Kurt/Dreamstime.com); Rosie O'Donnell and Kelli Carpenter (AP/Wide World Photos).

Copyright © 2007, by Salem Press, Inc.

All rights in this book are reserved. No part of this work may be used or reproduced in any manner whatsoever or transmitted in any form or by any means, electronic or mechanical, including photocopy, recording, or any information storage and retrieval system, without written permission from the copyright owner except in the case of brief quotations embodied in critical articles and reviews or in the copying of images deemed to be freely licensed or in the public domain. For information address the publisher, Salem Press, Inc., P.O. Box 50062, Pasadena, California 91115.

∞ The paper used in these volumes conforms to the American National Standard for Permanence of Paper for Printed Library Materials, Z39.48-1992 (R1997).

Some of the essays in this work originally appeared in *GLBT Life with Full Text*, an online subscription database distributed by EBSCO Publishing.

Library of Congress Cataloging-in-Publication Data

Great events from history. Gay, lesbian, bisexual, transgender events,
   1848-2006 / editorial board, Lillian Faderman ... [et al.].
      p. cm.
   Includes bibliographical references and index.
   ISBN-13: 978-1-58765-263-9 (set : alk. paper)
   ISBN-13: 978-1-58765-264-6 (v. 1 : alk. paper)
   ISBN-13: 978-1-58765-265-3 (v. 2 : alk. paper)
   ISBN-10: 1-58765-263-3 (set : alk. paper)
   ISBN-10: 1-58765-264-1 (v. 1 : alk. paper)
   ISBN-10: 1-58765-265-X (v. 2 : alk. paper)
   1. Sexual minorities--History. 2. Gays--History. 3. Gay rights--History.
   4. Gay community--History. I. Faderman, Lillian. II. Title: Gay, lesbian, bisexual, transgender events, 1848-2006.

HQ73.G74 2007
306.7609--dc22

2006028400

First Printing

PRINTED IN THE UNITED STATES OF AMERICA

Contents

Keyword List of Contents xlvii
List of Sidebars lxix

September, 1983, First National Lesbians of Color Conference Convenes 411
Spring, 1984, AIDS Virus Is Discovered. 413
October 9, 1984, San Francisco Closes Gay Bathhouses and Other Businesses. 417
November 6, 1984, West Hollywood Incorporates with Majority
   Gay and Lesbian City Council 419
December 4, 1984, Berkeley Extends Benefits to Domestic Partners of City Employees. 422
1985, GLAAD Begins Monitoring Media Coverage of Gays and Lesbians 424
1985, Lesbian Film *Desert Hearts* Is Released. 426
July 25, 1985, Actor Hudson Announces He Has AIDS 429
1986, *Bowers v. Hardwick* Upholds State Sodomy Laws 432
1986, Paula Gunn Allen Publishes *The Sacred Hoop* 435
January, 1986, South Asian Newsletter *Trikone* Begins Publication 438
September, 1986, AZT Treats People with AIDS 440
November, 1986, Californians Reject LaRouche's Quarantine Initiative 442
1987, Anzaldúa Publishes *Borderlands/La Frontera*. 446
1987, Asian Pacific Lesbian Network Is Founded 448
1987, *Compañeras: Latina Lesbians* Is Published 450
1987, Shilts Publishes *And the Band Played On* 453
1987, VIVA Is Founded to Promote Latina and Latino Artists. 455
March, 1987, Radical AIDS Activist Group ACT UP Is Founded. 458
April, 1987, Old Lesbians Organize for Change 462
May, 1987, *Lambda Rising Book Report* Begins Publication 464
May 30, 1987, U.S. Congressman Frank Comes Out as Gay 466
October 11, 1987, Second March on Washington for Lesbian and Gay Rights 469
October 14-17, 1987, Latin American and Caribbean Lesbian
   Feminist Network Is Formed 472
1988, *Macho Dancer* Is Released in the Philippines 474
January 1, 1988, Canada Decriminalizes Sex Practices Between Consenting Adults 477
March 20, 1988, *M. Butterfly* Opens on Broadway 479
May, 1988, Lavender Youth Recreation and Information Center Opens 482
June 27, 1988, Report of the Presidential AIDS Commission 485
October 11, 1988, First National Coming Out Day Is Celebrated 489
November 8, 1988, Oregon Repeals Ban on Antigay Job Discrimination 491
December 1, 1988, First World AIDS Day. 494
1989, Act Up Paris Is Founded. 496
1989, Vaid Becomes Executive Director of the National Gay and Lesbian Task Force. 498
1989-1990, Helms Claims Photographs Are Indecent 500
January 21, 1989, Death of Transgender Jazz Musician Billy Tipton 505
May 1, 1989, U.S. Supreme Court Rules Gender-Role Stereotyping Is Discriminatory. 508

GLBT Events

May 3, 1989, *Watkins v. United States Army* Reinstates Gay Soldier 510
June 2, 1989, Lambda Literary Award Is Created 512
December 10, 1989, ACT UP Protests at St. Patrick's Cathedral 514

1990, International Gay and Lesbian Human Rights Commission Is Founded 517
1990, United Lesbians of African Heritage Is Founded 519
1990-1993, Artists Sue the National Endowment for the Arts 520
1990, 1994, *Coming Out Under Fire* Documents Gay and Lesbian Military Veterans 522
March 20, 1990, Queer Nation Is Founded 524
June, 1990, BiNet USA Is Formed 527
July 26, 1990, Americans with Disabilities Act Becomes Law 530
December, 1990, Asian Lesbian Network Holds Its First Conference 533
1991, LeVay Postulates the "Gay Brain" 535
1991, Revisionist Criticism Recasts Sor Juana Inés de la Cruz 537
1991, Stone Publishes "A Posttranssexual Manifesto" 540
April 6, 1991, Asian Lesbians and Gays Protest Lambda Fund-Raiser 542
August, 1991, Leather Archives and Museum Is Founded 545
August 27, 1991, *The Advocate* Outs Pentagon Spokesman Pete Williams 547
September 29, 1991, California Governor Wilson Vetoes Antidiscrimination Bill 550
December 17, 1991, Minnesota Court Awards Guardianship to Lesbian Partner 552
December 30, 1991-February 22, 1993, Canada Grants Asylum
  Based on Sexual Orientation 555
1992, Canadian YMCA Extends Family Discounts to Gays and Lesbians 559
1992, Transgender Nation Holds Its First Protest 562
1992-2002, Celebrity Lesbians Come Out 565
1992-2006, Indians Struggle to Abolish Sodomy Law 568
April 27, 1992, Canadian Government Antigay Campaign Is Revealed 570
June, 1992, Feinberg Publishes *Transgender Liberation* 573
September 23, 1992, Massachusetts Grants Family Rights to Gay and Lesbian State Workers . . 576
October, 1992, Canadian Military Lifts Its Ban on Gays and Lesbians 579
November 3, 1992, Oregon and Colorado Attempt Antigay Initiatives 582
1993, Intersex Society of North America Is Founded 586
1993, Monette Wins the National Book Award for *Becoming a Man* 588
1993, *The Wedding Banquet* Is First Acclaimed Taiwanese Gay-Themed Film 591
1993-1996, Hawaii Opens Door to Same-Gender Marriages 593
March-April, 1993, Battelle Sex Study Prompts Conservative Backlash 596
April 24, 1993, First Dyke March Is Held in Washington, D.C. 598
April 25, 1993, March on Washington for Gay, Lesbian, and Bi Equal Rights and Liberation . . . 601
May 24, 1993, Achtenberg Becomes Assistant Housing Secretary 604
June 25, 1993, Clinton Appoints First AIDS Czar 606
September 21, 1993-April 21, 1995, Lesbian Mother Loses Custody of Her Child 608
November 30, 1993, Don't Ask, Don't Tell Policy Is Implemented 611
December 24, 1993-December 31, 1993, Transgender Man Brandon Teena
  Raped and Murdered 615
1994, Employment Non-Discrimination Act Is Proposed to U.S. Congress 618
1994, National Association of Lesbian and Gay Community Centers Is Founded 621

Contents

1994, Navratilova Honored for Her Career in Tennis 623
June, 1994, Stonewall 25 March and Rallies Are Held in New York City 627
August 6, 1994, Japanese American Citizens League Supports Same-Gender Marriage 629
September 16, 1994, U.N. Revokes Consultative Status International
   Lesbian and Gay Association 632
1995, *The Advocate* Outs Oscar Nominee Nigel Hawthorne. 634
1995, Athlete Louganis Announces He Is HIV-Positive 637
June 17, 1995, International Bill of Gender Rights Is First Circulated 639
December 4, 1995, Lesbian Couple Murdered in Oregon 641
1996, Hart Recognized as a Transgender Man 644
September 21, 1996, U.S. President Clinton Signs Defense of Marriage Act 646
1998, Transgender Scholarship Proliferates 650
April 2, 1998, Canadian Supreme Court Reverses Gay Academic's Firing 652
October 6-7, 1998, Gay College Student Shepard Is Beaten and Murdered 654
October 9-12, 1998, First International Retreat for Lesbian and Gay Muslims Is Held 657
December 3, 1998-February 25, 1999, Screening of *Fire* Ignites Violent Protests in India 660
October 27, 1999, *Littleton v. Prange* Withholds Survivor Rights from Transsexual Spouses 662
November, 1999, First Middle Eastern Gay and Lesbian Organization Is Founded. 664
December 20, 1999, *Baker v. Vermont* Leads to Recognition of Same-Gender Civil Unions 666

January 12, 2000, United Kingdom Lifts Ban on Gays and Lesbians in the Military 669
March 21, 2000, Hollywood Awards Transgender Portrayals in Film. 672
June 28, 2000, *Boy Scouts of America v. Dale* 675
April 20, 2001, Chinese Psychiatric Association Removes Homosexuality
   from List of Mental Disorders. 679
May 25, 2001, Japanese Human Rights Council Recommends Lesbian and Gay Rights 681
September 7, 2001, First Gay and Lesbian Television Network Is Launched in Canada 683
2002, Sylvia Rivera Law Project Is Founded 686
April 30, 2002, Transgender Rights Added to New York City Law 687
June 19, 2002, Gays and Lesbians March for Equal Rights in Mexico City 690
June 28, 2002, Irish American Lesbian Gains Canadian Immigrant Status 692
October 4, 2002, Transgender Teen Gwen Araujo Is Murdered in California 694
February 21, 2003, Australian Court Validates Transsexual Marriage 698
March, 2003-December, 2004, Transsexuals Protest Academic Exploitation 700
March 21, 2003, New Mexico Amends Its Human Rights Act 702
April, 2003, Buenos Aires Recognizes Same-Gender Civil Unions 705
June 17, 2003, and July 19, 2005, Canada Legalizes Same-Gender Marriage 707
June 26, 2003, U.S. Supreme Court Overturns Texas Sodomy Law. 710
July, 2003, Singapore Lifts Ban on Hiring Lesbian and Gay Employees 713
July, 2003, Wal-Mart Adds Lesbians and Gays to Its Antidiscrimination Policy 715
November 18, 2003, Massachusetts Court Rules for Same-Gender Marriage. 717
November 20, 2003, Transgender Day of Remembrance and Remembering Our Dead Project . . . 722
March 7, 2004, Robinson Becomes First Out Gay Bishop in Christian History 725
May 17, 2004, Transsexual Athletes Allowed to Compete in Olympic Games 728
November 18, 2004, United Kingdom Legalizes Same-Gender Civil Partnerships 731
April 4, 2005, United Kingdom's Gender Recognition Act Legalizes Transsexual Marriage 734

GLBT Events

June 30, 2005, Spain Legalizes Same-Gender Marriage 736
November 29, 2005, Roman Catholic Church Bans Gay Seminarians 738
January, 2006, Jiménez Flores Elected to the Mexican Senate 741
March 5, 2006, *Brokeback Mountain*, *Capote*, and *Transamerica* Receive Oscars 744

Bibliography 747
Electronic Resources 755
Chronological List of Entries 759
Category Index 767

Personages Index III
Subject Index X

KEYWORD LIST OF CONTENTS

Abortion and Extends Privacy Rights,
   Roe v. Wade Legalizes (Jan. 22, 1973) 252
Abzug and Koch Attempt to Amend the
   Civil Rights Act of 1964 (June 27, 1974) . . . 273
Academic and Activist Sues University of
   California for Discrimination, Lesbian
   (1982-1991). 395
Academic Exploitation, Transsexuals Protest
   (Mar., 2003-Dec., 2004) 700
Academic's Firing, Canadian Supreme Court
   Reverses Gay (Apr. 2, 1998) 652
Achtenberg Becomes Assistant Housing
   Secretary (May 24, 1993). 604
ACT UP Is Founded, Radical AIDS Activist
   Group (Mar., 1987). 458
Act Up Paris Is Founded (1989) 496
ACT UP Protests at St. Patrick's Cathedral
   (Dec. 10, 1989) 514
Activist Sues University of California for
   Discrimination, Lesbian Academic and
   (1982-1991). 395
Actor Hudson Announces He Has AIDS
   (July 25, 1985) 429
Advocate Outs Oscar Nominee Nigel
   Hawthorne, *The* (1995). 634
Advocate Outs Pentagon Spokesman Pete
   Williams, *The* (Aug. 27, 1991) 547
African Heritage Is Founded, United Lesbians
   of (1990) 519
AIDS, Actor Hudson Announces He Has
   (July 25, 1985) 429
AIDS, AZT Treats People with (Sept., 1986) . . . 440
AIDS, Gay-Related Immunodeficiency Is
   Renamed (July, 1982) 401
AIDS Activist Group ACT UP Is Founded,
   Radical (Mar., 1987). 458
AIDS Commission, Report of the Presidential
   (June 27, 1988) 485
AIDS Czar, Clinton Appoints First
   (June 25, 1993) 606
AIDS Day, First World (Dec. 1, 1988). 494
AIDS Epidemic, Reports of Rare Diseases
   Mark Beginning of (June 5 and
   July 3, 1981) 378
AIDS Virus Is Discovered (Spring, 1984) 413

Aldredge Dismisses Sodomy Charges Against
   Lesbians, *Thompson v.* (Jan. 12, 1939) 95
Alice Mitchell Found Guilty of Murdering
   Her Lover (Jan., 1892-July, 1892). 23
Allen Publishes *The Sacred Hoop*,
   Paula Gunn (1986) 435
Alyson Begins Publishing Gay and
   Lesbian Books (1980) 351
Amazon Bookstore Opens as First Feminist-
   Lesbian Book Shop (1970). 203
Amendment Fails State Ratification, Equal
   Rights (Mar. 22, 1972-June 30, 1982) 233
America," *Time* Magazine Issues "The
   Homosexual in (Oct. 31, 1969). 201
American Bar Association Calls for
   Repeal of Laws Against Consensual Sex
   (Aug., 1973) 258
American Conference of Homophile
   Organizations Convenes, First North
   (Feb. 19-20, 1966) 160
American Gay Literature, Golden Age of
   (1947-1948) 97
American Indian Visits Washington, D.C.,
   Two-Spirit (Jan.-June, 1886) 21
American Indians Is Founded, Gay (1975). . . . 285
Americans with Disabilities Act Becomes Law
   (July 26, 1990) 530
And the Band Played On, Shilts Publishes
   (1987). 453
Anita Bryant Campaigns Against Gay and
   Lesbian Rights (1977) 307
Anna Crusis Women's Choir Is Formed
   (Sept., 1975) 295
Antidiscrimination Bill, California Governor
   Wilson Vetoes (Sept. 29, 1991) 550
Antidiscrimination Laws, Local Governments
   Pass (1972-1973) 228
Antidiscrimination Policy, Wal-Mart Adds
   Lesbians and Gays to Its (July, 2003) 715
Antigay and Antilesbian Briggs Initiative Is
   Defeated (Nov. 7, 1978) 333
Antigay and Antilesbian Organizations
   Begin to Form (Mar. 5, 1974) 271
Antigay Campaign Is Revealed, Canadian
   Government (Apr. 27, 1992) 570

GLBT Events

Antigay Initiatives, Oregon and Colorado Attempt (Nov. 3, 1992) 582
Antigay Job Discrimination, Oregon Repeals Ban on (Nov. 8, 1988) 491
Antilesbian Briggs Initiative Is Defeated, Antigay and (Nov. 7, 1978) 333
Antilesbian Organizations Begin to Form, Antigay and (Mar. 5, 1974) 271
Antilesbian Witch Hunt, U.S. Navy Investigates the USS *Norton Sound* in (May-Aug., 1980) 357
Anzaldúa Publishes *Borderlands/La Frontera* (1987) 446
APA, Homosexuality Is Delisted by (Dec. 15, 1973) 265
APA Classifies Homosexuality as a Mental Disorder (1952) 111
Araujo Is Murdered in California, Transgender Teen Gwen (Oct. 4, 2002) 694
Archives and Museum Is Founded, Leather (Aug., 1991) 545
Archives Is Founded, First Gay and Lesbian (1975) 280
Archives Is Founded, Lesbian Herstory (Fall, 1973) 260
Argentina, Nuestro Mundo Forms as First Queer Organization in (1969) 187
Army Reinstates Gay Soldier, *Watkins v. United States* (May 3, 1989) 510
Army Reservist Ben-Shalom Sues for Reinstatement (1976-1990) 302
Artists, VIVA Is Founded to Promote Latina and Latino (1987) 455
Artists Sue the National Endowment for the Arts (1990-1993) 520
Arts, Artists Sue the National Endowment for the (1990-1993) 520
Asian Collective Is Founded, Lesbian and Gay (Oct. 12-15, 1979) 349
Asian Lesbian Network Holds Its First Conference (Dec., 1990) 533
Asian Lesbians and Gays Protest Lambda Fund-Raiser (Apr. 6, 1991) 542
Asian Newsletter *Trikone* Begins Publication, South (Jan., 1986) 438
Asian Pacific Lesbian Network Is Founded (1987) 448
Assistant Housing Secretary, Achtenberg Becomes (May 24, 1993) 604

Asylum Based on Sexual Orientation, Canada Grants (Dec. 30, 1991-Feb. 22, 1993) 555
Athlete Louganis Announces He Is HIV-Positive (1995) 637
Athletes Allowed to Compete in Olympic Games, Transsexual (May 17, 2004) 728
Australian Court Validates Transsexual Marriage (Feb. 21, 2003) 698
Autobiography *Zami* Is Published, Lorde's (1982) 392
Award Debuts, The Gay Book (June, 1971) 223
Award Is Created, Lambda Literary (June 2, 1989) 512
AZT Treats People with AIDS (Sept., 1986) . . . 440

Backlash, Battelle Sex Study Prompts Conservative (Mar.-Apr., 1993) 596
Baker v. Vermont Leads to Recognition of Same-Gender Civil Unions (Dec. 20, 1999) 666
Baldwin Publishes *Giovanni's Room* (1956) 135
Ban on Antigay Job Discrimination, Oregon Repeals (Nov. 8, 1988) 491
Ban on Gays and Lesbians, Canadian Military Lifts Its (Oct., 1992) 579
Ban on Gays and Lesbians in the Military, United Kingdom Lifts (Jan. 12, 2000) 669
Ban on Hiring Lesbian and Gay Employees, Singapore Lifts (July, 2003) 713
Bans Gay Seminarians, Roman Catholic Church (Nov. 29, 2005) 738
Bar Association Calls for Repeal of Laws Against Consensual Sex, American (Aug., 1973) 258
Barney Opens Her Paris Salon (Oct., 1909) 58
Bathhouses, Toronto Police Raid Gay (Feb. 5, 1981) 376
Bathhouses and Other Businesses, San Francisco Closes Gay (Oct. 9, 1984) . . . 417
Battelle Sex Study Prompts Conservative Backlash (Mar.-Apr., 1993) 596
Becoming a Man, Monette Wins the National Book Award for (1993) 588
Ben-Shalom Sues for Reinstatement, Army Reservist (1976-1990) 302
Benjamin International Gender Dysphoria Association Is Founded, Harry (1978) 320
Berkeley Extends Benefits to Domestic Partners of City Employees (Dec. 4, 1984) . . 422
Best-Seller List, *The Front Runner* Makes *The New York Times* (1974) 269

Bi Equal Rights and Liberation, March on Washington for Gay, Lesbian, and (Apr. 25, 1993) 601
Bilitis Founded as First National Lesbian Group in United States, Daughters of (1955) 132
BiNet USA Is Formed (June, 1990) 527
Bisexual Forum Is Founded (1974) 267
Bishop in Christian History, Robinson Becomes First Out Gay (Mar. 7, 2004) 725
Black Congresswoman from the South, Jordan Becomes First (Nov. 7, 1972) 239
Black Feminist Statement," Combahee River Collective Issues "A (Apr., 1977) 309
Body Politic, Toronto Police Raid Offices of *The* (Dec. 31, 1977) 318
Body Politic Begins Publication, *The* (Nov., 1971) 226
Book Award Debuts, The Gay (June, 1971) 223
Book Award for *Becoming a Man*, Monette Wins the National (1993). 588
Book Shop, Amazon Bookstore Opens as First Feminist-Lesbian (1970) 203
Books, Alyson Begins Publishing Gay and Lesbian (1980) 351
Bookshop Opens as First Gay Bookstore, Oscar Wilde Memorial (Fall, 1967) 180
Bookstore, Oscar Wilde Memorial Bookshop Opens as First Gay (Fall, 1967) 180
Bookstore Opens as First Feminist-Lesbian Book Shop, Amazon (1970) 203
Borderlands/La Frontera, Anzaldúa Publishes (1987). 446
Bowers v. Hardwick Upholds State Sodomy Laws (1986) 432
Boy Scouts of America v. Dale (June 28, 2000) . . 675
Brandon Teena Raped and Murdered, Transgender Man (Dec. 24, 1993-Dec. 31, 1993) 615
Briggs Initiative Is Defeated, Antigay and Antilesbian (Nov. 7, 1978) 333
British Television Series Airs, First Gay (1979-1981). 342
Broadway, *M. Butterfly* Opens on (Mar. 20, 1988). 479
Broadway, *The God of Vengeance* Opens on (Feb. 19, 1923). 66
Brokeback Mountain, Capote, and *Transamerica* Receive Oscars (Mar. 5, 2006). 744
Brown Publishes *Rubyfruit Jungle* (1973) 241
Bryant Campaigns Against Gay and Lesbian Rights, Anita (1977) 307
Buenos Aires Recognizes Same-Gender Civil Unions (Apr., 2003) 705

Cafeteria in San Francisco, Queer Youth Fight Police Harassment at Compton's (Aug., 1966) 163
California, Transgender Teen Gwen Araujo Is Murdered in (Oct. 4, 2002) 694
California Governor Wilson Vetoes Antidiscrimination Bill (Sept. 29, 1991) 550
Californians Reject LaRouche's Quarantine Initiative (Nov., 1986) 442
Canada, First Gay and Lesbian Television Network Is Launched in (Sept. 7, 2001) 683
Canada Decriminalizes Homosexual Acts (Aug. 26, 1969). 199
Canada Decriminalizes Sex Practices Between Consenting Adults (Jan. 1, 1988). 477
Canada Grants Asylum Based on Sexual Orientation (Dec. 30, 1991-Feb. 22, 1993). . . 555
Canada Legalizes Same-Gender Marriage (June 17, 2003, and July 19, 2005) 707
Canadian Gay Postal Workers Secure Union Protections (June 2, 1980) 360
Canadian Government Antigay Campaign Is Revealed (Apr. 27, 1992). 570
Canadian Immigrant Status, Irish American Lesbian Gains (June 28, 2002) 692
Canadian Military Lifts Its Ban on Gays and Lesbians (Oct., 1992). 579
Canadian Supreme Court Reverses Gay Academic's Firing (Apr. 2, 1998) 652
Canadian YMCA Extends Family Discounts to Gays and Lesbians (1992) 559
Candidate for Public Office, Sarria Is First Out Gay or Lesbian (1961) 149
Candidate for U.S. Congress, Kameny Is First Out (1971) 217
Capote, and *Transamerica* Receive Oscars, *Brokeback Mountain,* (Mar. 5, 2006). 744
Caribbean Lesbian Feminist Network Is Formed, Latin American and (Oct. 14-17, 1987) 472
Carnegie Hall, New York City Gay Men's Chorus Performs at (Dec. 8, 1981) 385
Carpenter Publishes *The Intermediate Sex* (1908) 55
Catholic Church Bans Gay Seminarians, Roman (Nov. 29, 2005). 738

Catholics Find Dignity, Gay (1969-1973) 189
CBS Airs *CBS Reports: The Homosexuals*
  (Mar. 7, 1967) 169
CBS Reports: The Homosexuals, CBS Airs
  (Mar. 7, 1967) 169
Celebrity Lesbians Come Out (1992-2002) 565
Charter of Human Rights and Freedoms, Quebec
  Includes Lesbians and Gays in Its
  (Dec. 19, 1977) 315
Child, Lesbian Mother Loses Custody of Her
  (Sept. 21, 1993-Apr. 21, 1995) 608
Chinese Psychiatric Association Removes
  Homosexuality from List of Mental Disorders
  (Apr. 20, 2001) 679
Choir Is Formed, Anna Crusis Women's
  (Sept., 1975) 295
Chorus Concert Tour, San Francisco Gay
  Men's (June 6-June 20, 1981) 380
Chorus Performs at Carnegie Hall, New York
  City Gay Men's (Dec. 8, 1981) 385
Choruses Is Formed, GALA (1981-1982) 373
Christian History, Robinson Becomes First
  Out Gay Bishop in (Mar. 7, 2004) 725
Church Bans Gay Seminarians, Roman
  Catholic (Nov. 29, 2005) 738
Church Is Founded, Metropolitan Community
  (Oct. 6, 1968) 184
City Council, West Hollywood Incorporates with
  Majority Gay and Lesbian (Nov. 6, 1984) . . . 419
City Employees, Berkeley Extends Benefits to
  Domestic Partners of (Dec. 4, 1984) 422
City of Night, Rechy Publishes (1963) 151
Civil Partnerships, United Kingdom Legalizes
  Same-Gender (Nov. 18, 2004) 731
Civil Rights Act of 1964, Abzug and Koch
  Attempt to Amend the (June 27, 1974) 273
Civil Rights Law, Wisconsin Enacts First
  Statewide Gay and Lesbian
  (Feb. 25, 1982) 397
Civil Service Commission Prohibits
  Discrimination Against Federal Employees,
  U.S. (July 3, 1975) 292
Civil Unions, *Baker v. Vermont* Leads to
  Recognition of Same-Gender
  (Dec. 20, 1999) 666
Civil Unions, Buenos Aires Recognizes
  Same-Gender (Apr., 2003) 705
Clinic Opens and Provides Gender Reassignment
  Surgery, First Gender Identity
  (Nov. 21, 1966) 165
Clinton Appoints First AIDS Czar
  (June 25, 1993) 606
Clinton Signs Defense of Marriage Act,
  U.S. President (Sept. 21, 1996) 646
College Student Shepard Is Beaten and
  Murdered, Gay (Oct. 6-7, 1998) 654
Color Conference Convenes, First National
  Lesbians of (Sept., 1983) 411
Color Press Is Founded, Kitchen Table:
  Women of (Oct., 1981) 383
Colorado Attempt Antigay Initiatives, Oregon
  and (Nov. 3, 1992) 582
Combahee River Collective Issues "A Black
  Feminist Statement" (Apr., 1977) 309
Come Out, Celebrity Lesbians (1992-2002) 565
Coming Out Day Is Celebrated, First National
  (Oct. 11, 1988) 489
Coming Out to Parents Is Published, First Novel
  About (1975) 283
Coming Out Under Fire Documents Gay and
  Lesbian Military Veterans (1990, 1994) 522
Commission Is Founded, International Gay and
  Lesbian Human Rights (1990) 517
Committee, Hirschfeld Founds the Scientific-
  Humanitarian (May 14, 1897) 36
Community Centers Is Founded, National
  Association of Lesbian and Gay (1994) 621
Compañeras: Latina Lesbians Is Published
  (1987) 450
Compton's Cafeteria in San Francisco, Queer
  Youth Fight Police Harassment at
  (Aug., 1966) 163
Conference, Asian Lesbian Network Holds
  Its First (Dec., 1990) 533
Conference Convenes, First National Lesbian
  (May, 1960) 144
Conference Convenes, First National Lesbians
  of Color (Sept., 1983) 411
Conference Convenes, First National Third
  World Lesbian and Gay
  (Oct. 12-15, 1979) 347
Conference Convenes, National Women's
  (Nov. 18-21, 1977) 311
Conference of Homophile Organizations
  Convenes, First North American
  (Feb. 19-20, 1966) 160
Congress, Employment Non-Discrimination
  Act Is Proposed to U.S. (1994) 618
Congress, Kameny Is First Out Candidate for
  U.S. (1971) 217

Congress, Studds Is First Out Gay Man in the
U.S. (July 14, 1983) 407
Congressman Frank Comes Out as Gay, U.S.
(May 30, 1987) 466
Congresswoman from the South, Jordan Becomes
First Black (Nov. 7, 1972) 239
Consensual Homosexual Sex, Illinois Legalizes
(1961). 147
Consensual Sex, American Bar Association Calls
for Repeal of Laws Against (Aug., 1973) . . . 258
Consensual Sex, The *Wolfenden Report* Calls
for Decriminalizing Private (Sept. 4, 1957) . . 142
Consenting Adults, Canada Decriminalizes
Sex Practices Between (Jan. 1, 1988) 477
Conservative Backlash, Battelle Sex Study
Prompts (Mar.-Apr., 1993) 596
Convention, Seneca Falls Women's Rights
(July 19-20, 1848). 1
Corydon, Gide Publishes the Signed Edition
of (1924) 69
Court Awards Guardianship to Lesbian Partner,
Minnesota (Dec. 17, 1991) 552
Court Distinguishes Between "Indecent" and
"Obscene," U.S. Supreme (July 3, 1978). . . . 327
Court Overturns Texas Sodomy Law, U.S.
Supreme (June 26, 2003) 710
Court Rules for Same-Gender Marriage,
Massachusetts (Nov. 18, 2003) 717
Court Rules Gender-Role Stereotyping Is
Discriminatory, U.S. Supreme
(May 1, 1989). 508
Court Rules in "Crimes Against Nature"
Case, U.S. Supreme (Nov. 17, 1975). 297
Court Supports Local Obscenity Laws, U.S.
Supreme (June 21, 1973) 255
Court Upholds Law Preventing Immigration of
Gays and Lesbians, U.S. Supreme
(May 22, 1967) 176
Court Validates Transsexual Marriage,
Australian (Feb. 21, 2003) 698
"Crimes Against Nature" Case, U.S. Supreme
Court Rules in (Nov. 17, 1975). 297
Criminalizes "Gross Indecency," United Kingdom
(1885) 18
Crusis Women's Choir Is Formed, Anna
(Sept., 1975) 295
Cuba Imprisons Gays, Revolutionary
(Nov., 1965) 157
Custody of Her Child, Lesbian Mother Loses
(Sept. 21, 1993-Apr. 21, 1995) 608

Czar, Clinton Appoints First AIDS
(June 25, 1993) 606

Dale, *Boy Scouts of America v.*
(June 28, 2000) 675
Daughters of Bilitis Founded as First National
Lesbian Group in United States (1955). . . . 132
Davis's Research Identifies Lesbian Sexuality as
Common and Normal (1929) 79
Dead Project, Transgender Day of Remembrance
and Remembering Our (Nov. 20, 2003) . . . 722
Death of Transgender Jazz Musician Billy Tipton
(Jan. 21, 1989) 505
Decriminalizes Homosexual Acts, Canada
(Aug. 26, 1969). 199
Decriminalizes Homosexual Sex, United
Kingdom (July 27, 1967) 178
Decriminalizes Sex Practices Between
Consenting Adults, Canada (Jan. 1, 1988) . . . 477
Decriminalizing Private Consensual Sex,
The *Wolfenden Report* Calls for
(Sept. 4, 1957) 142
Defense of Marriage Act, U.S. President Clinton
Signs (Sept. 21, 1996) 646
Del Martin Quits Gay Liberation Movement
(Nov. 28, 1970). 214
Der Eigene Is Published as First Journal on
Homosexuality (1896) 29
Desert Hearts Is Released, Lesbian Film
(1985). 426
Director of the National Gay and Lesbian
Task Force, Vaid Becomes Executive
(1989). 498
Disabilities Act Becomes Law, Americans with
(July 26, 1990) 530
Discounts to Gays and Lesbians, Canadian
YMCA Extends Family (1992) 559
Discrimination, Oregon Repeals Ban on Antigay
Job (Nov. 8, 1988) 491
Discrimination Against Federal Employees,
U.S. Civil Service Commission Prohibits
(July 3, 1975) 292
Discriminatory, U.S. Supreme Court Rules
Gender-Role Stereotyping Is
(May 1, 1989). 508
Diseases Mark Beginning of AIDS Epidemic,
Reports of Rare (June 5 and July 3, 1981) . . . 378
Disorder, APA Classifies Homosexuality as a
Mental (1952). 111

Domestic Partners of City Employees, Berkeley Extends Benefits to (Dec. 4, 1984) 422
Don't Ask, Don't Tell Policy Is Implemented (Nov. 30, 1993) 611
Don't Tell Policy Is Implemented, Don't Ask, (Nov. 30, 1993) 611
Dyke March Is Held in Washington, D.C., First (Apr. 24, 1993) 598
Dysphoria Association Is Founded, Harry Benjamin International Gender (1978) 320

Eigene Is Published as First Journal on Homosexuality, *Der* (1896) 29
Eisenhower Prohibits Federal Employment of Lesbians and Gays, U.S. President (Apr. 27, 1953) 129
Elected to the Mexican Senate, Jiménez Flores (Jan., 2006) 741
Election, Noble Is First Out Lesbian or Gay Person to Win State-Level (Nov. 5, 1974) . . . 277
Ellis Publishes *Sexual Inversion* (1897) 33
Employees, Berkeley Extends Benefits to Domestic Partners of City (Dec. 4, 1984) . . . 422
Employees, Singapore Lifts Ban on Hiring Lesbian and Gay (July, 2003) 713
Employees, U.S. Civil Service Commission Prohibits Discrimination Against Federal (July 3, 1975) 292
Employment Non-Discrimination Act Is Proposed to U.S. Congress (1994) 618
Employment of Lesbians and Gays, U.S. President Eisenhower Prohibits Federal (Apr. 27, 1953) 129
Epidemic, Reports of Rare Diseases Mark Beginning of AIDS (June 5 and July 3, 1981) 378
Equal Rights Amendment Fails State Ratification (Mar. 22, 1972-June 30, 1982) 233
Equal Rights and Liberation, March on Washington for Gay, Lesbian, and Bi (Apr. 25, 1993) 601
Equal Rights in Mexico City, Gays and Lesbians March for (June 19, 2002) 690
Eulenburg Affair Scandalizes Germany's Leadership, The (1907-1909) 52
Evelyn Hooker Debunks Beliefs That Homosexuality Is a "Sickness" (1953-1957) 126
Executive Director of the National Gay and Lesbian Task Force, Vaid Becomes (1989) 498

Exploitation, Transsexuals Protest Academic (Mar., 2003-Dec., 2004) 700

Faderman Publishes *Surpassing the Love of Men* (1981) 362
Families, and Friends of Lesbians and Gays Is Founded, Parents, (1981) 367
Family Discounts to Gays and Lesbians, Canadian YMCA Extends (1992) 559
Family Rights to Gay and Lesbian State Workers, Massachusetts Grants (Sept. 23, 1992) 576
Federal Employees, U.S. Civil Service Commission Prohibits Discrimination Against (July 3, 1975) 292
Federal Employment of Lesbians and Gays, U.S. President Eisenhower Prohibits (Apr. 27, 1953) 129
Feinberg Publishes *Transgender Liberation* (June, 1992) 573
Feminist-Lesbian Book Shop, Amazon Bookstore Opens as First (1970) 203
Feminist Network Is Formed, Latin American and Caribbean Lesbian (Oct. 14-17, 1987) . . . 472
Film, Hollywood Awards Transgender Portrayals in (Mar. 21, 2000) 672
Film, *The Wedding Banquet* Is First Acclaimed Taiwanese Gay-Themed (1993) 591
Film *Desert Hearts* Is Released, Lesbian (1985) 426
Films, Hollywood Bans "Sexual Perversion" in (1930's-1960's) 84
Fire Ignites Violent Protests in India, Screening of (Dec. 3, 1998-Feb. 25, 1999) 660
Firing, Canadian Supreme Court Reverses Gay Academic's (Apr. 2, 1998) 652
First Dyke March Is Held in Washington, D.C. (Apr. 24, 1993) 598
First Gay and Lesbian Archives Is Founded (1975) 280
First Gay and Lesbian Synagogue in the United States Is Formed (Mar., 1972-Mar., 1973) . . . 230
First Gay and Lesbian Television Network Is Launched in Canada (Sept. 7, 2001) 683
First Gay British Television Series Airs (1979-1981) 342
First Gay Games Are Held in San Francisco (Aug. 28, 1982) 405

Keyword List of Contents

First Gender Identity Clinic Opens and Provides Gender Reassignment Surgery (Nov. 21, 1966) 165

First International Retreat for Lesbian and Gay Muslims Is Held (Oct. 9-12, 1998) 657

First Lesbian and Gay Pride March in the United States (June 28, 1970) 212

First March on Washington for Lesbian and Gay Rights (Oct. 12-15, 1979) 344

First Middle Eastern Gay and Lesbian Organization Is Founded (Nov., 1999) 664

First National Coming Out Day Is Celebrated (Oct. 11, 1988) 489

First National Lesbian Conference Convenes (May, 1960) 144

First National Lesbians of Color Conference Convenes (Sept., 1983) 411

First National Third World Lesbian and Gay Conference Convenes (Oct. 12-15, 1979) . . . 347

First North American Conference of Homophile Organizations Convenes (Feb. 19-20, 1966) 160

First Novel About Coming Out to Parents Is Published (1975) 283

First Out Gay Minister Is Ordained (June 25, 1972) 236

First Student Homophile League Is Formed (Apr. 19, 1967) 172

First World AIDS Day (Dec. 1, 1988) 494

Flores Elected to the Mexican Senate, Jiménez (Jan., 2006) 741

Foster Publishes *Sex Variant Women in Literature* (1956) 138

Frank Comes Out as Gay, U.S. Congressman (May 30, 1987) 466

Freud Rejects Third-Sex Theory (1905) 46

Friedlaender Breaks with the Scientific-Humanitarian Committee (1906) 49

Friends of Lesbians and Gays Is Founded, Parents, Families, and (1981) 367

Front Runner Makes *The New York Times* Best-Seller List, *The* (1974) 269

GALA Choruses Is Formed (1981-1982) 373

Games Are Held in San Francisco, First Gay (Aug. 28, 1982) 405

Gay, U.S. Congressman Frank Comes Out as (May 30, 1987) 466

Gay Academic's Firing, Canadian Supreme Court Reverses (Apr. 2, 1998) 652

Gay American Indians Is Founded (1975) 285

Gay and Lesbian Archives Is Founded, First (1975) 280

Gay and Lesbian Books, Alyson Begins Publishing (1980) 351

Gay and Lesbian Center Is Founded, Los Angeles (Mar., 1971) 221

Gay and Lesbian City Council, West Hollywood Incorporates with Majority (Nov. 6, 1984) . . . 419

Gay and Lesbian Civil Rights Law, Wisconsin Enacts First Statewide (Feb. 25, 1982) 397

Gay and Lesbian Human Rights Commission Is Founded, International (1990) 517

Gay and Lesbian Immigration, U.S. Law Prohibits (1952-1990) 117

Gay and Lesbian Military Veterans, *Coming Out Under Fire* Documents (1990, 1994) 522

Gay and Lesbian Organization Is Founded, First Middle Eastern (Nov., 1999) 664

Gay and Lesbian Palimony Suits Emerge (1981) 365

Gay and Lesbian Rights, Anita Bryant Campaigns Against (1977) 307

Gay and Lesbian Rights, Karl Heinrich Ulrichs Speaks Publicly for (Aug. 29, 1867) 9

Gay and Lesbian Rights Movement, Stonewall Rebellion Ignites Modern (June 27-July 2, 1969) 192

Gay and Lesbian State Workers, Massachusetts Grants Family Rights to (Sept. 23, 1992) . . . 576

Gay and Lesbian Synagogue in the United States Is Formed, First (Mar., 1972-Mar., 1973) . . . 230

Gay and Lesbian Task Force, Vaid Becomes Executive Director of the National (1989) . . . 498

Gay and Lesbian Television Network Is Launched in Canada, First (Sept. 7, 2001) 683

Gay Asian Collective Is Founded, Lesbian and (Oct. 12-15, 1979) 349

Gay Association, U.N. Revokes Consultative Status of International Lesbian and (Sept. 16, 1994) 632

Gay Association Is Founded, International Lesbian and (Aug. 8, 1978) 330

Gay Bathhouses, Toronto Police Raid (Feb. 5, 1981) 376

Gay Bathhouses and Other Businesses, San Francisco Closes (Oct. 9, 1984) 417

Gay Bishop in Christian History, Robinson Becomes First Out (Mar. 7, 2004) 725

Gay Book Award Debuts, The (June, 1971) 223

liii

GLBT Events

Gay Bookstore, Oscar Wilde Memorial Bookshop Opens as First (Fall, 1967) 180

"Gay Brain," LeVay Postulates the (1991) 535

Gay British Television Series Airs, First (1979-1981) 342

Gay Catholics Find Dignity (1969-1973) 189

Gay College Student Shepard Is Beaten and Murdered (Oct. 6-7, 1998) 654

Gay Community Centers Is Founded, National Association of Lesbian and (1994) 621

Gay Conference Convenes, First National Third World Lesbian and (Oct. 12-15, 1979) 347

Gay Employees, Singapore Lifts Ban on Hiring Lesbian and (July, 2003) 713

Gay Games Are Held in San Francisco, First (Aug. 28, 1982) 405

Gay History Anthology, Katz Publishes First Lesbian and (1976) 300

Gay Latino Alliance Is Formed (1975-1983) . . . 290

Gay, Lesbian, and Bi Equal Rights and Liberation, March on Washington for (Apr. 25, 1993) . . . 601

Gay Liberation Front Is Formed (July 31, 1969) 195

Gay Liberation Movement, Del Martin Quits (Nov. 28, 1970) 214

Gay Literature, Golden Age of American (1947-1948) 97

Gay Man in the U.S. Congress, Studds Is First Out (July 14, 1983) 407

Gay Men's Chorus Concert Tour, San Francisco (June 6-June 20, 1981) 380

Gay Men's Chorus Performs at Carnegie Hall, New York City (Dec. 8, 1981) 385

Gay Minister Is Ordained, First Out (June 25, 1972) 236

Gay Muslims Is Held, First International Retreat for Lesbian and (Oct. 9-12, 1998) 657

Gay or Lesbian Candidate for Public Office, Sarria Is First Out (1961) 149

Gay Person to Win State-Level Election, Noble Is First Out Lesbian or (Nov. 5, 1974) 277

Gay Political Coalition, NACHO Formally Becomes the First (Aug. 11-18, 1968) 182

Gay Postal Workers Secure Union Protections, Canadian (June 2, 1980) 360

Gay Pride March in the United States, First Lesbian and (June 28, 1970) 212

Gay-Related Immunodeficiency Is Renamed AIDS (July, 1982) 401

Gay Rights, First March on Washington for Lesbian and (Oct. 12-15, 1979) 344

Gay Rights, Japanese Human Rights Council Recommends Lesbian and (May 25, 2001) . . 681

Gay Rights, Second March on Washington for Lesbian and (Oct. 11, 1987) 469

Gay Seminarians, Roman Catholic Church Bans (Nov. 29, 2005) 738

Gay Soldier, *Watkins v. United States Army* Reinstates (May 3, 1989) 510

Gay Task Force Is Formed, National (1973) . . . 246

Gay-Themed Film, *The Wedding Banquet* Is First Acclaimed Taiwanese (1993) 591

Gay Workplace Movement Is Founded, Lesbian and (1978) 323

Gay Writers Form the Violet Quill (1980-1981) 353

Gay Youth Protection Institute Is Founded, Lesbian and (1982) 387

Gays, Revolutionary Cuba Imprisons (Nov., 1965) 157

Gays, U.S. President Eisenhower Prohibits Federal Employment of Lesbians and (Apr. 27, 1953) 129

Gays and Lesbians, Canadian Military Lifts Its Ban on (Oct., 1992) 579

Gays and Lesbians, Canadian YMCA Extends Family Discounts to (1992) 559

Gays and Lesbians, GLAAD Begins Monitoring Media Coverage of (1985) 424

Gays and Lesbians, U.S. Supreme Court Upholds Law Preventing Immigration of (May 22, 1967) 176

Gays and Lesbians in the Military, United Kingdom Lifts Ban on (Jan. 12, 2000) 669

Gays and Lesbians March for Equal Rights in Mexico City (June 19, 2002) 690

Gays in Its Charter of Human Rights and Freedoms, Quebec Includes Lesbians and (Dec. 19, 1977) 315

Gays Is Founded, Parents, Families, and Friends of Lesbians and (1981) 367

Gays Protest Lambda Fund-Raiser, Asian Lesbians and (Apr. 6, 1991) 542

Gays to Its Antidiscrimination Policy, Wal-Mart Adds Lesbians and (July, 2003) 715

Gender Dysphoria Association Is Founded, Harry Benjamin International (1978) 320

Gender Identity Clinic Opens and Provides
Gender Reassignment Surgery, First
(Nov. 21, 1966). 165

Gender Reassignment Surgery, First Gender
Identity Clinic Opens and Provides
(Nov. 21, 1966). 165

Gender Recognition Act Legalizes Transsexual
Marriage, United Kingdom's
(Apr. 4, 2005). 734

Gender Rights Is First Circulated, International
Bill of (June 17, 1995) 639

Gender-Role Stereotyping Is Discriminatory,
U.S. Supreme Court Rules (May 1, 1989) . . . 508

George Jorgensen Becomes Christine Jorgensen
(Sept. 24, 1951). 108

Gerber Founds the Society for Human Rights
(Dec. 10, 1924). 72

Germany's Leadership, Eulenburg Affair
Scandalizes (1907-1909). 52

Gide Publishes the Signed Edition of *Corydon*
(1924) 69

Giovanni's Room, Baldwin Publishes (1956) . . . 135

GLAAD Begins Monitoring Media Coverage of
Gays and Lesbians (1985) 424

God of Vengeance Opens on Broadway, The
(Feb. 19, 1923). 66

Golden Age of American Gay Literature
(1947-1948) 97

Goodbye to Berlin, Isherwood Publishes
(1939) 92

Government Antigay Campaign Is Revealed,
Canadian (Apr. 27, 1992). 570

Governments Pass Antidiscrimination Laws,
Local (1972-1973) 228

Governor Wilson Vetoes Antidiscrimination Bill,
California (Sept. 29, 1991) 550

Gross Indecency, Oscar Wilde Is Convicted of
(May 25, 1895). 26

"Gross Indecency," United Kingdom Criminalizes
(1885) 18

Guardianship to Lesbian Partner, Minnesota
Court Awards (Dec. 17, 1991) 552

Hall Publishes *The Well of Loneliness* (1928). . . . 76

Harassment at Compton's Cafeteria in San
Francisco, Queer Youth Fight Police
(Aug., 1966) 163

Harry Benjamin International Gender Dysphoria
Association Is Founded (1978). 320

Hart Recognized as a Transgender Man
(1996). 644

Hawaii Opens Door to Same-Gender
Marriages (1993-1996) 593

Hawthorne, *The Advocate* Outs Oscar Nominee
Nigel (1995) 634

Helms Claims Photographs Are Indecent
(1989-1990). 500

Herstory Archives Is Founded, Lesbian
(Fall, 1973) 260

"Heterosexual," Kertbeny Coins the Terms
"Homosexual" and (May 6, 1868). 12

Hiring Lesbian and Gay Employees, Singapore
Lifts Ban on (July, 2003) 713

Hirschfeld Founds the Scientific-Humanitarian
Committee (May 14, 1897) 36

History Anthology, Katz Publishes First Lesbian
and Gay (1976) 300

Hitler's Night of the Long Knives (June 30-
July 1, 1934) 89

HIV-Positive, Athlete Louganis Announces
He Is (1995) 637

Hollywood Awards Transgender Portrayals in
Film (Mar. 21, 2000) 672

Hollywood Bans "Sexual Perversion" in Films
(1930's-1960's) 84

Hollywood Incorporates with Majority Gay
and Lesbian City Council, West
(Nov. 6, 1984) 419

Homophile League Is Formed, First Student
(Apr. 19, 1967) 172

Homophile Organizations Convenes, First
North American Conference of
(Feb. 19-20, 1966) 160

Homophobia in Women's Movement, Lavender
Menace Protests (May 1, 1970) 209

Homosexual Acts, Canada Decriminalizes
(Aug. 26, 1969) 199

"Homosexual" and "Heterosexual," Kertbeny
Coins the Terms (May 6, 1868) 12

Homosexual in America," *Time* Magazine Issues
"The (Oct. 31, 1969) 201

Homosexual Sex, Illinois Legalizes
Consensual (1961) 147

Homosexual Sex, United Kingdom
Decriminalizes (July 27, 1967). 178

Homosexuality, *Der Eigene* Is Published as
First Journal on (1896). 29

Homosexuality as a Mental Disorder, APA
Classifies (1952) 111

Homosexuality from List of Mental Disorders, Chinese Psychiatric Association Removes (Apr. 20, 2001) 679
Homosexuality Is a "Sickness," Evelyn Hooker Debunks Beliefs That (1953-1957) 126
Homosexuality Is Delisted by APA (Dec. 15, 1973) 265
Homosexuals, Nazis Persecute (1933-1945) 86
Hooker Debunks Beliefs That Homosexuality Is a "Sickness," Evelyn (1953-1957) 126
Housing Secretary, Achtenberg Becomes Assistant (May 24, 1993). 604
Hudson Announces He Has AIDS, Actor (July 25, 1985) 429
Human Rights, Gerber Founds the Society for (Dec. 10, 1924). 72
Human Rights Act, New Mexico Amends Its (Mar. 21, 2003) 702
Human Rights and Freedoms, Quebec Includes Lesbians and Gays in Its Charter of (Dec. 19, 1977) 315
Human Rights Campaign Fund Is Founded (Apr. 22, 1980) 355
Human Rights Commission Is Founded, International Gay and Lesbian (1990) 517
Human Rights Council Recommends Lesbian and Gay Rights, Japanese (May 25, 2001) . . . 681

Illinois Legalizes Consensual Homosexual Sex (1961). 147
Immigrant Status, Irish American Lesbian Gains Canadian (June 28, 2002). 692
Immigration of Gays and Lesbians, U.S. Supreme Court Upholds Law Preventing (May 22, 1967) 176
Immunodeficiency Is Renamed AIDS, Gay-Related (July, 1982) 401
Imprisons Gays, Revolutionary Cuba (Nov., 1965) 157
Indecency, Oscar Wilde Is Convicted of Gross (May 25, 1895). 26
Indecency," United Kingdom Criminalizes "Gross (1885) 18
Indecent, Helms Claims Photographs Are (1989-1990). 500
"Indecent" and "Obscene," U.S. Supreme Court Distinguishes Between (July 3, 1978) 327
India, Screening of *Fire* Ignites Violent Protests in (Dec. 3, 1998-Feb. 25, 1999) 660

Indian Visits Washington, D.C., Two-Spirit American (Jan.-June, 1886) 21
Indians Is Founded, Gay American (1975). 285
Indians Struggle to Abolish Sodomy Law (1992-2006). 568
Information Center Opens, Lavender Youth Recreation and (May, 1988) 482
Intermediate Sex, Carpenter Publishes *The* (1908) 55
International Bill of Gender Rights Is First Circulated (June 17, 1995) 639
International Gay and Lesbian Human Rights Commission Is Founded (1990) 517
International Gender Dysphoria Association Is Founded, Harry Benjamin (1978) 320
International Lesbian and Gay Association, U.N. Revokes Consultative Status of (Sept. 16, 1994). 632
International Lesbian and Gay Association Is Founded (Aug. 8, 1978) 330
International Retreat for Lesbian and Gay Muslims Is Held, First (Oct. 9-12, 1998). . . . 657
Intersex Society of North America Is Founded (1993). 586
Inversion, Westphal Advocates Medical Treatment for Sexual (1869) 16
Irish American Lesbian Gains Canadian Immigrant Status (June 28, 2002) 692
Isherwood Publishes *Goodbye to Berlin* (1939) 92

Japanese American Citizens League Supports Same-Gender Marriage (Aug. 6, 1994) 629
Japanese Human Rights Council Recommends Lesbian and Gay Rights (May 25, 2001). . . . 681
Jazz Musician Billy Tipton, Death of Transgender (Jan. 21, 1989) 505
Jiménez Flores Elected to the Mexican Senate (Jan., 2006) 741
Job Discrimination, Oregon Repeals Ban on Antigay (Nov. 8, 1988) 491
Jordan Becomes First Black Congresswoman from the South (Nov. 7, 1972) 239
Jorgensen Becomes Christine Jorgensen, George (Sept. 24, 1951) 108
Journal on Homosexuality, *Der Eigene* Is Published as First (1896). 29
Juana Inés de la Cruz, Revisionist Criticism Recasts Sor (1991) 537

Kameny Is First Out Candidate for U.S. Congress (1971). 217
Katz Publishes First Lesbian and Gay History Anthology (1976). 300
Kertbeny Coins the Terms "Homosexual" and "Heterosexual" (May 6, 1868). 12
Kinsey Publishes *Sexual Behavior in the Human Female* (1953) 121
Kinsey Publishes *Sexual Behavior in the Human Male* (1948). 103
Kitchen Table: Women of Color Press Is Founded (Oct., 1981). 383
Knives, Hitler's Night of the Long (June 30-July 1, 1934) 89
Koch Attempt to Amend the Civil Rights Act of 1964, Abzug and (June 27, 1974) 273

Lambda Fund-Raiser, Asian Lesbians and Gays Protest (Apr. 6, 1991). 542
Lambda Legal Authorized to Practice Law (Oct. 18, 1973) 263
Lambda Literary Award Is Created (June 2, 1989). 512
Lambda Rising Book Report Begins Publication (May, 1987). 464
LaRouche's Quarantine Initiative, Californians Reject (Nov., 1986). 442
Latin American and Caribbean Lesbian Feminist Network Is Formed (Oct. 14-17, 1987). . . . 472
Latina and Latino Artists, VIVA Is Founded to Promote (1987). 455
Latina Lesbians Is Published, *Compañeras:* (1987). 450
Latino Alliance Is Formed, Gay (1975-1983) . . . 290
Latino Artists, VIVA Is Founded to Promote Latina and (1987). 455
Lavender Menace Protests Homophobia in Women's Movement (May 1, 1970) 209
Lavender Youth Recreation and Information Center Opens (May, 1988) 482
Law, Americans with Disabilities Act Becomes (July 26, 1990) 530
Law, Indians Struggle to Abolish Sodomy (1992-2006). 568
Law, Lambda Legal Authorized to Practice (Oct. 18, 1973) 263
Law, Transgender Rights Added to New York City (Apr. 30, 2002) 687
Law, United Kingdom's Sexual Offences Act Becomes (Jan. 1, 1957). 140
Law, U.S. Supreme Court Overturns Texas Sodomy (June 26, 2003) 710
Law, Wisconsin Enacts First Statewide Gay and Lesbian Civil Rights (Feb. 25, 1982). 397
Law Censors Risque Theater, Wales Padlock (Feb., 1927) 74
Law Preventing Immigration of Gays and Lesbians, U.S. Supreme Court Upholds (May 22, 1967) 176
Law Prohibits Gay and Lesbian Immigration, U.S. (1952-1990) 117
Law Project Is Founded, Sylvia Rivera (2002). 686
Laws, *Bowers v. Hardwick* Upholds State Sodomy (1986) 432
Laws, Local Governments Pass Antidiscrimination (1972-1973). 228
Laws, U.S. Supreme Court Supports Local Obscenity (June 21, 1973) 255
Laws Against Consensual Sex, American Bar Association Calls for Repeal of (Aug., 1973) 258
Leather Archives and Museum Is Founded (Aug., 1991) 545
Leaves of Grass, Whitman Publishes (July 4, 1855) 3
Legalizes Consensual Homosexual Sex, Illinois (1961). 147
Legalizes Same-Gender Marriage, Spain (June 30, 2005) 736
Legalizes Transsexual Marriage, United Kingdom's Gender Recognition Act (Apr. 4, 2005). 734
Lesbian Academic and Activist Sues University of California for Discrimination (1982-1991). 395
Lesbian, and Bi Equal Rights and Liberation, March on Washington for Gay, (Apr. 25, 1993) 601
Lesbian and Gay Asian Collective Is Founded (Oct. 12-15, 1979) 349
Lesbian and Gay Association, U.N. Revokes Consultative Status of International (Sept. 16, 1994). 632
Lesbian and Gay Association Is Founded, International (Aug. 8, 1978) 330
Lesbian and Gay Community Centers Is Founded, National Association of (1994). 621
Lesbian and Gay Conference Convenes, First National Third World (Oct. 12-15, 1979) . . . 347

Lesbian and Gay Employees, Singapore Lifts
    Ban on Hiring (July, 2003) 713
Lesbian and Gay History Anthology, Katz
    Publishes First (1976) 300
Lesbian and Gay Muslims Is Held, First
    International Retreat for (Oct. 9-12, 1998) . . . 657
Lesbian and Gay Pride March in the United
    States, First (June 28, 1970) 212
Lesbian and Gay Rights, First March on
    Washington for (Oct. 12-15, 1979) 344
Lesbian and Gay Rights, Japanese Human
    Rights Council Recommends
    (May 25, 2001) 681
Lesbian and Gay Rights, Second March on
    Washington for (Oct. 11, 1987) 469
Lesbian and Gay Workplace Movement Is
    Founded (1978) 323
Lesbian and Gay Youth Protection Institute Is
    Founded (1982) 387
Lesbian Archives Is Founded, First Gay and
    (1975) 280
Lesbian Book Shop, Amazon Bookstore Opens
    as First Feminist- (1970) 203
Lesbian Books, Alyson Begins Publishing Gay
    and (1980) 351
Lesbian Candidate for Public Office, Sarria Is
    First Out Gay or (1961) 149
Lesbian Center Is Founded, Los Angeles Gay
    and (Mar., 1971) 221
Lesbian City Council, West Hollywood
    Incorporates with Majority Gay and
    (Nov. 6, 1984) 419
Lesbian Civil Rights Law, Wisconsin Enacts
    First Statewide Gay and (Feb. 25, 1982) . . . 397
Lesbian Conference Convenes, First National
    (May, 1960) 144
Lesbian Connection Begins Publication
    (Oct., 1974) 275
Lesbian Couple Murdered in Oregon
    (Dec. 4, 1995) 641
Lesbian Feminist Network Is Formed, Latin
    American and Caribbean
    (Oct. 14-17, 1987) 472
Lesbian Film *Desert Hearts* Is Released
    (1985) 426
Lesbian Gains Canadian Immigrant Status,
    Irish American (June 28, 2002) 692
Lesbian Group in United States, Daughters of
    Bilitis Founded as First National (1955) . . . 132
Lesbian Herstory Archives Is Founded
    (Fall, 1973) 260
Lesbian Human Rights Commission Is Founded,
    International Gay and (1990) 517
Lesbian Images, Rule Publishes (1975) 287
Lesbian Immigration, U.S. Law Prohibits Gay
    and (1952-1990) 117
Lesbian Military Veterans, *Coming Out Under
    Fire* Documents Gay and (1990, 1994) 522
Lesbian Mother Loses Custody of Her Child
    (Sept. 21, 1993-Apr. 21, 1995) 608
Lesbian Network Holds Its First Conference,
    Asian (Dec., 1990) 533
Lesbian Network Is Founded, Asian Pacific
    (1987) 448
Lesbian or Gay Person to Win State-Level
    Election, Noble Is First Out
    (Nov. 5, 1974) 277
Lesbian Organization Is Founded, First Middle
    Eastern Gay and (Nov., 1999) 664
Lesbian Palimony Suits Emerge, Gay and
    (1981) 365
Lesbian Partner, Minnesota Court Awards
    Guardianship to (Dec. 17, 1991) 552
Lesbian Periodical, *Vice Versa* Is Published as
    First (June, 1947-Feb., 1948) 101
Lesbian Rights, Anita Bryant Campaigns
    Against Gay and (1977) 307
Lesbian Rights, Karl Heinrich Ulrichs Speaks
    Publicly for Gay and (Aug. 29, 1867) 9
Lesbian Rights Movement, Stonewall Rebellion
    Ignites Modern Gay and (June 27-
    July 2, 1969) 192
Lesbian Sexuality as Common and Normal,
    Davis's Research Identifies (1929) 79
Lesbian State Workers, Massachusetts Grants
    Family Rights to Gay and
    (Sept. 23, 1992) 576
Lesbian Synagogue in the United States Is
    Formed, First Gay and (Mar., 1972-
    Mar., 1973) 230
Lesbian Task Force, Vaid Becomes Executive
    Director of the National Gay and (1989) . . . 498
Lesbian Television Network Is Launched in
    Canada, First Gay and (Sept. 7, 2001) 683
Lesbian Tide Publishes Its First Issue (1971) . . . 219
Lesbians, Canadian Military Lifts Its Ban on
    Gays and (Oct., 1992) 579
Lesbians, Canadian YMCA Extends Family
    Discounts to Gays and (1992) 559

Keyword List of Contents

Lesbians, GLAAD Begins Monitoring Media
Coverage of Gays and (1985) 424
Lesbians, *Thompson v. Aldredge* Dismisses
Sodomy Charges Against (Jan. 12, 1939) 95
Lesbians, U.S. Supreme Court Upholds Law
Preventing Immigration of Gays and
(May 22, 1967) 176
Lesbians and Gays, U.S. President Eisenhower
Prohibits Federal Employment of
(Apr. 27, 1953) 129
Lesbians and Gays in Its Charter of Human
Rights and Freedoms, Quebec Includes
(Dec. 19, 1977) 315
Lesbians and Gays Is Founded, Parents,
Families, and Friends of (1981) 367
Lesbians and Gays Protest Lambda Fund-Raiser,
Asian (Apr. 6, 1991) 542
Lesbians and Gays to Its Antidiscrimination
Policy, Wal-Mart Adds (July, 2003) 715
Lesbians Come Out, Celebrity (1992-2002) 565
Lesbians in the Military, United Kingdom Lifts
Ban on Gays and (Jan. 12, 2000) 669
Lesbians Is Published, *Compañeras: Latina*
(1987) 450
Lesbians March for Equal Rights in Mexico City,
Gays and (June 19, 2002) 690
Lesbians of African Heritage Is Founded, United
(1990) 519
Lesbians of Color Conference Convenes, First
National (Sept., 1983) 411
Lesbians Organize for Change, Old
(Apr., 1987) 462
LeVay Postulates the "Gay Brain" (1991) 535
Liberation Front Is Formed, Gay
(July 31, 1969) 195
Liberation Movement, Del Martin Quits Gay
(Nov. 28, 1970) 214
Literary Award Is Created, Lambda
(June 2, 1989) 512
Literature, Golden Age of American Gay
(1947-1948) 97
Littleton v. Prange Withholds Survivor Rights
from Transsexual Spouses (Oct. 27, 1999) . . . 662
Local Governments Pass Antidiscrimination
Laws (1972-1973) 228
Long Knives, Hitler's Night of the (June 30-
July 1, 1934) 89
Lorde's Autobiography *Zami* Is Published
(1982) 392

Los Angeles Advocate Begins Publication
(1967) 167
Los Angeles Gay and Lesbian Center Is
Founded (Mar., 1971) 221
"Los 41" in Mexico City, Police Arrest
(Nov. 17, 1901) 41
Louganis Announces He Is HIV-Positive,
Athlete (1995) 637

M. Butterfly Opens on Broadway
(Mar. 20, 1988) 479
Macho Dancer Is Released in the Philippines
(1988) 474
Magazine Begins Publication, *ONE* (1953) 124
Majority Gay and Lesbian City Council, West
Hollywood Incorporates with
(Nov. 6, 1984) 419
Manifesto, Radicalesbians Issues "The Woman
Identified Woman" (May 1, 1970) 206
Manifesto," Stone Publishes "The Posttranssexual
(1991) 540
March and Rallies Are Held in New York City,
Stonewall 25 (June, 1994) 627
March for Equal Rights in Mexico City, Gays
and Lesbians (June 19, 2002) 690
March in the United States, First Lesbian and
Gay Pride (June 28, 1970) 212
March Is Held in Washington, D.C., First
Dyke (Apr. 24, 1993) 598
March on Washington, Rustin Organizes the
(July 2-Aug. 28, 1963) 154
March on Washington for Gay, Lesbian, and
Bi Equal Rights and Liberation
(Apr. 25, 1993) 601
March on Washington for Lesbian and Gay
Rights, First (Oct. 12-15, 1979) 344
March on Washington for Lesbian and Gay
Rights, Second (Oct. 11, 1987) 469
Marriage, Australian Court Validates Transsexual
(Feb. 21, 2003) 698
Marriage, Canada Legalizes Same-Gender
(June 17, 2003, and July 19, 2005) 707
Marriage, Japanese American Citizens League
Supports Same-Gender (Aug. 6, 1994) 629
Marriage, Massachusetts Court Rules for Same-
Gender (Nov. 18, 2003) 717
Marriage, Spain Legalizes Same-Gender
(June 30, 2005) 736
Marriage, United Kingdom's Gender Recognition
Act Legalizes Transsexual (Apr. 4, 2005) . . . 734

Marriage Act, U.S. President Clinton Signs Defense of (Sept. 21, 1996) 646
Marriages, Hawaii Opens Door to Same-Gender (1993-1996). 593
Martin Quits Gay Liberation Movement, Del (Nov. 28, 1970). 214
Mary Edwards Walker Is Awarded the Medal of Honor (Nov. 11, 1865) 7
Massachusetts Court Rules for Same-Gender Marriage (Nov. 18, 2003) 717
Massachusetts Grants Family Rights to Gay and Lesbian State Workers (Sept. 23, 1992). 576
Mattachine Society Is Founded (1950). 106
Medal of Honor, Mary Edwards Walker Is Awarded the (Nov. 11, 1865) 7
Media Coverage of Gays and Lesbians, GLAAD Begins Monitoring (1985) 424
Medical Treatment for Sexual Inversion, Westphal Advocates (1869) 16
Mental Disorder, APA Classifies Homosexuality as a (1952) 111
Mental Disorders, Chinese Psychiatric Association Removes Homosexuality from List of (Apr. 20, 2001) 679
Metropolitan Community Church Is Founded (Oct. 6, 1968). 184
Mexican Revolution, Robles Fights in the (1912-1924) 61
Mexican Senate, Jiménez Flores Elected to the (Jan., 2006) 741
Mexico City, Gays and Lesbians March for Equal Rights in (June 19, 2002) 690
Mexico City, Police Arrest "Los 41" in (Nov. 17, 1901) 41
Michigan Womyn's Music Festival Holds Its First Gathering (Aug. 20-22, 1976) 304
Middle Eastern Gay and Lesbian Organization Is Founded, First (Nov., 1999) 664
Military, United Kingdom Lifts Ban on Gays and Lesbians in the (Jan. 12, 2000). 669
Military Lifts Its Ban on Gays and Lesbians, Canadian (Oct., 1992) 579
Military Veterans, *Coming Out Under Fire* Documents Gay and Lesbian (1990, 1994). . . 522
Milk, White Murders Politicians Moscone and (Nov. 27, 1978). 337
Minister Is Ordained, First Out Gay (June 25, 1972). 236
Minnesota Court Awards Guardianship to Lesbian Partner (Dec. 17, 1991). 552
Mitchell Found Guilty of Murdering Her Lover, Alice (Jan., 1892-July, 1892) 23
Monette Wins the National Book Award for *Becoming a Man* (1993) 588
Moral Majority Is Founded (1979). 339
Moscone and Milk, White Murders Politicians (Nov. 27, 1978). 337
Mother Loses Custody of Her Child, Lesbian (Sept. 21, 1993-Apr. 21, 1995) 608
Murdered, Gay College Student Shepard Is Beaten and (Oct. 6-7, 1998) 654
Murdered in California, Transgender Teen Gwen Araujo Is (Oct. 4, 2002) 694
Murdered in Oregon, Lesbian Couple (Dec. 4, 1995). 641
Murdering Her Lover, Alice Mitchell Found Guilty of (Jan., 1892-July, 1892) 23
Murders Politicians Moscone and Milk, White (Nov. 27, 1978). 337
Museum Is Founded, Leather Archives and (Aug., 1991) 545
Music Festival Holds Its First Gathering, Michigan Womyn's (Aug. 20-22, 1976) 304
Musician Billy Tipton, Death of Transgender Jazz (Jan. 21, 1989). 505
Muslims Is Held, First International Retreat for Lesbian and Gay (Oct. 9-12, 1998). 657

NACHO Formally Becomes the First Gay Political Coalition (Aug. 11-18, 1968) 182
Naiad Press Is Founded (1973). 244
National Association of Lesbian and Gay Community Centers Is Founded (1994) 621
National Book Award for *Becoming a Man*, Monette Wins the (1993). 588
National Coming Out Day Is Celebrated, First (Oct. 11, 1988) 489
National Endowment for the Arts, Artists Sue the (1990-1993). 520
National Gay and Lesbian Task Force, Vaid Becomes Executive Director of the (1989). 498
National Gay Task Force Is Formed (1973) . . . 246
National Lesbian Conference Convenes, First (May, 1960). 144
National Lesbian Group in United States, Daughters of Bilitis Founded as First (1955). 132

Keyword List of Contents

National Lesbians of Color Conference Convenes, First (Sept., 1983). 411

National Third World Lesbian and Gay Conference Convenes, First (Oct. 12-15, 1979) 347

National Women's Conference Convenes (Nov. 18-21, 1977) 311

Navratilova Honored for Her Career in Tennis (1994). 623

Navy Investigates the USS *Norton Sound* in Antilesbian Witch Hunt, U.S. (May-Aug., 1980) 357

Navy Launches Sting Operation Against "Sexual Perverts," U.S. (Mar. 15, 1919-1921). 63

Nazis Persecute Homosexuals (1933-1945). 86

New Mexico Amends Its Human Rights Act (Mar. 21, 2003). 702

New York City, Stonewall 25 March and Rallies Are Held in (June, 1994) 627

New York City Gay Men's Chorus Performs at Carnegie Hall (Dec. 8, 1981). 385

New York City Law, Transgender Rights Added to (Apr. 30, 2002). 687

New York Times Best-Seller List, *The Front Runner* Makes *The* (1974) 269

Newsletter *Trikone* Begins Publication, South Asian (Jan., 1986) 438

Night of the Long Knives, Hitler's (June 30-July 1, 1934) 89

Noble Is First Out Lesbian or Gay Person to Win State-Level Election (Nov. 5, 1974) 277

Non-Discrimination Act Is Proposed to U.S. Congress, Employment (1994) 618

North American Conference of Homophile Organizations Convenes, First (Feb. 19-20, 1966) 160

Norton Sound in Antilesbian Witch Hunt, U.S. Navy Investigates the USS (May-Aug., 1980). 357

Novel About Coming Out to Parents Is Published, First (1975). 283

Nuestro Mundo Forms as First Queer Organization in Argentina (1969) 187

"Obscene," U.S. Supreme Court Distinguishes Between "Indecent" and (July 3, 1978) . . . 327

Obscenity Laws, U.S. Supreme Court Supports Local (June 21, 1973). 255

Office, Sarria Is First Out Gay or Lesbian Candidate for Public (1961) 149

Old Lesbians Organize for Change (Apr., 1987). 462

Olivia Records Is Founded (1973) 249

Olympic Games, Transsexual Athletes Allowed to Compete in (May 17, 2004) 728

ONE, Inc., Is Founded (1952) 114

ONE Magazine Begins Publication (1953). 124

Oregon, Lesbian Couple Murdered in (Dec. 4, 1995). 641

Oregon and Colorado Attempt Antigay Initiatives (Nov. 3, 1992) 582

Oregon Repeals Ban on Antigay Job Discrimination (Nov. 8, 1988) 491

Organization in Argentina, Nuestro Mundo Forms as First Queer (1969) 187

Organizations Begin to Form, Antigay and Antilesbian (Mar. 5, 1974) 271

Organizations Convenes, First North American Conference of Homophile (Feb. 19-20, 1966) 160

Orientation, Canada Grants Asylum Based on Sexual (Dec. 30, 1991-Feb. 22, 1993) 555

Oscar Nominee Nigel Hawthorne, *The Advocate* Outs (1995). 634

Oscar Wilde Is Convicted of Gross Indecency (May 25, 1895). 26

Oscar Wilde Memorial Bookshop Opens as First Gay Bookstore (Fall, 1967). 180

Oscars, *Brokeback Mountain, Capote,* and *Transamerica* Receive (Mar. 5, 2006) 744

Out, Celebrity Lesbians Come (1992-2002) 565

Out as Gay, U.S. Congressman Frank Comes (May 30, 1987). 466

Out Candidate for U.S. Congress, Kameny Is First (1971) 217

Out Day Is Celebrated, First National Coming (Oct. 11, 1988) 489

Out Gay Bishop in Christian History, Robinson Becomes First (Mar. 7, 2004) 725

Out Gay Man in the U.S. Congress, Studds Is First (July 14, 1983) 407

Out Gay Minister Is Ordained, First (June 25, 1972) 236

Out Gay or Lesbian Candidate for Public Office, Sarria Is First (1961) 149

Out Lesbian or Gay Person to Win State-Level Election, Noble Is First (Nov. 5, 1974). 277

Out to Parents Is Published, First Novel About
  Coming (1975) 283
Outs Oscar Nominee Nigel Hawthorne, *The
  Advocate* (1995) 634
Outs Pentagon Spokesman Pete Williams, *The
  Advocate* (Aug. 27, 1991) 547

Pacific Lesbian Network Is Founded, Asian
  (1987). 448
Padlock Law Censors Risque Theater, Wales
  (Feb., 1927) 74
Palimony Suits Emerge, Gay and Lesbian
  (1981). 365
Pandora's Box Opens (1929) 81
Parents, Families, and Friends of Lesbians and
  Gays Is Founded (1981) 367
Parents Is Published, First Novel About Coming
  Out to (1975) 283
Paris Is Founded, Act Up (1989). 496
Paris Salon, Barney Opens Her (Oct., 1909) 58
Partners of City Employees, Berkeley Extends
  Benefits to Domestic (Dec. 4, 1984) 422
Partnerships, United Kingdom Legalizes Same-
  Gender Civil (Nov. 18, 2004) 731
Paula Gunn Allen Publishes *The Sacred Hoop*
  (1986). 435
Pentagon Spokesman Pete Williams, *The Advocate*
  Outs (Aug. 27, 1991) 547
Periodical, *Vice Versa* Is Published as First
  Lesbian (June, 1947-Feb., 1948) 101
Persecute Homosexuals, Nazis (1933-1945) 86
Perversion" in Films, Hollywood Bans "Sexual
  (1930's-1960's) 84
Perverts," U.S. Navy Launches Sting Operation
  Against "Sexual (Mar. 15, 1919-1921) 63
Philippines, *Macho Dancer* Is Released in the
  (1988). 474
Photographs Are Indecent, Helms Claims
  (1989-1990). 500
Police Harassment at Compton's Cafeteria in
  San Francisco, Queer Youth Fight
  (Aug., 1966) 163
Police Raid Gay Bathhouses, Toronto
  (Feb. 5, 1981). 376
Police Raid Offices of *The Body Politic*,
  Toronto (Dec. 31, 1977) 318
Political Coalition, NACHO Formally Becomes
  the First Gay (Aug. 11-18, 1968) 182
Politicians Moscone and Milk, White Murders
  (Nov. 27, 1978) 337

Postal Workers Secure Union Protections,
  Canadian Gay (June 2, 1980). 360
Posttranssexual Manifesto," Stone Publishes
  "The (1991). 540
Prange Withholds Survivor Rights from
  Transsexual Spouses, *Littleton v.*
  (Oct. 27, 1999). 662
President Clinton Signs Defense of Marriage
  Act, U.S. (Sept. 21, 1996) 646
President Eisenhower Prohibits Federal
  Employment of Lesbians and Gays, U.S.
  (Apr. 27, 1953) 129
Presidential AIDS Commission, Report of the
  (June 27, 1988) 485
Press Is Founded, Naiad (1973) 244
Privacy Rights, *Roe v. Wade* Legalizes Abortion
  and Extends (Jan. 22, 1973) 252
Private Consensual Sex, The *Wolfenden Report*
  Calls for Decriminalizing (Sept. 4, 1957) . . . 142
Protest, Transgender Nation Holds Its First
  (1992). 562
Protests in India, Screening of *Fire* Ignites Violent
  (Dec. 3, 1998-Feb. 25, 1999) 660
Psychiatric Association Removes Homosexuality
  from List of Mental Disorders, Chinese
  (Apr. 20, 2001) 679
Public Office, Sarria Is First Out Gay or Lesbian
  Candidate for (1961) 149
Publication, *Lambda Rising Book Report*
  Begins (May, 1987). 464
Publication, *Lesbian Connection* Begins
  (Oct., 1974). 275
Publication, *Los Angeles Advocate* Begins
  Publication (1967) 167
Publication, *ONE* Magazine Begins (1953) 124
Publication, South Asian Newsletter *Trikone*
  Begins (Jan., 1986) 438
Publication, *The Body Politic* Begins
  (Nov., 1971) 226
Published, *Compañeras: Latina Lesbians* Is
  (1987). 450
Published, Lorde's Autobiography *Zami* Is
  (1982). 392
Published, Novel About Coming Out to Parents
  Is First (1975). 283
Published, *This Bridge Called My Back* Is
  (1981). 370
Published as First Journal on Homosexuality,
  Der Eigene Is (1896). 29

Published as First Lesbian Periodical, *Vice Versa* Is (June, 1947-Feb., 1948) 101
Publishes *And the Band Played On*, Shilts (1987) 453
Publishes *Borderlands/La Frontera*, Anzaldúa (1987) 446
Publishes *City of Night*, Rechy (1963) 151
Publishes First Lesbian and Gay History Anthology, Katz (1976) 300
Publishes *Goodbye to Berlin*, Isherwood (1939) 92
Publishes Its First Issue, *Lesbian Tide* (1971) 219
Publishes *Leaves of Grass*, Whitman (July 4, 1855) 3
Publishes *Lesbian Images*, Rule (1975) 287
Publishes *Rubyfruit Jungle*, Brown (1973) 241
Publishes *Sex Variant Women in Literature*, Foster (1956) 138
Publishes *Sexual Behavior in the Human Female*, Kinsey (1953) 121
Publishes *Sexual Behavior in the Human Male*, Kinsey (1948) 103
Publishes *Sexual Inversion*, Ellis (1897) 33
Publishes *Surpassing the Love of Men*, Faderman (1981) 362
Publishes *The Intermediate Sex*, Carpenter (1908) 55
Publishes "The Posttranssexual Manifesto," Stone (1991) 540
Publishes *The Sacred Hoop*, Paula Gunn Allen (1986) 435
Publishes the Signed Edition of *Corydon*, Gide (1924) 69
Publishes *The Well of Loneliness*, Hall (1928) . . . 76
Publishes *Transgender Liberation*, Feinberg (June, 1992) 573
Publishes *Uranisme et Unisexualité*, Raffalovich (1896) 31
Publishing Gay and Lesbian Books, Alyson Begins (1980) 351

Q.E.D., Stein Writes (1903) 43
Quarantine Initiative, Californians Reject LaRouche's (Nov., 1986) 442
Quebec Includes Lesbians and Gays in Its Charter of Human Rights and Freedoms (Dec. 19, 1977) 315
Queer Nation Is Founded (Mar. 20, 1990) 524

Queer Organization in Argentina, Nuestro Mundo Forms as First (1969) 187
Queer Youth Fight Police Harassment at Compton's Cafeteria in San Francisco (Aug., 1966) 163

Radical AIDS Activist Group ACT UP Is Founded (Mar., 1987) 458
Radicalesbians Issues "The Woman Identified Woman" Manifesto (May 1, 1970) 206
Raffalovich Publishes *Uranisme et Unisexualité* (1896) 31
Raid Gay Bathhouses, Toronto Police (Feb. 5, 1981) 376
Raid Offices of *The Body Politic*, Toronto Police (Dec. 31, 1977) 318
Rallies Are Held in New York City, Stonewall 25 March and (June, 1994) 627
Raped and Murdered, Transgender Man Brandon Teena (Dec. 24, 1993-Dec. 31, 1993) 615
Ratification, Equal Rights Amendment Fails State (Mar. 22, 1972-June 30, 1982) 233
Reassignment Surgery, First Gender Identity Clinic Opens and Provides Gender (Nov. 21, 1966) 165
Rebellion Ignites Modern Gay and Lesbian Rights Movement, Stonewall (June 27-July 2, 1969) 192
Rechy Publishes *City of Night* (1963) 151
Records Is Founded, Olivia (1973) 249
Recreation and Information Center Opens, Lavender Youth (May, 1988) 482
Remembrance and Remembering Our Dead Project, Transgender Day of (Nov. 20, 2003) 722
Report of the Presidential AIDS Commission (June 27, 1988) 485
Reporter Covers Spanish-American War Revolts, Transgender (c. 1899) 39
Reports of Rare Diseases Mark Beginning of AIDS Epidemic (June 5 and July 3, 1981) . . . 378
Reservist Ben-Shalom Sues for Reinstatement, Army (1976-1990) 302
Retreat for Lesbian and Gay Muslims Is Held, First International (Oct. 9-12, 1998) 657
Revisionist Criticism Recasts Sor Juana Inés de la Cruz (1991) 537
Revolution, Robles Fights in the Mexican (1912-1924) 61

Revolutionary Cuba Imprisons Gays
 (Nov., 1965) 157
Rights, Anita Bryant Campaigns Against Gay
 and Lesbian (1977) 307
Rights, First March on Washington for Lesbian
 and Gay (Oct. 12-15, 1979) 344
Rights, Gerber Founds the Society for Human
 (Dec. 10, 1924). 72
Rights, Karl Heinrich Ulrichs Speaks Publicly
 for Gay and Lesbian (Aug. 29, 1867) 9
Rights, *Roe v. Wade* Legalizes Abortion and
 Extends Privacy (Jan. 22, 1973) 252
Rights, Second March on Washington for
 Lesbian and Gay (Oct. 11, 1987) 469
Rights Act, New Mexico Amends Its Human
 (Mar. 21, 2003) 702
Rights Added to New York City Law,
 Transgender (Apr. 30, 2002) 687
Rights Amendment Fails State Ratification,
 Equal (Mar. 22, 1972-June 30, 1982) 233
Rights and Liberation, March on Washington for
 Gay, Lesbian, and Bi Equal (Apr. 25, 1993) . . 601
Rights Campaign Fund Is Founded, Human
 (Apr. 22, 1980) 355
Rights Commission Is Founded, International
 Gay and Lesbian Human (1990) 517
Rights Council Recommends Lesbian and Gay
 Rights, Japanese Human (May 25, 2001) . . . 681
Rights from Transsexual Spouses, *Littleton v.
 Prange* Withholds Survivor
 (Oct. 27, 1999) 662
Rights in Mexico City, Gays and Lesbians March
 for Equal (June 19, 2002). 690
Rights Is First Circulated, International Bill of
 Gender (June 17, 1995). 639
Rights Law, Wisconsin Enacts First Statewide
 Gay and Lesbian Civil (Feb. 25, 1982) 397
Rights Movement, Stonewall Rebellion Ignites
 Modern Gay and Lesbian (June 27-
 July 2, 1969) 192
Rights to Gay and Lesbian State Workers,
 Massachusetts Grants Family
 (Sept. 23, 1992). 576
River Collective Issues "A Black Feminist
 Statement," Combahee (Apr., 1977) 309
Rivera Law Project Is Founded, Sylvia
 (2002). 686
Robinson Becomes First Out Gay Bishop in
 Christian History (Mar. 7, 2004) 725

Robles Fights in the Mexican Revolution
 (1912-1924) 61
Roe v. Wade Legalizes Abortion and Extends
 Privacy Rights (Jan. 22, 1973) 252
Roman Catholic Church Bans Gay Seminarians
 (Nov. 29, 2005). 738
Rubyfruit Jungle, Brown Publishes (1973). 241
Rule Publishes *Lesbian Images* (1975). 287
Rustin Organizes the March on Washington
 (July 2-Aug. 28, 1963) 154

Sacred Hoop, Paula Gunn Allen Publishes *The*
 (1986). 435
St. Patrick's Cathedral, ACT UP Protests at
 (Dec. 10, 1989) 514
Salon, Barney Opens Her Paris (Oct., 1909) 58
Same-Gender Civil Partnerships, United
 Kingdom Legalizes (Nov. 18, 2004) 731
Same-Gender Civil Unions, *Baker v. Vermont*
 Leads to Recognition of (Dec. 20, 1999). . . . 666
Same-Gender Civil Unions, Buenos Aires
 Recognizes (Apr., 2003) 705
Same-Gender Marriage, Canada Legalizes
 (June 17, 2003, and July 19, 2005). 707
Same-Gender Marriage, Japanese American
 Citizens League Supports (Aug. 6, 1994) . . . 629
Same-Gender Marriage, Massachusetts Court
 Rules for (Nov. 18, 2003) 717
Same-Gender Marriage, Spain Legalizes
 (June 30, 2005) 736
Same-Gender Marriages, Hawaii Opens Door to
 (1993-1996). 593
San Francisco, First Gay Games Are Held in
 (Aug. 28, 1982) 405
San Francisco, Queer Youth Fight Police
 Harassment at Compton's Cafeteria in
 (Aug., 1966) 163
San Francisco Closes Gay Bathhouses and
 Other Businesses (Oct. 9, 1984) 417
San Francisco Gay Men's Chorus Concert Tour
 (June 6-June 20, 1981) 380
Sarria Is First Out Gay or Lesbian Candidate
 for Public Office (1961) 149
Scholarship Proliferates, Transgender (1998) . . . 650
Scientific-Humanitarian Committee,
 Friedlaender Breaks with the (1906). 49
Scientific-Humanitarian Committee, Hirschfeld
 Founds the (May 14, 1897) 36
Screening of *Fire* Ignites Violent Protests in
 India (Dec. 3, 1998-Feb. 25, 1999). 660

Keyword List of Contents

Second March on Washington for Lesbian and Gay Rights (Oct. 11, 1987) 469

Seminarians, Roman Catholic Church Bans Gay (Nov. 29, 2005) 738

Senate, Jiménez Flores Elected to the Mexican (Jan., 2006) 741

Seneca Falls Women's Rights Convention (July 19-20, 1848) 1

Sex, American Bar Association Calls for Repeal of Laws Against Consensual (Aug., 1973) 258

Sex, Illinois Legalizes Consensual Homosexual (1961) 147

Sex, The *Wolfenden Report* Calls for Decriminalizing Private Consensual (Sept. 4, 1957) 142

Sex, United Kingdom Decriminalizes Homosexual (July 27, 1967) 178

Sex Practices Between Consenting Adults, Canada Decriminalizes (Jan. 1, 1988) 477

Sex Study Prompts Conservative Backlash, Battelle (Mar.-Apr., 1993) 596

Sex Variant Women in Literature, Foster Publishes (1956) 138

Sexual Behavior in the Human Female, Kinsey Publishes (1953) 121

Sexual Behavior in the Human Male, Kinsey Publishes (1948) 103

Sexual Inversion, Ellis Publishes (1897) 33

Sexual Inversion, Westphal Advocates Medical Treatment for (1869) 16

Sexual Offences Act Becomes Law, United Kingdom's (Jan. 1, 1957) 140

Sexual Orientation, Canada Grants Asylum Based on (Dec. 30, 1991-Feb. 22, 1993) 555

"Sexual Perversion" in Films, Hollywood Bans (1930's-1960's) 84

"Sexual Perverts," U.S. Navy Launches Sting Operation Against (Mar. 15, 1919-1921) 63

Sexuality as Common and Normal, Davis's Research Identifies Lesbian (1929) 79

Shepard Is Beaten and Murdered, Gay College Student (Oct. 6-7, 1998) 654

Shilts Publishes *And the Band Played On* (1987) 453

"Sickness," Evelyn Hooker Debunks Beliefs That Homosexuality Is a (1953-1957) 126

Singapore Lifts Ban on Hiring Lesbian and Gay Employees (July, 2003) 713

Society for Human Rights, Gerber Founds the (Dec. 10, 1924) 72

Sodomy Charges Against Lesbians, *Thompson v. Aldredge* Dismisses (Jan. 12, 1939) 95

Sodomy Law, Indians Struggle to Abolish (1992-2006) 568

Sodomy Law, U.S. Supreme Court Overturns Texas (June 26, 2003) 710

Sodomy Laws, *Bowers v. Hardwick* Upholds State (1986) 432

Soldier, *Watkins v. United States Army* Reinstates Gay (May 3, 1989) 510

Sor Juana Inés de la Cruz, Revisionist Criticism Recasts (1991) 537

South, Jordan Becomes First Black Congresswoman from the (Nov. 7, 1972) . . . 239

South Asian Newsletter *Trikone* Begins Publication (Jan., 1986) 438

Spain Legalizes Same-Gender Marriage (June 30, 2005) 736

Spanish-American War Revolts, Transgender Reporter Covers (c. 1899) 39

Spouses, *Littleton v. Prange* Withholds Survivor Rights from Transsexual (Oct. 27, 1999) 662

State-Level Election, Noble Is First Out Lesbian or Gay Person to Win (Nov. 5, 1974) 277

State Ratification, Equal Rights Amendment Fails (Mar. 22, 1972-June 30, 1982) 233

State Sodomy Laws, *Bowers v. Hardwick* Upholds (1986) 432

State Workers, Massachusetts Grants Family Rights to Gay and Lesbian (Sept. 23, 1992) . . 576

Statewide Gay and Lesbian Civil Rights Law, Wisconsin Enacts First (Feb. 25, 1982) 397

Stein Writes *Q.E.D.* (1903) 43

Stereotyping Is Discriminatory, U.S. Supreme Court Rules Gender-Role (May 1, 1989) 508

Sting Operation Against "Sexual Perverts," U.S. Navy Launches (Mar. 15, 1919-1921) . . . 63

Stone Publishes "The Posttranssexual Manifesto" (1991) 540

Stonewall Rebellion Ignites Modern Gay and Lesbian Rights Movement (June 27-July 2, 1969) 192

Stonewall 25 March and Rallies Are Held in New York City (June, 1994) 627

Studds Is First Out Gay Man in the U.S. Congress (July 14, 1983) 407

Student Homophile League Is Formed, First (Apr. 19, 1967) 172

GLBT Events

Student Shepard Is Beaten and Murdered, Gay College (Oct. 6-7, 1998). 654
Sue the National Endowment for the Arts, Artists (1990-1993). 520
Sues University of California for Discrimination, Lesbian Academic and Activist (1982-1991). 395
Suits Emerge, Gay and Lesbian Palimony (1981). 365
Supreme Court Distinguishes Between "Indecent" and "Obscene," U.S. (July 3, 1978). 327
Supreme Court Overturns Texas Sodomy Law, U.S. (June 26, 2003) 710
Supreme Court Reverses Gay Academic's Firing, Canadian (Apr. 2, 1998) 652
Supreme Court Rules Gender-Role Stereotyping Is Discriminatory, U.S. (May 1, 1989) 508
Supreme Court Rules in "Crimes Against Nature" Case, U.S. (Nov. 17, 1975) 297
Supreme Court Supports Local Obscenity Laws, U.S. (June 21, 1973) 255
Supreme Court Upholds Law Preventing Immigration of Gays and Lesbians, U.S. (May 22, 1967) 176
Surgery, First Gender Identity Clinic Opens and Provides Gender Reassignment (Nov. 21, 1966). 165
Surpassing the Love of Men, Faderman Publishes (1981). 362
Survivor Rights from Transsexual Spouses, *Littleton v. Prange* Withholds (Oct. 27, 1999) 662
Sylvia Rivera Law Project Is Founded (2002) . . . 686
Synagogue in the United States Is Formed, First Gay and Lesbian (Mar., 1972- Mar., 1973) 230

Taiwanese Gay-Themed Film, *The Wedding Banquet* Is First Acclaimed (1993). 591
Task Force, Vaid Becomes Executive Director of the National Gay and Lesbian (1989) . . . 498
Task Force Is Formed, National Gay (1973) . . . 246
Teen Gwen Araujo Is Murdered in California, Transgender (Oct. 4, 2002) 694
Teena Raped and Murdered, Transgender Man Brandon (Dec. 24, 1993-Dec. 31, 1993) 615
Television Network Is Launched in Canada, First Gay and Lesbian (Sept. 7, 2001) 683

Television Series Airs, First Gay British (1979-1981). 342
Tennis, Navratilova Honored for Her Career in (1994) 623
Texas Sodomy Law, U.S. Supreme Court Overturns (June 26, 2003) 710
Theater, Wales Padlock Law Censors Risque (Feb., 1927) 74
Third-Sex Theory, Freud Rejects (1905) 46
Third World Lesbian and Gay Conference Convenes, First National (Oct. 12-15, 1979) 347
This Bridge Called My Back Is Published (1981). 370
Thompson v. Aldredge Dismisses Sodomy Charges Against Lesbians (Jan. 12, 1939). . . . 95
Time Magazine Issues "The Homosexual in America" (Oct. 31, 1969). 201
Tipton, Death of Transgender Jazz Musician Billy (Jan. 21, 1989) 505
Toronto Police Raid Gay Bathhouses (Feb. 5, 1981). 376
Toronto Police Raid Offices of *The Body Politic* (Dec. 31, 1977). 318
Transamerica Receive Oscars, *Brokeback Mountain, Capote,* and (Mar. 5, 2006) 744
Transgender Day of Remembrance and Remembering Our Dead Project (Nov. 20, 2003). 722
Transgender Jazz Musician Billy Tipton, Death of (Jan. 21, 1989) 505
Transgender Liberation, Feinberg Publishes (June, 1992). 573
Transgender Man, Hart Recognized as a (1996). 644
Transgender Man Brandon Teena Raped and Murdered (Dec. 24, 1993-Dec. 31, 1993) . . . 615
Transgender Nation Holds Its First Protest (1992). 562
Transgender Portrayals in Film, Hollywood Awards (Mar. 21, 2000) 672
Transgender Reporter Covers Spanish-American War Revolts (c. 1899) 39
Transgender Rights Added to New York City Law (Apr. 30, 2002) 687
Transgender Scholarship Proliferates (1998) . . . 650
Transgender Teen Gwen Araujo Is Murdered in California (Oct. 4, 2002) 694
Transsexual Athletes Allowed to Compete in Olympic Games (May 17, 2004) 728

Keyword List of Contents

Transsexual Marriage, Australian Court
  Validates (Feb. 21, 2003). 698
Transsexual Marriage, United Kingdom's
  Gender Recognition Act Legalizes
  (Apr. 4, 2005). 734
Transsexual Spouses, *Littleton v. Prange*
  Withholds Survivor Rights from
  (Oct. 27, 1999). 662
Transsexuals Protest Academic Exploitation
  (Mar., 2003-Dec., 2004) 700
Treatment for Sexual Inversion, Westphal
  Advocates Medical (1869). 16
Trikone Begins Publication, South Asian
  Newsletter (Jan., 1986). 438
Two-Spirit American Indian Visits Washington,
  D.C. (Jan.-June, 1886). 21

Ulrichs Speaks Publicly for Gay and Lesbian
  Rights, Karl Heinrich (Aug. 29, 1867) 9
U.N. Revokes Consultative Status of International
  Lesbian and Gay Association
  (Sept. 16, 1994). 632
Union Protections, Canadian Gay Postal Workers
  Secure (June 2, 1980). 360
Unions, *Baker v. Vermont* Leads to Recognition
  of Same-Gender Civil (Dec. 20, 1999). 666
Unions, Buenos Aires Recognizes Same-Gender
  Civil (Apr., 2003). 705
United Kingdom Criminalizes "Gross Indecency"
  (1885) 18
United Kingdom Decriminalizes Homosexual
  Sex (July 27, 1967). 178
United Kingdom Legalizes Same-Gender Civil
  Partnerships (Nov. 18, 2004). 731
United Kingdom Lifts Ban on Gays and Lesbians
  in the Military (Jan. 12, 2000) 669
United Kingdom's Gender Recognition Act
  Legalizes Transsexual Marriage
  (Apr. 4, 2005). 734
United Kingdom's Sexual Offences Act Becomes
  Law (Jan. 1, 1957) 140
United Lesbians of African Heritage Is Founded
  (1990). 519
United States, Daughters of Bilitis Founded as
  First National Lesbian Group in (1955) 132
United States, First Lesbian and Gay Pride
  March in the (June 28, 1970). 212
United States Army Reinstates Gay Soldier,
  Watkins v. (May 3, 1989). 510

United States Is Formed, First Gay and Lesbian
  Synagogue in the (Mar., 1972-Mar., 1973). . . 230
University of California for Discrimination,
  Lesbian Academic and Activist Sues
  (1982-1991). 395
Uranisme et Unisexualité, Raffalovich Publishes
  (1896) 31
U.S. Civil Service Commission Prohibits
  Discrimination Against Federal Employees
  (July 3, 1975). 292
U.S. Congress, Employment Non-Discrimination
  Act Is Proposed to (1994) 618
U.S. Congress, Kameny Is First Out Candidate for
  (1971). 217
U.S. Congress, Studds Is First Out Gay Man in
  the (July 14, 1983) 407
U.S. Congressman Frank Comes Out as Gay
  (May 30, 1987). 466
U.S. Law Prohibits Gay and Lesbian Immigration
  (1952-1990). 117
U.S. Navy Investigates the USS *Norton Sound* in
  Antilesbian Witch Hunt (May-Aug., 1980) . . . 357
U.S. Navy Launches Sting Operation Against
  "Sexual Perverts" (Mar. 15, 1919-1921) 63
U.S. President Clinton Signs Defense of
  Marriage Act (Sept. 21, 1996) 646
U.S. President Eisenhower Prohibits Federal
  Employment of Lesbians and Gays
  (Apr. 27, 1953). 129
U.S. Supreme Court Distinguishes Between
  "Indecent" and "Obscene" (July 3, 1978) . . . 327
U.S. Supreme Court Overturns Texas Sodomy
  Law (June 26, 2003) 710
U.S. Supreme Court Rules Gender-Role
  Stereotyping Is Discriminatory
  (May 1, 1989). 508
U.S. Supreme Court Rules in "Crimes Against
  Nature" Case (Nov. 17, 1975) 297
U.S. Supreme Court Supports Local Obscenity
  Laws (June 21, 1973). 255
U.S. Supreme Court Upholds Law Preventing
  Immigration of Gays and Lesbians
  (May 22, 1967) 176
USS *Norton Sound* in Antilesbian Witch Hunt,
  U.S. Navy Investigates the
  (May-Aug., 1980) 357

Vaid Becomes Executive Director of the National
  Gay and Lesbian Task Force (1989) 498

GLBT EVENTS

Vermont Leads to Recognition of Same-Gender Civil Unions, *Baker v.* (Dec. 20, 1999) 666
Veterans, *Coming Out Under Fire* Documents Gay and Lesbian Military (1990, 1994) 522
Vice Versa Is Published as First Lesbian Periodical (June, 1947-Feb., 1948) 101
Violet Quill, Gay Writers Form the (1980-1981) 353
Virus Is Discovered, AIDS (Spring, 1984) 413
VIVA Is Founded to Promote Latina and Latino Artists (1987) 455

Wales Padlock Law Censors Risque Theater (Feb., 1927) 74
Walker Is Awarded the Medal of Honor, Mary Edwards (Nov. 11, 1865) 7
Wal-Mart Adds Lesbians and Gays to Its Antidiscrimination Policy (July, 2003) 715
War Revolts, Transgender Reporter Covers (c. 1899) 39
Washington, Rustin Organizes the March on (July 2-Aug. 28, 1963) 154
Washington, D.C., First Dyke March Is Held in (Apr. 24, 1993) 598
Washington, D.C., Two-Spirit American Indian Visits (Jan.-June, 1886) 21
Washington for Gay, Lesbian, and Bi Equal Rights and Liberation, March on (Apr. 25, 1993) 601
Washington for Lesbian and Gay Rights, First March on (Oct. 12-15, 1979) 344
Washington for Lesbian and Gay Rights, Second March on (Oct. 11, 1987) 469
Watkins v. United States Army Reinstates Gay Soldier (May 3, 1989) 510
Wedding Banquet Is First Acclaimed Taiwanese Gay-Themed Film, *The* (1993) 591
Well of Loneliness, Hall Publishes *The* (1928) . . . 76
West Hollywood Incorporates with Majority Gay and Lesbian City Council (Nov. 6, 1984) . . . 419
Westphal Advocates Medical Treatment for Sexual Inversion (1869) 16
White Murders Politicians Moscone and Milk (Nov. 27, 1978) 337
Whitman Publishes *Leaves of Grass* (July 4, 1855) 3
Wilde Is Convicted of Gross Indecency, Oscar (May 25, 1895) 26

Wilde Memorial Bookshop Opens as First Gay Bookstore, Oscar (Fall, 1967) 180
Williams, *The Advocate* Outs Pentagon Spokesman Pete (Aug. 27, 1991) 547
Wilson Vetoes Antidiscrimination Bill, California Governor (Sept. 29, 1991) 550
Wisconsin Enacts First Statewide Gay and Lesbian Civil Rights Law (Feb. 25, 1982) . . . 397
Wolfenden Report Calls for Decriminalizing Private Consensual Sex, The (Sept. 4, 1957) 142
Woman Identified Woman" Manifesto, Radicalesbians Issues "The (May 1, 1970) . . . 206
Women of Color Press Is Founded, Kitchen Table: (Oct., 1981) 383
Women's Choir Is Formed, Anna Crusis (Sept., 1975) 295
Women's Conference Convenes, National (Nov. 18-21, 1977) 311
Women's Movement, Lavender Menace Protests Homophobia in (May 1, 1970) 209
Women's Rights Convention, Seneca Falls (July 19-20, 1848) 1
Womyn's Music Festival Holds Its First Gathering, Michigan (Aug. 20-22, 1976) 304
Workers, Massachusetts Grants Family Rights to Gay and Lesbian State (Sept. 23, 1992) . . . 576
Workplace Movement Is Founded, Lesbian and Gay (1978) 323
World AIDS Day, First (Dec. 1, 1988) 494
Writers Form the Violet Quill, Gay (1980-1981) 353
Writes *Q.E.D.*, Stein (1903) 43

YMCA Extends Family Discounts to Gays and Lesbians, Canadian (1992) 559
Youth Fight Police Harassment at Compton's Cafeteria in San Francisco, Queer (Aug., 1966) 163
Youth Protection Institute Is Founded, Lesbian and Gay (1982) 387
Youth Recreation and Information Center Opens, Lavender (May, 1988) 482

Zami Is Published, Lorde's Autobiography (1982) 392

List of Sidebars

Achtenberg, Senate Hearings on the Nomination of Roberta (*primary source*) 605
Act to Amend the Canadian Human Rights Act, An (*primary source*) 361
AIDS Epidemic, Reagan on the (*primary source*) 486
AIDS Memorial Quilt (*sidebar*) 471
Al-Fatiha Mission Statement (*sidebar*) 658
American Airlines, Statement of Equal Opportunity (*sidebar*) 324
American Women, Declaration of (1977) (*primary source*) 313
Americans with Disabilities Act (*primary source*) 531
Andrew Johnson's Presentation Speech (*primary source*) 8
Anti-Harassment Policy for Schools, Model (*primary source*) 389
Araujo's Mother: "Life After Gwen" (*primary source*) 696
Archives, Lesbian Herstory: Statement of Principles (*sidebar*) 261
Arenas, Reinaldo (*biographical sidebar*) 158
"Armed Forces, Homosexuality and the" (*primary source*) 670
Asch, Sholem (*biographical sidebar*) 68
Asian Lesbian and Gay Coalition Statement (*primary source*) 543

Baehr v. Lewin (*primary source*) 594
Baker v. Vermont (*primary source*) 668
Barney, Natalie Clifford (*biographical sidebar*) 59
Battelle Study, The (*primary source*) 597
Bérubé, Allan (*biographical sidebar*) 523
Bill of Gender Rights, International (*primary source*) 640
Bill of Rights for Lesbian, Gay, Bisexual, and Transgender Students (*primary source*) 388
"Black Feminist Statement, A" (*primary source*) 310
Bottoms v. Bottoms (*primary source*) 609
Bowers v. Hardwick (*primary source*) 433
Boy Scouts of America v. Dale (*primary source*) 677
Breaking the Surface (*primary source*) 638

Briggs Initiative (*primary source*) 334
Brocka, Lino (*filmography*) 475
Brooks, Louise (*biographical sidebar*) 82
"But I Am Not a Housewife" (*primary source*) 136

California Supreme Court Rules on Spousal Benefits for Lesbian Couple (*sidebar*) 560
Canadian Criminal Code, Section 159 (*primary source*) 478
Canadian Human Rights Act, An Act to Amend the (*primary source*) 361
Child, U.N. Convention on the Rights of (1990) (*primary source*) 633
"Christ, We Are One Body In" (*primary source*) 237
Church, In Conversation with the (*primary source*) 145
City and the Pillar, The (*primary source*) 97
Civil Marriage Act, Canadian (*primary source*) 708
Civil Partnership Act (*primary source*) 731
Clinton's Order Against Discrimination in Federal Government Employment (1998) (*primary source*) 619
Community Centers, National Association of Lesbian and Gay, Mission Statement (*sidebar*) 621
Composing Women (*primary source*) 296
Conduct-Based Policy for Gays and Lesbians in the Military, A (*primary source*) 613
Convention on the Rights of the Child, United Nations (1990) (*primary source*) 633
Conversation with the Church, In (*primary source*) 145
Criminal Code, Canadian, Section 159 (*primary source*) 478
Criminal Law Amendment Act (1885) (*primary source*) 19
Cruz, Sor Juana Inés de la (*biographical sidebar*) 538

Declaration of American Women (1977) (*primary source*) 313
Defense of Marriage Act (*primary source*) 647

Defrocking of Elizabeth Stroud, The
    (*sidebar*)................. 727
Democratic National Convention, Jordan's
    Keynote Speech Before the 1976
    (*primary source*)............. 240
*Diagnostic and Statistical Manual of Mental
    Disorders* (*primary source*).......... 112
DignityUSA: Statement of Position and Purpose
    (*sidebar*)................. 190
Disabilities Act, Americans with (*primary
    source*).................. 531
Discrimination, Order Against, Commonwealth
    of Massachusetts (*primary source*)...... 577
Discrimination in Federal Government
    Employment, Clinton's Order Against (1998)
    (*primary source*)............. 619
Douglas v. Canada (*primary source*)....... 580

Elizabeth Stroud, The Defrocking of (*sidebar*).. 727
Employment, Clinton's Order Against
    Discrimination in Federal Government (1998)
    (*primary source*)............. 619
Employment, "Notoriously Disgraceful Conduct"
    and Government (*primary source*)....... 130
Equal Rights Amendment, Fifteen States That
    Failed to Ratify the (*table*).......... 233

Faderman, Lillian (*biographical sidebar*)..... 363
Federation of Gay Games, Concept and Purpose
    (*sidebar*)................. 406
Fourteen U.S. States with Laws Against Sodomy
    Prior to the 2003 *Lawrence v. Texas* Ruling
    (*table*).................. 710
Friedan on the Lesbian-Rights Resolution
    (*primary source*)............. 314

Gay Games, Federation of, Concept and Purpose
    (*sidebar*)................. 406
"Gay Manifesto, A" (*primary source*)....... 196
Gays and Lesbians in the Military, A Conduct-
    Based Policy for (*primary source*)....... 613
"Gays and Lesbians in the Military, Clinton's
    Remarks Announcing the New Policy on,"
    (*primary source*)............. 614
Gays and the Priesthood, Roman Catholic
    Church: Instruction On 739
"Gender Identity Disorder," as Defined in the
    *Diagnostic and Statistical Manual of Mental
    Disorders-IV* (*primary source*)........ 563

Gender Identity Disorders, Standards of Care for
    (2001) (*primary source*)........... 321
Gender Recognition Act (*primary source*).... 735
Gender Rights, Bill of, International (*primary
    source*).................. 640
German Criminal Code, Paragraph 175 (1871)
    (*primary source*)............. 36
German Criminal Code, Paragraph 175 (1935)
    (*primary source*)............. 88
Gide, André (*biographical sidebar*)........ 70
GLAAD, Select Milestones (*sidebar*)....... 425
Goodridge v. Department of Public Health
    (*primary source*)............. 718
Government Employment, "Notoriously
    Disgraceful Conduct" and (*primary source*).. 130
Guardianship of Sharon Kowalski, Ward, In re
    (*primary source*)............. 553
"Güera, La": An Excerpt from *This Bridge Called
    My Back* (*primary source*).......... 372
Guiding Principles of the Transgender Day of
    Remembrance (*sidebar*)........... 723

Hawthorne "Acting Out" (*sidebar*)........ 635
History of the Pride Institute (*sidebar*)...... 279
"Homosexuality and the Armed Forces"
    (*primary source*)............. 670
"Homosexuality as a Clinical Entity Does Not
    Exist" (*primary source*)........... 127
"How It All Began" (*primary source*)...... 371
Human Rights, Society for, Charter (1924)
    (*primary source*)............. 73
Human Rights Act: An Amendment, New
    Mexico's (*primary source*).......... 703
Human Rights and Freedoms, Quebec Charter of
    (*primary source*)............. 316
Hwang, David Henry (*biographical sidebar*)... 481

"I Am Someway the Lesbian Woman"
    (*primary source*)............. 139
"I Sing the Body Electric" (*primary
    source*).................. 4
Immigration and Nationality Act, McCarran-
    Walter (1952) (*primary source*)........ 119
In re Guardianship of Sharon Kowalski, Ward
    (*primary source*)............. 553
Indian Penal Code (1860) (*primary source*)... 569
Instruction on Gays and the Priesthood, Roman
    Catholic Church (*primary source*)....... 739
Intermediate Sex, The (*primary
    source*).................. 56

LIST OF SIDEBARS

International Bill of Gender Rights (*primary source*) 640
International Lesbian and Gay Association, Aims and Objectives (*sidebar*) 331
Introduction to *Sexual Inversion*, An (*primary source*) 33
IOC Statement on Sex Reassignment in Sports (*primary source*) 729
Isherwood, Christopher (*biographical sidebar*) ... 93

Japanese American Citizens League (*sidebar*) ... 630
Jordan's Keynote Speech Before the 1976 Democratic National Convention (*primary source*) 240

Kinsey, Alfred (*biographical sidebar*) 104
Kowalski, Ward, In re Guardianship (*primary source*) 553
Kramer, Larry (*biographical sidebar*) 460

Lavender Youth Recreation and Information Center, Mission and Vision Statement (*sidebar*) 483
Lawrence v. Texas (*primary source*) 711
Lesbian and Gay Association, International, Aims and Objectives (*sidebar*) 331
Lesbian and Gay Coalition Statement, Asian (*primary source*) 543
Lesbian and Gay Community Centers, National Association of, Mission Statement (*sidebar*) 621
Lesbian Couple, California Supreme Court Rules on Spousal Benefits for (*sidebar*) 560
Lesbian, Gay, Bisexual, and Transgender Students, Bill of Rights for (1990) (*primary source*) 388
Lesbian Herstory Archives: Statement of Principles (*sidebar*) 261
"Lesbian Is the Rage of All Women, A" (*primary source*) 210
Lesbian Rights Resolution, Friedan on the (*primary source*) 314
"Lesbian Woman, I Am Someway the" (*primary source*) 139
LeVay, Simon (*biographical sidebar*) 536
Louganis: "What If I'm Bleeding?" (*primary source*) 638
"Love Between Women" (*primary source*) 288

McCarran-Walter Immigration and Nationality Act (1952) (*primary source*) 119

March, Remembering the, Twenty-Five Years Later (*sidebar*) 345
March on Washington, Vaid Speaks at the 1993 (*primary source*) 499
Marriage Act, Civil, Canadian (*primary source*) 708
Marriage Act, Defense of (*primary source*) 647
Massachusetts, Commonwealth of, Order Against Discrimination (*primary source*) 577
Measure 8, Ballot Question and Explanation, Oregon (*primary source*) 492
Mehta, Deepa (*biographical sidebar*) 661
Metropolitan Community Church, Statement of Faith (*sidebar*) 185
Military, A Conduct-Based Policy for Gays and Lesbians in the (*primary source*) 613
Mitchell Murder Case, The Psychology of the (*primary source*) 24
Model Anti-Harassment Policy for Schools (*primary source*) 389
Motion Picture Production Code (1930) (*primary source*) 85
Murder Case, The Psychology of the Mitchell (*primary source*) 24

National Association of Lesbian and Gay Community Centers, Mission Statement (*sidebar*) 621
National Gay and Lesbian Task Force: Strategies and Directions (*sidebar*) 247
New Mexico's Human Rights Act: An Amendment (*primary source*) 703
New York City's Local Law 3 (*primary source*) 688
Nomination of Roberta Achtenberg, Senate Hearings on the (*primary source*) 605
"Notoriously Disgraceful Conduct" and Government Employement (*primary source*) 130

"On Prettiness" (*primary source*) 99
On Sexual Inversion, An Introduction to (*primary source*) 33
ONE's Articles of Incorporation (*primary source*) 115
Order Against Discrimination, Commonwealth of Massachusetts (*primary source*) 577
"Our Obligation To Love People" (*primary source*) 191

Paragraph 175 (1871) (*primary source*) 36
Paragraph 175 (1935) (*primary source*) 88
Paris Adult Theatre I v. Slaton
    (*primary source*) 256
Penal Code, Indian (1860) (*primary source*). . . . 569
Pink Triangle Press, Mission Statement
    (*sidebar*). 227
"Piss Christ," U.S. Senators Decry Serrano's
    (*primary source*) 503
Plato on Third Sex (*primary source*) 48
Pride Institute, History of the (*sidebar*) 279
Priesthood, Roman Catholic Church: Instruction
    on Gays and the (*primary source*) 739
Proposition 64 (*primary source*) 444
Psychology of the Mitchell Murder Case
    (*primary source*) 24

Quebec Charter of Human Rights and Freedoms
    (*primary source*) 316

Reagan on the AIDS Epidemic
    (*primary source*) 486
Rechy, John (*biographical sidebar*) 152
"Refugee," United Nations Definition of (1951)
    (*primary source*) 555
"Remarks Announcing the New Policy on Gays
    and Lesbians in the Military, Clinton's"
    (*primary source*) 614
Remembering the March, Twenty-Five Years
    Later (*sidebar*) 345
Rights, International Bill of Gender (*primary
    source*) 640
Roe v. Wade (*primary source*) 253
Roman Catholic Church: Instruction on Gays
    and the Priesthood (*primary source*) 739
Romer v. Evans: From the Dissenting
    Opinion (*primary source*). 584
Romer v. Evans: From the Majority
    Opinion (*primary source*). 583
Rose v. Locke (*primary source*) 298

Schools, Model Anti-Harassment Policy for
    (*primary source*) 389
Senate Hearings on the Nomination of Roberta
    Achtenberg (*primary source*) 605
Sex Reassignment in Sports, IOC Statement
    (*primary source*) 729
Sexual Inversion, What Is? (*primary source*) . . . 34
Shilts, Randy (*biographical sidebar*). 454

Signorile, Michelangelo (*biographical
    sidebar*) 548
Social Group Defined by the Canadian Supreme
    Court (*primary source*) 557
Society for Human Rights, Charter (1924)
    (*primary source*) 73
Sor Juana Inés de la Cruz (*biographical
    sidebar*) 538
Spousal Benefits for Lesbian Couple, California
    Court Rules on (*sidebar*) 560
*Standards of Care for Gender Identity
    Disorders* (*primary source*) 321
Statement to Congress, Studds's
    (*primary source*) 408
States with Laws Against Sodomy Prior to the
    2003 *Lawrence v. Texas* Ruling, U.S.
    (*table*) 710
Stein, Gertrude (*biographical sidebar*) 44
Studds's Statement to Congress, Personal
    Statement of Rep. Gerry (*primary source*) . . . 408

Third Sex, Plato on (*primary source*) 48
Transgender Day of Remembrance, Guiding
    Principles of the (*sidebar*). 723
Trikone's Mission Statement (*sidebar*) 439

U.N. Convention on the Rights of the Child
    (1990) (*primary source*) 633
United Nations Convention Definition of
    "Refugee" (1951) (*primary source*). 555
United States Army III, Watkins v.
    (*primary source*) 511
Urning Nature (*primary source*). 10
U.S. Senators Decry Serrano's "Piss Christ"
    (*primary source*) 503

Vaid Speaks at the 1993 March on Washington
    (*primary source*) 499

Watkins v. United States Army III (*primary
    source*) 511
"We Are One Body In Christ" (*primary
    source*) 237
West, Mae (*biographical sidebar*). 75
What Is Sexual Inversion? (*primary source*) 34
Wilde from Prison (*primary source*) 27

Zami (*primary source*) 393

Great Events from History

Gay, Lesbian, Bisexual, Transgender Events

1848-2006

September, 1983
FIRST NATIONAL LESBIANS OF COLOR CONFERENCE CONVENES

The First National Lesbians of Color Conference formed as a means to confront the conflicts among issues of sexuality, gender, race, ethnicity, and class in white-dominated lesbian and lesbian feminist organizations. The discussions led to the founding of several organizations for lesbians of color around the United States and more awareness within the lesbian rights movement in general about racism.

LOCALE: Malibu, California
CATEGORIES: Race and ethnicity; feminism; organizations and institutions

SUMMARY OF EVENT

Lesbians of color always have been active in social justice movements, including the movements for lesbian and women's rights. Their lives at the intersection of oppressions—racism, sexism, classism, and homophobia—has made it difficult, however, to choose sexuality and gender over race and ethnicity. Some lesbians of color have opted to form their own groups separate from white lesbian groups and cogender groups for LGBTI (lesbian, gay, bisexual, transgender, and intersex) people of color. The First National Lesbians of Color Conference held in Malibu, California, in September of 1983 came as a result of activism that began in the early 1970's.

One of the earliest known groups for lesbians of color was Salsa Soul Sisters of New York City (formed November, 1974). More than thirty years later, the group is known as African Ancestral Lesbians United for Societal Change (AALUSC). Latin American Lesbians (formed June, 1974) was a short-lived group that met in the Highland Park area of Los Angeles. In 1975 the cogender group Gay American Indians was cofounded by Barbara Cameron and others in San Francisco. In the mid-1970's a social group called Debreta's was active in Los Angeles. Debreta's organizers Deborah Johnson and her partner Bobreta Franklin were activists who also had ties to white LGBT power brokers. Debreta's became an entry point for African American lesbians who wanted to participate in an activist environment. In the 1980's, Asian Pacific Islander lesbians began forming groups such as Asian Lesbians of the East Coast and Asian/Pacific Lesbians—Los Angeles.

In 1973, at the historic West Coast Lesbian Conference, held in Los Angeles, lesbians of color from San Francisco (primarily African American) presented one of the earliest workshops on racism in the lesbian rights movement. Present at the workshop was Del Martin, who had cofounded with her long-time partner Phyllis Lyon, Daughters of Bilitis (DOB), the first lesbian group in the United States (1955). Martin acknowledged that in her travels around the United States she had found not one lesbian group that had managed to successfully deal with the racism.

While many white lesbians focused on sexism as the root oppression, lesbians of color faced a more complex obstacle: the racism of white lesbians; the sexism and racism of white gay men; and the sexism and homophobia of their own communities of color. Classism was often intertwined with racism because stereotypes often equate people of color with poverty.

In 1978, the National Lesbian Feminist Organization (NLFO) founding conference was held in Santa Monica, also in California. Few lesbians of color had been invited as delegates and major conflicts soon broke out over the lack of delegate diversity. The problem was solved by recruiting those women of color who were present as visitors or staff to be voting delegates. The conference passed a resolution stipulating that in the NLFO, women of color were to hold half of the officer positions and half of the votes on decision-making committees. The NLFO did not last long but its policy of racial and ethnic parity had some effect nationally within lesbian groups and organizations and in the planning of conferences.

Shortly after the NLFO conference, lesbians of color, some of whom had attended the conference, formed Lesbians of Color (LOC) Los Angeles. A similar group formed in San Francisco. LOC Los Angeles, made up of African Americans and Latinas mostly but also of Asians and Native Americans, met on Sundays at the Alcoholism Center for Women. The group offered workshops on racism and sponsored social events and consciousness-raising discussions. LOC members also worked in alliance with heterosexual groups and white lesbian groups on issues such as farmworker rights, apartheid in South Africa, and homophobia.

LOC Los Angeles actively participated in a major historical LGBT event—the first March on Washington for Lesbian and Gay Rights in October of 1979. Earlier that year, LGBT grassroots activists began planning a march even as mainstream LGBT groups warned that the time was not right for such an event. The grassroots activists met in Houston and voted to have lesbians of color lead the march. LGBT activists of color also began to plan the first National Third World Gay and Lesbian Conference, scheduled for Harambee House (at Howard University) before the march.

At the people of color conference, arguments arose when Native Americans and Asian Pacific Islander attendees, all of whom were fewer in number, correctly argued that their issues were being ignored. Heated debates ensued but in the end, the people of color contingent marched together. The LOC Los Angeles banner can be seen on the 1979 March on Washington's official black-and-white poster. People of color who spoke at the march and later rally included Audre Lorde and Juanita Ramos (Díaz-Cotto).

In the early 1980's, Latinas formed a support group that would gather after the general LOC meetings. In May of 1982, LOC members attended the Califia Women of Color gathering. Califia was a white women's group known for its weeklong campouts and its intense workshops against racism and classism. It was following the Califia gathering of 1982 that LOC women decided to organize the First National Lesbians of Color Conference; a camp in Malibu had been selected as the conference site. Conference participants included more than two hundred women of color. The introduction to the conference program read, in part, "This first National Conference of Lesbians of Color is dedicated to all of our sisters who are struggling for justice, dignity and the freedom to live full, productive lives of choice."

The themes of the conference workshops spanned a wide spectrum of issues, including identity, spirituality, politics, and culture. The list of workshop presenters included many women of color who were also political activists: Gloria Anzaldúa, Paula Gunn Allen, Beth Brant, Andrea Canaan, Joy Harjo, Nancy Reiko Sato, Naomi Littlebear, Kwambe OmDahda, Aleida Rodríguez, Luisah Teish, Nellie Wong, Merle Woo, and Mitsuye Yamada.

The group had argued about whether or not the conference should be a political or a cultural event. National Radical Women, a socialist group, wanted the former and criticized the planners for not emphasizing that agenda. However, many of the women did not agree with this critique. They were activists who did not want to align with what was perceived as a socialist agenda, but they did want to spend time with other women of color in a safe environment, away from racism, sexism, and homophobia. There also were intense discussions about whether or not straight women of color should be at the conference and also concerning complex issues of skin color.

At the closing gathering, Kwambe OmDahda and Rha Medeen read a statement to bring the conference participants together: "When you go home you owe it to yourself and to all the sisters at this conference to create an atmosphere that deals with the issues that rose over this past weekend.... Take responsibility to create or join groups dedicated to issues unique to us as people of color, as womyn and as lesbians." LOC continued to meet for several more years after the conference before disbanding.

SIGNIFICANCE

In general, white-dominated lesbian groups were not proactive about addressing racism in the lesbian rights movement, even after the empowering National Lesbians of Color Conference in Malibu in 1983. One exception, however, was a group of lesbian activists called White Women Against Racism (WWAR). The Los Angeles group met during the 1980's, offered antiracism workshops for white women, and wrote a column for the *Lesbian News*, a periodical still in circulation. WWAR faced derisive comments from lesbians who did not believe racism was a problem within the lesbian community.

—*Yolanda Retter*

FURTHER READING

Alaniz, Yolanda, and Nellie Wong, eds. *Voices of Color*. Seattle, Wash.: Red Letter Press, 1999.

Lorde, Audre. "I Am Your Sister: Black Women Organizing Across Sexualities." Freedom Organizing Pamphlet Series 3. Latham, N.Y.: Kitchen Table: Women of Color Press, 1985.

Retter, Yolanda. "Lesbian (Feminist) Los Angeles, 1970-1990: An Exploratory Ethnohistory." 1995. http://www.usc.edu/isd/archives/queerfrontiers/queer/papers/retter.html.

Russell, Valerie. "Racism and Sexism, a Collective Struggle: A Minority Woman's Point of View." (n.d.) http://scriptorium.lib.duke.edu/wlm/racesex/.

"Short Takes: Los Angeles, California." *The Advocate*, September 15, 1983, 62.

Thompson, Becky. "Multiracial Feminism: Recasting the Chronology of Second Wave Feminism." *Feminist Studies* 28, no. 2 (2002).

SEE ALSO: Nov. 7, 1972: Jordan Becomes First Black Congresswoman from the South; 1975: Gay American Indians Is Founded; 1975-1983: Gay Latino Alliance Is Formed; Apr., 1977: Combahee River Collective Issues "A Black Feminist Statement"; Nov. 18-21, 1977: National Women's Conference Convenes; Oct. 12-15, 1979: First National Third World Lesbian and Gay Conference Convenes; Oct. 12-15, 1979: Lesbian and Gay Asian Collective Is Founded; 1981: *This Bridge Called My Back* Is Published; Oct., 1981: Kitchen Table: Women of Color Press Is Founded; 1982: Lorde's Autobiography *Zami* Is Published; 1987: Anzaldúa Publishes *Borderlands/La Frontera*; 1987: *Compañeras: Latina Lesbians* Is Published; 1990: United Lesbians of African Heritage Is Founded.

Spring, 1984
AIDS VIRUS IS DISCOVERED

French and U.S. officials announced that scientists in their respective countries had isolated what was believed to be the virus, or pathogen, that causes AIDS: human immunodeficiency virus, or HIV. The question of which team from which country was the first to isolate and name a virus, however, spurred years of intense international debate. The French, who isolated a virus as early as January of 1983, had been reluctant to make their announcement because they were unsure of the sufficiency of their findings.

LOCALE: Washington, D.C.; Paris, France
CATEGORIES: HIV-AIDS; science; health and medicine; organizations and institutions; government and politics

KEY FIGURES

Robert Gallo (b. 1937), medical doctor, National Cancer Institute

Margaret M. Heckler (b. 1931), former secretary, U.S. Department of Health and Human Services

Luc Montagnier (b. 1932), virologist at Pasteur Institute, Paris

Jay A. Levy (b. 1938), medical doctor, Cancer Research Institute, University of California, San Francisco

SUMMARY OF EVENT

By 1984, the U.S. Centers for Disease Control had recorded four thousand cases of AIDS since it began tracking the disease in 1981. Despite the best efforts of physicians, half of the patients diagnosed had died already. With various hypotheses about how the virus was spread, many people were concerned for their health. Scientists remained baffled by the long-lasting disease, which presented the unique challenge of a long delay between exposure to the causal agent and the onset, years later, of immune system failure.

In April, 1984, French scientists announced the discovery of a virus called lymphadenopathy-associated virus (LAV), identified as a possible cause of AIDS. They had isolated the virus in January of 1983. This team, led by virologist Luc Montagnier of the Pasteur Institute, was optimistic but cautious. Montagnier and colleagues judged their findings insufficient to claim definitively that LAV caused AIDS.

In a press conference one week later, Secretary Margaret Heckler of the U.S. Department of Health and Human Services announced that U.S. scientists had uncovered the virus that, evidence suggested, was the causal pathogen for the disease. She reported that the virus was not LAV, as the French team thought; rather, it was a variant of a known human cancer virus, the human T-cell leukemia/lymphotrophic virus type III (HTLV-III), which had been discovered by Robert Gallo of the National Institutes of Health. (Gallo already had applied to patent HTLV-III with the U.S. Patent Office.) Heckler stated further that her hope was that a blood test would be developed within six months and that a vaccine would be ready for testing within two years.

The intent of Heckler's statement likely was to provide hope in the face of uncertainty. She characterized Gallo's findings as "the triumph of science over a dreaded disease." Her statement, however, contained scientific and historical inaccuracies, which would come to cause a major international rift in the field of human immunodeficiency virus (HIV) research for

Microphotographs of HTLV-III (top) and LAV, the differently named though identical virus—later called HIV—believed to cause AIDS. LAV was isolated by Luc Montagnier in 1983 and HTLV-III was isolated by Robert Gallo in 1984. Montagnier and Gallo are considered codiscoverers of HIV. (AP/Wide World Photos)

AIDS Virus Is Discovered

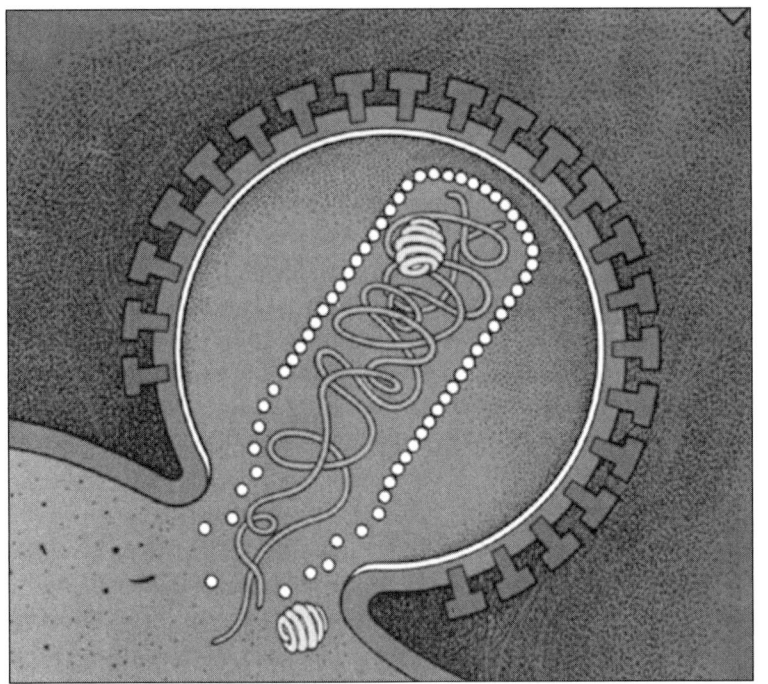

An early schematic of HIV. (National Institutes of Health)

years to come. The primary contention resulting from Heckler's announcement was the question of who, in fact, should be rightfully credited with discovering the virus that causes AIDS, and thus, who should reap the benefits: Montagnier or Gallo, France or the United States? Earlier, the labs of Gallo and Montagnier had shared blood samples and preliminary data, so before this announcement, they were collaborators to some degree. Later, however, legal debates changed them into adversaries.

It was clear, through the use of electron microscopy, that the respective viruses they found were different. Although hotly debated in the public sphere, what remained scientifically unclear, initially, was the question, Which scientist's findings were accurate? At stake were the reputations of Gallo and Montagnier within the scientific community as well as the extent of the contribution to science and medicine made by their respective countries. Furthermore, discovering and patenting the pathogen that would almost certainly serve as the basis for an AIDS test could yield a significant personal profit.

To address the legal and scientific furor that ensued, U.S. president Ronald Reagan and French prime minister Jacques Chirac announced jointly in 1987 that Gallo and Montagnier would be considered the codiscoverers of HIV. This was the first instance of scientific debate settled publicly at the highest level of government. Eventually, Gallo and Montagnier would come forward with their own accounts of what happened. Despite considerable evidence, and likely because of the public debate, more than a decade would pass before there was widespread agreement that HIV is the cause of AIDS.

Significance

Although identifying and isolating the pathogen responsible for causing AIDS was an important first step in the battle against this virus, a final victory over AIDS remains elusive. A blood test for HIV infection was developed and became available commercially in the summer of 1985, contrary to Heckler's hope that a test would be developed within six months (meaning early 1985). Since the mid-1980's, a number of possible vaccines have been tested, but all have been found to be ineffective in controlling the spread of the disease.

In hindsight, it is known that Heckler's 1984 statement was naively optimistic at best, according to Gallo, and, more gravely, a brazen attempt to best the French and garner undue praise and royalties for the United States, according to Montagnier. Undeniably, Gallo's earlier, basic scientific work was foundational because it developed the techniques required to isolate and cultivate in the lab quantities of HIV necessary for an adequate study of the virus; that is, Gallo's earlier work made possible the widespread discovery of HIV. However, it was Montagnier who first correctly identified the virus that causes AIDS, which had been renamed "HIV," from HTLV-III, in 1986.

Independently and simultaneously, Jay Levy of the University of California, San Francisco, confirmed the presence of HIV in patients displaying AIDS symptoms as well as patients who were asymptomatic HIV carriers. Levy managed to avoid the public controversy and thus his contributions are usually overlooked. Rancorous public and scientific debate ensued, which called into question the specific discovery of the cause of AIDS, shaking the scientific method's confident reliance on logic.

The significance of identifying the HIV pathogen cannot be overstated, however. With this knowledge, the scientific community proved definitively that HIV causes AIDS (debates continue, however). Scientists and others developed an accurate HIV test, safeguarded the blood supply, and began to squelch the hysteria about modes of transmission.

—*David W. Pantalone*

FURTHER READING

Fan, Hung, Ross F. Conner, and Luis P. Villarreal. *AIDS: Science and Society*. 4th ed. Boston: Jones & Bartlett, 2004.

_____. *The Biology of AIDS*. 4th ed. Boston: Jones & Bartlett, 2000.

Garrett, Laurie. *The Coming Plague: Newly Emerging Diseases in a World Out of Balance*. New York: Farrar, Straus and Giroux, 1994.

Mayer, Kenneth H., and H. F. Pizer, eds. *The Emergence of AIDS: The Impact on Immunology, Microbiology, and Public Health*. Washington, D.C.: American Public Health Association, 2000.

Snow, Bill, ed. *HIV Vaccine Handbook: Community Perspectives on Participating in Research, Advocacy, and Progress*. New York: AIDS Vaccine Advocacy Coalition, 1999.

Wain-Hobson, S., J. P. Vartanian, M. Henry, N. Chenciner, et al. "LAV Revisited: Origins of the Early HIV-1 Isolates from Institut Pasteur." *Science* 252 (1991): 961-964.

SEE ALSO: June 5 and July 3, 1981: Reports of Rare Diseases Mark Beginning of AIDS Epidemic; July, 1982: Gay-Related Immunodeficiency Is Renamed AIDS; Oct. 9, 1984: San Francisco Closes Gay Bathhouses and Other Businesses; July 25, 1985: Actor Hudson Announces He Has AIDS; Sept., 1986: AZT Treats People with AIDS; Mar., 1987: Radical AIDS Activist Group ACT UP Is Founded; June 27, 1988: Report of the Presidential AIDS Commission; Dec. 1, 1988: First World AIDS Day; 1989: Act Up Paris Is Founded; June 25, 1993: Clinton Appoints First AIDS Czar.

October 9, 1984
SAN FRANCISCO CLOSES GAY BATHHOUSES AND OTHER BUSINESSES

The head of the San Francisco Health Department closed fourteen gay bathhouses and other businesses, including bookstores, movie theaters, and sex clubs, after investigators saw at those businesses what they believed were sexual acts that were high risk for HIV transmission. The regulatory approach caused extensive debates as gay activists raised civil liberty issues.

LOCALE: San Francisco, California
CATEGORIES: Civil rights; HIV-AIDS; health and medicine

KEY FIGURES
Mervyn Silverman, medical doctor and San Francisco's public health director
Roy L. Wonder, Superior Court judge
Dianne Feinstein (b. 1933), mayor of San Francisco

SUMMARY OF EVENT
On April 9, 1984, Mervyn Silverman, San Francisco's public health director, banned sexual activity in fourteen of the city's bathhouses, bookstores, movie theaters, and sex clubs. He stated, "What we are doing today is taking steps to eliminate bathhouses as places of sexual encounters between individuals. . . . That doesn't mean the elimination of such places. What we are trying to do is reduce the spread of AIDS."

Acquired immunodeficiency syndrome, or AIDS, a fatal disease that in 1984 had been in the public eye for at most five years and was mainly affecting homosexual men, is primarily spread through sexual contact. By 1984, 477 San Franciscans had AIDS and 175 had died.

The reaction to the restrictions was divided. Some accepted the measure as a possible way to prevent the spread of the virus (human immunodeficiency virus, or HIV) believed to cause AIDS.

Others feared that increased regulations meant increased discrimination against gay male communities. The question of civil liberties versus public health regulations was debated among activists, politicians, and media.

Public health officials first began targeting bathhouses in 1983 as a way to control AIDS. Bathhouses and sex clubs were primarily designed for multiple sexual encounters; finding numerous contacts in a short amount of time meant more opportunities to become infected. While some considered closing the bathhouses completely, others felt that the activities within the baths would merely move outside to parks and public toilets, where access to condoms was nonexistent. Initial city efforts to curb high-risk sex at these establishments, however, had limited success.

To test the effectiveness of the ban, undercover private investigators inspected the establishments during the summer of 1984. They witnessed, according to Silverman, a "blatant disregard for the health of their patrons and of the community." Bathhouses were profiting by permitting high-risk sexual contacts. Given the transmissible disease, sexually active men were at risk. Officials had hoped that gay men, knowing the health hazards, would voluntarily reduce anonymous sexual contacts. They also had believed bathhouse owners would take action to stop certain sex practices.

On October 9, 1984, Silverman ordered nine bathhouses and five bookstores and theaters to close. Sexual activity, which was not in compliance with the April ordinance, was still taking place. At that time, 723 San Franciscans had AIDS. San Francisco mayor Dianne Feinstein stated, "I am absolutely convinced that the public health would be better served by closure of the bathhouses."

Owners of several of the bathhouses filed suit to block the authorities from carrying out the order, contending that it was unconstitutional. On October

15, 1984, Superior Court judge William E. Mullins ordered the bathhouses to close temporarily until a hearing could take place. Although First Amendment rights kept the bookstores and theaters open, the bathhouses became known as a health menace. Five bathhouses asked the state's First District Court of Appeal to let them reopen pending a hearing with regard to permanent closure. The appeals court refused.

On November 28, Superior Court judge Roy L. Wonder lifted the temporary restraining order but imposed strict limitations on sexual behavior. Bathhouse operators who allowed their establishments to remain open were forced to hire employees to monitor sexual activity and remove anyone who engaged in high-risk activity: sex acts that involve the exchange of bodily fluids, as defined by the San Francisco AIDS Foundation. Private rooms were banned, and the doors to cubicles and booths were to be removed. Establishments were under orders to assign monitors to patrol the premises and remove patrons who violated the regulations. The numbers had indicated that 817 San Franciscans had AIDS, and 358 had died from the disease.

Bathhouse owners, some hoping to maintain their highly profitable businesses, were willing to regulate sexual activity in public areas. Many did hire monitors and remove orgy rooms. Posters went up to inform patrons of what constituted safer versus high-risk sex. Most owners, however, refused to remove the doors from the rooms, saying that they would not spy on their patrons. They argued that activity in the cubicles was protected by privacy rights set forth in the California constitution. The creation of a "sex police" made many uncomfortable, and they had difficulty removing paying patrons. After Judge Wonder's ruling, many bathhouses closed as business declined, but a few remained open.

Significance

Gay bathhouses were important in the emergence of a gay male community in the twentieth century, giving patrons the safety and freedom with which to explore multiple relations. These "legal" spaces played a significant role in gay liberation and the development of a gay identity.

To many gays, publicizing the activities at the baths meant airing dirty laundry in public. Some in the gay population were concerned about individual rights and confidentiality. To these men, the closing of the baths was an attack on a gay lifestyle, a political more than public health issue. Many argued that the gay community had the right to make its own decisions.

Silverman, who left his job in January of 1985, maintained that he had acted responsibly in the face of the serious threat presented by the disease. "As I read medical history," he said, "there has been no modern disease with the deep social impact of AIDS. Polio was frightening and tragic, but even that disease did not carry all the social implications of AIDS."

The conflict between some gay leaders and city authorities on how to contain AIDS, amid fears and anxieties, created heated debate and recriminations. Some still feel that the bathhouses should have been closed immediately. Others believe that a stronger educational approach would have been more effective, one that reached the portion of the gay population who sought and might well continue to seek multiple or communal sexual engagements. The latter group holds that, rather than focusing on the sites of sexual encounters, everyone would have benefited more from efforts to communicate the value of practicing safer sex.

Because of the long incubation period for the AIDS virus—years and sometimes decades—it is difficult to determine the impact of the efforts of the San Francisco authorities, as well as those in other cities with large gay populations who learned from San Francisco and followed its lead. However, by late 1985, instances of sexually transmitted diseases including rectal gonorrhea were down. AIDS began receiving mass media attention, and the use of condoms during sexual intercourse began to increase. Many gay men made major changes in their lives to slow the spread of AIDS.

—Ira Tattelman

Further Reading

Dritz, Selma K., and Mervyn F. Silverman. *The AIDS Epidemic in San Francisco: The Medical*

Response, 1981-1984. Vol. 1. Berkeley: Regents of the University of California, 1995.

Fan, Hung, Ross F. Conner, and Luis P. Villarreal. *AIDS: Science and Society*. 4th ed. Boston: Jones & Bartlett, 2004.

Mayer, Kenneth H., and H. F. Pizer, eds. *The AIDS Pandemic: Impact on Science and Society*. San Diego, Calif.: Elsevier/Academic, 2005.

_____. *The Emergence of AIDS: The Impact on Immunology, Microbiology, and Public Health*. Washington, D.C.: American Public Health Association, 2000.

Shilts, Randy. *And the Band Played On: Politics, People, and the AIDS Epidemic*. New York: St. Martin's Press, 1987.

Woods, William J., and Diane Binson, et al., eds. *Gay Bathhouses and Public Health Policy*. New York: Harrington Park Press, 2003.

SEE ALSO: June 5 and July 3, 1981: Reports of Rare Diseases Mark Beginning of AIDS Epidemic; July, 1982: Gay-Related Immunodeficiency Is Renamed AIDS; Spring, 1984: AIDS Virus Is Discovered; July 25, 1985: Actor Hudson Announces He Has AIDS; Sept., 1986: AZT Treats People with AIDS; Mar., 1987: Radical AIDS Activist Group ACT UP Is Founded; June 27, 1988: Report of the Presidential AIDS Commission; Dec. 1, 1988: First World AIDS Day; June 25, 1993: Clinton Appoints First AIDS Czar.

November 6, 1984
WEST HOLLYWOOD INCORPORATES WITH MAJORITY GAY AND LESBIAN CITY COUNCIL

West Hollywood voters approved cityhood and elected a majority gay and lesbian city council, making the municipality the first "gay city" in the United States.

LOCALE: West Hollywood, California
CATEGORIES: Government and politics; laws, acts, and legal history

KEY FIGURES
John Heilman,
Steve Schulte, and
Ron Stone, West Hollywood city council members
Valerie Terrigno, mayor of West Hollywood

SUMMARY OF EVENT
Residents of West Hollywood, an area of Los Angeles County of less than two square miles, is sandwiched between the city of Beverly Hills and Hollywood (a district of the city of Los Angeles). West Hollywood voters chose to incorporate as an independent city on November 6, 1984, creating what has often been referred to as a "gay Camelot."

Before incorporation, West Hollywood was already known as a haven for gays and lesbians—but especially for gay men—who frequent the gay nightclubs, shops, and organizations clustered, especially, around the western portion of the city's Santa Monica Boulevard. The area is also known as "Boystown." Because West Hollywood was, before its incorporation, a loosely governed part of greater Los Angeles County, the Los Angeles Police Department did not have jurisdiction in the area. This enabled nightclubs and bars on Sunset Boulevard (the Sunset Strip) to operate with fewer regulations than did clubs in adjacent Hollywood and Mid-City—a situation that was also favorable to many gay and lesbian businesses.

In the 1920's, the Sunset Strip had been a trendy area for silent-film stars, and it flourished in the 1940's with nightclubs such as the legendary Trocadero. In the 1960's, West Hollywood became a center for the countercultural rock music scene in Southern California, and by the 1970's, gay residents and entrepreneurs had begun to buy inexpensive real estate in the area, building a gay ghetto similar to those in San Francisco's Castro district and New York City's Greenwich Village. According to historian Moira Rachel Kenney, "Today, West Hollywood reflects all of these preincorporation cultures—hippie, rock, Hollywood star, and gay."

West Hollywood in 1984 was populated mostly by older adults and by gay men, 90 percent of whom were renters. Confronted with the prospect of losing their rent control and of overdevelopment, as well as lacking solid local representation at the county level, the 1984 incorporation drive was motivated more by the desire to maintain rent controls and curb development than by the dream of creating a "gay city." Ron Stone, a local gay activist and the incorporation-drive founder, wrote in the *LA Weekly*, a local, independent newspaper, that, "All this sub-dividing and separation makes West Hollywood a prime target for development. With no local government to turn to or take control of, citizens of the area who want to retain the village-like characteristics that attracted them in the first place have had a difficult time of it."

Although West Hollywood's gay and lesbian leadership first resisted incorporation, believing that the county's "neglect" was useful for gay and lesbian residents, eventually they were convinced that supporting the incorporation of a "gay city" would likely be a good idea. Their efforts were bolstered by the Coalition for Economic Survival (CES), a tenants' rights group that advocated rent control and brought older adults and nongay renters to the table. On November 6, West Hollywood residents voted to incorporate as an independent city, and they elected a five-member city council, a council with the first gay and lesbian majority in the nation.

On November 29, the new city council, including out gay members John Heilman and Steve Schulte and out lesbian member Valerie Terrigno, officially declared the birth of West Hollywood. The council chose Terrigno as West Hollywood's mayor, making her the first mayor in the nation who was out as either lesbian or gay.

West Hollywood's city council quickly passed a series of progressive measures to reward those who voted for incorporation—older adult renters and gays and lesbians. The council immediately established a rent-hike freeze, and in June of 1985, passed a rent-control law that was one of the strictest in the United States. The council also banned discrimination against gays and lesbians, established domestic partnership benefits for city employees, and established the first civil union registry in the nation. In one now-legendary example of West Hollywood's commitment to gay and lesbian rights, the entire city council marched to a local restaurant, Barney's Beanery, to call for the removal of a sign it had that stated, "Fagots [sic] Stay Out."

The early days of incorporated West Hollywood were also marked by growing pains as new city leaders learned how to deal with a fledgling bureaucracy, the demands of local constituents, and internal controversy. In August of 1985, Mayor Terrigno had ceded her position to John Heilman after several weeks of a public power struggle over the duties of the largely ceremonial position of mayor. Also, in April of 1986, after being convicted for embezzling funds prior to her filling her city position, Terrigno resigned from office.

SIGNIFICANCE

According to historian Moira Rachel Kenney in her book *Mapping Gay L.A.* (2001), the incorporation of West Hollywood marks a transition in the LGBT rights movement in Los Angeles from focusing on short-term crisis management to creating longer-term community institutions by allying with other local groups, such as the older adults and the immigrant Russians who make up major portions of the West Hollywood population. In 1999, out of a population of 37,000, 19 percent were elderly and 10 to 15 percent were Russian immigrants.

West Hollywood, however, remains a city composed largely of gay, white men, with lesbians and queers of color making up a minority of the population; many lesbians and many queers of color do visit the city, but mostly on weekends. Despite the city's history of supporting rent control, a 1999 state law allowed landlords to set rents at market rates after tenants vacated their apartments. Skyrocketing rents, as a result, have made West Hollywood financially out of reach for most middle- and lower-income people.

Economic developments have made West Hollywood a relatively exclusive neighborhood, but it has long since been established as a progressive city government that aims to serve its residents. West Hollywood, for example, was one of the first local governments to support sanctions against South Africa because of apartheid.

Benjamin Forest argues that West Hollywood's identity as a new city was entwined with the construction of a new gay identity that included progressive politics and an orientation toward entertainment and consumption. While this new identity did not challenge existing political or social systems to any great extent, it did seek to demarginalize LGBT people and bring them more toward the center.

—*Malinda Lo*

FURTHER READING

Braun, Stephen. "West Hollywood, One Year Later." *Los Angeles Times*, December 1, 1985, A1.

Forest, Benjamin. "West Hollywood as Symbol: The Significance of Place in the Construction of a Gay Identity." *Environment and Planning D: Society and Space* 13 (1995): 133-157.

Kenney, Moira Rachel. *Mapping Gay L.A.: The Intersection of Politics and Place*. Philadelphia: Temple University Press, 2001.

Moos, Adam. "The Grassroots in Action: Gays and Seniors Capture the Local State in West Hollywood, California." In *The Power of Geography*, edited by Jennifer Wolch and Michael Dear. Boston: Unwyn Hyman, 1989.

Ward, Jane. "Producing 'Pride' in West Hollywood: A Queer Cultural Capital for Queers with Cultural Capital." *Sexualities* 6, no. 1 (2003): 65-94.

SEE ALSO: 1972-1973: Local Governments Pass Antidiscrimination Laws; June 21, 1973: U.S. Supreme Court Supports Local Obscenity Laws; Aug., 1973: American Bar Association Calls for Repeal of Laws Against Consensual Sex; Dec. 19, 1977: Quebec Includes Lesbians and Gays in Its Charter of Human Rights and Freedoms; Nov. 27, 1978: White Murders Politicians Moscone and Milk; Dec. 4, 1984: Berkeley Extends Benefits to Domestic Partners of City Employees; Apr., 2003: Buenos Aires Recognizes Same-Gender Civil Unions.

December 4, 1984
BERKELEY EXTENDS BENEFITS TO DOMESTIC PARTNERS OF CITY EMPLOYEES

Berkeley, California, became the first U.S. city to extend health and other employee benefits to the gay and lesbian domestic partners of city employees.

LOCALE: Berkeley, California
CATEGORIES: Civil rights; government and politics

SUMMARY OF EVENT
On December 4, 1984, the city council of Berkeley, California, adopted a policy allowing unmarried employees to enroll their domestic partners for health and dental benefits, as well as to take sick leave or bereavement leave for situations involving their domestic partners. With this policy Berkeley became the first municipality in the United States to provide such benefits to its employees. The plan was negotiated as part of the contract between the city and its unionized employees and extended to all employees, so by adopting the contract, the city council effectively adopted the domestic partnership plan.

Two years earlier, the city and county of San Francisco board of supervisors had adopted a domestic partnership program for its employees, but it was vetoed by Mayor Dianne Feinstein, so it never took effect. Feinstein also resisted proposals to adopt a domestic partnership benefits plan in 1984 after receiving recommendations from a committee she had appointed. A modified plan was adopted in San Francisco in 1989, but it was overturned in a referendum by voters that same year. In 1990, a domestic partners registry was established and city employees became eligible to cover domestic partners on their health plans, but both of those moves were first subjected to unsuccessful referenda.

A few other cities adopted domestic partnership benefit plans in the 1980's, the largest of which was Seattle, Washington. Small cities, such as West Hollywood, California, which approved the idea of providing domestic partnership benefits in 1985, found it difficult to implement their decisions because private insurers would not sell them the appropriate insurance policies. The earliest cities usually had to be self-insured to provide such coverage. Beginning in the 1990's, however, a number of insurance companies developed products for both public and private sector employees that offered the option of domestic partnership coverage.

Local governments also had to face legal questions from groups opposed to offering domestic partnership benefit programs. In almost every state in which at least one city, county, or school district has offered employees a domestic partnership benefit option, a lawsuit has been filed charging that the local entity exceeded its powers under that state's laws or constitution. The charge is usually either that the city is trying to create a marital relationship that only the state is allowed to create or that there is no authority for the city to offer such benefits, and therefore the offer should not be allowed.

In most cases, these arguments have not persuaded the state courts, although in Minnesota, Massachusetts, and Virginia, the courts did find that local governments could not offer domestic partnership benefits. In 2004, cases were pending in Pennsylvania, Louisiana, and Ohio. In other states—including Florida, Georgia, Colorado, New York, Arizona, Maine, Maryland, Washington, North Carolina, Illinois, and California—the state courts found that the cities did have authority to adopt such programs. About half the states, however, still have no local governments that offer domestic partnership benefits.

In establishing domestic partnership benefit programs, government employers, like private employers, have had to make some choices. How will domestic partnerships be defined? How are they established? What benefits will be offered? One of the major differences between public and private employers is in the way each entity decides who is eligible to form a domestic partnership. In the private sector, most employers opt to limit domestic partnerships to same-gender couples only on the theory that opposite-gender couples could make themselves eligible for benefits by marrying. In the public sector, because of legal concerns about both sex discrimination and sexual-orientation discrimination, most public employers allow both same-gender and opposite-gender couples to form domestic partnerships. In the cities that offer health benefits and keep statistics, opposite-gender domestic partnerships almost always outnumber same-gender domestic partnerships.

As for the "eligibility" requirements, most domestic partnership regulations look similar to those imposed on parties who want to get married, except for the gender of the partners. Typically the parties must be age eighteen or older, mentally competent, and not related by blood. Unlike marriage requirements, however, most have some requirement that the parties share a residence and have lived together for a specified period to establish their "domestic" partnership. Most domestic partnerships can be dissolved simply if only one party declares the partnership is ended and files paperwork to that effect. Most jurisdictions set a period of time that must pass after one domestic partnership is dissolved before a person can establish a new one.

In deciding which benefits to offer, more jurisdictions offer what are sometimes called "soft benefits," such as the ability to take sick leave or bereavement leave to attend to a partner, rather than "hard benefits" like health, dental, and vision insurance, which often require the employer to pay a third party for the benefits. Even fewer jurisdictions with domestic partnership benefit programs go so far as to allow employees to designate domestic partners as eligible for survivors' benefits of pensions earned by an employee, the way a surviving widow or widower would be, though a few public employers have begun to do this.

SIGNIFICANCE

The city of Berkeley's successful adoption of domestic partnership benefits began a trend that has reached the point where, according to the Human Rights Campaign, more than two hundred cities and counties offered some form of domestic partnership benefits as of June 1, 2006. These public-sector domestic partnership programs have become models for the private sector as well.

—*Charles W. Gossett*

FURTHER READING

DeLeon, Richard. "San Francisco and Domestic Partners: New Fields of Battle in the Culture War." In *Culture Wars and Local Politics*, edited by Elaine B. Sharp. Lawrence: University Press of Kansas, 1999.

Gossett, Charles W. "Domestic Partnership Benefits: Public Sector Patterns." *Review of Public Personnel Administration* 14, no. 1 (Winter, 1994): 64-84.

SEE ALSO: 1972-1973: Local Governments Pass Antidiscrimination Laws; June 21, 1973: U.S. Supreme Court Supports Local Obscenity Laws; Aug., 1973: American Bar Association Calls for Repeal of Laws Against Consensual Sex; Dec. 19, 1977: Quebec Includes Lesbians and Gays in Its Charter of Human Rights and Freedoms; Nov. 27, 1978: White Murders Politicians Moscone and Milk; Nov. 6, 1984: West Hollywood Incorporates with Majority Gay and Lesbian City Council; Apr., 2003: Buenos Aires Recognizes Same-Gender Civil Unions.

1985
GLAAD Begins Monitoring Media Coverage of Gays and Lesbians

The Gay and Lesbian Alliance Against Defamation, or GLAAD, promotes accurate and fair media coverage of lesbian, gay, bisexual, and transgender persons, and ensures that representations are not defamatory or biased. The organization has had a significant impact on how media report LGBT-related news and other stories and how the entertainment industry depicts LGBT persons on television and radio, and in film, music videos, computer games, online communities, and even comics.

Locale: New York, New York
Categories: Organizations and institutions; publications

Key Figures
Vito Russo (1946-1990), film historian, activist, cofounder of ACT UP, and cofounder of GLAAD
Joan Nestle (b. 1940), author, founder of the Lesbian Herstory Archives, and cofounder of GLAAD
Jewelle Gomez (b. 1948), poet and cofounder of GLAAD

Summary of Event
The Gay and Lesbian Alliance Against Defamation, or GLAAD, whose motto is "Fair, Accurate and Inclusive Representation," was founded in late 1985 during a meeting in a New York City apartment. The founders, Vito Russo, Joan Nestle, Jewelle Gomez, and other activists organized to protest defamatory coverage of the HIV-AIDS pandemic in the *New York Post*.

The grassroots organization grew into a national advocacy group but its focus moved from news to entertainment media. Joan Garry, who had worked in the entertainment industry, was GLAAD's president from 1997 to 2005, and, as of 2006, the organization's president is Neil G. Giuliano.

GLAAD has offices in New York City, Los Angeles, San Francisco, and other cities, and it serves regional and local interests. In addition to being a media watchdog, GLAAD works to destigmatize same-gender sexuality, to temper heterosexism, and to end discrimination based on sexual orientation and gender identity.

Among the many programs offered by GLAAD is AM/FM Activism, launched in 2001, which provides an online kit for developing antidefamation campaigns in local communities. Because GLAAD cannot launch these campaigns in every local community, the kit provides local organizers with the tools and other resources to counter defamation, especially on local radio. A community network can be created with other activists in the area. This program was initiated after a successful alliance between GLAAD and local community activists in the campaign against Laura Schlessinger. The goal in this campaign had been to protest Schlessinger's antigay rhetoric on her TV show, *Dr. Laura*. GLAAD provided resources, contacts, and tips. Major strategies included letter writing campaigns and mediation with local managers of TV stations. In March of 2001, the show was canceled.

Significance
GLAAD was founded during a time when lesbians and gays faced defamation and ridicule in the media. Newspapers printed heterosexist stories on its front pages, and the entertainment industry produced blatantly stereotypical images of lesbians and gays on television. Since the time of GLAAD's inception in 1985, negative and imbalanced portrayals of LGBT communities have decreased and LGBT visibility has increased. Lesbian and gay stories and issues are now covered in national and local news publications, in film, on television, and in nearly every other type of media.

Gay and Lesbian Alliance Against Defamation: Select Milestones
• **1987:** *The New York Times* changed its editorial policy to use the word "gay" instead of "homosexual."
• **1988:** Comedian Bob Hope made a public service announcement condemning antigay violence after he had used the word "fag" as a guest on *The Tonight Show*.
• **1989:** *Daily Variety* agreed to list survivors of same-gender couples in obituaries.
• **1991:** Hallmark Cards withdrew the word "lesbian" from its list of banned words.
• **1992:** A campaign against antigay rap music led to public service announcements produced by Mercury Records.
• **1993:** Received an ADDY Award from the American Advertising Federation for a billboard campaign of a lesbian couple expecting a child. The ad had been placed in neighborhoods throughout California.
• **1994:** Ensured the airing of an episode of the sitcom *Roseanne* that had two women kissing each other.
• **1995:** Protested Snapple Beverage Company's sponsorship of the television show *The Rush Limbaugh Show*. Quaker Oats (Snapple's parent company) responded by not renewing its advertising contract with the show.
• **1996:** CBS-TV fired sports commentator Ben Wright after GLAAD protested his sexist and heterosexist remarks about two male golfers.
• **1997:** Supported the Walt Disney Company throughout the Southern Baptists' boycott of Disney for its fair treatment of lesbians and gays in employment and in its media.
• **1998:** Joined a broad-based coalition of LGBT and allied organizations, family advocates, psychiatrists, and other mental-health professionals to denounce fraudulent ads encouraging "conversion" of lesbians and gays.
• **1999:** Demanded that *Merriam-Webster's Collegiate Thesaurus* remove derogatory epithets such as "faggot," "pansy," and "fruit" from its publication.
• **2000:** Exposed the antigay defamation of radio talk-show host Laura Schlessinger as well as the antigay hate lyrics of hip-hop singer Eminem.
• **2001:** Promoted LGBT intellectual activism and awarded fellowships to eight scholars.
• **2002:** Worked with the American Civil Liberties Union on media strategy for comedian and TV-host Rosie O'Donnell's campaign against Florida's antigay and antilesbian adoption law.
• **2003:** Began shaping media discussion of same-gender marriage rights.
• **2004:** Published the Republican and Democratic parties platforms on gay and lesbian equity and had media outlets cover the discriminatory policy language of the Republican platform.
• **2005:** An antigay and antilesbian group was countered by leading negotiations with Ford Motor Company. The company issued a policy statement of its commitment to the LGBT community.

GLAAD staff and volunteers have not only led the way in changing how lesbians and gays are portrayed on the screen and in the news but also have been a major resource for entertainment and news media decision makers wishing to change their approach to covering LGBT persons. *Entertainment Weekly* named GLAAD one of "Hollywood's 100 most powerful entities," and the *Los Angeles Times* said that GLAAD is "possibly the most successful organization lobbying the media for inclusion." In addition to its media advocacy, GLAAD holds an annual media awards event to recognize those who have played significant roles in advancing the image of LGBT people in the news media and in entertainment.

—Ski Hunter

Further Reading

Bell, David, and Gil Valentine. *Mapping Desire: Geographies of Sexuality*. New York: Routledge, 1995.

Cruickshank, Margaret. *The Gay and Lesbian Liberation Movement*. New York: Routledge, 1992.

Gay and Lesbian Alliance Against Defamation. *GLAAD Media Reference Guide*. 7th ed. New York: Author, 2006.

Gross, Larry. *Up from Invisibility: Lesbians, Gay Men, and the Media in America*. New York: Columbia University Press, 1991.

Longmire, L., and L. Merrill. *Under the Tongue: Gender, Power, and the Word*. Westport, Conn.: Greenwood Press, 1998.

National Lesbian and Gay Journalists Association. http://www.nlgja.org.

Padilla, Y. C. *Gay and Lesbian Rights Organizing: Community-Based Strategies*. Binghamton, N.Y.: Haworth, 2004.

Singer, D., and J. L. Singer. *Handbook of Children and the Media*. Thousand Oaks, Calif.: Sage, 2001.

See also: 1930's-1960's: Hollywood Bans "Sexual Perversion" in Films; Mar. 7, 1967: CBS Airs *CBS Reports: The Homosexuals*; Oct. 31, 1969: *Time* Magazine Issues "The Homosexual in America"; July 3, 1978: U.S. Supreme Court Distinguishes Between "Indecent" and "Obscene"; 1979-1981: First Gay British Television Series Airs; June 5 and July 3, 1981: Reports of Rare Diseases Mark Beginning of AIDS Epidemic; 1985: Lesbian Film *Desert Hearts* Is Released; July 25, 1985: Actor Hudson Announces He Has AIDS; 1992-2002: Celebrity Lesbians Come Out; Mar. 21, 2000: Hollywood Awards Transgender Portrayals in Film; Sept. 7, 2001: First Gay and Lesbian Television Network Is Launched in Canada; Mar. 5, 2006: *Brokeback Mountain, Capote,* and *Transamerica* Receive Oscars.

1985
Lesbian Film *Desert Hearts* Is Released

Desert Hearts was the first positive and widely distributed film portrayal of a lesbian relationship. Its box office success, however, was followed first by another decade of traditional, negative film depictions of lesbians, but the film later inspired independent filmmakers to offer less-stereotypical depictions of lesbians and lesbian sexuality.

Locale: United States
Categories: Cultural and intellectual history; literature; arts

Key Figures
Donna Deitch (b. 1945), American film director
Patricia Charbonneau (b. 1959), American actor
Helen Shaver (b. 1951), American actor

Summary of Event
The screening of *Desert Hearts* in the United States in 1985 marked the first positive representation of a lesbian relationship in mainstream movie theaters. Earlier films with lesbian characters tended to end in tragedy or death. Films such as *The Children's Hour* (1961) depicted a lesbian character's suicide; *Personal Best* (1982) has a main female character leaving her lesbian lover for a man; and *Silkwood* (1983) ends with the isolation and loneliness of a lesbian character played by singer and actor Cher.

Donna Deitch, the director of *Desert Hearts*, explained to *Ms.* magazine in 1986 that "At the time I bought the rights to the book, there hadn't been a film about a relationship between two women that hadn't ended in suicide, like 'The Children's Hour,' or in a bisexual triangle. I wanted to make just a love story, like any other love story between a man and a woman, handled in a frank and real way."

Deitch's quest to film a lesbian romance began in 1979, when she bought the rights to Jane Rule's 1964 novel *The Desert of the Heart*. Although Deitch was a novice filmmaker at the time and had only a few film-school productions on her resume, she knew early on that a major Hollywood production company was not likely to finance her film; so she spent more than two years raising money to make the film by selling $1,000 shares in the movie to interested investors, many of whom were lesbian or gay. Her fund-raising efforts reaped in a budget that reportedly ranged from between $850,000 and $1.5 million, an amount that limited the number of filmable takes and scenes in the thirty-one-day shooting schedule.

Poster for Desert Hearts *(1985).*

Set in 1950's Reno, Nevada, *Desert Hearts* tells the story of Vivian Bell (Helen Shaver), a thirty-five-year-old literature professor from Columbia University in New York City, who travels to Reno to obtain a quick, no-hassle divorce from her husband. Planning to stay at a dude ranch for six weeks, Vivian meets the younger, free-spirited, and out lesbian Cay Rivers (Patricia Charbonneau), who works at a local casino. Vivian and Cay are opposites in a number of ways: Vivian is ten years older and represents the more conservative East Coast; Cay represents the open-minded West. Also, Vivian has just emerged from a sexually repressed heterosexual relationship, whereas Cay is out as a lesbian. Vivian is depicted in a more "traditional" role with long hair, feminine dress, and feminine mannerisms; Cay is shown with shorter hair and a casual self-assurance that mark her as more butch, or masculine, than femme.

Lesbian viewers reacted positively to *Desert Hearts*, which has become a classic and iconic lesbian film. It was nominated for the Grand Jury Prize at the Sundance Film Festival in 1986, but many academic critics dismissed the film as too mainstream and not radical enough in its representation of lesbian sexuality.

SIGNIFICANCE

Desert Hearts was a box-office success but was not followed by more mainstream lesbian romance films. Instead, in the following decade, films had stereotypical lesbian or bisexual serial killers (*Basic Instinct*, 1992) and psychopaths (*Single White Female*, 1991) or had forced female friendships—lesbian subtexts—in films such as *Fried Green Tomatoes* (1991) or *Thelma and Louise* (1991).

Some independent films did include positive portrayals of lesbian relationships, including *Claire of the Moon* (1992), but mainstream box-office success did not return until the mid-1990's, with the release of several movies featuring lesbian characters. Rose Troche's *Go Fish* (1994) is a love story about two young Chicago lesbians that, despite an estimated $15,000 budget, ended up grossing approximately $2.4 million. Maria Maggenti's *Incredibly True Adventure of Two Girls in Love* (1995) is a teen romance in the tradition of John Hughes that features two girls instead of a straight couple in a classic opposites-attract story line.

In 1996, the Wachowski brothers' adventure-heist movie *Bound* features Gina Gershon as a lesbian former convict who falls for a Mafia gangster's girlfriend (Jennifer Tilly). Lisa Cholodenko's critically acclaimed *High Art* (1998) is a drama about a lesbian photographer played by Ally Sheedy. In 1999, Jamie Babbit's campy comedy *But I'm a Cheerleader* tells the story of a teen lesbian who is sent to summer camp to learn how to be straight. The year 2004 saw the Sundance Film Festival premiere of Angela Robinson's action-adventure comedy *D.E.B.S.*, which features a lesbian romance between girls who are also spies. The film was widely released in 2005.

Many of the directors of lesbian films have gone

on to work in television instead of continuing to work exclusively in film. Deitch directed the lesbian-friendly television drama *The Women of Brewster Place* (1989). Similarly, Troche, Maggenti, Cholodenko, Babbit, and Robinson went on to direct or write network and cable television programs. The successful lesbian-themed television series *The L Word*, which debuted in 2004 and remains a strong draw for many cross-over viewers, featured episodes written by Troche and Guinevere Turner (both of *Go Fish* fame).

Although *Desert Hearts* was not immediately followed by more films with positive representations of lesbians, it did signal the beginning of a trend toward films produced and directed by lesbian filmmakers.

—Malinda Lo

FURTHER READING

Benshoff, Harry M., and Sean Griffin. *Queer Images: A History of Gay and Lesbian Film in America.* Lanham, Md.: Rowman & Littlefield, 2006.

Berenstein, Rhona J. "Where the Girls Are: Riding the New Wave of Lesbian Feature Films." *GLQ: A Journal of Lesbian and Gay Studies* 3 (1996): 125-137.

Darren, Alison. *Lesbian Film Guide.* New York: Cassell, 2000.

Kabir, Shameen. *Daughters of Desire: Lesbian Representations in Film.* Washington, D.C.: Cassell, 1998.

Kort, Michele. "Independent Filmmaker Donna Deitch Controls Her Whole Show." *Ms.*, November, 1985, 66-67.

Russo, Vito. *The Celluloid Closet: Homosexuality in the Movies.* Rev. ed. New York: Harper & Row, 1987.

Stacey, Jackie. "'If You Don't Play, You Can't Win': *Desert Hearts* and the Lesbian Romance Film." In *Immortal, Invisible: Lesbians and the Moving Image*, edited by Tamsin Wilton. New York: Routledge, 1995.

Tasker, Yvonne. "Pussy Galore: Lesbian Images and Lesbian Desire in the Popular Cinema." In *The Good, the Bad, and the Gorgeous: Popular Culture's Romance with Lesbianism*, edited by Diane Hamer and Belinda Budge. London: Pandora, 1994.

Weiss, Andrea. *Vampires and Violets: Lesbians in Film.* New York: Penguin, 1993.

SEE ALSO: 1930's-1960's: Hollywood Bans "Sexual Perversion" in Films; Mar. 7, 1967: CBS Airs *CBS Reports: The Homosexuals*; Oct. 31, 1969: *Time* Magazine Issues "The Homosexual in America"; 1975: Rule Publishes *Lesbian Images*; 1979-1981: First Gay British Television Series Airs; June 5 and July 3, 1981: Reports of Rare Diseases Mark Beginning of AIDS Epidemic; 1985: GLAAD Begins Monitoring Media Coverage of Gays and Lesbians; July 25, 1985: Actor Hudson Announces He Has AIDS; 1988: *Macho Dancer* Is Released in the Philippines; 1992-2002: Celebrity Lesbians Come Out; Mar. 21, 2000: Hollywood Awards Transgender Portrayals in Film; Sept. 7, 2001: First Gay and Lesbian Television Network Is Launched in Canada; Mar. 5, 2006: *Brokeback Mountain, Capote,* and *Transamerica* Receive Oscars.

July 25, 1985
ACTOR HUDSON ANNOUNCES HE HAS AIDS

Film star Rock Hudson publicly acknowledged he had AIDS, an announcement that led to increased public awareness about the then-mysterious disease, about being HIV-positive or having AIDS, and about homosexuality in general. AIDS would no longer be a silent epidemic.

LOCALE: Los Angeles, California; Paris, France
CATEGORIES: HIV-AIDS; health and medicine; arts

KEY FIGURES
Rock Hudson (1925-1985), American actor, died from AIDS-related complications
Tom Clark (b. 1930), Hudson's partner for seventeen years
Marc Christian (b. 1953), Hudson's companion and sometime partner in his later years
Letantia Bussell, Hudson's dermatologist, first confirmed that Hudson had AIDS

SUMMARY OF EVENT
Rock Hudson was considered a remarkably able, dedicated, and gifted actor. Many actors assume roles completely counter to their personalities offscreen or offstage, but Hudson had difficulty doing that. He was versatile, and he could perform both comic and dramatic roles. In addition to film, he adapted well to acting in television dramas and to the stage.

Hudson also was an intensely private person, and had been closeted about his sexuality throughout his career. By rushing into a marriage of convenience in 1955 with his agent's secretary, Phyllis Gates, he quashed rumors, which were probably untrue, that he was having an affair with fellow actor Jim Nabors. His union with Gates lasted slightly more than two years. Hudson and Gates separated and then were divorced in August, 1958.

A heartthrob whose pictures adorned the bedroom walls of many, Hudson was often seen in public with women, and rumors regarding his imminent matrimonial plans circulated for years. Hudson had no intention of remarrying, and he remained noncommittal when reporters fired personal questions at him during interviews.

In 1968, Tom Clark moved into Hudson's house in Beverly Hills and became his lover. Marc Christian became Hudson's lover as well, toward the end of Hudson's life, and Christian remained with him until Hudson's death. After his death, Christian filed a suit against Hudson's estate and was initially awarded $14 million in damages, having alleged that Hudson had had sex with him when he knew he was suffering from AIDS. The Hudson estate contested the jury award and finally reached an out-of-court settlement with Christian.

Hudson was born Roy Harold Scherer, Jr., in Winnetka, Illinois, on November 17, 1925. His parents separated when he was four years old and eventually divorced. His mother married Wallace Fitzgerald in 1932, after which Hudson changed his last name to Fitzgerald, the name he used until he went to Hollywood seeking an acting career. His agent, Henry Willson, insisted that he change his name to something more arresting than Roy Fitzgerald. Ultimately Roy Fitzgerald became Roc Hudson. Then, at Hudson's insistence, he changed his name, again, to Rock Hudson.

An early indication that Hudson was suffering from AIDS was his rapid weight loss, which he first attributed to anemia. He shed some fifty pounds unwillingly. Also, a large, persistent pimple appeared on his neck. Finally, his dermatologist, Letantia Bussell, performed a needle biopsy on the pimple. On June 2, 1984, she informed Hudson that the pimple was a manifestation of Kaposi's sarcoma, a rare cancer and a complication of AIDS.

Three days later, on June 5, Hudson had the pimple excised by a plastic surgeon. The surgeon performed further biopsies on the specimen and on a nearby lymph node. These biopsies, along with Hudson's rapid weight loss, confirmed Bussell's initial diagnosis. Hudson was initially in a state of

Rock Hudson. (AP/Wide World Photos)

denial, and he insisted on telling those who asked that he was suffering from anemia. Knowing that AIDS was universally construed as an affliction associated with gays only, Hudson declined to reveal publicly that he had AIDS. The only people with whom he shared his diagnosis were close friends Mark Miller and George Nader, whom he swore to secrecy. He did not share the diagnosis with Marc Christian, who was living with him at the time.

In the fall of 1984, Hudson was to begin filming six episodes of the television drama *Dynasty*, a show to which he had agreed to act in during a trip to France in August. Esther Shapiro, co-creator and executive producer of *Dynasty*, talked with Hudson at the Deauville Film Festival in France and urged him to make this commitment. He accepted her offer, thinking that it would take his mind off his physical problems. During his visit to France, he had participated in experimental treatments being conducted in Paris with HPA-23, a new antiviral drug that offered some hope of eliminating or, at minimum, suppressing HIV-AIDS.

Dominique Dormont, a leading expert in experimental HIV-AIDS treatments, working at the famed Pasteur Institute, began Hudson on a treatment of HPA-23. In the fourth week of treatment, extensive tests showed no trace of the AIDS virus in Hudson's blood, but Dormont warned that the virus had merely been suppressed, not eliminated. Dormont told Hudson how important it was to continue treatment, but Hudson said that the filming of *Dynasty* would prevent him from returning before February. It turned out that he did not see Dormont again until July, after he collapsed in Paris. By then it was too late to resume the HPA-23 treatment.

By late October, 1984, after the filming of the *Dynasty* episodes had begun, Hudson had lost another ten pounds, suggesting that the HPA-23 treatment was losing its effect. His friends urged him to bow out of his acting commitment, but he was determined to stay with the show. His early performances in *Dynasty* were so strong that the producers exercised their option to film four episodes beyond the six to which they had been committed.

Episode six of the series involved a scene in which Hudson was to kiss actor Linda Evans. Hudson had reservations about the kissing scene but he also knew that refusing to perform might have forced him to reveal his condition. He went through with the scene and was later severely criticized for putting Evans at risk. At this early point in the AIDS crisis, little was known about the virus and how it was transmitted. People feared casual contact with those who were HIV-positive or with those who had been suffering from the disease. Hudson, however, reduced the risk of passing the virus to Evans by kissing Evans with his lips wiped clear of saliva and tightly pursed.

On July 15, 1985, Hudson flew to Carmel, California, to appear on Doris Day's new show called *Doris Day's Best Friends*. He was in such dire physical condition that Day offered to release him from his commitment, but Hudson insisted on proceeding with the show. Day, realizing that Hudson was near death, was devastated. Hudson, his health deteriorating, flew to Paris on July 21 to seek additional treatment. A liver scan revealed that his liver was badly compromised and word circulated that he was suffering from liver cancer. On July 25, a French publicist, Yanou Collart, held a press conference sanctioned by Hudson and his friend Mark Miller to announce that the actor had AIDS. Hudson had become the first high-profile American to acknowledge he had the disease.

So quiet had Hudson been about his condition that when the media released the news, even those closest to him—Clark, Elizabeth Taylor, Martha Raye, Carol Burnett—had not been informed and were learning about it for the first time. With this story came news that Hudson was gay. As late as the end of May, 1985, he had categorically denied to Christian that he had AIDS or cancer.

Following his collapse in Paris and after finding out the futility of further treatment with HPA-23, Hudson knew that he was dying, but he wanted to die at home. Severely weakened, he chartered an aircraft for $250,000 and, on July 30, 1985, returned to Los Angeles and was taken by helicopter to the University of California, Los Angeles, Medical Center. He remained hospitalized until August 25, the day that Clark and other friends insisted he be permitted to return to his home in nearby Beverly Hills. At his home, he had a private nurse, household staff, and friends. Many friends visited him during his last month of life. He died quietly on the morning of October 2 after having coffee with Clark, who had supported Hudson by staying with him for more than one month.

Significance

Media coverage of Rock Hudson's illness and death, like the media coverage of his life, was extensive. Because he was the first well-known celebrity to die of AIDS, public interest in the disease grew, and with that interest came information about the realities of the virus and how it is passed between people, about being HIV-positive, and the disease itself. HIV is transmitted in three ways: through the exchange of body fluids, usually during unprotected sex; by means of blood transfusions; or by sharing hypodermic needles used to inject substances into the blood stream. Information had been reaching the public through the media that neither HIV, nor AIDS, was communicable through casual contact.

After Hudson's "coming out," many people began to reassess their views about homosexuality. Some categorically condemned Hudson for his sexual orientation but others developed a more charitable attitude, realizing that he had made a notable contribution to popular culture through his acting and that his homosexuality, although it ran counter to the convictions of many Americans, was a private matter.

Following his death, many of Hudson's friends in the film industry called for increased AIDS research and assistance for those who had the disease. Prominent supporters included Hudson's close friends Taylor, Burnett, and Raye. The studios, although still wanting discretion from actors, began asserting less pressure on gay and lesbian actors to appear heterosexual outside their work by dating or marrying members of the opposite gender.

—*R. Baird Shuman*

Further Reading

Clark, Tom, with Dick Kleiner. *Rock Hudson, Friend of Mine*. New York: Pharos Books, 1990.

Gates, Phyllis, and Bob Thomas. *My Husband, Rock Hudson: The Real Story of Rock Hudson's Marriage to Phyllis Gates*. Garden City, N.Y.: Doubleday, 1987.

Hudson, Rock, and Sara Davidson. *Rock Hudson: His Story*. New York: William Morrow, 1986.

Oppenheimer, Jerry, and Jack Vitek. *Idol Rock Hudson: The True Story of an American Film Hero*. New York: Villard, 1986.

Parker, John. *Five for Hollywood*. Secaucus, N.J.: Carol, 1991.

Royce, Brenda Scott. *Rock Hudson: A Bio-Bibliography*. Westport, Conn.: Greenwood Press, 1995.

See also: 1930's-1960's: Hollywood Bans "Sexual Perversion" in Films; June 5 and July 3, 1981: Reports of Rare Diseases Mark Beginning of AIDS Epidemic; July, 1982: Gay-Related Immunodeficiency Is Renamed AIDS; Spring, 1984: AIDS Virus Is Discovered; Sept., 1986: AZT Treats People with AIDS; Mar., 1987: Radical AIDS Activist Group ACT UP Is Founded; June 27, 1988: Report of the Presidential AIDS Commission; Dec. 1, 1988: First World AIDS Day; 1989: Act Up Paris Is Founded; June 25, 1993: Clinton Appoints First AIDS Czar.

1986
Bowers v. Hardwick Upholds State Sodomy Laws

The U.S. Supreme Court's decision in Bowers v. Hardwick *upheld the state of Georgia's power to criminalize private, consensual, adult sexual relations between men.*

Locale: Atlanta, Georgia
Categories: Laws, acts, and legal history; civil rights; crime

Key Figures

Michael J. Bowers, attorney general of Georgia, 1981-1997
Michael Hardwick (1954-1991), bartender
Harry A. Blackmun (1908-1999), associate justice of the United States, 1970-1994
Warren E. Burger (1907-1995), chief justice of the United States, 1969-1986
Lewis F. Powell (1907-1998), associate justice of the United States, 1972-1987
John Paul Stevens (b. 1920), associate justice of the United States from 1975
Byron White (1917-2002), associate justice of the United States, 1962-1993

Summary of Event

In August, 1982, Atlanta police arrived at the home of a twenty-eight-year-old gay bartender, Michael Hardwick. They were lawfully admitted into the apartment by a roommate of the respondent for the purpose of serving Hardwick with an arrest warrant for failure to appear in court on an unrelated charge (drinking in public). The arrest warrant was later found to have been invalid. While attempting to serve the warrant, the police officers entered Hardwick's bedroom and found him engaged in oral sex with another man. The law enforcement officials arrested both men under Georgia's sodomy statute.

The district attorney for the county of Fulton, Georgia, declined to prosecute. However, Hardwick was issued a warning that the sodomy charges would be brought in the future if the respondent did not stay out of trouble for a period of seven years. Hardwick, in turn, filed suit against Michael Bowers, attorney general of the state of Georgia, charging that Georgia's sodomy statute was unconstitutional. A sodomy conviction in Georgia carried a maximum punishment of twenty years in prison. After hearings in the Federal District Court for the District of Northern Georgia and the U.S. Court of Appeals, the case moved to the U.S. Supreme Court on a writ of certiorari.

The closely divided Court ruled 5-4 against the respondent, Hardwick, and for the petitioner, Michael J. Bowers, attorney general of Georgia. Five opinions were filed in this case: the majority ruling (Justice Byron White), two minority concurring decisions (Chief Justice Warren E. Burger and Justice Lewis F. Powell), and two dissenting opinions (one by Justice Harry A. Blackmun, the other by Justice John Paul Stevens).

The fundamental issue in *Bowers v. Hardwick* (1986) was the right to privacy. The Supreme Court had previously ruled in *Griswold v. Connecticut* (1965) that, although the U.S. Constitution does not enumerate a specific "right to privacy," the provisions of the Bill of Rights, taken together, created certain penumbras, or zones of privacy, within which the government may not intervene. The First, Third, Fourth, and Ninth Amendments to the Constitution established an implied right to privacy in

> **BOWERS V. HARDWICK: KEY EXCERPTS**
>
> *From the majority opinion:*
> (a) The Constitution does not confer a fundamental right upon homosexuals to engage in sodomy....
> (b) Against a background in which many States have criminalized sodomy and still do, to claim that a right to engage in such conduct is "deeply rooted in this Nation's history and tradition" or "implicit in the concept of ordered liberty" is, at best, facetious.
> (c) There should be great resistance to expand the reach of the Due Process Clauses to cover new fundamental rights....
> (d) The fact that homosexual conduct occurs in the privacy of the home does not affect the result.
> (e) Sodomy laws should not be invalidated on the asserted basis that majority belief that sodomy is immoral is an inadequate rationale to support the laws....
>
> Respondent... asserts that the result should be different where the homosexual conduct occurs in the privacy of the home....
>
> Stanley did protect conduct that would not have been protected outside the home, and it partially prevented the enforcement of state obscenity laws; but the decision was firmly grounded in the First Amendment. The right pressed upon us here has no similar support in the text of the Constitution, and it does not qualify for recognition under the prevailing principles for construing the Fourteenth Amendment. Its limits are also difficult to discern. Plainly enough, otherwise illegal conduct is not always immunized whenever it occurs in the home. Victimless crimes, such as the possession and use of illegal drugs, do not escape the law where they are committed at home.... And if respondent's submission is limited to the voluntary sexual conduct between consenting adults, it would be difficult, except by fiat, to limit the claimed right to homosexual conduct while leaving exposed to prosecution adultery, incest, and other sexual crimes even though they are committed in the home. We are unwilling to start down that road.
>
> Even if the conduct at issue here is not a fundamental right, respondent asserts that there must be a rational basis for the law and that there is none in this case other than the presumed belief of a majority of the electorate in Georgia that homosexual sodomy is immoral and unacceptable. This is said to be an inadequate rationale to support the law. The law, however, is constantly based on notions of morality....
>
> Accordingly, the judgment of the Court of Appeals is Reversed.
>
> *Concurring opinion:* I join the Court's opinion, but I write separately to underscore my view that in constitutional terms there is no such thing as a fundamental right to commit homosexual sodomy.
>
> *Dissenting opinion:* This case is no more about "a fundamental right to engage in homosexual sodomy," as the Court purports to declare, than Stanley v. Georgia was about a fundamental right to watch obscene movies.... Rather, this case is about "the most comprehensive of rights and the right most valued by civilized men," namely, "the right to be let alone."...
>
> I believe we must analyze respondent Hardwick's claim in the light of the values that underlie the constitutional right to privacy. If that right means anything, it means that, before Georgia can prosecute its citizens for making choices about the most intimate aspects of their lives, it must do more than assert that the choice they have made is an "'abominable crime not fit to be named among Christians.'"

marital relations. Any law, regulation, ruling, or statute that conflicted with this right to privacy was unconstitutional.

In the 1973 Supreme Court ruling in *Roe v. Wade*, the justices expanded the foundation of the right to privacy by adding the Fifth and Fourteenth Amendments to those already cited in *Griswold*. The right to privacy, the Court said, was educed from the guarantees of the Fifth Amendment and the due process clause of the Fourteenth Amendment. Abortion, therefore, fell under the penumbra of the right to privacy implied in the Bill of Rights and extended those protections to apply to the states as well as the federal government.

In *Bowers v. Hardwick* the majority ruled that the right to privacy did not extend to private, consensual adult same-gender sodomy. Justice White, writing for the majority, held that "[t]he Constitution does not confer a fundamental right upon homosexuals to engage in sodomy." The Court further ruled that it was disinclined to discover new rights within the embrace of the due process clause of the Fourteenth Amendment. That the behavior in question (sodomy) occurred in the privacy of the home did not matter to the Court. Finally, the Court determined that the opinion that a majority of Georgians disapproved of homosexual sodomy as immoral and unacceptable was a rational basis in law for Georgia's sodomy statute.

In his concurring decision, Chief Justice Burger noted that the Constitution guarantees no fundamental right to practice homosexual sodomy. The real question, according to Burger, concerned the scope of the state's police powers and whether that authority enabled the state to regulate private, consensual, adult homosexual relations. He argued it did.

Justice Powell, also concurring, ruled that there was, indeed, no substantive right at issue in the case that was protected by due process under the Fourteenth Amendment. He worried that there may be a violation of the guarantee against cruel and unusual punishment, observing that violation of Georgia's sodomy statute carried a maximum penalty of twenty years in prison. However, Powell concluded that no breach of the Eighth Amendment existed in this particular case because Hardwick had been neither convicted nor sentenced under the statute.

In his dissent, Justice Blackmun held that the case had nothing to do with a fundamental right to practice homosexual sodomy. Rather, the statute impinged upon an even more basic privilege: the right of an individual to be let alone. Essentially, Georgia's sodomy law prohibited individuals from making their own choices about what adult consensual sexual activity they may or may not engage in within the privacy of their own homes. This, Blackmun ruled, was an unconscionable infringement of individual rights.

Justice Stevens disagreed with the ruling opinion, noting that a majority governing interest cannot be construed to deny the minority of their rights.

Moreover, the Georgia statute was a violation of the liberty that the due process clause of the Fourteenth Amendment protected. The penumbral zone created by the Fourteenth Amendment included homosexual sodomy.

SIGNIFICANCE

The legacy of *Bowers v. Hardwick* was twofold. First, the 5-4 ruling reflected the divisive nature of American attitudes toward homosexuality in the last decades of the twentieth century. Second, the decision set back the movement toward legal equality and gay and lesbian rights for almost two decades. Legal parity between gay and lesbian Americans and their heterosexual counterparts would not be achieved until the Supreme Court decision in *Lawrence v. Texas* (2003).

Michael Hardwick did not live to see his case overturned. He reportedly died on June 13, 1991, in Gainesville, Florida, after battling AIDS. Michael J. Bowers, the Georgia attorney general, became embroiled in another gay rights litigation matter when he was sued by Robin Shahar in 1991 for illegally withdrawing a job offer after he had learned the lawyer was a lesbian and was planning a commitment ceremony with her partner. Eventually, the Supreme Court refused to hear her case. In 1997, Bowers was exposed for being in an adulterous affair with a secretary while running for governor. He lost his gubernatorial bid.

—*Keith Carson*

FURTHER READING

Caserio, Robert L. "Supreme Court Discourse v. Homosexual Fiction." In *Displacing Homophobia: Gay Male Perspectives in Literature and Culture*, edited by Ronald R. Butters, John M. Clum, and Michael Moon. Durham, N.C.: Duke University Press, 1989.

Curry, Lynne. *The Human Body on Trial: A Handbook with Cases, Laws, and Documents*. Santa Barbara, Calif.: ABC-CLIO, 2002.

Hickey, Adam. "Between Two Spheres: Comparing State and Federal Approaches to the Right to Privacy and Prohibitions Against Sodomy." *Yale Law Review* 111, no. 4 (January, 2002): 993-1030.

Murdoch, Joyce, and Deb Price. *Courting Justice: Gay Men and Lesbians v. the Supreme Court*. New York: Basic Books, 2001.

Richards, David A. J. *The Case for Gay Rights: From Bowers to Lawrence and Beyond*. Lawrence: University Press of Kansas, 2005.

Rubenstein, William B., ed. *Lesbians, Gay Men, and the Law*. New York: New Press, 1994.

"Sodomy Laws Around the World." http://www.sodomylaws.org.

See also: May 6, 1868: Kertbeny Coins the Terms "Homosexual" and "Heterosexual"; 1885: United Kingdom Criminalizes "Gross Indecency"; Jan. 12, 1939: *Thompson v. Aldredge* Dismisses Sodomy Charges Against Lesbians; Sept. 4, 1957: The *Wolfenden Report* Calls for Decriminalizing Private Consensual Sex; 1961: Illinois Legalizes Consensual Homosexual Sex; Jan. 22, 1973: *Roe v. Wade* Legalizes Abortion and Extends Privacy Rights; Aug., 1973: American Bar Association Calls for Repeal of Laws Against Consensual Sex; Oct. 18, 1973: Lambda Legal Authorized to Practice Law; Nov. 17, 1975: U.S. Supreme Court Rules in "Crimes Against Nature" Case; Jan. 1, 1988: Canada Decriminalizes Sex Practices Between Consenting Adults; 1992-2006: Indians Struggle to Abolish Sodomy Law; June 26, 2003: U.S. Supreme Court Overturns Texas Sodomy Law.

1986
Paula Gunn Allen Publishes *The Sacred Hoop*

Paula Gunn Allen, a specialist in American Indian/Native American studies, published The Sacred Hoop *as a challenge to the Anglo-European erasure of indigenous American beliefs about gender and sexuality.*

Locale: United States
Categories: Publications; race and ethnicity; feminism; literature; transgender/transsexuality

Key Figure
Paula Gunn Allen (Paula Marie Francis; b. 1939), Laguna Pueblo scholar of Native American sexuality and gender history and women's studies

Summary of Event
In 1986, Native American scholar and lesbian Paula Gunn Allen published *The Sacred Hoop: Recovering the Feminine in American Indian Traditions*, the first collection of essays in which gender issues and sexuality are examined from an American Indian perspective. The book combines autobiography with historical narrative, poetry, literary

Paula Gunn Allen. (© Tama Rothschild)

analysis, and myth, and explores how homophobia, sexism, and racism have significantly distorted how American Indian cultures are perceived and interpreted. *The Sacred Hoop* is of added significance to lesbian, gay, and transgender history because Allen comes out as lesbian in the book's introduction.

Allen, born Paula Marie Francis in 1939 in Cubero, New Mexico, has a Laguna Pueblo-Lakota Sioux-Scottish mother and a Lebanese American father. She is a member of the Laguna Pueblo tribe. She spent much of her childhood absorbing the stories and beliefs of the female-centered Pueblo culture from her mother and grandmother. As a result, Allen's thinking has been deeply influenced by the Native American experience. Allen, who received her bachelor's degree in English in 1966 and a master of fine arts degree in creative writing in 1968, both from the University of Oregon, also earned a doctorate in American studies with an emphasis in Native American studies from the University of New Mexico in 1976. She retired as a professor of English and American Indian Studies at the University of California, Los Angeles, in 1999. In both nonfiction and fiction, Allen has addressed Native American lesbian and gay ways of life. Along with *The Sacred Hoop*, she has written poetry and novels and has edited several collections.

The Sacred Hoop journeys to the roots of American Indian cultures to find ways to challenge patriarchal constructions of gender identity. Native American cultures once celebrated people who were "two-spirited," that is, individuals, found in most tribes, who would now be called lesbian, gay, bisexual, or transgender. The Kaska culture would designate as a boy one girl in a family of only girls. The new "son" would dress in male clothing and then would function in the Kaska male role for the rest of his life. The Yuma culture had a tradition of gender designation based on dreams; a female who dreamed of weapons would become a male for all practical purposes. A Cocopah girl who chose to play with boys or with boys' objects such as a bow and arrow would become a male functionary. Among the Mohave, the *hwame,* or lesbian, took a male name and was in all respects subject to ritual male taboos such as avoidance of contact with a menstruating wife. The *hwame*'s wife was considered not a *hwame* but simply a woman. The Navajo considered lesbians an asset to their culture, and the Mohave, Quinault, Apache, Ojibwa, and Eskimo all viewed homosexuals as a natural and necessary part of society.

This fluid definition and understanding of "gender" had been quickly dismissed and forgotten by European settlers. Allen reports that in the centuries following European colonization of the New World, American Indian tribes have seen a progressive shift from gynocentric, egalitarian, ritual-based social systems to secularized systems closely imitative of the European patriarchal system. Patriarchy is harmful to gender-bending and rule-breaking gays and lesbians, whereas female-centered social systems, also called matriarchies, accord honor to a diversity of people, including gays, lesbians, and those who are transgender; patriarchy, on the other hand, values masculinity and sameness. Female-centered societies and cultures are focused on social responsibility rather than on privilege. To the pre-Columbian American Indians who originated this female-centered system, it was a way of life to recognize and respect diversity rather than enforce conformity and sameness. Allen's notion of gynocentrism is not the same as the idea of a matriarchy, however, in which females dominate males. To Allen, the genders operate in the context of balance and mutual respect.

European colonizers of the Americas also had been threatened by Native American culture because it was a culture of decisive, self-directing females and nurturing, pacifist males. To achieve total conquest, the Europeans needed to establish and practice a patriarchal social and cultural system. Along with the devaluation of women in patriarchy comes the devaluation of traditional spiritual leaders, and, largely because of their ritual power and status, the devaluation of lesbian and gay tribal members as leaders, shamans, healers, or ritual participants. Virtually all sexual customs among the tribes had been changed by colonialism, including marital, premarital, homosexual, and ritual sexual practices. Allen argues that this loss of tradition and memory, in particular the erasure of tribal gynocentric belief systems, represents the root of oppression.

SIGNIFICANCE

Paula Gunn Allen was one of the most prominent American Indian intellectuals and writers of the twentieth century. Her scholarship on Native American understandings of "two-spirits" represents some of the most significant work on the subject, laying the groundwork for more research in this area. Despite increased scholarly interest in women of color, Allen's feminist writings have not attracted the attention they deserve. Scholars such as AnaLouise Keating have attributed this lack of attention to what many believe is the extreme nature of Allen's views.

Reflecting Allen's background as a feminist of color who came of age politically in the 1960's, Allen takes a separatist stance grounded in a rigidly gynocentric American Indian life perspective. She has been criticized for taking what some consider to be a monolithic, essentializing view of spiritual forces and the feminine in American Indian traditions. In addition, because she conceives of an inner self that often receives guidance from the supernatural, Allen has been further challenged for perpetuating romantic images of a mythic tribal universe to which Euro-America can securely escape in a desire to find an exotic, authentic Native Other.

Allen nevertheless has made visible the lives of lesbians, gays, bisexuals, and transgender people from the past. She has written these individuals into Native American history. In doing so, she has helped to undermine the notion that homosexuality is an "unnatural" concept.

—*Caryn E. Neumann*

FURTHER READING

Allen, Paula Gunn. *Off the Reservation: Reflections on Boundary-busting Border-crossing Loose Canons*. Boston: Beacon Press, 1998.

_____. *The Sacred Hoop: Recovering the Feminine in American Indian Traditions*. 1986. New preface. Boston: Beacon Press, 1992.

Anderson, Kim. *A Recognition of Being: Reconstructing Native Womanhood*. Toronto, Ont.: Second Story Press, 2000.

Bloom, Harold, ed. *Native American Women Writers*. Philadelphia: Chelsea House, 1998.

Hansen, Elizabeth. *Paula Gunn Allen*. Boise, Idaho: Boise State University Press, 1990.

Jacobs, Sue-Ellen, Wesley Thomas, and Sabine Lang, eds. *Two-spirit People: Native American Gender Identity, Sexuality, and Spirituality*. Urbana: University of Illinois Press, 1997.

Keating, AnaLouise. *Women Reading Women Writing: Self-Invention in Paula Gunn Allen, Gloria Anzaldúa, and Audre Lorde*. Philadelphia: Temple University Press, 1996.

Pulitano, Elvira. *Toward a Native American Critical Theory*. Lincoln: University of Nebraska Press, 2003.

SEE ALSO: Jan.-June, 1886: Two-Spirit American Indian Visits Washington, D.C.; 1975: Gay American Indians Is Founded; Oct. 12-15, 1979: First National Third World Lesbian and Gay Conference Convenes; Oct., 1981: Kitchen Table: Women of Color Press Is Founded; Sept., 1983: First National Lesbians of Color Conference Convenes.

January, 1986
SOUTH ASIAN NEWSLETTER *TRIKONE* BEGINS PUBLICATION

The publication and distribution of Trikone, *the newsletter of the group of the same name, set in motion the creation of an international network of support groups for gay, lesbian, bisexual, and transgender South Asians. The newsletter became* Trikone Magazine *in 1993 and remains in circulation.*

LOCALE: Palo Alto, California
CATEGORIES: Publications; organizations and institutions

KEY FIGURES
Arvind Kumar (b. 1956), cofounder of *Trikone* and the organization
Suvir Das, cofounder of *Trikone* and the organization

SUMMARY OF EVENT
In the 1980's, the lesbian and gay community in the San Francisco Bay Area was vibrant. There were dozens of bars, restaurants, and shops serving the social needs of a thriving population of lesbians and gays. Additionally, out of the horrors of the HIV-AIDS crisis came lesbian and gay support groups as well as new knowledge of the basics of political organizing. Yet, for some individuals who were seeking social and political connections with those with similar ethnic and cultural backgrounds, this scene was less than ideal.

After finishing graduate school in 1982, Arvind Kumar, originally from India, moved to Palo Alto, California. Although he participated in the activities of several lesbian and gay groups at local universities, as well as activities sponsored by groups such as Pacific Friends—aimed expressly at Asians and Pacific Islanders—Kumar felt that some sort of cultural connection was missing between him and other gay men. Specifically, he was looking for an organization that provided a supportive space where he could meet other gays and lesbians who, like himself, were of South Asian (Indian, Pakistani, Bangladeshi, Sri Lankan, Nepalese, Bhutanese, Burmese [Myanmar], Tibetan, Maldivian, and Afghani) descent.

In the early 1980's, there were no groups or publications explicitly for lesbians and gays from South Asia. While *Anamika,* a newsletter for South Asian lesbian and bisexual women, began publication in 1985, it soon folded.

In late 1985, Kumar met fellow Indian Suvir Das and the two struck up a friendship. Eventually, they determined that unless they organized their own group for individuals of South Asian descent, they would never meet others with a similar sociocultural background. In January of 1986, using the existing lesbian and gay periodicals in the San Francisco Bay Area as models, the two began publishing a newsletter. They chose to name the newsletter *Trikone*, Sanskrit for "triangle," as a reminder of past injustices (the triangle was used to identify lesbians and gays in Nazi concentration camps) as well as a symbol of gay and lesbian pride and unity.

Because there was no network for lesbian and gay South Asians, Kumar and Das did not have a mailing list for the newsletter, thus they sent the inaugural issue to local and national lesbian and gay newspapers and magazines as well as to the publishers of mainstream Indian-run newspapers around the United States. Issues also were sent to individuals in India and to other areas of South Asia for distribution. Almost immediately, *Trikone* began serving as an umbrella under which lesbian, gay, bisexual, and transgender individuals of South Asian descent could gather, regardless of gender, class, religion, or national origin.

As the newsletter was being published, the social-support group, also called Trikone, was being formed by the small number of men who had worked on the newsletter. Subsequently, members of this group marched in the June, 1986, gay and lesbian pride parade in San Francisco, which provided, perhaps for the first time, a public face to the lesbian and gay South Asian community.

> **TRIKONE'S MISSION STATEMENT**
>
> Through social and political activities, Trikone offers a supportive, empowering, and non-judgmental environment, where queer South Asians can meet, make connections, and proudly promote awareness and acceptance of their sexuality in society. Trikone actively works against all forms of oppression based on race, gender, class, and other identities.
>
> Trikone works toward the following goals:
>
> Bring people of South Asian heritage together in a friendly, supportive, and non-judgmental environment.
>
> Promote awareness, visibility and acceptance of alternative sexuality in society.
>
> Trikone proudly affirms both its South Asian identity as well as its sexuality.
>
> Oppose discrimination based on race, gender, class, and other identities.

In April of 1993, the newsletter became a glossy quarterly called *Trikone Magazine* (www.trikone.org), and it has since won critical acclaim. It can be found in bookshops as well as on the library shelves of colleges and universities in the United States and in South Asia. The magazine features editorials, letters, news, poetry, artwork, fiction, interviews, film and book reviews, classified ads, and more. Topics cover interracial relationships and marriage, youth and aging, arts and entertainment, and immigration. Additionally, each issue of *Trikone Magazine* features an important resource section that includes Web sites of interest, lists of other relevant publications, and South Asian contacts—both international and domestic. In February of 1995, Trikone's board elected cogender cochairs, creating a more gender-inclusive organization that reflected the group's diversity.

SIGNIFICANCE

Trikone, and the group that formed by those who worked on assembling the newsletter, has inspired the formation of other groups using "Trikone" in their names. These include Trikone-Tejas (Texas), Trikone-Northwest (Seattle), and Trikone-Atlanta. Other gay and lesbian South Asian organizations that followed in the footsteps of the "original" Trikone include Gay Bombay, South Asian Network (SAN), South Asian Lesbian and Gay Association of New York (SALGA), and Satrang (formerly Trikone-Los Angeles), to name just a few.

As further testament to the influence of Trikone, organizations aimed at cultural groups other than South Asian have emerged across the United States and around the world as well. Examples include the Gay and Lesbian Armenian Society (GALAS), Los Angeles Greek Gay and Lesbian Association, and the Iranian Lesbian/Gay and Bisexual Community (known as HOMAN).

The diligence of Arvind Kumar, Suvir Das, and the other founding members of *Trikone* has inspired the founding of a number of social, political, cultural, and support organizations around the world whose purpose is to empower South Asian lesbians, gays, bisexuals, transgender individuals, and those questioning their sexuality.

—*Robert F. Phillips*

FURTHER READING

Eng, David, and Alice Y. Hom. *Q & A: Queer in Asian America*. Philadelphia: Temple University Press, 1998.

Kumar, Arvind, and Suvir Das. "First Editorial." *Trikone* 1 (1986): 10.

Paranjape, Makarand, ed. *Diaspora: Theories, Histories, Texts*. New Delhi, India: Indialong, 2001.

Ratti, Rakesh, ed. *A Lotus of Another Color: An Unfolding of the South Asian Gay and Lesbian Experience*. Boston: Alyson, 1993.

Shankar, Lavina Dhingra, and Rajini Srikanth, eds. *A Part, Yet Apart: South Asians in Asian America*. Philadelphia: Temple University Press, 1998.

SEE ALSO: 1975: Gay American Indians Is Founded; Oct. 12-15, 1979: First National Third World Lesbian and Gay Conference Convenes; Sept., 1983: First National Lesbians of Color Conference Convenes; 1987: Asian Pacific Lesbian Network Is Founded; 1987: VIVA Is Founded to Promote Latina and Latino Artists; Oct. 14-17, 1987: Latin American and Caribbean Lesbian Feminist Network Is Formed; 1990: United Lesbians of African Heritage Is Founded; Dec., 1990: Asian Lesbian Network Holds Its First Conference; Apr. 6, 1991: Asian Lesbians and Gays Protest Lambda Fund-Raiser; Oct. 9-12, 1998: First International Retreat for Lesbian and Gay Muslims Is Held; Nov., 1999: First Middle Eastern Gay and Lesbian Organization Is Founded.

September, 1986
AZT TREATS PEOPLE WITH AIDS

Because of promising findings, the U.S. Food and Drug Administration ended a clinical trial of AZT early and released the experimental drug so that it could be prescribed to people with AIDS.

LOCALE: Washington, D.C.
CATEGORIES: HIV-AIDS; health and medicine; science; organizations and institutions; marches, protests, and riots

KEY FIGURES
Janet Rideout, organic chemist and codiscoverer of AZT's effectiveness in fighting HIV
Samuel Broder, research scientist, National Cancer Institute, who helped find AZT's role in fighting HIV
Hiroaki Mitsuya (b. 1950), research scientist, National Cancer Institute, who helped find AZT's role in fighting HIV
Robert Yarchoan (b. 1950), research scientist, National Cancer Institute, who helped find AZT's role in fighting HIV
Larry Kramer (b. 1935), playwright, novelist, and gay rights activist

SUMMARY OF EVENT
Azidothymidine, or AZT (now called zidovudine), was developed first during the 1960's by scientists in the United States using National Cancer Institute (NCI) funding, and when many scientists thought that human cancers were caused by infectious agents (retroviruses). Consistent findings dispelled these beliefs, so research on AZT was stopped.

In 1985, NCI scientist Hiroaki Mitsuya published the first report of AZT's successful effects against AIDS in humans. Mitsuya and colleagues Samuel Broder, Robert Yarchoan, and Burroughs-Wellcome chemist Janet Rideout, showed that AZT interferes with the functioning of the virus's reverse transcriptase enzyme, an enzyme the virus needs if it is to insert its RNA into the DNA of the host cell. Scientists found that AZT does not destroy the AIDS virus per se. Rather, the drug incapacitates the virus's reproductive capabilities, thus delaying disease progression. This was the first documented instance of the effectiveness of an antiretroviral medication in humans. Based on these data, and at Mitsuya's urging, AZT was selected over other potential medication for continued study by NCI.

The early clinical trials of AZT for use against AIDS were sponsored jointly by NCI and the pharmaceutical company Burroughs-Wellcome (now GlaxoSmithKline). Initial, promising findings led to a larger, multisite, placebo-controlled trial of AZT in 282 patients who had either recently had *pneumocystis carinii* pneumonia or were diagnosed with AIDS-related complex (that is, had a compromised immune system and a history of multiple AIDS-defining illnesses). This study was to follow participants, each receiving either AZT or placebo, for twenty-four weeks, but to the pleasant surprise of scientists and people living with AIDS, the study was terminated several months ahead of schedule, in September of 1986.

An interim analysis of the data performed by an independent scientific advisory board showed promising but preliminary effects of AZT on mortality, with significantly greater short-term survival rates in the HIV-infected patients receiving AZT compared to placebo. Institutional ethics boards that oversee medical and behavioral research generally take the drastic step of stopping a trial early only when the trial shows unequivocal benefit or unacceptable toxicity. In this study, only one patient who received AZT had died, but there were nineteen deaths among patients receiving the placebo. Still, this step was particularly surprising since only 10 percent of the patients (27 of 282) had been observed for the full duration of the study. These strong results marked the first major success in the fight against AIDS.

One week later, the U.S. Food and Drug Administration (FDA) approved a plan to offer AZT to the study participants who had been receiving the placebo pills. Soon after the clinical trial was stopped, Burroughs-Wellcome purchased the AZT formula and filed for a patent in the United States. In January, 1987, more than three thousand HIV-infected individuals began receiving AZT.

With the recommendation of FDA scientists, as well as the support of the FDA's independent Anti-Infective Drugs Advisory Committee, the agency officially approved AZT for use against AIDS in March, 1987, and then as a preventive treatment (for example, for hospital employees accidentally stuck by syringes containing HIV-infected blood) in 1990. In 1994, AZT was approved for use in HIV-infected pregnant women and in newborn babies of HIV-infected mothers.

SIGNIFICANCE

Burroughs-Wellcome was granted a patent for AZT, giving the company a monopoly in the U.S. market and allowing the company to sell the drug for more than twelve times its production cost. Consumers and advocates were incensed. Generally, high drug prices reflect a pharmaceutical company's attempt to recoup the cost of developing and testing a drug, but in this case, those initial costs were covered by taxpayers through NCI funding. Lawsuits that garnered heavy press coverage ensued, claiming that the AZT patent was invalid, but a U.S. federal appeals court in 1994 ruled in favor of the drug company.

In response to apathy from the U.S. government and from drug companies, gay activist Larry Kramer founded the AIDS Coalition to Unleash Power (ACT UP), which boasted tens of thousands of members, organized into 140 chapters worldwide at the organization's peak in the late 1980's. With the slogans "Silence = Death" and "Knowledge = Power," ACT UP used extreme and radical measures to gain visibility and, in particular, to convince Burroughs-Wellcome to increase the availability of AZT and make it less expensive. Early tactics included a large protest at the New York Stock Exchange and a "die in" (where protesters sat in a city street during rush hour), which brought lower Manhattan traffic to a near standstill.

Despite the success of the initial study, later studies showed that AZT was having no positive effect against AIDS progression. A heated international debate ensued about whether AZT was helpful or a waste of time and money and whether it was causing more health problems than it prevents. With the rise of other antiretroviral medications, that controversy diminished, but not before it gave birth to the AIDS "rethinker" movement, which claims, in spite of overwhelming scientific evidence, that HIV does not cause AIDS. Led by biologist Peter Duesberg, AIDS "denialists" gained currency especially in the 1990's in Africa, as government leaders used this movement to justify their positions to downplay the seriousness of the widespread AIDS epidemic in their countries.

AZT's intense side effects and a complicated dosing schedule (for example, every four hours) meant that it was difficult to adhere to the drug regimen. Those taking the drug would end up developing a resistance to it, which would weaken the drug's effectiveness over time. Eventually, virtually all persons with AIDS who were treated long term with AZT alone (called AZT monotherapy) developed an increased resistance to AZT through viral mutations. Using knowledge gained from the biological mechanism of AZT, however, scientists subsequently developed other drugs, and combination therapy would prove most effective at controlling, at least to some degree, the disease's effects.

—*David W. Pantalone*

Further Reading

Barnes, D. M. "Promising Results Halt Trial of Anti-AIDS Drug." *Science* 234 (1986): 15-16.

Duesberg, Peter H. *Inventing the AIDS Virus*. Washington, D.C.: Regnery, 1996.

Ezzell, Carol. "Hope in a Vial: Will There Be an AIDS Vaccine Anytime Soon?" *Scientific American* 186 (June, 2002): 38-45.

Fischl, M. A., D. D. Richman, M. H. Grieco, et al. "The Efficacy of Azidothymidine (AZT) in the Treatment of Patients with AIDS and AIDS-Related Complex: A Double-Blind, Placebo-Controlled Trial." *New England Journal of Medicine* 317, no. 4 (1987): 185-191.

Kramer, Larry. *Reports from the Holocaust: The Making of An AIDS Activist*. New York: St. Martin's Press, 1989.

Roleff, Tamara L., ed. *AIDS: Opposing Viewpoints*. San Diego, Calif.: Greenhaven Press, 2003.

See also: June 5 and July 3, 1981: Reports of Rare Diseases Mark Beginning of AIDS Epidemic; July, 1982: Gay-Related Immunodeficiency Is Renamed AIDS; Spring, 1984: AIDS Virus Is Discovered; July 25, 1985: Actor Hudson Announces He Has AIDS; Nov., 1986: Californians Reject LaRouche's Quarantine Initiative; 1987: Shilts Publishes *And the Band Played On*; Mar., 1987: Radical AIDS Activist Group ACT UP Is Founded; June 27, 1988: Report of the Presidential AIDS Commission; Dec. 1, 1988: First World AIDS Day; June 25, 1993: Clinton Appoints First AIDS Czar.

November, 1986
Californians Reject LaRouche's Quarantine Initiative

California voters rejected Proposition 64, which would have allowed health officials to quarantine people with AIDS. The campaign in support of the initiative was funded by Lyndon LaRouche, a political extremist using fear of AIDS as a wedge issue.

Also known as: Proposition 64; Prevent AIDS Now Initiative Committee (PANIC)
Locale: California
Categories: Laws, acts, and legal history; HIV-AIDS; civil rights

Key Figures

Lyndon LaRouche (b. 1922), unofficial sponsor of California's Proposition 64
Khushro Ghandhi, proposition sponsor and California director for LaRouche's National Democratic Policy Committee
Brian Lantz, proposition sponsor and LaRouche movement leader
William E. Dannemeyer (b. 1929), U.S. representative from California who supported the measure
Dianne Feinstein (b. 1933), mayor of San Francisco who opposed the measure
Diane Abbitt and
Peter Scott, gay and lesbian rights activists and chairpersons of the No on 64 campaign
David Mixner (b. 1946), gay rights activist and political consultant

Summary of Event

If passed, California's Proposition 64 would have made persons with HIV-AIDS subject to quarantine by public health directors. Officially the ballot initiative was sponsored by Khushro Ghandhi, the California director for the National Democratic

Policy Committee of political extremist and writer Lyndon LaRouche, and Brian Lantz, leader of the LaRouche movement in the Southwest. LaRouche formed the Prevent AIDS Now Initiative Committee (PANIC) to collect signatures for the measure in 1985 and campaign for its passage throughout 1986.

Opponents of the measure had argued that Proposition 64 was a direct attack on gays and lesbians by LaRouche, who had railed against gays and lesbians in his political writings. In fact, one of LaRouche's key advisers had pointed out that the measure was primarily meant to affect "nonheterosexuals" and those persons described as belonging to "classic risk groups," which presumably meant homosexuals, intravenous drug users, and racial and ethnic minorities.

Independent analysis of the measure suggested that the proposal would declare AIDS to be an infectious, contagious, and communicable disease and that the condition of being a carrier of the human T-cell leukemia/lymphotrophic virus type III (HTLV-III) was an infectious, contagious, and communicable condition. This classification would require that both be placed on the list of reportable diseases and conditions maintained by the director of California's health services department. Subsequently, both would be subject to quarantine and isolation statutes and regulations. In addition, persons infected with a disease-causing organism could be excluded from schools and from food-handling jobs. These measures could be applied to persons merely *suspected* of having the infection or the disease.

If broadly interpreted, the measure could have cost the state hundreds of millions of dollars per year. GLBT activists also had argued that the same internment camps used to harbor Japanese Americans during World War II would have been used to intern those identified as "carriers." Given the draconian nature of the measure, public support was low, 31 to 56 percent, and changed little throughout the campaign.

Beyond LaRouche and his followers, supporters of the measure included Republican representative William E. Dannemeyer, California state senator John T. Doolittle, and several California medical doctors. Dannemeyer would go on to sponsor measures with similar provisions in legislation introduced in the U.S. House of Representatives. In total, $370,000 had been spent by proponents to collect signatures and to campaign for the measure.

The measure was opposed by the No on 64—Stop LaRouche coalition of gay rights, medical, and civil rights organizations, including the California Medical Association. The No on 64 campaign was chaired by Diane Abbitt and Peter Scott. David Mixner was hired to run the campaign, and Larry Sprenger became its treasurer. High-profile politicians from both parties opposed the measure, including California's Republican governor George Deukmejian, U.S. senators Alan Cranston (Democrat) and Pete Wilson (Republican), Senate candidate Ed Zschau (Republican), San Francisco mayor Dianne Feinstein (Democrat), and Los Angeles mayor Tom Bradley (Democrat), who was also a candidate for governor. The measure was also opposed by a number of Hollywood stars, including the otherwise conservative Bob Hope. Indeed, by the middle of the summer in 1986, even the chair of the state Republican Party had come out against the

A button from the No on 64 campaign.

> **PROPOSITION 64**
>
> *Ballot Summary:* [This proposition] Declares that AIDS is an infectious, contagious and communicable disease and that the condition of being a carrier of the HTLV-III virus is an infectious, contagious and communicable condition. Requires both be placed on the list of reportable diseases and conditions maintained by the director of the Department of Health Services. Provides that both are subject to quarantine and isolation statutes and regulations. Provides that Department of Health Services personnel and all health officers shall fulfill the duties and obligations set forth in specified statutory provisions to preserve the public health from AIDS.
>
> *Section 1.* The purpose of this Act is to:
>
> A. Enforce and confirm the declaration of the California Legislature set forth in Health and Safety Code Section 195 that acquired immune deficiency syndrome (AIDS) is serious and life threatening to men and women from all segments of society, that AIDS is usually lethal and that it is caused by an infectious agent with a high concentration of cases in California;
>
> B. Protect victims of acquired immune deficiency syndrome (AIDS), members of their families and local communities, and the public health at large; and
>
> C. Utilize the existing structure of the State Department of Health Services and local health officers and the statutes and regulations under which they serve to preserve the public health from acquired immune deficiency syndrome (AIDS).
>
> *Section 2.* Acquired immune deficiency syndrome (AIDS) is an infectious, contagious and communicable disease and the condition of being a carrier of the HTLV-III virus is an infectious, contagious and communicable condition and both shall be placed and maintained by the director of the Department of Health Services on the list of reportable diseases and conditions mandated by Health and Safety Code Section 3123. . . .

measure, and only a handful of elected officials had supported it.

The 71 to 29 percent defeat of the measure came after the opposing coalition spent almost $2.8 million on its campaign, more than six times what the proponents spent. Analysis suggests that the measure's opponents were successful because they framed the decision as a civil rights issue, but also because so many political elites, both liberal and conservative, spoke out against Proposition 64 early in the campaign.

SIGNIFICANCE

As part of the No on 64—Stop LaRouche coalition, the Lobby for Individual Freedom and Equality (LIFE Lobby) was created in 1986. Originally called the LIFE AIDS Lobby, the group was spawned by the coalition that had formed No on 64, including the Municipal Elections Committee of Los Angeles and the Los Angeles Gay and Lesbian Center. Founders of the group included Diane Himes, John Duran, and David Kessler.

Even though the measure failed, Proposition 64 paved the way for three additional HIV-AIDS-related ballot initiatives in California. The first, Proposition 69, which appeared on the June, 1988, ballot, was also sponsored by followers of LaRouche. The measure, among other things, would have made it possible for public health directors to quarantine persons with HIV-AIDS. The list of supporters and opponents was virtually the same as for Proposition 64. Opponents spent only $700,000 to defeat the measure by a 68 to 32 percent margin.

The second measure, Proposition 96, allowed for testing persons arrested for sex crimes and persons who might have exposed emergency workers to HIV. The test results would remain confidential. Framed largely as a law-and-order rather than an AIDS or gay rights issue, the measure was sponsored and financed by Los Angeles County sheriff Sherman Block and appeared on the November, 1988, ballot. Supporters of the previous AIDS measures were not publicly active in this campaign. With little general opposition, the measure passed with 62 percent in favor and 38 percent against.

Many suggest Proposition 96 passed because it

was framed as a law-and-order measure and because GLBT activists had focused their attention on another AIDS measure on the same ballot. This measure, Proposition 102, was sponsored by Representative Dannemeyer and tax crusader Paul Gann through their organization, the Stop AIDS Initiative Committee. Among other things, the measure would have required doctors to report the names of persons testing positive for HIV-AIDS to government health officials. The initiative also would have required health officials to contact the sexual partners of persons testing positive and made it a felony for an HIV-positive person to donate blood or engage in prostitution.

Proponents spent almost $700,000 in support of the measure, while opposition groups spent $800,000 on their campaign. U.S. surgeon general C. Everett Koop joined those opposed to the measure one week before the election—an action, many argued, that helped to turn public opinion against the measure. Although 72 percent of California adults supported the measure in July, 1988, support dropped to 58 percent in September, and dropped again to 51 percent in October, just before the election. The initiative was defeated 66 to 34 percent.

The failure of Proposition 102 and the defeat of Propositions 64 and 69 brought an end to attempts to place harsh restrictions on persons with HIV-AIDS. No other state has since considered similar measures at the ballot box, and California voters had made their preferences clear. However, these measures did distract GLBT activists from larger fights over AIDS funding, civil rights, and grassroots organizing. Also, some have suggested that these measures inspired related state and congressional legislation introduced between 1986 and 1990.

Although the measures did drain GLBT resources, the creation of LIFE Lobby ensured that anti-GLBT and AIDS measures in the state legislature would face significant opposition through the late 1990's. LIFE also created a separate think tank, The Institute, which conducted policy relevant research for the political arm of the group.

—*Donald P. Haider-Markel*

FURTHER READING

Adam, Barry D. *The Rise of a Gay and Lesbian Movement*. Rev. ed. New York: Twayne, 1995.

Berlet, Chip, and Joel Bellman. *Lyndon LaRouche: Fascism Wrapped in an American Flag*. Cambridge, Mass.: Political Research Associates, 1989.

Haider-Markel, Donald P. "AIDS and Gay Civil Rights: Politics and Policy at the Ballot Box." *American Review of Politics* 20 (Winter, 1999): 349-375.

King, Dennis. *Lyndon LaRouche and the New American Fascism*. New York: Doubleday, 1989.

Le Poire, Beth A., Carol K. Sigelman, Lee Sigelman, and Henry C. Kenski. "Who Wants to Quarantine Persons with AIDS? Patterns of Support for California's Proposition 64." *Social Science Quarterly* 71 (1990): 239-249.

Rimmerman, Craig A. *From Identity to Politics: The Lesbian and Gay Movements in the United States*. Philadelphia: Temple University Press, 2002.

Shilts, Randy. *And the Band Played On: Politics, People, and the AIDS Epidemic*. New York: St. Martin's Press, 1987.

Vaid, Urvashi. *Virtual Equality: The Mainstreaming of Gay and Lesbian Liberation*. New York: Anchor Books, 1995.

SEE ALSO: 1933-1945: Nazis Persecute Homosexuals; Feb. 5, 1981: Toronto Police Raid Gay Bathhouses; June 5 and July 3, 1981: Reports of Rare Diseases Mark Beginning of AIDS Epidemic; July, 1982: Gay-Related Immunodeficiency Is Renamed AIDS; Spring, 1984: AIDS Virus Is Discovered; Oct. 9, 1984: San Francisco Closes Gay Bathhouses and Other Businesses; July 25, 1985: Actor Hudson Announces He Has AIDS; Sept., 1986: AZT Treats People with AIDS; Mar., 1987: Radical AIDS Activist Group ACT UP Is Founded; June 27, 1988: Report of the Presidential AIDS Commission; Dec. 1, 1988: First World AIDS Day; June 25, 1993: Clinton Appoints First AIDS Czar.

1987
Anzaldúa Publishes *Borderlands/La Frontera*

Chicana lesbian feminist Gloria Anzaldúa published Borderlands/La Frontera, *a foundational work that combines scholarly research, personal narrative, and indigenous world views to reinterpret history and culture.*

Locale: San Francisco, California
Categories: Race and ethnicity; literature; publications; feminism

Key Figure
Gloria Anzaldúa (1942-2004), Chicana writer and scholar

Summary of Event

Gloria Anzaldúa was one of the first Chicanas to publicly come out as lesbian and to incorporate her cultural roots and queer sexuality within her writings. Published in 1987, *Borderlands/La Frontera: The New Mestiza* analyzes the psychological, historic, and political conflict inherent along the physical border between the United States and Mexico and the metaphoric borders among individuals living in the border regions.

Written in poetry and prose in English, with a mixture of Spanish, Tex-Mex Spanglish, and Nahuatl, *Borderlands/La Frontera* features Anzaldúa's childhood in the Rio Grande Valley of southern Texas, where she was a migrant worker and learned to speak English at nine years old. Anzaldúa's personal narrative, combined with scholarly research, political commentary, and in-depth references to mythology, spirituality, and indigenous heritage, broke with the scholarly conventions of the time in both structure and content. While not directed solely at academic readers, *Borderlands/La Frontera* nonetheless challenged an academy that privileged Eurocentric curricula, lacked instruction in the lives of people of color, barely represented the works of authors "of color," and had limited people of color as faculty.

Detailing the injustice and harsh realities of the lives of Mexicans on both sides of the border, Anzaldúa recounts and critiques the colonization of Mexico by the United States. In particular, she focuses on the difficulty and complexity of existing simultaneously in a land with two languages and two cultures, an existence reflected throughout the text by her practice of code-switching without providing English translations. She reaffirms Chicano Spanish as a living language and calls on Chicanos to embrace their indigenous roots as part of being mestiza or mestizo (of mixed indigenous and European ancestry). She also challenges the Chicano movement's sexism, and cites homophobia and the "fear of going home" as reasons why Chicanas are hesitant to come out of the closet within their community.

Anzaldúa foregrounds a Chicano culture that had been marginalized, and she connects it to its indigenous Mexican roots. However, she does not merely glorify Aztec history—she reinterprets it, and challenges and revises the meanings assigned to certain icons. For example, she takes prominent female figures who had been cast as traitors in Mexican history—Malintzin, Coatlicue, and La Llorona—and presents them as powerful deities. Coatlicue, for instance, is reclaimed as the archetypal, serpent, Earth goddess of life and death, who rules the unconscious mind and is the feminine sexual basis of life.

Anzaldúa's "new mestiza" exists in the consciousness of the borderlands, taking inventory of her cultural inheritance, discarding its tainted aspects, and creating a new way of perceiving reality. The new mestiza is a plural personality with flexible boundaries and a transformative being who is in continual creative motion. While the theorization of *mestizaje* is outstanding in *Borderlands/La Frontera*, Anzaldúa's major goal in writing the book was to use her convergent and divergent thinking processes to mobilize her people and her oppressors toward social justice.

Prior to publishing *Borderlands/La Frontera*, Anzaldúa coedited with Cherríe Moraga the ground-

The cover of Anzaldúa's Borderlands/La Frontera *(1987).* (Aunt Lute Books)

breaking multicultural feminist anthology *This Bridge Called My Back: Writings by Radical Women of Color*, published in 1981 (an expanded and revised edition was published in 2002 by Third Woman Press). Anzaldúa has continued her distinctive blend of creative and academic discourse by editing a series of anthologies. She has merged ideology with different genres, including the anthology of poetry, creative prose, and academic writings she edited in 1990 called *Making Face, Making Soul/Haciendo Caras: Creative and Critical Perspectives by Women of Color*. Other works include the 2002 anthology coedited with AnaLouise Keating, *This Bridge We Call Home: Radical Visions for Transformation*, which include the writings not only of women of color but also men and Caucasians. Much of Anzaldúa's life and personal philosophies are documented in *Interviews/Entrevistas*, an edited collection of memoir-like interviews. She died in 2004 from diabetes-related complications.

SIGNIFICANCE

Borderlands/La Frontera is an important and popular book that has remained in print with small independent publishers. It was named one of the 100 Best Books of the Century by the magazines *Utne Reader* and *Hungry Mind Review*, and *Library Journal* selected it as one of the 38 Best Books of 1987.

Borderlands/La Frontera has had a remarkable impact on the academy. It has validated personal experience and unconventional approaches to scholarly research and continues to call for an interdisciplinary approach to higher education. It diversified the conventions of literary criticism and became a central text for cultural theory, women's studies, American studies, and queer studies, among others. It supported the presence of people of color in the academy and championed the use of multicultural texts and perspectives in the classroom. Within and beyond the classroom, *Borderlands/La Frontera* also contributed to the theorization of identity formation for women of color.

—tatiana de la tierra

FURTHER READING

Anzaldúa, Gloria E. *Borderlands/La Frontera: The New Mestiza*. San Francisco, Calif.: Spinsters/Aunt Lute Books, 1987. Second edition published in 1999 by Aunt Lute Books.

———, ed. *Making Face, Making Soul/Haciendo Caras: Creative and Critical Perspectives by Women of Color*. San Francisco, Calif.: Aunt Lute Books, 1990.

Anzaldúa, Gloria, and AnaLouise Keating, eds. *This Bridge We Call Home: Radical Visions for Transformation*. New York: Routledge, 2002.

Anzaldúa, Gloria, and Cherríe Moraga, eds. *This Bridge Called My Back: Writings by Radical Women of Color*. New York: Kitchen Table: Women of Color Press, 1981.

Arredondo, Gabriela F., et al., eds. *Chicana Feminisms: A Critical Reader. Durham, N.C.: Duke University Press, 2003.

Browdy de Hernandez, Jennifer, ed. *Women Writing Resistance: Essays on Latin America and the Caribbean*. Cambridge, Mass.: South End Press, 2003.

Keating, AnaLouise, ed. *Interviews/Entrevistas: Gloria E. Anzaldúa*. New York: Routledge, 2000.

Saldivar-Hull, Sonia. *Feminism on the Border: Chicana Gender Politics and Literature*. Berkeley: University of California Press, 2000.

SEE ALSO: Apr., 1977: Combahee River Collective Issues "A Black Feminist Statement"; Oct. 12-15, 1979: First National Third World Lesbian and Gay Conference Convenes; 1981: *This Bridge Called My Back* Is Published; Oct., 1981: Kitchen Table: Women of Color Press Is Founded; 1982: Lorde's Autobiography *Zami* Is Published; Sept., 1983: First National Lesbians of Color Conference Convenes; 1986: Paula Gunn Allen Publishes *The Sacred Hoop*; 1987: Asian Pacific Lesbian Network Is Founded; 1987: *Compañeras: Latina Lesbians* Is Published; 1987: VIVA Is Founded to Promote Latina and Latino Artists; Oct. 14-17, 1987: Latin American and Caribbean Lesbian Feminist Network Is Formed; 1990: United Lesbians of African Heritage Is Founded; Jan., 2006: Jiménez Flores Elected to the Mexican Senate.

1987
ASIAN PACIFIC LESBIAN NETWORK IS FOUNDED

The Asian Pacific Lesbian Network was formed after Asian lesbian women came together for the second lesbian and gay march on Washington. The network supports and empowers lesbian, bisexual, and transgender Asian women through increased visibility, building leadership within the community, and by developing resources.

LOCALE: Washington, D.C.; Sonoma and San Francisco, California

CATEGORIES: Organizations and institutions; race and ethnicity

KEY FIGURES

Doreena Wong, attorney, cofounder of the network

June Chan, cofounder of the network

Trinity Ordona, Filipina activist, gave the keynote address at the network's first retreat

SUMMARY OF EVENT

The United States in the early 1980's saw the growth of support groups and informal networks for Asian and Pacific Islander (API) lesbians and gays, primarily in urban areas such as San Francisco and New York. About one hundred API lesbians from all over the United States met at the 1987 National March on Washington for Lesbian and Gay Rights in the nation's capitol. This group included members from organizations such as Asian Pacifica Sisters in San Francisco, D.C. Asian Lesbians, Asian Lesbians of the East Coast, and the South Asian Gay and Lesbian Association from New York. The march—which energized API participants, especially those who lived outside urban areas and did not have access to API-focused support groups—marked the first time that API lesbians in particular had organized to participate in a national event.

The Asian Pacific Lesbian Network, now called the Asian & Pacific Islander Lesbian, Bisexual Women, and Transgender Network (APLBTN) had been in the planning stages in 1987 when API women discussed founding the network. The women founded the network after meeting at the home of a cofounder and after participating in the first West Coast Asian Pacific Lesbian Retreat in Sonoma, California, and in the first Asian Pacific Gay and Lesbian Conference in San Francisco.

Two of the founders were Doreena Wong, a Chinese American attorney who has been a part of APLBTN since the network's founding, and June Chan, who cofounded Asian Lesbians of the East Coast (ALOEC) in 1983. The first national meeting of the APLBTN was in October, 1988, in Washington, D.C., when API lesbians from nine cities around the United States gathered to form a mission statement for the organization.

One of the first activities of the APLBTN was the First National Asian Pacific Lesbian Retreat in Santa Cruz, California, during Labor Day weekend in 1989. The theme of the retreat was "Coming Together, Moving Forward." More than 150 API lesbians and bisexual women from around the United States and Canada attended the retreat. There were also a handful of international participants, those from England, Malaysia, and the Philippines. Trinity Ordona, a Filipina activist, gave the opening address of the retreat, stressing the continued oppression faced by API's in both the lesbian community and the Asian American community. She added that, importantly, the retreat was a political solution to that oppression.

Retreat workshops focused on a variety of issues, including internalized oppression and fighting the common stereotype of Asians as the "model minority." There were also workshops on alcoholism and recovery in the API lesbian community and coping with mixed heritage. Originally, the retreat was billed as an "Asian/Pacific" lesbian gathering, but during the course of the retreat, the terminology changed to "Asian/Pacifica" to reflect the inclusion of all members.

Retreat participants expressed a sense of relief at being in an environment that was lesbian *and* API focused, but there were also tensions about exclusion within the organization, specifically the focus on Eastern Asians at the exclusion of Pacific Islanders and South Asians. For example, retreat organizers were criticized about the way the brochures and T-shirts pictured East Asian women only. There were also concerns about including bisexuals. The retreat ended with a serious discussion of the network's goals and the planning of the next APLBTN retreat, which was to be in Hawaii.

Significance

The APLBTN helped spread the formation of API-focused support groups and political networks outside large urban centers. It created a central organization to connect all the various existing and newly developed API lesbian organizations throughout the United States. Many women were able to connect with other API lesbians at the first retreat. The social isolation faced by API lesbians within both the Asian American community and the lesbian community has often kept API lesbians apart.

Many women of color have criticized lesbians for their racism and for excluding them from the debate regarding issues that affect women of color predominately, such as economic oppression. APLBTN responded to these criticisms by creating a forum for discussion and political action. Also, South Asians and Pacific Islanders, such as Hawaiians, in particular, were critical that they were included in the early days of APLBTN in name only. The network has since addressed issues of inclusion and exclusion within the API community. In particular, they have addressed the high visibility of Japanese and Chinese American lesbian API's.

—*Amy Stone*

Further Reading

Chung, Cristy, Alison Kim, and A. Kaweah Lemeshewsky, eds. *Between the Lines: An Anthology by Pacific/Asian Lesbians of Santa Cruz, California*. Santa Cruz, Calif.: Dancing Bird Press, 1987.

Eng, David L., and Alice Y. Hom, eds. *Q & A: Queer in Asian America*. Philadelphia: Temple University Press, 1998.

Hom, Alice. "Addressing Differences: A Look at the 1989 Asian Pacific Lesbian Network Retreat, Santa Cruz." In *Privileging Positions: The Sites of Asian American Studies*, edited by Gary Y. Okihiro, et al. Pullman: Washington State University Press, 1995.

Hune, Shirley, and Gail M. Nomura, eds. *Asian/Pacific Islander American Women: A Historical Anthology*. New York: New York University Press, 2003.

Islam, Naheed. "Naming Desire, Shaping Identity:

Tracing the Experiences of Indian Lesbians in the United States." In *A Patchwork Shawl: Chronicles of South Asian Women in America*, edited by Shamita Das Dasgupta. New Brunswick, N.J.: Rutgers University Press, 1998.

Kumashiro, Kevin K., ed. *Restoried Selves: Autobiographies of Queer Asian-Pacific-American Activists.* New York: Harrington Park Press, 2004.

Lim-Hing, Sharon, ed. *The Very Inside: An Anthology of Writing by Asian and Pacific Islander Lesbian and Bisexual Women.* Toronto, Ont.: Sister Vision Press, 1994.

Ordona, Trinity A. "Coming Out Together: An Ethnohistory of the Asian and Pacific Islander Queer Women's and Transgendered People's Movement of San Francisco." Unpublished Ph.D. dissertation, University of California, Santa Cruz, 2000.

_____. "In Our Own Way: A Roundtable Discussion." *Amerasia Journal* 20, no. 1 (1994): 137-147.

Williams-León, Teresa. "The Convergence of Passing Zones: Multiracial Gays, Lesbians, and Bisexuals of Asian Descent." In *The Sum of Our Parts: Mixed-Heritage Asian Americans*, edited by Teresa Williams-León and Cynthia L. Nakashima. Philadelphia: Temple University Press, 2001.

SEE ALSO: 1969: Nuestro Mundo Forms as First Queer Organization in Argentina; 1975: Gay American Indians Is Founded; Oct. 12-15, 1979: First March on Washington for Lesbian and Gay Rights; Oct. 12-15, 1979: Lesbian and Gay Asian Collective Is Founded; 1981: *This Bridge Called My Back* Is Published; 1982-1991: Lesbian Academic and Activist Sues University of California for Discrimination; Sept., 1983: First National Lesbians of Color Conference Convenes; 1987: VIVA Is Founded to Promote Latina and Latino Artists; Oct. 14-17, 1987: Latin American and Caribbean Lesbian Feminist Network Is Formed; 1990: United Lesbians of African Heritage Is Founded; Dec., 1990: Asian Lesbian Network Holds Its First Conference; Oct. 9-12, 1998: First International Retreat for Lesbian and Gay Muslims Is Held; Nov., 1999: First Middle Eastern Gay and Lesbian Organization Is Founded.

1987
COMPAÑERAS: LATINA LESBIANS IS PUBLISHED

Oral histories, interviews, and creative writing make up the collection Compañeras, *the first anthology of the writings, artwork, and oral histories of Latina lesbians.* Compañeras *led to the publication of another influential collection of work by lesbian women of color:* Chicana Lesbians.

LOCALE: New York, New York; San Francisco, California

CATEGORIES: Literature; publications; race and ethnicity; organizations and institutions

KEY FIGURE
Juanita Ramos (Juanita Díaz-Cotto; b. 1953), editor of the anthology

SUMMARY OF EVENT
Compañeras: Latina Lesbians, a collection of writings, oral histories, and artwork by Latina lesbians published in 1987, was the first of work of its kind. The anthology was conceived as a response to the isolation and invisibility of Latina lesbians in the United States. Its editor, Juanita Ramos (pseudonym for Juanita Díaz-Cotto), is a black Puerto Rican lesbian activist who has been living in the New

York City region since the early 1960's. Since the late 1970's, she has been active in lesbian and gay organizations such as El Comité Homosexual Latinoamericano (The Latin American Homosexual Committee) and the Coalition for Lesbian and Gay Rights. She also was an organizer for the 1979 National March on Washington for Lesbian and Gay Rights.

Confronted with the racism and classism of predominantly Anglo, middle-class organizations, Ramos sought to create autonomous projects for Latina lesbians. She noted that very few Latina lesbians had been published in lesbian-focused books and journals and envisioned an anthology of the works of Latina lesbians. Along with Digna Landrove de la O, Ramos formed the Colectiva Lesbiana Latinoamericana (Latin American Lesbian Collective) in 1980 and sought material for the anthology. While the collective did grassroots networking within the communities in New York City and San Francisco, it was difficult to get a sufficient amount of original creative writing from Latina lesbians. To remedy the problem, Ramos offered potential contributors the option of presenting their life experiences via oral histories. She interviewed more than twenty women from New York City and San Francisco. While the collective eventually dissolved, Ramos continued gathering and editing the material for the anthology.

A number of fund-raising events were held to support the production of *Compañeras*. Organizations from Brooklyn and Manhattan assisted with raising funds for the project; these organizations included the Lesbian Herstory Archives, Lesbians Rising at Hunter College, and the restaurant La Papaya. Supporters in San Francisco organized a fund-raising dance featuring the all-women salsa band La Orquesta Sabrosita. In addition, funds were solicited and received from the North Star Fund, the Astraea Foundation, the Lucius and Eva Eastman Fund, Inc., and the Chicago Resource Center.

After encountering resistance from women's publishers and commercial presses related to the editing process, Ramos formed the Latina Lesbian History Project, which published the first edition of *Compañeras* in 1987. This edition features the writings, oral histories, and artwork of forty-seven women who were born in ten different countries. The book is organized thematically by sections such as The Other Side, Coming Out, Lovers and Friends, Families, and The Struggle Continues, the last of which alludes to the difficulties of straddling the dual Latina and lesbian identity in the midst of a racist, sexist, and homophobic society.

A second edition of the book was published by Routledge in 1994, and a the third edition, published in 2004 by the Latina Lesbian History Project, contains an expanded section in Spanish by sixteen additional women from an additional four countries. This newer section focuses on identity formation and lesbian-feminist movements in Latin America.

Compañeras documents the lives of a variety of Latina lesbians, from a young Chicana prostitute and junkie to a Nicaraguan immigrant who struggles with the memory of a closeted love. Latin American activists are also well-documented, such as the Mexican politician Patria Jiménez Flores and founding lesbian activists in Argentina, Ecuador, Costa Rica, and the Dominican Republic. Many of the international interviews took place during several of the Latin American, lesbian-feminist Encuentros. The anthology includes an extensive introduction by Chilean lesbian writer Mariana Romo-Carmona (whose books were later published by the Latina Lesbian History Project). Writings in the book include Spanish, English, and Spanglish. While the preface and introduction appear in both Spanish and English, other texts appear as first written and submitted to the editor or in the language spoken during a given oral history.

Many of the women who wrote or were interviewed for the collection used their first names or a pseudonym for publication, reflecting the homophobia of the time and of the fear of coming out publicly. Among the writers who named themselves and who eventually published in other journals, anthologies, musical recordings, or in books of their own were Gina Anderson, Rosita Angulo Libre de Marulanda, Gloria Evangelina Anzaldúa, Ochy Curiel, tatiana de la tierra, Yuderkys Espinosa, Hilda Hidalgo, Nemir Matos-Cintrón, Naomi Littlebear Morena, Juana María Paz, Migdalia Reyes, and Mariana Romo-Carmona.

SIGNIFICANCE

Compañeras: Latina Lesbians is characteristic of early literature by women and lesbians of color who politicized the fusion of race, ethnicity, and sexuality. Their declarative statements of identity were influenced by social movements of the 1960's and 1970's, such as the movements for civil rights, women's rights, gay and lesbian rights, and the Mexican labor struggle.

Another anthology, influenced by the work in *Compañeras*, was published in 1991. Edited by Carla Trujillo, *Chicana Lesbians: The Girls Our Mothers Warned Us About*, features poetry, fiction, essays, and artwork in English, Spanish, and Spanglish by twenty-five Chicana (Mexican American) contributors. *Chicana Lesbians* similarly presents the varieties of language, class, education, color, and culture among Chicana lesbians. Other significant Latina lesbian publishing projects are the magazines *esto no tiene nombre* (1991-1994; this has no name) and *conmoción* (commotion, or in motion). These magazines published poetry, fiction, essays, reviews, interviews, comics, and artwork by more than eighty Latina lesbians from the United States and abroad, with the writings alternating in Spanish, English, and Spanglish as well. Some of the contributors to *esto no tiene nombre* and *conmoción* included Latina lesbians who were published in *Compañeras* and in *Chicana Lesbians* originally.

—*tatiana de la tierra*

FURTHER READING

De la tierra, tatiana. "Activist Latina Lesbian Publishing: *esto no tiene nombre* and *conmoción*." In *I Am Aztlán: The Personal Essay in Chicano Studies*, edited by Chon A. Noriega and Wendy Belcher. Los Angeles: University of California, Chicano Studies Research Center, 2004.

Ramos, Juanita, ed. *Compañeras: Latina Lesbians, An Anthology*. New York: Latina Lesbian History Project, 2004.

Trujillo, Carla, ed. *Chicana Lesbians: The Girls Our Mothers Warned Us About*. Berkeley, Calif.: Third Woman Press, 1991.

SEE ALSO: Apr., 1977: Combahee River Collective Issues "A Black Feminist Statement"; Oct. 12-15, 1979: First National Third World Lesbian and Gay Conference Convenes; 1981: *This Bridge Called My Back* Is Published; Oct., 1981: Kitchen Table: Women of Color Press Is Founded; 1982: Lorde's Autobiography *Zami* Is Published; Sept., 1983: First National Lesbians of Color Conference Convenes; 1986: Paula Gunn Allen Publishes *The Sacred Hoop*; 1987: Anzaldúa Publishes *Borderlands/La Frontera*; 1987: Asian Pacific Lesbian Network Is Founded; 1987: VIVA Is Founded to Promote Latina and Latino Artists; Oct. 14-17, 1987: Latin American and Caribbean Lesbian Feminist Network Is Formed; 1990: United Lesbians of African Heritage Is Founded; Jan., 2006: Jiménez Flores Elected to the Mexican Senate.

1987
SHILTS PUBLISHES *AND THE BAND PLAYED ON*

Randy Shilts, in his groundbreaking book And the Band Played On, *documented the beginning of the AIDS epidemic with a critical view of the U.S. government, gay community leaders, and American mass media. The book was the first report on the epidemic to reach a wide, general readership.*

LOCALE: New York, New York; San Francisco, California; Atlanta, Georgia; Washington, D.C.
CATEGORIES: Literature; HIV-AIDS; publications; health and medicine

KEY FIGURES
Randy Shilts (1952-1994), reporter for the *San Francisco Chronicle* and author of three books on gay and lesbian issues
Ronald Reagan (1911-2004), president of the United States, 1981-1989, in office during the first eight years of the AIDS epidemic
Gaëtan Dugas (1952/1953-1984), Québécois flight attendant whom Shilts claimed was "patient zero" in the epidemic

SUMMARY OF EVENT
Randy Shilts's book *And the Band Played On: Politics, People, and the AIDS Epidemic*, based on more than one thousand interviews and research spanning five years, provided a chronicle of the early years of the AIDS epidemic to everyday Americans. In the years immediately preceding its 1987 publication, much of the country had little understanding of this new disease, which in the early years had appeared mostly among homosexual men. Panic over the containment and prevention of AIDS gripped the country. People with AIDS or suspected to have AIDS found themselves turned away from hospitals, evicted from apartments, and even barred from public swimming pools with increasing frequency during this panic.

And the Band Played On, initially rejected for publication by more than one dozen potential publishers, offered an explanation of the early AIDS crisis and a cast of characters responsible for its spread in the United States. Climbing to the top of best-seller lists in 1987, Shilts's easy to read and engagingly written book educated and calmed mainstream America. *And the Band Played On* was a finalist for the National Book Award in nonfiction and won Shilts the American Society of Journalists and Authors Outstanding Author Award in 1988. In 1993, Hollywood adapted *And the Band Played On* into a television movie that initially aired on the Home Box Office network.

The book was as much about chronicling the early AIDS crisis as it was about assigning responsibility for the unchecked spread of the disease. Shilts placed President Ronald Reagan at the center of government inaction and showed Reagan's unwillingness to discuss the epidemic in public. He

Randy Shilts, 1977. (AP/Wide World Photos)

also explored the administration's tactic of ignoring the growing public health problems of the early 1980's. Reagan's homophobia and indifference, according to Shilts, resulted in government delays in granting research funding, education, and drug approval. In *And the Band Played On*, Reagan was as much the villain of the early 1980's as the AIDS virus itself.

However, in *And the Band Played On*, Reagan and the federal government did not work alone; Shilts also indicted a full cast of scientific researchers, bathhouse owners, gay activists, and even some people with AIDS. Throughout the book, Shilts suggested that AIDS was somehow a result of the overt sexuality of 1970's gay liberation, an interpretation that drew much criticism from the gay community. One of the most controversial members of Shilts's cast was Québécois flight attendant Gaëtan Dugas, whom Shilts dubbed "patient zero." According to Shilts, Dugas was almost single-handedly responsible for the introduction and spread of HIV to numerous gay communities around the world. Epidemiologists, many of whom Shilts chronicles in the book, disavowed the notion of a patient zero upon the release of the book and pointed to more complicated explanations for the spread of HIV.

While controversial and flawed in places, *And the Band Played On* arguably served as the most influential book about AIDS in the 1980's. No other book matched its accessibility or popularity in mainstream America.

Upon handing in the final version of the book manuscript, Shilts tested positive for HIV antibodies, the virus that causes AIDS. He kept his HIV status secret until 1993, when he became very ill; keeping his HIV status secret was a decision which drew criticism from the gay community. Shilts died of complications of AIDS in 1994.

SIGNIFICANCE

Randy Shilts's interpretation of events surrounding the early AIDS epidemic spawned a number of controversies and debates among activists, scientists, gay and lesbian community leaders, and, later, historians. While informed by facts and interviews, *And the Band Played On* reflects the anger and politics brewing in the gay community in the mid-1980's as well as the scientific unknowns about HIV-AIDS.

Many who bore the brunt of blame in *And the Band Played On* also faced the rage and protests of groups like AIDS Coalition to Unleash Power (ACT UP) and Lesbian Avengers. These groups, which had formed around the same time as the book's release, gained momentum as the book became popular, and in the years following 1987 witnessed some of the largest victories for AIDS activists. Using civil disobedience and lobbying, activists fought for and won fast-track approval for

RANDY SHILTS

On the day in 1987 he completed the manuscript for *And the Band Played On*, a landmark study of AIDS in the gay community, Randy Shilts learned that he was HIV-positive. He had been tested one year earlier but directed his physician to withhold the results of the tests until he had completed his book; he feared that learning he was HIV-positive could unduly influence his writing. Shilts would become known as the person who first brought the HIV-AIDS epidemic to widespread public attention. Although he knew he was HIV-positive already in 1987, he did not go public with this information until 1993.

Shilts, the first openly gay reporter on the staff of the *San Francisco Chronicle*, had published *The Mayor of Castro Street: The Life and Times of Harvey Milk* (1982), the story of the San Francisco supervisor murdered by a homophobic former police officer and supervisor, Dan White. Even as his health declined, Shilts also worked on *Conduct Unbecoming*, a study of the treatment of gays and lesbians in the military, published in 1993. Shilts's illness, which medications had controlled well for several years, erupted into full-blown AIDS in August, 1992, when he developed AIDS-related pneumonia.

As his health deteriorated, Shilts was forced to dictate the last pages of *Conduct Unbecoming* from the hospital where he was being treated for a collapsed lung. He then developed Kaposi's sarcoma and essentially remained at the home he shared with his partner Barry Barbieri in California's Sonoma County. Barbieri was at Shilts's bedside when he died on February 17, 1994.

AIDS medications, increased research funding, protective legislation, and education. Ronald Reagan had left office in 1988; he would be the only AIDS-era president not to have an AIDS platform.

While not directly responsible for all of these advancements, *And the Band Played On* publicized the issues surrounding AIDS and heightened awareness and understanding of the disease among everyday people. This increased awareness resulted as much from Shilts's public presence as it did from the book itself: Upon the book's release, Shilts toured the country, giving numerous speeches, appearing on morning television talk shows, and giving interviews that broadcast over radio. While AIDS, by 1987, had made the cover of many national publications such as *Time*, *Newsweek*, and *The New York Times*, Shilts's book was the first journalistic work of such magnitude written for a wide audience.

—Catherine P. Batza

FURTHER READING

Berkowitz, Richard. *Stayin' Alive: The Invention of Safe Sex*. Cambridge, Mass.: Westview Press, 2003.

Crimp, Douglas. *Melancholia and Moralism: Essays On AIDS and Queer Politics*. Cambridge, Mass.: MIT Press, 2002.

_____, ed. *AIDS: Cultural Analysis, Cultural Activism*. Cambridge, Mass.: MIT Press, 1988.

Shilts, Randy. *And the Band Played On: Politics, People, and the AIDS Epidemic*. New York: St. Martin's Press, 1987.

_____. "Patient Zero: The Man Who Brought the AIDS Epidemic to California." *California* 12, no. 10 (October, 1987): 96-99, 149-151, 160.

SEE ALSO: June 5 and July 3, 1981: Reports of Rare Diseases Mark Beginning of AIDS Epidemic; July, 1982: Gay-Related Immunodeficiency Is Renamed AIDS; Spring, 1984: AIDS Virus Is Discovered; Oct. 9, 1984: San Francisco Closes Gay Bathhouses and Other Businesses; July 25, 1985: Actor Hudson Announces He Has AIDS; Sept., 1986: AZT Treats People with AIDS; Nov., 1986: Californians Reject LaRouche's Quarantine Initiative; Mar., 1987: Radical AIDS Activist Group ACT UP Is Founded; June 27, 1988: Report of the Presidential AIDS Commission; Dec. 1, 1988: First World AIDS Day; June 25, 1993: Clinton Appoints First AIDS Czar.

1987
VIVA IS FOUNDED TO PROMOTE LATINA AND LATINO ARTISTS

Latino lesbian and gay artists in Los Angeles countered a lack of representation in the Los Angeles arts community by founding the organization VIVA, Lesbian and Gay Latino Artists.

LOCALE: Los Angeles, California
CATEGORIES: Organizations and institutions; arts; race and ethnicity

KEY FIGURES

Roland Palencia (Rolando Palencia), activist and founding member of VIVA

Luis Alfaro, performance artist and founding member of VIVA

Mike Moreno, visual artist and founding member of VIVA

Aleida Rodríguez, writer and founding member of VIVA

Marcus Kuiland-Nazario, performance artist and founding member of VIVA

Summary of Event

VIVA, Lesbian and Gay Latino Artists, was founded in 1987 as a nonprofit arts organization. Based in Los Angeles, the idea for the organization was conceived by activist Roland (Rolando) Palencia. Palencia had said about the group's formation that he "had been going to a lot of museums. When I went to the Latino community, not much was gay; when I went to the gay and lesbian exhibits, not much was Latino. I thought: Wouldn't it be incredible if we had all those creative minds breaking down all those barriers?" Joining Palencia were like-minded individuals, including Mike Moreno (a visual artist), writer Aleida Rodríguez, and performance artists Marcus Kuiland-Nazario and Luis Alfaro. Alfaro would later receive a MacArthur Foundation fellowship, the so-called "genius award."

VIVA, working at the intersection of nationality, sexuality, and art, focused on bringing together and empowering lesbian, gay, and Latino/a artists who had been forgotten by or dismissed from the Los Angeles art community. To increase visibility within the wider LGBT community, the organization also worked with individuals such as gay activist Morris Kight and with organizations such as the Los Angeles Gay and Lesbian Center. VIVA also made use of the widely distributed Spanish language newspaper, *La Opinión*, to address issues of homophobia within the Latino community.

VIVA had the structural and administrative support of Gay and Lesbian Latinos Unidos (GLLU), the major Latino/a activist group in Los Angeles at the time. By 1990, VIVA was one of the largest gay and lesbian Latino/a groups in Los Angeles, second only to GLLU, with a budget of $120,000 and three employees paid through grant money from the city of Los Angeles, the United States Conference of Mayors, Apple Computers, and gay and lesbian organizations.

Within the first six months of its creation, VIVA's membership grew from five to fifty artists. The group saw a growing number of nationally recognized, self-identified gay and lesbian Latino/a artists join them, including comedian Monica Palacios, visual artists Miguel Angeles Reyes and Teddy Sandoval, writer Terri de la Peña, and photographers Laura Aguilar and Becky Villaseñor. In addition, VIVA highlighted the work of artists such as Beto Araiza, Paul Bonin-Rodríguez, Cherríe Moraga, Ric Oquita, Gloria Anzaldúa, Nao Bustamante, Al Luján, David Acosta-Posada, David Zamora Casa, and Michael Martínez by hosting performances, readings, and exhibitions. In December, 1988, VIVA featured its first artist by presenting Roberto Ochoa Schutz's bilingual play *Santo Union*, which examined issues of coming out and interracial relationships. The following year, VIVA inaugurated an annual awards event.

VIVA hosted a variety of events, including an artists reception series, which held solo events for featured artists, and also an artists roundtable series, which has invited well-known artists to discuss their work and lead workshops for other artists. VIVA also organized a Queer Latino film festival and panel in coordination with OutFest, the annual Los Angeles gay and lesbian film festival. In 1993, the vibrant organization held twenty-one events, and between 1994 and 1995, VIVA also held a residency at Beyond Baroque Literary Center in the Venice district of Los Angeles.

VIVA also produced a literary journal (*VIVA Arts Quarterly*), which featured Latino artists, poetry, fiction, excerpts of performances, and news about the organization. While largely produced by and featuring VIVA members, the *VIVA Arts Quarterly* also provided a forum for unaffiliated artists and writers, including Jeanne Córdova and tatiana de la tierra. Journal issue themes included "Food and Fetish," "Sexy and Spiritual," "Passion and Protest," and "Natural/Unnatural."

VIVA also worked to address the culture and politics of art. It partnered with the AIDS Program Office of the County of Los Angeles to manage a large scale AIDS project that disseminated information about HIV-AIDS in the gay, lesbian, and bisexual Latino/a community, primarily through a guerrilla theater project called Teatro VIVA—Early Intervention Program. Teatro VIVA used comedic and frank skits to encourage individuals to get tested for HIV. The theater group gave performances at, among other sites, Cal-Arts (an advanced art school) in Valencia, California; East Los Angeles College; the L.A. Gay and Lesbian Center; and San Diego City College. The group included actors Frank Castorena, Refugio Guevara, and Ron Sandoval, and the project directors were Monica Palacios and Luis Alfaro, performing the work of Los Angeles writers Guillermo Reyes, Albert Antonio Araiza, Nancy de Los Santos, Rosanna Staffa, Rufugio Guevara, and many others.

To bring visibility to Latina lesbian concerns, VIVA also produced the multimedia event *Chicks and Salsa*, created by visual artist and poet Dyan Garza and writer and performer Monica Palacios in 1992, and featured performers such as Gina Acuña, Christina Pascal Fernández, and Aida Pineda. *Chicks and Salsa*, VIVA's only women-focused production, was the organization's most successful event. It was often performed in West Hollywood in collaboration with Lesbian Visibility Week.

VIVA remained involved with several LGBT organizations throughout Los Angeles, including Lesbianas Unidas, and the National LGBT Latino organization, LLEGO. VIVA also worked in collaboration with Los Angeles city agencies such as the Cultural Affairs Department. VIVA was the organizational chair of the board of the Gay Men of Color Consortium, which included the Black Gay and Lesbian Leadership Forum, Minority AIDS Project, Asian Pacific Lesbian and Gays, and Bienestar Latino AIDS Center. The Gay Men of Color Consortium produced artwork and literature about health and HIV awareness for people of color.

In 1990, VIVA received the president's award from Christopher Street West, organizers of the annual LGBT pride event in Los Angeles, and the Gay and Lesbian Community Services Award from GLUU. VIVA received the Artes de México Festival Committee Award in 1991 for the exhibit *VIVA's México: Too Many Centuries of Denial, Invisibility and Silence*, and the Community Service Award from the Gay and Lesbian Alliance Against Defamation (GLAAD), a media watchdog group, in 1993.

In the early twenty-first century, VIVA approached the women of Tongues to resume the VIVA legacy. Tongues, a grassroots cultural organization, addresses the social, cultural, and political issues that especially concern queers and people of color. In 2000, Tongues premiered the electronic magazine *Tongues* and, in 2001, the print version. *Tongues* highlights queer women of color writers, artists, activists, and academics, and participates in a number of social justice projects.

Significance

From the 1980's through to the early twenty-first century, VIVA had been deeply involved in the Los Angeles art scene as well as in the gay and lesbian community. When VIVA became one of the largest Latino/a gay and lesbian organizations in Los Angeles, it fulfilled its mission to bring visibility to Latino/a artists who had until then been ignored by the general arts community. Many of the Latino/a artists highlighted by VIVA went on to gain national recognition. VIVA's successful history demonstrates the need for gays and lesbians of color to form separate groups in which they can address specific issues with the goal of raising awareness in all communities.

—*Joy Novak*

Further Reading

Costa, María Dolores, ed. *Latina Lesbian Writers and Artists*. New York: Harrington Park Press, 2003.

Darder, Antonia, and Rodolfo D. Torres, eds. *The Latino Studies Reader: Culture, Economy, and Society*. Malden, Mass.: Blackwell, 1998.

"Natural/Unnatural." *VIVA Arts Quarterly* (Winter/Spring/Summer, 1995).

"Sexy and Spiritual." *VIVA Arts Quarterly* (Fall, 1993/Winter, 1994).

VIVA Papers. University of California, Los Angeles, Chicano Studies Research Center Library. Finding aid available at http://www.oac.cdlib.org/institutions/ark:/13030/kt187015vw.

Wolman, Karen Dale. "Gay y Latino en Los Angeles." *Frontiers*, September 28, 1990, 25-31.

See also: 1975-1983: Gay Latino Alliance Is Formed; 1987: Anzaldúa Publishes *Borderlands/La Frontera*.

March, 1987
RADICAL AIDS ACTIVIST GROUP ACT UP IS FOUNDED

Gay activists founded the AIDS Coalition to Unleash Power, better known as ACT UP, a radical and confrontational street-action group demanding public and governmental attention to the HIV-AIDS epidemic. ACT UP's actions helped change social views and awareness about HIV-AIDS, helped change drug policy and reduce drug costs for those with HIV-AIDS, and promoted the care and well-being of those with the disease.

LOCALE: New York, New York
CATEGORIES: HIV-AIDS; civil rights; government and politics; health and medicine; marches, protests, and riots; organizations and institutions

KEY FIGURE
Larry Kramer (b. 1935), American playwright, novelist, and gay rights activist, who inspired the founding of ACT UP

SUMMARY OF EVENT

In early March, 1987, Larry Kramer presented the best speech of his career as a gay activist at a meeting at New York City's Gay and Lesbian Community Center. Kramer had called upon gays to demand that the U.S. government increase its attention to the HIV (human immunodeficiency virus) and AIDS (acquired immunodeficiency syndrome) crisis, which had begun to devastate America's gay population, and to take concrete steps to stem the tide. On this day, the AIDS Coalition to Unleash Power (ACT UP) was born.

Kramer spoke of the difficulties physicians encountered in obtaining new drugs for treating the disease. He urged his audience to demand that the Food and Drug Administration (FDA) accelerate the testing procedures for HIV-AIDS medications and to pressure the pharmaceutical industry to speed up its research to find drugs for treating and even eradicating the disease. He urged governmental controls that would make such drugs affordable for the average person with AIDS, because such drugs would have required substantial government subsidies because of the high cost of medical and pharmaceutical research.

Kramer was outraged that both the general public and the government dragged its feet in dealing with the rapidly developing crisis. In the late 1980's, even after actor Rock Hudson announced in 1985 he had AIDS, the public considered HIV-AIDS a gay disease unworthy of much public support or governmental attention. Indeed, politicians realized that supporting HIV-AIDS research could become a political liability for them given the homophobia and otherwise negative attitudes and views about GLBT people.

Kramer was adamant in his attempts to arouse a lethargic public and a White House avoiding the epidemic. Throughout the United States, Kramer's two fundamental slogans—"Knowledge = Power" and "Silence = Death"—became rallying cries for LGBT and AIDS activists.

In 1981, when the epidemic was in its earliest, and misunderstood, stages, Kramer had cofounded Gay Men's Health Crisis (GMHC), based in New York City, and was actively involved in its day-to-day operations until 1983, when he came under fire from the organization. His article, "1,112 and Counting," appeared in the March 14-17, 1983, issue of *New York Native* and was widely disseminated in gay publications throughout the country. In this article, Kramer verified 1,112 cases of HIV-AIDS and 418 deaths.

Some members of the gay community, still apathetic regarding the disease, accused Kramer of overstating its dangers and of running the risk of creating a national panic and intensified homophobia. Such criticism did not deter Kramer. Because of the firestorm his article generated and because of concerns about his reportedly abrasive personality and inflammatory language, he was, in 1983, ousted from his leadership role in the GMHC.

ACT UP and other protesters outside the Houston Astrodome in 1992, site of the Republican National Convention. The activists are staging a "die-in." (AP/Wide World Photos)

Kramer's abrasiveness and intemperate language helped spark the ACT UP movement. He did not shrink from confrontation or from extremism, contending that a crisis like the HIV-AIDS pandemic often calls for extreme measures; the louder and more forceful he was in making his case, the more uncomfortable and, he hoped, conciliatory the government would become. He made little effort himself to be conciliatory, convinced that the more his opponents feared him, the more he could accomplish.

These tactics, which attracted attention to Kramer and ACT UP's cause, in time alienated the people who initially were on his side. Communication theorists point out that when diction fraught with unpleasant implications is used in such situations, the expectations that the listener has of the speaker and of the occasion may become lopsided, as they did in this case.

After 1983, relieved of his responsibilities with the GMHC, Kramer was able to devote more time to his writing. He focused his attention on turning out one of the earliest plays about AIDS, *The Normal Heart* (1985), which was well received by audiences and critics. It ran for more than one year on Broadway and helped those who saw the play begin to appreciate problems faced by gay people in the United States at that time.

It was not until Kramer's speech at New York City's Gay and Lesbian Community Center in the spring of 1987 that his activism became most radical. Kramer convinced his audience to join him in establishing ACT UP. This organization, which used unconventional and sometimes ethically questionable tactics, including the outing of public officials who were not open about their homosexuality, proved threatening to not only many people in the mainstream but also many moderate gay activists. In some cases, however, these tactics proved effective.

ACT UP spread rapidly from its beginnings in New York City. Soon, chapters were established throughout the United States, mostly centered in urban areas such as Boston, Philadelphia, Atlanta, Chicago, Milwaukee, Minneapolis, St. Louis, Denver, Phoenix, Los Angeles, San Francisco, and Seattle. The AIDS crisis was growing and was beginning also to affect heterosexuals. Nevertheless, many people blamed the disease on gay sex and had little sympathy for gays, feeling threatened by them because of public misconceptions about how AIDS was transmitted.

From its outset, quite in keeping with Kramer's mandates, the ACT UP movement was to focus on nonviolent civil disobedience. Kramer was willing to use attention-getting tactics, but he did not sanction violence in achieving this end.

On March 28, 1989, under Kramer's leadership, ACT UP rallied more than three thousand people in front of New York's City Hall, which had been ACT UP's largest rally. In September of 1989, ACT UP demonstrators had chained themselves to the balcony railing of the New York Stock Exchange, an institution considered symbolic of poor, uncaring values and greed. The demonstrators blew loud horns and unfurled a banner that called for the sale of the pharmaceutical company Burroughs-Wellcome (now GlaxoSmithKline) for charging outrageous prices for the drug AZT, which it manufactured. The company lowered its price for the drug to $6,400 per year four days after the protest.

In December, 1989, ACT UP members chained themselves to the pews in St. Patrick's Cathedral on New York's Fifth Avenue and almost drowned out the sermon being preached by Cardinal O'Connor, with shouts of "bigot," "murderer," and "defiler of the Eucharist." The protest group WHAM!, Women's Health Action and Mobilization, cosponsored the "Stop the Church" protest, which also included 4,500 protesters outside the church.

Ironically, ACT UP members eventually found Kramer's tactics difficult to justify and found him impossible to work with on a long-term basis. Just as members of GMHC had turned on Kramer and ousted him from the organization, members of ACT UP rallied against him and made his future with the group tenuous.

By 1990, Kramer was convinced that the battle to fight

LARRY KRAMER

Larry Kramer was the first and, arguably, the most outspoken voice in the fight against acquired immunodeficiency syndrome (AIDS). His plays and essays were written to educate gay men as well as government, media, and education officials about improved medical research, health care, and prevention of AIDS. The son of George L. and Rea (Wishengrad) Kramer, he was born in Connecticut but moved to Washington, D.C., in 1941. He hated his father, who abused him both physically and emotionally for being a "sissy." Kramer felt isolated during his formative years, not only because of his Jewish heritage but also because he had begun to express his homosexuality, although with fear and guilt. The process of accepting his homosexuality began in 1953, his freshman year at Yale University, when he had an affair with one of his professors. He sought psychiatric help, which soon led him to the realization that he could not change his sexual orientation.

Throughout his writing career, even as a screenwriter, Kramer focused on matters relating to homosexuality. His 1969 screenplay of D. H. Lawrence's novel *Women in Love* emphasized Lawrence's thinly veiled dealings with homosexuality in that novel. Kramer emphasized this in his film version. His controversial gay novel, *Faggots*, although not a critical or artistic success, has stayed in print almost continuously since its publication in 1978 and is said to have sold close to half a million copies. In it, as in his unhappy experience with the bureaucracy of the Gay Men's Health Crisis, are found intimations of themes explored in his two most radical plays, *The Normal Heart* (1985), which has evoked comparisons to Henrik Ibsen's *En folkefiende* (pb. 1882; *An Enemy of the People*, 1890), and *The Destiny of Me* (pr. 1992, pb. 1993). Kramer's nonfiction also emphasizes the inroads that AIDS has made on the lives of all Americans.

AIDS had been lost. He stepped down from the ACT UP leadership, and the group continued to function without him. Branches sprang up throughout the country, each with its own unique agenda, often quite different from Kramer's original intent. The organization believed it had lost its significance in the 1990's because the AIDS pandemic was coming under greater control, even though no cure had been found. Safer sex, bywords in the gay community, substantially reduced the number of AIDS cases during the last decade of the twentieth century.

Significance

The Treatment Action Group (TAG), a nonprofit organization founded in January, 1992, is an outgrowth of ACT UP. TAG encourages AIDS research and ensures that those with AIDS are cared for and that they receive effective treatment. TAG meets regularly with public health officials and with pharmaceutical companies to determine the most efficient ways of coping with HIV-AIDS. TAG has lobbied successfully to get the Food and Drug Administration to permit the compassionate use of unapproved drugs for patients who have no realistic hope of recovery. Because time is of the essence for those who have AIDS, the organization also encouraged the FDA to accelerate drastically the process of testing and approving new drugs.

Because many who had AIDS have died and many more continue to manage the disease successfully with medications, the initial work of ACT UP has been minimized somewhat and the functions of the organization and its branches have changed to meet current needs. AIDS, however, is a global problem, particularly in Africa, Asia, and Russia. The ACT UP model has been adapted around the world, to local conditions, and applied with a small amount of success.

Some nations, notably South Africa and Brazil, have waived the patent protection of some drugs crucial to the successful management of AIDS. This has become a highly controversial issue, but while the legalities are being worked out, many people suffering from AIDS have received medications they could not otherwise afford.

It was not until 2004 that the U.S. government awakened to the reality that HIV-AIDS represents a global emergency that will affect everyone alive today if it is not controlled. AIDS is now considered a global human-welfare and health issue. The message of Larry Kramer from the 1980's has been heard, making him perhaps the most prominent figure in the fight against HIV-AIDS during the last two decades of the twentieth century.

—R. Baird Shuman

Further Reading

ACT UP/NY Women and AIDS Book Group. *Women, AIDS, and Activism*. Boston: South End Press, 1990.

Bayer, Ronald, and David L. Kirp, eds. *AIDS in the Industrialized Democracies: Passion, Politics, and Policies*. New Brunswick, N.J.: Rutgers University Press, 1992.

Cohen, Peter. *Love and Anger: Essays on AIDS, Activism, and Politics*. New York: Haworth Press, 1998.

Cvetkovich, Ann. "AIDS Activism and Public Feelings: Documenting ACT UP's Lesbians." In *An Archive of Feelings: Trauma, Sexuality, and Lesbian Public Cultures,* by Ann Cvetkovich Durham, N.C.: Duke University Press, 2003.

Grmek, Mirko D. *The History of AIDS: Emergence and Origin of a Modern Pandemic*. Princeton, N.J.: Princeton University Press, 1990.

Hilderbrand, Lucas. "Retroactivism." *GLQ: A Journal of Lesbian and Gay Studies* 12, no. 2 (2006): 303-317.

Kramer, Larry. *Reports from the Holocaust: The Making of an AIDS Activist*. New York: St. Martin's Press, 1989.

Mass, Lawrence D. *We Must Love One Another or Die: The Life and Legacies of Larry Kramer*. New York: St. Martin's Press, 1997.

Shepard, Benjamin, and Ronald Hayduk, eds. *From ACT UP to the WTO: Urban Protest and Community Building in the Era of Globalization*. New York: Verso, 2002.

Stockdill, Brett. *Activism Against AIDS: At the Intersections of Sexuality, Race, Gender, and Class*. Boulder, Colo.: Lynne Rienner, 2003.

SEE ALSO: July 31, 1969: Gay Liberation Front Is Formed; June 5 and July 3, 1981: Reports of Rare Diseases Mark Beginning of AIDS Epidemic; July, 1982: Gay-Related Immunodeficiency Is Renamed AIDS; Spring, 1984: AIDS Virus Is Discovered; Oct. 9, 1984: San Francisco Closes Gay Bathhouses and Other Businesses; July 25, 1985: Actor Hudson Announces He Has AIDS; Sept., 1986: AZT Treats People with AIDS; Nov., 1986: Californians Reject LaRouche's Quarantine Initiative; 1987: Shilts Publishes *And the Band Played On*; June 27, 1988: Report of the Presidential AIDS Commission; Dec. 1, 1988: First World AIDS Day; 1989: Act Up Paris Is Founded; Dec. 10, 1989: ACT UP Protests at St. Patrick's Cathedral; Mar. 20, 1990: Queer Nation Is Founded; June 25, 1993: Clinton Appoints First AIDS Czar.

April, 1987
OLD LESBIANS ORGANIZE FOR CHANGE

Old Lesbians Organizing for Change was created to address the invisibility of self-described "older" lesbians within society in general and within the women's and lesbian rights movements in particular. The organization has reclaimed the word "old" as a form of empowerment, rejecting euphemisms such as "senior" to show that being old is not a problem.

LOCALE: Los Angeles, California
CATEGORIES: Organizations and institutions; feminism

KEY FIGURES

Barbara Macdonald (1913-2000), writer, social worker, activist, helped inspire the founding of OLOC
Shevy Healey (1922-2001), cofounder of OLOC, writer, psychologist, and activist
Vera Martin, cofounder of OLOC, civil rights worker and lesbian activist, and former civil service manager
Betty Shoemaker (1918-2002), founding member of OLOC, bookstore owner, and activist

SUMMARY OF EVENT

There are conflicting reports as to when Old Lesbians Organizing for Change (OLOC) was founded. There is no question, however, that a precursor to OLOC was the West Coast Conference of Older Lesbians, held at California State University, Dominguez Hills, in April of 1987. Older lesbians, defined by the group as those age sixty and up, believed they were being forgotten not only by society in general but also by the women's movement.

Barbara MacDonald's book *Look Me in the Eye: Old Women, Aging, and Ageism* (1983), cowritten with her domestic partner Cynthia Rich, included the essay "Open Letter to the Women's Movement," which condemned the movement's exclusion and dismissal of older women. Some say that this work was a major foundation for the first older lesbians' conference, which led, ultimately, to the formation of OLOC. Some believe that it was MacDonald's words especially that inspired the cofounders to take matters into their own hands. Shevy Healey, another cofounder of the conference as well as the OLOC, was an activist with personal and professional interests in ageism.

More than 150 older lesbians were present at the first OLOC meeting in Los Angeles, which was a success. In 1989, when the conference met for the third time, this time in San Francisco, OLOC had been fully established, and it had an organizational structure. Some individuals claim that the name "Old Lesbians Organizing for Change" was actually adopted at this San Francisco meeting, but others date the organization's beginnings to the 1987 meeting. Whatever the case, the group developed a mission statement in 1989 and started a newsletter, the *OLOC Reporter*, in 1990. The Horizons Foundation (a funding agency for gay and lesbian causes) supported the first two conferences with grants.

SIGNIFICANCE

Old Lesbians Organizing for Change has expanded into a national organization, and its headquarters are in Athens, Ohio. Its membership is open to lesbians sixty years of age and older, and those who are younger than age sixty are welcome as supporters. The organization holds "gatherings," rather than annual national meetings, and has had major gatherings in 1996, 1999, 2002, and 2006. With grant funding, OLOC sponsors the Arden Eversmeyer Old Lesbian Oral Herstory Project, which seeks autobiographical information from lesbians over the age of seventy. The OLOC has been represented at the White House Conference on Aging, by the National Gay and Lesbian Task Force, and by other major groups working to include older people in their outreach. Many older lesbians indicate that the OLOC has been one of the most meaningful organizations to which they have belonged.

OLOC is adamantly in favor of using the word "old," instead of euphemisms such as "golden," "senior," or "elder," to describe its membership. OLOC leadership has continually justified using "old" in the organization's title, reclaiming the word, in a way, to avoid age oppression. The euphemisms are considered patronizing, as if the term "old" were a dirty word. The OLOC has made it clear that older lesbians are vital to the lesbian and women's rights movements.

As of 2004, OLOC had a speakers' bureau, a mission statement, a planned-giving brochure, a travel directory, chapters in many states in the east, west, and south, as well as chapters in Canadian provinces. The organization continues to work toward its stated goals, which include the following:

> We are committed to empowering old lesbians in the common struggle to:
> 1. Confront ageism within our own and the larger community
> 2. Explore who we are and name our oppression
> 3. Analyze our experience of ageism by sharing our individual stories
> 4. Develop and disseminate educational material
> 5. Facilitate formation of new groups and stimulate existing groups to confront ageism
> 6. Make our presence a visible force in the women's movement and in the lesbian community

The statement continues with the words, "We celebrate our differences and affirm our diversity."

—*Mary Ware*

FURTHER READING

Adleman, Jeanne, et al., eds. *Lambda Gray: A Practical, Emotional, and Spiritual Guide for Gays and Lesbians Who Are Growing Older*. North Hollywood, Calif.: Newcastle, 1993.

Anderson, Pokey. "Rebels and Survivors: The Life Stories from Four of Our Lesbian 'Ancestors.'" *OutSmart*. http://www.outsmartmagazine.com/issue/i03-01/lesbian.html.

Boxer, Andrew. "Gay, Lesbian, and Bisexual Aging into the Twenty-First Century: An Overview and Introduction." *Journal of Gay, Lesbian and Bisexual Identity* 2, nos. 3/4 (1997).

Cahill, Sean, Ken South, and Jane Spade. *Outing Age: Public Policy Issues Affecting Gay, Lesbian, Bisexual, and Transgender Elders*. Policy Institute of the National Gay and Lesbian Task Force Foundation. http://www.ngltf.org/downloads/outingage.pdf.

Healey, Shevy. "Diversity with a Difference: On Being Old and Lesbian." *Journal of Gay and Lesbian Social Services* 1, no. 1 (1994).

Lyon, Phyllis, and Del Martin. "Aging, a Season of Grace: The Old Lesbian." In *Positively Gay: New Approaches to Gay and Lesbian Life*, edited by Betty Berzon, foreword by Barney Frank. 3d ed. Berkeley, Calif.: Celestial Arts, 2001.

MacDonald, Barbara. *Look Me in the Eye: Old Women, Aging, and Ageism*. San Francisco, Calif.: Spinsters Ink, 1983.

Old Lesbians Organizing for Change. http://www.oloc.org.

"Women and Aging: An Anthology." In *Calyx: A*

Journal of Art and Literature by Women 9, nos. 2/3 (Winter, 1986).

SEE ALSO: 1955: Daughters of Bilitis Founded as First National Lesbian Group in United States; May 27-30, 1960: First National Lesbian Conference Convenes; Fall, 1973: Lesbian Herstory Archives Is Founded; 1990, 1994: *Coming Out Under Fire* Documents Gay and Lesbian Military Veterans; July 26, 1990: Americans with Disabilities Act Becomes Law.

May, 1987
LAMBDA RISING BOOK REPORT BEGINS PUBLICATION

The Lambda Rising Book Report, *the first publication dedicated to reviewing books by, for, and about the lesbian, gay, bisexual, and transgender communities, has led to an expanded market for GLBT literature and an increase in the acquisition of GLBT-themed books of all genres in libraries around the United States.*

ALSO KNOWN AS: *Lambda Book Report*
LOCALE: Washington, D.C.
CATEGORIES: Publications; literature; organizations and institutions

KEY FIGURES
Deacon Maccubbin, founder and owner of Lambda Rising bookstore and founder of the *Report*
Robert Dirmeyer, first editor of the *Report*
Jane Troxell, second editor of the *Report*
Jim Marks, founder of Lambda Literary Foundation and publisher of the *Report*

SUMMARY OF EVENT
In 1974, Deacon Maccubbin had founded Lambda Rising bookstore in Washington, D.C., one of the first and most successful gay bookstores in the United States at the time. Thirteen years later, during the blossoming of GLBT literature in the 1980's, Maccubbin founded the *Lambda Rising Book Report* (or, simply, the *Report*), the first publication devoted to reviewing GLBT books.

Maccubbin, who served as the *Report*'s publisher for several years, started the journal because information about gay-related publications was not readily available to librarians and booksellers in 1987. As Lambda Rising's owner, he knew firsthand that publishers did not effectively advertise their GLBT books. A political activist and bibliophile, Maccubbin also wanted to increase GLBT literacy with the *Report*. As with his bookstore, he said he created the *Report* as a mission, not as a means for profit.

Comparable in format to *The New York Times Book Review*, the *Report* features bimonthly reviews of contemporary GLBT literature, articles often written by authors themselves. Each issue also contains special features and lists of best-selling paperback and hardcover books for men and women. Like other GLBT publications at the time, the *Report* also provided space for GLBT advertisements. Unlike other publications, however, the *Report* has maintained its focus on GLBT literature and the spread of literacy throughout the community.

The first issue of the *Report* was published in May of 1987. Robert Dirmeyer was the journal's first editor, but after only a few issues, Jane Troxell took over and served as editor until 1993. For several issues, the *Report* was distributed as an insert in larger GLBT publications, such as the *Washington Blade* and *Frontiers*. Maccubbin had arranged this method of distribution in order to reach a larger audience. He accomplished his goal resoundingly: The *Report* had a circulation of nearly 100,000 in 1987, whereas the circulation was one-tenth that size in 2004.

In 1990, the *Report* changed from a tabloid format to a magazine format, and the magazine's name was changed to *Lambda Book Report*. Not coincidentally, in 1996, the bookstore disassociated itself from the journal for two reasons: the high cost of maintaining the publication, and the *Report* staff's mission of literacy. So the *Report* was handed over to the Lambda Literary Foundation, a nonprofit organization founded by Jim Marks, who had been a staff member on the *Report* and who became the magazine's publisher. Also, with the 1996 ownership transfer the *Report* became a monthly.

SIGNIFICANCE
Founded during the apex of the HIV-AIDS crisis and only five months before the massive AIDS protest on the nation's capital in October, 1987, the *Lambda Rising Book Report* provided a source of community solidarity and edification during a politically tempestuous decade. Because of anti-GLBT backlash caused by paranoia and naïveté about HIV-AIDS, much of the media exposure in 1987 was negative. The *Report*, however, offered positive reading. It publicized the literary accomplishments of lesbians and gays for a national audience, and its neutral political tone, particularly compared with that of activist magazines such as *OutWeek*, revealed the versatility of the efflorescent GLBT press and offered a less-combative—though liberating in its own right—national voice from a GLBT journal.

Also, according to Maccubbin's mission statement, the *Report* allowed gays and lesbians to purchase reading material that was otherwise not carried in libraries or major bookstores. Aside from Lambda Rising bookstore in Washington, D.C., Oscar Wilde Memorial Bookshop in New York City, and A Different Light bookstore in Los Angeles, most bookstores did not carry GLBT literature, especially nonfiction and specialty books. Lesbian and lesbian-feminist books were being sold by women's bookstores, however, since the early 1970's. Accordingly, the *Report* aimed to bring the whole of contemporary GLBT writing to the reading public's attention.

At the same time, the journal helped to rectify the absence of GLBT books available through such venues. Since many libraries required that their acquisitions first be reviewed by a national publication, and since publishers were not communicating well with booksellers about the GLBT books they published, libraries and booksellers needed a national journal that reviewed GLBT books in a timely manner. Fulfilling this need, the *Report* became well known as the best source for reviews of GLBT materials. It remains the best single source of such reviews.

At a time when GLBT literature was growing in both quantity and quality, the *Report* also played a significant role in launching the careers of many writers. E. Lynn Harris, for example, sent an unsolicited, self-published manuscript of his first book, *Invisible Life*, to editor Jane Troxell, who then assigned a review of the book for the *Report*. Harris's career then blossomed, and he became one of the most popular and respected GLBT authors writing in the last half of the twentieth century. The *Report* also gave many GLBT writers an opportunity to write reviews, conduct and publish interviews, and write other articles for a national publication.

—*Sam See*

FURTHER READING
Groff, David. "Queer Publishing: Between the Covers." *Poets & Writers* 21, no. 3 (1993): 48-55.
Ridinger, Robert B. Marks. "So's Your Old Lady: Naming Patterns in the Gay and Lesbian Press." *Journal of Homosexuality* 28, no. 4 (1994).
Streitmatter, Rodger. *Unspeakable: The Rise of the Gay and Lesbian Press in America*. Winchester, Mass.: Faber and Faber, 1995.
Weeks, Linton. "Bookseller's Success Speaks Volumes: Lambda Rising Owner Helped Bring Gay Literature Out of the Closet." *The Washington Post*, April, 2003, p. C-1.

SEE ALSO: 1896: *Der Eigene* Is Published as First Journal on Homosexuality; June, 1947-Feb., 1948: *Vice Versa* Is Published as First Lesbian Periodical; 1953: *ONE* Magazine Begins Publication; 1967: *Los Angeles Advocate* Begins Publication; Fall, 1967: Oscar Wilde Memorial

Bookshop Opens as First Gay Bookstore; 1970: Amazon Bookstore Opens as First Feminist-Lesbian Book Shop; 1971: *Lesbian Tide* Publishes Its First Issue; June, 1971: The Gay Book Award Debuts; Nov., 1971: *The Body Politic* Begins Publication; Oct., 1974: *Lesbian Connection* Begins Publication; Dec. 31, 1977: Toronto Police Raid Offices of *The Body Politic*; 1980: Alyson Begins Publishing Gay and Lesbian Books; Jan., 1986: South Asian Newsletter *Trikone* Begins Publication; June 2, 1989: Lambda Literary Award Is Created.

May 30, 1987
U.S. Congressman Frank Comes Out as Gay

Massachusetts representative Barney Frank was the second member of Congress to come out as gay but the first to do so willingly. He has been re-elected by his district many times since coming out and has been a champion for civil and gay and lesbian rights.

LOCALE: Washington, D.C.
CATEGORY: Government and politics

KEY FIGURES
Barney Frank (b. 1940), U.S. representative from Newton, Massachusetts
John Robinson, reporter for the *Boston Globe*, who broke the story of Frank's coming out

SUMMARY OF EVENT
There is a long history in politics of closeted gays and lesbians fearing scandal if their sexual orientation became known publicly. During the 1980's, it was common knowledge in the professional workplace on Capitol Hill that some members of Congress were gay or lesbian, but this was not a subject that was openly discussed or otherwise commented upon. Careers could be ruined, and those dependent upon the ballot box for their positions saw discretion as the better part of valor. A series of events led Barney Frank to question this complicity, and he took a stand in acknowledging his sexual orientation to the press without shame.

In the first week of May, 1987, the Gary Hart/Donna Rice scandal broke. The scandal revealed an extramarital affair by Gary Hart, the leading Democratic candidate for president, which increased scrutiny of politicians' private lives by the media and destroyed Hart's promising campaign. Republican representative Stewart B. McKinney of Connecticut died the same week of complications resulting from AIDS, and these unrelated events created an atmosphere of heightened gossiping and journalistic inquiry into the private sexual lives of politicians. Frank had been increasingly open about his sexuality, coming out to more and more associates, but he had maintained that journalistic pondering about his private life was inappropriate, and it diverted attention away from the political and social issues he was championing.

Another factor motivating Frank's disclosure was the 1986 publication of *The Gentleman from Maryland: The Conscience of a Gay Conservative* by Republican Robert Bauman. Bauman had left Congress in disgrace in 1981 after being arrested and receiving a suspended six-month sentence for soliciting a sixteen-year-old male prostitute, and the book was essentially an apologia, recounting a sordid life. However, in the book, Bauman asserted that he was not the only congressman with "homosexual tendencies," and he made reference to Frank anonymously but in such a way that it was just a matter of time before reporters would begin to ask specific questions.

Frank had quipped that as a left-handed Jew he was quite used to being different. He realized that formal disclosure of his sexuality would give his

A Barney Frank campaign letter from July, 1972, which reads, in part, "The following constitutes my views on proper government policy towards homosexuals...." (William J. Canfield Papers, Northeastern University Library)

mance. He believed that coming out would stop his ongoing fear of being outed by someone else. To come out, he granted an interview with a newspaper reporter for the *Boston Globe*, John Robinson.

The May 30, 1987, issue of the *Boston Globe* included a front-page story on Frank, in which he acknowledged that he is gay. The story was based on an hour-long interview Robinson had with Frank on Capitol Hill. Kay Longcope wrote a follow-up piece that the *Globe* published the next day.

SIGNIFICANCE

Coming out was a watershed event for Frank. He not only survived the exposure but also has been returned several times to office by his constituents. In the meantime, his seniority has placed him on powerful committees. Immediately following his disclosure, a study was conducted to determine the views of his Massachusetts constituents; they were found to be supportive of Frank, and were generally unconcerned or unsurprised about his sexual orientation. For every letter of criticism he received for coming out came six letters of support. In the election that followed his coming out, his Republican opponent tried to make Frank's sexuality a negative issue, but Frank nevertheless garnered 70 percent of the vote.

Frank had to deal with his own scandal in late 1989, however. He called for an investigation by the House Ethics Committee when it was learned that a former employee of his had been running a prostitution ring from Frank's home. In the end, even though right-wing conservatives wanted to

future political opponents the tool of homophobia. Still, he had the precedent of Representative Gerry Studds, who had been forced to acknowledge that he was gay in 1983 after a scandal with a congressional page. Studds received a formal censure from the House, but he nonetheless was returned twice to office by his constituents. Frank decided the time was right to come out and to emphasize that his sexual orientation was not relevant to his job perfor-

censure or expel Frank because of the scandal, the House voted to reprimand him instead, and he was cleared of any knowledge of the prostitution ring. He was, however, held accountable for fixing some traffic tickets the employee had received while using the congressman's car.

Frank persevered, using his wisdom and political acumen to fight for civil rights and social justice. He went on to become the highest ranking Democratic member of the Financial Services Committee in 2003 and the chair of the Subcommittee on the Constitution. In this latter role, he delivered a memorable, thoughtful, and effective speech on May 13, 2004, against the proposed constitutional amendment to ban same-gender marriage in the United States, a proposal that was defeated.

Frank has broken barriers, and he serves as a model for young gay and lesbian politicians eager to enter public service. He demonstrated that if one gets the job done, and done well, many voters will support a candidate regardless of his or her sexual orientation. In 2005, he was the highest ranking, out gay political figure in the United States.

—*Scot M. Guenter*

Further Reading

Frank, Barney. *Speaking Frankly: What's Wrong with the Democrats and How To Fix It*. New York: Times Books/Random House, 1992.

Hertzog, Mark. *The Lavender Vote: Lesbians, Gay Men, and Bisexuals in American Electoral Politics*. New York: New York University Press, 1996.

Marcus, Eric. *Making Gay History: The Half Century Fight for Lesbian and Gay Civil Rights*. New York: Perennial, 2002.

Rayside, David. *On the Fringe: Gays and Lesbians in Politics*. Ithaca, N.Y.: Cornell University Press, 1998.

Yeager, Ken. *Trailblazers: Profiles of America's Gay and Lesbian Elected Officials*. New York: Haworth Press, 1999.

See also: 1961: Sarria Is First Out Gay or Lesbian Candidate for Public Office; 1971: Kameny Is First Out Candidate for U.S. Congress; Nov. 5, 1974: Noble Is First Out Lesbian or Gay Person to Win State-Level Election; Nov. 27, 1978: White Murders Politicians Moscone and Milk; July 14, 1983: Studds Is First Out Gay Man in the U.S. Congress; Nov. 6, 1984: West Hollywood Incorporates with Majority Gay and Lesbian City Council; Aug. 27, 1991: *The Advocate* Outs Pentagon Spokesman Pete Williams; May 24, 1993: Achtenberg Becomes Assistant Housing Secretary.

October 11, 1987
SECOND MARCH ON WASHINGTON FOR LESBIAN AND GAY RIGHTS

The Second National March on Washington for Lesbian and Gay Rights brought more than one-half-million marchers and protesters to the nation's capital and signaled major shifts in both strategy and visibility for the strengthening lesbian, gay, bisexual, and transgender rights movement not only in the United States but also around the world.

LOCALE: Washington, D.C.
CATEGORIES: Marches, protests, and riots; organizations and institutions; civil rights

KEY FIGURES
Cleve Jones (b. 1954), organizer of the AIDS quilt project
Troy Perry (b. 1940), reverend and founder of the Metropolitan Community Church, conducted a commitment ceremony for thousands of same-gender couples
Karen Thompson (b. 1947), and
Sharon Kowalski, lesbian couple who had been fighting for same-gender and disability rights

SUMMARY OF EVENT
The Second National March on Washington for Lesbian and Gay Rights was only the second national lesbian and gay march on the nation's capital (the first, in 1979, attracted about eighty thousand people), but the October 11, 1987, event situated lesbian and gay civil rights as part of the long tradition of protest marches on Washington. Marches on Washington reach back to at least the 1890's. The marches have been particularly resonant since the 1963 March on Washington for Jobs and Freedom, led by Dr. Martin Luther King, Jr., and organized by gay African American Bayard Rustin.

The 1987 lesbian and gay march emerged as a grassroots organization overseen by a national steering committee of approximately fifty members. This steering committee was made up of four members from eleven national districts, each reflecting gender parity and including at least one person of color, in addition to a national board of seven members representing specific constituencies (for example, the disabled, seniors, college students, and so forth). The 1987 steering committee crafted a bold mission statement demanding such things as the legal recognition of lesbian and gay relationships, the repeal of all laws criminalizing homosexuality, a federal ban on discrimination on the basis of sexual orientation and on HIV-AIDS status, the right to reproductive freedom and the end of racism in the United States, and the expansion of funding for HIV-AIDS education, treatment, research, and patient care.

This broad mandate by the national committee inspired an elaborate catalog of events affiliated with the march across the entirety of the Columbus Day holiday weekend. These events included a morning rally sponsored by the People of Color caucus, a concert by fourteen Lesbian/Gay Bands of America, and a conference hosted by the National Leather Association (which was held in the U.S. Treasury Department building).

At "The Wedding" on the afternoon of Saturday, October 10, several thousand committed, same-gender couples arrived on the steps of the Internal Revenue Service building singing "we're going to the chapel and we're gonna get married." The crowd heard Karen Thompson speak about her custody battle over her disabled partner, Sharon Kowalski, before Reverend Troy Perry conducted a commitment ceremony for thousands of couples.

The NAMES Project Foundation's AIDS Memorial Quilt was unveiled on the morning of October 11. Founded by Cleve Jones and other San Francisco community activists in June of 1987, NAMES gathered quilt panels from Los Angeles, San Francisco, and New York and, using donated materials, equipment, and labor, crafted the 1,920 panels memorializing people whose deaths were AIDS-related. Displayed on the National Mall, the quilt was laid out on a space greater than that of a football field.

Hundreds of thousands of LGBT individuals marched from the Ellipse (south of the White House) to the Lincoln Memorial, where they were addressed by Jesse Jackson, Whoopi Goldberg, Ginny Appuzzo, United Farm Workers (UFW) president César Chávez, and National Organization for Women (NOW) president Eleanor Smeal, among others. Event organizers anticipated somewhere between 100,000 and 250,000 marchers, but the more than 500,000 marchers who were there (most later estimates put the crowd somewhere near 650,000) defied all expectations, especially those of the National Park Service, which had released its pre-event estimate of 200,000 marchers to the media, unrevised. There were contingents from all fifty states and a host of foreign nations as well.

The largest act of civil disobedience since the Vietnam era took place on Tuesday, October 13. Protesting the spate of U.S. Supreme Court decisions that refused to decriminalize homosexuality, more than three thousand protesters "sat in" on the steps of the Supreme Court. In turn, groups of twenty or so people would stand, circle hands, be arrested, and be led off by capitol police wearing riot gear and rubber gloves. More than six hundred individual protesters were arrested that morning, even as LGBT people called upon their elected representatives.

SIGNIFICANCE

Many groups point to the 1987 March on Washington for Lesbian and Gay Rights as the event that inspired their sustained engagement and involvement in grassroots activism throughout the later 1980's and early 1990's. The NAMES Project expanded immediately, literally tripling in size during the four-month national tour of twenty cities that followed its unveiling at the march. National Coming Out Day (October 11) was founded as an annual testament to the power of the march and its visibility. Civil disobedience, especially as practiced by ACT UP (the AIDS Coalition to Unleash Power), emerged as a crucial activist strategy during the years following the march. A host of national professional associations of teachers, lawyers, journalists, and others had been organized after the march as well. Likewise, at colleges and universities, and even in small towns, grassroots organizations and publications began to flourish.

However, the 1987 march provided an organizing impetus for conservative anti-GLBT groups, too, including activists at the American Family Association (AFA), who interpreted the march's mission statement as an articulation of the overriding agenda of the LGBT movement. In the early 1990's, the AFA elaborated on its interpretation of the mission statement in *The Gay Agenda*, a series of videos, and through public information events targeting religious and conservative voters across the United States.

The march affirmed the national viability of gay and lesbian culture and community, and the

The AIDS Memorial Quilt was first unveiled in 1987 in front of the Washington Monument. (National Institutes of Health)

> **THE AIDS MEMORIAL QUILT**
>
> The NAMES Project Foundation AIDS Memorial Quilt was conceived in 1985 and physically unveiled at the National Mall in Washington, D.C., the day of the Second March on Washington for Lesbian and Gay Rights (October 11, 1987). The quilt was produced to memorialize those who had died from AIDS-related complications. The quilt idea arose when gay rights activist Cleve Jones finished a candlelight march honoring slain San Francisco supervisor Harvey Milk and Mayor George Moscone. Jones and his fellow marchers attached to the walls of the San Francisco federal building the placards they were carrying of the names of friends who had died of AIDS. Stepping back, Jones saw the quilt-like effect of the cards. By the following year, Jones, friend Mike Smith, and several others created the NAMES Project Foundation.
>
> The quilt was unveiled with more than nineteen hundred panels. In direct response to this historic first unveiling, the quilt was taken on a four-month tour across the United States to raise awareness and give many the opportunity to create their own panels of remembrance to add to the foundation's legacy. By the end of the first tour the quilt had tripled its size. A second tour in 1989 doubled the number of cities visited across the United States and Canada and included fund-raising campaigns for AIDS service organizations.
>
> The last year the AIDS Memorial Quilt was displayed in its entirety was 1996. Since that time new panels have been added, numbering more than forty-five thousand in 2006 and weighing more than fifty-four tons. NAMES Project Foundation local chapters have been established across the United States with more than forty quilt affiliates around the world. Warehoused since 2001 in a climate-controlled building in Atlanta, Georgia, portions of the quilt can be found on display all over the world at any given time.

seriousness of its political activism. The strategies of civil disobedience, affirmation of same-gender relationships, and advocacy for federal action regarding HIV-AIDS would emerge as the defining features of LGBT activism in the years to follow.

—*Brian Eugenio Herrera*

FURTHER READING

Bernstein, Mary. "Celebration and Suppression: The Strategic Uses of Identity by the Lesbian and Gay Movement." *American Journal of Sociology* 103 (1997): 531-565.

Jones, Cleve, with Jeff Dawson. *Stitching a Revolution: The Making of An Activist*. San Francisco, Calif.: HarperSanFrancisco, 2001.

Marcus, Eric. *Making Gay History: The Half Century Fight for Lesbian and Gay Equal Rights*. New York: Harper Perennial, 2002.

Pope, Lisa, et al. *One Million Strong: The 1993 March on Washington for Lesbian, Gay, and Bi Equal Rights*. New York: Alyson, 1993.

Rimmerman, Craig. *From Identity to Politics: The Lesbian and Gay Movements in the United States*. Philadelphia: Temple University Press, 2001.

SEE ALSO: July 2-Aug. 28, 1963: Rustin Organizes the March on Washington; Aug., 1966: Queer Youth Fight Police Harassment at Compton's Cafeteria in San Francisco; June 27-July 2, 1969: Stonewall Rebellion Ignites Modern Gay and Lesbian Rights Movement; July 31, 1969: Gay Liberation Front Is Formed; May 1, 1970: Lavender Menace Protests Homophobia in Women's Movement; June 28, 1970: First Lesbian and Gay Pride March in the United States; Oct. 12-15, 1979: First March on Washington for Lesbian and Gay Rights; Mar., 1987: Radical AIDS Activist Group ACT UP Is Founded; Oct. 11, 1988: First National Coming Out Day Is Celebrated; Dec. 10, 1989: ACT UP Protests at St. Patrick's Cathedral; Mar. 20, 1990: Queer Nation Is Founded; Apr. 24, 1993: First Dyke March Is Held in Washington, D.C.; Apr. 25, 1993: March on Washington for Gay, Lesbian, and Bi Equal Rights and Liberation; June, 1994: Stonewall 25 March and Rallies Are Held in New York City; June 19, 2002: Gays and Lesbians March for Equal Rights in Mexico City.

October 14-17, 1987
LATIN AMERICAN AND CARIBBEAN LESBIAN FEMINIST NETWORK IS FORMED

The first lesbian-feminist Encuentro, or encounter, was held in Mexico to establish a network of like-minded women in Latin America and the Caribbean. Although not without controversy over the inclusion of Latinas and Chicanas from the United States, and despite some problems with privacy and security and with religious and local governmental groups, the Encuentro was successful, empowering, and pathbreaking nonetheless.

LOCALE: Cuernavaca, Mexico
CATEGORIES: Cultural and intellectual history; organizations and institutions; feminism

SUMMARY OF EVENT
The idea for a specifically feminist and lesbian Encuentro came out of the 1985 International Lesbian Conference in Geneva, Switzerland. Women at the conference had envisioned a network for lesbian feminists from Latin America and the Caribbean that would emerge from the various feminist Encuentros that had taken place since 1981. The First Latin American and Caribbean Lesbian-Feminist Encuentro would take place in Cuernavaca, Mexico, from October 14 through October 17, 1987, at a private hacienda outside Mexico City.

The lesbian-feminist Encuentro had been scheduled to take place one week prior to the fourth feminist Encuentro in Taxco, Mexico. At the Encuentro were 250 lesbian women from Chile, Peru, Brazil, Argentina, Colombia, Nicaragua, Panama, Honduras, Puerto Rico, the Dominican Republic, and Costa Rica. Latinas and Chicanas also came from the United States, and a small number of non-Latinas who attended were from the United States, Canada, and Europe. Many participants also attended the feminist Encuentro the following week.

Women interested in attending the conference were required to write an essay about their knowledge of lesbian sexuality and of feminism. These essays were read by members of the Latina Americana Lesbiana (LAL) organizing committee, which selected the participants based on their essays. The rates for attending the conference varied according to regional classifications, which caused some dissension. Lesbians from Latin America and the Caribbean were charged $50 to attend; lesbians who were from Latin America and the Caribbean but who lived in other countries were charged $80-$120; and non-Latinas were charged $150-$250.

Concerned that the police or local residents would disrupt the gathering, the LAL planned the event with as little local publicity as possible. This prevented them, however, from seeking regional funding, and, consequently, from helping to fund the travel expenses for lesbians in Latin America and the Caribbean. For these funds, they approached organizations and individuals in Europe and the United States. Lacking, however, were adequate amounts of food, housing, volunteers, and funds during the conference. As a security measure, only three members of LAL knew the exact location of the Encuentro until the last minute. Bus drivers who transported participants from Mexico City to Cuernavaca were informed that they were en route to a Christian women's retreat. Security guards were stationed around the perimeter of the central venue, and attendees were asked to refrain from public "displays" of their sexuality, including political and affectional, when they were outside the gathering site.

Lesbians who attended the Encuentro resided onsite and in nearby hotels and private residences. The conference program included workshops on topics such as lesbian motherhood, self-defense, sexuality, health, spirituality, relationships, documentation, organizing strategies, and monogamy versus nonmonogamy.

A plenary was the main event of each day, and they turned out to be the major sites of debate and conflict as well. At issue, in particular, was the creation of the network for lesbians from Latin America and the Caribbean specifically. Participants were divided about who could join the network, how it would be established, the criteria for inclusion, and how the network would serve lesbians who lived great distances from each other. The strongest disagreement came over whether or not to include Latinas and Chicanas from the United States. While some considered U.S. Latinas and Chicanas outsiders who lived in a privileged country and who could thus misuse their votes if they were included in the network, others recognized that there was a popular misunderstanding of U.S. Latinas and Chicanas. In the original voting, U.S. Chicanas and Latinas were not accepted into the network, a position that was reversed after heated and emotional debate and mediation.

The first gathering also included about fifteen women who were not Latina or Chicana. While permitted to attend, they were not welcomed by some of the participants. There also was concern that the five attending members of the International Lesbian Information Service, organizers of the conference in Geneva, would take control of the network. At the same time, internal disputes divided the organizers, especially involving those with a Marxist-Leninist political philosophy.

SIGNIFICANCE

Despite internal conflicts and concerns with security, privacy, and local government and religious intolerance, the first lesbian-feminist Encuentro was still a successful, historic event. The first Encuentro laid the groundwork for future gatherings in Peru (1989), Costa Rica (1990), Puerto Rico (1992), Argentina (1995), Brazil (1998), and Mexico (2004).

Encuentros that had been affected by unique, local circumstances and the political climate of the time included the gathering in Costa Rica in 1990. Threats from religious and governmental organizations and local residents hampered the gathering after news of the event was leaked to the media. In 1992, some lesbians from Latin America and the Caribbean had difficulty attending the Encuentro in Puerto Rico because of U.S. immigration restrictions. This conference included many participants from the United States, but because their participation was initially rejected by Mexican and Latin American lesbians during the debates about the network's formation, the future participation of lesbian Latinas, especially Chicanas, was impacted greatly. Despite being relatively close to the southwestern United States geographically, not many Chicanas attended the sixth Encuentro in Mexico in 2004.

Over time, the network that was established at the first Encuentro faded. However, with the Internet and the Web, another type of "network" has since flourished, providing a simple and cost-effective means of communication among lesbians from around the world. Furthermore, lesbian feminists from Latin America and the Caribbean still attend feminist Encuentros.

—tatiana de la tierra

FURTHER READING

De la tierra, tatiana. "Latin American Lesbian-Feminists: Together in Mexico." *Visibilities* (September/October, 1988): 8-11.

Díaz-Cotto, Juanita. "Lesbian-Feminist Activism and Latin American Feminist Encuentros." In *Sexual Identities, Queer Politics*, edited by Mark Blasius. Princeton, N.J.: Princeton University Press, 2001.

Likosky, Stephan, ed. *Coming Out: An Anthology of International Gay and Lesbian Writings*. New York: Pantheon Books, 1992. Includes the articles "Mexico: From 'First Encounter of Lesbians and Feminists'" and "Man Royals and Sodomites: Some Thoughts on the Invisibility of Afro-Caribbean Lesbians."

Randall, Margaret. *Our Voices, Our Lives: Stories of Women from Central America and the Caribbean*. Monroe, Maine: Common Courage Press, 1995.

Reyes, Migdalia. "The Latin American and Caribbean Feminist/Lesbian Encuentros: Crossing the Bridge of Our Diverse Identities." In *This Bridge We Call Home: Radical Visions for Transformation*, edited by Gloria E. Anzaldúa and Ana-Louise Keating. New York: Routledge, 2002.

See also: Nov. 17, 1901: Police Arrest "Los 41" in Mexico City; 1912-1924: Robles Fights in the Mexican Revolution; Nov., 1965: Revolutionary Cuba Imprisons Gays; 1969: Nuestro Mundo Forms as First Queer Organization in Argentina; Nov. 18-21, 1977: National Women's Conference Convenes; Oct. 12-15, 1979: First National Third World Lesbian and Gay Conference Convenes; June 19, 2002: Gays and Lesbians March for Equal Rights in Mexico City; Apr., 2003: Buenos Aires Recognizes Same-Gender Civil Unions; Jan., 2006: Jiménez Flores Elected to the Mexican Senate.

1988
Macho Dancer Is Released in the Philippines

Film director and social activist Lino Brocka made gay film history by using Macho Dancer *to agitate and shed light on the governments of Ferdinand Marcos and Corazon Aquino, whose devastating economic policies forced many poor young Filipino males into prostitution. Despite repeated attempts by the Philippine government to censor his work, Brocka continued to fight for free artistic expression.*

Locale: Philippines
Categories: Arts; civil rights; government and politics; economics

Key Figures

Lino Brocka (1940-1991), director of *Macho Dancer*
Allan Paole, star of *Macho Dancer*
Ferdinand Marcos (1917-1984), tenth president of the Republic of the Philippines
Corazon Aquino (b. 1933), eleventh president of the Republic of the Philippines

Summary of Event

Famed international film director Lino Brocka was the only out, gay, public figure in the conservative Philippines when his film *Macho Dancer* was released in 1988. The movie made gay history by shedding light on how the inadequate and corrupt conservative regimes of Ferdinand Marcos and Corazon Aquino, which continued to support U.S. military bases in the Philippines, forced poor young Filipino males into prostitution.

Based on a true story, the confrontational *Macho Dancer* explores the lives of young men stuck in Manila's "red-light" world of brothels and sexual slavery. The character Pol (Allan Paole), a young Filipino man barely out of his teens, seeks a better life for his family after his lover, a U.S. Army soldier, the sole support of Pol's family, abandons him and returns to the United States. Pol soon realizes that he has to support his family, and that he has to resort to prostitution to make money. He leaves his home in the mountainous countryside and moves to the large city of Manila, the capital of the Philippines, where he finds work as a go-go boy and male prostitute. In Manila, Pol meets Noel (Daniel Fernando), whose sister has been abducted to work in a brothel. The two form an intense sexual relationship, and when Noel is violently killed, Pol finds he must avenge his lover's murder. He moves back to the countryside alone.

Director Brocka's own background prepared him for presenting films that depict many marginalized sectors of society: the poor, prostitutes, and drug addicts. He, too, grew up in a poor and rural area in the Philippine countryside. Before moving to San Francisco, California, where he worked helping the homeless, he studied to be a Mormon missionary. He also taught in Hawaii and worked in a leper colony before returning to the Philippines, where he wrote scripts for and directed the Philippine Educational Theater Association (PETA).

From the beginning of his directorial career,

LINO BROCKA FILMOGRAPHY, 1970-1991

1970
Wanted: Perfect Mother
Santiago

1971
Tubog Sa Ginto (Dipped in Gold/Gold-plated)
Now
Lumuha Pati Mga Anghel (Even the Angels Cried)
Cadena De Amor (Chain of Love)
Stardoom

1972
Villa Miranda
Cherry Blossoms

1974
Tinimbang Ka Ngunit Kulang (Weighed but Found Wanting)
Tatlo, Dalawa, Isa (Three, Two, One)

1975
Maynila, Sa Mga Kuko Ng Liwanag (Manila in the Claws of Lights/Manila in the Claws of Neon Lights)
Dung-aw (Peasants Lament)

1976
Lunes, Martes, Miyerkules, Huwebes, Biyernes, Sabado, Linggo (Monday, Tuesday, Wednesday, Thursday, Friday, Saturday, Sunday)
Insiang

1977
Tahan Na Empoy, Tahan (Stop Crying, Little Boy)
Tadhana: Ito Ang Lahing Pilipino—Reform Movement Episode (History of the Filipino Race)
Inay (Mother)

1978
Mananayaw (The Dancer)
Ang Tatay Kong Nanay (My Father, My Mother)
Gumising Ka Maruja (Wake up Maruja)
Hayop Sa Hayop (Beast to Beast)
Rubia Servios

1979
Init (Heat)
Ina, Kapatid, Anak (Mother, Sister, Daughter)
Jaguar Ina Ka Ng Anak Mo (You Are the Mother of Your Child/Whore of a Mother)

1980
Nakaw Na Pag-ibig (Stole Love)
Angela Markado Bona

1981
Burgis
Kontrobersyal (Controversial)
Hello, Young Lovers
Binata Si Mister, Dalaga Si Misis (The Husband Is a Bachelor, the Wife Is a Maiden)
Caught in the Act

1982
Px
In Dis Corner (In This Corner)
Palipat-lipat, Papalit-palit (Keep on Changing, Keep on Moving)
Mother Dear
Cain at Abel (Cain and Abel)

1983
Strangers in Paradise
Hot Property

1984
Bayan Ko: Kapit Sa Patalim (My Country: Gripping the Knife's Edge)
Adultery (Aida Macaraeg Case No. 7892)
Akin Ang Iyong Katawan (Your Body Is Mine Experience)

1985
Miguelito, Ang Batang Rebelde (Miguelito, the Rebel Boy)
White Slavery
Ano Ang Kulay Ng Mukha Ng Diyos Napakasakit Kuya Eddie

1987
Maging Akin Ka Lamang (If Only You Could Be Mine)
Pasan Ko Ang Daigdig (I Carry the World)

1988
Macho Dancer
Tatlong Mukha Ng Pag-ibig—"Ang Silid" (The Three Faces of Love—"The Room" Episode)
Natutulog Pa Ang Diyos (God Is Still Asleep)

1989
Kailan Mahuhugasan Ang Kasalanan (When Will the Sin Be Washed Away)
Orapronobis (Fight for Us)
Babangon Ako't Dudurugin Kita (I Will Rise and Crush You)

1990
Kung Tapos Na Ang Kailanman (At the End of Eternity)
Gumapang Ka Sa Lusak (Dirty Affair)
Hahamakin Ang Lahat (Despise Everything)
How Are the Kids
Biktima (Victim)
Ama, Bakit Mo Ako Pinabayaan (Father, Why Have You Forsaken Me)

1991
Sa Kabila Ng Lahat (No Matter What)
Kislap Sa Dilim (Sparkle in the Dark)
Makiusap Sa Diyos (Plead with God)

Brocka, who is often compared to gay directors Rainer Werner Fassbinder and Pier Paolo Pasolini, won quick international acclaim. In all, he made more than seventy films, addressing social as well as political concerns. For example, there can be little doubt that the American soldier who abandoned Pol, the young Filipino hero in *Macho Dancer*, represents Brocka's condemnation of the American military bases in the Philippine Islands and the corrupt Marcos and Aquino governmental regimes, which supported their presence. Brocka became so critical of President Marcos, who declared martial law in 1972 and formed a dictatorship in 1973, that his films had to be smuggled out of the country. Despite imprisonment for sixteen days in 1984, the director heroically continued to fight all forms of censorship by continuing his controversial filmmaking.

His earlier films, including his first, *Wanted: Perfect Mother* (1970), brought to light the plight of orphans in the Philippines. In *Maynila* (1975) and *Jaguar* (1979), Brocka criticizes the corrupt Marcos government by depicting the true economic concerns of the Filipino people. In *Angela Markado Bona* (1980), he attacks the extravagant lives of movie stars, and his *Kontrobersyal* (1981) condemns pornography. *Bayan Ko* (1984), was so critical of the country that the Philippine government disowned it when it earned an entry in the 1984 Cannes Film Festival. Brocka, however, won the Ramon Magsaysay Award for Journalism, Literature and Creative Communication Arts in 1985, awarded to Brocka by a Philippines' based foundation for "making cinema a vital social commentary, awakening public consciousness to disturbing realities of life among the Filipino poor."

SIGNIFICANCE

Lino Brocka's *Macho Dancer* inspired an entirely new film genre. To take one example, Filipino Mel Chionglo's *Burlesk King* (1999) was critically referred to as a "macho dancer" film, crediting the significance of Brocka's work to that of Chionglo.

Also, *Macho Dancer*, in Tagalog with English subtitles, brought international attention to the excellence of Philippine cinema. In can be argued that because of Brocka's filmmaking and the work it inspired, Manila is now acclaimed worldwide as one of the cities that produces the best in Third World cinema. *Macho Dancer* is considered historically significant in gay film history as well because it was the first film in Third World cinema to address homosexuality.

—*M. Casey Diana*

FURTHER READING

Dyer, Richard. *Now You See It: Studies on Lesbian and Gay Film*. New York: Routledge, 2002.

Hadleigh, Boze. *The Lavender Screen: The Gay and Lesbian Films—Their Stars, Makers, Characters, and Critics*. New York: Citadel Press, 2001.

Kalaw-Tirol, Lorna. *Above the Crowd* (Profiles of Famous Filipinos). Manila, the Philippines: Anvil, 2000.

SEE ALSO: 1929: *Pandora's Box* Opens; 1930's-1960's: Hollywood Bans "Sexual Perversion" in Films; 1985: Lesbian Film *Desert Hearts* Is Released; Mar. 20, 1988: *M. Butterfly* Opens on Broadway; 1993: *The Wedding Banquet* Is First Acclaimed Taiwanese Gay-Themed Film; 1995: *The Advocate* Outs Oscar Nominee Nigel Hawthorne; Mar. 5, 2006: *Brokeback Mountain, Capote,* and *Transamerica* Receive Oscars.

January 1, 1988
CANADA DECRIMINALIZES SEX PRACTICES BETWEEN CONSENTING ADULTS

Among amendments to section 159 of the Canadian criminal code, sodomy and anal intercourse between consenting adults age eighteen and older were eliminated as criminal offenses.

LOCALE: Ottawa, Ontario, Canada
CATEGORIES: Civil rights; laws, acts, and legal history; government and politics

KEY FIGURES
Pierre Trudeau (1919-2000), federal minister of justice, later prime minister
Henry Halm, U.S. citizen convicted in 1990 for sodomy and child endangerment, challenged a deportation order in 1993
Marvin Catzman, Ontario court of appeals justice
Rosalie Silberman Abella, Ontario court of appeals justice
Susanne R. Goodman, Ontario court of appeals justice

SUMMARY OF EVENT
In 1967, Pierre Trudeau introduced the sexual offenses reform bill, which, in 1969, amended Section 159 of the Canadian criminal code and decriminalized "private," consensual same-gender sex, which had been articulated in law as "gross indecency" between adults. As a result, LGBT Canadians could acknowledge their sexuality without that sexuality being considered criminal behavior.

However, this liberal recommendation was ineffectual and buried under many antigay and antilesbian provisions. Not only was the age of consent for gay sex twenty-one years of age, higher than for heterosexuals, but also the criminal code left many gay-oriented criminal offenses on the books. The code merely rearranged the offenses under the structure of "homosexual offences." Offenses that remained on the books included buggery (a reference to anal intercourse), indecent assault on male by male or female by female, acts of "gross indecency" between men, procuring and attempts to procure acts of gross indecency between males, persistent solicitation, importuning of males by males for immoral purposes, and violations of indecency by-laws. In addition, the report and subsequent laws contained language criminalizing homosexuality in the military and prohibiting marriage between same-gender couples.

In the early 1980's, there had been an increase in social and political activism and in published articles calling for further amendments to the criminal code with regard to sexuality. The discourse indicated a concern over the language that addressed anal intercourse. Proponents of legal change demonstrated anger over unfair discrepancies in the age of consent between heterosexual and homosexual sex.

In 1985, Canada's parliament prepared to adopt Bill C-15, which added further amendments to section 159. The amendments were adopted and went into effect on January 1, 1988. The age of consent was lowered from twenty-one years of age to fourteen years of age for most sexual acts in private by two unmarried persons. The old offenses of gross indecency and buggery were repealed. The bill, however, sent mixed messages to LGBT people. The age of consent for anal intercourse between unmarried persons remained eighteen. Those who perform anal sex with persons under age eighteen or in a public place would risk a possible ten-year prison sentence.

The new age of consent, particularly for same-gender sex, still roused fear among conservative members of Parliament. In the hopes of appeasing these fears and of strengthening the laws to protect children from abuse, a new law was introduced to accompany the lower age of consent. This new offense made punishable by up to five years in prison

> **FROM THE CANADIAN CRIMINAL CODE, SECTION 159**
>
> *Anal intercourse*
> 159. (1) Every person who engages in an act of anal intercourse is guilty of an indictable offence and liable to imprisonment for a term not exceeding ten years or is guilty of an offence punishable on summary conviction.
>
> *Exception*
> (2) Subsection (1) does not apply to any act engaged in, in private, between
> (a) husband and wife, or
> (b) any two persons, each of whom is eighteen years of age or more, both of whom consent to the act.
>
> *Idem*
> (3) For the purposes of subsection (2),
> (a) an act shall be deemed not to have been engaged in in private if it is engaged in in a public place or if more than two persons take part or are present; and
> (b) a person shall be deemed not to consent to an act
>   (i) if the consent is extorted by force, threats or fear of bodily harm or is obtained by false and fraudulent misrepresentations respecting the nature and quality of the act, or
>   (ii) if the court is satisfied beyond a reasonable doubt that the person could not have consented to the act by reason of mental disability.

the act of obtaining or attempting to obtain sex with a minor in exchange for food, housing, clothing, money, drugs, or alcohol.

SIGNIFICANCE

The decriminalization of adult consensual sex in Canada in 1988 furthered LGBT equality. Those portions of section 159 that were less than friendly to lesbians and gays motivated activists to continue fighting for full equality. One point of contention was the higher age of consent for anal intercourse. Activists worked tirelessly in the judicial system to challenge section 159.

In 1995, a Canadian federal court, in *Halm v. Canada* (*Minister of Employment and Immigration*), reviewed a deportation case involving a U.S. citizen who jumped bail after being convicted of sodomy and child endangerment in 1990. The court decided that Canadian law was contrary to section 159 of the country's charter for two reasons: It had an adverse and disparate impact on homosexual men and it discriminated on the basis of age. One justice (the only woman) ruled that the law "arbitrarily disadvantages gay men by denying to them until they are eighteen a choice available at the age of fourteen to those who are not gay, namely, their choice of sexual expression with a consenting partner with whom they are not married."

Another case, *R. v. M. (C.)* (1995), concerning a heterosexual couple, was decided in the Ontario Court of Appeals. At trial, the judge decided that section 159 was contrary to section 7 of the charter and that it was discriminatory to prevent an accused from offering a defense of "consent" to acts of anal intercourse with a young person. According to the court, section 159 violated the charter's equality rights guarantee when it discriminated based on sexual orientation (Justice Abella) and based on age (Justices Goodman and Catzman).

As a result of these cases and the hard work of activists, on March 1, 1995, section 159 of the criminal code was struck down.

In the late 1990's and early twenty-first century, however, the tide turned regarding age of consent laws. Ironically, whereas LGBT activists fought in the 1970's and 1980's for the abolition of the age of consent, the fight in the early part of the twenty-first century has been more about opposing forces that want to raise it. A government announcement made in late 1999 had called for a review of the age of consent laws in the hopes of changing the age of consent for all sexual acts to sixteen or even eighteen. The discourse in support of the change cited the need to protect children from abuse.

—*Daniel-Raymond Nadon*

Further Reading

Lahey, Kathleen A. *Are We "Persons" Yet? Law and Sexuality in Canada*. Buffalo, N.Y.: University of Toronto Press, 1999.

MacDougall, Bruce. *Queer Judgements: Homosexuality, Expression, and the Courts in Canada*. Buffalo, N.Y.: University of Toronto Press, 2000.

McLeod, Donald W. *Lesbian and Gay Liberation in Canada: A Selected Annotated Chronology, 1964-1975*. Toronto, Ont.: ECW Press/Homewood Books, 1996.

Smith, Miriam. *Lesbian and Gay Rights in Canada: Social Movements and Equality Seeking, 1971-1999*. Buffalo, N.Y.: University of Toronto Press, 1999.

Warner, Tom. *Never Going Back: A History of Queer Activism in Canada*. Buffalo, N.Y.: University of Toronto Press, 2002.

See also: May 6, 1868: Kertbeny Coins the Terms "Homosexual" and "Heterosexual"; 1885: United Kingdom Criminalizes "Gross Indecency"; Jan. 12, 1939: *Thompson v. Aldredge* Dismisses Sodomy Charges Against Lesbians; Sept. 4, 1957: The *Wolfenden Report* Calls for Decriminalizing Private Consensual Sex; 1961: Illinois Legalizes Consensual Homosexual Sex; Jan. 22, 1973: *Roe v. Wade* Legalizes Abortion and Extends Privacy Rights; Aug., 1973: American Bar Association Calls for Repeal of Laws Against Consensual Sex; Oct. 18, 1973: Lambda Legal Authorized to Practice Law; Nov. 17, 1975: U.S. Supreme Court Rules in "Crimes Against Nature" Case; 1986: *Bowers v. Hardwick* Upholds State Sodomy Laws; 1992-2006: Indians Struggle to Abolish Sodomy Law; June 26, 2003: U.S. Supreme Court Overturns Texas Sodomy Law.

March 20, 1988
M. Butterfly Opens on Broadway

Based on a true story, David Henry Hwang's play about a male Chinese agent who dupes a French diplomat into believing he is a woman won three Tony Awards for theatrical excellence. Also, M. Butterfly is the first universally acclaimed Asian American play.

Locale: New York, New York
Categories: Arts; literature; race and ethnicity

Key Figures
David Henry Hwang (b. 1957), Asian American playwright
B. D. Wong (b. 1962), Asian American actor
John Lithgow (b. 1945), American actor

Summary of Event

David Henry Hwang's *M. Butterfly* is loosely based on the true story of French diplomat Bernard Boursicot, who carried on a twenty-year relationship with a Chinese man, Shi Pei Pu, all the while believing that the Communist agent was really a female opera singer. When Boursicot was charged with treason in 1986, he claimed that only then was he aware of the truth.

Hwang, fascinated with this story, proceeded to write a play based on it. Seeing parallels to Giacomo Puccini's opera *Madama Butterfly* (1904, 1907), Hwang incorporated elements from the opera into *M. Butterfly* to create a piece that explores both the cultural stereotypes of East versus West and concepts of gender and sexuality.

In Hwang's play, René Gallimard is a French civil servant working at the embassy in China. He meets Song Liling, whom he believes to be female, and falls in love. Gallimard finds himself trapped in a sort of fantasy world, reinforced by Song, who actually is a man but relishes being treated as a woman. Their relationship is rooted in Gallimard's inherent prejudice, which allows him to see Song as a subservient and pleasing geisha; all the while, Song plays into this stereotype in order to solicit governmental secrets, which he then passes on to the Chinese government. Eventually, all is revealed and the Chinese spy is sentenced to a labor camp for sexual deviancy, while Galliard commits suicide, echoing the ending of *Madama Butterfly*, rather than face the truth that his relationship was a homosexual one.

M. Butterfly opened on March 20, 1988, to rave reviews. The original cast featured John Lithgow as Gallimard and B. D. Wong as Song Liling. Previously known as Bradley Darryl Wong, Wong changed his name to B. D. at the request of the producers so that when his name appeared in publicity and playbills, the secret about Song Liling would remain intact. Wong won universal praise in his gender-bending role, garnering numerous awards, including a Tony Award for supporting actor. He went on to work in both film and television, notably as a priest in *Oz* (Home Box Office), but is still perhaps best known for his groundbreaking work in *M. Butterfly*.

M. Butterfly is largely considered to be the first universally acclaimed Asian American play. It won the Pulitzer Prize for Drama in 1989, the Tony Award for Best Play and Best Director, New York Drama Desk and Outer Critics Circle Awards, and the John Gassner Award for the season's outstanding new playwright. It ran for 777 performances on Broadway, and broke box-office records when it transferred to London's Shaftsbury Theatre. In 1993, the play was made into a feature film directed by David Cronenberg.

David Henry Hwang.

SIGNIFICANCE

The impact of *M. Butterfly* lies in its exposé of biases against not only Asians but also gays and lesbians and those who are transgender. Historically, Asian Americans have been largely unrepresented in American media, except for culturally insensitive stereotypes. This, combined with mistrust due to Japan's involvement in World War II and the tendency for Asian Americans to live in culturally homogenous neighborhoods, meant that Asians were "invisible" to most Americans. This started to change in the 1960's, when ethnic and cultural groups began asserting their voices and when the first Asian American theater, East West Players, opened in Los Angeles in 1965. East West Players is still a leader in Asian American theater and houses the David Henry Hwang Theatre.

When Hwang began writing, he was one of a small handful of Asian American playwrights. His work dealt largely with the Asian American experience, and with *M. Butterfly* he was able to blend the styles of Japanese Kabuki theater and Chinese opera with Western opera and re-

David Henry Hwang

David Henry Hwang has been a prominent playwright for the American stage since the early 1980's. Best known for *M. Butterfly*, Hwang typically questions traditional racial and gender stereotypes, complicates notions of cultural identity, and chronicles the Asian American experience in the United States.

The son of banker Henry Yuan Hwang and piano professor Dorothy Yu (Huang) Hwang, Hwang grew up in Los Angeles in the 1960's and 1970's. His parents were both immigrant Chinese Americans. As a child, Hwang studied classical violin for ten years and later played jazz beginning in his college years, a musical upbringing and calling that influenced many of his dramatic works, most notably *M. Butterfly*, which melds Giacomo Puccini's opera *Madama Butterfly* (1904) with a historical account of French-Chinese espionage, sexual liaison, and imprisonment. Later, Hwang would collaborate with Philip Glass, writing librettos for Glass's musical compositions.

Hwang's family practiced a blend of Asian and Christian fundamentalism, and he was brought up in a conservative household. His mother and father's faith and politics influenced his dramatic works, in which the certainty of his characters' beliefs in definable identities and absolute truths is often surprisingly and completely deconstructed. Hwang began recording stories of his family at an early age. At ten, he composed a novel about his dying grandmother's life memories, material which would become the basis for his 1996 drama, *Golden Child*.

In 1987, Hwang cofounded both the Theatre Communications Group and the Stanford Asian American Theatre Group. He has been a member of the board of trustees for Pitzer College since 1990. He sits on the board of directors for the Dramatists Guild and the Writers Guild of America. In 1994 he was appointed by President Bill Clinton to the President's Committee on the Arts and Humanities.

---

alism. Artistically, his play excited audiences by synthesizing disparate theatrical elements with an examination of prejudices about gender and sexuality.

In Hwang's play, Song Liling comments wryly on sexual stereotyping. She says, "Only a man knows how a woman is supposed to act." This sense of irony is presented throughout the piece, as the audience sees how Gallimard fetishizes both Song's Asian-ness and her gender. It is not biology but social predispositions that lead Gallimard to believe Song is a woman. Indeed, Hwang asserts, imperialism exists not just geographically but socially, and *M. Butterfly* challenges the audience, who for the first three-quarters of the play does not learn that Song is a man, to investigate their own biases regarding gender and sexuality. Hwang drives home the point that the root of all prejudices is the same, and that the eradication of one prejudice holds promise for the eradication of all prejudices.

Perhaps because he is heterosexual, Hwang has not been applauded by the gay community as much as he deserves. Although his theories against prejudice strongly support gay and lesbian rights, he is rarely identified first as an important contributor to GLBT literature and drama. B. D. Wong, on the other hand, wrote and published a book in 2003, *Following Foo (The Electronic Adventures of the Chestnut Man): A Memoir*, based on his experiences adopting a child while in a gay relationship. His memoir brought him national attention and recognition by the GLBT community, though it did little to break down cultural prejudices.

Hwang will likely be remembered solely for his work advancing Asian American dramatic literature rather than as an important proponent of gender and sexual equality. However, his play *M. Butterfly* remains an important and highly honored play in the canon of gay-themed work.

—Tom Smith

Further Reading

"David Henry Hwang." Video recording, ABC News Productions. Princeton, N.J.: Films for the Humanities and Sciences, 2004.

DiGaetani, John Louis. "*M. Butterfly:* An Interview with David Henry Hwang." *TDR* 33 (1989): 141-153.

Hwang, David Henry. *M. Butterfly*. New York: New American Library, 1988.

Savran, David. "David Hwang." In *In Their Own*

Words: Contemporary American Playwrights, by David Savran. New York: Theatre Communications Group, 1988.

Shimakawa, Karen. "'Who's to Say?' Or, Making Space for Gender and Ethnicity in *M. Butterfly*." *Theatre Journal* 45 (1993): 349-361.

Skloot, Robert. "Breaking the Butterfly: The Politics of David Henry Hwang." *Modern Drama* 33 (1990): 59-66.

Street, Douglas. *David Henry Hwang*. Boise, Idaho: Boise State University, 1989.

Watt, Stephen, and Gary A. Richardson, comps. "Mr. Butterfly." In *American Drama: Colonial to Contemporary*. Fort Worth, Tex.: Harcourt Brace College, 1995.

Wiegmann, Mira. *The Staging and Transformation of Gender Archetypes in "A Midsummer Night's Dream," "M. Butterfly," and "Kiss of the Spider Woman."* Lewiston, N.Y.: Edwin Mellen Press, 2003.

SEE ALSO: Feb. 19, 1923: *The God of Vengeance* Opens on Broadway; 1993: *The Wedding Banquet* Is First Acclaimed Taiwanese Gay-Themed Film.

May, 1988
LAVENDER YOUTH RECREATION AND INFORMATION CENTER OPENS

The Lavender Youth Recreation and Information Center, developed to provide social and recreational activities to lesbian, gay, bisexual, transgender, and questioning youth in San Francisco, California, was the first program in the United States that focused primarily on providing social and recreational activities to queer and questioning youth.

LOCALE: San Francisco, California
CATEGORY: Organizations and institutions

KEY FIGURES
Beth Kivel, center cofounder and first director
Donna Ozawa, center cofounder

SUMMARY OF EVENT

In May of 1988, Beth Kivel and Donna Ozawa met for lunch at Quincy's sandwich shop on Market Street in the civic center area of San Francisco. During lunch, they talked about their high school coming-out experiences. Kivel came out in Tyler, Texas, in 1978 and was targeted with verbal harassment and physical threats of violence; Ozawa came out in San Francisco and felt isolated and alone. In the course of their conversation, they began to imagine what life might be like if there was a positive place for queer youth to gather and engage in social and recreational activities. They jotted down their ideas on the back of a brown paper bag. This "brown paper bag" became the blueprint for the creation of the Lavender Youth Recreation and Information Center (LYRIC). LYRIC was the first organization of its kind in the United States.

After Kivel and Ozawa wrote up their plan, they began to talk with like-minded folks, namely a social worker named Ruth Hughes and a nurse named Mary Goulart, who worked at Larkin Street, a drop-in center for homeless and runaway youth. They asked young people to join them in a brainstorming session about how to make life better for queer youth. Ruth suggested organizing a dance, and the group concurred. Over the summer, an ad hoc group composed of youth and adults came together. The group recruited friends, housemates, and lovers to give money and time for the event, which was scheduled for October, 1988, and raised $1,000 for the dance, which was held on October 15 at the Met-

> **LAVENDER YOUTH RECREATION AND INFORMATION CENTER: MISSION AND VISION STATEMENT**
>
> LYRIC's mission is to build community and inspire positive social change through education enhancement, career training, health promotion, and leadership development with lesbian, gay, bisexual, transgender, queer, and questioning youth, their families, and allies of all races, classes, genders, and abilities.
>
> LYRIC envisions a diverse society where LGBTQQ youth are embraced for who they are and encouraged to be who they want to be. By working towards social justice and supporting young leaders, their families and allies, LYRIC is building a world that honors, respects and appreciates LGBTQQ youth and their contributions.

ropolitan Community Church (MCC) in the Castro District. The dance was sponsored by several advocacy and youth-serving and community-serving agencies, including Coleman Advocates for Children and Youth, Larkin Street Medical Clinic, Castro Lions Club, and Jackson Street Youth Group. The dance also was meant to get young people involved in the planning and implementation of more social and recreational activities. Toward that end, the group developed a survey to give out to young people, asking them two main questions: Do you want more social, recreational events? and, Are you willing to be a part of the planning process for these events? Participants also were asked how they heard about the event and where they lived.

Forty people attended the dance, advertised as a clean-and-sober event for young people up to age twenty-three. Approximately twenty chaperones attended—representatives from youth agencies, teachers, social service agencies, and homeless youth shelters. The service providers were amazed at the high turnout and heartened to think that this event might signal the beginning of more programs and services for queer youth, because the main city-sponsored program at the time was a therapy-based group, called "The Center for Special Problems."

After the dance, meetings were held with both youth and adults interested in continuing the work. Two of the first youth volunteers were sixteen-year-old Olga Texidor, who would later become a paid employee, and twenty-two-year-old Kristen Hoffmeister. They worked side by side with other youth and adults who planned, implemented, and evaluated more dances, social, recreational events, and fund-raisers. All of the work was being done by volunteers.

Within one year of the first dance, Alfonso Diaz, Vincent Fuqua, and Mark Chekal, and adult allies Joe Hosking, Steve Sims, Ishmael Torres, and Danny Barutta (the second director of LYRIC), among others, began a weekly rap group for young men. A similar group for young women began with support from adult allies Regina Gabrielle (the third director of LYRIC), Roma Guy, Jamie, Kathy Bollinger, Barbara Blinnick, and youth volunteers Olga Texidor and Jonna Hensley. The two rap groups, along with quarterly dances, a softball team in the San Francisco Gay Softball League, picnics, hikes, and camping trips, became central to the program. To fund these activities, the group held grassroots fund-raisers, including bake sales in the Castro and annual pancake-breakfast fund-raisers, cosponsored with Gay/Lesbian Outreach to Elders (GLOE) at MCC.

Along the way, the group adopted the name, Lavender Youth Recreation and Information Center, which reflected their hopes for an actual space. In 1990, Judith Stevenson, director of Operation Concern (OC), a counseling center for the LGBT community, provided LYRIC with office space; OC also served as LYRIC's fiscal agent. Stevenson, and John Wilhite, submitted the first grant on LYRIC's behalf to the San Francisco Department of Public Health, HIV-AIDS Prevention Education Program. This grant was followed by support from the San Francisco Foundation, and former mayor Art Agnos worked with LYRIC to secure funding from his office to pay for Kivel to become the first director of the program.

In 1991, LYRIC moved into a space at The Women's Building, and in the same year LYRIC was featured in an NBC-TV affiliate (KRON) documentary, "Growing Up and Coming Out." Also in 1991, LYRIC formed an advisory board composed of youth and adults, and it received support from leaders such as Carmen Vazquez, Greg Day, Kristen Bachler, and San Francisco board of supervisors members Roberta Achtenberg and Carole Migden.

During a one-year period, Kivel wrote more than one dozen grants, and, in 1992, she left LYRIC to pursue a doctorate; Danny Barutta took over as LYRIC's second director, with a budget of $250,000. In 1993, Roberta Achtenberg secured funds for LYRIC to purchase a three-story Victorian house in the Castro District.

SIGNIFICANCE

Between 1988 and 1992, a committed group of young people and adults worked together to transform an idea into a reality. This informal group became an institution that continues to thrive with a staff of fourteen and an annual budget of more than $1 million.

—*Beth D. Kivel*

FURTHER READING

Bass, Ellen, and Kate Kaufman. *Free Your Mind: The Book for Gay, Lesbian, and Bisexual Youth—And Their Allies*. New York: HarperPerennial, 1996.

Gay Straight Alliance Network. http://www.gsanetwork.org/.

Huegel, Kelly. *GLBTQ: The Survival Guide for Queer and Questioning Teens*. Minneapolis, Minn.: Free Spirit, 2003.

National Youth Advocacy Coalition. http://www.nyacyouth.org/index.html.

Parents, Families, and Friends of Lesbians and Gays. *Be Yourself: Questions and Answers for Gay, Lesbian, and Bisexual Youth*. http://www.pflag.org.

Rich, Jason R. *Growing Up Gay in America: Informative and Practical Advice for Teen Guys Questioning Their Sexuality and Growing Up Gay*. Boston: Franklin Street Books, 2002.

Ryan, Caitlin. *Lesbian and Gay Youth*. New York: Columbia University Press, 1998.

SEE ALSO: Aug., 1966: Queer Youth Fight Police Harassment at Compton's Cafeteria in San Francisco; Mar., 1971: Los Angeles Gay and Lesbian Center Is Founded; 1982: Lesbian and Gay Youth Protection Institute Is Founded; 1994: National Association of Lesbian and Gay Community Centers Is Founded.

June 27, 1988
REPORT OF THE PRESIDENTIAL AIDS COMMISSION

U.S. president Ronald Reagan appointed a commission to study and address HIV-AIDS in the United States, but he rejected most of its recommendations. The framework for a national policy was built under his successor, George H. W. Bush, and was expanded under Bill Clinton.

ALSO KNOWN AS: Presidential Commission on the Human Immunodeficiency Virus Epidemic; Watkins Commission
LOCALE: United States
CATEGORIES: HIV-AIDS; organizations and institutions; health and medicine; science; government and politics; laws, acts, and legal history

KEY FIGURES
James Watkins, chair of the presidential AIDS commission, 1987-1988
C. Everett Koop, U.S. surgeon general, 1981-1989
Ronald Reagan (1913-2004), U.S. president, 1981-1989
George H. W. Bush (b. 1924), U.S. president, 1989-1993
Bill Clinton (b. 1946), U.S. president, 1993-2001

SUMMARY OF EVENT

U.S. president Ronald Reagan appointed the Presidential Commission on the Human Immunodeficiency Virus Epidemic (later named the Watkins Commission) on June 24, 1987, which was late in his second term and at least six years into the HIV-AIDS epidemic. His delayed response likely stemmed from his political ideology and practice. The conservative philosophy of the 1980's delegated domestic issues to the states and localities: the federal government was considered by conservatives to be the problem, not the solution. Thus, for too long, the Reagan administration assumed that states, localities, and charities would shoulder the burdens of HIV-AIDS.

Most critical in retarding any federal action, however, was the evangelical Christian view that HIV-AIDS is a providential punishment for the alleged "sins" of male homosexuality, "sins" that had become openly practiced and destigmatized in the previous decade. Evangelical Christians began to make up an increasing share of likely voters, and Reagan's appeals to traditional values had made evangelicals desert fellow evangelical Jimmy Carter (U.S. president, 1977-1981, and a Democrat) in 1980. Although Reagan himself was not a born-again Christian and did not personally share the more extreme homophobia and hatred of gays and lesbians of the Christian Right, his administration pandered to evangelicals by ignoring the epidemic, largely because of its "sinful" nature, which should never be mentioned among or to Christians.

Yet as much as the White House pretended that the epidemic was not serious, several factors undermined the opportunistic stance of governmental indifference. Personal friends of the Reagans, including actor Rock Hudson and entertainer Liberace, had died from AIDS complications. Their deaths started to change the president's mind about the disease. There were growing public pressures to do something, even within the Republican Party, Representative Stewart McKinney of Connecticut, the second-ranking Republican on the House Banking Committee and a married father of five, had died of AIDS in May of 1987, belying the myth that the disease affected the politically marginal constituencies of promiscuous gay men, drug addicts, and Haitian refugees; this changed public opinion about the people who could be impacted by the epidemic. Suddenly, the door opened to a handful of open-minded pragmatists, who then laid the groundwork for the restrained and moderate federal responses of presidents George H. W. Bush, Bill Clinton, and George W. Bush.

When the scope of the catastrophe could no longer be denied, appointees of Reagan, such as Surgeon General C. Everett Koop and Admiral James D. Watkins, pushed the administration and that of his successor, George H. W. Bush, to be proactive in combating HIV-AIDS, that is, to be more active than conventional conservative wisdom had envisioned. Rejecting rigid right-wing ideology, Koop issued a 1986 report that advocated for a greater federal role in both patient treatment and preventive education. Shocking cultural conservatives, he urged the ubiquitous use of condoms in addition to abstinence, and the U.S. Public Health Service promptly sent out a mass mailing with that commonsense message. Koop preferred a constructive rather than a punitive federal role, rejecting the quarantine of those with AIDS—as was being done in Cuba—or any nationwide list of those who were HIV-positive. Quarantines and lists facilitated what some thought would be *necessary* segregation or discrimination.

As surgeon general, Koop wielded little actual power, but his recommendations (as well as the predictable conservative chorus in opposition to them) led Reagan and his advisers to appoint the commission with Executive Order 12601 in the summer of 1987. The president's choice for chair was Watkins, who later admitted to knowing nothing about HIV-AIDS before his appointment. Most of the rest of the commission's members consisted of scientists and physicians involved in AIDS research and treatment, with a few ideologues thrown in to appease cultural conservatives worried about Koop's embrace of the use of condoms. Presidential commissions usually are convenient vehicles to table issues until after a term in office has ended, and they rarely lead to radical changes. The Watkins Commission, as this body would come to be known, started out similarly and predictably, and its initial composition offered little comfort to HIV-AIDS activists clamoring for a real, comprehensive effort. The independent and no-nonsense personality of the commission's chair, nevertheless, came back to haunt those in the administration hoping to prolong the era of malign neglect.

Before issuing its final report on June 27, 1988, the Watkins Commission actually did its homework. It held many hearings and site visits, allowing ordinary people as well as experts to speak truth to power. The commission uncovered frequent instances of irrational discrimination against those who were HIV-positive, discrimination the administration had earlier dismissed. The commission concluded that both ignorance and indifference had accelerated and prolonged the spread of HIV-AIDS. Based upon its investigation of the grassroots, the commission recommended nearly six hundred over-

---

REAGAN ON THE AIDS EPIDEMIC

I have just been briefed on the unanimous report of the Commission on the Human Immunodeficiency Virus Epidemic by Adm. James D. Watkins, the Commission's Chairman. The report represents an impressive effort and significantly increases our level of understanding to deal with AIDS. To begin implementing this report, I am today directing Dr. Ian Macdonald, a distinguished physician and my Special Assistant for Drug Policy, to present to me within 30 days a course of action that takes us forward. At Admiral Watkins' suggestion, I have also directed Dr. Macdonald to include among his priorities consideration of specific measures to strengthen implementation of the policy guidance from "AIDS in the Workplace," recently issued by the Office of Personnel Management. The report embraces the major concepts my administration laid out over a year ago: to be compassionate towards victims of the disease; to care for them with dignity and kindness; and at the same time, to inform and educate our citizens so that we can prevent the further spread of the disease. There is a direct relationship between drug abuse and the spread of the HIV virus that becomes AIDS. It is critical that particular attention be focused on this relationship now, while developing a national consensus on additional anti-drug abuse measures.

I want to express my sincere appreciation to Admiral Watkins and all of the Commission participants for their perseverance and diligence in completing their work. It is my hope that we can continue to approach this problem, which is more than a medical crisis or a public health threat, in a thoughtful and bipartisan manner.

Source: Statement on the Report of the Presidential Commission on the Human Immunodeficiency Virus Epidemic, June 27, 1988.

due, specific ways to combat HIV-AIDS, steps that included the establishment of what came to be called the National Commission on AIDS, which was to carry on the presidential commission's work into the next decade; produce national antidiscrimination legislation; expand drug treatment programs; mandate a "cleaner" national blood supply; and earmark more money for case management and preventive education.

Significance

Reagan rejected most of these recommendations in early August of 1988, opting instead for his own scaled-down plan of action. He refused to consider a national antidiscrimination law to protect people with HIV-AIDS. Instead, he ordered that federal employees should not fire or harass other federal employees who had HIV-AIDS but still were able to work. To Reagan, if HIV-positive federal employees could not work, they could be terminated with cause. Private businesses, trade unions, and public schools were asked to follow his functional example voluntarily so that no new federal intrusion into the marketplace would be necessary.

Similarly, Reagan refused to increase funding for drug treatment as recommended by the commission. Reflecting the contempt of social conservatives for what they viewed as a permissive society, Reagan was much more interested in punishing addicts and users in his "war on drugs" than in expanding the drug treatment programs that he believed were "coddling" the offenders. Worried about the "innocent victims" of the epidemic rather than the dreaded higher-risk groups, the president called for better screening of blood and blood products, encouraging people to think about donating their own blood before elective surgery or to have blood available for emergency surgery.

Reagan, and then his successor, Bush, did acquiesce in the formation of a National Commission on AIDS in 1989, which had a four-year mandate. This time, ten of the fifteen members of the commission were appointed by the Democratic majority Congress, with the remaining five being the sitting secretaries of Health and Human Services, Defense, and Veteran's Affairs, plus two more presidential picks. Because of congressional involvement, this commission had even less patience with right-wing ideology than did the Watkins Commission, as it issued fifteen reports, usually critical of the indifference or timidity of the Reagan and Bush administrations in dealing with the epidemic. It made many more site visits than its immediate predecessor, covering topics from HIV among African Americans and Asian Americans to client care at Southern California AIDS service organizations to how Belle Glade and Miami in southern Florida tried to stem the tide of infection.

The commission's final report, *AIDS: An Expanding Tragedy* (1993), had two main recommendations: One, leaders at all levels of U.S. government need to end their silence on the epidemic, and, two, the president should spearhead a consistent, broad, lucid, and properly funded national policy on HIV-AIDS. Bill Clinton's AIDS czars, AIDS conferences, and his White House Office of National AIDS Policy would have more power on paper than his immediate predecessor's national commission, but all involved shared frustration and disappointment at the lack of follow-through in reference to their suggestions to do more.

While the national commission was frequently critical of his policies, George H. W. Bush, however, was more sympathetic toward people with HIV-AIDS than was Reagan at any time. The epitome of noblesse oblige, he endorsed a "kinder, gentler" approach to governing that would be recycled by his son as "compassionate conservatism" ten years later. Unlike his son, fortunately, he would not be held hostage by the tenets of evangelical Christianity. Accordingly, the Bush administration that followed Reagan would construct the basic outlines of AIDS policies that Bill Clinton and George W. Bush would follow, piecemeal compromises that tried to address the still-expanding tragedy without being fully underwritten or increased when necessary.

Most significant was George H. W. Bush's signing in 1990 of two landmark pieces of legislation that promised to help people with HIV-AIDS: the Americans with Disabilities Act (ADA) and the Ryan White Comprehensive AIDS Resources Emergency (CARE) Act. Among many other things, the ADA outlawed the pervasive discrimination based upon HIV status that the Watkins Commission had first uncovered. Like other people with disabilities, the two acts stated that the seropositive could not be discriminated against in employment and public accommodations and could insist that reasonable accommodations be tailored for them at their workplaces. Bush, however, was not instrumental in extending federal legal protections to people with HIV-AIDS, but, also, he did not veto these key provisions.

The Ryan White Act provided federal funds for case management and any FDA-approved drug that patients with HIV-AIDS might require to improve or extend their lives. With Bush's guidance, Congress then appropriated $220.5 million for the Ryan White programs in its first year, a sum that only scratched the surface in meeting the needs of the many local AIDS service organizations that spent and distributed the money.

Clinton would greatly increase funding for the Ryan White programs, but it would never be enough to keep up with the "expanding tragedy." As more effective drugs prolonged the lives of those infected after 1996, the emergency nature of the epidemic passed only to reemerge as a chronic sea of poverty that required even more money than the fiscally prudent Clinton was willing to spend.

Also, George H. W. Bush in 1991 signed what would be the groundwork for presidential AIDS policies in two other areas: the Housing Opportunities for Persons with AIDS Act (HOPWA) and new Social Security rules to secure disability benefits for HIV-positive citizens. HOPWA addressed the relationship between catastrophic illness and homelessness in urban areas, offering much-needed emergency assistance for poor people with HIV-AIDS, and their families.

During the 1990's, HOPWA funding would wax and eventually wane, but the quick-fix nature of the program was not designed to fix the long-term cultural roots of poverty and their impact on the spread of the epidemic. The Social Security rules allowed HIV-positive individuals without AIDS to qualify for disability benefits. Yet, as the epidemic affected increasingly poor and young members of ethnic and racial minority groups in the 1990's, those benefits designed for middle-class workers remained elusive or inadequate for the majority of those newly infected.

Presidential AIDS policy on the domestic side really has not gone beyond the reforms of 1990 and 1991. Clinton may have postured to feel the pain better than Reagan and the Bushes, but he left little more than dashed hopes about a more coordinated and comprehensive federal effort. Excitement about new cocktails of drugs in 1996 and 1997 gave way to a resigned sense of complacency by 2000, stymieing any large-scale "Manhattan Project" response to HIV-AIDS long called for by activists and patients. Clinton's scandals jeopardized any domestic reforms, let alone those that appealed to the poor and marginal.

Finally, international, not domestic, AIDS concerns became preeminent in Clinton's second term and then under George W. Bush. AIDS was declared a national security threat in 2000, but that failed to generate any more attention to the unresolved crisis in the United States. Indeed, as the costs for the Iraq war mounted in 2004, the first programs to be cut were Ryan White and HOPWA. On the international front, one might hope that enlightened self-interest will continue to increase U.S. funding of HIV-AIDS treatment and prevention in Africa, the Caribbean, and Asia, funding that did increase substantially under Clinton and his successor. Yet given the fitful and incomplete track record of the U.S. government at home in reference to HIV-AIDS, no one should hold their breath.

—*Charles H. Ford*

FURTHER READING

Behrman, Greg. *The Invisible People: How the U.S. Has Slept Through the Global AIDS Pandemic, the Greatest Humanitarian Catastrophe of Our Time*. New York: Free Press, 2004.

Kaiser Foundation. *Kaiser Daily HIV-AIDS Report: AIDS at 20* (June 4-8, 2001). http://www.kaisernetwork.org/dailyreports/aidsat20.cfm.

Koop, C. Everett. *Koop: The Memoirs of America's Family Doctor*. New York: Random House, 1991.

National Institutes of Health, Archives and Modern Manuscripts Program, History of Medicine Division. Complete listing of the presidential and national commissions' archival records (Collection no. MS C 544). http://www.nlm.nih.gov/hmd/manuscripts/ead/ncaids544.html#series1.

Shilts, Randy. *And the Band Played On: Politics, People, and the AIDS Epidemic*. New York: St. Martin's Press, 1987.

Smith, Raymond A., ed. *Encyclopedia of AIDS: A Social, Political, Cultural, and Scientific Record of the HIV Epidemic*. New York: Penguin Books, 2001.

Willinger, Barbara L., and Alan Rice, eds. *A History of AIDS Social Work in Hospitals: A Daring Response to an Epidemic*. Binghamton, N.Y.: Haworth Press, 2003.

See also: June 5 and July 3, 1981: Reports of Rare Diseases Mark Beginning of AIDS Epidemic; July, 1982: Gay-Related Immunodeficiency Is Renamed AIDS; Spring, 1984: AIDS Virus Is Discovered; July 25, 1985: Actor Hudson Announces He Has AIDS; Sept., 1986: AZT Treats People with AIDS; Mar., 1987: Radical AIDS Activist Group ACT UP Is Founded; Dec. 1, 1988: First World AIDS Day; July 26, 1990: Americans with Disabilities Act Becomes Law; June 25, 1993: Clinton Appoints First AIDS Czar.

October 11, 1988
First National Coming Out Day Is Celebrated

National Coming Out Day, the first of which was held in 1988, encourages lesbian, gay, bisexual, and transgender individuals to come out—and not just on National Coming Out Day—to themselves, their families and friends, their peers and classmates, their coworkers, and society in general.

Locale: Washington, D.C.
Categories: Marches, protests, and riots; organizations and institutions

Key Figures

Rob Eichberg, cofounder of National Coming Out Day
Jean O'Leary (b. 1948), cofounder of National Coming Out Day
Lynn Shepodd, founding-year organizer and executive director in 1990
Pilo Bueno, national coordinator in 1989

Summary of Event

On October 11, 1987, half a million people marched on Washington, D.C., for gay and lesbian equality, the second GLBT march in the nation's capital. Along with the march, the now-famous AIDS Quilt was displayed for the first time in public, and several independent LGBT rights organizations formed, including the idea for a group to plan what would come to be called National Coming Out Day (NCOD).

Several months after the march, at a meeting held just outside Washington, D.C., Rob Eichberg, founder of a workshop for personal growth, and Jean O'Leary, then head of National Gay Rights Advocates, came up with an idea to help promote LGBT visibility and awareness: National Coming Out Day, to be held annually on the anniversary of the second march on Washington, October 11.

The first NCOD, October 11, 1988, was organized by O'Leary and her staff out of the offices of the National Gay Rights Advocates in West Hollywood, California. The event's staff chose an image of a figure emerging from an opened closet door, created by activist Sean Strub and artist Keith Haring, as the NCOD logo. The logo has since come to represent "coming out" more generally. The first NCOD was recognized in eighteen states and received media attention from *USA Today*, *CNN*, *National Public Radio*, and *The Oprah Winfrey Show*.

Pilo Bueno was hired as NCOD national coordinator in 1989. By this time, twenty-one states recognized NCOD, and media attention grew as well. In 1990, Lynn Shepodd was hired as the NCOD executive director. Also, more than 150 publications printed the Strub and Haring image, and the event was celebrated in all fifty states and in seven foreign countries.

A key moment came in 1993, when the Human Rights Campaign (HRC), then called the Human Rights Campaign Fund, merged with National Coming Out Day. The HRC had a larger pool of resources to promote and expand the event. One of the first steps was to turn NCOD into a year-round campaign that would help people with the often-difficult and complicated process of coming out. HRC also began implementing media campaigns involving celebrities such as Amanda Bearse, the out lesbian actor who played Marcy on the TV show *Married with Children*.

Over the years, supportive celebrities have included Candace Gingrich, Chastity Bono, Cher, Melissa Etheridge, k.d. lang, Cyndi Lauper, Ani DiFranco, Olympic diver Greg Louganis, Ellen DeGeneres and her mother Betty, Latin American talk-show star Christina Seralegui, Anne Heche, Patrick Bristow, Dick Sargent, Dan Butler, and athlete Billy Bean, among many others. The efforts and support of these celebrities has been key in promoting the event in the media and for fund-raising. Most notably, a benefit CD, "Being Out Rocks," was released in 2002, featuring the music of eighteen musicians, with all proceeds being donated to the HRC Foundation.

In addition to celebrity spokespersons, NCOD has seen businesses, cities, and college campuses celebrate the day in a variety of ways. Colleges and universities have been particularly key in organizing events. Rallies, media advertisements, letters to local newspapers, dances, chalkings, diversity training seminars, and even three-dimensional closets from which to emerge have all been used to promote awareness.

Although there is no particular way to celebrate, a different theme is chosen each year to bring unity to NCOD events. The first year's theme was "Take the Next Step." The goal was to encourage people to "take the next step" in their own coming-out process. This meant that if a person were out to no one, that person could "take the next step" and maybe come out to a friend or family member; or if that individual were out to friends and family, that person could perhaps "take the next step" and come out at work; or, if a person were out entirely, that individual could engage in civil disobedience. The idea was that regardless of where an individual was in his or her coming out process, that person could forever "take the next step." Other themes have included "You've Got the Power. Register. Vote" in 1996, "Come Out to Congress" in 1999, and "It's a Family Affair" in 2004.

SIGNIFICANCE

National Coming Out Day has become a widely recognized sort of holiday for the LGBT community and its allies, but NCOD is also serious and empowering because the act of coming out is a lifelong one that helps increase GLBT visibility and awareness. Coming out as lesbian, gay, bisexual, transgender, or questioning is important not only for those who are entirely in "the closet" but also for those who are out.

—*Michael Ryan*

FURTHER READING

Brown, Michael P. *Closet Space: Geographies of Metaphor from the Body to the Globe*. New York: Routledge, 2000.

Curtis, Wayne, ed. *Revelations: A Collection of Gay Male Coming Out Stories*. Boston: Alyson, 1988.

Eichberg, Rob. *Coming Out: An Act of Love*. New York: Plume, 1991.

Signorile, Michelangelo. *Outing Yourself: How to Come Out as Lesbian or Gay to Your Family, Friends, and Coworkers*. New York: Fireside, 1996.

Wolfe, Susan J., and Julia Penelope Stanley, eds. *The Coming Out Stories*. Watertown, Mass.: Persephone Press, 1980.

SEE ALSO: 1975: First Novel About Coming Out to Parents Is Published; Apr. 22, 1980: Human Rights Campaign Fund Is Founded; 1981: Parents, Families, and Friends of Lesbians and Gays Is Founded; Oct. 11, 1987: Second March on Washington for Lesbian and Gay Rights.

November 8, 1988
OREGON REPEALS BAN ON ANTIGAY JOB DISCRIMINATION

Oregon voters repealed a 1987 executive order by Governor Neil Goldschmidt that had banned discrimination on the basis of sexual orientation. The measure's success paved the way for antigay initiatives around the United States in the early 1990's, but it also mobilized a new nationwide movement for lesbian and gay civil rights.

ALSO KNOWN AS: Measure 8
LOCALE: Oregon
CATEGORIES: Civil rights; laws, acts, and legal history

KEY FIGURES
Neil Goldschmidt (b. 1940), Democratic governor of Oregon
Liz Kaufman, gay and lesbian rights activist
Lon T. Mabon, conservative activist who founded the Oregon Citizens Alliance

SUMMARY OF EVENT

In 1987, gay and lesbian activists in Oregon followed the lead of activists in other states and lobbied Democratic governor Neil Goldschmidt to sign Executive Order 87-20, which banned employment discrimination on the basis of sexual orientation in the state executive branch. Many have suggested that Goldschmidt supported the GLBT community because GLBT activists had played a significant role in his election. The GLBT groups, such as the informal Portland Town Council, that mobilized in the state, were centered mostly in a few cities. The cities of Portland and Eugene had passed analogous civil rights measures earlier, and similar bills had been introduced in the state legislature since 1973, but Eugene's law had been repealed by ballot initiative in May, 1978.

Lon T. Mabon and other conservative activists saw the governor's executive order as a clear sign that gay activists were helping to bring about moral decline in America. Mabon, who had been part of a Christian movement to change abortion laws and build a national grassroots campaign for "family values," formed a group in Oregon called the Oregon Citizens Alliance (OCA). Mabon had seen the movement fail on some pro-life ballot initiatives and was convinced that gay issues could galvanize Christian conservatives in the state and around the country.

Through the OCA, Mabon announced in 1988 that he would collect signatures for a ballot initiative to repeal Goldschmidt's executive order. The OCA was able to collect more than 118,000 signatures in nine weeks, ensuring that the proposal would reach the ballot. The proposal was certified as Measure 8.

GLBT activists seemed almost unconcerned, and their public comments suggested they were confident they could control the elements of the debate and defeat the measure in November. A group called Oregonians for Fairness (OFF) was formed, with Liz Kaufman managing the campaign against the measure. OFF was able to raise $375,000, obtain endorsements from political elites, and produce professional ads that described the measure as a "witch hunt" without using terms such as gay or lesbian. Public opinion polls suggested that the measure would be defeated, and some writers have suggested that the OFF campaign became complacent. In fact, the group simply followed the traditional

> **MEASURE 8, BALLOT QUESTION AND EXPLANATION**
>
> *Question:* Shall voters revoke Governor's authority to ban discrimination, based on sexual orientation, in state executive department employment and services?
>
> *Explanation:* Enacts new law. Revokes Governor's order which bans discrimination, based on sexual orientation, both in executive branch employment and in carrying out executive branch duties within state government. Measure 8 provides that no state official shall forbid taking personnel action against a state employee because of the employee's sexual orientation. Measure permits state officials to forbid taking personnel actions against state employees based on nonjob related factors. For the purposes of this measure, sexual orientation means heterosexuality, homosexuality, or bisexuality.

campaign model, beginning most of their activity after Labor Day, in early September. Leaders of OFF have also suggested that no one believed the OCA could collect enough signatures, and once they did, GLBT activists had only twelve weeks to respond.

Meanwhile, the OCA had formed a campaign group called the No Special Rights Committee. This marked the first time that the phrase "special rights" had been used in anti-GLBT campaigns; it would come into wide use by the early 1990's. The name of the group was effective because it implied that gays and lesbians had obtained rights above and beyond those of other citizens through the governor's executive order, and every media report about Measure 8 would inadvertently project its supporters' message simply by stating the committee's name. This technique ensured that the OCA shaped how the issue was presented to the public, which is a key element of any ballot initiative fight.

On November 8, 1988, Measure 8 passed 53 percent (626,751) to 47 percent (561,355). The vote stunned GLBT activists and set the stage for dozens of local anti-GLBT initiatives in Oregon and several statewide initiatives outside Oregon in the 1990's.

Significance

On November 12, 1992, the Oregon Court of Appeals struck down Measure 8 as unconstitutional, but by this time, the benefits and damages to the GLBT movement had taken effect. In terms of benefits, the passage of Measure 8 taught GLBT activists in Oregon and elsewhere three lessons. First, activists needed to start campaigns early and not become complacent, regardless of what public-opinion polls indicate; it became clear that poll respondents can harbor biases that they do not want to reveal to poll takers. Second, a base of support must be built both within and beyond the GLBT community; the movement should present a united front, but the clear public support of political elites is also needed. Third—and this point is much debated—although a campaign should focus on broad themes, such as the right to privacy and basic human rights, avoiding the use of terms such as "gay," "lesbian," or "homosexual" may confuse the public and alienate the GLBT community.

The GLBT movement in Oregon also benefited from the measure because the campaign helped lead to the formation of new GLBT groups. For example, AFTER 8 was formed by women who wanted to mobilize the GLBT community in the months following the measure's passage, and the group eventually was active in all parts of the state. An even larger group, Right to Privacy (RTP), formed in the wake of the election defeat. RTP was the first permanent statewide group in Oregon, and it would soon face the Oregon Citizens Alliance again at the ballot box. Indeed, the success of the OCA is credited for generating additional anti-GLBT initiatives throughout Oregon at the local level, at the state level, and in states such as Idaho and Colorado. Although Colorado's Amendment 2—which prohibited any governmental body from adopting any ordinance offering claims of "any minority status, quota preferences, protected status or claim of discrimination" to gay, lesbian, or bisexual Coloradans—became nationally known, in part because it passed and none of the other statewide initiatives did, the real battle following the 1988 vote took place within Oregon.

GLBT activists struck back in Oregon by convincing Portland to expand its sexual orientation antidiscrimination law and encouraging the Oregon senate to pass a gay civil rights law in 1991. The OCA battled back by passing several local anti-GLBT initiatives in 1991 and 1992 and placing a new initiative (Measure 9) on the state ballot in 1992 that would have prevented any government in the state from adopting laws that ban discrimination based on sexual orientation. Measure 9 failed after GLBT groups raised $2.1 million to defeat it, but the OCA was successful in passing more than twenty-four local initiatives in 1993 and 1994. The state legislature supported the OCA's efforts, and in 1994 the OCA introduced another anti-GLBT initiative, Measure 13.

By 1994, however, GLBT activists were running a very polished and professional $1.8 million campaign against the OCA's efforts and easily defeated Measure 13. High-profile political elites and religious leaders in the state opposed both Measures 9 and 13, even though the OCA dominated the state's Republican Party in the early 1990's. Meanwhile, many GLBT activists rallied around a new GLBT group, Basic Rights Oregon (BRO), following the defeat of Measure 9. BRO has effectively blocked anti-GLBT initiatives in the state since 1994.

—Donald P. Haider-Markel

FURTHER READING

Bernstein, Mary. "Celebration and Suppression: The Strategic Uses of Identity by the Lesbian and Gay Movement." *American Journal of Sociology* 103, no. 3 (1997): 531-565.

Bull, Chris, and John Gallagher. *Perfect Enemies: The Religious Right, the Gay Movement, and the Politics of the 1990's*. New York: Crown, 1996.

Gay Writers Group. *It Could Happen to You: An Account of the Gay Civil Rights Campaign in Eugene, Oregon*. Boston: Alyson, 1983.

Gregg, Ronald. "Queer Representation and Oregon's 1992 Anti-Gay Ballot Measure: Measuring the Politics of Mainstreaming." In *Between the Sheets, in the Streets: Queer, Lesbian, Gay Documentary*, edited by Chris Holmlund and Cynthia Fuchs. Minneapolis: University of Minnesota Press, 1997.

Haider-Markel, Donald P., and Kenneth J. Meier. "Legislative Victory, Electoral Uncertainty: Explaining Outcomes in the Battles over Lesbian and Gay Civil Rights." *Review of Policy Research* 20, no. 4 (2003): 671-690.

Rimmerman, Craig A. *From Identity to Politics: The Lesbian and Gay Movements in the United States*. Philadelphia: Temple University Press, 2002.

Stein, Arlene. *The Stranger Next Door: The Story of a Small Community's Battle over Sex, Faith, and Civil Rights*. Boston: Beacon Press, 2001.

Thompson, Mark, ed. *The Long Road to Freedom*. New York: St. Martin's Press, 1994.

Witt, Stephanie L., and Suzanne McCorkle, eds. *Anti-Gay Rights Initiatives: Assessing Voter Initiatives*. Westport, Conn.: Greenwood Press, 1997.

SEE ALSO: 1972-1973: Local Governments Pass Antidiscrimination Laws; Mar. 5, 1974: Antigay and Antilesbian Organizations Begin to Form; June 27, 1974: Abzug and Koch Attempt to Amend the Civil Rights Act of 1964; July 3, 1975: U.S. Civil Service Commission Prohibits Discrimination Against Federal Employees; 1977: Anita Bryant Campaigns Against Gay and Lesbian Rights; 1978: Lesbian and Gay Workplace Movement Is Founded; Nov. 7, 1978: Antigay and Antilesbian Briggs Initiative Is Defeated; Nov. 27, 1978: White Murders Politicians Moscone and Milk; 1979: Moral Majority Is Founded; Nov., 1986: Californians Reject LaRouche's Quarantine Initiative; Nov. 3, 1992: Oregon and Colorado Attempt Antigay Initiatives; Mar.-Apr., 1993: Battelle Sex Study Prompts Conservative Backlash; 1994: Employment Non-Discrimination Act Is Proposed to U.S. Congress; Dec. 4, 1995: Lesbian Couple Murdered in Oregon; Mar. 21, 2003: New Mexico Amends Its Human Rights Act; June 26, 2003: U.S. Supreme Court Overturns Texas Sodomy Law.

December 1, 1988
First World AIDS Day

World AIDS Day was created as a global response to the crises surrounding the HIV-AIDS pandemic. An international meeting of health ministers unanimously approved the adoption of the day of commemoration and education, and they did so also to counter the common belief that AIDS was a "gay disease."

Locale: Worldwide
Categories: HIV-AIDS; organizations and institutions; civil rights; health and medicine; marches, protests, and riots

Summary of Event

In January, 1988, the World Summit of Ministers of Health on Programmes for AIDS Prevention met in London, with representatives from 140 national governments. The conference was the first broad admission by national governments in an international setting that AIDS was a serious world health problem that needed to be addressed and confronted. The idea for a World AIDS Day came out of this meeting, and the first event was held on December 1, 1988. Each year since, December 1 has been recognized as World AIDS Day.

International collaboration against AIDS had been exceedingly slow. The London meeting happened approximately eight years after AIDS had been recognized among gay men in California and New York. Because AIDS had been identified first as a disease affecting a stigmatized group, resources against the illness were mobilized slowly. Ronald Reagan, then president of the United States, did not speak about AIDS publicly until September of 1985, when he made a brief statement in response to a reporter's question. His first public speech that mentioned AIDS was in February of 1986, by which time there had been about sixteen thousand deaths from AIDS in the United States alone.

In May, 1988, the Forty-first World Health Assembly, in Geneva, Switzerland, passed resolution WHA41.24 ("Avoidance of Discrimination in Relation to HIV-infected People and People with AIDS"). At this assembly, the Global Programme on AIDS of the World Health Organization (WHO) endorsed the London Declaration on AIDS Prevention (passed by the World Summit of Ministers of Health on Programmes for AIDS Prevention in 1988), which had determined that World AIDS Day should be held every year in December.

Further support for World AIDS Day came on October 27, 1988, when the United Nations General Assembly passed a resolution providing support and publicity for both WHO's earlier resolution and the original London Declaration of World AIDS Day.

Significance

The international resolutions gave credibility to the concept of World AIDS Day. The first event had the theme "A World United Against AIDS." In the United States, the resolutions seemed to make it clear that the federal government intended to help fund AIDS research and to publicize information about AIDS prevention and treatment. AIDS activists, however, had been so disturbed by the federal government's indifference to the epidemic and lack of care concerning the disease that many showed their frustrations on World AIDS Day instead of using the day as a solemn reminder of the disease and its effects.

Still, organizations and individuals joined together to promote HIV-AIDS awareness and to encourage speedier governmental action in approving treatment options. Also, the NAMES Project Foundation's AIDS Memorial Quilt was exhibited for the first time in conjunction with World AIDS Day. Quilt panels have been displayed in cities around the United States and the world.

During the third World AIDS Day, in 1990, public attention focused on women and HIV and the increasing cases of AIDS among women (African American women have been especially affected). Many activists had argued for years that women and

First World AIDS Day

"Stop AIDS. Keep the Promise." World AIDS Day poster, 2005. (Courtesy, World AIDS Campaign)

girls were being ignored and forgotten by AIDS education, prevention, and treatment programs.

World AIDS Day is always a political event, and this was especially the case after the World AIDS Day conference of 1994, when U.S. surgeon general Joycelyn Elders resigned. Elders had spoken publicly about sex education in schools and included what turned out to be a controversial suggestion that masturbation was healthy and should perhaps be included in sex education classes as a way to prevent HIV and AIDS. When her remarks were publicized, she was urged by President Clinton to resign and thus lost her job.

By 1995, there had been some improvements in HIV-AIDS prevention and treatment, but the disease had become the highest ranked cause of death among Americans ages twenty-five to forty-four. The illness continues to affect African Americans at rates higher than other groups. Stigma against HIV infection and against those with AIDS persists, although prejudice has diminished somewhat through the years. World AIDS Day has played a role in this progress.

—Susan J. Wurtzburg

FURTHER READING

Feldman, Douglas A., ed. *Global Aids Policy*. Westport, Conn.: Bergin & Garvey, 1994.

Grmek, Mirko D. *History of AIDS: Emergence and Origin of a Modern Pandemic*. Princeton, N.J.: Princeton University Press, 1993.

Jennings, M. Kent, and Ellen Ann Anderson. "The Importance of Social and Political Context: The Case of AIDS Activism." *Political Behavior* 25, no. 2 (2003): 177-199.

Smith, Raymond A., ed. *Encyclopedia of AIDS: A Social, Political, Cultural, and Scientific Record of the HIV Epidemic*. New York: Penguin Books, 2001.

Stockdill, Brett C. *Activism Against AIDS: At the Intersections of Sexuality, Race, Gender, and Class*. Boulder, Colo.: Lynne Rienner, 2003.

Willinger, Barbara I., and Alan Rice, eds. *A History of AIDS Social Work in Hospitals: A Daring Response to an Epidemic*. New York: Haworth Press, 2003.

SEE ALSO: Aug. 8, 1978: International Lesbian and Gay Association Is Founded; June 5 and July 3, 1981: Reports of Rare Diseases Mark Beginning of AIDS Epidemic; July, 1982: Gay-Related Immunodeficiency Is Renamed AIDS; Spring, 1984: AIDS Virus Is Discovered; July 25, 1985: Actor Hudson Announces He Has AIDS; Sept., 1986: AZT Treats People with AIDS; Mar., 1987: Radical AIDS Activist Group ACT UP Is Founded; June 27, 1988: Report of the Presidential AIDS Commission; 1990: International Gay and Lesbian Human Rights Commission Is Founded; June 25, 1993: Clinton Appoints First AIDS Czar; Sept. 16, 1994: U.N. Revokes Consultative Status of International Lesbian and Gay Association; June 17, 1995: International Bill of Gender Rights Is First Circulated; Oct. 9-12, 1998: First International Retreat for Lesbian and Gay Muslims Is Held.

1989
Act Up Paris Is Founded

French journalists familiar with the American radical activist group ACT UP founded a uniquely French organization that brought together a coalition of individuals, straight and gay, who were dissatisfied with French politics to protest the government's record on AIDS and its indifference to the plight of all French citizens.

Locale: Paris, France
Categories: Health and medicine; HIV-AIDS; marches, protests, and riots; organizations and institutions

Key Figures
Didier Lestrade, French journalist
Christophe Martet, French journalist
Joëlle Bouchet, French mother of a hemophiliac and HIV-positive son

Summary of Event

From a Paris apartment in 1989, novice activists inspired by the radical American group AIDS Coalition to Unleash Power (ACT UP), began to transform AIDS and gay and lesbian politics in France. The new French group even imported ACT UP's famous black T-shirt with a pink triangle when its members marched in their first lesbian and gay pride parade. This approach was risky, as many still believed that AIDS had been brought to France by gay men who had visited New York.

Despite flirting with American-style activism and American-inspired symbols, Act Up Paris (lowercase letters intentional) grew to reflect a different model of activism. Distinctly French, it tackled issues that ACT UP in the United States did not emphasize, remained distant from the government and pharmaceutical industry, and joined a coalition of those dissatisfied with mainstream French politics. In the process, Act Up Paris laid the foundation for the election of the first gay mayor of a major city anywhere in the world. Bertrand Delanoë, an out gay man, became mayor of Paris in 2001.

In 1987, journalist Didier Lestrade had arrived in New York to research a travel article for a gay publication. It was the year in which American activists, angered by government inaction on AIDS, were founding ACT UP. Lestrade found hope in their anger and militancy, their refusal to accept that nothing could be done to slow the spread of AIDS, their efforts to speed research on a cure, and their attempts to encourage treatment of those with the disease. Lestrade blamed the spread of AIDS in France on government and medical establishment homophobia. Returning to Paris, Lestrade brought together a like-minded group of gay men, numbering a few dozen.

In 1989, another French journalist, Christophe Martet, moved to New York and joined ACT UP there. Diagnosed HIV-positive, Martet had left his job as an economics reporter with French television. In New York, he found new hope as he came to sympathize with the activist claim that industry profiteering was also at the heart of the AIDS crisis. If Lestrade represented one brand of gay and AIDS activism in France, Martet represented another. Lestrade and his supporters made building a strong gay community a centerpiece of their struggle against the disease and targeted many of their actions and efforts within the community itself. Martet, however, immediately identified with other activists who thought AIDS was a symptom of a variety of failures in French government. In fact, the first person Martet met at the organization was Joëlle Bouchet, whose son, Ludovic, was infected with HIV through blood products used to treat hemophilia.

Working together, Bouchet, Martet, Cleews Vellay, and others made the French government's early inaction on blood safety a symbol for all the failures in responding to AIDS. While other hemophiliacs had filed criminal accusations against the administrators of the blood supply system, Act Up Paris was the first to launch an accusation against the former prime minister, Laurent Fabius, who presided over early AIDS policy from 1984 to 1986. Act Up accused Fabius of murder and demanded that he be investigated and prosecuted for his crimes. Act Up was so successful that, in the period after the group launched its accusations in January, 1992, attendance grew at weekly meetings from approximately forty to more than several hundred. The group was sought out by French journalists, who were surprised to find gay AIDS activists marching alongside hemophiliacs.

Both Lestrade and Martet represent approaches to AIDS and gay politics very different from those that had been attempted before. French political values, called Republicanism, demonize organizations that make demands based on race, religion, or sex/gender. All French people, according to Republicanism, are equally entitled to the rights and protections of citizenship, so there is no need to claim any "special protections" from the government. (The rhetoric of "special rights" is used in the United States.) Early gay activism in the 1970's called for a right to be different, and AIDES, still the largest AIDS service provider in France, was founded by gay men who refused to make homosexuality an issue in fighting the disease. Martet called on gay men to join with others who suffered from government indifference, while Lestrade, by contrast, argued for a stronger gay community.

Significance

With Act Up Paris's growth in membership, it was clear that Martet's argument had won. When he was elected president of the organization, he counted on new activists who would challenge government policies on prevention and treatment, official indifference to the needs of immigrants, the expulsion of undocumented immigrants suffering from the disease, and the failure to decriminalize drug use as part of AIDS prevention. Joined by many straight women and a few straight men, Act Up Paris began to work with a variety of organizations on the left, including those fighting globalization and demanding increasing rights for workers, women, the poor, and others marginalized because of their race, ethnicity, class, or gender.

By the end of the 1990's, this strategy worked. While many tied to the establishment still attacked gay and AIDS activists as the "tools" of some foreign conspiracy and a danger to French Republicanism, a broad segment of the public began to respect Act Up's commitment to a broader agenda, including the election of an HIV-negative heterosexual woman as the president of the organization in 2000. By demanding the prosecution of a powerful Socialist Party politician such as Fabius on behalf of hemophiliacs, Act Up demonstrated that gays were concerned about the well-being of all French citizens. By joining with organizations on the left critical of left- and right-wing governments alike, they proved that gays could place their values above partisan politics. By pointing out that the government's failure to protect gay men from AIDS was also a failure to protect France in general, they demonstrated a measure of patriotism that many in the government did not seem to possess.

This approach enabled Bertrand Delanoë, considered the rather bland leader of the Socialist Party in Paris, to position himself, because of his homosexuality, as a political outsider despite his ties to the government. While other Socialists failed to win election when they called for political reform, Delanoë's call for greater participation in decision making rang true.

—*Michael J. Bosia*

Further Reading

Agar, James N. "Writing = Life: Breaking the Silence on the 'Histoire' of AIDS in France." *French Cultural Studies* 9, no. 27 (October, 1998): 411.

Lestrade, Didier. *Act Up: Une Histoire*. Paris: Denoël, 2000.

Shepard, Benjamin, and Ronald Hayduk. *From ACT UP to the WTO: Urban Protest and Community Building in the Era of Globalization*. New York: Verso, 2002.

Smith, Raymond A., ed. *Encyclopedia of AIDS: A Social, Political, Cultural, and Scientific Record of the HIV Epidemic*. New York: Penguin Books, 2001.

Stockdill, Brett. *Activism Against AIDS: At the Intersections of Sexuality, Race, Gender, and Class*. Boulder, Colo.: Lynne Rienner, 2003.

SEE ALSO: July 31, 1969: Gay Liberation Front Is Formed; Aug. 8, 1978: International Lesbian and Gay Association Is Founded; July, 1982: Gay-Related Immunodeficiency Is Renamed AIDS; Spring, 1984: AIDS Virus Is Discovered; Mar., 1987: Radical AIDS Activist Group ACT UP Is Founded; Dec. 1, 1988: First World AIDS Day; Dec. 10, 1989: ACT UP Protests at St. Patrick's Cathedral.

1989
Vaid Becomes Executive Director of the National Gay and Lesbian Task Force

Urvashi Vaid became the first person of color to run a mainstream national civil rights organization for the GLBT community when she assumed leadership of the National Gay and Lesbian Task Force. She took part in direct political action and advocated for a multiracial and cogender movement.

LOCALE: Washington, D.C.
CATEGORIES: Organizations and institutions; government and politics

KEY FIGURE
Urvashi Vaid (b. 1958), executive director of the National Gay and Lesbian Task Force, 1989-1992

SUMMARY OF EVENT

Born in India in 1958, Urvashi Vaid moved to the United States when she was eight years old. At an early age, she was reading voraciously and became politically active, participating in antiwar marches and giving speeches at age twelve. Vaid began political organizing in college, addressing the discrimination she felt as a woman and a person of color. In 1983, she graduated from law school at Northeastern University in Boston. Hired by the American Civil Liberties Union, she initiated the National Prisons Project, which worked with prisoners who were HIV-positive.

In 1985, Vaid began her involvement with the National Gay and Lesbian Task Force (NGLTF), one of the most influential GLBT rights organizations in the United States, and served on its board of directors. In 1986, she became NGLTF's director of public information and brought to the position a new degree of professionalism and media savvy.

In 1989, she was appointed executive director, becoming the first person of color to run a mainstream national civil rights organization for the GLBT community. Vaid tripled the NGLTF's operating budget while beginning major public outreach programs, and she cofounded NGLTF's Creating Change conference, the only national gay and lesbian political conference. Vaid resigned from her position in 1992 to work on her book, *Virtual Equality: The Mainstreaming of Gay and Lesbian Liberation* (1995), but would return to NGLTF in 1997 as the director of public information for an additional three years.

SIGNIFICANCE

The choice of Urvashi Vaid to lead NGLTF was an endorsement of her political agenda, which would help shape the GLBT movement in the following decade. Her multifaceted agenda consisted of four key points: direct political action, multiracial and cogender politics, building coalitions, and fighting the right wing.

Alongside Queer Nation and ACT UP (AIDS Coalition to Unleash Power), NGLTF under Vaid used direct-action strategy to end homophobia and

> **VAID SPEAKS AT THE 1993 MARCH ON WASHINGTON**
>
> The Christian supremacists are wrong spiritually when they demonize us. . . . [They] are wrong morally . . . because justice is moral, and prejudice is evil; because truth is moral and the lie of the closet is the real sin. . . . [We] must prove the religious right wrong politically. . . . We believe in democracy, in many voices co-existing in peace, and people of all faiths living together in harmony. . . . Our opponents believe in monotheism. . . . One law, the Old Testament. . . . Democracy battles theism. . . . We've got to march from Washington into action at home. I challenge every one of you, straight or gay, . . . to fight the Right. We have got to match [their] power . . . vote for vote, dollar for dollar. Get involved! Volunteer! . . . The gay rights movement . . . is not a lifestyle. . . . [It] is an integral part of the American promise of freedom. . . . We stand for freedom as we have yet to know it, and we will not be denied.
>
> *Source:* Excerpted from Gifts of Speech: Women's Speeches from Around the World. http://gos.sbc.edu/w/vaid.html.

heterosexism and to break the silence concerning the AIDS epidemic's effect on the GLBT community. Vaid wrote in *Virtual Equality* of "the shock of ACT UP's 1989 Stop the Church demonstration against the [Roman] Catholic Church" and "the red-and-black posters citing the AIDS death toll so far and asking 'Where Was George [H. W. Bush]?'" In 1990, Vaid interrupted President Bush's first and only AIDS policy speech at the National Community AIDS Partnership meeting, protesting his inactivity as she held up a sign reading "Remember Gay People with AIDS." Vaid was escorted outside. Because of her action, she "incurred the wrath of conservatives" in the GLBT movement.

Vaid's work focuses on multiracial and "multigendered" politics that challenge racism, sexism, homophobia, and other kinds of social and cultural biases in the mainstream society in general and the GLBT movement in particular. In an interview for *Vanity Fair*, she described the nature of her work: "The movement I work in might be called a gay and lesbian movement, but its mission is the liberation of all people." Vaid realized that most gay and lesbian people neither understand nor value the importance of multiracial and multi-issue politics. In *Virtual Equality*, she asks, rhetorically,

> If we are . . . a diverse, multicolored, many-gendered, multisexual rainbow of a people, then why should an attempt to bring up racism and sexism in our movement become a matter of dispute? . . . Why do we still try to find 'one of each' for our conference, meeting, board, . . . ?

During her tenure at NGLTF, there were incidents of racial and gender intolerance, but Vaid refused to "neuter and derace (erase)" herself in order to be heard: "I am, after all, who I am: the first Indian and person of color to run a mainstream gay and lesbian group."

Multiculturalism and building coalitions were Vaid's strategies for the movement's success and for fostering understanding about race and gender. Gay and lesbian organizations worked on racism and sexism "because it was the right thing to do, because gay people of color and lesbians were directly affected, and because to do otherwise would be hypocritical, since we so often asked nongay organizations to support gay rights." Thanks to Vaid's strategies, a prestigious national civil rights lobby, the Leadership Conference on Civil Rights, in 1992 endorsed the idea of federal nondiscrimination legislation for gays and lesbians.

Vaid had two strategies to fight the right wing. First, she advocated the public debate on sexuality.

> Gay and lesbian sexuality remains the biggest obstacle to our full acceptance as human beings by the dominant heterosexual culture. We are hated because of how, with whom, and how much (mythic or real) we do it. To win against the right wing, we have to fight back on the sexual battleground, not run away from it. . . . [W]e threaten the myth of universal heterosexuality simply by our existence in every culture, color, and time. . . . [W]e disrupt the sexist order that decrees women exist for the pleasure and service of men. . . . [O]ur movement represents the liberation of the most powerful and untamed motivating force in human life: desire.

Second, as she stated in her speech at the 1993 March on Washington for Lesbian, Gay and Bi Equal Rights and Liberation, the movement must address Christian bigotry against LGBT persons.

—Bassam Kassab

FURTHER READING
D'Emilio, John. *Making Trouble: Essays on Gay History, Politics, and the University.* New York: Routledge, 1992.
_____. *The World Turned: Essays on Gay History, Politics, and Culture.* Durham, N.C.: Duke University Press, 2002.
D'Emilio, John, William Turner, and Urvashi Vaid. *Creating Change: Sexuality, Public Policy, and Civil Rights.* New York: St. Martin's Press, 2002.
Vaid, Urvashi. *Virtual Equality: The Mainstreaming of Gay and Lesbian Liberation.* New York: Anchor Books, 1995.

SEE ALSO: 1950: Mattachine Society Is Founded; 1952: ONE, Inc., Is Founded; 1955: Daughters of Bilitis Founded as First National Lesbian Group in United States; May 27-30, 1960: First National Lesbian Conference Convenes; Feb. 19-20, 1966: First North American Conference of Homophile Organizations Convenes; Apr. 19, 1967: First Student Homophile League Is Formed; Aug. 11-18, 1968: NACHO Formally Becomes the First Gay Political Coalition; July 31, 1969: Gay Liberation Front Is Formed; June 28, 1970: First Lesbian and Gay Pride March in the United States; Nov. 28, 1970: Del Martin Quits Gay Liberation Movement; 1973: National Gay Task Force Is Formed; Oct. 18, 1973: Lambda Legal Authorized to Practice Law; Mar. 5, 1974: Antigay and Antilesbian Organizations Begin to Form; 1977: Anita Bryant Campaigns Against Gay and Lesbian Rights; Apr. 22, 1980: Human Rights Campaign Fund Is Founded.

1989-1990
HELMS CLAIMS PHOTOGRAPHS ARE INDECENT

The homoerotic and otherwise controversial images of photographers Robert Mapplethorpe and Andres Serrano, and the work of other artists, became flash points in a cultural and legislative battle over public funding for the arts in the United States.

LOCALE: Washington, D.C.; Cincinnati, Ohio
CATEGORIES: Arts; government and politics; laws, acts, and legal history; organizations and institutions; religion

KEY FIGURES
Robert Mapplethorpe (1946-1989), art photographer
Andres Serrano (b. 1950), art photographer
Donald Wildmon (b. 1938), founder and head of the American Family Association and reverend
Jesse Helms (b. 1921), Republican senator, North Carolina
Dennis Barrie, director of the Contemporary Arts Center, Cincinnati, Ohio
John E. Frohnmayer, National Endowment for the Arts chair
Christina Orr-Cahall, director of the Corcoran Gallery of Art, Washington, D.C.

SUMMARY OF EVENT
By the late 1980's, the Christian Right had gained significant influence in U.S. politics and had become increasingly critical of what it considered excessive liberalism and permissiveness in American culture. Cultural battles raged around religion in public life, homosexuality, and the arts.

In early 1989, the Reverend Donald Wildmon, head of the conservative American Family Association headquartered in Tupelo, Mississippi, began a campaign against *Piss Christ*, a photograph by artist Andres Serrano depicting a crucifix submerged in a jar of urine. Wildmon called the work an example of "anti-Christian bigotry." Critics were particularly incensed that Serrano had received $15,000 in indirect funding from the National Endowment for the Arts (NEA), a federal government agency founded in 1965 by President Lyndon B. Johnson "to create and sustain . . . a climate encouraging freedom of thought, imagination, and inquiry."

The furor over *Piss Christ* soon expanded to include works with homoerotic content and those deemed anti-American. Among the critics' main targets was a retrospective exhibition of the work of gay photographer Robert Mapplethorpe, who died of complications from AIDS in March, 1989. Titled *The Perfect Moment*, the exhibition was created by the Institute of Contemporary Art in Philadelphia, funded in part with $30,000 from the NEA. The show included a representative sample of Mapplethorpe's fine-art photography, much of which featured flowers, classical nudes, and portraits of celebrities (including bodybuilder Lisa Lyon and Mapplethorpe's former roommate, singer Patti Smith). Among the selections, however, were candid photographs of young children with their genitals visible, as well as the *X Portfolio*, a collection of several images showing gay-male sadomasochism, including one of the artist with a bullwhip protruding from his anus. Even with these images, *The Perfect Moment* had already shown in Philadelphia and Chicago, garnering little notice outside the art world.

After Wildmon held a press conference in the spring of 1989 denouncing Serrano's and Mapplethorpe's work, the controversy moved into the halls of Congress. One the Senate floor, senators Jesse Helms (R-NC) and Alfonse D'Amato (R-NY) criticized the work, with D'Amato deriding *Piss Christ* as a "deplorable, despicable display of vulgarity." Helms had previously raised the ire of GLBT activists in 1987, when he proposed an amendment—which came to be known as "no promo homo"—that prohibited the use of federal funds for AIDS education and prevention materials or activities that "promote, encourage, or condone, directly or indi-

Andres Serrano. (Hulton Archive/Getty Images)

rectly, homosexual activities or intravenous use of illegal drugs." In May, Helms, D'Amato, and more than two dozen other senators sent a letter of outrage to outgoing NEA chairman Hugh Southern. More than one hundred members of the House of Representatives, led by Representative Dick Armey (R-TX), soon followed suit, demanding that the NEA end its sponsorship of "morally reprehensible trash" and requesting new grant guidelines that would "pay respect to public standards of taste and decency."

In June, 1989, Christina Orr-Cahall, director of the Corcoran Gallery of Art in Washington, D.C., canceled a scheduled showing of *The Perfect Moment*, hoping to avoid exacerbating the NEA controversy and endangering the museum's funding. However, the move had the opposite effect. Artists, students, civil libertarians, and GLBT activists were angered by the cancellation. Several artists vowed to boycott the museum, and activists (including members of ACT UP) held pickets and projected some of Mapplethorpe's most controversial images onto the facade of the Corcoran building. A small arts organization called the Washington Project for the Arts (which in 1996 merged with the Corcoran) took on the exhibition, which was attended by some fifty thousand people. The furor generated by the cancellation ultimately led to Orr-Cahall's resignation.

Throughout the summer and fall, debate over the NEA and the nature of appropriate public art continued in the legislature and in the media as Congress considered reauthorization of the agency. Southern defended the NEA's practice—mandated in its authorizing legislation—of allowing grantee organizations to select funding recipients based on artistic criteria, "even though sometimes the work may be deemed controversial and offensive to some individuals." Although conservatives such as Representative Dana Rohrabacher (R-CA) demanded that the NEA lose *all* funding, arts champions including Representative Sidney Yates (D-IL) and Senator Claiborne Pell (D-RI) prevailed, and the agency retained its funding level of about $170 million—less a deduction of $45,000, representing the combined amount of support for Serrano and the Mapplethorpe exhibition.

Cultural conservatives were not satisfied, however. That summer, Helms introduced an amendment in the Senate, which passed on a voice vote, banning the use of NEA funding to

> promote, disseminate or produce obscene or indecent materials, including but not limited to depictions of sadomasochism, homoeroticism, the exploitation of children, or individuals engaged in sex acts; or material which denigrates the objects or beliefs of the adherents of a particular religion or non-religion.

The House of Representatives did not adopt the Helms amendment as written, but in October, the two houses approved compromise legislation that retained much of its language and intent. The compromise measure (passed by a vote of 382-41 in the House and 62-35 in the Senate) mirrored U.S. Supreme Court legal language, banning "obscene" but not "indecent" materials, and only those which "taken as a whole, do not have serious literary, artistic, political, or scientific value." To implement the new restrictions, the NEA began requiring that prospective recipients certify in advance that the money they received would not be used to produce obscene materials.

Controversy continued to surround Mapplethorpe's work the following year, as religious and antipornography groups opposed the exhibition of *The Perfect Moment* at Cincinnati's Contemporary Arts Center (CAC). On opening day, April 7, 1990, the Hamilton County sheriff arrested CAC director Dennis Barrie and seized seven photographs deemed to be obscene, as demonstrators protested outside the museum. Barrie and the CAC were indicted by a grand jury for pandering obscenity and for "illegal use of a minor in nudity-oriented material," but U.S. District Court judge Carl Rubin issued a preliminary injunction prohibiting local authorities from interfering with the exhibition, which ran for several weeks and drew record-breaking crowds.

The case against Barrie and the CAC went to trial the following fall. The city prosecutor, Frank Prouty, argued that communities had the right to determine their own standards for acceptable art. The lawyers for the defense, H. Louis Sirkin and Marc D. Mezibov, countered that the works were constitutionally protected in the light of the Supreme Court's 1973 *Miller v. California* ruling. Several art experts and museum directors testified for the defense, while antipornography consultant Judith Reisman acted as a witness for the prosecution. On October 5, after two hours of deliberation, a jury acquitted Barrie and the CAC. The jurors found that although the images on trial "appeal to the prurient interest" and were "patently offensive," they did not lack literary, artistic, political, or scientific value, and thus were protected under the First Amendment.

The events in Cincinnati transpired against the backdrop of continued controversy over funding for the arts. In 1990, Congress required the NEA to take into account "general standards of decency and re-

> **U.S. SENATORS DECRY SERRANO'S "PISS CHRIST"**
>
> U.S. Senate, Washington, D.C.,
> May 18, 1989
> Mr. Hugh Southern, Acting Chairman
> National Endowment for the Arts
> Washington, D.C.
>
> Dear Mr. Southern:
>
> We recently learned of the Endowment's support for a so-called "work of art" by Andres Serrano entitled "Piss Christ." We write to express our outrage and to suggest in the strongest terms that the procedures used by the Endowment to award and support artists be reformed.
>
> The piece in question is a large and vivid photograph of Christ on a crucifix submerged in the artist's urine. This work is shocking, abhorrent and completely undeserving of any recognition whatsoever. Millions of taxpayers are rightfully incensed that their hard-earned dollars were used to honor and support Serrano's work.
>
> There is a clear flaw in the procedures used to select art and artists deserving of taxpayers' support. That fact is evidenced by the Serrano work itself. Moreover, after the artist was selected and honored for his "contributions" to the field of art, his work was exhibited at government expense and with the imprimatur of the Endowment.
>
> This matter does not involve freedom of artistic expression—it does involve the question whether American taxpayers should be forced to support such trash.
>
> And finally, simply because the Endowment and the Southeastern Center for Contemporary Art (SECCA) did not have a direct hand in choosing Serrano's work, does not absolve either of responsibility. The fact that both the Endowment and the SECCA with taxpayer dollars promoted this work as part of the Awards in Visual Arts exhibition, is reason enough to be outraged.
>
> We urge the Endowment to comprehensively review its procedures and determine what steps will be taken to prevent such abuses from recurring in the future. We await your response.
>
> Sincerely,
>
> Alfonse D'Amato, Bob Kerrey, Warren R. Rudman, Rudy Boschwitz, Dennis Deconcini, Pete Wilson, Bob Dole, Chuck Grassley, James A. McClure, John Heinz, Wendell Ford, Howell Heflin, Harry Reid, Richard Shelby, John W. Warner, Larry Pressler, Conrad Burns, Tom Harkins, Trent Lott, Jesse Helms, John McCain, Arlen Specter, Steve Symms
>
> *Source: Congressional Record*, May 18, 1989.

spect for the diverse beliefs and values of the American public" when awarding grants. A number of additional artists, institutions, and exhibitions came under fire, including bisexual performance artist and former porn star Annie Sprinkle (who invited audience members to view her cervix with a speculum as part of her Post-Porn Modernist show), and Witness: Against Our Vanishing, an exhibition of AIDS-related art with catalog copy by gay artist David Wojnarowicz (who sued the American Family Association for using his work in their propaganda without his permission).

In June, 1990, appointed NEA chairman John E. Frohnmayer withheld grants from four solo performance artists, Karen Finley, John Fleck, Holly Hughes, and Tim Miller—respectively, a feminist, a gay man, a lesbian, and a gay man—because of the sexual content of their work. The NEA Four, as they came to be popularly called, sued the federal government, setting off a long legal battle. In 1993, a federal judge in Los Angeles struck down the NEA decency clause as unconstitutionally vague, a decision that was upheld by the Ninth Circuit Court of Appeals in 1996. The Clinton administration appealed, and *NEA v. Finley* made its way to the Supreme Court, which, in June, 1998, reversed the lower court ruling and allowed the decency provision to stand.

Significance

The controversy surrounding Mapplethorpe's work sent shock waves through the art world. According to William Ivey, NEA chairman from 1998 to 2001, the Mapplethorpe controversy "let the genie out of the bottle and demonstrated the power of images in creating political conflict around artistic work." Yet, rather than suppressing homoerotic art, the controversy made Mapplethorpe a household name and launched representations of gay male sexuality, interracial sex, sadomasochism, and AIDS into the spotlight. While some mainstream arts organizations succumbed to the chilling effects of censorship, many radical artists became more defiant, producing ever more explicit and challenging work. In the years to come, homoerotic, sadomasochistic, and AIDS-related imagery would become a staple of consumer advertising, utilized by companies such as Calvin Klein, Benneton, and Abercrombie & Fitch.

Also, the controversy over sacrilegious and homoerotic art occurred at a time when the United States was undergoing a profound cultural debate. At the 1992 Republican National Convention in Houston, Texas, Christian Coalition founder Patrick Buchanan went so far as to declare a religious and cultural war. The conservative upsurge peaked in 1994 with the election of a Republican majority in Congress for the first time in decades. The combined influence of the Christian Right and fiscal conservatives concerned about the bloated federal budget succeeded in slashing the NEA budget by nearly 40 percent in 1995-1996. Grants to individual artists were discontinued, a larger proportion of funding was disbursed through local and state arts councils, and more money was devoted to arts education programs for children.

Conservatives never succeeded in gutting the agency as some had hoped, however; after hitting a low in 2000, the agency's funding slowly rebounded, reaching $120 million in 2004. Since the mid-1990's, a bipartisan consensus has emerged in favor of the NEA and public arts funding. Controversy over sexually explicit material has largely shifted to the Web, which has been the focus of indecency and obscenity legislation since the mid-1990's.

By highlighting what was at stake, the Mapplethorpe controversy brought artists, academics, and GLBT activists together to oppose censorship and demand continued public funding for the arts and humanities. Faced with the grassroots strength of the Christian Right, progressive and cultural activists became politicized themselves, and they formed a united front to oppose the conservative agenda.

—*Liz Highleyman*

Further Reading

Bolton, Richard. *Culture Wars: Documents from the Recent Controversies in the Arts*. New York: New Press, 1992.

Danto, Arthur. *Playing with the Edge: The Photographic Achievement of Robert Mapplethorpe*. Berkeley: University of California Press, 1996.

Dubin, Steven. *Arresting Images*. New York: Routledge, 1992.

Duggan, Lisa, and Nan D. Hunter. *Sex Wars: Sexual Dissent and Political Culture*. New York: Routledge, 1995.

Frohnmayer, John. *Leaving Town Alive: Confessions of an Arts Warrior*. New York: Houghton Mifflin, 1993.

Meyer, Richard. *Outlaw Representation: Censorship and Homosexuality in Twentieth-Century American Art*. New York: Oxford University Press, 2002.

Vance, Carol S. "The War on Culture." *Art in America*, September, 1989.

Wallis, Brian, Marianne Weems, and Philip Yenawine, eds. *Art Matters: How the Culture Wars Changed America*. New York: New York University Press, 1999.

White, Edmund. *Arts and Letters*. San Francisco, Calif.: Cleis Press, 2004.

See also: Mar. 5, 1974: Antigay and Antilesbian Organizations Begin to Form; 1990-1993: Artists Sue the National Endowment for the Arts.

January 21, 1989
DEATH OF TRANSGENDER JAZZ MUSICIAN BILLY TIPTON

Billy Tipton, who was named Dorothy Lucille Lipton at birth and who lived the first nineteen years of his life as a woman, lived fifty-five years as a man. He had a career in music, was married five times to women, and adopted and helped raise three sons. His gender at birth was revealed at his death.

LOCALE: Spokane, Washington
CATEGORIES: Transgender/transsexuality; arts

KEY FIGURE
Billy Tipton (1914-1989), jazz musician

SUMMARY OF EVENT
When Billy Tipton died of hemorrhaging ulcers in 1989, a paramedic revealed something very few people knew—that Tipton had the body of a seventy-four-year-old woman; only Tipton's first wife knew that he was transgender. As he left no will, diary, or letters articulating his reasons for why he stopped living as Dorothy at the age of nineteen and started living as Billy for the rest of his life, others have since spoken for the musician in articles, a biography, plays, an opera, and a novel.

After the divorce of his parents, neither of whom wanted custody of Dorothy (Billy) or her (his) brother, the children were sent from Oklahoma City to live with two aunts in Kansas City. Young Dorothy already had shown talent for playing piano by ear, but it was Aunt Bess who saw to it that her niece received formal instruction in piano, violin, and saxophone starting at the age of fourteen. After graduating from high school, Dorothy moved back to Oklahoma City to live with her mother, single again after a divorce from her second husband.

The Depression made the couple desperate economically, so Dorothy set her sights on making a living in the music world. Oklahoma City in the 1930's was full of dance halls and honky-tonks that needed musicians, but nineteen-year-old Dorothy could find work only at a seedy dive, a job that did not last long because male customers did not want a woman piano player. Dorothy then heard of a traveling band that needed a saxophone player. Knowing full well that touring bands never traveled with female players, Dorothy enlisted the help of her cousins to cut her hair, bind her breasts, and devise a costume. Dorothy (as Billy Tipton) got the job.

For a time in Oklahoma City, Tipton lived on extreme sides of the gender binary by dressing in male clothing but living as a female musician. A shaping influence on his new identity was a veteran of dance marathons, a bisexual woman named Non Earl Harrell. Although the exact nature of Tipton's relationship with Harrell remains unclear, it is known that they lived together in Oklahoma City and registered as husband and wife when they rented a house. When Tipton got his first real job in 1935, going on the road with the Banner Playboys—an eight-piece band—Harrell's presence helped to confirm for others Tipton's heterosexuality and masculinity. Fifteen years older than Tipton, Harrell had life and business experience that proved instrumental in her young companion's maturation as a performer.

Tipton continued to get better jobs, and, even after Harrell moved on in 1943, Tipton was not without a companion for long. Later that year, he married a female singer named June, who sang with many of the bands that he played for until 1946. During World War II, Tipton would explain to others that because he had been injured at the age of twelve after being kicked by a horse, his lingering injury made him ineligible for the armed services. He also used this story to explain to his wives and girlfriends why he wore bandages constantly around his chest and groin, thereby masking his female anatomy.

Eighteen-year-old Betty Cox met the dashing thirty-two-year-old Tipton in 1946. Even though they had no official ceremony, Betty changed her driver license name to "Tipton," and the couple presented themselves as husband and wife for the next seven years. Serving to confirm Tipton's successful

The cover of Diane Wood Middlebrook's book, Suits Me: The Double Life of Billy Tipton *(1998). (Courtesy, Houghton Mifflin)*

performance of his masculine gender, Betty had seen Tipton shave every morning, and band members recall hearing lovemaking from Tipton's hotel room when the band was on the road. Betty told biographer Diane Middlebrook that Tipton would toss a condom out of bed after they made love.

In 1951, Tipton formed the Billy Tipton Trio with two men in their early twenties. At the age of thirty-six, Tipton needed to surround himself with youthful men to better frame his boyish appearance (he was 5 feet, 4 inches in height). The trio successfully played in Elks clubs and at Veterans of Foreign Wars posts, and resorts, traveling constantly throughout the western United States. Betty left Tipton, however, when she got tired of life on the road.

The Billy Tipton Trio recorded an album in 1956, followed by *Billy Tipton Plays Hi-Fi on the Piano*, which earned them a four-week gig at a Reno, Nevada, hotel, where stars such as Liberace were booked year-round. The trio's slick professionalism prompted management to offer them the position as house band. Much to the surprise of his partners, Tipton said no to the lucrative offer, explaining that he wanted to take a day job in a musical booking agency and settle down. Middlebrook suggests that Tipton was wary of too much visibility in a place such as Reno, where any number of acquaintances from his gender-bending days in Oklahoma City, or indeed his past as Dorothy, might unravel the elaborate persona he had developed. After twenty years in show business, Tipton not only had proved his musical talent but also was well-regarded as an entertainer, artistic director, and business manager. As much as Tipton wanted to perform, perhaps he feared exposure and recognition as well. In 1958 he set his sights much lower and headed for Spokane, Washington, with his new wife, Maryann. Betty earlier had left him.

In Spokane, Tipton became a successful agent, continued to play music at night locally, and maintained his masculinity by peppering his act with antigay slurs and by avoiding Spokane's gay nightclub. He and Maryann split when Maryann discovered he was having an affair with a stripper named Kitty Kelly, "The Irish Venus."

Tipton and Kitty Kelly were married with a forged marriage license in 1962, and they adopted three sons. At Kitty's insistence, the couple never had sex, but she reported later that the marriage was a good one until pressures resulting from raising teenage boys and Tipton's reduced earnings resulted in the couple's separation in 1980. Slowed down by age and arthritis, Tipton lived out the rest of his years in a mobile home with his youngest son.

Significance

Billy Tipton's name lives on not only in biographies, plays, operas, and novels but also in the Billy Tipton Memorial Saxophone Quartet. Featuring five female jazz artists who blend jazz, punk, funk, and world music, the group issued four albums before reconfiguring itself into the Tiptons in 2003 but retaining its identity as an all-female saxophone quartet.

Scholar Marjorie Garber suggests that the only thing remarkable about the Billy Tipton story is "that it caught the fancy of the media and the public," noting that history contains scores of accounts of lifelong cross-dressers whose gender at birth was "discovered" only at their deaths. Garber rejects various versions of the "progress narrative" theory of transvestism, which argues that Tipton (and other cross-dressers) lived as a man to secure employment, succeed in a patriarchal world, or realize or fulfill some deep-seated personal goal, such as, in Tipton's case, becoming a jazz musician. Arguments against the progress narrative point out that Tipton abandoned his professional music career in 1958 at the age of forty-four; opponents to the theory have asked an important question: Why, then, after his career had ended, would it be essential for Tipton to continue to live as a man (publicly and privately), to marry a woman, and to raise his adoptive sons to know him as "dad," if he did not *self-identify* as a man in the first place?

The progress narrative also does not account for sexuality. If Tipton and Non Earl Harrell, a woman-born-woman, had sex, then they had *lesbian* sex because they were both women; Tipton, although he dressed as a man, lived as a female musician at this time. Tipton and his other wives and girlfriends, however, were not "technically" in lesbian relationships because the women reportedly thought they were making love to a man. As playwright David Henry Hwang suggests in his opera *M. Butterfly*, "Happiness is so rare that our mind can turn somersaults to protect it." Billy Tipton's life is testimony not only to the power of the performance of gender but also to the personal desire to live the gender (and sexuality) of one's choice.

—*Bud Coleman*

FURTHER READING

Brubach, Holly. "Swing Time." Review of *Suits Me: The Double Life of Billy Tipton* (1998) by Diane Wood Middlebrook. *The New York Times Book Review*, June 28, 1998, p. 7, 9.

Bullough, Vern L., and Bonnie Bullough. *Cross Dressing, Sex, and Gender*. Philadelphia: University of Pennsylvania Press, 1993.

Garber, Marjorie. *Vested Interests: Cross-Dressing and Cultural Anxiety*. New York: Routledge, 1992.

Hadleigh, Boze. *Sing Out! Gays and Lesbians in the Music World*. New York: Barricade Books, 1997.

Halberstam, Judith. "Telling Tales: Brandon Teena, Billy Tipton, and Transgender Biography." In *Passing: Identity and Interpretation in Sexuality, Race, and Religion*, edited by Maria Carla Sanchez and Linda Schlossberg. New York: New York University Press, 2001.

Hwang, David Henry. *M. Butterfly*. New York: New American Library, 1988.

Kay, Jackie. *Trumpet*. New York: Pantheon, 1999.

Middlebrook, Diane Wood. *Suits Me: The Double Life of Billy Tipton*. New York: Houghton Mifflin, 1998.

Smith, Cinitia. "One False Note in a Musician's Life." *The New York Times*, June 2, 1998, p. B1, B4.

SEE ALSO: Jan.-June, 1886: Two-Spirit American Indian Visits Washington, D.C.; 1912-1924: Robles Fights in the Mexican Revolution; Sept. 24, 1951: George Jorgensen Becomes Christine Jorgensen; Dec. 24, 1993-Dec. 31, 1993: Transgender Man Brandon Teena Raped and Murdered; June 17, 1995: International Bill of Gender Rights Is First Circulated; 1996: Hart Recognized as a Transgender Man; 1998: Transgender Scholarship Proliferates; Mar. 21, 2000: Hollywood Awards Transgender Portrayals in Film; 2002: Sylvia Rivera Law Project Is Founded; Apr. 30, 2002: Transgender Rights Added to New York City Law; Feb. 21, 2003: Australian Court Validates Transsexual Marriage; May 17, 2004: Transsexual Athletes Allowed to Compete in Olympic Games; Apr. 4, 2005: United Kingdom's Gender Recognition Act Legalizes Transsexual Marriage.

May 1, 1989
U.S. SUPREME COURT RULES GENDER-ROLE STEREOTYPING IS DISCRIMINATORY

The U.S. Supreme Court affirmed that the prohibition in Title VII of the Civil Rights Act of 1964 against discrimination "because of" sex, or gender, extended to discrimination based on gender-role stereotypes. The decision has been interpreted by scholars and others as extendable to the rights of lesbians and gays as well because sexuality and sexual expression are kinds of gender-role stereotypes.

ALSO KNOWN AS: *Price Waterhouse v. Hopkins*
LOCALE: Washington, D.C.
CATEGORIES: Laws, acts, and legal history; civil rights; transgender/transsexuality

KEY FIGURE
Ann B. Hopkins (b. 1943), original plaintiff in the case

SUMMARY OF EVENT
Ann B. Hopkins joined the accounting firm of Price Waterhouse in 1978. After a successful tenure as senior manager in its office of government services, Hopkins was nominated for partnership in 1982. Her nomination was placed on hold in 1983, however, and she was later informed that her candidacy would not be renewed in the next cycle. She resigned from the firm on January 17, 1984, and subsequently filed suit for discrimination.

The legal fight, known as *Price Waterhouse v. Hopkins* (1989), began with the first trial in federal district court in 1985 and was not concluded until a second appeal to the Circuit Court of Appeals in Washington, D.C., in 1990. All courts hearing this case, including the U.S. Supreme Court, agreed that Hopkins had been the victim of gender stereotyping. Accounts described her as a brusque, aggressive woman, given at times to coarse language. The primary legal issue focused on whether these characteristics, which would have been tolerated or applauded in a man, were viewed negatively because Hopkins is a woman. The firm objected to the foul language not because it was foul but "because it's a lady using foul language." Hopkins was advised "to take 'a course at charm school'" and to "walk more femininely, talk more femininely, dress more femininely, wear makeup, have her hair styled, and wear jewelry."

Because Price Waterhouse's rejection of Hopkins "stemmed from an impermissibly cabined view of proper behavior of women," it had violated the prohibition in Title VII of the Civil Rights Act of 1964 against discrimination because of sex (or gender). The legal challenges to this finding related not to the extension of gender discrimination to include gender-role stereotypes but to more arcane legal details, such as the proper burdens of proof. If Price Waterhouse could show by a preponderance of the evidence that it would have made the same partnership decisions about Hopkins even absent the biased evaluations, she would not have been entitled to relief.

Finding that Price Waterhouse failed to make this showing, the federal courts ultimately ordered the firm to make Hopkins a partner, with retroactive benefits to the date of July 1, 1983, the date she would have become a partner had she not been discriminated against. In addition, she received $371,175 in back pay and interest, as well as attorney fees. This loophole for employers who discriminated was closed in 1991 by a congressional amendment to the act. Under the new law, a violation occurs whenever a prohibited consideration motivates an employment decision, regardless of the presence of permissible considerations.

SIGNIFICANCE
The *Price Waterhouse* case is best known for its extension of "sex" (gender) in Title VII employment cases to include gender-role stereotypes. This out-

come was surprisingly uncontroversial in the opinions. As the Supreme Court said, "in forbidding employers to discriminate against individuals because of their sex, Congress intended to strike at the entire spectrum of disparate treatment of men and women resulting from sex stereotypes."

This holding has, however, been invoked in ways that Congress surely did not intend. On one hand, Title VII has repeatedly been held not to extend employment protections to gays and lesbians. It is for this reason that the Employment Non-Discrimination Act (ENDA) is considered to be a high priority by advocacy groups such as the Human Rights Campaign (HRC). On the other hand, requiring males to be sexually attracted to females, and vice versa, arguably represents another sex/gender stereotype, or assumption. Under that argument, gays and lesbians are already protected under Title VII through the cumulative holdings of *Price Waterhouse* and other Supreme Court opinions, such as *Oncale v. Sundowner* (1998). Decisions suggesting this possibility include the following:

Heller v. Columbia Edgewater Country Club (2002), which denied summary judgment where a lesbian employee had sued her employer. The employer had allegedly discharged the woman because she did not conform to her supervisor's notions of how a woman ought to behave.

Nicolas v. Azteca Restaurant Enterprises, Inc. (2001), involving abuse of a male restaurant employee by his male workmates, including references to him as "she" and "her" and insults because he did not have sexual intercourse with a female friend. These actions were, for purposes of Title VII, "because of sex" because the abuse reflected a belief that the employee did not act as a man was supposed to act.

Rene v. MGM Grand Hotel, Inc. (2002), which held that whether a harasser was motivated by hostility toward an employee's sexual orientation is irrelevant for purposes of a Title VII claim.

This split in approaches toward the advancements of civil rights for gays and lesbians is captured by the debate between Andrew Koppelman and Edward Stein. These legal scholars differ as to whether discrimination against gays and lesbians can be reduced to gender discrimination. Stein asserts that gay and lesbian rights are *sui generis* and that any attempt to equate antigay discrimination with a special case of gender discrimination will lose some of the unique harms gays and lesbians experience. Koppelman argues that gender discrimination arguments for gay and lesbian rights require the least legal innovation to achieve the ultimate goal of full equality for all citizens, and is thus the one most likely to persuade courts.

—*James M. Donovan*

FURTHER READING

Hopkins, Ann Branigar. *So Ordered: Making Partner the Hard Way*. Amherst: University of Massachusetts Press, 1996.

Koppelman, Andrew. "Defending the Sex Discrimination Argument for Lesbian and Gay Rights: A Reply to Edward Stein." *UCLA Law Review* 49 (2001): 519-538.

_____. "Why Discrimination Against Lesbians and Gay Men Is Sex Discrimination." *New York University Law Review* 69 (1994): 197-287.

MacKinnon, Catharine A., and Reva B. Siegal, eds. *Directions in Sexual Harassment Law*. New Haven, Conn.: Yale University Press, 2004.

Stein, Edward. "Evaluating the Sex Discrimination Argument for Lesbian and Gay Rights." *UCLA Law Review* 49 (2001): 471-518.

SEE ALSO: July 3, 1975: U.S. Civil Service Commission Prohibits Discrimination Against Federal Employees; 1978: Lesbian and Gay Workplace Movement Is Founded; 1982-1991: Lesbian Academic and Activist Sues University of California for Discrimination; Sept. 21, 1993-Apr. 21, 1995: Lesbian Mother Loses Custody of Her Child; 1994: Employment Non-Discrimination Act Is Proposed to U.S. Congress; June 28, 2000: *Boy Scouts of America v. Dale*; June 26, 2003: U.S. Supreme Court Overturns Texas Sodomy Law.

May 3, 1989
Watkins v. United States Army Reinstates Gay Soldier

In the final ruling of a seven-year legal battle, a federal court of appeals ordered the reinstatement of U.S. Army sergeant Perry Watkins, who had been dismissed from the military because of his sexual orientation.

Locale: San Francisco, California
Categories: Military; laws, acts, and legal history; civil rights

Key Figures
Perry Watkins (1949-1996), U.S. Army sergeant and later drag entertainer
Harry Pregerson, judge, U.S. Court of Appeals
William Norris, judge, U.S. Court of Appeals

Summary of Event

When Perry Watkins, an African American, was drafted in 1967, he replied "yes" on a questionnaire that asked enlistees if they were gay or if they had same-gender sexual attractions. Despite the U.S. Army's long-standing policy of excluding homosexuals and bisexuals, Watkins was admitted as a soldier. The next year, when he was investigated for engaging in prohibited homosexual conduct, he admitted in an affidavit that the allegations were true. The Army, nevertheless, dropped the investigation because of insufficient evidence.

In 1975, a board of officers, with full knowledge that Watkins was gay, recommended his retention. His associates testified that his sexuality had neither created problems nor interfered with his duties. In 1979, because of his earlier admission of homosexual conduct, an Army board revoked his security clearance, but later that same year the Army accepted him for another three-year enlistment. His evaluations indicated that his service had consistently been exemplary in every way.

In 1981, after the election of Ronald Reagan as U.S. president, the Army issued a new and stricter regulation mandating the discharge of all homosexuals regardless of their merit. Pursuant to this stern directive, an Army board recommended discharging Watkins, but then a district judge prohibited the discharge on the basis that it would constitute double jeopardy. The judge reasoned that the charges against Watkins in 1981 were the same as those in 1975.

In 1982, Watkins was refused reenlistment in the Army because "of his self-admitted homosexuality as well as homosexual acts." Later that year, a district court admonished the Army for refusing to re-enlist him. The court based its ruling on the legal doctrine of equitable estoppel, which means that the Army's unfair conduct precluded the service from asserting a right that it otherwise would have had (illustrating the maxim, "he who seeks equity, must do equity"). When appealed in *Watkins v. United States Army I* (1983), however, a panel of the court of appeals overruled the district court's injunction. The case was then remanded to the district court, which ruled explicitly that the Army regulations did not violate the U.S. Constitution.

The new ruling allowed for another appeal. In *Watkins v. United States Army II* (1988), a panel of the court of appeals reversed the ruling and held that the Army's reenlistment regulations violated the equal protection clause of the Fourteenth Amendment to the U.S. Constitution. At the Army's request, the court of appeals agreed to grant a full court review of the issues of the case. The American Civil Liberties Union and the American Psychological Association submitted friend-of-the-court briefs, which argued in favor of upholding the panel's ruling of 1988.

In *Watkins v. United States Army III* (1989), the majority of the justices ignored the 1988 ruling and upheld the 1982 judgment of the district court, which equitably estopped (barred) the Army from refusing to enlist Watkins. Speaking for the majority, Judge Harry Pregerson declared that the Army's unfairness in the matter constituted "affirmative misconduct." During the fourteen years of Watkins's career, Pregerson argued, the Army had given Watkins

> **WATKINS V. UNITED STATES ARMY III**
>
> *Pregerson, Circuit Judge:* The United States Army denied Sgt. Perry J. Watkins reenlistment solely because he is a homosexual. The Army refused to reenlist Watkins, a 14-year veteran, even though he had been completely candid about his homosexuality from the start of his Army career, even though he is in all respects an outstanding soldier, and even though the Army, with full knowledge of his homosexuality, had repeatedly permitted him to reenlist in the past. The Army did so despite its long-standing policy that homosexuality was a nonwaivable disqualification for reenlistment.
>
> The issue before the en banc court is whether the Army may deny reenlistment to Watkins solely because of his acknowledged homosexuality. . . .
>
> *Conclusion*
>
> This is a case where equity cries out and demands that the Army be estopped from refusing to reenlist Watkins on the basis of his homosexuality. We therefore reinstate the district court's October 5, 1982 Order estopping the Army from relying on its reenlistment regulation as a bar to Sgt. Watkins' reenlistment. . . .
>
> *Norris, Circuit Judge, concurring in the judgment:* I concur in the judgment requiring the Army to reconsider Sgt. Watkins' reenlistment application without regard to his homosexuality. I cannot join the majority's opinion, however, because I agree with the dissent that the judgment cannot rest on the doctrine of equitable estoppel. The Supreme Court has declined to approve the invocation of equitable estoppel against the government even in cases where the facts are no less sympathetic than the facts in Sgt. Watkins' case. . . .
>
> In my view, Watkins is entitled to relief because the Army denied him the equal protection of the laws by discharging and refusing to reenlist him solely on the basis of his homosexuality.

incorrect information about his right to reenlist in eight administrative reviews. After having overlooked the reenlistment regulations so often, "equity cries out and demands" that the Army be stopped from barring Watkins from continuing his career. Four judges dissented from the ruling and voted in favor of the Army's position.

The majority found that it was not necessary to address the constitutional question. Two concurring members of the court, however, would have preferred to decide the case on the basis of the principle of equal protection. Judge William Norris wrote an especially strong opinion, which argued that the Army's ban on homosexuality was unconstitutional because it discriminated "against homosexuals on the basis of their sexual orientation."

President George H. W. Bush attempted to have *Watkins v. United States Army III* reversed, but the U.S. Supreme Court declined to review the decision, which meant that it stood. As soon as Watkins was reinstated, he then retired from the Army with retroactive pay, full retirement benefits, and an honorable discharge. Watkins became a popular female impersonator under the drag name of "Simone." He died in Tacoma, Washington, of AIDS-related complications in 1996. His life was explored in the documentary *The Perry Watkins Story*, which appeared in 1997.

Significance

Because *Watkins v. United States Army III* was based on the narrow issue of equitable estoppel, the case did not challenge the Army's general ban on gays and lesbians, and, consequently, it did not have far-reaching affects. Judge Norris's concurring opinion, however, based squarely on the equal protection principle, would have had great ramifications, for it would have prohibited the armed forces from promulgating the Don't Ask, Don't Tell policy. Although not binding, such opinions often influence public opinion as well as the thinking of other judges.

Even with the case's limited impact, the story of Perry Watkins served to put a human face on the struggle of gays and lesbians wishing to be part of the U.S. armed forces. A courageous man who refused to lie about his identity, Watkins performed his duties with distinction while risking his career for the cause of promoting gay and lesbian rights in the military.

—*Thomas Tandy Lewis*

Further Reading

Belkin, Aaron, and Geoffrey Batteman. *Don't Ask, Don't Tell: Debating the Gay Ban in the Military*. Boulder, Colo.: Lynne Rienner, 2003.

Dyer, Kate. *Gays in Uniform: The Pentagon Secret Report*. Boston: Alyson, 1990.

Lehring, Gary. *Officially Gay: The Political Construction of Sexuality in the U.S. Military*. Philadelphia: Temple University Press, 2003.

Rimmermann, Craig. *Gay Rights, Military Wrongs: Political Perspectives on Lesbians and Gays in the Military*. New York: Taylor & Francis, 1996.

Shawver, Lois. *And the Flag Was Still There: Straight People, Gay People, and Sexuality in the U.S. Military*. Binghamton, N.Y.: Haworth Press, 1995.

Shilts, Randy. *Conduct Unbecoming: Gays and Lesbians in the U.S. Military*. 1994. New ed. New York: St. Martin's Griffin, 2005.

See also: 1912-1924: Robles Fights in the Mexican Revolution; Mar. 15, 1919-1921: U.S. Navy Launches Sting Operation Against "Sexual Perverts"; July 3, 1975: U.S. Civil Service Commission Prohibits Discrimination Against Federal Employees; 1976-1990: Army Reservist Ben-Shalom Sues for Reinstatement; May-Aug., 1980: U.S. Navy Investigates the USS *Norton Sound* in Antilesbian Witch Hunt; 1990, 1994: *Coming Out Under Fire* Documents Gay and Lesbian Military Veterans; Aug. 27, 1991: *The Advocate* Outs Pentagon Spokesman Pete Williams; Oct., 1992: Canadian Military Lifts Its Ban on Gays and Lesbians; Nov. 30, 1993: Don't Ask, Don't Tell Policy Is Implemented; Jan. 12, 2000: United Kingdom Lifts Ban on Gays and Lesbians in the Military.

June 2, 1989
Lambda Literary Award Is Created

The Lambda Literary Award was created to fill the gap left by mainstream publishers who did not recognize writing by, for, and about lesbians, gays, bisexuals, and transgender persons. The award, also called the "Lammy," stimulated the development and maturation of creative talent in all genres of GLBT writing.

Locale: Washington, D.C.
Categories: Literature; publications; organizations and institutions

Key Figures

Deacon Maccubbin, owner of Lambda Rising bookstore and creator of the award
Edmund White (b. 1940), writer who gave the first awards' lecture
Jewelle Gomez (b. 1948), poet and keynote speaker at the first ceremony
Armistead Maupin (b. 1944), author of the *Tales of the City* series and emcee of the first ceremony

Summary of Event

The first annual Lambda Literary Award banquet, sponsored by the periodical *Lambda Book Report*, was timed to coincide with the convention of the American Booksellers Association. The ceremony, held on June 2, 1989, at the Hyatt Regency Hotel on Capitol Hill in Washington, D.C., marked the beginning of the first formal recognition extended exclusively to writing by GLBT authors in a ceremony by the publishing industry. The awards have served as a stimulus to the growth of all components of this literary genre since that time.

Not surprisingly, the idea for the award, soon to be known as the "Lammy," originated in one of the oldest GLBT bookstores in the United States, Lambda Rising in Washington, D.C., founded in 1974, and its bimonthly trade journal, the *Lambda Book Report*. In 1987, store owner Deacon Maccubbin and two of his staff members had discussed the absence of works by exclusively GLBT authors from the then-extant array of literature awards.

An announcement of the proposed new award and calls for nominations for the competition in twelve categories was sent through notices in the *Lambda Book Report*, which at the time had been widely distributed as an insert in local GLBT newspapers and through private subscriptions. Fifty-three recommended works issued by thirty-one publishers in the classes of GLBT nonfiction, fiction, small presses, poetry, first novels, mystery and science fiction, and AIDS-related works, by fifty-eight different authors published in 1988, were nominated. The work of some individuals, such as Betty Berzon, Allan Hollinghurst, Karen Thompson, Judy Grahn, and Michael Nava, was submitted under more than one category.

During the ceremony, author Edmund White delivered the first Bill Whitehead Lecture, named for the editor who assisted White and many other LGBT authors in placing their work with mainstream publishing houses. The lecture was awarded by the Publishing Triangle, founded in 1988 as a caucus of lesbians and gays working in the publishing industry. White called upon the writers' community to continue "the recording of our remarkable differences."

The event was emceed by writer Armistead Maupin, creator of the popular *Tales of the City* series. Especially memorable was the keynote address by poet Jewelle Gomez, who sharply criticized gay and lesbian writers for going to major houses seeking what she termed "mainstream heterosexual acceptance." She admonished the audience to "stay tough when the going gets soft."

Given their multiple nominations, the winning of six of the twelve awards by Michael Nava, Dorothy Alison, and Paul Monette was exciting if not totally surprising. Monette's personal volume *Borrowed Time: An AIDS Memoir* took both the AIDS and gay men's nonfiction categories. The poetry award went to the collection *Gay and Lesbian Poetry in Our Time*, while the editor's award was presented by Jane Troxelll to *Why Can't Sharon Kowalski Come Home?*

The publisher's service award went to Sasha Alyson of Alyson Publications, both for his decade-long support of LGBT literature and for his coordination of the project that produced the free book *You Can Do Something About AIDS*. Less-familiar award recipients included Antoinette Azolakov for her lesbian mystery novel *Skiptrace*, Sarah Lucia Hoagland for the nonfiction work *Lesbian Ethics*, and Madelyn Arnold for *Bird-Eyes*, the winner as a lesbian first novel.

Significance

The creation of the Lambda Literary Award, although not the first award for GLBT writing, was the first to address *specifically* a rapidly diversifying genre of GLBT writing in all its forms. It provided a forum for publicizing new works and emerging creative talents. In 1989, the categories of humor, children's and young adult books, and anthologies were added. What distinguishes the Lambda Award from the award of the American Library Association's Gay, Lesbian, Bisexual, and Transgendered Round Table, inaugurated in 1970, is the Lambda's broad framework in determining recipients. The award categories are far more specific than those of the American Library Association.

On May 1, 1996, the Lambda Literary Foundation was incorporated in Washington, D.C., as a national organization dedicated to promoting the cause of GLBT literature and recognizing new writers. The foundation had managed the Lambda Book Award and ceremony, published the *Lambda Book Report* and the *James White Review*, and presented the Lambda Literary Festival, an annual writer's conference, until it ended operations in 2005. The foundation has been embroiled in a controversy after it selected for an award a book on male to female (MTF) transsexuality that had been denounced by transgender and transsexual activists and others for its problematic portrayals of MTF individuals and for its "junk science."

—*Robert Ridinger*

Further Reading

Sullivan, Mark. "Alison, Monette, Nava Take Home Double 'Lammys.'" *Washington Blade*, June 9, 1989, 23, 29.

_____. "Presenting the 'Lammys.'" *Washington Blade*, May 26, 1989, 23, 25.

Weeks, Linton. "Bookseller's Success Speaks Volumes: Lambda Rising Owner Helped Bring Gay Literature Out of the Closet." *The Washington Post*, April, 2003, p. C1.

SEE ALSO: July 4, 1855: Whitman Publishes *Leaves of Grass*; May 25, 1895: Oscar Wilde Is Convicted of Gross Indecency; 1924: Gide Publishes the Signed Edition of *Corydon*; 1939: Isherwood Publishes *Goodbye to Berlin*; 1947-1948: Golden Age of American Gay Literature; 1956: Baldwin Publishes *Giovanni's Room*; 1963: Rechy Publishes *City of Night*; June, 1971: The Gay Book Award Debuts; 1974: *The Front Runner* Makes *The New York Times* Best-Seller List; 1975: First Novel About Coming Out to Parents Is Published; 1980: Alyson Begins Publishing Gay and Lesbian Books; 1980-1981: Gay Writers Form the Violet Quill; May, 1987: *Lambda Rising Book Report* Begins Publication; 1993: Monette Wins the National Book Award for *Becoming a Man*.

December 10, 1989
ACT UP PROTESTS AT ST. PATRICK'S CATHEDRAL

More than five thousand activists held a massive protest called Stop the Church at St. Patrick's Cathedral in New York City, rallying against the Roman Catholic Church interfering in public policy on abortion, same-gender sexuality, and HIV-AIDS. The action did not lead to reform within the Church but it helped place ACT UP on the cultural map and likely influenced subsequent public policy.

ALSO KNOWN AS: Stop the Church
LOCALE: New York, New York
CATEGORIES: Marches, protests, and riots; HIV-AIDS; religion; civil rights; government and politics; health and medicine; laws, acts, and legal history; organizations and institutions

KEY FIGURES
Victor Mendolia and
Vincent Gagliostro, Stop the Church organizers
John Joseph O'Connor (1920-2000), archbishop of New York, 1984-2000

SUMMARY OF EVENT
The AIDS Coalition to Unleash Power (ACT UP) was formed in New York City in March of 1987. In less than three years, the group had issued studies, testified at government hearings, and conducted loud, attention-grabbing protests that changed the face of the HIV-AIDS epidemic in the United States. The action known as Stop the Church, however, even before it began, was considered the group's most controversial protest yet.

ACT UP was taking on the powerful and influential Roman Catholic Archdiocese of New York City. There were myriad reasons why the Church was being targeted. Even before the HIV-AIDS epidemic emerged, Scripture had been used by the Church to justify generations of hatred and violence against gays and lesbians. Since the early 1970's, the New York Archdiocese had been consistently vocal in its public opposition to lesbian and gay rights, often sending representatives to city hall to oppose a city GLBT rights bill.

When the HIV-AIDS epidemic began to affect the residents of New York City, the Church offered two faces to the public. One welcomed HIV-positive people and those with AIDS into its Church-sponsored hospitals and hospices. Much had been made of Cardinal John Joseph O'Connor, emptying the bedpans of people with AIDS. At the same time, however, the Church devised several roadblocks in the fight against the epidemic. First, Church factions insisted that AIDS was God's retribution against homosexuality (despite the medical fact that millions of heterosexual Africans were also infected at this time in the epidemic's history). Second, Church officials lobbied against frank sex education about HIV-AIDS in public schools, insisting that abstinence be the only focus. Third, Church officials lobbied against condom distribution in schools and against clean needle exchange for intravenous-drug users. The Church continued to condemn homosexuality, even as the sheer reality of the large number of deaths from the epidemic turned public opinion in favor of gays. For example, a Vatican encyclical (1986) written by then-Cardinal Joseph Ratzinger (now Pope Benedict XVI), concerning the pastoral care of gay people, called homosexuality, "an intrinsic moral evil."

Stop the Church organizers Victor Mendolia and Vincent Gagliostro knew that a demonstration against so formidable a foe would need reinforcements. ACT UP partnered with the New York-based WHAM! (Women's Health Action and Mobilization), a group that opposed the Roman Catholic Church for its ongoing opposition to public contraception, sex education in schools, and legal access to an abortion. Cardinal O'Connor had stated his support of Operation Rescue, a Radical Right, Christian group that, among other actions, blocked the entrances to reproductive health clinics, where abortions were performed. Members of several other AIDS, GLBT, and pro-choice groups pledged support and promised to participate.

Stop the Church was months in the planning. ACT UP held several orientation sessions to explain the many issues that motivated this protest, since there was dissent even among the ranks about taking on the Church. ACT UP's media committee sent out several press releases and other communications to journalists in the weeks leading up the protest, explaining its complex issues and providing facts and figures to support the protester's arguments.

The demonstration began on December 10 at 9:30 A.M., so that it would coincide with St. Patrick's Cathedral's Sunday morning Mass. A protest fact sheet distributed to passersby read, "Stop Church Interference in Our Lives/Cardinal O'Connor has eagerly stepped into the political arena breaking the barrier separating Church and State! December 10th we bring our anger to his doorstep!" More than five thousand activists were present, many holding protest signs, as scores of police officers controlled the area with barricades.

One group of ACT UP protesters, acting under their own volition as "an affinity group," entered St. Patrick's and interrupted the mass by loudly voicing ACT UP's objections. Some chained themselves to the pews, while others lay down in the aisles. Television cameras inside the cathedral that morning documented the chaos and beamed to the world the image of Cardinal O'Connor sitting in his chair, one hand covering his head. One ACT UP member, a former altar boy named Tom Keane, accepted a wafer during Communion but crumbled it, saying, "Withholding safe sex education is murder." The demonstration lasted more than three hours, and 111 people were arrested, 43 of whom were inside the cathedral.

SIGNIFICANCE

The disruption inside the cathedral commanded even more media attention following the protest, but the media swept aside ACT UP's messages about why they were protesting the Roman Catholic Church and why they had rallied at St. Patrick's Cathedral. Using religious jargon, media reported that the cathedral had been "desecrated" by activists. In the days that followed, numerous GLBT and AIDS groups, seeking to distance themselves from ACT UP, issued critical statements about the demonstration.

In the meantime, media interest did not wane; ACT UP was contacted by journalists from around the world. In the face of mounting censure from local politicians and religious leaders, ACT UP and WHAM! held an emergency press conference two days later in Manhattan. Before cameras and a standing-room-only crowd of reporters, activists reiterated why they demonstrated and made no apology for the controversial action inside the cathedral. Protest coorganizer Gagliostro said, "I don't care if people are offended. People [with AIDS] are dying."

However, the protest caused rancor among ACT UP members: Some were proud of the actions, and others felt the group had gone too far with the "secret" protest inside. However members felt about it, the protest put ACT UP on the international map. Talk-show host Phil Donahue subsequently asked ACT UP members to appear on his show. Even *The New York Times*, long criticized by ACT UP for its uneven HIV-AIDS reportage, ran a feature story on January 3, 1990, by Jason DeParle, "Rash, Rude, and Effective, Act-Up Helps Change AIDS Policy." The feature was a powerful public vindication of the beleaguered organization.

If numbers are any indication, the landmark protest at St. Patrick's made ACT UP the most visible activist organization in the city. Weekly meetings, which typically drew between two hundred and three hundred people, soon swelled to nearly one thousand and had to move from New York's GLBT community center to Cooper Union, across town. For months afterward, police officers would patrol St. Patrick's during Sunday Mass. Years later, however, one would be hard-pressed to find any Catholic Church policy reform stemming directly from the controversial demonstration, but Stop the Church made ACT UP a force to be reckoned with in the fight against AIDS, government indifference, and religious condemnation.

—*Jay Blotcher*

Further Reading

Crimp, Douglas. *Melancholia and Moralism: Essays on AIDS and Queer Politics*. Cambridge, Mass.: MIT Press, 2002.

Crimp, Douglas, with Adam Rolston. *AIDS Demo Graphics*. Seattle, Wash.: Bay Press, 1990.

Edwards, Jeffrey. "AIDS, Race, and the Rise and Decline of a Militant Oppositional Lesbian and Gay Politics in the U.S." *New Political Science* 22 (2000): 485-506.

Kramer, Larry. *Reports from the Holocaust: The Making of an AIDS Activist*. New York: St. Martin's Press, 1989.

Shepard, Benjamin, and Ronald Hayduk. *From ACT UP to the WTO: Urban Protest and Community Building in the Era of Globalization*. New York: Verso, 2002.

Smith, Raymond A., ed. *Encyclopedia of AIDS: A Social, Political, Cultural, and Scientific Record of the HIV Epidemic*. New York: Penguin Books, 2001.

Stockdill, Brett. *Activism Against AIDS: At the Intersections of Sexuality, Race, Gender, and Class*. Boulder, Colo.: Lynne Rienner, 2003.

See also: Aug., 1966: Queer Youth Fight Police Harassment at Compton's Cafeteria in San Francisco; June 27-July 2, 1969: Stonewall Rebellion Ignites Modern Gay and Lesbian Rights Movement; July 31, 1969: Gay Liberation Front Is Formed; June 28, 1970: First Lesbian and Gay Pride March in the United States; Oct. 12-15, 1979: First March on Washington for Lesbian and Gay Rights; Mar., 1987: Radical AIDS Activist Group ACT UP Is Founded; 1989: Act Up Paris Is Founded; Mar. 20, 1990: Queer Nation Is Founded; Apr. 24, 1993: First Dyke March Is Held in Washington, D.C.; Nov. 29, 2005: Roman Catholic Church Bans Gay Seminarians.

1990
INTERNATIONAL GAY AND LESBIAN HUMAN RIGHTS COMMISSION IS FOUNDED

Through advocacy, documentation, coalition building, public education, and technical assistance, the International Gay and Lesbian Human Rights Commission has worked to secure and protect the rights and safety of people across the world who are abused or discriminated against because of their sexual orientation, gender identity, or HIV-AIDS status.

LOCALE: San Francisco, California; Moscow, U.S.S.R. (now Russia)
CATEGORIES: Organizations and institutions; civil rights; laws, acts, and legal history

KEY FIGURES
Julie Dorf, commission cofounder and first executive director
Roman Kalinin, Russian activist and commission cofounder

SUMMARY OF EVENT
Activists in the United States and the Soviet Union (now Russia) founded the International Gay and Lesbian Human Rights Commission (IGLHRC) in 1990, a nonprofit and nongovernmental organization (NGO). Julie Dorf, the commission's cofounder and first executive director, conceived the idea for the commission while doing academic research in what was then the USSR. Dorf interviewed men imprisoned under the now-repealed Article 121, an antisodomy law in Russia that carried a penalty of five years in prison.

At the time of the founding of IGLHRC, the gay and lesbian rights movement in the former USSR was in its infancy. Roman Kalinin was a Russian activist who helped found the Moscow Union of Gays and Lesbians and who published *Tema*, the first gay and lesbian newspaper in the USSR. The KGB (the Soviet secret service) routinely harassed Kalinin, breaking into his house, stealing documents with the names of other gays and lesbians, interrogating him, and even informing his parents of his sexuality.

IGLHRC worked initially to repeal Article 121 (which was eventually abolished in 1993) and the antisodomy laws in twenty-five U.S. states and the District of Columbia. Addressing the violent threat experienced by gays and lesbians around the world would become the commission's main focus. In 1991, IGLHRC organized the first-ever delegation to the USSR, complete with conferences, demonstrations, and a film festival. IGLHRC now works in places where support is lacking; therefore, it works outside the United States, Canada, and Western Europe as well. The commission works in partnership with groups around the world, including the Americas, Africa, the Middle East, and Asia, to document human rights abuses and advocate for social change.

IGLHRC's programs can be broken into three categories. The first is its "emergency response" program, which documents and responds to human rights violations on the basis of sexual orientation, gender identity, and HIV-AIDS status, and provides assistance to those seeking asylum. The second program covers "human rights education," in which the commission trains and provides technical assistance to its international partners. The third program is called "linking human rights and social movements," in which IGLHRC promotes the adoption and development of "sexual rights as human rights" frameworks in communities around the world. The IGLHRC presses government officials, international organizations, and the mainstream media to accept that sexual and gender identity rights are basic human rights.

SIGNIFICANCE
The reach of the International Gay and Lesbian Human Rights Commission is far and wide, as it intends. In addition to protecting lesbians, gays, bisexuals, transgender individuals, and those who are

HIV-positive or who have AIDS, the commission helps to monitor abuse and discrimination against sexual minorities. The commission, for example, cosponsored the International Tribunal on Human Rights Violations Against Sexual Minorities, a group of international human rights experts who called on the United Nations (U.N.) to designate a special investigator to monitor human rights violations based on sexual and gender orientation.

IGLHRC also attended the U.N. Fourth World Conference on Women in Beijing, China, in 1995 to pressure organizers to address issues of concern to lesbian and bisexual women. By staging a direct action within the weeklong conference, the commission hoped to have "sexual orientation" mentioned in the government delegates' 147-page Platform for Action, which spelled out the delegations' priorities for women into the twenty-first century. Unfortunately, after an all-night deliberation session, the phrase did not make it into the document's antidiscrimination clause. Nonetheless, IGLHRC's continued pressure on the U.N. has been successful in other ways. In 2004, IGLHRC successfully lobbied the U.N. to hear arguments that sexual orientation is a human right that deserves protection.

IGLHRC works with other international human rights organizations as well. Some activists argue that it was IGLHRC's pressure on Amnesty International (A.I.) that spurred A.I. to start addressing sexual and gender orientation as a human rights issue. Others point out that several regional A.I. offices had called for the inclusion of sexual minorities *before* IGLHRC had been formed. In either case, it is clear that IGLHRC has had a large impact on mainstream organizations and public institutions in highlighting human rights violations and pressuring these organizations and government officials to address and act on them.

In 1994, the administration of U.S. president Bill Clinton ordered that U.S. immigration laws allow foreigners persecuted abroad because of their sexuality to receive political asylum in the United States. Gay U.S. representative Barney Frank said he was acting on an appeal from IGLHRC when he requested the order.

Since its founding, IGLHRC has mobilized a worldwide network of activists, politicians, and citizens through e-mail alerts, press releases, and demonstrations. Among its achievements, the commission organized the first gay pride events in the USSR in 1991. The commission also publishes reports detailing human rights abuses around the world. IGLHRC is one of the few organizations taking part in a worldwide coalition to build solidarity and exchange advocacy strategies within international movements that fight against discrimination and abuse on the basis of sexual orientation, gender identity, and HIV-AIDS status. Overall, the IGLHRC has made huge inroads in the fight to secure the full enjoyment of the human rights of all people.

—*Jenn Rosen*

FURTHER READING

International Gay and Lesbian Human Rights Commission. http://www.iglhrc.org/.

International Tribunal on Human Rights Violations Against Sexual Minorities. San Francisco, Calif.: International Gay and Lesbian Human Rights Commission, 1995.

Ridinger, Robert. *Speaking for Our Lives: Historic Speeches and Rhetoric for Gay and Lesbian Rights, 1892-2000*. New York: Harrington Park Press, 2004.

Rosenbloom, Rachel, ed. *Unspoken Rules: Sexual Orientation and Women's Human Rights*. San Francisco, Calif.: International Gay and Lesbian Human Rights Commission, 1995.

Stychin, Carl, and Didi Herman, eds. *Law and Sexuality: The Global Arena*. Minneapolis: University of Minnesota Press, 2001.

Tuller, David, and Dan Levy. "The Movement Gains Strength: Gay Rights on a Worldwide Front." *San Francisco Chronicle*, August 24, 1992, p. A1.

SEE ALSO: Aug. 8, 1978: International Lesbian and Gay Association Is Founded; Dec. 1, 1988: First World AIDS Day; Sept. 16, 1994: U.N. Revokes Consultative Status of International Lesbian and Gay Association; June 17, 1995: International Bill of Gender Rights Is First Circulated; Oct. 9-12, 1998: First International Retreat for Lesbian and Gay Muslims Is Held.

1990
UNITED LESBIANS OF AFRICAN HERITAGE IS FOUNDED

United Lesbians of African Heritage formed in response to a need for an organization dedicated to the visibility, unity, and empowerment of black lesbians.

LOCALE: Los Angeles, California
CATEGORIES: Organizations and institutions; race and ethnicity

KEY FIGURES
Lisa Powell,
Saundra Tignor, and
Yolanda Whittington, cofounders of United Lesbians of African Heritage

SUMMARY OF EVENT

In March of 1989, a group in Los Angeles began to meet regularly with the goal of planning a black lesbian conference. The impetus for the meetings was the lack of women's programming at the National Black Gay & Lesbian Leadership Forum Conference. The early seeds were planted at these meetings for the formation of United Lesbians of African Heritage (ULOAH). Through the following several months, and after many community meetings, it became clear that the black lesbian community needed an organization that could address effectively the broad range of issues that affected the lives of women who were black and lesbian. The early issues and concerns were wide-ranging, from activism to building coalitions to health and wellness, to name just a few. Even in a large metropolitan area such as Los Angeles, there had been no organization dedicated to serving black lesbians.

ULOAH was founded as a nonprofit organization in 1990 by Lisa Powell, Saundra Tignor, and Yolanda Whittington. It is the only organization of its type in Southern California and one of only a few in the United States. ULOAH has a staff of four, including a full-time executive director.

SIGNIFICANCE

ULOAH serves a growing, yet vastly underserved, community of black lesbians and is committed to combating discrimination and prejudice against black lesbians, prejudice and discrimination that comes from stigmas against the intersecting identities of race, gender, and sexual orientation.

The primary goals of ULOAH, whose slogan is "Making the world safe for black lesbians," have been to build self-esteem, to challenge heterosexism and other forms of oppression, and to work for lasting social change through visibility, education, and advocacy. Some of the organization's programs have included "ULOAH University," workshops, speakers, panel discussions, and training sessions designed to increase black lesbian activism and leadership. ULOAH/YES (Young, Empowered Sistahs) is a program that foster leadership among young black lesbians (ages sixteen to twenty-six). Strong Sistahs/Sweet Success is a ULOAH program that aims to decrease obesity and increase physical activity among black lesbians, and ULOAH provides social support to black lesbians ages fifty and older. Furthermore, ULOAH organizes Sistahfest, an annual four-day educational and cultural festival. In keeping with ULOAH's mission, the Family Reunion program focuses on increasing understanding of black LGBT persons within non-LGBT communities and institutions such as churches and schools.

—*Patricia E. Clark*

FURTHER READING

Asanti, Ta'Shia. "The New ULOAH: Black Lesbian Organization Expands Its Vision in 2003." *Lesbian News*, February, 2003, 16.

_____. "ULOAH's Black Lesbian Vagina Dialogues." *Lesbian News*, August, 2001, 30.

Douglas, Kelly Brown. *Sexuality and the Black Church: A Womanist Perspective*. Maryknoll, N.Y.: Orbis Books, 1999.

Johnson, E. Patrick, and Mae G. Henderson, eds. *Black Queer Studies: A Critical Anthology*. Dur-

ham, N.C.: Duke University Press, 2005.
Lorde, Audre. *I Am Your Sister: Black Women Organizing Across Sexualities*. Freedom Organizing Pamphlet Series 3. Latham, N.Y.: Kitchen Table: Women of Color Press, 1985.
Mason-John, Valerie, ed. *Talking Black: Lesbians of African and Asian Descent Speak Out*. New York: Cassell, 1995.
Smith, Rhonda. "To the Front Line." *Washington Blade*, April 20, 2001, 1.

SEE ALSO: Apr., 1977: Combahee River Collective Issues "A Black Feminist Statement"; Oct. 12-15, 1979: First National Third World Lesbian and Gay Conference Convenes; 1981: *This Bridge Called My Back* Is Published; Oct., 1981: Kitchen Table: Women of Color Press Is Founded; 1982: Lorde's Autobiography *Zami* Is Published; Sept., 1983: First National Lesbians of Color Conference Convenes.

1990-1993
ARTISTS SUE THE NATIONAL ENDOWMENT FOR THE ARTS

The National Endowment for the Arts revoked grants to four performance artists, singled out for their sexually explicit and feminist work. The subsequent trial became a universal rallying cry against censorship in the arts in the United States.

ALSO KNOWN AS: *Finley v. National Endowment for the Arts* (1992)
LOCALE: Washington, D.C.
CATEGORIES: Arts; laws, acts, and legal history; government and politics; organizations and institutions; feminism

KEY FIGURES
Karen Finley, feminist performance artist
John Fleck, performance artist
Holly Hughes (b. 1955), feminist performance artist
Tim Miller (b. 1958), performance artist
John E. Frohnmayer, former chair of the National Endowment for the Arts
Jesse Helms (b. 1921), Republican senator, North Carolina

SUMMARY OF EVENT

In 1989, solo performance artists Karen Finley, Holly Hughes, John Fleck, and Tim Miller received grants from the National Endowment for the Arts (NEA). Each artist's work dealt with sexuality; Hughes, Fleck, and Miller focused their work on homosexuality specifically. Videos of their work, however, had been shown to the National Council, a body of presidential appointees who oversee all grants awarded by the NEA. Council members, saying they were shocked by the content of the performances, immediately revoked funding. Their decision was upheld by NEA chair John E. Frohnmayer, who feared that if he did not placate conservatives in Congress and revoke the grants to the four artists, NEA funding would be slashed.

In 1990, Congress, led by the vocal and conservative North Carolina senator Jesse Helms, amended a statute requiring the NEA chairperson to consider "general standards of respect and decency for the diverse beliefs and values of the American public" before awarding grants. In essence, this gave both the NEA and the National Council the authority to deny funds based on what they felt constituted "indecent" art. There were no specific guidelines set forth for what was to be considered indecent; many felt that homosexual content alone was enough to deny funding. The four solo artists, by this time referred to as the NEA 4, sued, claiming that the decency clause violated their First Amendment rights to free speech and was a form of artistic censorship.

The trial set off a firestorm of protest within the

arts community. Arts organizations such as the National Campaign for Freedom of Expression, the Rockefeller Foundation, and the National Association of Artists' Organizations joined with the American Civil Liberties Union in supporting and assisting the performance artists in their lawsuit.

During evidence gathering for the case, the NEA deadline for new grants approached. Numerous artists, as a form of protest, submitted work they felt sure would not be accepted under the decency clause. Unsure how the final court battle would play out, the NEA chose to deny funding to these artists, claiming the applicants' work lacked artistic merit; the artists were rejected, the NEA said, not because of any indecency in their work.

In 1993, the trial judge ruled in favor of the NEA 4, declaring the decency clause was both unconstitutionally vague and overly broad. The artists' grants were reinstated, including court costs. On appeal, the U.S. Court of Appeals for the Ninth Circuit determined as well that the clause was vague and that it violated the First Amendment.

The NEA 4 trial, which had been more than a simple case protesting denied funding, became a universal rallying cry against censorship in the arts. The concept that one could tell good art from bad art when one saw it, as declared by Jesse Helms, was widely debated. In terms of gay and lesbian rights, an important declaration was made that homosexual content in art is not indecent by definition. This declaration, coming at the height of the AIDS epidemic, was a positive step toward the social acceptance of homosexuality.

Unfortunately, the victory was short-lived. Ultimately, the case, now called *National Endowment for the Arts et al. v. Finley et al.* (1998), was appealed to the U.S. Supreme Court, as conservatives fought to maintain criteria that would allow them to deny funding of art they felt was not in the best interest of the American populace. On June 25, 1998, in an 8 to 1 ruling, the Supreme Court upheld the right of the NEA to consider decency standards when awarding art grants. This criteria remains in effect, although it remains broad and vague for the express purpose of allowing subjective assessment of art.

Significance

The court rulings have impacted the lives of the four solo artists. While Finley and Miller have applied for and received NEA grants since the trial, Hughes and Fleck have refused to reapply. All four continue to give presentations about their experiences and the devastating effect governmental censorship can have on art, especially art with GLBT and feminist content and imagery.

In 1992, after personal attacks from both sides of the debate, Frohnmayer stepped down from his post as NEA chair and then worked as an attorney and author. He lectured about the controversy, and much of his writing focuses on the arts and politics.

The NEA, after years of funding cuts and attempts by Republicans to eliminate the endowment altogether, still struggles to administer grant awards. In 2004, solo artists had been receiving a tiny percentage of awards only: Most grants go to large, established organizations and programs focusing on children and minority groups. Visual artists have had to support themselves solely through their work, and midsize and smaller performance companies have had to shut their doors. Funding for work with gay, lesbian, or feminist content has been all but eliminated in lieu of work that reaches "larger" populations.

The NEA 4 case has often been used as a precedent in other cases of arts discrimination. For example, in the late 1990's and the first years of the twenty-first century, the case has been used to force schools and colleges to allow GLBT groups on campus if that school or college allows religious groups on campus.

—*Tom Smith*

Further Reading

Dubin, Steven C. *Arresting Images: Impolite Art and Uncivil Actions*. New York: Routledge, Chapman, and Hall, 1992.

Lassell, Michael. "NEA Four Survive a Year of Uproar." *The Advocate*, December 3, 1991, 76-78.

Meyer, Richard. *Outlaw Representation: Censorship and Homosexuality in Twentieth-Century American Art*. New York: Oxford University Press, 2002.

Wallis, Brian, Marianne Weems, and Philip Yenawine, eds. *Art Matters: How the Culture Wars Changed America.* New York: New York University Press, 1999.

SEE ALSO: May 25, 1895: Oscar Wilde Is Convicted of Gross Indecency; Feb. 19, 1923: *The God of Vengeance* Opens on Broadway; 1929: *Pandora's Box* Opens; Mar. 5, 1974: Antigay and Antilesbian Organizations Begin to Form; Mar. 20, 1988: *M. Butterfly* Opens on Broadway; 1989-1990: Helms Claims Photographs Are Indecent.

1990, 1994
COMING OUT UNDER FIRE DOCUMENTS GAY AND LESBIAN MILITARY VETERANS

Independent filmmakers and scholars uncovered the experiences of gays and lesbians who served in the military during World War II. Allan Bérubé's book Coming Out Under Fire *and Arthur Dong's documentary with the same name told of the lives of gays and lesbians in the military and those labeled sex or psychological perverts by the armed services.*

LOCALE: New York, New York; Los Angeles, California
CATEGORIES: Civil rights; military; laws, acts, and legal history; organizations and institutions; arts

KEY FIGURES
Allan Bérubé, American researcher and author
Arthur Dong (b. 1953), independent documentary filmmaker
Phyllis Abry (1920-1993), veteran radio technician, U.S. Women's Army Corps, World War II
Marvin Liebman (1923-1997), special services veteran, U.S. Army Air Corps, World War II, and conservative author
Tom Reddy, special services veteran, U.S. Marine Corps, World War II

SUMMARY OF EVENT
In his book *Coming Out Under Fire: The History of Gay Men and Women in World War Two* (1990), Allan Bérubé detailed the lives of forgotten lesbians and gays who served in World War II. *Coming Out Under Fire* was one of the first works to explore and document the history of pre-Stonewall gays and lesbians in the United States, tying their sacrifices to the lives of all Americans and allies during World War II. Bérubé's book highlights stories from interviews, letters, and diaries, and brings to light previously declassified military documents.

Arthur Dong adapted Bérubé's material for his documentary *Coming Out Under Fire* (1994) just after the Don't Ask, Don't Tell policy was adopted by the U.S. military in 1993. Beginning during World War II, lesbians and gays were labeled and discharged as sex perverts. This policy was made more stringent during the McCarthy era after the war. Don't Ask, Don't Tell was meant to lessen these strictures, but in practice, it has resulted in the discharge of more lesbians, gays, and bisexuals (as well as those presumed to be so) from the military, with a loss of benefits and, at times, with a liability to pay back the government for the costs involved in their training.

Dong's film uses archival documentary footage and interviews with nine lesbian and gay World War II veterans from many backgrounds who served in a wide variety of military positions. The World War II era, for example, was a time when soldiers could be accused of psychological perversions for writing campy letters in the style of short-story

ALLAN BÉRUBÉ

At the height of civil unrest in 1968, Allan Bérubé was attending the University of Chicago. Following roommate Roy Guttman's death in a racial incident, he left the university and the city. He set out on a personal journey of discovery and coming out. He would settle in San Francisco's counterculture Haight-Ashbury district in 1974.

Jonathan Ned Katz's *Gay American History* inspired Bérubé's writing career. At the time, little had been written about gay U.S. history. What materials did exist either were covered up, censored, or destroyed. Bérubé joined other like-minded historians and helped establish the San Francisco Lesbian and Gay History Project.

A friend of Bérubé discovered a box with hundreds of letters exchanged among gay Missouri soldiers. The letters captured his heart. Over the next decade Bérubé devoted most of his time to sharing the undocumented history of gay and lesbian soldiers in World War II. He subsidized his endeavor producing a slide show on gay and lesbian veterans and presenting it at colleges and gay and lesbian community centers across the United States. His dogged determination resulted in his book *Coming Out Under Fire* (1990).

Bérubé received the 1991 Lambda Literary Award for nonfiction for the groundbreaking work, a work often referred to in 1993 U.S. Senate hearings concerning gays and lesbians in the military. Also, the book was adapted as a television documentary directed by Arthur Dong in 1994. Bérubé, who was awarded a "genius grant" by the MacArthur Foundation in 1996, planned to use the $300,000 grant to study gays who worked on the majestic ocean liners of the 1930's and 1940's. These men helped found the Cooks and Stewards Union, which protected their rights.

---

writer and humorist Dorothy Parker, addressing one another as "darling." Some were able to work the system, while others were drummed out with undesirable discharges, bearing a stigma that likely affected the rest of their lives.

The film documents the experiences of Marvin Liebman, Phyllis Abry, and Tom Reddy, among others. Liebman was investigated and discharged as a "psychological pervert." He was a Republican policymaker and fund-raiser until he came out in 1990. Abry managed to have a lesbian lover the entire time she was in the military but later married a man and had children. Reddy often appeared in drag in shows to boost the morale of the marines with humor. He received an honorable discharge.

After making *Coming Out Under Fire*, Dong's far-reaching interests in the U.S. government's control over its citizens, and his general interest in fighting homophobia, led him to create other groundbreaking documentary films. *Licensed to Kill* (1997) explores the reasons why some men bash and murder gay men. The film also supports Dong's, and others', general thesis that antigay behavior, like any prejudice or hatred, is learned. The convicted men Dong interviewed were not misfits, outcasts, fanatics, or lunatics. Instead, the men's attitudes and behaviors reflect the deeply disturbing homophobia and hatred held by many Americans. The interviewee's stories tell of the ways this antigay behavior is nurtured and molded by social conditioning. One interviewee states that his junior-high-school librarian taught him that homosexuality was wrong. Another inmate recalls how he was told that gays were weak and would therefore not fight back. A third said he was supported by words in the Bible.

SIGNIFICANCE

Bérubé's *Coming Out Under Fire* was the first opportunity for many of the gay and lesbian veterans of World War II to see in print a history of their accomplishments and their daily lives, as well as an account of how they coped while in the military. The book includes personal testimonies of the many ways gays and lesbians constructed their lives, loves, and social and support groups in a time when living as lesbian or gay was not just challenging but also illegal under various civil and military laws.

Dong's documentary films are tools for creating change, for they confront and deconstruct not only U.S. government—including military—policy that excludes an entire class of individuals from civil protection and rights but also social and religious proscriptions against same-gender sexuality and couplings.

Bérubé and Dong have been given numerous awards for their works. Bérubé was a fellow of the MacArthur Foundation and received a Lambda Literary Award and an award from the Monette/Horwitz Trust, among others. Dong has received a George Foster Peabody Award, two GLAAD media awards, three Sundance Film Festival awards, and also an award from the Monette/Horwitz Trust, among others. Dong's work has been nominated five times for Emmy Awards. These accolades have particular, resonant meaning in a society that gets much of its information from visual media.

—Dan Luckenbill

FURTHER READING

Bérubé, Allan. *Coming Out Under Fire: The History of Gay Men and Women in World War Two.* New York: Free Press, 1990.

Carpenter, C. Tyler, and Edward H. Yeatts. *Stars Without Garters! The Memoirs of Two Gay GI's in WWII.* San Francisco, Calif.: Alamo Square Press, 1996.

Meyer, Leisa D. "The Myth of Lesbian (In)Visibility: World War II and the Current 'Gays in the Military' Debate." In *Modern American Queer Theory*, edited by Allida M. Black. Philadelphia: Temple University Press, 2001.

Thomson, Patricia. "The Documentary in Action." http://fundfilm.org/for_grant/for_grant_article6_all.htm.

SEE ALSO: Mar. 15, 1919-1921: U.S. Navy Launches Sting Operation Against "Sexual Perverts"; July 3, 1975: U.S. Civil Service Commission Prohibits Discrimination Against Federal Employees; 1976-1990: Army Reservist Ben-Shalom Sues for Reinstatement; May-Aug., 1980: U.S. Navy Investigates the USS *Norton Sound* in Antilesbian Witch Hunt; May 3, 1989: *Watkins v. United States Army* Reinstates Gay Soldier; Aug. 27, 1991: *The Advocate* Outs Pentagon Spokesman Pete Williams; Oct., 1992: Canadian Military Lifts Its Ban on Gays and Lesbians; Nov. 30, 1993: Don't Ask, Don't Tell Policy Is Implemented; Jan. 12, 2000: United Kingdom Lifts Ban on Gays and Lesbians in the Military.

March 20, 1990
QUEER NATION IS FOUNDED

Driven by the success of the radical activist group ACT UP, and frustrated by what was believed to be the liberal, assimilationist focus of the lesbian and gay rights movement, a new queer rights protest group—Queer Nation—was formed by veteran political activists. Queer Nation had a simple, direct mandate: queer visibility.

LOCALE: New York, New York

CATEGORIES: Organizations and institutions; civil rights; government and politics; marches, protests, and riots

KEY FIGURES
Alan Klein,
Karl Soehnlein,
Michelangelo Signorile, and
Tom Blewitt, organizers of Queer Nation

SUMMARY OF EVENT
Queer Nation (QN) was formed for reasons more pragmatic than idealistic. Foremost among them was that ACT UP/New York, another queer activist group, had an unwieldy agenda of social issues. QN, in part, was formed to help with this agenda. ACT UP had been drawing several hundreds of in-

Queer Nation/Houston and ACT UP/Golden Gate protesters in August, 1992, outside a hotel in Houston, Texas, where Moral Majority founder Jerry Falwell was speaking. (Hulton Archive/Getty Images)

dividuals to weekly meetings by 1990, its third year in existence. ACT UP's success in achieving social change had sparked an influx of new members and, accordingly, a broader mandate.

Originally formed by gays and lesbians, ACT UP had once effortlessly tackled gay and lesbian politics as well as HIV-AIDS concerns. As the epidemic's demographics changed, however, so did the makeup of ACT UP. New members called for activist muscle to be thrown behind different crises, including HIV in prisons; infection among heterosexual women, blacks, and Latinos; and needle exchange. What became an occasional request from the floor for protests for gay and lesbian rights was facing growing resistance.

Four longtime ACT UP members—Alan Klein, Karl Soehnlein, Michelangelo Signorile, and Tom Blewitt—were concerned about what they considered a deadlock and began meeting privately. They felt that a number of problems germane to gays and lesbians were going unchallenged, including a leap in gay-bashing incidents in New York City and around the United States; a rash of homophobic rap lyrics by hip-hop singers; and a *60 Minutes* television commentary by Andy Rooney, who explained without apology how gay people made him feel uneasy. QN's organizers felt that tackling these issues required direct-action tactics that were of a caliber like that of ACT UP. A new group would have to be formed. On March 20, 1990, sixty people attended a meeting at the New York City Gay and Lesbian Community Services Center, also the birthplace of ACT UP. Many who showed up at this first public meeting were ACT UP veterans who had become "burned out" and no longer attended weekly meetings.

Mindful of the bureaucracy that had been dogging ACT UP, many demanded that the new group be untethered by majority votes or consensus. Some even disdained a name for the new venture. The bid for anarchy was soon forgotten, though, and the group was dubbed Queer Nation. Its simple mandate was a commitment to queer visibility. Drawing from the lessons of ACT UP, from others fighting for civil rights, and from its savvy talent for eye-catching graphics, new group members groomed QN's look from the start: Members wore black T-shirts with a huge yellow Q and the message "Get used to it!" This was shorthand for the group's rallying cry, "We're here. We're queer. Get used to it!"

By mid-April of 1990, QN had a battery of tactics. "Nights Out" involved "invasions" of straight hangouts throughout Manhattan. The Queer Shopping Network distributed progay and pro-lesbian pamphlets at exurban malls. This edgy mix of politics and camp humor was reminiscent of the early days of ACT UP/New York.

QN's early main focus was on the rise in gay bashing. The group was galvanized in its first month when a pipe bomb exploded at Uncle Charlie's Downtown, a West Village gay bar in New York City, injuring three people. The next evening, QN mobilized one thousand protesters to demand a full police investigation. (Years later, it was determined that the bar blast had been committed by a faction of the terrorist group al-Qaeda.) QN also marched on politicians who opposed a state antibias bill, which lingered for years because conservatives refused to honor the clause protecting sexual orientation.

In June of 1990, QN held a march in Manhattan against antiqueer violence, which drew fifteen hundred people. Marching from the West Village to the East Village, the group demanded local police and state government action to stop the increase in bias-motivated attacks. QN's greatest contribution to the war on gay bashing occurred later that summer. After a Latino man from Queens was beaten to death in a Jackson Heights schoolyard, police wanted to write it off as a drug deal gone wrong, but QN, working with the New York City Lesbian & Gay Anti-Violence Project, brought the murder of Julio Rivera to national prominence, forcing an investigation that resulted in convictions for three men who lured Rivera to his death with the promise of sex.

QN commanded extensive media attention from the start, especially from reporters who had initially ignored ACT UP and then scrambled when the group rose to prominence. Several members of the group appeared on the cover of the *Village Voice*, a weekly alternative newspaper, and became the focus of a feature story by Guy Trebay that chronicled the group's urban exploits. Much was made of the group's name, a co-opting of an old epithet that rankled both queers and straight people. By summer, QN chapters were thriving in Boston, Philadelphia, Los Angeles, San Francisco, and Montreal.

By the middle of 1991, the energy of QN had inexplicably faltered. Weekly meetings, which once drew two hundred people, were attracting just one-tenth that number. The four founders had backed off from the group around this time, pleading exhaustion. QN groups in other cities also reported "battle-fatigue." By 1993, the founding organization had morphed into a weekly encounter group for crossdressers and transsexuals, before it disbanded.

Significance

Queer Nation's shock troops popularized the postmodern queer aesthetic that began with ACT UP. Masculine gay boys, femme lesbians, and punkish, tattooed hybrids of each—wearing protest T-shirts, decals, and buttons—became the new standard for the queer "look." Within five years, straight suburban kids would co-opt the earrings and tattoos of QN.

While it had a relatively short existence, QN thrived at a time when queer cultural tropes became a part of the mainstream; more queer-themed books, films, and TV shows had found their way to the nonqueer world. QN energized mainstream queer rights groups, such as the Gay and Lesbian Alliance Against Defamation (GLAAD) and the Human Rights Campaign (HRC), which became more aggressive in the wake of QN. QN also inspired queer student activism on college and university campuses around the country. Furthermore, the founding chapter of QN spun off two contingents: the Lesbian Avengers and The Pink Panthers. The Pink Panthers patrolled queer neighborhoods nightly to discourage bias attacks.

How will QN be remembered? The answer came to light in 2003 at a New York University seminar. Academics explained how the establishment of the group fit into a continuum of sexual identity politics. However, QN cofounder Alan Klein was on the panel, and he offered the nuts-and-bolts reason for its creation.

—*Jay Blotcher*

FURTHER READING

Berlant, Lauren, and Elizabeth Freeman. "Queer Nationality." *boundary 2* 19, no. 1 (Spring, 1992): 149-180.

Bérubé, Allan, and Jeffrey Escoffier. "Queer/Nation." *OutLook* (Winter, 1991): 12-23.

Cunningham, Michael. "If You're Queer and You're Not Angry in 1992, You're Not Paying Attention." *Mother Jones* (May/June, 1992): 60-68.

Duggan, Lisa. "Making It Perfectly Queer." In *Sex Wars: Sexual Dissent and Political Culture*, edited by Lisa Duggan and Nan Hunter. New York: Routledge, 1995.

Signorile, Michelangelo. *Queer in America: Sex, the Media, and the Closets of Power*. New York: Random House, 1993.

Trebay, Guy. "In Your Face." *Village Voice*, August 14, 1990.

Warner, Michael, ed. *Fear of a Queer Planet: Queer Politics and Social Theory*. Minneapolis: University of Minnesota Press, 1993.

SEE ALSO: July 31, 1969: Gay Liberation Front Is Formed; May 1, 1970: Radicalesbians Issues "The Woman Identified Woman" Manifesto; June 28, 1970: First Lesbian and Gay Pride March in the United States; Mar. 5, 1974: Antigay and Antilesbian Organizations Begin to Form; Oct. 12-15, 1979: First March on Washington for Lesbian and Gay Rights; Mar., 1987: Radical AIDS Activist Group ACT UP Is Founded; 1989: Act Up Paris Is Founded; Dec. 10, 1989: ACT UP Protests at St. Patrick's Cathedral; Sept. 29, 1991: California Governor Wilson Vetoes Antidiscrimination Bill; 1992: Transgender Nation Holds Its First Protest; Apr. 24, 1993: First Dyke March Is Held in Washington, D.C.

June, 1990
BiNet USA Is Formed

BiNet USA was founded at a time when lesbian and gay groups were encouraged—by emerging bisexual, queer, and transgender activism and by an intellectual movement known as queer theory—to become more inclusive not only of bisexuals but also of transgender people.

ALSO KNOWN AS: National Bisexual Network; North American Multicultural Bisexual Network
LOCALE: San Francisco, California
CATEGORIES: Organizations and institutions; feminism

KEY FIGURES
Lucy Friedland and
Liz Nania, activists who first called for a national bisexual network
Lani Kaahumanu (b. 1943), organizer and writer

SUMMARY OF EVENT

The fortunes of the bisexual movement, which first developed in the early 1970's, have shifted along with changes in gay and lesbian politics and identity. While in the early days of gay liberation the movement was seen to encompass anyone who had same-gender desires, this began to change as gays and lesbians increasingly regarded themselves as a distinct minority. As a result, bisexuals were often perceived as "fence sitters" and pressured to "choose sides." In addition, some bisexual women became alienated from lesbian-feminist communities as lesbian separatism took hold in the 1970's. Also, the issue of what constituted "acceptable" lesbian sexual practice reached its height during the so-called "sex wars" among feminists in the early 1980's.

Among the first organized bisexual groups were New York City's National Bisexual Liberation Group (formed in 1972), New York's Bisexual Forum (founded in 1974), and the San Francisco Bisexual Center (opened in 1976). Along with these newly organized groups came a wave of magazine and newspaper articles that appeared in the mid-1970's in the mainstream press. Also in the 1970's, many of the most popular books on bisexuality were published, including Bernhardt Hurwood's *The Bisexuals* (1970), Janet Bode's *View from Another Closet: Exploring Bisexuality in Women* (1976), and Fred Klein's *The Bisexual Option: A Concept of One-Hundred Percent Intimacy* (1978).

A new wave of bisexual organizing emerged in the mid-1980's, largely spearheaded by feminist women. Among the earliest such groups were the Boston Bisexual Women's Network (BBWN), San Francisco's BiPol, and Chicago's Action Bi-Women, all begun in 1983. In 1987, two BBWN members, Lucy Friedland and Liz Nania, distributed a flyer that read, "Are We Ready for a National Bisexual Network?" The response was encouraging. In October, about seventy-five activists gathered at the Mayflower Hotel in Washington, D.C., for the first-ever national meeting of bisexuals. The group also participated in the October 11, 1987, March on Washington for Gay and Lesbian Rights behind a BBWN banner proclaiming "Bisexual Pride—Gay Liberation is Our Liberation."

This gathering inspired activists to discuss the formation of a national bisexual organization, at first informally called the National Bisexual Network. The first International Directory of Bisexual Groups was produced to facilitate national and international networking. BiPol offered its post office box as a contact address, receiving two shopping bags worth of supportive mail. Local groups met to discuss the incipient national network, and proposals were discussed via mail and telephone.

In June, 1990, this networking culminated in the first national bisexual conference, hosted by BiPol in San Francisco, which drew some 450 attendees. After three days of discussion, participants formally launched the North American Multicultural Bisexual Network. From its inception, the network adopted a grassroots focus and a consensus-based structure, and it was committed to feminist and antiracist principles. At the network's first organizing meeting in Seattle in July, 1991, participants adopted a shorter, more recognizable name: BiNet USA, the Bisexual Network of the USA.

The early 1990's saw the bisexual movement's greatest growth as new groups continued to spring up across the country. In 1992, bisexual activists, working with gay and lesbian allies, organized a successful campaign for bisexual inclusion in what became known as the 1993 March on Washington for Lesbian, Gay and Bi Equal Rights and Liberation. At the April 25 march, an estimated one thousand people were part of the bisexual contingent. At the rally that followed, BiPol's Lani Kaahumanu, a former lesbian activist, was the first person to speak on behalf of the bisexual community at a national gay and lesbian event, although she was the last speaker to take the stage.

BiNet continued to grow throughout the 1990's, spawning local chapters and reaching a membership of about one thousand. The network launched the Bisexual Youth Initiative in 1995, met with the White House gay and lesbian community liaison in 1996, hosted the first National Institute on Bisexuality and HIV-AIDS in 1998, and participated in the National Gay and Lesbian Task Force's "Equality Begins at Home" campaign in March of 1999. The network also focused on bisexual media activism, assisting with a July, 1995, *Newsweek* cover story on bisexuality, and collaborating with the Gay and Lesbian Alliance Against Defamation (GLAAD) on a bisexual visibility Web site. BiNet, however, had perhaps its greatest impact in helping to foster local organizing among bisexuals.

From the start, BiNet USA was beset by tensions between grassroots activists who decried encroaching bureaucracy and those who favored a more traditional organizational structure. In 2001, the network selected Venetia Porter as its first executive director and took steps to secure an office in San Francisco's new LGBT Community Center. However, the organization experienced a series of setbacks, including the diversion of both funding and activist attention following the September 11, 2001, terrorist attacks. As a result, the national office was never fully occupied and Porter was let go. In 2004, BiNet maintained a skeletal board and a Web site, but it is essentially on a long-term hiatus.

SIGNIFICANCE

During the late 1980's and much of the 1990's, bisexual activists for the most part focused on persuading gay and lesbian organizations to be inclusive of bisexuals. At the same time, social changes were afoot that would lead to greater acceptance of bisexuality. The early 1990's saw the birth of a mixed-gender queer activist movement that emphasized sexual and gender diversity, and the burgeoning transgender movement called into question traditional boundaries of gender and sexual orientation. The same decade also witnessed the popularization of queer theory in academia, which stressed the fluid and socially constructed nature of sexuality and gender.

The 1990's also saw a growth in bisexual literature, including Lani Kaahumanu and Loraine Hutchins's *Bi Any Other Name: Bisexual People Speak Out* (1991) and *Bisexual Politics: Theories, Queries, and Visions* (1995), edited by Naomi Tucker. There also was increased visibility in higher education and mainstream media.

While BiNet USA never achieved anywhere near the prominence of the major national gay and lesbian groups, the gay and lesbian movement expanded to include bisexuals. By the beginning of the twenty-first century, hundreds of gay and lesbian groups had added "bisexual" and "transgender" to their names and mission statements, much as the gay movement had started to include "lesbian" in its names in the 1970's and 1980's.

—*Liz Highleyman*

FURTHER READING

Hutchins, Loraine, and Lani Kaahumanu. *Bi Any Other Name: Bisexual People Speak Out*. Boston: Alyson, 1991.

Ochs, Robyn, and Liz Highleyman. "Bisexual Movement." In *Lesbian Histories and Cultures*, edited by Bonnie Zimmerman. New York: Garland, 2000.

Raymond, Dannielle, and Liz Highleyman. "Brief Timeline of Bisexual Activism in the United States." In *Bisexual Politics: Theories, Queries, and Visions*, edited by Naomi Tucker. Binghamton, N.Y.: Harrington Park Press, 1995.

Storr, Merl, ed. *Bisexuality: A Critical Reader*. New York: Routledge, 1999.

Udis-Kessler, Amanda. "Identity/Politics: A History of the Bisexual Movement." In *Bisexual Politics: Theories, Queries, and Visions*, edited by Naomi Tucker. Binghamton, N.Y.: Harrington Park Press, 1995.

SEE ALSO: May 6, 1868: Kertbeny Coins the Terms "Homosexual" and "Heterosexual"; June 27-July 2, 1969: Stonewall Rebellion Ignites Modern Gay and Lesbian Rights Movement; 1974: Bisexual Forum Is Founded.

July 26, 1990
AMERICANS WITH DISABILITIES ACT BECOMES LAW

Gay and lesbian community-based civil rights and HIV-AIDS organizations joined in a broad coalition that demanded sweeping civil rights legislation protecting individuals with disabilities, including persons with HIV and AIDS. The Americans with Disabilities Act, signed into law in 1990, includes as protected those persons who are HIV-positive or who have AIDS.

LOCALE: Washington, D.C.
CATEGORIES: Civil rights; HIV-AIDS; laws, acts, and legal history

KEY FIGURES
Dan Burton, Republican U.S. representative, Indiana
Jim Chapman, Democratic U.S. representative, Texas
Chai Feldblum, attorney with the American Civil Liberties Union AIDS Project
Jean McGuire, executive director, AIDS Action Council
Jesse Helms (b. 1921), Republican U.S. senator, North Carolina
Tim McFeely, executive director of the Human Rights Campaign Fund

SUMMARY OF EVENT

Enacted on July 26, 1990, the Americans with Disabilities Act (ADA) provides legal protection against discrimination for individuals with disabilities in a wide range of settings, including employment and public accommodations. It also includes provisions for access to services.

Passage of the ADA was the result of a broad coalition, including Patrisha Wright of the Disability Rights Education & Defense Fund and Ralph Neas of the Leadership Council on Civil Rights. Chai Feldblum, a lawyer with the American Civil Liberties Union (ACLU), was a key architect of the legislation, while Tim McFeely of the Human Rights Campaign Fund (now called the Human Rights Campaign), a gay lobbying organization, and Jean McGuire and Tom Sheridan of the AIDS Action Council were the leading representatives for those with HIV-AIDS. Senator Ted Kennedy's chief staff member on HIV-AIDS issues, Michael Iskowitz, also had a prominent role in the ADA's passage.

Although intended to provide broad protection to all persons with disabilities, the ADA also was a response to the HIV-AIDS epidemic, in its eighth year when the ADA was introduced in Congress in 1989. Widespread discrimination against people with HIV-AIDS resulted in recommendations, such as that of the Presidential Commission on the Human Immunodeficiency Virus Epidemic (1988), for strong legal protection. A bill that would have protected from discrimination only individuals with HIV, but not other disabilities, was introduced in 1987 but did not have adequate support. Instead, HIV-AIDS advocates joined with other disability rights advocates to pass the ADA.

The ADA received significant bipartisan support in Congress as well as support from the administration of President George H. W. Bush. Some conservative legislators, however, attacked the ADA because it included protection for persons who had what many conservatives considered disabilities that were morally objectionable. Ultraconservative Republican senator Jesse Helms, a leading opponent of gay and lesbian rights, objected to the ADA's inclusion of, in his words, "people who are HIV-positive, most of whom are drug addicts or homosexuals or bisexuals." Representative Dan Burton opposed the ADA because it was, according to him, "a last ditch attempt of the remorseless sodomy lobby to achieve its national agenda before the impending decimation of AIDS destroys its political clout."

Despite these objections, Congress rejected amendments to the bill that would have excluded homosexuals or bisexuals with HIV-AIDS. Congress did agree, however, to amendments that excluded "transvestism," transsexualism, and gender-

> **AMERICANS WITH DISABILITIES ACT**
>
> *Findings and Purposes*
> (a) *Findings.* The Congress finds that
> (1) some 43,000,000 Americans have one or more physical or mental disabilities, and this number is increasing as the population as a whole is growing older;
> (2) historically, society has tended to isolate and segregate individuals with disabilities, and, despite some improvements, such forms of discrimination against individuals with disabilities continue to be a serious and pervasive social problem;
> (3) discrimination against individuals with disabilities persists in such critical areas as employment, housing, public accommodations, education, transportation, communication, recreation, institutionalization, health services, voting, and access to public services;
> (4) unlike individuals who have experienced discrimination on the basis of race, color, sex, national origin, religion, or age, individuals who have experienced discrimination on the basis of disability have often had no legal recourse to redress such discrimination;
> (5) individuals with disabilities continually encounter various forms of discrimination, including outright intentional exclusion, the discriminatory effects of architectural, transportation, and communication barriers, overprotective rules and policies, failure to make modifications to existing facilities and practices, exclusionary qualification standards and criteria, segregation, and relegation to lesser services, programs, activities, benefits, jobs, or other opportunities;
> (6) census data, national polls, and other studies have documented that people with disabilities, as a group, occupy an inferior status in our society, and are severely disadvantaged socially, vocationally, economically, and educationally;
> (7) individuals with disabilities are a discrete and insular minority who have been faced with restrictions and limitations, subjected to a history of purposeful unequal treatment, and relegated to a position of political powerlessness in our society, based on characteristics that are beyond the control of such individuals and resulting from stereotypic assumptions not truly indicative of the individual ability of such individuals to participate in, and contribute to, society;
> (8) the Nation's proper goals regarding individuals with disabilities are to assure equality of opportunity, full participation, independent living, and economic self-sufficiency for such individuals; and
> (9) the continuing existence of unfair and unnecessary discrimination and prejudice denies people with disabilities the opportunity to compete on an equal basis and to pursue those opportunities for which our free society is justifiably famous, and costs the United States billions of dollars in unnecessary expenses resulting from dependency and nonproductivity.
> (b) *Purpose. It is the purpose of this Act*
> (1) to provide a clear and comprehensive national mandate for the elimination of discrimination against individuals with disabilities;
> (2) to provide clear, strong, consistent, enforceable standards addressing discrimination against individuals with disabilities;
> (3) to ensure that the Federal Government plays a central role in enforcing the standards established in this Act on behalf of individuals with disabilities; and (4) to invoke the sweep of congressional authority, including the power to enforce the fourteenth amendment and to regulate commerce, in order to address the major areas of discrimination faced day-to-day by people with disabilities.

identity disorder from protection. While the U.S. Senate initially included homosexuality and bisexuality in this same list, the House of Representatives concluded that homosexuality and bisexuality are not impairments and therefore are not disabilities. These amendments were necessary for passage of the ADA. While the provision regarding homosexuality and bisexuality is legally insignificant because such identities are not covered as disabilities under the ADA, the provisions excluding "transvestism," transsexualism, and gender-identity disorder are legally significant.

During final consideration of the ADA, Representative Jim Chapman introduced an amendment that allowed individuals with "an infectious or communicable disease of public health significance" to be excluded from jobs involving food handling. This was intended to allow employers to exclude employees with HIV. Because there is no risk of HIV transmission in food preparation, this provision would have perpetuated the unfair prejudice that the ADA was intended to end. At a White House meeting in which Tim McFeely, McGuire, and Sheridan represented the AIDS community, ADA supporters agreed that if the food handler provision were included, they would withdraw their support, thus killing the ADA. This dispute was resolved, however, when Senator Orrin Hatch introduced a compromise amendment drafted by ACLU lawyer Feldblum. The compromise required the secretary of Health and Human Services to issue a list of infectious diseases that can be transmitted by food handling. (HIV has never appeared on that list.) The Hatch amendment was accepted, the ADA passed Congress, and President Bush signed it into law on July 26, 1990.

SIGNIFICANCE

The Americans with Disabilities Act has been widely hailed as the "Bill of Rights" for people with disabilities. Before the ADA, federal protection against disability-based discrimination was limited to federal agencies, federal contractors, or recipients of federal financial assistance. After the ADA, protection extended far more widely, taking within its sweep private-sector employers, businesses such as restaurants and hotels, professional offices such as those of physicians and attorneys, and transportation and communication services.

The ADA's definition of "disability" is not specific to any medical condition but is instead generic. Under the ADA, a person has a disability if he or she has a physical or mental impairment that results in a substantial limitation on a major life activity. The ADA not only protects persons with actual disabilities; it also covers persons perceived to have a disability or who have a record of having a disability but in fact are not disabled. For example, a man fired from his job because his employer believes he has AIDS, when in fact he does not, is nevertheless able to sue his employer for discrimination under the ADA.

Much to the disappointment of its proponents, the ADA often has been interpreted narrowly by the courts. In 1998, the U.S. Supreme Court ruled in *Bragdon v. Abbott* that asymptomatic HIV infection is a disability based on the plaintiff's inability to bear children because of her HIV infection. Although judicial interpretation of the ADA is sometimes narrower than that intended by Congress, the ADA has nevertheless had a profoundly positive impact on the lives of individuals with HIV-AIDS and others with disabilities.

—David W. Webber

FURTHER READING

Colker, Ruth. "The ADA's Journey Through Congress." *Wake Forest Law Review* 39, no. 1 (2004).

Feldblum, Chai. "The Art of Legislative Lawyering and the Six Circles Theory of Advocacy." *McGeorge Law Review* 34, no. 785 (2003).

National Council on Disability. "Equality of Opportunity: The Making of the Americans with Disabilities Act." July 26, 1997. http://www.ncd.gov/newsroom/publications/1997/equality.htm.

Webber, David W. "Legislative History in Regard to HIV." In *AIDS and the Law*, edited by David W. Webber. New ed. New York: Aspen, 2005.

Wright, Patrisha. "When to Hold 'Em and When to Fold 'Em: Lessons Learned from Enacting the Americans with Disabilities Act." Disability Rights Education and Defense Fund. http://www.dredf.org/international/paper_w-w.html.

SEE ALSO: June 27, 1988: Report of the Presidential AIDS Commission; Dec. 17, 1991: Minnesota Court Awards Guardianship to Lesbian Partner; 1994: Employment Non-Discrimination Act Is Proposed to U.S. Congress.

December, 1990
ASIAN LESBIAN NETWORK HOLDS ITS FIRST CONFERENCE

The Asian Lesbian Network gathered for its first conference in Bangkok, Thailand, marking the first formal, regional meeting of lesbians in Asia.

LOCALE: Bangkok, Thailand
CATEGORIES: Organizations and institutions; race and ethnicity

KEY FIGURE
Anjana Tang Suvarnananda, founder of the Asian Lesbian Network

SUMMARY OF EVENT
The Asian Lesbian Network (ALN) emerged out of an international gathering in Geneva, Switzerland, in 1986, an event that had been sponsored by the International Lesbian Information Service (ILIS) and had attracted more than eight hundred lesbians from around the world, including ALN founder Anjana Tang Suvarnananda. The ILIS supported the founding of ALN shortly after the gathering in Switzerland.

Suvarnananda was a key figure in promoting the budding ALN, as she traveled around Asia to do outreach work with lesbians in Singapore and the Philippines and was in constant contact with lesbians in countries such as India, Sri Lanka, and Bangladesh. One of the first activities of the ALN was a conference hosted by Anjaree, a Thai lesbian organization, in Bangkok in December of 1990.

Thai lesbians who described themselves as "women who love women" founded Anjaree in 1986. *Anjaree*, which means "someone who follows non-conformist ways," is an indigenous term that comes close to describing women's same-gender attraction. The word was chosen because there is no descriptive Thai term for "lesbian." Most Thai women, however, do not use "anjaree" to describe themselves but rather refer to themselves as "tomboys" (*tom*) or "ladies" (*dee*, or *dy*). *Tom* and *dee* relationships are in some ways analogous to butch-femme relationships in the Western world.

Organizers first faced difficulties trying to create the ALN conference in Thailand. Problems and concerns included the hesitancy of many Asian women who are sexually attracted to women to use the word "lesbian" to describe themselves. Suvarnananda suggested in a letter to ILIS that part of the difficulty of organizing ALN was the perception that lesbian sexuality had been imported from the West and was not indigenous to Asia.

The conference's opening reception was well attended by more than two hundred Thai *toms* and *dees*, in addition to conference registrants. Attendees of the workshops included thirty-six Asians living in Asia (seven of whom were Thai organizers), nine Asians living outside Asia, and nine non-Asians living within Asia (two of whom were Anjaree volunteers). Workshops throughout the weekend focused on questions of visibility, organization expansion, and the development of an Asian lesbian identity. One of the workshops raised questions about the hierarchy of power among *toms* and *dees* in Thailand, along with how to negotiate traditional Thai ideas about what it means to be unmarried.

The plenary session on the final day of the conference, "The Future of the ALN," raised the question of who belongs in the Asian Lesbian Network. There was dissension among participants about whether or not non-Asians should be included in the organization or the conference. Non-Asian lesbians left the room voluntarily when this question came up, and the conversation continued; it ended without agreement.

The first issue of the ALN newsletter reported details of the conference, including the disagreement over whether or not non-Asians could or should participate in ALN. The newsletter resolved the issue by stating that ALN Nippon (Japan) would organize the second conference and members would decide among themselves who should be included. ALN Nippon resolved this issue in December, 1992, by holding two concurrent conferences in Tokyo, one for Asian lesbians only and a concurrent retreat open to all lesbians regardless of ethnicity.

SIGNIFICANCE

The Asian Lesbian Network conference was the first formal meeting of Asian lesbians. ALN later had an impact on the U.N. Fourth World Conference on Women, which was held in Beijing, China, in 1995. ALN members helped to educate other women at the conference by encouraging them to see lesbian issues as important women's movement issues.

Also, the ALN conference decreased the social isolation felt by Asian lesbians from many countries, and it provided a venue for newly formed lesbian groups to network and exchange information. Even though a few Asian countries, such as Japan and Thailand, had emerging lesbian communities at the time of the conference, many countries had no organizations or support groups, let alone bars, for lesbians. In Thailand, Anjaree had been the only formal organization, and in Indonesia, there was just one gay and lesbian group for the entire country.

The ALN conference also raised issues that would continue throughout the history of the ALN, namely, issues concerning the connection between Western culture and lesbian sexuality and identity, an association that marks lesbian sexuality and identity as "phenomena" imported from the West. The second issue was how to incorporate (or not incorporate) into ALN the non-Asian lesbians who live in Asia. It was argued that by including non-Asian lesbians in ALN, the ALN would be stigmatized by the Asian world, given the association of lesbian sexuality with the West. Others argued that it was possible that non-Asians would co-opt and dominate ALN. The Japanese community, in particular, which had a non-Asian lesbian community of more than one hundred women and a handful of events and organizations, had experienced conflict over the benefits and disadvantages of including non-Asian lesbians in Japanese lesbian events.

—*Amy Stone*

FURTHER READING

Anderson, Shelley. "Tomboys, Ladies, and Amphibians." *Connexions* 29 (1989).

Anjaree. "Anjaree—Toward Lesbian Visibility." *Connexions* 46 (1994).

Kase, Alleson. "Asian Lesbians Speak: A Conference Report." *Off Our Backs* 22, no. 8 (August, 1992): 8.

Sinnott, Megan J. *Toms and Dees: Transgender Identity and Female Same-Sex Relationships in Thailand*. Honolulu: University of Hawaii Press, 2004.

Thongthiraj, Took Took. "Toward a Struggle Against Invisibility: Love Between Women in Thailand." *Amerasia Journal* 20, no. 1 (1994): 45-58.

SEE ALSO: 1969: Nuestro Mundo Forms as First Queer Organization in Argentina; 1975: Gay American Indians Is Founded; Oct. 12-15, 1979: First March on Washington for Lesbian and Gay Rights; Oct. 12-15, 1979: Lesbian and Gay Asian Collective Is Founded; 1981: *This Bridge Called My Back* Is Published; 1982-1991: Lesbian Academic and Activist Sues University of California for Discrimination; Sept., 1983: First National Lesbians of Color Conference Convenes; 1987: Asian Pacific Lesbian Network Is Founded; 1987: VIVA Is Founded to Promote Latina and Latino Artists; Oct. 14-17, 1987: Latin American and Caribbean Lesbian Feminist Network Is Formed; 1990: United Lesbians of African Heritage Is Founded; Oct. 9-12, 1998: First International Retreat for Lesbian and Gay Muslims Is Held; Nov., 1999: First Middle Eastern Gay and Lesbian Organization Is Founded.

1991
LeVay Postulates the "Gay Brain"

A widely publicized study comparing the brains of gay and heterosexual men led to a debate over the nature of same-gender attraction and the role of biological studies in understanding sexuality.

Locale: California
Categories: Science; health and medicine

Key Figure
Simon LeVay (b. 1943), neuroscientist

Summary of Event

The end of the twentieth century saw an explosion of interest in the cognitive, genetic, and neurologic bases of complex behaviors like language, reasoning, and human sexuality. In the midst of this interest came one the first contemporary studies on possible biological correlates of same-gender attraction and affection.

In 1991, Simon LeVay, a neuroscientist who earlier had been affiliated with the Salk Institute for Biological Studies in San Diego, California, published an article in the journal *Science* reporting on a postmortem analysis of the sizes of the hypothalamuses of the brains in gay men, heterosexual men, and women whose sexual orientations were unknown. The hypothalamus, located deep in the brain, helps regulate many of the body's automatic functions, such as breathing, temperature, hunger, and water intake. The hypothalamus also plays a primary role in controlling the secretion of hormones, such as those that regulate growth, production of ova and sperm, and lactation.

One of the structures within the hypothalamus, the medial preoptic region (MPR), appears to be associated with male-typical sexual behavior in rats and monkeys. Studies have shown that hormone levels influence the structure and function of the MPR throughout development, including during fetal development in utero. These studies have also shown that the size of the MPR differs as a function of sex: females have a smaller MPR than males.

LeVay conducted a postmortem analysis of the size of the MPR in three groups of people: heterosexual men, gay men, and women whose sexual orientations were unknown. LeVay found that the size of gay men's MPR was smaller than that of heterosexual men and comparable in size to that of women. LeVay interpreted this as an indication that same-gender attraction in men has a biological basis. Specifically, he argued that his finding was broadly consistent with theories of sexual orientation that posit that gay men had experienced different hormonal levels while in utero. These hormone levels influence the structure and function of different areas of the brain, including the MPR, which could lead to same-gender attraction in adulthood.

The reaction to LeVay's findings was mixed. Some people reacted positively, claiming that LeVay's finding was evidence that same-gender attraction and affection were inevitable and should therefore not be judged as morally or ethically deviant lifestyle "choices." Others applauded LeVay for extending biological research to include studies of sexual diversity and for formulating explicit hypotheses about the nature of sexual orientation that could be tested with data that had been collected in controlled, experimental settings.

Considerable negative reaction followed LeVay's study as well. Many people felt that LeVay's findings ran strongly contrary to their personal experience of having overtly and consciously chosen same-gender attraction. Other people criticized LeVay for having what they perceived to be the motive of reducing diversity in human behaviors to simple genetic differences and, in doing so, discounting a large body of literature suggesting that social identities are actively constructed. Still others criticized LeVay's methodology. All of the gay men and many of the heterosexual men in LeVay's sample had died of AIDS. People questioned whether this sample was sufficiently representative of the entire population of gay and heterosexual men to draw general conclusions about the nature of same-gender attraction.

Simon LeVay

Simon LeVay was born in 1943 in Oxford, England. His academic training at Cambridge University (B.A., 1966), the University of Göttingen (Ph.D., 1971), and Harvard University Medical School (postdoctoral fellowship, 1972-1974) focused on the natural sciences and neuroanatomy. His early career research at Harvard University and the Salk Institute for Biological Studies in San Diego, California, examined the visual cortex—the part of the brain that processes visual stimuli—in animals.

LeVay gained wide recognition in 1991 with his article "A Difference in Hypothalamic Structure Between Heterosexual and Homosexual Men," which showed differences between self-identified gay and heterosexual men in the size of a structure in the brain, postmortem. These findings spurred a spirited public debate on the bases of gay, lesbian, and bisexual identities. Some interpreted LeVay's finding as a persuasive argument against the conjecture that individuals choose their sexual identities. Others criticized aspects of LeVay's methodology, particularly because all of the gay men whose brains he examined had died of AIDS-related complications.

LeVay's original article was followed by two books on the biological aspects of sexuality: *The Sexual Brain* (1993) and *Queer Science: The Use and Abuse of Research into Homosexuality* (1996). This research can be credited for initiating a wide-reaching public debate on the science of sexuality that continues to this day. More recently, LeVay developed a GLB-focused community education institute in Los Angeles, consulted with NASA on developing plans and strategies for investigating extraterrestrial life, and engaged in a variety of adjunct teaching assignments and guest lectures.

Significance

The years since Simon LeVay's original finding have seen an increase in research quantifying the relative contribution of biological and social factors in same-gender attraction. Although not in direct response to LeVay's research, these studies have continued many of the debates that LeVay's study began.

For example, later studies purport to have found further support for the hypothesis that same-gender attraction is related to prenatal hormonal levels. Research has found differences as a function of sexual orientation in the way that the inner ear responds to sound. These responses, called otoacoustic emissions, are related to hormonal levels. Books by Joan Roughgarden and Bruce Bagemihl have proposed alternative accounts of same-gender attraction in the context of biological diversity. In particular, these works have sought to show that same-gender attraction is not an aberrant condition that results from atypically high hormone levels but is instead a natural consequence of sexual diversity within organisms and communities.

Much of the criticism of LeVay's study has occurred during a time when older debates on whether "nature" or "nurture" predominates in development have been replaced by newer theories in which complex behaviors are seen to emerge as the consequence of interactions among biological and social conditions as well as cognitive abilities. Ultimately, these theories provide a framework in which to understand sexuality as the product of input and experience in conditions of diverse biological and cognitive predispositions.

—Benjamin Munson

Further Reading

Bagemihl, Bruce. *Biological Exuberance: Animal Homosexuality and Natural Diversity*. New York: St. Martin's Press, 1998.

Eisenberg, Leon. "The Social Construction of the Human Brain." *American Journal of Psychiatry* 152 (1995): 1563-1575.

Elman, Jeffrey L., Elizabeth A. Bates, Mark H. Johnson, Annette Karmiloff-Smith, Domenico Parisi, and Kim Plunkett. *Rethinking Innateness: A Connectionist Perspective on Development*. Cambridge, Mass.: MIT Press, 1996.

LeVay, Simon. "A Difference in Hypothalamic Structure Between Heterosexual and Homosexual Men." *Science* 253 (1991): 1034-1037.

_____. *The Sexual Brain*. Cambridge, Mass.: MIT Press, 1993.

McFadden, Dennis, and Edward D. Pasanen. "Spontaneous Otoacoustic Emissions in Heterosexuals, Homosexuals, and Bisexuals." *Journal of the Acoustical Society of America* 105 (1999): 2403-2413.

Roughgarden, Joan. *Evolution's Rainbow: Diversity, Gender, and Sexuality in Nature and People*. Berkeley: University of California Press, 2004.

SEE ALSO: May 6, 1868: Kertbeny Coins the Terms "Homosexual" and "Heterosexual"; 1869: Westphal Advocates Medical Treatment for Sexual Inversion; 1897: Ellis Publishes *Sexual Inversion*; May 14, 1897: Hirschfeld Founds the Scientific-Humanitarian Committee; 1905: Freud Rejects Third-Sex Theory; 1906: Friedlaender Breaks with the Scientific-Humanitarian Committee; 1908: Carpenter Publishes *The Intermediate Sex*; 1929: Davis's Research Identifies Lesbian Sexuality as Common and Normal; 1948: Kinsey Publishes *Sexual Behavior in the Human Male*; 1952: APA Classifies Homosexuality as a Mental Disorder; 1953: Kinsey Publishes *Sexual Behavior in the Human Female*; 1953-1957: Evelyn Hooker Debunks Beliefs That Homosexuality Is a "Sickness"; June 5 and July 3, 1981: Reports of Rare Diseases Mark Beginning of AIDS Epidemic; Spring, 1984: AIDS Virus Is Discovered.

1991
REVISIONIST CRITICISM RECASTS SOR JUANA INÉS DE LA CRUZ

The revisionist critical anthology Feminist Perspectives on Sor Juana Inés de la Cruz *treats the best-known intellectual of colonial Latin America as a writer of woman-centered works who negotiated the strictures placed on her gender and the proscriptions of her Roman Catholic faith.*

LOCALE: United States
CATEGORIES: Race and ethnicity; literature; publications; feminism; religion; cultural and intellectual history

KEY FIGURES
Sor Juana Inés de la Cruz (1648-1695), Mexican poet, writer, and intellectual
Stephanie Merrim, feminist scholar
Dorothy Schons, pioneer of Sor Juana studies in the 1920's
Asunción Lavrín, feminist scholar
Octavio Paz (1914-1998), Mexican poet and biographer

Sor Juana Inés de la Cruz. (Library of Congress)

Summary of Event

In the late 1980's and early 1990's, academics from a variety of disciplines and specialties uncovered protofeminist or even Sapphic tones in the works of women writers who either were ignored by most critics or were dismissed as conservative or conventional by the first waves of feminist scholarship. In the 1960's and 1970's, many feminist researchers had lauded only those women writers of the past whose tactics and ideas resembled more modern agendas. Then, with the growing acceptance of feminist criticism and theory within universities, came feminist criticism and theory's application to seemingly more traditional figures.

Sor Juana Inés de la Cruz was no exception. She had always been appreciated for her intellect, but her Baroque, Catholic, and Mexican background had dissuaded most scholars from seeing her as the first feminist of the Americas. Colonial Latin America did not appear to be a stage for such an independent voice. Despite the pioneering work of Dorothy Schons, first published in 1926 and later reprinted in Stephanie Merrim's 1991 anthology *Feminist Perspectives on Sor Juana Inés de la Cruz*, many critics and historians praised Sor Juana's exceptional talent without pursuing fully some of the woman-centered messages in her plays, poems, and autobiography.

Octavio Paz's famous biography *Sor Juana Inés de la Cruz: O, Las trampas de la fe* (1982; *Sor Juana: Or, The Traps of Faith*, 1988) looked at Sor Juana as a woman, but not as a writer; it would take Merrim's anthology and later her monograph *Early Modern Women's Writing and Sor Juana Inés de la Cruz* (1999) to complete the academic assessment of Sor Juana as not only a fascinating woman but also a significant and telling writer. This revisionist criticism—joined simultaneously by other scholars and a feature-length film by María Luisa Bemberg in 1990, *Yo, la peor de todas*—sought to decipher Sor Juana's often coded and ambiguous imagery and wording to reveal glimpses of the free-spirited intellectual inside the pious nun.

From this scholarship, Sor Juana emerges with a kind of split personality. As Merrim points out in one of her two contributions to the anthology, Sor Juana's plays always had the same plot and similar characters. Each one of her plays revolves around a woman's internal struggle, perhaps paralleling the struggle within herself over whether to toe the line or break free from male supremacy. The free spirit in Sor Juana's dramas, Merrim notes, tends to win in the end, even if she pays a heavy price.

Asunción Lavrín's essay "Unlike Sor Juana: The Model Nun in the Religious Literature of Colonial Mexico" notes that Sor Juana, unlike her protagonists, eventually submitted to authority unconditionally in her religious crisis of 1693, but not be-

---

Sor Juana Inés de la Cruz

Sor Juana Inés de la Cruz was a Mexican literary virtuoso who was called the "tenth muse" during her lifetime and who is generally considered the most important writer of colonial Spanish America. At her best, she was able to manipulate the often unwieldy and intricate language of the Spanish Baroque, with its rich heritage from the Golden Age, into expressions of delicate, feminine vision and sensibility. Her aesthetic documentation of the search for knowledge, love, and God is the most complete personal and artistic record of any figure from the colonial period.

Sor Juana's love poetry appears to reflect frustrating and painful experiences prior to her entry into the convent at about the age of seventeen. Few of the poems are concerned with fulfillment or the intimate communication of personal feelings; most are, instead, variations on the themes of ambivalence and disillusionment in love.

It is not difficult to dwell on the more romantic side of the "tenth muse," to use certain of her poems to enhance the image of a jilted, precocious, disenchanted teenage intellectual sequestering herself in a convent and spending her life in extremely elaborate sublimation. Her most famous pieces contribute to such an image, but as the reader is exposed to a wider spectrum of her talents, a more balanced picture emerges; a trajectory of maturation becomes visible in which Catholicism and the Baroque are means to the self-fulfillment and self-expression originally thwarted in her youth by her lack of social position and her fascination with scholarship.

fore she pushed the envelope of the permissible in seventeenth century Mexico. Indeed, Lavrín notes how Sor Juana differed from most nuns for most of her life. Lavrín argues that Sor Juana, unlike most of her contemporaries, enthusiastically wrote for an audience, sought the public limelight, was bored with convent gossip and rules, and spoke on topics other than her faith. She did so until 1693, then returned for the last two years of her life to tradition and the acceptable.

Sor Juana commandeered and recast conventional plots and forms to put forth a subversive message. Looking at her outwardly staid "Reply to Sister Philotea" and also her memorable poem "First Dream," Josefina Ludmer's "Tricks of the Weak" essay uncovers Sor Juana's main survival strategies of not letting those in power over her know that oftentimes she knew more than they did. Two other contributors, Electa Arenal and Georgina Sabat-Rivers, connect the soul's final defeat by the body in Sor Juana's "First Dream" with the famous nun's own ultimately unsuccessful efforts to be intellectually unimpaired by temporal and thus male-dominated concerns. Furthermore, in Ester Gimbernat de González's essay, Sor Juana takes on the male poet's venerable role of speaking through female characters in some of her love sonnets, but then she confidently breaks with tradition by underscoring that she is not male and yet she is still the one in control.

These literary critics tended to downplay Sor Juana's religiosity in favor of her reasoning. Like most biographers, Schons and Merrim agree that Sor Juana chose convent life because she believed, wisely, that it was the only life for a woman in the Baroque era that allowed reflection without the pressures and distractions of husband and children. They also agree that she involuntarily stopped her writing and criticism in 1693 due to the heavy-handed overreaction of certain church officials who were both threatened by Sor Juana's gift for discourse and debate and empowered by the death of her main male patron, the Marquis de la Laguna. To Merrim especially, a conventional return to God had nothing to do with Sor Juana's decision. Another work, by Pamela Kirk—*Sor Juana Inés de la Cruz: Religion, Art, and Feminism* (1998)—takes Sor Juana more seriously as a truly religious figure without obscuring or dismissing her gynocentric, or woman-identified, tendencies.

Significance

While exploring the feminist tones in Sor Juana Inés de la Cruz's work, Stephanie Merrim and the anthology's other scholars did not spend much time on analyzing the lesbian "potential" in some of Sor Juana's passages. For the Sapphic in this genius, one still has to turn to María Luisa Bemberg's film *Yo, la peor de todas*. Bemberg depicts a sultry, physical side to the famous nun as the author of passionate verses addressed to her favorite vicereine, who takes on the role of sexual aggressor as well as patron.

The critical feminist scholarship on the life and works of Sor Juana helps to explain how and why she largely spurned and then suddenly embraced (after 1693) the passivity, inactivity, and resignation expected of a nun in seventeenth century Mexico.

—*Charles H. Ford*

Further Reading

Kirk, Pamela. *Sor Juana Inés de la Cruz: Religion, Art, and Feminism.* New York: Continuum Press, 1998.

Merrim, Stephanie. *Early Modern Women's Writing and Sor Juana Inés de la Cruz.* Nashville, Tenn.: Vanderbilt University Press, 1999.

_____, ed. *Feminist Perspectives on Sor Juana Inés de la Cruz.* Detroit, Mich.: Wayne State University Press, 1991.

Paz, Octavio. *Sor Juana: Or, The Traps of Faith.* Translated by Margaret Sayers Pedén. Cambridge, Mass.: Belknap Press, 1988.

Scott, Nina M. "Sor Juana and Her World." *Latin American Research Review* 29, no. 1 (1994): 143-154.

See also: 1956: Foster Publishes *Sex Variant Women in Literature*; Fall, 1973: Lesbian Herstory Archives Is Founded; 1975: Rule Publishes *Lesbian Images*; June 19, 2002: Gays and Lesbians March for Equal Rights in Mexico City; Nov. 29, 2005: Roman Catholic Church Bans Gay Seminarians.

1991
Stone Publishes "A Posttranssexual Manifesto"

Allucquére Rosanne Stone's cogent reply to writings by lesbian feminists, who had argued against gender-variance, established scholarly and public debate about gender identity and the nature of gender reassignment and led to a new openness among transgender persons.

Locale: New York, New York
Categories: Transgender/transsexuality; cultural and intellectual history; publications

Key Figures
Allucquére Rosanne Stone, transgender theorist and university professor
Janice Raymond, feminist university professor
Kate Bornstein (b. 1948), writer and transgender performance artist
Leslie Feinberg (b. 1949), writer and transgender activist

Summary of Event
Throughout the 1970's, assimilationist as well as separatist agendas polarized the character of moderate queer culture, creating an increasingly intolerant atmosphere for gender-variant people, including transsexuals. Lesbian-feminist writer Robin Morgan, for example, in her keynote address at the 1973 West Coast Lesbian Conference, denounced Beth Elliott, who is transgender and was then vice president of the San Francisco chapter of the lesbian organization Daughters of Bilitis, as "an opportunist, an infiltrator, and a destroyer—with the mentality of a rapist." In 1977, radical feminists demanded that Olivia Records, a producer of music by and for women, dismiss transsexual audio engineer Allucquére Rosanne (Sandy) Stone (recruited for her experience with high-profile musicians at A&M Records), or they would boycott the company.

The situation reached a head in 1979, when Janice Raymond published a version of her doctoral dissertation in which she asserted that "the problem of transsexuality would best be served by morally mandating it out of existence." Raymond's work provided academic clout for existing prejudice, and although replete with factual errors, anger, and overt paranoia, Raymond's book, *The Transsexual Empire: The Making of the She-Male* (1979), simultaneously raised substantive critiques of sociopolitical aspects of male-to-female (MTF) gender reassignment and the medical protocol that governs such transitions.

Stone's "The 'Empire' Strikes Back: A Posttranssexual Manifesto" (pb. 1991), a response to Raymond presented at a conference eight years after Raymond's *The Transsexual Empire*, squarely engages, and then transcends, Raymond's critique on its own grounds, placing it in a broader, postmodern context. Utilizing the textual theory of French philosopher Jacques Derrida, and proceeding also from the poststructuralist philosophy, critical social archaeology, and politics of *résistance* of the French critic Michel Foucault, Stone generated a "counter-discourse" to the hegemony of essentialism—a theory that individuals have "essential," or natural, personal attributes—shown in the works of Raymond and others, with a teleology that fragments and reconstitutes the elements of sex and gender, including eroticism. Stone's deconstruction (further drawing on the work of scholars Judith Butler and Judith Shapiro and utilizing concepts of border theory, dissonance, and the political economy of the human body) lays bare the modern division between social and personal arenas of performance, highlights the totalizing power of institutional medicine, and expresses the dynamic interrelational association between queer and straight, and organic and manufactured, identities.

In cultures that authoritatively and thoroughly circumscribe all aspects of being human, Stone postulates that transsexuality highlights a politicized arena. This arena includes the fact of the ultimate and radical unknowability of the subject (the individual), which can be explored authentically and with the power and possibility of surprise.

Significance

Stone's confrontation with Raymond's work on semantic/didactic/rhetorical levels helped to open the field of transgender scholarship, balanced lopsided radical rants, and established a true debate. Stone's direct engagement provided an "openness," an air of disclosure beyond the call merely for individual transsexual "self-outing." It remains a question whether Stone's work alone effected, or even served as a bellwether for, sustained discourse concerning transgenderism. It is certain, however, that her manifesto crystallized and conveyed certain aspects of gender discourse both within and beyond the confines of the queer community, namely in the areas of theory, politics, and medicine.

Stone simultaneously questioned and subverted binary thinking by arguing that there exists a unified, coexisting plurality of genders within personal and public realms. This hybridity introduced a crisis for paradigms that insist on the singularity of identity, internal sufficiency, and normative knowledge because hybridity offers both a raison d'être and a mode of articulation that makes intelligible a space of new possibilities for gender expression and for living one's gender. Stone proposed a radical hermeneutic, a violation of gender boundaries.

Perhaps the most socially recognizable effect of Stone's manifesto of gender fluidity and hybridity was that the transgender and lesbian and gay communities in the 1990's reconnected. Stone accomplished this coming together by arguing about the endless ways one can express gender. Genderqueer youth, especially, have accepted the often moment-to-moment fluidity of gender and sexual identities, and they have expressed this visual, linguistic, and erotic play as "genderfuck." Certainly the most famous and adept practitioner of this art is Kate Bornstein, who explicitly, in her work *Gender Outlaw: On Men, Women, and the Rest of Us* (1994), credits the possibility of "hir" "cut-and-paste" gender identity to Stone's work.

Related to these theoretical watersheds, Stone initiated a crucial political turn within the queer community in the United States that had all but disappeared since 1968/1969 (when queer politics was characterized and represented by a strong drag queen and transgender presence during the Stonewall Rebellion in New York City). Stone has theorized a politics of inclusion and unification versus fragmentation and exclusion. Her renovated politics disputes the oversimplification that comes with the idea of singular and clear-cut female and male identities and the idea that there exists a completely uniform men's and women's history. Stone, instead, advocates the integrity of multiple, and at times seemingly paradoxical, identities.

Her work asserts, particularly under the stewardship of transgender activists and writers Leslie Feinberg and Riki Wilchins, that oppression based on sex, gender identification, and sexual orientation are intricately linked; that unity is of paramount importance; and that integrity and honesty (although rare) is valuable, and that efforts toward that end should be supported. Thus, "queerness," in the light of Stone's work, is not about narrowly defined politics or sex or gender or sexuality or history (forms of self-imposed colonialism). Instead, queerness is about intersecting the identities that are unique to each individual.

Raymond's arguments highlight the dishonesty inherent in the medicalization of transsexuality, where the prescribed treatment includes the blurring of a person's biological and social history. Furthermore, Stone, by urging transsexuals to be open and affirming of their transgressive character and complex gender histories, instituted a break with prescribed medical treatment and helped to build an informed transgender community. Subsequently, a transgender movement has coalesced and articulated the need for reform of the medical and legal systems. Notably, transgender persons have demanded their inclusion in civil-liberties legislation (especially the proposed Employment Non-Discrimination Act, which had been introduced in Congress in 1994 but has yet to pass), and have called for the removal of "gender identity disorder" as a psychopathology from the American Psychiatric Association's *Diagnostic and Statistical Manual of Mental Disorders* (DSM).

—*Matthew Steven Carlos*

Further Reading

Bornstein, Kate. *Gender Outlaw: On Men, Women, and the Rest of Us*. New York: Routledge, 1994.

Califia, Pat. *Sex Changes: The Politics of Transgenderism*. San Francisco, Calif.: Cleis Press, 1997.

Ekins, Richard, and Dave King, eds. *Blending Genders: Social Aspects of Cross-Dressing and Sex-Changing*. New York: Routledge, 1996.

Feinberg, Leslie. *Trans-Liberation: Beyond Pink or Blue*. Boston: Beacon Press, 1998.

Meyerowitz, Joanne. *How Sex Changed: A History of Transsexuality in the United States*. Cambridge, Mass.: Harvard University Press, 2002.

Raymond, Janice G. *The Transsexual Empire: The Making of the She-Male*. Boston: Beacon Press, 1979.

Stone, Sandy. "The 'Empire' Strikes Back: A Posttranssexual Manifesto." In *Body Guards: The Cultural Politics of Gender Ambiguity*, edited by Julia Epstein and Kristina Straub. New York: Routledge, 1991. Available at http://www.sandystone.com/empire-strikes-back.

See also: 1973: Olivia Records Is Founded; 1992: Transgender Nation Holds Its First Protest; June, 1992: Feinberg Publishes *Transgender Liberation*; Apr. 2, 1998: Canadian Supreme Court Reverses Gay Academic's Firing; Mar., 2003-Dec., 2004: Transsexuals Protest Academic Exploitation; Nov. 20, 2003: Transgender Day of Remembrance and Remembering Our Dead Project.

April 6, 1991
Asian Lesbians and Gays Protest Lambda Fund-Raiser

Members of the Asian Lesbians of the East Coast (ALOEC) and Gay Asian and Pacific Islander Men of New York (GAPIMNY) led a demonstration against a fund-raiser held by the LGBT rights organization Lambda Legal Defense and Education Fund at a preview performance of Miss Saigon, *a musical the activist groups and others considered racist, sexist, and otherwise dehumanizing.*

Locale: New York, New York
Categories: Marches, protests, and riots; arts; organizations and institutions; cultural and intellectual history

Key Figures
Milyoung Cho, protester and activist
Yoko Yoshikawa, protester and activist
Tom Stoddard, executive director of Lambda Legal

Summary of Event

Miss Saigon, a Broadway musical that premiered in London's West End in 1989, immediately caused controversy. An adaptation of Puccini's *Madama Butterfly*, the musical, by Claude-Michel Schönberg and Alain Boubil, and produced and directed by Cameron MacIntosh, tells the story of Kim, a Vietnamese prostitute who falls in love with a U.S. soldier and bears his child. The soldier is ordered back to the United States, but Kim remains loyal to him, even when he marries a white woman from the United States. The couple returns to Southeast Asia and finds Kim and her child. Kim commits suicide so her son can be raised by the soldier and his wife in the United States.

On April 6, 1991, members of the Asian Lesbians of the East Coast (ALOEC) and Gay Asian and Pacific Islander Men of New York (GAPIMNY) demonstrated against a fund-raiser being held by the Lambda Legal Defense and Education Fund—a GLBT rights organization—in conjunction with a preview performance of *Miss Saigon*. Like *Ma-*

> **ASIAN LESBIAN AND GAY COALITION: STATEMENT TO LAMBDA**
>
> We call upon you to recognize that Lambda's use of a racist and sexist play is blatantly hypocritical and unprincipled. The monies you raise from *Miss Saigon* will disappear by the end of your fiscal year, but we contend every day with the exploitative and dehumanizing stereotypes and violence perpetuated by *Miss Saigon*.
>
> We call upon Lambda to recognize its responsibility as an organization of cutting-edge civil rights litigation, to put itself on the line for anti-sexist, anti-racist activism, in solidarity with all of us committed to social change.

dama Butterfly, *Miss Saigon* is an Orientalist fable that reinforces the view of Western dominance over the East and reflects "a nostalgia for white European racial and cultural supremacy." The libretto contained numerous anti-Asian epithets and slurs, including "greasy Chinks" and "slits." Although many actors of Asian descent were cast in the show, Jonathan Pryce, a white British actor, was cast as the main male character of Asian descent. Pryce performed with eyelid prosthetics and tinted foundation—in "yellow-face."

Individuals of Asian descent and antiracist groups had been protesting the Broadway opening of *Miss Saigon* when ALOEC and GAPIMNY learned that Lambda and New York City's Lesbian and Gay Community Services Center (LGCSC) were holding their annual fund-raisers in conjunction with performances of *Miss Saigon*. ALOEC and GAPIMNY met in December of 1990 and formed a coalition to convince Lambda and the LGCSC to cancel their fund-raisers. Lambda's event was scheduled for April and LGCSC's event was scheduled for October, so the coalition decided to approach Lambda first. They sent a letter to Lambda, detailing their concerns and asking the group to cancel their event. Lambda refused to cancel but agreed to meet with representatives of the coalition on February 19, 1991. The coalition's opening statement clearly described its position and demands.

Lambda's executive director, Tom Stoddard, explained that the organization had already invested in the fund-raiser and that canceling would be difficult. Also, Lambda had been depending on the event to provide 10 percent of its annual budget. The discussion that followed had been heated and polarized. A white male member of Lambda declared that *Miss Saigon* was not racist, according to a white friend who had seen it. When Lambda's Carol Buell began a statement with, "Well, when *Miss Saigon* is dead and buried . . . ," protester Milyoung Cho responded, "Men yell 'Suzy Wong' at me in the streets now and that came out 20 years ago!" Tsuhyang Chen compared the play's use of the terms "greasy Chinks" and "slits" to the derogatory of the words "faggots" and "dykes," and asked Lambda board members how they would feel if they had paid to hear gays and lesbians so described. Ron Johnson, an African American Lambda board member, suggested offering forums on racism to Lambda's board members as part of the *Miss Saigon* fund-raiser. Lambda refused to cancel the fund-raiser. Stoddard confirmed the refusal by fax a few days later.

While negotiating with Lambda, the coalition had kept its protests within the LGBT communities, calling upon progressive LGBT people of all races and ethnicities to address institutional racism, including within their own communities. At this juncture, the coalition moved to public dialogue and protest so that Lambda would feel continued pressure to cancel the fund-raiser, and the coalition planned to greet donors with a demonstration if Lambda failed to cancel.

Joining the coalition were activists from other LGBT groups, including members of ACT UP, Brooklyn Women's Martial Arts, Gay Men of African Descent, Kambal sa Lusog, Las Buenas Amigas, Latino Gay Men of New York, Men of All Colors Together, Other Countries, Queer Nation, Salsa Soul Sisters, South Asian Lesbians and Gay Men, We Wah, and Bar Chee Ampe. Seven female Lambda staff members sent a letter to the board, urging them to cancel the fund-raiser and offering to have their salaries reduced to offset any financial loss to the organization. Mariana Romo-Carmona, Lambda's public education coordinator, resigned in protest. In California, Gay Asian and Pacific Alliance and Asian Pacifica Sisters pressured Lambda's Los Angeles office. The renowned poet and social justice leader Audre Lorde refused to accept Lambda's Liberty Award and said, "Until the real nugget of what racism and sexism is all about comes through to the white lesbian and gay community, this thing is going to keep happening all over again." The strength and clarity of these efforts led to a meeting in March of 1991, in which the LGCSC—but not Lambda—agreed to cancel its fund-raiser.

The Center's decision did not garner approval from all LGBT communities. Anonymous fliers calling the coalition homophobic were left at the Center on March 29, when a forum on the *Miss Saigon* controversy was held. In the *Village Voice*, a New York alternative newspaper, Don Shewey called the coalition's protests "more p.c.-than-thou gay-bashing." Furthermore, the controversy raged in the letters section of *Outweek* magazine.

By February, the coalition had begun to plan a second protest for the opening night of *Miss Saigon*. It hoped to engage communities of Asian and Pacific Islander descent and to clarify that its protest was against *Miss Saigon* and not against Lambda itself. Members of Asian Pacific Alliance for Creative Equality, Youth for Philippine Action, the Coalition Against Anti-Asian Violence, the Japanese American Citizen's League, the Pan Asian Repertory Theater, the Chinese Progressive Association, and various student groups joined the coalition.

The April 6, 1991, demonstration at the Lambda fund-raiser was attended by approximately five hundred people, predominantly progressive LGBT people of all races and leftist people of Asian and Pacific Islander descent. It was rumored that Tom Stoddard had told the police he expected a large, possibly violent demonstration. Protesters first were stopped about a block from the theater by police, who tried to keep them out of the view of theatergoers. Because the group was large, however, they were able to move across the street from the theater. The police arrested and removed six demonstrators—Haftan Eckholdt, Joe Pressley, Chris Hansen, Simon Howard-Stewart, Karl Jagbundhansingh, and John Kusakabe—and charged them with disorderly conduct. Kusakabe and Pressley later reported being beaten by police while in custody.

Shortly before the start of the show, two attendees gave their $100 tickets to Milyoung Cho and Yoko Yoshikawa. The two activists entered the theater and waited until Jonathan Pryce came on stage, at which point they began shouting, "This play is racist and sexist! Lambda is racist and sexist!" Although the two were quickly removed from the theater, the activists were pleased that the show had not been able to proceed without interruption.

The second demonstration, on April 11, 1991, did not attract as many protesters, and the police successfully confined the demonstrators to cordoned off sections of pavement. The media presence, however, was much greater than for the first demonstration. The coverage did not address the LGBT leadership of the coalition, and one television reporter asked a demonstrator, "What do lesbians and gay men have to do with protesting *Miss Saigon*?" The exchange took place off camera.

Significance

The protests did not close down *Miss Saigon*, though Lambda promised to be more aware of racism. The coalition experienced tension around sexual orientation while working with communities of Asian and Pacific Islander descent and tensions around race working with LGBT groups—experiences common for politically active LGBT people of color. The organizers felt, however, that the success of their alliance-building provided a model for future community development, a model in which "a complex identity is not only valued, but becomes a foundation for unity."

—*Gwendolyn Alden Dean*

Further Reading

"Inquirer Editorial: Heated Celebration." *Philippine Daily Inquirer*, October 1, 2000. http:// www.geocities.com/Hollywood/Prop/6137/ archives/ october2000/inquirer1001.html.

Said, Edward. *Orientalism*. New York: Random House, 1979.

Wernisch, Alexandra. "'Madame Butterfly,' 1887

Through 1989: A Stereotype and Its Challenge." *Austrian Association for American Studies.* http://www.sbg.ac.at/aaas/conf/aaas1999/abstracts/wernisch.htm.

Yoshikawa, Yoko. "The Heat Is On *Miss Saigon* Coalition: Organizing Across Race and Sexuality." In *The State of Asian America: Activism and Resistance in the 1990's*, edited by Karin Aguilar-San-Juan. Boston: South End Press, 1994.

SEE ALSO: Oct. 18, 1973: Lambda Legal Authorized to Practice Law.

August, 1991
LEATHER ARCHIVES AND MUSEUM IS FOUNDED

Longtime activist Chuck Renslow founded the first formally organized archival collection of art, artifacts, ephemera, and other materials relating specifically to the history and subculture of the leather lifestyle.

LOCALE: Chicago, Illinois
CATEGORIES: Organizations and institutions; arts

KEY FIGURES
Chuck Renslow, businessperson and leather community activist
Anthony De Blase, writer and publisher of *Drummer* magazine
Joseph Bean, leather community columnist, artist, and writer

SUMMARY OF EVENT
The Leather Archives and Museum began as an assemblage of the various media artworks of the late graphic artist Dom Orejudos (better known in the erotic-art world as Etienne) in the possession of his partner, Chicago activist Chuck Renslow. As a longtime member of the leather community at both the local and national levels, owner of the famous Gold Coast bar, and organizer with Orejudos of the International Mr. Leather contest in 1979, Renslow was acutely aware of the devastation being wreaked on this population by the AIDS pandemic and the resultant loss of much historical information on the global and postwar American leather world, as well as its personalities, organizations, and subcultures.

While recognizing the work already done by local and regional gay and lesbian archives and libraries toward retrieval of LGBT histories, Renslow envisioned a separate collection devoted solely to the subculture of leatherfolk, a coherent community not well reflected in existing special libraries on sexuality. Among the leaders of the American and Canadian leather communities who answered his call to form the first board of directors and coordinate various preservation and historical projects was Anthony De Blase, then publisher of *Drummer* magazine and prominent writer of S/M fiction (fiction with a theme of sadomasochism), who had designed the blue, black, and red "leather flag" that had quickly become a global symbol of the leather community after its debut in 1989.

The Leather Archives and Museum was formally incorporated in August of 1991 in the state of Illinois, taking as its mission "the compilation, preservation and maintenance" of artifacts and printed and visual media documenting the "leather lifestyle and related lifestyles (including but not limited to the Gay and Lesbian communities), history, archives and memorabilia for historical, educational and research purposes." The gay community gradually came to know about the archives through publicity in such internationally circulated periodicals as *The Leather Journal* and the dissemination of information through existing networks of regional leather conferences and contests. The archives also had consciousness-raising exhibits at the annual International Mr. Leather competition in Chicago.

In 1996, the archives opened its first storefront space on Clark Street, beginning a period of rapid expansion augmented by the appointment in 1997 of well-known writer and artist Joseph Bean as executive director and the search for a permanent facility. In 1999, the archives found a former synagogue and community theater building on Greenview Avenue near Loyola University in northern Chicago, and the archives started a capital campaign for its purchase; the campaign ended, successfully, in August of 2004. This effort was totally financed by leatherfolk from around the world, who worked together on an unprecedented scale over a period of seven years, with no external funding of any kind.

From its inception, the archives moved to establish professional links within the library and archival professions, both through the personal contacts of staff librarians and formal presentations at the conventions of the American Library Association and the Society for American Archivists. At the national level, in 2000, the Leather Archives joined the Subject Authority Cooperative Program run by the Library of Congress (LOC), which allowed it to propose new headings for the Library of Congress classification system, based upon its own materials. The archives would be able to suggest changes to headings already in use by the LOC.

Although begun with a collection of drawings and paintings, the holdings of the archives quickly diversified into more than twenty-six categories of materials, including organization bylaws, minutes, colors, insignias, and friendship pins, as well as items of clothing and uniforms, artworks (including two spectacular statues from the now-defunct Mineshaft bar in New York City and a collection of leather roses, each made by a different craftsperson). It also includes photographs, event memorabilia, documentary and popular films and videos, books, and magazines, all arranged into a highly distinctive library collection of several thousand volumes.

The oral history collection includes nearly one hundred interviews with leather men and leather women of all orientations and, in some cases, has the only primary biographical source material extant for them. The archives houses also the largest collection in North America of the artwork of Etienne, and its special collections are home to materials from several organizations, among them the International Gay Rodeo Association and the National Leather Association. Use of the collection has been strong from the beginning, ranging from activists to graduate students from the Art Institute of Chicago, Indiana University's Kinsey Institute, and other schools.

Significance

The Leather Archives and Museum, the first formal multimedia collection documenting the histories of GLBT leatherfolk and leather subculture, is a critical resource for researchers and the general public. It is part of a network of lesbian and gay archives around the world.

—*Robert Ridinger*

Further Reading

Bean, Joseph. "Speech at the Dedication of the Leather Archives and Museum, February 20, 2000." In *Speaking for Our Lives: Historic Speeches and Rhetoric for Gay and Lesbian Rights, 1892-2000*. Binghamton, N.Y.: Harrington Park Press, 2004.

Carmichael, James V., Jr. "'They Sure Got to Prove It on Me': Millennial Thoughts on Gay Archives, Gay Biography, and Gay. . . ." *Libraries & Culture* 35, no. 1 (Winter, 2000).

Leather Archives & Museum. http://www.leatherarchives.org.

"Leather Archives Burns Mortgage." *Leather Journal* 174 (September, 2004).

Ridinger, Robert. "Things Visible and Invisible: The Leather Archives and Museum." *Journal of Homosexuality* 43, no. 1 (2002): 1-9.

Thompson, Mark, ed. *Leatherfolk: Radical Sex, People, Politics, and Practice*. 10th anniversary edition. Los Angeles: Alyson, 2001.

See also: 1952: ONE, Inc., Is Founded; Fall, 1973: Lesbian Herstory Archives Is Founded; 1975: First Gay and Lesbian Archives Is Founded.

August 27, 1991
THE ADVOCATE OUTS PENTAGON SPOKESMAN PETE WILLIAMS

Assistant secretary of defense and Pentagon spokesperson Pete Williams was outed as gay by The Advocate *magazine, embarrassing his employer, the U.S. Defense Department, which has a policy prohibiting lesbians, gays, and bisexuals from serving openly in the military.*

LOCALE: Washington, D.C.
CATEGORIES: Government and politics; military; publications

KEY FIGURES
Pete Williams, assistant secretary of defense for public affairs, U.S. Department of Defense
Michelangelo Signorile (b. 1960), freelance journalist
Richard B. Cheney (b. 1941), U.S. secretary of defense, and vice president of the United States, 2001-

SUMMARY OF EVENT
When a photograph of Assistant Secretary of Defense Pete Williams appeared on the cover of the August 27, 1991, issue of *The Advocate*, a national gay and lesbian newsmagazine, the Pentagon's chief press spokesperson became the latest in a string of celebrities and government officials to be "outed" to the public. The headline accompanying William's photograph read, "Did this man . . . Ruin 2,000 Lives? Know About the Suicides? Waste Taxpayers' Millions on Military Witch-hunts? The outing of Assistant Secretary of Defense Pete Williams."

Media scholar Larry Gross has traced the practice of political outing—revealing the sexuality of closeted lesbians or gays against their will—to practices in imperial Germany during the early 1900's. The threat of outing as a political tool briefly resurfaced during the McCarthy hearings in the 1950's. Outing also occurred in the early 1990's, when gay journalists, who historically had protected the lives of closeted lesbian and gay notables, began to resent the hypocrisy of powerful and politically connected lesbians and gays who either refused to use their influence to help with issues important to the gay and lesbian community or, worse, actively worked against these interests.

Michelangelo Signorile, who wrote the article on Williams, had pioneered the practice of outing public officials when he worked at *OutWeek*, a now-defunct gay and lesbian magazine. Signorile had been buoyed by the publicity the article received as well as the controversy it generated.

Williams had become a highly visible member of the administration of President George H. W. Bush during the Gulf War in 1991. During the height of the war, Williams's name was in newspapers and his face was on television screens almost daily. Less visible to the general public was his gay identity, although it had been well known in Washington circles for some time. Williams was generally well liked and respected within the Beltway, and he had been mentioned as a possible White House press secretary.

Williams's professional career had begun on the other side of the cameras and microphones in the 1970's as a reporter for a television station in his hometown of Casper, Wyoming. From there, he went to Washington to serve as press secretary for Wyoming congressman Richard Cheney. When Cheney went to the Defense Department as secretary in 1989, Williams went with him as his chief public affairs officer. His favored status in the Department of Defense, however, coincided with an increasingly aggressive Pentagon policy of exposing and discharging members of the military who were thought to be lesbian or gay, including a number of highly decorated officers. By one estimate, the number of discharged service personnel had topped ten thousand during the 1980's.

The Defense Department directive declaring that "homosexuality is incompatible with military service" and claiming that the presence of lesbians and gays in the armed forces "adversely affects the ability of the military services to maintain discipline, good order and morale" actually dates to 1943, though enforcement for much of that time was lax and inconsistent.

While *The Advocate*, which has been published since 1967, is generally considered to be a respected and credible chronicler of events and issues within the lesbian and gay communities, its readership outside those communities is sparse. The treatment of the story by more mainstream media varied. Many newspapers, including *The Washington Post*, and the major television networks refused to pick up the story. Other media reported that a major figure within the Defense Department had been outed but did not identify Williams by name. A few, such as the *Oakland Tribune* and the *Detroit News*, printed the story with a photograph of Williams.

After the story broke, Secretary Cheney said he would not ask Williams to resign. Williams himself refused all comment. When asked at a Pentagon briefing whether he was gay, he said he was paid to discuss government policy, not his personal life.

SIGNIFICANCE

Though rumors of closeted homosexuality had swirled around celebrities and political figures for years, Pete Williams's face was arguably the most familiar of those gays outed during the late 1980's and early 1990's. His almost nightly presence on television screens in living rooms across the country during the Gulf War brought heightened visibility, likewise, to the controversial practice of outing.

The coverage of *The Advocate* story by other media, most of which chose not to mention Williams by name, fueled the debate over the ethics of outing and, more broadly, over the proper journalistic boundaries between public and private. Historically, reporters assigned to cover governmental bodies and officials—whether at the local, state, or federal level—had kept the personal secrets of those about whom they wrote, sexual and otherwise. However, the combination of increased media competition, audience appetite for voyeuristic celebrity stories, and younger journalists unwilling to play by the rules of the old boys' network had made the boundaries permeable, if not obsolete.

It can be argued that the fallout from the Williams story had far broader public policy implications. Together with the increased activism by groups opposed to the ban on military service by lesbians and gays, the seeming hypocrisy in the Pentagon—on one hand, aggressively discharging both open and closeted gays and lesbians from the service ranks and, on the other hand, employing a

---

MICHELANGELO SIGNORILE

Born in New York City in 1960 into a blue-collar Italian family, Michelangelo Signorile grew up in Brooklyn and on Staten Island. During the late 1970's, he studied journalism at the Newhouse School of Public Communications at Syracuse University. After returning to New York City in the 1980's, he became an influential voice in gay politics and in educating the public about issues dealing with acquired immunodeficiency syndrome, or AIDS.

In 1989, Signorile, with Gabriel Rotello, founded *OutWeek Magazine*. In addition to addressing a variety of issues associated with the gay and lesbian community, Signorile used the magazine specifically to promote the practice of "outing," the revealing of a person's sexual orientation. Signorile, soon known as the "pioneer of outing," contended that when the homosexuality of public figures was relevant to a bigger story, those public figures should be outed. In 1990, he exposed publishing giant Malcolm Forbes. Many newspapers reported the story as shocking, scandalous, and unethical. After becoming a columnist for *The Advocate* in the early 1990's, Signorile outed U.S. assistant secretary of defense Pete Williams. Later, Signorile outed gossip columnist Liz Smith and other public figures.

Signorile has written a number of groundbreaking books, including *Queer in America* (1993), *Outing Yourself* (1995), *Life Outside* (1998), and *Hitting Hard* (2005). He hosts a daily talk show on the *OutQ* channel on Sirius Satellite Radio, writes a weekly column for the *New York Press*, and has been instrumental in changing journalistic practices in the United States. His work, although controversial, has helped to make it easier for ordinary individuals to reveal their sexual orientation.

closeted gay as its chief public face—placed the question of that policy's fairness front and center. Only months later, presidential candidate Bill Clinton would campaign against the ban in the 1992 election. His efforts to fulfill that campaign pledge in early 1993 were met by hostility from key members of Congress, forcing him reluctantly to support the superficially fairer Don't Ask, Don't Tell policy.

For Williams, the incident proved to be a mixed blessing. Though public disclosure of his homosexuality and the defeat of George H. W. Bush in 1992 effectively precluded him from advancing his career as media spokesperson for the executive branch, his new visibility and Washington contacts prompted NBC News to hire him in 1993 as a Washington-based correspondent covering the Justice Department and the U.S. Supreme Court. As of 2006, he was still a television correspondent in Washington.

—*Bruce E. Drushel*

FURTHER READING

Carr, C. "Why Outing Must Stop." *Village Voice*, March 19, 1990, p. 37.

Cassidy, John. "'Outing' Claims Pentagon Victim." *Sunday Times*, August 11, 1991.

Gross, Larry. "Contested Closets: The Politics and Ethics of Outing." In *The Columbia Reader on Lesbians and Gay Men in Media, Society, and Politics*, edited by Larry Gross and James D. Woods. New York: Columbia University Press, 1999.

Signorile, Michelangelo. "How I Brought Out Malcolm Forbes—And the Media Blinked." *Village Voice*, April 3, 1990, p. 23-24.

———. *Queer in America: Sex, the Media, and the Closets of Power*. Madison: University of Wisconsin Press, 2003.

SEE ALSO: 1967: *Los Angeles Advocate* Begins Publication; Mar. 7, 1967: CBS Airs *CBS Reports: The Homosexuals*; Oct. 31, 1969: *Time* Magazine Issues "The Homosexual in America"; July 14, 1983: Studds Is First Out Gay Man in the U.S. Congress; 1985: GLAAD Begins Monitoring Media Coverage of Gays and Lesbians; July 25, 1985: Actor Hudson Announces He Has AIDS; Mar., 1987: Radical AIDS Activist Group ACT UP Is Founded; May 30, 1987: U.S. Congressman Frank Comes Out as Gay; Oct. 11, 1988: First National Coming Out Day Is Celebrated; 1992-2002: Celebrity Lesbians Come Out; Nov. 30, 1993: Don't Ask, Don't Tell Policy Is Implemented; 1995: *The Advocate* Outs Oscar Nominee Nigel Hawthorne; 1995: Athlete Louganis Announces He Is HIV-Positive.

September 29, 1991
CALIFORNIA GOVERNOR WILSON VETOES ANTIDISCRIMINATION BILL

California governor Pete Wilson reneged on a campaign promise to protect gays and lesbians from employment discrimination when he vetoed AB-101, a bill that would have prohibited employers from discriminating in hiring and promotion on the basis of a person's sexual orientation. His veto drew weeks of street protests and rallies in California and around the country.

ALSO KNOWN AS: AB-101
LOCALE: Sacramento, San Francisco, and Los Angeles, California
CATEGORIES: Laws, acts, and legal history; civil rights; marches, protests, and riots

KEY FIGURES
Pete Wilson (b. 1933), governor of California, 1991-1999
Terry B. Friedman, Democratic assemblyman and author of AB-101
John J. Duran, attorney and cochair of the Lobby for Individual Freedom and Equality, or LIFE Lobby, a key sponsor of AB-101

SUMMARY OF EVENT
Pete Wilson, who had been a U.S. senator representing California, was known as a moderate Republican and had less than full support from the more conservative right wing of the Republican Party. When he ran for governor in 1990 against the popular former San Francisco mayor, Democrat Dianne Feinstein (now a U.S. senator), he ran on the tailcoat of Proposition 115, the Crime Victims Justice Reform Act, which helped him solidify his credentials as "tough on crime" and gain favor with more conservative Republicans. Wilson seemed to be walking a very tight line, trying to woo the votes of both conservative Republicans and moderate Republicans and Democrats.

During the heated gubernatorial campaign, Wilson made promises to gays and lesbians, stating that he would sign any legislation before him that outlawed employment discrimination on the basis of sexual orientation. Many gay and lesbian Californians supported his run based on his campaign promises. In late September, 1991, the state senate passed AB-101, a bill authored by Assemblyman Terry B. Friedman. The bill would have added sexual orientation as a protected class under California's nondiscrimination law; it passed by one vote and went to the governor for his signature. Gay and lesbian Californians had looked forward to the signing of the bill based on Wilson's campaign promises.

On September 29, 1991, Governor Wilson, feeling the pressures of conservative Republicans who found him to be pro-tax and antifamily, vetoed AB-101. He stated that existing laws afforded lesbians and gays ample protection against discrimination, although he added that he was "tempted to sign the legislation to protect gays from a tiny minority of mean-spirited, gay-bashing bigots." His political savvy failed to garner many rewards from conservative groups such as the Traditional Values Coalition, led by the Reverend Lou Sheldon, who said he was pleased but withheld his full support of the governor. Other conservatives criticized the governor for implying that gays and lesbians needed protection from a tiny minority of bigots. It seemed that few on either side were happy with Wilson's veto, least of all gay and lesbian Californians, who had believed his promises and supported his campaign.

California gay and lesbian communities erupted in the wake of Wilson's veto. Their sense of betrayal flowed into the streets as thousands protested and rebelled in San Francisco, Sacramento, and Los Angeles. Protesters decried Wilson as a spineless politician thinking only of his presidential aspirations. In San Francisco, crowds marched to the Old State House, where police were not prepared with riot gear. The crowds overwhelmed the officers, using bricks and two-by-fours to destroy stained-glass windows in their rage. The crowd set fire to the building and chanted anti-Wilson slogans as it burned. In Los Angeles, protesters marched through the streets, disrupted and stopped traffic, and held multiple nonviolent protests over several weeks, well into the month of November.

SIGNIFICANCE

Governor Wilson had managed to sandwich himself politically between two powerful California constituencies, the conservative right of the Republican Party and the progressive left of the Democratic Party. Though he would serve as governor until 1999, he would never find his footing as he tried to assuage both constituencies. Wilson's political career turned sharply to the right, as signaled by his veto. Wilson heard the voices of angry gays and lesbians, but he was swayed by conservative Republicans, who continued to eschew his middle-of-the-road, tax-and-spend politics. The right sustained its pressure on Wilson at the same time that protesters made their anger known to Wilson at gatherings throughout the state. John J. Duran, an Anaheim attorney and cochair of the Lobby for Individual Freedom and Equality (LIFE Lobby) (a key sponsor of AB-101), contended that Wilson's veto led to questions about his political stances. Duran said that "Wilson absolutely caved in to the far right of his own party and to fundamentalists on gay rights. What else then? Abortion? What else will the right hold him hostage to?"

The people of California would pass a proposition modeled after AB-101 by a 2-1 margin. In 1992, Wilson signed into legislation AB-2601, authored by Assemblyman Friedman. AB-2601, similar to AB-101, added sexual orientation as a protected class in the state's labor code. Wilson signed the legislation, noting that it afforded "a wholly adequate remedy to those suffering discrimination and is responsive . . . to the need for fairness to innocent employers and their employees." The gay and lesbian communities disagreed and fought for legislation during his second session that would transfer responsibility for enforcing workplace discrimination protections for gays and lesbians to the Department of Fair Employment and Housing, the same department that handled all other forms of discrimination. Gay and lesbian advocates argued that a law of protection existed and no one knew how to use it. Wilson vetoed the bill on October 13, 1997.

During his years as governor, Wilson supported Proposition 187, legislation denying state-financed benefits to illegal immigrants; vetoed several pieces of gay rights legislation, including a 1994 domestic partnership bill; attempted to block the regents of the University of California from providing domestic partnership benefits to their employees; and significantly shifted to the political right. Though Wilson had dreams of a presidential run, his inconsistency with promises and his stance on Proposition 187, a position that Republicans later called a mistake, ended his dreams.

—*Jennifer Self*

FURTHER READING

Berstein, Dan. "Initiatives Are at the Top of Politicians' List of Favorite Things." *Sacramento Bee*, August 5, 1996.

D'Emilio, John. "Gay Politics and Community in San Francisco Since World War II." *Socialist Review* 55 (January/February, 1981): 77-104.

_____. *Making Trouble: Essays on Gay History, Politics, and the University*. New York: Routledge, 1992.

Gewertz, Catherine, and George Frank. "Wilson Criticized by Both Sides After Gay Rights Bill Veto." *Los Angeles Times*, October 1, 1991, p. 1.

Harris, Scott, and George Ramos. "Gay Activists Vent Rage over Wilson's Veto Protest." *Los Angeles Times*, October 1, 1991, p. 3.

Kaiser, Charles. *The Gay Metropolis: 1940-1996*. New York: Houghton Mifflin, 1997.

Marcus, Eric. *Making History: The Struggles for Gay and Lesbian Equal Rights, 1945-1990, an Oral History*. New York: HarperCollins, 1992.

Murphy, Dean, and Victor Merina. "March by One Thousand Gay Activists Halts Business Protest." *Los Angeles Times*, October 6, 1991, p. 5.

"Rights Watch: Political Veto." Editorial. *Los Angeles Times*, October 1, 1991, p. 6.

See also: Apr. 27, 1953: U.S. President Eisenhower Prohibits Federal Employment of Lesbians and Gays; 1972-1973: Local Governments Pass Antidiscrimination Laws; June 27, 1974: Abzug and Koch Attempt to Amend the Civil Rights Act of 1964; July 3, 1975: U.S. Civil Service Commission Prohibits Discrimination Against Federal Employees; 1978: Lesbian and Gay Workplace Movement Is Founded; June 2, 1980: Canadian Gay Postal Workers Secure Union Protections; Dec. 4, 1984: Berkeley Extends Benefits to Domestic Partners of City Employees; Nov. 8, 1988: Oregon Repeals Ban on Antigay Job Discrimination; May 1, 1989: U.S. Supreme Court Rules Gender-Role Stereotyping Is Discriminatory; Sept. 23, 1992: Massachusetts Grants Family Rights to Gay and Lesbian State Workers; 1994: Employment Non-Discrimination Act Is Proposed to U.S. Congress; Apr. 2, 1998: Canadian Supreme Court Reverses Gay Academic's Firing; July, 2003: Singapore Lifts Ban on Hiring Lesbian and Gay Employees; July, 2003: Wal-Mart Adds Lesbians and Gays to Its Antidiscrimination Policy.

December 17, 1991
Minnesota Court Awards Guardianship to Lesbian Partner

Karen Thompson, the lesbian partner of Sharon Kowalski, a disabled woman unable to care for herself after she had been paralyzed in a vehicle accident, was named Kowalski's guardian by the Minnesota Court of Appeals. The decision ended an eight-year legal struggle for guardianship between Thompson and Kowalski's parents.

Locale: Minnesota
Categories: Laws, acts, and legal history; civil rights

Key Figures
Sharon Kowalski, partner of Karen Thompson
Karen Thompson (b. 1947), partner and guardian of Sharon Kowalski
Donald and Della Kowalski, parents of Sharon Kowalski
Karen Tomberlin, former guardian and Kowalski family friend

Summary of Event
On November 13, 1983, Sharon Kowalski, then twenty-seven years old, was driving her niece and nephew home when the car they were in was struck head-on by a car driven by a man who was drunk. Sharon's four-year-old niece was killed in the collision, and Sharon arrived at the hospital in St. Cloud, Minnesota, with a severe head injury and in a coma. Karen Thompson, Sharon's lesbian partner of nearly four years at the time, arrived at the hospital after receiving a call from Donald Kowalski, Sharon's father, who notified her of the accident. Karen saw a sign in the intensive care unit that stated that "family members" were the only ones who could visit a patient within the unit.

From all appearances, this innocuous sign at the door to the intensive care unit would not predict what would follow. Four years earlier, on December 17, 1979, Sharon and Karen exchanged rings and committed themselves to each other; few knew of their relationship. They bought a house together, and each had a life-insurance policy naming the other as beneficiary. However, because Karen was not legally "family," hospital regulations prevented her from seeing her seriously injured partner. Hours passed, until a priest said he would check on Sharon's status. A doctor emerged and informed Karen that Sharon had devastating injuries, including a severe injury to her head and multiple orthope-

> **FROM *IN RE GUARDIANSHIP OF SHARON KOWALSKI*, WARD**
>
> Appellant Karen Thompson challenges the trial court's denial of her petition for guardianship of Sharon Kowalski, and the court's award of guardianship to Karen Tomberlin. We reverse and remand for appointment of Karen Thompson as guardian. . . .
>
> *Issue*
>
> Did the trial court abuse its discretion in denying appellant's petition for guardianship of Sharon Kowalski? . . .
>
> *Conclusion*
>
> While the trial court has wide discretion in guardianship matters, this discretion is not boundless. The Minnesota guardianship statutes are specific in their requirement that factual findings be made on a guardian's qualifications. The statutes also consistently require the input of the ward where possible. Upon review of the record, it appears the trial court clearly abused its discretion in denying Thompson's petition and naming Tomberlin guardian instead.
>
> All the medical testimony established that Sharon has the capacity reliably to express a preference in this case, and she has clearly chosen to return home with Thompson if possible. This choice is further supported by the fact that Thompson and Sharon are a family of affinity, which ought to be accorded respect.
>
> Thompson's suitability for guardianship was overwhelmingly clear from the testimony of Sharon's doctors and caretakers. At the same time, evidence of Tomberlin's qualifications was not in the record. Moreover, Tomberlin's status as a neutral party was undermined by evidence of her close ties to the Kowalskis and her expressed intention to relocate Sharon, contrary to the doctors' recommendations that Sharon have a less-restrictive environment near Thompson.
>
> We reverse the trial court and grant Thompson's petition. While under Minn.Stat. Section 525.56, subd. 1, a guardian always remains subject to court control, it should be made clear that this court is also reversing specific restrictions on the guardian's decision-making power that might be read into the trial court order. She is free to make whatever decisions she and the doctors feel are necessary to achieve Sharon's best interests, including decisions regarding Sharon's location. Thompson is, however, directed to continue efforts at accommodating visitation between Sharon and the Kowalskis, without unreasonable restrictions.
>
> *Decision*
>
> The trial court abused its discretion in denying Thompson's petition where there was uncontradicted expert testimony as to appellant's suitability, and where there was insufficient evidence as to the qualifications or neutrality of the named guardian. We remand for an order, consistent with this opinion, appointing Karen Thompson guardian.
>
> Reversed and remanded.

dic injuries; her recovery, if she survived, would be long term. Karen was allowed to visit her partner for five minutes.

Later that night, Sharon's parents, Donald and Della Kowalski, arrived from northern Minnesota, having learned earlier that evening that their granddaughter (Sharon's niece) had died in the accident. During the next month, Sharon's parents and Karen spent as much time as they could at the hospital, with Sharon's parents occasionally staying with Karen at her and Sharon's home. The Kowalskis did not know that their daughter and Karen were partners.

Eventually, the Kowalskis began to question the amount of time Karen was spending with their daughter, who remained in a coma. They told Karen they were planning to move Sharon closer to them and that they could best care for their daughter. Karen struggled with what to do and then decided, with the support of a counselor at the hospital, to write Sharon's parents and explain their lesbian relationship.

Karen's expression of love and hope for Sharon quickly turned into a legal and emotional nightmare as the Kowalskis reacted angrily to her letter. On March 2, 1984, Karen petitioned for appointment as Sharon's guardian, essentially revealing publicly for the first time that she and Sharon were partners; Donald Kowalski immediately cross-petitioned for appointment. A probate court concluded that Sharon was incapacitated and, on April 25, 1984, appointed her father her guardian, but on the condition that Karen would retain visitation rights and have access to Sharon's medical records.

In 1984, Sharon was moved three times, eventually residing in a nursing home in Hibbing, Minnesota, hundreds of miles from her home outside St.

Cloud. Despite the travel and relocations, Sharon began to show signs of improvement, while Karen's effort to communicate with the Kowalskis continued to deteriorate. On November 1, 1984, a temporary restraining order was issued against Karen, with motions of guardianship heard in May of 1985. On July 23, 1985, a district court judge ordered Donald Kowalski sole guardian, and within twenty-four hours he terminated visitation rights for Karen; her visit with Sharon in August of 1985 would be her last for three and one-half years.

Legal proceedings over guardianship and whether Sharon was receiving proper therapy continued in local, state, and federal courts, as Karen, a very private person, began to speak out with support from women's, lesbian, and disability rights groups. Karen's lawyer petitioned the court in September of 1987 for a medical evaluation of Sharon. In May of 1988, the district court judge ordered a medical evaluation to take place in Duluth, Minnesota, and doctors determined that Sharon wanted to see Karen. On February 4, 1989, the two women reunited for the first time since 1985.

Donald Kowalski, citing a heart condition and deteriorating health, resigned as his daughter's guardian in May of 1990. On April 23, 1991, denying Karen's petition for guardianship, the court named Karen Tomberlin, a family friend, as Sharon's guardian. Then, on December 17, 1991, twelve years to the day after Sharon and Karen exchanged rings, the Minnesota Court of Appeals granted Karen Thompson guardianship of Sharon Kowalski. The appeals court ruled that Sharon "has the capacity reliably to express a preference in this case, and she has clearly chosen to return home with Thompson," and the court also recognized their lesbian relationship, stating, "This choice is further supported by the fact that Thompson and Sharon are a family of affinity, which ought to be accorded respect." Sharon's homecoming took place on April, 1993, after the Minnesota Supreme Court refused to hear Tomberlin's appeal.

SIGNIFICANCE

From the moment Karen Thompson arrived at the hospital to see her partner Sharon, she had no legal rights. This happened, all too often, during the HIV-AIDS crisis (and still happens today) when long-time companions, there to provide comfort and help make decisions about care, were denied access. Karen's gaining guardianship was hailed as a victory for lesbian and gay rights, but Karen, who was quoted after the decision in the *Los Angeles Times*, said, "today's decision is not a victory. It is a right decision, a just decision that should have been made eight years ago."

Karen's eight-year legal struggle highlighted the need for same-gender couples to seek legal recognition of their domestic partnership, including receiving "spousal" benefits from the employers of their partners, for ending discrimination in the workplace, for the legal right to marry or to form a civil union, and for domestic partnership laws in general, including rights of visitation, guardianship, and custody.

—*John Boyd*

FURTHER READING

Charles, Casey. *The Sharon Kowalski Case: Lesbian and Gay Rights on Trial*. Lawrence: University Press of Kansas, 2003.

Hansen, Mark. "Gay-Rights Victory." *ABA Journal* 78 (March, 1992): 22.

Hayden, Curry, Denis Clifford, and Frederick Hertz. *A Legal Guide for Lesbian and Gay Couples*. Berkeley, Calif.: Nolo Press, 2004.

In re Guardianship of Sharon Kowalski, Ward. Court of Appeals of Minnesota. 478 N.M. 2d 790; 1991. http://www.danpinello.com/Kowalski2.htm.

Lewin, Tamar. "Disabled Woman's Care Given to Lesbian Partner." *The New York Times*, December 18, 1991, p. A26.

Thompson, Karen, and Julie Andrzejewski. *Why Can't Sharon Kowalski Come Home?* San Francisco, Calif.: Spinsters Ink/Aunt Lute, 1988.

SEE ALSO: 1981: Gay and Lesbian Palimony Suits Emerge; July 26, 1990: Americans with Disabilities Act Becomes Law; Sept. 21, 1993-Apr. 21, 1995: Lesbian Mother Loses Custody of Her Child; Dec. 20, 1999: *Baker v. Vermont* Leads to Recognition of Same-Gender Civil Unions.

December 30, 1991-February 22, 1993
Canada Grants Asylum Based on Sexual Orientation

Canada extended refugee protection to men and women who feared persecution in their home countries because of their sexual orientation.

Locale: Canada
Categories: Civil rights; laws, acts, and legal history; government and politics

Key Figures

N. (K.U.), pseudonym for gay man from Bangladesh who applied for refugee status in Canada
Jorge Alberto Inaudi, gay man from Argentina who applied for refugee status in Canada
Marcelo Tenorio, gay man from Brazil who applied for refugee protection in the United States

Summary of Event

Jorge Alberto Inaudi fled Argentina in March, 1990, after he had been arrested outside a gay bar. While in detention, Inaudi was severely beaten, raped, and tortured with electric shocks by police officers. For years, he also had been blackmailed and assaulted by police, evicted by landlords, and fired by employers. He made his way to Canada and requested asylum to avoid being returned to the persecution he had suffered as a gay man in Argentina.

Inaudi had hoped to take advantage of an international treaty on asylum, the 1951 United Nations Convention Relating to the Status of Refugees, which binds Canada, the United States, and many other industrialized countries. Under the convention, states had agreed not to return any individual to a territory where his or her life or freedom would be threatened. Canada signed the convention in 1969. As of September, 2004, 142 states had ratified the convention.

The 1951 convention does not, however, protect all of the world's refugees. A person must meet the definition of a "refugee" as set forth in the international treaty. According to the convention, a "refugee" means a person who has a well-founded fear of persecution for reasons of race, religion, nationality, membership in a particular social group, or political opinion. Persons seeking asylum must therefore satisfy a two-pronged legal test. They must first demonstrate a well-founded fear of persecution, which is generally defined as a threat to life or security of the person, serious violations of human rights, or severe discrimination. Second, refugees must link the persecution they fear to their race, religion, nationality, membership in a particular social group, or political opinion. If any person satisfies the definition of a refugee, Canada and other signatory states have an international obligation not to return the person to the country where he or she may face persecution.

The convention does not list sexual orientation as a ground upon which a refugee could claim asylum. Nevertheless, as early as the 1980's, human rights abuses against sexual minorities led some gays and lesbians to flee to countries that provide refugee protection. In making the case for asylum,

---

United Nations Definition of "Refugee" (1951)

Chapter I
General Provisions
Article 1. Definition of the term "refugee"
  A. For the purposes of the present Convention, the term "refugee" shall apply to any person who: ... (2) As a result of events occurring before 1 January 1951 and owing to well-founded fear of being persecuted for reasons of race, religion, nationality, membership of a particular social group or political opinion, is outside the country of his nationality and is unable, or owing to such fear, is unwilling to avail himself of the protection of that country; or who, not having a nationality and being outside the country of his former habitual residence as a result of such events, is unable or, owing to such fear, is unwilling to return to it.

gays and lesbians tried to argue that their persecution was based on political opinion, membership in a social group, or a combination of both. However, sexual orientation was not considered to fit any of the definitions of "refugee" already listed in the convention. Few of the first lesbian and gay refugees were successful in their asylum claims.

That changed on January 6, 1992, in Canada, when Inaudi was granted refugee status there based on his sexual orientation. Believed to be the first successful gay or lesbian refugee claim in Canada, Inaudi's case was widely publicized around the world as a breakthrough in refugee law for gays and lesbians.

In reality, the first Canadian decision to grant asylum to a gay man was released several days before the Inaudi decision. On December 30, 1991, in a case referred to as *Re N. (K.U.)*, the Immigration and Refugee Board of Canada granted asylum to a Bengali man who testified that he feared persecution in Bangladesh because he was a homosexual. The gay man testified that Bengali authorities had become aware of his homosexuality when he was caught having sex with another man. He avoided arrest by bribing a security guard and police officer. However, after continuing to receive several threatening phone calls from a police officer, he fled the country and arrived in Canada on June 16, 1990. In supporting his claim for refugee status, the Immigration and Refugee Board concluded that there was a reasonable chance that the Bengali man would be subject to severe and excessive punishment because of his homosexual practices. While his identity was kept confidential, the Bengali man had in effect made the first successful refugee claim in Canada to be based on sexual orientation. However, Inaudi's case was the one that received wide media coverage and subsequently influenced asylum rules in several other countries around the world.

Significance

Despite progress made in several countries, the human rights situation for sexual minorities around the world was bleak in the 1980's and remains so into the twenty-first century. In many countries, homosexuality is considered a mental disease by the medical profession, penalized as a crime by the law, and condemned as a sin by religion. Some countries continue to execute individuals for their homosexuality. In other countries, while executions are not the norm, criminalization of consensual same-gender relations is still common. Even when not criminalized or pathologized, gays and lesbians are provided with little protection from harassment and persecution. Most countries do not extend protection against discrimination to lesbians and gays in the workforce. Government restrictions are also placed on the freedom of expression of lesbians and gays, and community publications are regularly shut down. Gay and lesbian groups are consistently denied the right to freedom of assembly.

While an increasing number of gays and lesbians are fleeing the egregious human rights abuses against sexual minorities in their countries, refugee law in safer countries does not explicitly provide protection for sexual minorities. The legal responsibility to provide protection is engaged only if a person meets the definition of a refugee as provided for in the convention. In 1991, the main obstacle facing gay and lesbian refugees was proving that the persecution they feared was based on one of the five enumerated grounds: race, religion, nationality, membership in a particular group, or political opinion.

In Canada, most gay and lesbian refugees had argued that the persecution they face was based on their membership in a particular social group, namely homosexuals. While N. (K.U.) and Jorge Alberto Inaudi were able to convince the Immigration and Refugee Board members that gays and lesbians constitute a particular social group for the purposes of refugee law, many other refugees failed to make that case. Immigration and Refugee Board members adjudicating these claims took a variety of approaches to the question of whether lesbians and gays form a particular social group for the purposes of the convention's definition of a refugee. It was not until a Supreme Court of Canada decision in *Canada v. Ward* (February 22, 1993) that the scope of a social group was clearly defined to include sexual orientation.

Canada v. Ward was not about a gay refugee claimant. However, in the course of deciding

> **"SOCIAL GROUP" DEFINED BY THE CANADIAN SUPREME COURT**
>
> Social group is not defined in the Immigration Act. I believe, therefore, that the words should be given their ordinary and usual meaning. The Oxford Dictionary defines social as "capable of being associated or united." Clearly homosexuals are capable of being associated or united. The same dictionary defines group as "a number of persons classed together on account of a certain degree of similarity." Homosexuals are classed together on account of a certain degree of similarity, i.e., that they are attracted to persons of their own gender. I therefore find that homosexuals, be they male or female, are members of a particular social group.

whether an Irish terrorist organization constituted a particular social group for the purposes of refugee law, the Canadian Supreme Court set forth a definition of social groups that determined, at the same time, that gays and lesbians could make refugee claims based on their membership in a particular social group because sexual orientation was an innate or unchangeable personal characteristic.

The decision settled Canadian refugee law relating to the issue of sexual orientation: Women and men who fear persecution because of homosexuality clearly fall within the enumerated grounds of persecution in the refugee convention. The holding in *Canada v. Ward* was quickly adopted in subsequent decisions of the Immigration and Refugee Board regarding sexual orientation. Since 1993, several hundred gays and lesbians have successfully claimed refugee status in Canada. In 1994, a Costa Rican lesbian who was assaulted by police was granted asylum; this decision is believed to be the first case of a woman obtaining refugee status in Canada based on her sexual orientation. Canada has also led the way in recognizing the asylum claims of transgender people. On July 4, 1994, the Immigration and Refugee Board released a decision in which it granted asylum status to an Iranian male-to-female transgender person.

The positive decisions in Canada established precedents that had an impact on refugee cases internationally. In the United States, the first widely publicized gay asylum case involved Brazilian Marcelo Tenorio. Tenorio had fled Brazil after being severely assaulted and stabbed outside a gay discotheque in Rio de Janeiro. On July 23, 1993, an immigration judge relied on the *Inaudi* case from Canada to find that Tenorio was a member of a particular social group and was deserving of refugee protection. In *In re Pitcherskaia*, a Russian lesbian was denied asylum in the United States despite having been beaten by militia and forced into involuntary psychiatric confinement. In her successful 1996 appeal to the United States Court of Appeals for the Ninth Circuit, lawyers representing several human rights organizations argued on her behalf that the refugee law in the United States should follow the Canadian precedents in *Inaudi* and *Ward*. In New Zealand, on August 30, 1995, the Refugee Status Appeal Authority had granted refugee status to an Iranian gay man after relying on the decision of the Supreme Court of Canada in *Ward*.

Many other states followed Canada's lead and began interpreting the convention to extend asylum to women and men fleeing persecution based on their sexual orientation. Decisions in countries such as Australia, Austria, Belgium, Denmark, Finland, Germany, the Netherlands, and Sweden have found that homosexual men and women constitute a "social group" for the purposes of refugee protection. Ireland enacted a refugee law in 1995 that explicitly mentions sexual orientation in defining membership in a particular social group.

Since 1991, there has been a growing volume of sexual orientation-based asylum cases in Western industrialized states. While the early groundbreaking decisions in Canada determined the ground upon which gays and lesbians can claim asylum—namely their membership in a particular social group—many other questions remain unresolved. Since the *N. (K.U.)* and *Inaudi* cases, sexual minorities have faced other challenges in gaining asylum in countries such as Canada and the United States. Claimants must prove that they face persecution, not simply discrimination, and the line between the two situations can be difficult to determine. Claimants must also prove that authorities from their country of origin are unable or unwilling to protect them and that they have no other safe refuge inside their country. Finally, jurisdictions like Australia traditionally have required that gay and lesbian claimants explain why they cannot exercise discretion in giving expression to their homosexuality and therefore avoid persecution. Nevertheless, in the early 1990's, the groundbreaking Canadian decisions in the *N. (K.U.)*, *Inaudi*, and *Ward* cases opened the door to asylum protection for thousands of sexual minorities around the world.

—Nicole LaViolette

FURTHER READING

Brook, James. "In Live-and-Let-Live Land, Gay People Are Slain." *The New York Times*, August 12, 1993.

Farnsworth, Clyde. "Argentine Homosexual Gets Refugee Status in Canada." *The New York Times*, January 22, 1992.

LaViolette, Nicole. "The Immutable Refugees: Sexual Orientation in *Ward v. Canada*." *University of Toronto Faculty of Law Review* 55, no. 1 (1997): 1.

Levy, Sydney, ed. *Asylum Based on Sexual Orientation: A Resource Guide*. San Francisco, Calif.: International Gay and Lesbian Human Rights Commission, 1996.

McClure, Heather, Christopher Nugent, and Lavi S. Soloway. *Preparing Sexual-Orientation Based Asylum Claims: A Handbook for Advocates and Asylum Seekers*. Chicago: Heartland Alliance for Human Needs and Human Rights, 1997.

Park, Jin S. "Pink Asylum: Political Asylum Eligibility of Gay Men and Lesbians Under U.S. Immigration Policy." *UCLA Law Review* 42 (1995): 1069.

Rosskopf, Ralf, ed. *Agents and Victims: Nongovernmental and Gender-Related Persecution in International and National Law*. Treatises on Migration and Refugee Problems 1. Berlin: BWV, 2004.

Walker, Kristen. "Sexuality and Refugee Status in Australia." *International Journal of Refugee Law* 12, no. 2 (2000): 175.

SEE ALSO: 1972-1973: Local Governments Pass Antidiscrimination Laws; Dec. 19, 1977: Quebec Includes Lesbians and Gays in Its Charter of Human Rights and Freedoms; June 2, 1980: Canadian Gay Postal Workers Secure Union Protections; Jan. 1, 1988: Canada Decriminalizes Sex Practices Between Consenting Adults; Apr. 27, 1992: Canadian Government Antigay Campaign Is Revealed; Oct., 1992: Canadian Military Lifts Its Ban on Gays and Lesbians; Apr. 2, 1998: Canadian Supreme Court Reverses Gay Academic's Firing; June 28, 2002: Irish American Lesbian Gains Canadian Immigrant Status; June 17, 2003, and July 19, 2005: Canada Legalizes Same-Gender Marriage.

1992
CANADIAN YMCA EXTENDS FAMILY DISCOUNTS TO GAYS AND LESBIANS

The Toronto and Ottawa YMCAs began offering family membership rates to same-gender couples, providing them some rights that heterosexual couples had taken for granted.

LOCALE: Ottawa and Toronto, Canada
CATEGORIES: Organizations and institutions; laws, acts, and legal history; civil rights

SUMMARY OF EVENT

Two YMCAs in Canada, one in Toronto and the other in Ottawa, agreed in 1992 to extend family membership rates to same-gender couples. The Ottawa YMCA changed its policy in the fall, prompted, in part, by an Ottawa man who had been refused a family membership for himself and his partner. Family memberships were $200 less than two individual memberships. Following suit, the Toronto YMCA changed its policy soon thereafter.

Both policy changes had been part of a movement by employers, organizations, and governments that had recognized the legal and social rights of same-gender relationships in Canada. The Ottawa YMCA also had responded to an Ontario Human Rights Commission Board of Inquiry ruling in 1992, which ordered the provisional government to provide survivor benefits for same-gender partners. Companies, municipalities, colleges and universities, and many other organizations across Canada and the United States have since been recognizing same-gender couples as family relationships.

In June of 2006, the Human Rights Campaign, the largest gay, lesbian, bisexual, and transgender rights organization in the United States, reported that several thousand private employers and colleges and universities provide health insurance coverage to an employee's domestic partner. In 1992, Lotus Corporation became the first publicly traded company in the United States to offer benefits to GLBT couples. As of June 1, 2006, 51 percent of *Fortune* 500 companies provided domestic partner benefits and 86 percent included sexual orientation in their policies against discrimination. Among cities and counties, more than two hundred offered domestic partner benefits (through June 1, 2006).

Across Canada, provinces have registered same-gender and common-law relationships. In 2001, Nova Scotia formally recognized gay and lesbian couples as domestic partners, and one year later, Quebec gave parental rights to lesbians and gays in the province. In 1999, Ontario and Quebec passed legislation providing homosexual couples many of the same benefits enjoyed by heterosexual couples, amending more than one hundred provincial statutes and regulations. In late 2004, the Supreme Court of Canada recognized marriage for same-gender couples.

Changes have also occurred at some of the most exclusive country clubs in the United States. In San Diego, for example, a lesbian couple had filed suit against the Bernardo Heights Country Club, claiming that they were denied full membership privileges because they are not married. The California Supreme Court ruled in their favor in August, 2005. In Atlanta, a similar complaint was filed by a gay couple with the city's Human Relations Commission. Many country clubs in Massachusetts are following the lead of the state of Massachusetts and changing their policies on marriage to give same-gender couples the same privileges as heterosexuals.

Although there has been a backlash to the legalizing of same-gender marriage in the state of Massachusetts, including the federal Defense of Marriage Act (DOMA) signed by U.S. president Bill Clinton in 1996, as well as a constitutional amendment proposed by U.S. president George W. Bush in 2004 and again in 2006 to define marriage as between a man and a woman, much of the change is being driven by shifting demographics. The once-prevalent married-couple households made up only half of U.S. households in 2004, and the once-common married couple with kids, which included about every residence one century ago, represents less than 25 percent of the nation's households.

From tax rates, company benefits, pensions, and country-club memberships to social security and hospital visitation, these perks were designed around marital unions. The U.S. Census Bureau reports that very soon the nation's nearly ninety million single households will be the new majority. Even though companies across Canada and the United States are implementing benefits for same-gender couples, they are also accommodating family benefits to include domestic partners, extended family members, and sometimes even grown children. The impetus for changes in country-club privileges is being driven, in part, not only by same-gender couples but also by longtime members, primarily widows and widowers who now have live-in partners.

Quietly, on January 12, 2004, the governor of the state of New Jersey signed into law a bill that provides gay and lesbian couples some benefits that married couples enjoy, including tax advantages, hospital visiting privileges, the right to claim a partner on state income tax filings, and other benefits previously denied same-gender couples. New Jersey has followed the lead of countries that include Canada, Denmark, Germany, Sweden, Portugal, and the Netherlands, in passing laws that recognize same-gender couples. On October 25, 2006, the New Jersey Supreme Court ruled that same-gender couples are entitled to the same legal rights as heterosexual married couples. The state of Vermont legalized same-gender civil unions in 2000, and California, since January 1, 2005, has provided some legal rights to same-gender couples who are registered with the state as domestic partners.

It remains to be seen, however, what steps the U.S. government will take in recognizing same-gender relationships at the federal level, but in the meantime, local and state jurisdictions around the country are taking steps to do so.

SIGNIFICANCE

The decision by two YMCAs in Canada to extend family memberships to same-gender couples is part of a larger trend occurring throughout the United States and Canada—the legal recognition of same-gender couples. Not only are the courts recognizing same-gender relationships, but so too are municipalities, states and provinces, companies, and organizations. Like the case with YMCAs in Canada, YMCA members in the United States are demanding and, in many cases, winning family mem-

---

CALIFORNIA SUPREME COURT RULES ON SPOUSAL BENEFITS FOR LESBIAN COUPLE

The California Supreme Court ruled on August 1, 2005, that California businesses must give registered domestic partners the same benefits and privileges that it extends to married couples. The ruling was the first on the state's domestic partner law, which took effect on January 1, 2005.

The case, *Koebke v. Bernardo Heights Country Club*, involved B. Birgit Koebke and Kendall French, partners since 1993 and registered domestic partners since 2000, and the Bernard Heights Country Club of San Diego County. Koebke, a member of the club since 1987, had on numerous occasions attempted to obtain membership privileges for French that are offered to spouses of married members, but the club had refused.

California first established a registry for domestic partners (same-gender couples of any age and opposite-gender couples in which one partner is older than age sixty-two may register) in 1999 and expanded by the California Domestic Partners Rights and Responsibilities Act of 2003, which granted to domestic partners most of the rights of spouses. In citing the act, the court declared that an important goal of the act is to "create substantial legal equality between domestic partners and spouses."

The decision expanded the protection provided by the state's Unruh Civil Rights Act, which prohibits discrimination based on sex, race, color, religion, ancestry, national origin, disability, or medical condition, to same-gender couples, but only if they are registered with the state as domestic partners.

bership rights for their same-gender partners.

Changes for legal recognition are important for same-gender couples; they also are important for children. Approximately 34 percent of lesbian couples and 22 percent of gay couples are raising children under the age of eighteen. Without legal protection, children of same-gender couples have less rights and protection than other children, and as a 2003 Human Rights Campaign report indicates, civil unions (a proposed alternative to marriage) only provide state-level protections. The report has identified 1,138 rights, benefits, and protections that are provided by the federal government for married couples that are not guaranteed for same-gender couples in civil unions.

—John Boyd

FURTHER READING

Bernstein, Robert A. *Families of Value: Personal Profiles of Pioneering Lesbian and Gay Parents*. New York: Marlowe, 2005.

Cahill, Sean, Mitra Ellen, and Sarah Tobias. *Family Policy: Issues Affecting Gay, Lesbian, Bisexual, and Transgender Families*. New York: National Gay and Lesbian Task Force Policy Institute, 2003. http://www.thetaskforce.org/reslibrary/.

Chambers, Marcia. "At Country Clubs, Gay Members Want All Privileges for Partners." *The New York Times*, September 21, 2004, p. D2.

Conlin, Michell, and Jessi Hempel. "UnMarried America." *Business Week*, October 20, 2003, 106.

Hayden, Curry, Denis Clifford, and Frederick Hertz. *A Legal Guide for Lesbian and Gay Couples*. Berkeley, Calif.: Nolo Press, 2004.

Lahey, Kathleen A. *Are We "Persons" Yet? Law and Sexuality in Canada*. Buffalo, N.Y.: University of Toronto Press, 1999.

Policy on Discrimination of Harassment Because of Sexual Orientation. Ontario Human Rights Commission. Approved January 11, 2000. http://www.ohrc.on.ca/english/code/.

"Same-Sex Marriage: A Selective Bibliography of the Legal Literature." Law Library, Rutgers School of Law. http://law-library.rutgers.edu/SSM.html.

Smith, Miriam. *Lesbian and Gay Rights in Canada: Social Movements and Equality Seeking, 1971-1999*. Buffalo, N.Y.: University of Toronto Press, 1999.

SEE ALSO: Dec. 4, 1984: Berkeley Extends Benefits to Domestic Partners of City Employees; Dec. 17, 1991: Minnesota Court Awards Guardianship to Lesbian Partner; Sept. 23, 1992: Massachusetts Grants Family Rights to Gay and Lesbian State Workers; July, 2003: Singapore Lifts Ban on Hiring Lesbian and Gay Employees.

1992
TRANSGENDER NATION HOLDS ITS FIRST PROTEST

Transgender Nation staged its first major action at the 1993 American Psychiatric Association convention to protest the APA's classification of "transsexuality" as a mental illness. In the short span in which the group was active, it was instrumental in bringing transgender issues to the forefront of queer political consciousness and for inspiring the formation of new groups focused on transgender rights.

LOCALE: San Francisco, California
CATEGORIES: Organizations and institutions; transgender/transsexuality; civil rights; marches, protests, and riots

KEY FIGURES
Anne Ogborn, transsexual activist and organizer of Transgender Nation
Jamison Green (b. 1948), transsexual activist, board chair of Gender Education and Advocacy
Susan Stryker, transsexual historian and activist, member of Transgender Nation
Christine Tayleur, transsexual activist, member of Transgender Nation

SUMMARY OF EVENT
Transgender Nation was first organized in 1992 by male-to-female (MTF) transsexual Anne Ogborn. The group's first action was a major protest at the annual convention of the American Psychiatric Association (APA) at the Moscone Center in downtown San Francisco. Several demonstrators at the conference center on May 23, 1993, including Ogborn, were arrested for defacing public property and disturbing the peace that day. Christine Tayleur, a member of Transgender Nation, described in an interview during the protest that she had been institutionalized at the age of fourteen because she cross-dressed, and while institutionalized, she had been administered medication. "They call it treatment. I call it torture," she was quoted as saying by the *San Francisco Chronicle* in its next-day report of the demonstration.

Female-to-male (FTM) activist Jamison Green recalled in his memoir that he had talked to psychiatrists at a transgender education booth inside the Moscone Center as the protesters demonstrated outside. According to Green, many of the psychiatrists were more inclined to speak to him because they wanted to understand why the protesters were outside. "The two strategies worked together," he wrote, noting that the presence of Transgender Nation demonstrators outside the convention enabled transgender educators inside to make headway in conversations with APA members.

The protest was reminiscent of the "gay invasion" demonstration at the APA meeting in San Francisco on May 14, 1970, in which activists demanded that homosexuality be depathologized and dropped from the APA's *Diagnostic and Statistical Manual of Mental Disorders* (DSM). Similarly, transgender protesters at the 1993 action called for the removal of "gender identity disorder," "transvestic fetishism," and "transsexualism" as mental illnesses listed in the DSM. While "homosexuality" was removed as a diagnosis in 1973, and "egodystonic homosexuality" was removed in 1986, "transsexuality" and related diagnoses remain in the latest version of the manual, nearly fifteen years after the Moscone Center protest.

Transgender Nation modeled its actions after the in-your-face activism of Queer Nation and ACT UP (AIDS Coalition to Unleash Power), speaking out publicly on behalf of transgender civil rights and to combat transphobia. The group drew support from the expanding queer political movement of the early 1990's, forging connections among drag communities, transsexuals, and the emerging group of queer activists earlier identified as part of the lesbian, gay, and bisexual communities. For example, on February 13, 1994, members of Transgender Nation and the drag action-group Sisters of Perpetual Indulgence gathered together to stage an action at

> ### "GENDER IDENTITY DISORDER," AS DEFINED IN THE
> ### *DIAGNOSTIC AND STATISTICAL MANUAL OF MENTAL DISORDERS-IV*
>
> In boys, the cross gender identification is manifested by a marked preoccupation with traditionally feminine activities. They may have a preference for dressing in girls' or women's clothes or may improvise such items from available materials when genuine articles are unavailable. Towels, aprons, and scarves are often used to represent long hair or skirts. There is a strong attraction for the stereotypical games and pastimes of girls. They particularly enjoy playing house, drawing pictures of beautiful girls and princesses, and watching television or videos of their favorite female characters. Stereotypical female-type dolls, such as Barbie, are often their favorite toys, and girls are their preferred playmates. When playing "house," these boys role-play female figures. Most commonly "mother roles," and often are quite preoccupied with female fantasy figures. they avoid rough-and-tumble play and competitive sports and have little interest in cars and trucks or other non-aggressive but stereotypical boy's toys. They may express a wish to be a girl and assert that they will grow up to be a woman. They may insist on sitting to urinate and pretend not to have a penis by pushing it in between their legs. More rarely, boys with Gender Identity Disorder may state that they find their penis or testes disgusting, that they want to remove them, or that they have, or wish to have, a vagina.
>
> Girls with Gender Identity Disorder display intense negative reactions to parental expectations or attempts to have them wear dresses or other feminine attire. Some may refuse to attend school or social events where such clothes may be required. They prefer boy's clothing and short hair, are often misidentified by strangers as boys, and may ask to be called a boy's name. Their fantasy heroes are most often powerful male figures, such as Batman or Superman. These girls prefer boys as playmates, with whom they share interests in contact sports, rough-and-tumble play and traditional boyhood games. They show little interest in dolls or any form of feminine dress up or role-play activity. A girl with this disorder may occasionally refuse to urinate in a sitting position. She may claim that she has or will grow a penis and may not want to grow breasts or menstruate. She may assert that she will grow up to be a man. Such girls typically reveal marked cross-gender identification in role-play, dreams and fantasies.
>
> *Source:* Excerpted from Transsexual Road Map. http://www.tsroadmap.com/info/gender-identity-disorder.html.

Nordstrom's, a department store in downtown San Francisco, to protest the company's transphobia.

In 1994, the group worked for inclusion of "transgender" in the title of San Francisco's annual Freedom Day Parade, and also lobbied at a public hearing on the issue on May 12 for a city ordinance prohibiting transgender discrimination. Both measures were ultimately successful, taking effect the following year, in 1995. By that time, Transgender Nation had already folded, as had Queer Nation before it. Historian Susan Stryker credits Transgender Nation with breaking political ground for successor groups such as Transexual Menace and It's Time, America, groups that "went on to play a larger role in the national political arena."

SIGNIFICANCE

As a direct action group, Transgender Nation was the first known action-oriented political group to organize for transgender civil rights. Emerging from San Francisco's radical queer communities of political activists in the early 1990's, the group drew inspiration from the Bay Area's long history of protest for gay and lesbian rights, AIDS activism, and the "in-your-face" actions of Queer Nation and ACT UP.

The mainstream media coverage of the Moscone Center protest against the APA's continued listing of transsexuality as a mental illness was undoubtedly one of the first demonstrations to focus on transgender rights. At the APA demonstration, furthermore, the direct action and civil disobedience of protesters outside the convention paved the way for transgender educators working on the inside to promote awareness and understanding of the problems surrounding the published diagnoses of transsexuality and related conditions as mental illnesses in the DSM.

Transgender Nation's efforts to make transgender issues visible came at a time when the debate concerning transgender inclusion in gay, lesbian, and bisexual movements was heating up. In this respect, San Francisco activists played a leading role in the drive to include transgender people as part of the new queer political agenda. On the national scene, transgender activists lost the battle to include the word "transgender" in the 1993 March on Washington for Lesbian, Gay, and Bi Equal Rights and Liberation. Two years later, though, San Francisco pride organizers added the term to the literature of the Freedom Day Parade there, and city officials signed into law what was at the time just the fourth city ordinance in the country to protect transgender individuals from discrimination.

Although the APA demonstration itself did not result in a change in the DSM, the cumulative impact of Transgender Nation's actions from 1992 to 1994 helped establish transgender concerns as a bona fide element of a new queer political agenda, and they even brought transgender issues to the attention of the country.

—*K. Surkan*

FURTHER READING

Califia, Patrick. *Sex Changes: The Politics of Transgenderism*. 2d ed. San Francisco, Calif.: Cleis Press, 2003.

Currah, Paisley, and Shannon Minter. *Transgender Equality: A Handbook for Activists and Policymakers*. New York: National Gay and Lesbian Task Force Policy Institute, 2000.

Diagnostic and Statistical Manual of Mental Disorders: DSM-IV. Washington, D.C.: American Psychiatric Association, 1994.

Green, Jamison. *Becoming a Visible Man*. Nashville, Tenn.: Vanderbilt University Press, 2004.

Olszewski, Lori. "Transsexuals Protest at Psychiatry Meeting." *San Francisco Chronicle*, May 24, 1993, p. A13.

Stryker, Susan. "Transgender Activism." *GLBTQ: An Encyclopedia of Gay, Lesbian, Bisexual, Transgender, and Queer Culture*. http://www.glbtq.com/social-sciences/transgender_activism.html.

Stryker, Susan, and Jim Van Buskirk. *Gay by the Bay*. San Francisco, Calif.: Chronicle Books, 1996.

SEE ALSO: Sept. 24, 1951: George Jorgensen Becomes Christine Jorgensen; Aug., 1966: Queer Youth Fight Police Harassment at Compton's Cafeteria in San Francisco; Nov. 21, 1966: First Gender Identity Clinic Opens and Provides Gender Reassignment Surgery; July 31, 1969: Gay Liberation Front Is Formed; Dec. 15, 1973: Homosexuality Is Delisted by APA; 1978: Harry Benjamin International Gender Dysphoria Association Is Founded; Mar. 20, 1990: Queer Nation Is Founded; June, 1992: Feinberg Publishes *Transgender Liberation*; 1993: Intersex Society of North America Is Founded; June 17, 1995: International Bill of Gender Rights Is First Circulated; 1996: Hart Recognized as a Transgender Man; 1998: Transgender Scholarship Proliferates; Apr. 30, 2002: Transgender Rights Added to New York City Law; Mar., 2003-Dec., 2004: Transsexuals Protest Academic Exploitation; Nov. 20, 2003: Transgender Day of Remembrance and Remembering Our Dead Project; Mar. 5, 2006: *Brokeback Mountain, Capote,* and *Transamerica* Receive Oscars.

1992-2002
CELEBRITY LESBIANS COME OUT

Marking a new first for the LGBT movement, country and pop singer k. d. lang became the first major female recording artist to come out as lesbian, followed by rock star Melissa Etheridge, comedian and talk-show host Ellen DeGeneres, comedian and talk-show host Rosie O'Donnell, and others.

LOCALE: United States
CATEGORIES: Cultural and intellectual history; arts

KEY FIGURES
k. d. lang (b. 1961), Canadian country and pop singer
Melissa Etheridge (b. 1961), American rock and folk singer
Ellen DeGeneres (b. 1958), American comedian, actor, and talk-show host
Rosie O'Donnell (b. 1962), American comedian and talk-show host

SUMMARY OF EVENT

In 1992, tennis star Martina Navratilova was the only out lesbian celebrity, and mainstream America was still grappling with the HIV-AIDS crisis, which exploded in the 1980's and took the life of actor Rock Hudson in 1985. It was in a relatively conservative climate, at the end of the Ronald Reagan and George H. W. Bush administrations, that k. d. lang became the first major celebrity to officially come out as lesbian.

Although lang released several successful country music albums before 1992, including the Grammy Award-winning *Absolute Torch and Twang* (1989), her androgynous appearance—which had often been described by the mainstream media as "strange"— and her outspokenness on vegetarianism alienated much of the mostly conservative Nashville music industry. After struggling with the country music industry for several years, lang decided to take her career in a different direction in 1992 with the pop crossover album *Ingénue*. She accompanied this album with an interview in the national gay and lesbian newsmagazine *The Advocate*, in which she publicly confirmed that she was a lesbian.

Admitting that she had long hesitated to come out because she was concerned about the way her mother would react, lang's decision was heralded by the National Gay and Lesbian Task Force as "a whole new era of possibility for celebrities." Indeed, lang's coming out was not followed by a negative backlash, and in 1993 she was on the cover of mainstream magazine *Vanity Fair* dressed in a man's suit and sitting in a barber's chair, with supermodel Cindy Crawford, in very feminine at-

The provocative cover of the August, 1993, issue of Vanity Fair, *with singer k. d. lang and former supermodel Cindy Crawford.*

tire, appearing to give her a facial shave.

Lang's continued success after coming out signaled the beginning of a period of more openness, as other lesbian celebrities also began to come out. At the 1993 Triangle Ball during the time of President Bill Clinton's inauguration, rock star Melissa Etheridge announced that she too was lesbian. In comparison to lang, whose first major interview about being lesbian was with a GLBT publication, Etheridge was featured in *People* magazine, reflecting her more mainstream, middle-America audience.

In an interview with *The Advocate* soon after coming out, Etheridge noted, "k. d. and myself, we came out after a certain amount of success. . . . I hope that by us doing that and other artists doing that, the teenagers growing up now who are bound for entertainment or whatever feel that they can actually come out and still not have any extra difficulty climbing to the top." Despite the relatively positive support that Etheridge and lang received from the mainstream press and their fans, it was another four years before another celebrity would follow in their footsteps and come out too.

In the fall of 1996, rumors began circulating that the character of Ellen Morgan on the sitcom *Ellen* was going to come out as lesbian on the show, and that the actor playing the character—comedian Ellen DeGeneres—was also going to come out. The airing of the now-famous "Puppy Episode" in April, 1997, was followed by intense media hype, so DeGeneres's coming-out had dwarfed the buzz that accompanied lang's and Etheridge's announcements. The episode included guest appearances from lang and Jenny Shimizu, as well as an appearance by LGBT-friendly Oprah Winfrey as Ellen's psychologist.

The "Puppy Episode" was followed by DeGeneres on the cover of *Time* magazine with the words "Yep, I'm Gay," and the conservative Reverend Jerry Falwell famously deriding her as "Ellen De*Generate*." Although ratings for the coming-out episode skyrocketed, the sitcom failed to maintain high ratings and was canceled after the following season. At the same time, Ellen's much-publicized relationship with actor Anne Heche dominated the entertainment press, resulting in criticism that both DeGeneres and her sitcom were "too gay." DeGeneres continued to work in the years following the cancellation of *Ellen*, but her next major project, another sitcom titled *The Ellen Show*, also failed. By the time her relationship with Heche ended in 2000, her career had experienced a notable decline.

During the late 1990's, comedian and talk-show host Rosie O'Donnell was also rumored to be lesbian, and she even joked with DeGeneres about being "Lebanese" just before DeGeneres came out. However, O'Donnell did not announce she was lesbian until 2002, after her talk show had ended. In an interview with journalist Diane Sawyer for ABC TV's *Primetime Live*, O'Donnell explained that she did not want to talk about her sexual orientation unless there was reason to, and she had found the reason in a child custody case from Florida involving two gay fathers who were denied the ability to adopt their foster son because they were gay. Well known

Ellen DeGeneres, 1995. (AP/Wide World Photos)

for being an adoptive mother herself, O'Donnell wanted to show that gay and lesbian parents make good parents, and after coming out she became active in supporting the rights of GLBT parents.

SIGNIFICANCE

While it is impossible to determine how celebrities coming out has affected the private lives of gays and lesbians—who have long been denied many positive, public role models—it is clear that mainstream media reaction has been mixed. Although lang and Etheridge did not suffer a significant backlash, they were also pop stars, who are often expected to be overtly sexual in a way that actors or comedians are not. In addition, lang and Etheridge have recorded music with lyrics not explicitly lesbian in theme, and have thus avoided "offending" some listeners.

DeGeneres and O'Donnell, television personalities known to mainstream audiences for being friendly and nonthreatening, did suffer a certain amount of backlash after they came out. O'Donnell faced criticism for months after coming out because she was involved in a court case involving the dissolution of her magazine, but she was also criticized for cutting her hair short and "looking like" a lesbian. DeGeneres made a successful comeback to television with a popular daytime talk show that debuted in September, 2003, and continued as an Emmy-Award winning program into 2006, but she was also criticized by the GLBT press for not being vocal enough about GLBT rights and issues. O'Donnell joined the popular morning talk show *The View* in 2006.

Despite these mixed results, less-known lesbian, gay, and bisexual actors, comedians, and singers have benefited from the actions of lang, Etheridge, DeGeneres, and O'Donnell. While many actors remain closeted, and because there still is a taboo against gay male actors (especially if they are out), after 2000, several younger female actors have made no secret that they are lesbian or bisexual or, even, "questioning," and have suffered few if any repercussions.

—*Malinda Lo*

FURTHER READING

Allen, Louise. *The Lesbian Idol: Martina, k. d., and the Consumption of Lesbian Masculinity*. London: Cassell, 1997.

Bennetts, Leslie. "k. d. lang Cuts It Close." *Vanity Fair*, August, 1993, 94-99, 142-146.

Capsuto, Steven. *Alternate Channels: The Uncensored Story of Gay and Lesbian Images on Radio and Television, 1930's to the Present*. New York: Ballantine Books, 2000.

Handy, Bruce. "Yep, I'm Gay." *Time*, April 14, 1997, 80-86.

Keller, James R., and Leslie Stratyner, eds. *The New Queer Aesthetic on Television: Essays on Recent Programming*. Jefferson, N.C.: McFarland, 2006.

Lemon, Brendan. "k. d.: A Quiet Life." *The Advocate*, June 16, 1992, 34-46.

Tropiano, Stephen. *The Prime Time Closet: A History of Gays and Lesbians on TV*. New York: Applause Theatre & Cinema Books, 2002.

Walters, Barry. "Melissa Etheridge: Rocking the Boat." *The Advocate*, September 21, 1993.

SEE ALSO: 1930's-1960's: Hollywood Bans "Sexual Perversion" in Films; Mar. 7, 1967: CBS Airs *CBS Reports: The Homosexuals*; Oct. 31, 1969: *Time* Magazine Issues "The Homosexual in America"; 1973: Olivia Records Is Founded; Aug. 20-22, 1976: Michigan Womyn's Music Festival Holds Its First Gathering; 1979-1981: First Gay British Television Series Airs; June 5 and July 3, 1981: Reports of Rare Diseases Mark Beginning of AIDS Epidemic; 1985: GLAAD Begins Monitoring Media Coverage of Gays and Lesbians; 1985: Lesbian Film *Desert Hearts* Is Released; July 25, 1985: Actor Hudson Announces He Has AIDS; Mar. 21, 2000: Hollywood Awards Transgender Portrayals in Film; Sept. 7, 2001: First Gay and Lesbian Television Network Is Launched in Canada; Mar. 5, 2006: *Brokeback Mountain, Capote,* and *Transamerica* Receive Oscars.

1992-2006
INDIANS STRUGGLE TO ABOLISH SODOMY LAW

Two petitions challenging India's antisodomy law had been dismissed by the Delhi high court, but the battle to remove the discriminatory law continues as the Indian Supreme Court ordered the high court in March, 2006, to reconsider the case and the constitutionality of the law.

ALSO KNOWN AS: Section 377
LOCALE: New Delhi, India
CATEGORIES: Laws, acts, and legal history; civil rights; government and politics

SUMMARY OF EVENT

India's LGBT movement began in the 1980's. In 1990, *Bombay Dost*, the first Indian gay magazine, carried an article in its second issue about the country's sodomy law. India's British rulers introduced this law—Section 377 of the Indian Penal Code—in 1860 (see sidebar). No systematic persecution or punishment of same-gender desire occurred in precolonial India; laws and practices varied widely, and same-gender relationships were discussed and even celebrated in premodern literature. The new law has led to few convictions, but it is widely used by extortionists and police to blackmail gays and also to threaten women who marry each other by customary rites.

On August 11, 1992, AIDS Bhedbhav Virodhi Andolan (the AIDS antidiscrimination movement), known as ABVA, which had published the pathbreaking 1991 report "Less than Gay," held the first protest in India condemning police use of Section 377. This protest, at the New Delhi police headquarters, occurred after police arrested eighteen persons at a popular cruising site.

In March of 1994, after prison authorities, citing Section 377, refused to make condoms available to prisoners, ABVA filed a public interest petition in the Delhi high court, asking for repeal of Section 377 on the grounds that it violates fundamental, constitutional rights to life, liberty, and nondiscrimination, and obstructs HIV-AIDS prevention. The petition was admitted on February 8, 1995. It came up for hearing in March, 2001, and was dismissed without arguments, probably because ABVA, the only major HIV-AIDS organization in India that is entirely unfunded and is run by unpaid volunteers, was unaware it had finally come up for hearing, and thus failed to appear.

In the 1990's, global attention to HIV-AIDS enabled greater public discussion of homosexuality, governmental and foreign funding became available, and many HIV-AIDS organizations appeared in India. The Indian women's movement also began to take cognizance of the growing LGBT movement. In 1997, Sakshi, a women's rights organization, asked the supreme court of India to define "sexual intercourse" as used in rape laws, and the court directed the law commission to review these laws. In its report (March, 2000), the commission recommended expanding laws relating to rape, sexual assault, and child abuse, and making them gender neutral; it also recommended deleting Section 377, solely on the grounds that including same-gender rape in the rape laws would render 377 unnecessary.

Some women's rights, civil liberties, and LGBT organizations began to discuss strategies for changing the law, including introducing a bill in Parliament. The groups, however, were deeply divided because some women's organizations, like the All India Democratic Women's Association (AIDWA), wanted Section 377 rewritten to exclude consensual sex and include a wide variety of possible sexual abuses, including male-male and female-female nonconsensual sexual contact, while most gay and lesbian organizations wanted the demand for deletion of Section 377 to be separated from any demand for sexual assault legislation.

In July of 2001, the office of Bharosa Trust, an HIV-AIDS organization in Lucknow, was raided, and the police filed charges against the trust under several laws, including Section 377. On December 7, 2001, Naz Foundation (India) Trust, an HIV-

> **INDIAN PENAL CODE (1860)**
>
> Whoever voluntarily has carnal intercourse against the order of nature with any man, woman or animal, shall be punished with imprisonment for life, or with imprisonment of either description for a term which may extend to ten years, and shall also be liable to fine.
>
> *Explanation:* Penetration is sufficient to constitute the carnal intercourse necessary to the offence described in this section.
>
> *Comment:* This section is intended to punish the offense of sodomy, buggery and bestiality. . . .
>
> *Source:* IndiaLawInfo. http://www.indialawinfo.com/bareacts/ipc.html.

AIDS organization, and Lawyers Collective (whose HIV-AIDS unit was set up in 1998) jointly filed a petition in the Delhi high court, asking that Section 377 apply only to sexual assault of children. Like the ABVA petition, this petition pointed out that Section 377 violates constitutional rights to life, liberty, and nondiscrimination, and has a devastating impact on HIV-AIDS-prevention work. The petition was admitted on January 15, 2003.

This second petition received widespread media attention, and it garnered support from Indian celebrities in different fields. In the August 26, 2002 hearing, the solicitor general's office claimed that homosexuality is unnatural, immoral, and opposed to India's conservative culture. Justice R. S. Sodhi responded by asking whether homosexuality is not natural for homosexuals, whether ideas of morality do not change, and whether India is conservative more in theory than in practice. In its September, 2003, written response, the government of India quoted the 42nd Law Commission Report to claim that Indian society disapproves of homosexuality; it also claimed that Section 377 has been used to punish child abuse primarily. Several groups, including AIDWA, protested these claims.

On September 3, 2004, the court had dismissed the petition on the grounds that since the petitioners were not being prosecuted under Section 377, they had no cause of action against it. This contradicted the court's admission not only of this petition but also the earlier petition by the ABVA. More than one year later, on February 3, 2006, however, the Indian Supreme Court ordered the Delhi high court to reconsider the case and rule on the constitutionality of Section 377.

SIGNIFICANCE

The petitions against India's antisodomy law galvanized social action groups and spurred public discussion of GLBT rights. Legislation to overturn Section 377 could soon be introduced in the legislature as well.

Several lower courts have ruled in favor of the cohabiting rights of female couples who married by customary rites and who had been threatened with prosecution under Section 377. On March 8, 2006, a local Indian court allowed two young women to live together as a lesbian couple after months of fighting law enforcement, family, and the courts over their right to do so. The parents of one of the women had falsely claimed that their daughter had been kidnapped by her lover, but after it had been found that the claim was untrue, the two were free to live together legally. The court refused to consider their relationship a violation of Section 377. This case sets a precedent for the gay and lesbian rights movement in India, and is part of a changing atmosphere in the country enabling GLBT people to fight for their civil rights.

—*Ruth Vanita*

FURTHER READING

AIDS Bhedbhav Virodhi Andolan. *For People Like Us*. New Delhi, India: ABVA, 1999.

Bhaskaran, Suparna. "The Politics of Penetration: Section 377 of the Indian Penal Code." In *Queering India*, edited by Ruth Vanita. New York: Routledge, 2002.

Bhat, Srikant. "Indian Law and the Homosexual." *Bombay Dost* no. 2 (1990).

David, Robin. "Court Order on Gay Relationship Now a Precedent." *Times of India*, March 30, 2006. http://timesofindia.indiatimes.com/articleshow/1471374.cms.

"Gay Community Hails SC [Supreme Court] Decision." *Times of India*, February 4, 2006. http://timesofindia.indiatimes.com/articleshow/msid-1400349.cms.

Narrain, Arvind. *Queer: Despised Sexuality, Law, and Social Change.* Bangalore, India: Books for Change, 2004.

Ratti, Rakesh, ed. *A Lotus of Another Color: An Unfolding of the South Asian Gay and Lesbian Experience.* Boston: Alyson, 1993.

Vanita, Ruth. *Love's Rite: Same-Sex Marriage and Its Antecedents in India.* New York: Palgrave, 2005.

Vanita, Ruth, and Saleem Kidwai. *Same-Sex Love in India.* New York: Palgrave, 2000.

SEE ALSO: May 6, 1868: Kertbeny Coins the Terms "Homosexual" and "Heterosexual"; 1885: United Kingdom Criminalizes "Gross Indecency"; Jan. 12, 1939: *Thompson v. Aldredge* Dismisses Sodomy Charges Against Lesbians; Sept. 4, 1957: The *Wolfenden Report* Calls for Decriminalizing Private Consensual Sex; 1961: Illinois Legalizes Consensual Homosexual Sex; Jan. 22, 1973: *Roe v. Wade* Legalizes Abortion and Extends Privacy Rights; Aug., 1973: American Bar Association Calls for Repeal of Laws Against Consensual Sex; Oct. 18, 1973: Lambda Legal Authorized to Practice Law; Nov. 17, 1975: U.S. Supreme Court Rules in "Crimes Against Nature" Case; 1986: *Bowers v. Hardwick* Upholds State Sodomy Laws; Jan. 1, 1988: Canada Decriminalizes Sex Practices Between Consenting Adults; June 26, 2003: U.S. Supreme Court Overturns Texas Sodomy Law.

April 27, 1992
CANADIAN GOVERNMENT ANTIGAY CAMPAIGN IS REVEALED

Documents released in 1992 under Canada's Access to Information Act revealed a national search for homosexuals in the 1950's and 1960's by the Canadian government, namely the Royal Canadian Mounted Police. The campaign, under the guise of national security, targeted nearly nine thousand individuals and led to the dismissal of hundreds of people from government service who were assumed to be lesbian or gay.

LOCALE: Ottawa, Canada
CATEGORIES: Civil rights; government and politics; laws, acts, and legal history

KEY FIGURES
Brian Mulroney (b. 1939), prime minister of Canada, 1984-1993
Gary Kinsman and
Patrizia Gentile, coauthors of a 1998 report that brought widespread attention to the campaign
Robert Wake, psychology professor, Carleton University

SUMMARY OF EVENT
Canadian national security documents, released in April of 1992 under Canada's Access to Information Act, detail the Royal Canadian Mounted Police (RCMP) campaign against gays and lesbians during the Cold War. Speaking before the House of Commons on April 27, 1992, shortly after the documents had been released, Prime Minister Brian Mulroney said, "this would appear to be one of the great outrages and violations of fundamental human liberties that one would have seen for an extended period of time."

For nearly one decade, beginning in the 1950's, the RCMP, claiming that homosexuality constituted a security threat, waged an investigation to name individuals in the Canadian government believed to be gay or lesbian. A decade later, thousands of names, primarily in the Ottawa region, would be on file, two-thirds of whom were not civil servants; and hundreds would lose their jobs.

During World War II and continuing through the Cold War, the RCMP and the Canadian Department of National Defense routinely dismissed "discovered" homosexuals within their organizations by claiming that homosexuals were susceptible to blackmail by foreign intelligence agencies. Homosexuals were also classified as having "psychopathic personalities" and, like chronic delinquents, drug addicts, and alcoholics, were considered unfit for service.

Beginning in 1959, the RCMP began searching other government departments for those persons believed to be homosexual. By 1962, more than eight hundred men and women had been identified as suspected and confirmed homosexuals in thirty-three government departments and agencies. The released documents, now the property of the Canadian Security and Intelligence Service, prove also that persons not holding public service positions were investigated by the RCMP and the Security Panel (a committee formed to coordinate security efforts). The RCMP maintained that talking to civilians might give them names of homosexuals currently working in the government and that these civilians might at some time apply for government jobs.

The RCMP also funded a project in the early 1960's by Robert Wake, a psychologist from Carleton University, which reportedly could determine if a person was gay or lesbian. Part of the project was a test based upon the Pupillary Response Test, first developed at the University of Chicago in 1960. Wake would have test subjects peer at provocative pictures through an opening in a box while their pupils were photographed at half-second intervals. Known at the "fruit machine" by the RCMP and funded for nearly four years, the project was disbanded in the late 1960's, having been a failure and proving to be one of the most bizarre revelations in the released documents.

By the end of 1968, the RCMP had the names of nearly nine thousand suspected homosexuals on file. The RCMP relied on informants to help identify those who were suspect in the hopes of moving them to the "confirmed" category. Security police put in place by the RCMP would then either transfer the individuals to lower-level positions, or have them fired.

Gary Kinsman, a sociology professor at Laurentian University in Sudbury, Ontario, showed that nearly four hundred individuals lost their jobs. Kinsman had coauthored a 1998 research report based on the national security documents released in 1992 and on interviews conducted with persons directly affected by the campaign.

Homosexuals would continue to be removed from the military and the RCMP throughout the 1970's and 1980's, and, as Kinsman points out, "the security campaign was never officially called off. It simply became less tenable." Calls for greater tolerance and broader rights became more prevalent in the 1980's, but it would not be until 1992 that the Canadian military officially ended its policy of dismissing gays and lesbians from service. The Canadian Security Intelligence Service still can make recommendations against security clearance for homosexuals.

SIGNIFICANCE

Government documents released in Ottawa in April of 1992 showed that at the highest levels of the Canadian government, homosexuals were spied upon, were fired from their jobs, and had their careers ruined under the guise of national security. Prime Minister Mulroney said, "the passage of time certainly does not make it any less odious." Time did, however, put the spotlight on existing policies and treatment of lesbians and gays in Canada.

Citizens demanded the elimination of discrimination against lesbians and gays, called for an amendment to the Canadian Human Rights Act (which the Canadian Human Rights Commission first called for in the 1970's), and called for an end to the ban on gays and lesbians in the military. Sexual orientation was added to the Human Rights Act in 1996, and the ban on gays and lesbians serving in the military officially was ended in November of 1992.

The initial release of the government documents received minimal media coverage, and not until Mulroney spoke publicly in the House of Commons was there extensive press coverage of what the security documents revealed. Lacking, too, was a face on those persons whose rights were violated.

The destructive impact of the RCMP investigations on individual lives had became apparent especially after the 1998 release of the report *In the Interests of the State: The Anti-Gay, Anti-Lesbian National Security Campaign in Canada*, by Kinsman and coauthor Patrizia Gentile. Furthermore, individuals came forward to talk about their experiences, putting a face on the witch hunts.

—*John Boyd*

FURTHER READING

Ferguson, Sue. "Tale of a Witch Hunt." *Macleans* 114, no. 26 (2001): 34-36.

Kinsman, Gary. "The Canadian Cold War on Queers: Sexual Regulation and Resistance." In *Love, Hate, and Fear in Canada's Cold War*, edited by Richard Cavell. Buffalo, N.Y.: University of Toronto Press, 2004.

Kinsman, Gary, Dieter K. Buse, and Mercedes Steedman, eds. *Whose National Security? Canadian State Surveillance and Creation of Enemies*. Toronto, Ont.: Between the Lines Press, 2000.

Kinsman, Gary, and Patrizia Gentile. *In the Interests of the State: The Anti-Gay, Anti-Lesbian National Security Campaign in Canada, A Preliminary Research Report*. Sudbury, Ont.: Laurentian University, 1998.

Robinson, Daniel J., and David Kimmel. "The Queer Career of Homosexual Security Vetting in Cold War Canada." *Canadian Historical Review* 75, no. 3 (1994): 319-345.

Sawatsky, John. *Men in the Shadows: The RCMP Security Service*. Toronto, Ont.: Doubleday Canada, 1980.

SEE ALSO: 1885: United Kingdom Criminalizes "Gross Indecency"; Mar. 15, 1919-1921: U.S. Navy Launches Sting Operation Against "Sexual Perverts"; Aug. 26, 1969: Canada Decriminalizes Homosexual Acts; 1972-1973: Local Governments Pass Antidiscrimination Laws; Dec. 19, 1977: Quebec Includes Lesbians and Gays in Its Charter of Human Rights and Freedoms; June 2, 1980: Canadian Gay Postal Workers Secure Union Protections; Jan. 1, 1988: Canada Decriminalizes Sex Practices Between Consenting Adults; Dec. 30, 1991-Feb. 22, 1993: Canada Grants Asylum Based on Sexual Orientation; Oct., 1992: Canadian Military Lifts Its Ban on Gays and Lesbians; Apr. 2, 1998: Canadian Supreme Court Reverses Gay Academic's Firing; June 17, 2003, and July 19, 2005: Canada Legalizes Same-Gender Marriage.

June, 1992
FEINBERG PUBLISHES *TRANSGENDER LIBERATION*

Leslie Feinberg's pamphlet inspired transgender politics and activism by placing transgender oppression within a historical context and by calling for an inclusive community of gender-variant people. The pamphlet is the first publication to use the word "transgender" to represent all gender-variant people.

LOCALE: New York, New York
CATEGORIES: Publications; transgender/transsexuality; civil rights

KEY FIGURE
Leslie Feinberg (b. 1949), author and transgender activist who self-identifies as "a masculine, lesbian, female-to-male cross-dresser and transgenderist"

SUMMARY OF EVENT
In June of 1992, *World View Forum* published *Transgender Liberation: A Movement Whose Time Has Come*, a twenty-two-page pamphlet written by transgender activist Leslie Feinberg. In the opening paragraph, Feinberg wrote, "This pamphlet is an attempt to trace the historic rise of an oppression that, as yet, has no commonly agreed name. We are talking here about people who defy the 'man'-made boundaries of gender." Thus, the focus of the pamphlet is twofold: It is a historical account of gender variance, and it is an attempt to give a name to the transgender community.

Feinberg posited that, historically, "Transgender is a very ancient form of human expression that pre-dates oppression," and she outlines its existence as early as 25,000 B.C.E. As a Marxist, Feinberg used this historical account to illustrate that "when societies were not ruled by exploiting classes that rely on divide-and-conquer tactics, 'cross-gendered' youths, women and men on all continents were respected members of their communities." She then shows how both societal laws and religious doctrines were introduced to transform the natural existence of transgender individuals into a seemingly unnatural and even reviled existence.

Transgender Liberation used the word "transgender" to represent *all* gender-variant people, the first time the term was used in publication as a term of inclusiveness. Feinberg outlined the importance of a shared language that honors transgender people, that is, of a language of pride that validates those who face this oppression. Feinberg argued also for the importance of connecting the gender-variant and sex-minority communities so that together people can work to battle bigotry, hatred, and brutality.

For Feinberg, connecting the communities also means recognizing that not all lesbians and gays are "cross"-gendered and that not all transgender people are lesbian or gay. Feinberg states that, "In reality the two huge communities are like circles that only partially overlap. While the oppressions within these two powerful communities are not the same, we face a common enemy. Gender-phobia—like racism, sexism and bigotry against lesbians and gays men—is meant to keep us divided. Unity can only increase our strength." Within a historical context, this call to action paralleled the emergence of the AIDS crisis, which mandated a reorientation of sexual-identity politics in the late 1980's and early 1990's, consequently requiring alliances among different social groups affected by the epidemic. Creating these alliances required these groups to address systemic social problems, including poverty, racism, and sexism. It was through these alliances that transgender issues entered broader struggles for social justice and equal treatment.

SIGNIFICANCE
The coupling of transgender concerns with a Marxist perspective has not lived on as the pamphlet's legacy, but what has lived on is the work's locating of transgender issues within a social justice agenda. Forming shortly after its publication was a San Francisco-based activist group called Transgender

Leslie Feinberg. (Courtesy, Beacon Press)

Nation, part of the gay and lesbian activist group Queer Nation. Transgender Nation was the first group to express a newly militant political movement using the term "transgender." The group got the attention of the media in 1993 by organizing a protest at the annual meeting of the American Psychiatric Association, focusing on the APA's classifying of transgenderism and "gender identity disorder" as pathologies. Transgender Nation paved the way for other groups, such as Transgender Menace and It's Time, America, to continue its mandate and play larger roles in national politics.

In *Transgender Liberation*, Feinberg wrote that the transgender community has "also given careful thought to our use of pronouns, striving for both clarity and sensitivity in a language that only allows for two sexes." While the issue of language-use is not addressed in depth in the pamphlet, Feinberg has challenged gender-binary language in other forums to incorporate alternate pronouns such as "hir" rather than "her" and "his" and "ze" or "sie" rather than "he" or "she."

Feinberg has published additional nonfiction works about transgender issues, including *Transgender Warriors* (1996) and *Trans Liberation: Beyond Pink or Blue* (1998). She also wrote a novel called *Stone Butch Blues* (1993). Feinberg also is a leader in the Workers World Party, a cofounder of Rainbow Flags for Mumia, an organizer with the International Action Center, and is at the forefront of the movement bringing transgender health issues to the attention of the medical community. Feinberg's activism and writings continue to examine oppression against transgender people and how it intersects with capitalism and with racism, sexism, and other oppressions.

Some individuals have criticized both Feinberg's definition of transgender and the connections she draws between transgender persons and gays, lesbians, and bisexuals. Furthermore, there are concerns about the implicitly lesbian and gay framework of transgender writing and political action, in general, within Anglo-American contexts. As queer theory has entered academia, many have embraced its inclusion of transgender issues. Some, however, have pushed for transgender studies that are not tied to gay, lesbian, and bisexual studies, because many transgender people do not embrace GLB identities and politics. Regarding the definition of the word "transgender," some contend that its umbrella-like usage and universalizing potential obscures meaningful differences within the community itself. Opponents of the seemingly "all-inclusive" term argue that it fails to recognize the differences among transsexuals, drag kings and queens, cross-dressers, those who are gender-ambiguous, and other gender-variant people.

Nonetheless, since the publication of *Transgender Liberation*, the term "transgender," and transgender as a concept, has become well-established within the academy, politics, and public-health arenas. Moreover, it has been recognized by mainstream media and popular culture (for example, the 1999 film *Boys Don't Cry,* about the rape and murder of transgender man Brandon Teena in 1993, garnered a

Best Actress Oscar for actor Hilary Swank and a Best Supporting Actress nomination for Chloe Sevigny). As a result of the current wave of transgender activism that started in part because of Feinberg's publication, transgender issues have been brought closer to the forefront of social movements and political action, resulting in the passage of transgender civil rights legislation and policies in several municipalities, states, and businesses around the United States.

—*Kim Hackford-Peer*

FURTHER READING

Bornstein, Kate. *Gender Outlaw: On Men, Women, and the Rest of Us*. New York: Routledge, 1994.

Feinberg, Leslie. *Stone Butch Blues*. Ithaca, N.Y.: Firebrand Books, 1993.

_____. *Trans Liberation: Beyond Pink or Blue*. Boston: Beacon Press, 1998.

_____. "Transgender Liberation: A Movement Whose Time Has Come." In *Materialist Feminism: A Reader in Class, Difference, and Women's Lives*, edited by Rosemary Hennessey and Chrys Ingraham. New York: Routledge, 1997.

_____. *Transgender Warriors: Making History from Joan of Arc to RuPaul*. Boston: Beacon Press, 1996.

Gilbert, Michael, ed. *International Journal of Transgenderism* 4, no. 3 (July/September, 2000). Special issue, "What Is Transgender?" http://www.symposion.com/ijt/index.htm.

Halberstam, Judith. *In a Queer Time and Place: Transgender Bodies, Subcultural Lives*. New York: New York University Press, 2005.

SEE ALSO: Sept. 24, 1951: George Jorgensen Becomes Christine Jorgensen; Aug., 1966: Queer Youth Fight Police Harassment at Compton's Cafeteria in San Francisco; Nov. 21, 1966: First Gender Identity Clinic Opens and Provides Gender Reassignment Surgery; July 31, 1969: Gay Liberation Front Is Formed; Dec. 15, 1973: Homosexuality Is Delisted by APA; 1978: Harry Benjamin International Gender Dysphoria Association Is Founded; Mar. 20, 1990: Queer Nation Is Founded; 1992: Transgender Nation Holds Its First Protest; 1993: Intersex Society of North America Is Founded; June 17, 1995: International Bill of Gender Rights Is First Circulated; 1996: Hart Recognized as a Transgender Man; 1998: Transgender Scholarship Proliferates; Apr. 30, 2002: Transgender Rights Added to New York City Law; Mar., 2003-Dec., 2004: Transsexuals Protest Academic Exploitation; Nov. 20, 2003: Transgender Day of Remembrance and Remembering Our Dead Project; Mar. 5, 2006: *Brokeback Mountain, Capote,* and *Transamerica* Receive Oscars.

September 23, 1992
MASSACHUSETTS GRANTS FAMILY RIGHTS TO GAY AND LESBIAN STATE WORKERS

The governor of Massachusetts was the first governor in the United States to sign an executive order granting lesbian and gay state workers the same bereavement and family leave rights as heterosexual workers.

LOCALE: Boston, Massachusetts

CATEGORIES: Laws, acts, and legal history; civil rights; government and politics

KEY FIGURE

William F. Weld (b. 1945), Republican governor of Massachusetts, 1991-1997

SUMMARY OF EVENT

In 1992, Massachusetts governor William F. Weld signed Executive Order 340, "Providing for Non-Discriminatory Benefit Policies for Employees of the Commonwealth," with the intention of protecting Massachusetts state workers from employment-related discrimination on the basis of sexual orientation. Because there already had been a non-discrimination law on the books that established Massachusetts's obligation to extend protections based on sexual orientation (as of November, 1989), it followed that the state had to ensure that its employment policies "are in harmony with the established obligations of Chapter 151B" of Executive Order 340.

The 1992 executive order called for expanded bereavement and family leave rights for the same-gender domestic partners of state employees. Although its wording appeared to extend these benefits to all state workers, the employee population actually impacted was small; only those at the senior level of management were eligible. The order also defined the characteristics of those gay and lesbian relationships that would qualify for the newly mandated extension of benefits to same-gender domestic partners. Next, it stated that the commonwealth's personnel administration department was to administer the necessary regulations and policies.

The executive order laid the foundation for a groundswell of grassroots efforts to chip away at systemic homophobia and discrimination. However, arguably the most critical of benefits—that of health insurance coverage—continued to be exempt from efforts to provide equitable benefits to the spousal equivalents of gay and lesbian state workers.

The Group Insurance Commission, the body that administers health insurance programs for all state employees, was on record stating that extension of health benefits to domestic partners could not occur "until and unless Chapter 32A of the General Laws which defines eligible dependents, is amended by the Legislature." Thus, a two-tiered system of benefits continued to be upheld—one for heterosexual employees and their families, and an inferior one for gay and lesbian employees in "spousal equivalent" relationships.

The grassroots efforts and coalition-building activities to advocate for equitable same-gender domestic partnership benefits included initiatives by state employee ad hoc groups, collective bargaining units, and community-based organizations such as Gay and Lesbian Advocates and Defenders (GLAD) and the Massachusetts Gay and Lesbian Political Caucus, to address the gap in the state insurance laws (including the annual introduction of related bills to the legislature over approximately one dozen years); and the establishment of domestic-partnership registries in Provincetown, Boston, and Cambridge, allowing for those city employees to gain domestic-partnership benefits coverage.

Along the way, as roadblocks were circumvented, new obstacles appeared. For example, a 1999 court ruling found that Boston did not have the power to expand the reach of state insurance laws

> **ORDER AGAINST DISCRIMINATION, COMMONWEALTH OF MASSACHUSETTS**
>
> *Providing for Non-discriminatory Benefit Policies For Employees of the Commonwealth*
>
> 1. For purposes of this executive order, "relationship of mutual support" means a relationship between two individuals, each unmarried, and competent to contract, characterized by mutual caring and emotional support; an agreement to share basic living expenses; a sharing of living quarters and an intent to do so indefinitely; a mutual assumption of responsibility for each other's welfare; and a mutual expectation that the relationship is exclusive and will endure over time.
>
> 2. The Department of Personnel Administration shall, no later than November 1, 1992, promulgate such regulations and policies as are necessary to eliminate discrimination on the basis of sexual orientation in the benefits provided to employees under its jurisdiction. Benefits shall include the following:
>
>   a. An employee of the Commonwealth shall be entitled to a maximum of four calendar days of paid "bereavement" leave, upon the death of a family member or of a person with whom the employee has a relationship of mutual support.
>
>   b. An employee of the Commonwealth shall be allowed to use up to 10 days of accrued sick leave in the event of the serious illness of a family member or of a person with whom the employee has a relationship of mutual support.
>
> 3. An employee of the Commonwealth claiming leave benefits on account of the illness or death of a person with whom the employee has a relationship of mutual support must, as a condition of receiving such leave benefits, certify to the Department of Personnel Administration the existence of his or her relationship of mutual support.

by including domestic partners in the group health system, rescinding benefits that had been provided. Also, GLAD noted in an overview of the state's benefits, when such benefits were provided, "unlike benefits provided to an employee's spouse, workplace benefits provided to an employee's domestic partner are counted as taxable income to the employee." The bottom line seemed to be that attempts to extend equal "family" benefits to gay and lesbian state workers was impossible without changing existing laws, and that efforts to impact legislation had repeatedly failed. It became increasingly clear that the route most likely to be successful would be one that was grounded in challenging the legal interpretations of existing antidiscrimination laws to allow Massachusetts gay and lesbian couples to marry legally.

Significance

Ultimately, the grassroots struggle in Massachusetts over this particular area of GLBT civil rights led to the 2003 Supreme Judicial Court decision to legalize same-gender marriage in Massachusetts. Although no longer governor, Weld had a hand in this as well: In 1996, he had appointed Justice Margaret H. Marshall, who wrote the majority opinion in the 2003 decision. This change in the state's marriage laws, which went into effect May 17, 2004, not only allowed gay and lesbian state employees who were legally married to have equal access to health benefits but also set the stage for many other state-controlled rights to be extended to gay and lesbian citizens, and their legally recognized spouses.

Governor Weld's signing of the executive order to grant lesbian and gay state workers bereavement and family leave rights set in motion a series of events that have kept the Commonwealth of Massachusetts at the forefront of the GLBT civil rights movement in the United States. His actions included establishing a Governor's Commission on Gay and Lesbian Youth, signing legislation to prohibit discrimination in Massachusetts public schools against students based on their sexual orientation (both of which gave rise to a groundbreaking, national model for creating a safe environment in schools for gay and lesbian students, including the establishment of a network of Gay-Straight Alliances (GSAs); expanding hate crimes and housing antidiscrimination laws to include gays and lesbians; and appointing out gay and lesbian state officials. These actions laid the groundwork for a state environment ideal for advancing gay and lesbian civil rights.

Although Executive Order 340 was very limited legally, its symbolic importance was significant. Governor Weld's willingness to sign this and other gay-rights executive orders early in his tenure as governor established him as a maverick within his political party. As a "big tent" Republican, his positions in support of gay and lesbian civil rights and abortion rights brought him into the national spotlight and raised the ire of party conservatives. He was named "Hetero Hero" by the national gay and lesbian newsmagazine *The Advocate*, and he graced its cover in 1993.

—*Emily Ferrara*

FURTHER READING

Hunter, Nan D., Courtney G. Joslin, and Sharon M. McGowan. *The Rights of Lesbians, Gay Men, Bisexuals, and Transgendered People (American Civil Liberties Union Handbook)*. 4th ed. Carbondale: Southern Illinois University Press, 2004.

Nava, Michael, and Robert Dawidoff. *Created Equal: Why Gay Rights Matter to America*. New York: St. Martin's Press, 1995.

Richards, David A. J. *Identity and the Case for Gay Rights: Race, Gender, Religion as Analogies*. Chicago: University of Chicago Press, 1999.

Rimmerman, Craig A., Kenneth D. Wald, and Clyde Wilcox. *The Politics of Gay Rights*. Chicago: University of Chicago Press, 2000.

SEE ALSO: Apr. 27, 1953: U.S. President Eisenhower Prohibits Federal Employment of Lesbians and Gays; 1972-1973: Local Governments Pass Antidiscrimination Laws; June 27, 1974: Abzug and Koch Attempt to Amend the Civil Rights Act of 1964; July 3, 1975: U.S. Civil Service Commission Prohibits Discrimination Against Federal Employees; 1978: Lesbian and Gay Workplace Movement Is Founded; June 2, 1980: Canadian Gay Postal Workers Secure Union Protections; Dec. 4, 1984: Berkeley Extends Benefits to Domestic Partners of City Employees; Nov. 8, 1988: Oregon Repeals Ban on Antigay Job Discrimination; May 1, 1989: U.S. Supreme Court Rules Gender-Role Stereotyping Is Discriminatory; Sept. 29, 1991: California Governor Wilson Vetoes Antidiscrimination Bill; 1994: Employment Non-Discrimination Act Is Proposed to U.S. Congress; Apr. 2, 1998: Canadian Supreme Court Reverses Gay Academic's Firing; July, 2003: Singapore Lifts Ban on Hiring Lesbian and Gay Employees; July, 2003: Wal-Mart Adds Lesbians and Gays to Its Antidiscrimination Policy.

October, 1992
CANADIAN MILITARY LIFTS ITS BAN ON GAYS AND LESBIANS

Expecting an unfavorable ruling from the Supreme Court of Canada, the Canadian armed forces negotiated a settlement with lesbian soldier Michelle Douglas, which encouraged the Canadian attorney general to lift the government's ban on gays and lesbians in the military.

LOCALE: Ottawa, Ontario, Canada
CATEGORIES: Military; civil rights; government and politics; laws, acts, and legal history

KEY FIGURES

Michelle Douglas, servicemember
Graham Haig, servicemember
Joshua Birch, servicemember
Kim Campbell, Canadian attorney general who lifted the ban

SUMMARY OF EVENT

Before 1992, Canada had banned gays and lesbians from serving in its armed forces, a ban outlined in Administrative Order 19-20. The Canadian Forces (CF) did not allow the enlistment or commission of gays and lesbians who were out, and any service personnel found to be gay or lesbian were dismissed. Soldiers were required to notify leadership about all suspected or known gay and lesbian personnel. A special investigations unit had been formed to handle the resulting court cases.

The CF policy on lesbian and gay servicemembers came under increasing judicial and political scrutiny after the passage of the Canadian Human Rights Act (CHRA) in 1978 and the Canadian Charter of Rights and Freedoms in 1985. While the CHRA did not explicitly cover sexual orientation, it required employers to justify exclusionary or restrictive policies. The charter, similar to the U.S. Bill of Rights, also did not include sexual orientation in its list of prohibited grounds of discrimination. Section 15 of the charter did, however, enable the restriction of other forms of discrimination if so ruled by the courts.

Following the adoption of the charter, the CF launched a study of the issue of lesbians and gays in the military. Following its results, the ban was slightly modified. Under this change, the CF would not knowingly enroll gays and lesbians. If soldiers were "discovered" or announced themselves to be gay or lesbian, they would be asked to leave but would not be dismissed. Those who chose to stay, however, would not be eligible for training courses, security clearances, transfers, promotions, or re-enlistment. The CF already had removed from regulations the obligation of servicemembers to report on suspicions that another solider may be lesbian or gay.

In 1986, Canadian courts served as the battleground for ending this modified policy. In one case, *Stiles v. The Queen*, a soldier was denied an important transfer because he was gay; the case was settled. A second case, *Bordeleau v. Canada*, escalated the conflict. Bordeleau was dismissed from the CF because he was gay. The dismissal, he argued, violated the charter. In June, 1989, the court ruled that Bordeleau "may have a reasonable cause of action since discrimination under the Charter is not limited only to the categories listed." The CF did not respond.

In 1992, two important cases prompted the courts, the legislature, and the military to reconsider the ban. The first case, *Haig v. Canada*, pitted Graham Haig, an Ottawa gay activist, and Joshua Birch, a former Canadian air force (CAF) captain, against the Canadian forces. The CAF refused to promote Birch because he was gay. The CHRA refused to investigate policy because sexual orientation was not included in it. In June, 1992, the Ontario Court of Appeals weighed in and demanded that the CHRA was to be "interpreted, applied and administrated as though it contained sexual orientation as a prohibitive ground of discrimination and read as if sexual orientation was specifically included in it." The government did not appeal, and the precedent would soon be cited in a number of other cases.

> ### FROM DOUGLAS V. CANADA
>
> This [case] was an action for damages and declaratory relief following the plaintiff's release from the Armed Forces. The plaintiff, an officer, accepted release from the Canadian Armed Forces after admitting that she was a lesbian. The alternative was to be retained with severe career restrictions: ineligibility for promotion, conversion of existing terms of service, posting outside the geographic area, further training, and transfer to the reserve force. Although, shortly before trial, the parties agreed upon a disposition including terms of a declaratory judgment which provided that plaintiff's Charter, section 15 rights had been denied and that the defendant's policies regarding service of homosexuals in the Canadian Forces were contrary to the Charter, reasons for judgment were prepared in that this case may take on greater significance than the typical out-of-court settlement.
>
> Held, the draft judgment as agreed upon by the parties should be signed. . . .
>
> In this action, commenced by statement of claim filed in January 1990, the plaintiff claims damages and declaratory relief following her severance from the Canadian Armed Forces in which she had formerly served as an officer.
>
> Shortly before trial of the action was scheduled to commence, the parties through counsel agreed on settlement of the matter including the terms of a declaratory judgment relating in part to the relief claimed by the plaintiff.
>
> The draft judgment as agreed upon between them was presented to me at the hearing scheduled for the trial and after brief consideration, I signed that judgment as presented and requested by the parties.
>
> I did not render oral reasons at the time. However, because the circumstances are somewhat unusual, because the judgment might hereafter be given more significance than a resolution between parties ordinarily warrants, and because the process raises an issue of policy where Charter [Canadian Charter of Rights and Freedoms] questions are raised, these reasons are now recorded and filed. . . .

The most significant case was filed in 1992 by Michelle Douglas, who had been expelled because she was a lesbian. Douglas charged that Administrative Order 19-20 was inconsistent with the charter. She also argued her dismissal undermined her right to freedom of association. An adjudicator agreed, and ordered that Douglas be reinstated to her position.

A series of appeals ensued, with each side scoring victories. However, as the final lawsuit was about to be heard, the armed forces capitulated and, citing Haig, negotiated a settlement. Shortly thereafter, in October, Attorney General Kim Campbell (later prime minister) relented and lifted the ban against gays and lesbians in the military. A Canadian court agreed with and adopted the settlement on December 1 (*Douglas v. Canada*).

Significance

Various studies by different Canadian government agencies between 1992 and 1995 found that heterosexual soldiers were increasingly accepting of gay and lesbian personnel and that military effectiveness was not affected. The studies also found gay soldiers reported a good working relationship with their heterosexual peers, reports of sexual harassment dropped 46 percent, there was no increase in disciplinary problems, and gay bashing incidents in the military dropped significantly.

The process of lifting the ban, and the subsequent studies, served as a strong example for other countries throughout the world. Shortly after Canada lifted the ban, Australia followed suit. As part of his 1992 presidential campaign, Bill Clinton promised to do the same with the U.S. armed forces. However, soon after he took office in 1993, Clinton was undermined by the Republican-led Congress, and instead created a much maligned compromise known as Don't Ask, Don't Tell. New Zealand lifted its ban in 1993, and South Africa did the same in 1998. Following the examples set by Canada and the European Union, the government of Great Britain also lifted its ban on gay and lesbian servicemembers in 2000. Taiwan followed suit in 2002. The only country to move backward, Russia, added further restrictions on gay and lesbian personnel in 2003.

On another front, section 15 of the Canadian charter, which secures equal rights for all Canadians without regard to sexual orientation, was strengthened by lifting the military ban. Because the antidiscrimination clause grew stronger, Canada was well positioned to initiate groundbreaking laws regarding same-gender marriage (which is now legal in Canada) and other gay and lesbian rights concerns.

—*Daniel-Raymond Nadon*

FURTHER READING

Belkin, Aaron, and Jason McNichol. "Effects of the 1992 Lifting of Restrictions on Gay and Lesbian Service in the Canadian Forces: Appraising the Evidence." April, 2000. Center for the Study of Sexual Minorities in the Military, University of California, Santa Barbara. http://www.gaymilitary.ucsb.edu/Publications/CanadaPub1.htm#_Toc475351398.

Bindman, Stephen. "Military Opens Its Arms to Gays: New Policy Lifts Ban on Hiring, Promotion of Homosexuals." *The Gazette* (Montreal), October 10, 1993, p. B1.

Jackson, Paul. *One of the Boys: Homosexuality in the Military During World War II*. Montreal, Ont.: McGill-Queen's University Press, 2004.

Lahey, Kathleen A. *Are We "Persons" Yet? Law and Sexuality in Canada*. Buffalo, N.Y.: University of Toronto Press, 1999.

MacDougall, Bruce. *Queer Judgements: Homosexuality, Expression, and the Courts in Canada*. Buffalo, N.Y.: University of Toronto Press, 2000.

Smith, Miriam. *Lesbian and Gay Rights in Canada: Social Movements and Equality Seeking, 1971-1999*. Buffalo, N.Y.: University of Toronto Press, 1999.

Warner, Tom. *Never Going Back: A History of Queer Activism in Canada*. Buffalo, N.Y.: University of Toronto Press, 2002.

SEE ALSO: Mar. 15, 1919-1921: U.S. Navy Launches Sting Operation Against "Sexual Perverts"; July 3, 1975: U.S. Civil Service Commission Prohibits Discrimination Against Federal Employees; 1976-1990: Army Reservist Ben-Shalom Sues for Reinstatement; May-Aug., 1980: U.S. Navy Investigates the USS *Norton Sound* in Antilesbian Witch Hunt; May 3, 1989: *Watkins v. United States Army* Reinstates Gay Soldier; 1990, 1994: *Coming Out Under Fire* Documents Gay and Lesbian Military Veterans; Aug. 27, 1991: *The Advocate* Outs Pentagon Spokesman Pete Williams; Nov. 30, 1993: Don't Ask, Don't Tell Policy Is Implemented; Jan. 12, 2000: United Kingdom Lifts Ban on Gays and Lesbians in the Military.

November 3, 1992
OREGON AND COLORADO ATTEMPT ANTIGAY INITIATIVES

Oregon and Colorado faced referenda limiting the rights of gays, lesbians, and bisexuals. Oregon's Measure 9 was defeated at the polls, but Colorado's Amendment 2 passed. Amendment 2 was subsequently declared unconstitutional by the U.S. Supreme Court. The Court's ruling marks the first time the nation's high court acknowledged gays and lesbians as citizens deserving of some degree of civil rights.

ALSO KNOWN AS: Measure 9; Amendment 2; *Romer v. Evans* (1996)
LOCALE: Oregon; Colorado
CATEGORIES: Laws, acts, and legal history; government and politics

KEY FIGURES
Jean Dubofsky, attorney who argued against Amendment 2 before the U.S. Supreme Court
Richard G. Evans, lead plaintiff in the Amendment 2 case
Roy Romer (b. 1928), governor of Colorado and defendant in the Amendment 2 case

SUMMARY OF EVENT
At the 1992 Republican National Convention, Christian Coalition founder Pat Robertson referred to a "cultural war" in the United States. Later that year, that cultural war was dramatically enacted in statewide campaigns about gay and lesbian rights in Oregon and Colorado. Conservative organizations in both states gathered signatures to place referenda on the November 3, 1992, statewide ballots.

The Oregon Citizens Alliance proposed ballot Measure 9, the more extreme of the two referenda, which grouped homosexuality with pedophilia, sadism, and masochism, declaring all to be "abnormal, wrong, unnatural, and perverse." The measure required that governmental entities, including public schools, promote this view of homosexuality, especially to youth, and prohibited governmental efforts to "promote, encourage, or facilitate" homosexuality (or pedophilia, sadism, or masochism). Colorado for Family Values proposed Amendment 2, which prohibited any governmental body from adopting any ordinance offering claims of "any minority status, quota preferences, protected status or claim of discrimination" to gay, lesbian, or bisexual (GLB) Coloradans. Amendment 2 effectively nullified existing antidiscrimination ordinances in the state and prohibited the enactment of any such ordinances in the future.

The campaigns against gay rights in the two states drew on the same printed materials and a video, *The Gay Agenda*, all of which exploited long-standing stereotypes of GLB people and antipathy toward them. The campaigns divided each state, with the two sides engaging in vitriolic accusations. Antigay hate crimes were reported in both states, but the atmosphere grew especially heated in Oregon, where churches were desecrated, serious threats against GLB campaign workers were commonplace, and two people—a lesbian and a gay man—were killed when their house was torched by arsonists. Despite such tensions, GLB people from Oregon and Colorado came out in significant numbers and many heterosexual allies, including major public figures, took visible stands for GLB people and their rights.

The election results were split. Oregon voters rejected Measure 9, 56.5 to 43.5 percent; Colorado voters endorsed Amendment 2, 53 to 47 percent. In the aftermath of its loss in the 1992 election, the Oregon Citizens Alliance sponsored a variety of antigay referenda at the county level as well as subsequent statewide referenda. During the same period, GLB people in Oregon built an organization designed not only to fight such ballot measures but also to build a comprehensive pro-gay movement in the state.

Colorado's GLB community was similarly galvanized after the passage of Amendment 2. The first order of business was to activate pre-election contingency plans for a judicial challenge to Amend-

> ### *ROMER V. EVANS* (1996): FROM THE MAJORITY OPINION
>
> *Justice Kennedy delivered the opinion of the Court:* Amendment 2, in explicit terms, does more than repeal or rescind these provisions. It prohibits all legislative, executive or judicial action at any level of state or local government designed to protect the named class, a class we shall refer to as homosexual persons or gays and lesbians. The amendment reads: "No Protected Status Based on Homosexual, Lesbian, or Bisexual Orientation. Neither the State of Colorado, through any of its branches or departments, nor any of its agencies, political subdivisions, municipalities or school districts, shall enact, adopt or enforce any statute, regulation, ordinance or policy whereby homosexual, lesbian or bisexual orientation, conduct, practices or relationships shall constitute or otherwise be the basis of or entitle any person or class of persons to have or claim any minority status, quota preferences, protected status or claim of discrimination. This Section of the Constitution shall be in all respects self-executing." . . . Sweeping and comprehensive is the change in legal status effected by this law. So much is evident from the ordinances that the Colorado Supreme Court declared would be void by operation of Amendment.
>
> Homosexuals, by state decree, are put in a solitary class with respect to transactions and relations in both the private and governmental spheres. The amendment withdraws from homosexuals, but no others, specific legal protection from the injuries caused by discrimination, and it forbids reinstatement of these laws and policies. . . .
>
> Amendment 2 fails, indeed defies, even this conventional inquiry. First, the amendment has the peculiar property of imposing a broad and undifferentiated disability on a single named group, an exceptional and, as we shall explain, invalid form of legislation. Second, its sheer breadth is so discontinuous with the reasons offered for it that the amendment seems inexplicable by anything but animus toward the class that it affects; it lacks a rational relationship to legitimate state interests. . . .
>
> Amendment 2 confounds this normal process of judicial review. It is at once too narrow and too broad. It identifies persons by a single trait and then denies them protection across the board. The resulting disqualification of a class of persons from the right to seek specific protection from the law is unprecedented in our jurisprudence. The absence of precedent for Amendment 2 is itself instructive; "[d]iscriminations of an unusual character especially suggest careful consideration to determine whether they are obnoxious to the constitutional provision." . . .
>
> A second and related point is that laws of the kind now before us raise the inevitable inference that the disadvantage imposed is born of animosity toward the class of persons affected. "[I]f the constitutional conception of 'equal protection of the laws' means anything, it must at the very least mean that a bare . . . desire to harm a politically unpopular group cannot constitute a legitimate governmental interest." . . .
>
> We must conclude that Amendment 2 classifies homosexuals not to further a proper legislative end but to make them unequal to everyone else. This Colorado cannot do. A State cannot so deem a class of persons a stranger to its laws. Amendment 2 violates the Equal Protection Clause, and the judgment of the Supreme Court of Colorado is affirmed.
>
> It is so ordered.

ment 2. The legal team, headed by Jean Dubofsky, initiated the case that ultimately became *Romer v. Evans* (1996). Colorado governor Roy Romer, who ironically had publicly opposed Amendment 2 prior to his election, chose to defend it against a post-election legal challenge. "Evans" was Richard G. Evans, one of seven individuals who, along with the cities of Boulder, Denver, and Aspen and the Boulder Valley School District, were plaintiffs in the case.

On January 15, 1993, Colorado district judge Jeffrey Bayless granted an injunction: Amendment 2 would not go into effect until the courts heard arguments and rendered a decision about its constitutionality. Later that year, the Colorado Supreme Court upheld the injunction and, after a full trial on the merits of the case, declared Amendment 2 unconstitutional on December 14, 1993.

The state of Colorado appealed the case to the U.S. Supreme Court, and arguments were heard in October of 1995. In a decision written by Justice Anthony Kennedy and handed down on May 20, 1996, the Court declared Amendment 2 unconstitutional. The ruling argued that the amendment violated the constitutional right to equal protection and lacked a rational basis for singling out GLB people. Justice Antonin Scalia penned a scathing dissent on behalf of himself and two other justices. Their dis-

> **ROMER V. EVANS (1996): FROM THE DISSENTING OPINION**
>
> *Dissenting opinion by Justice Scalia:* The Court has mistaken a Kulturkampf for a fit of spite. The constitutional amendment before us here is not the manifestation of a "'bare . . . desire to harm'" homosexuals, ante, at 13, but is rather a modest attempt by seemingly tolerant Coloradans to preserve traditional sexual mores against the efforts of a politically powerful minority to revise those mores through use of the laws. That objective, and the means chosen to achieve it, are not only unimpeachable under any constitutional doctrine hitherto pronounced (hence the opinion's heavy reliance upon principles of righteousness rather than judicial holdings); they have been specifically approved by the Congress of the United States and by this Court.
>
> In holding that homosexuality cannot be singled out for disfavorable treatment, the Court contradicts a decision, unchallenged here, pronounced only 10 years ago, see Bowers v. Hardwick, . . . (1986), and places the prestige of this institution behind the proposition that opposition to homosexuality is as reprehensible as racial or religious bias. Whether it is or not is precisely the cultural debate that gave rise to the Colorado constitutional amendment (and to the preferential laws against which the amendment was directed).
>
> Since the Constitution of the United States says nothing about this subject, it is left to be resolved by normal democratic means, including the democratic adoption of provisions in state constitutions.
>
> This Court has no business imposing upon all Americans the resolution favored by the elite class from which the Members of this institution are selected, pronouncing that "animosity" toward homosexuality . . . is evil. I vigorously dissent. . . .
>
> Today's opinion has no foundation in American constitutional law, and barely pretends to. The people of Colorado have adopted an entirely reasonable provision which does not even disfavor homosexuals in any substantive sense, but merely denies them preferential treatment. Amendment 2 is designed to prevent piecemeal deterioration of the sexual morality favored by a majority of Coloradans, and is not only an appropriate means to that legitimate end, but a means that Americans have employed before. Striking it down is an act, not of judicial judgment, but of political will. I dissent.

sent notwithstanding, Amendment 2 never took legal effect in Colorado.

SIGNIFICANCE

The success of the campaign against Oregon's Measure 9 suggests that antigay politics could be effectively countered. On the other hand, the passage of Colorado's Amendment 2 demonstrated that some American voters were capable of expressing bias toward GLB people at the ballot box. This fact caused significant pain, fear, and anger in Colorado and in other states. Furthermore, the election demonstrated that appeals to "special rights" were especially effective and difficult to counter. The campaign and election also suggested the potential gains for conservatives in pursuing antigay measures, because they provided a means to raise money and galvanize voters. In retrospect, these measures were a harbinger of the subsequent practice of using GLB rights as political wedge issue.

Conservatives were inspired by Amendment 2 to propose similar antigay ordinances in a variety of locations; many petition drives never made it to the ballot box, but some did. However, these efforts were met with intensive and widespread organizing by GLB communities. These campaigns challenged many people in Colorado, in Oregon, and throughout the nation to come out and to take explicit public stands on behalf of GLB rights. Some GLB communities began to look more seriously at the internal divisions that hampered their efforts—divisions based on such factors as race, gender, the degree to which a person was out, and rural-urban differences. The awareness of the very real dangers posed by prejudice against GLB people prompted many heterosexuals to support GLB rights. Oregon and Colorado became models of what was possible—for better and for worse.

The Supreme Court decision declaring Amendment 2 unconstitutional also had significant legal impacts that went beyond the case in question. For the first time in history, the nation's top judicial authority had acknowledged and delimited antigay prejudice. Also, the majority decision in the case represented a new way of speaking about GLB people, one that regarded them as citizens worthy of respect and civil rights. These two shifts laid a foundation for judicial rulings very different from tradition.

—*Glenda M. Russell*

FURTHER READING

Haider-Markel, Donald P., and Kenneth J. Meier. "Legislative Victory, Electoral Uncertainty: Explaining Outcomes in the Battles over Lesbian and Gay Civil Rights." *Review of Policy Research* 20, no. 4 (2003): 671-690.

Herman, Didi. *The Antigay Agenda*. Chicago: University of Chicago Press, 1997.

Hunter, Nan D. "Proportional Equality: Readings of *Romer*." *Kentucky Law Journal* 89 (2001): 885-910.

Jacobs, Andrew. "*Romer* Wasn't Built in a Day: The Subtle Transformation on Judicial Argument over Gay Rights." *Wisconsin Law Review* (1996): 893-969.

Keen, Lisa, and Suzanne B. Goldberg. *Strangers to the Law: Gay People on Trial*. Ann Arbor: University of Michigan Press, 1998.

Murdoch, Joyce, and Deb Price. *Courting Justice: Gay Men and Lesbians v. the Supreme Court*. New York: Basic Books, 2001.

Russell, Glenda M. *Voted Out: The Psychological Consequences of Anti-Gay Politics*. New York: New York University Press, 2000.

Stein, Arlene. *The Stranger Next Door*. Boston: Beacon Press, 2004.

SEE ALSO: 1972-1973: Local Governments Pass Antidiscrimination Laws; 1973: National Gay Task Force Is Formed; Mar. 5, 1974: Antigay and Antilesbian Organizations Begin to Form; June 27, 1974: Abzug and Koch Attempt to Amend the Civil Rights Act of 1964; July 3, 1975: U.S. Civil Service Commission Prohibits Discrimination Against Federal Employees; 1977: Anita Bryant Campaigns Against Gay and Lesbian Rights; 1978: Lesbian and Gay Workplace Movement Is Founded; Nov. 7, 1978: Antigay and Antilesbian Briggs Initiative Is Defeated; Nov. 27, 1978: White Murders Politicians Moscone and Milk; 1979: Moral Majority Is Founded; Nov., 1986: Californians Reject LaRouche's Quarantine Initiative; Mar.-Apr., 1993: Battelle Sex Study Prompts Conservative Backlash; 1994: Employment Non-Discrimination Act Is Proposed to U.S. Congress; Dec. 4, 1995: Lesbian Couple Murdered in Oregon; Mar. 21, 2003: New Mexico Amends Its Human Rights Act; June 26, 2003: U.S. Supreme Court Overturns Texas Sodomy Law.

1993
INTERSEX SOCIETY OF NORTH AMERICA IS FOUNDED

The Intersex Society of North America, founded in 1993 by intersex activist Cheryl Chase, revealed the often secretive genital surgeries and gender reassignments of intersexed infants. The organization has brought intersexuality into public discussion and has advocated for increased sensitivity and understanding within the medical profession.

LOCALE: Seattle, Washington
CATEGORIES: Organizations and institutions; health and medicine; science

KEY FIGURE
Cheryl Chase (b. 1956), founder of the Intersex Society of North America

SUMMARY OF EVENT

It is believed that one out of every two thousand children are born intersexed, that is, with ambiguous genitalia. Because the 1950's was the height of Freudian psychiatry, which, among other things, placed great emphasis on the significance of external genitalia to "normal" human growth and maturation, the medical profession thought that the answer to ambiguous genitalia was to operate quickly to ensure that the child's genitals would look as "normal" as possible.

The procedure often was kept secret from the child's parents to further the chances of reinforcing the "assigned" gender. When parents were informed, they often were given partial information. Many were told that their child's genitals did not fully form, and that surgery was required to "fix" the "anomaly." Most doctors did not tell parents that the surgery was essentially experimental, nor did they inform parents that their child could be wounded physically and emotionally. For decades, the surgical procedures and their secrecy were common practice.

In the 1990's, intersex activists, as they came to be known, began speaking out against these unquestioned medical interventions. Activists came together after obtaining their medical records or experiencing sexual or medical problems and then learning about their medical histories. The main thing that united them was the anger they shared about how they were treated: Their variant or ambiguous genitalia was treated like a disease or an anomaly (hence the term "ambiguous") and was "fixed" in secrecy.

At the time, there was little actual research data to back up the activists' claims of secrecy by the medical profession, but that did not stop Cheryl Chase, the first person to break the silence surrounding the cosmetic genital surgery of intersexed individuals. Chase founded the Intersex Society of North America (ISNA) in 1993, which has since brought light to the experience of intersexed individuals and has altered the way medical professionals approach intersex births.

Chase was born intersexed, so doctors thought the best thing to do was to label Chase a boy. Her parents named her Charlie, but eighteen months later doctors "reassigned" her as a girl. Chase's parents were counseled by doctors to have their daughter's clitoris removed, to change her name, and to relocate to a town where nobody knew the family. This surgery left Chase with a permanent loss of sexual sensation and an inability to reach orgasm.

According to its Web site, the ISNA "is devoted to systemic change to end shame, secrecy, and unwanted genital surgeries for people born with an anatomy that someone decided is not standard for male or female." The organization's program includes diagnosis, gender assignment, peer and professional counseling, and support for patients wanting surgery and who are mature enough to make informed decisions about the procedure. The ISNA has a patient-centered approach to care, and its agenda (the first sentence of each item below) is educational in focus:

1. *Intersexuality is basically a problem of stigma and trauma, not gender.* It is the social importance given to nonambiguous gender that makes doctors feel that they are doing the "right thing" by performing surgeries and keeping them secret. The real harm though comes from the stigma and trauma intersexed individuals face.

2. *Parents' distress must not be treated by surgery on the child.* It is clear that parents also need psychological and emotional support, but decisions about the care of the child must be made only with the child's best interest in mind.

3. *Professional mental health care is essential.* Currently only a small percentage of persons with intersex conditions receive professional psychological support either as children or as adults.

4. *Honest, complete disclosure is good medicine.* Parents need full disclosure from the medical profession about their intersexed children to help make informed medical decisions, and patients need full disclosure to help them understand their intersexed bodies. Full disclosure normalizes rather than stigmatizes intersexuality.

5. *All children should be assigned as boy or girl, without early surgery.* Assigning gender at birth is a legal and social requirement, but surgery is not, and, therefore, it should not be performed automatically. The newborn's gender should be assigned only after a comprehensive examination and diagnosis, based on the best guess for the most likely gender development of the child.

Significance

A body of scholarship on intersexuality has emerged because of ISNA's activism. Historian Alice Dreger, psychologist Suzanne Kessler, and biologist Anne Fausto-Sterling have all written important works that complement ISNA's positions. Breaking the silence about intersexed people and their families, and the scholarship, have resulted in significant changes in the medical approach to intersexuality. The impact that ISNA's work has made on the medical profession is by and large its greatest contribution and has helped to make the lives of intersexed individuals less shameful and secretive.

The ISNA has brought intersexuality into mainstream media. A popular online magazine, *Slate*, in an article called "The Cutting Edge," discussed the positive ways that Texas Children's Hospital is dealing with intersex births. Also, ISNA board members and staff have been called upon by diverse media to discuss the topic.

—Kim Hackford-Peer

Further Reading

Atkins, Dawn. *Looking Queer.* New York: Haworth Press, 1998.

Chase, Cheryl. "Hermaphrodites with Attitude: Mapping the Emergence of Intersex Political Activism." *GLQ: A Journal of Lesbian and Gay Studies* 4, no. 2 (1998). Reprinted in *The Transgender Issue*, edited by Susan Stryker. Durham, N.C.: Duke University Press, 1998.

Cohen-Kettenis, Peggy Tine, and Friedemann Pfafflin. *Transgenderism and Intersexuality in Childhood and Adolescence: Making Choices.* Thousand Oaks, Calif.: Sage, 2003.

Colapinto, John. *As Nature Made Him: The Boy Who Was Raised as a Girl.* New York: HarperCollins, 2000.

Dreger, Alice. "'Ambiguous Sex' or Ambivalent Medicine?" Ethical Issues in the Medical Treatment of Intersexuality. *Hastings Center Report* 28, no. 3 (1998): 24-35.

_____. *Hermaphrodites and the Medical Invention of Sex.* Cambridge, Mass.: Harvard University Press, 1998.

_____, ed. *Intersex in the Age of Ethics.* Frederick, Md.: University Publishing Group, 1999.

Fausto-Sterling, Anne. *Sexing the Body: Gender Politics and the Construction of Sexuality.* New York: Basic Books, 2000.

Hegarty, Peter, and Cheryl Chase. "Intersex Activism, Feminism, and Psychology." In *Queer Theory*, edited by Iain Morland and Annabelle Willox. New York: Palgrave Macmillan, 2005.

James, Stanlie M., and Claire C. Robertson, eds. *Genital Cutting and Transnational Sisterhood: Disputing U.S. Polemics.* Urbana: University of Illinois Press, 2002.

Koyama, Emi, comp. *Introduction to Intersex Activism: A Guide for Gay, Lesbian, Bi, and Trans Allies.* Petaluma, Calif.: Intersex Society of North America, 2001.

Preves, Sharon. *Intersex and Identity: The Contested Self*. New Brunswick, N.J.: Rutgers University Press, 2003.

Sharpe, Andrew N. *Transgender Jurisprudence: Dysphoric Bodies of Law*. London: Cavendish, 2002.

See also: Nov. 21, 1966: First Gender Identity Clinic Opens and Provides Gender Reassignment Surgery; 1978: Harry Benjamin International Gender Dysphoria Association Is Founded; 1992: Transgender Nation Holds Its First Protest.

1993
Monette Wins the National Book Award for *Becoming a Man*

While living with AIDS, Paul Monette wrote Becoming a Man: Half a Life Story *to provide solace and meaning for gays and lesbians who grew up closeted and alone.*

Locale: Los Angeles, California; New York, New York

Categories: Literature; publications; HIV-AIDS

Key Figures
Paul Monette (1945-1995), writer
Roger Horwitz (1941-1986), attorney, Monette's lover
Winston Wilde (b. 1958), psychotherapist, surviving lover of Monette
Ned Rorem (b. 1923), composer and diarist
Roger Bourland (b. 1952), composer
J. D. McClatchy (b. 1945), poet and literary critic

Summary of Event
Becoming a Man: Half a Life Story (1992) was written when Paul Monette was dying of AIDS. He composed the book on a computer and left no printed manuscripts, such was the compelling haste of the project, meant to help others through exorcising his own agonies of living in the closet until his late twenties.

He writes in the memoir of having no story to tell in the years he was in the closet. He had crushes on straight men, "golden Adonises" who comprised "a Parthenon frieze of heroic male flesh parading to the showers after practice." He formed emotional and physical relations with women. This behavior was all too typical in the years when all realms of society stigmatized homosexuality: law, medicine, religion, psychiatry. His interior life was agonized because he could not tell the truth, but he would not know how to speak if he could, because there were so few examples of how to speak.

Monette was born into a working- and middle-class family but was able to attend prestigious schools: Phillips Academy, Andover as a day student, and Yale University on a scholarship. In his adolescence, Monette delineates a cultural attitude of the day. It was okay to be very effeminate—and usually the butt of jokes—but there was no place for a more masculine-acting homosexual. This quandary would not be resolved until the 1970's, after gay liberation.

At Yale he wrote his thesis on Alfred, Lord Tennyson's *In Memoriam* (1850) without acknowledging its homoerotic overtones, another aspect of the silence of the closet. In his youth he wrote poetry and attracted the attention of various poets and poet critics.

A trip to Sea Island, Georgia, with poet J. D. (Sandy) McClatchy gave Monette the setting for a sex scene in his first novel. Discussions with McClatchy showed Monette that there was not just gay sex but a gay sensibility. This writing breakthrough led to his coming out completely. In 1974 in Boston

Paul Monette, receiving his National Book Award medal in 1992. (AP/Wide World Photos)

at Rudy Kikel's place, with Kikel's friend Craig Rowland, Monette met his ideal accepting gay male, the "laughing man" who would reciprocate his love, Roger Horwitz.

Horwitz had received a doctorate in comparative literature and a law degree, both from Harvard. In 1977, Monette and Horwitz moved to Los Angeles, where they led a privileged life among an accepting lesbian and gay subculture. Horwitz's stepbrother was Sheldon Andelson, also gay, a businessman who was appointed a University of California regent.

Monette had stopped writing poetry, but before Horwitz's death Monette wrote well-received novels in the genres of romance and comedy. His first novel, *Taking Care of Mrs. Carroll*, appeared in the annus mirabilis, or wonderful year, of gay fiction, 1978, when gay novels were also published by East Coast writers Edmund White, Larry Kramer, and Andrew Holleran. Gay publishing had progressed a great deal by that time, and Monette's novel appeared in part in the slick gay male erotica magazine *Blueboy*, with appropriate illustrations by Stavrinos.

Horwitz's death from AIDS compelled Monette to produce works different from his early, lighter works. A book about Horwitz's death, *Borrowed Time: An AIDS Memoir* (1988), put into words the experiences of thousands of persons living with AIDS or caring for someone with AIDS. Monette then wrote a book of poems to Horwitz, *Love Alone: Eighteen Elegies for Rog* (1988); a novel about survivors of partners who died of AIDS, *Afterlife* (1990); and another novel about AIDS, *Halfway Home* (1991).

SIGNIFICANCE

Monette's circles in Los Angeles gay life were more than social. He and Horwitz supported such pioneering institutions as the Los Angeles Gay and Lesbian Center.

While written U.S. literary history is still centered on the East Coast and New York City, Monette was a writer living in and writing about his adopted city, Los Angeles. He tells his stories with details and settings that enrich the city's larger social and cultural history.

Monette used his considerable public speaking talent to promote his work, especially his AIDS writings, and helped to create the audience and even the acceptance for his memoirs. *Borrowed Time* was nominated for a National Book Award, and *Becoming a Man* won the award a few years later. His abilities also made him a community spokesman on numerous topics of protest, such as the Roman Catholic Church's condemnation of homosexuality.

For his books on Horwitz's dying of AIDS, Monette received an almost unprecedented amount of fan mail. Monette brought out into the open and articulated for others what at the beginning of the AIDS pandemic few could express.

Several composers have set Monette's AIDS

writings to music and thus enlarged their original impact. Ned Rorem used the poem "Here" from *Love Alone*, while Roger Bourland used a portion of the prose foreword to that volume, "Love Is All You Need." Bourland's work was written for the Gay Men's Chorus of Los Angeles, another example of interrelated gay cultural influences.

In the years remaining to him, Monette had two other lovers, Stephen Kolzak, a casting director who also died of AIDS, and Winston Wilde, who would become a psychotherapist. Monette then wrote several compelling short works and poems, including a touching memoir of an older lesbian friend, along with works that move in a more spiritual direction, such as the essay "My Priests," which appeared in *Last Watch of the Night: Essays Too Personal and Otherwise* (1994). One of his last public appearances was to speak at St. Thomas Episcopal Church, Hollywood, to inspire an audience overflowing the sanctuary.

Before Monette's death, director Monte Bramer began his documentary film *Paul Monette: The Brink of Summer's End*. Released in 1996, the film won the 1997 Sundance Festival Audience Award for a documentary. Monette's brother, Robert, and Kolzak, Wilde, and numerous others appear in the film to give him homage as brother, lover, friend, writer, and activist.

—*Dan Luckenbill*

Further Reading

Kermode, Lloyd Edward. "Using Up Words in Paul Monette's AIDS Elegy." In *Response to Death: The Literary Work of Mourning*, edited by Christian Riegel. Edmonton: University of Alberta Press, 2005.

Monette, Paul. *Afterlife*. New York: Crown, 1990.

_____. *Becoming a Man: Half a Life Story*. New York: Harcourt Brace Jovanovich, 1992.

_____. *Borrowed Time: An AIDS Memoir*. New York: Harcourt Brace Jovanovich, 1988.

_____. *Last Watch of the Night: Essays Too Personal and Otherwise*. New York: Harcourt Brace, 1994.

_____. *Love Alone: Eighteen Elegies for Rog*. New York: St. Martin's Press, 1988.

Robinson, Paul. *Gay Lives: Homosexual Autobiography from John Addington Symonds to Paul Monette*. Chicago: University of Chicago Press, 1999.

Román, David. "Paul Monette." In *Contemporary Gay American Novelists*, edited by Emmanuel S. Nelson. Westport, Conn.: Greenwood Press, 1993.

See also: July 4, 1855: Whitman Publishes *Leaves of Grass*; May 25, 1895: Oscar Wilde Is Convicted of Gross Indecency; 1924: Gide Publishes the Signed Edition of *Corydon*; 1939: Isherwood Publishes *Goodbye to Berlin*; 1947-1948: Golden Age of American Gay Literature; 1956: Baldwin Publishes *Giovanni's Room*; 1963: Rechy Publishes *City of Night*; June, 1971: The Gay Book Award Debuts; 1974: *The Front Runner* Makes *The New York Times* Best-Seller List; 1975: First Novel About Coming Out to Parents Is Published; 1980: Alyson Begins Publishing Gay and Lesbian Books; 1980-1981: Gay Writers Form the Violet Quill; May, 1987: *Lambda Rising Book Report* Begins Publication; June 2, 1989: Lambda Literary Award Is Created.

1993
THE WEDDING BANQUET IS FIRST ACCLAIMED TAIWANESE GAY-THEMED FILM

A unique comedy revolving around cross-cultural, sexual, national, and family issues, The Wedding Banquet *was an immediate commercial and critical success, launching Taiwanese filmmaker Ang Lee's career. Also, Lee won an Oscar and a Golden Globe for Best Director for the gay-themed 2005 film* Brokeback Mountain *in 2006.*

LOCALE: Taiwan; China; United States
CATEGORIES: Arts; race and ethnicity; cultural and intellectual history

KEY FIGURES
Ang Lee (b. 1954), Taiwanese cowriter, producer, and director of *The Wedding Banquet*
Winston Chao (b. 1960), Taiwanese model who played Wai Tung, the gay Asian character
Ah-Leh Gua (b. 1944), veteran Taiwanese actor who played the role of Wai Tung's mother
Sihung Lung (1930-2002), veteran Taiwanese actor who portrayed Wai Tung's father
May Chin, Taiwanese singing star who played Wei Wei, the bride
Mitchell Lichtenstein (b. 1956), American actor who played Simon, Wai Tung's lover

SUMMARY OF EVENT
The Wedding Banquet was the most profitable film of 1993. Earning more than twenty-three times its budget, the film had a higher return-to-cost ratio than Steven Spielberg's *Jurassic Park*, which opened the same year. In addition to being Taiwan's biggest box-office hit, *The Wedding Banquet* made $7 million in the United States and $30 million worldwide.

Shot on location in New York City, *The Wedding Banquet* tells the story of Wai Tung (Winston Chao), a gay Taiwanese man who has been living with his Caucasian lover Simon (Mitchell Lichtenstein) for five years in Manhattan. Wai Tung is a successful real estate entrepreneur who is happy in his long-term relationship. However, he has hidden his homosexuality from his elderly parents, Mr. and Mrs. Gao (Sihung Lung and Ah-Leh Gua), who are hoping for a grandchild from Wai Tung, their only child. Determined to find a wife for him, they have registered him with computer dating-services in Taiwan.

Meanwhile, Wai Tung has trouble collecting rent from his tenant Wei Wei, a struggling visual artist from Shanghai, China. An undocumented immigrant, Wei Wei (May Chin) is in danger of being deported, so she is desperate to obtain a green card or gain legal status through marriage. Simon suggests a solution: If Wai Tung and Wei Wei become married legally, then Wai Tung's parents would be satisfied that he had found a bride, Wei Wei would get her green card, and Wai Tung and Simon could continue their relationship. However, this deception leads to hilarious complications and more deception when Wai Tung's parents come to America to plan their son's wedding. Wai Tung fools his parents into thinking he and Wei Wei are living in Simon's home and that Simon is the landlord.

The Gaos are disappointed with the simple wedding ceremony at city hall. Following the ceremony, Simon invites everyone to dinner at the best Chinese restaurant in Manhattan. The restaurant owner recognizes Mr. Gao as his former army commander and offers to host an extravagant wedding banquet. Wai Tung and Wei Wei soon become intoxicated and later make love in the newlywed suite.

Wei Wei discovers she is pregnant, and Simon becomes angry. When Simon and Wai Tung argue, Mr. Gao, who actually understands some English, realizes that Simon and Wai Tung are lovers. Mr. Gao suffers a mild stroke. In the hospital waiting room, Wai Tung tells his mother that he is gay, but Mrs. Gao asks that he keep it a secret from his father. Wei Wei had planned to have an abortion but changes her mind.

As Mr. Gao recuperates, Simon helps him with physical therapy. One day, Mr. Gao tells Simon that he accepts him as Wai Tung's companion, but he asks Simon to never tell Wai Tung, Mrs. Gao, or Wei Wei that he (Mr. Gao) knows. Wei Wei asks Simon to be a second father for her and Wai Tung's child, and the movie ends happily with the Gaos returning to Taiwan, expecting a grandchild.

SIGNIFICANCE

In addition to its remarkable commercial success, *The Wedding Banquet* received widespread critical acclaim. In 1993, it won numerous awards. At the Berlin International Film Festival, it won the top prize, the Golden Bear, for best picture. At the Locarno Film Festival, it received the audience choice award. At the Golden Horse Film Festival (Taiwan's equivalent of the Academy Awards), the film won awards for best picture, best screenplay, best director, best supporting actress, and best supporting actor. It also received the Golden Space Needle awards for best film and best director at the 1993 Seattle International Film Festival. In 1993, at both the Academy Awards and the Golden Globe Awards, *The Wedding Banquet* was nominated for best foreign-language film. At the 1994 Homer Awards, the film was a nominee for best foreign-language film of the year.

With *The Wedding Banquet*, Ang Lee achieved international recognition and financial success that firmly established his place in film history. His 2005 film *Brokeback Mountain*, about long-term love between two cowboys, garnered for Lee a best director Golden Globe and an Oscar.

The Wedding Banquet was the first Taiwanese film in which two men kissed; Lee's cross-cultural gay film, however, was not the usual superficial or often derogatory presentation of stereotypical gay and Asian characters. Instead, Lee created a unique comedy about national, cultural, individual, and family identities in conflict. The intricate development of plot and characters made it a film that appealed to mainstream audiences worldwide. In Taiwan, international critical acclaim led to government support and incentives for the Taiwanese filmmaking industry. *The Wedding Banquet* was released in video and DVD formats for the mass market.

—*Alice Myers*

FURTHER READING

Berry, Chris, and Feii Lu, eds. *Island on the Edge: Taiwan New Cinema and After*. Hong Kong: Hong Kong University Press, 2005.

Berry, Michael. "Ang Lee: Freedom in Film." In *Speaking in Images: Interviews with Contemporary Chinese Filmmakers*, by Michael Berry. New York: Columbia University Press, 2005.

Cheshire, Ellen. *Ang Lee*. Harpenden, England: Pocket Essentials, 2001.

Feng, Peter X., ed. *Screening Asian Americans*. New Brunswick, N.J.: Rutgers University Press, 2002.

Hamamoto, Darrell Y., and Sandra Liu, eds. *Countervisions: American Film Criticism*. Philadelphia: Temple University Press, 2000.

Lee, Ang, et al. "*Eat Drink Man Woman*," and "*The Wedding Banquet*." In *Two Films by Ang Lee*. Woodstock, N.Y.: Overlook Press, 1994.

Lewis, Jon, ed. *The End of Cinema as We Know It: American Film in the Nineties*. New York: New York University Press, 2001.

Summerfield, Ellen, and Sandra Lee. *Seeing the Big Picture: Exploring American Cultures on Film*. Yarmouth, Maine: Intercultural Press, 2001.

SEE ALSO: 1929: *Pandora's Box* Opens; 1930's-1960's: Hollywood Bans "Sexual Perversion" in Films; 1985: Lesbian Film *Desert Hearts* Is Released; 1988: *Macho Dancer* Is Released in the Philippines; Mar. 20, 1988: *M. Butterfly* Opens on Broadway; 1995: *The Advocate* Outs Oscar Nominee Nigel Hawthorne; Mar. 5, 2006: *Brokeback Mountain, Capote,* and *Transamerica* Receive Oscars.

1993-1996
Hawaii Opens Door to Same-Gender Marriages

Hawaii's Supreme Court ruled in 1993 that a state law banning same-gender couples from marrying violated the state's constitution, allowing the case against the state to proceed. The ruling, reaffirmed in 1996 in the circuit court, led to not only lesbian and gay marriages in the state but also to antigay backlash, a constitutional amendment in 1998 banning same-gender marriage, and a 1999 decision by the state supreme court outlawing same-gender marriage.

Locale: Hawaii
Categories: Laws, acts, and legal history; civil rights; government and politics

Key Figures
Kevin Chang, circuit court justice who ruled on the constitutionality of Hawaii's marriage law
Newt Gingrich (b. 1943), House majority leader in the mid-1990's, who was a major backer of the federal Defense of Marriage Act (DOMA)
Ninia Baehr,
Genora Dancel,
Tammy Rodrigues,
Antoinette Pregil,
Pat Lagon, and
Joseph Melilio, sued Hawaii for the right to marry

Summary of Event

In 1996, judge Kevin Chang of the Hawaii circuit court made history when he ruled in favor of three same-gender couples who wished to marry in that state. The case began in 1990, when Ninia Baehr, her partner Genora Dancel, and two other same-gender couples decided to challenge, on state constitutional grounds, a Hawaii law forbidding gay and lesbian marriage.

The six filed a lawsuit in 1991, arguing, in *Baehr v. Lewin* (later renamed *Baehr v. Miike*) that the state constitution, in its due process and equal protection clauses, guaranteed that same-gender couples could marry in the same manner as heterosexual couples. They also argued that limiting marriage to that between a man and a woman violated the state constitution because it was sex discrimination. In 1993, the Hawaii Supreme Court agreed, and the couples were allowed to challenge the law in court, leading to Chang's historic decision.

However, after Chang's 1996 decision, public opinion in Hawaii turned against gay and lesbian marriage, and opponents of the ruling immediately began an effort in Hawaii's legislature to amend the state constitution to specifically outlaw same-gender marriage. In 1998, Hawaii's voters overwhelmingly approved the amendment, so the state had to appeal Chang's 1996 ruling on behalf of the voters. Therefore, because of the amendment to the state constitution, in 1999, Hawaii's Supreme Court had to overturn Chang's 1996 decision and rule in favor of the prohibitive law.

At the national level in 1996, as a direct result of Chang's decision, conservative House speaker Newt Gingrich spearheaded the Defense of Marriage Act (DOMA), which defined "marriage" as being between one man and one woman. The bill passed the House of Representatives by an overwhelming vote of 346 to 67 and the Senate by a vote of 85 to 14; President Bill Clinton then agreed to sign it. DOMA represented an effort to prevent other states from following Hawaii's lead and making gay and lesbian marriage legal. DOMA did not prohibit any state from legalizing same-gender marriage, but made it optional for other states to recognize such marriages, or not. Conservative Christians dominated the national arguments, and Gingrich and other leaders argued that same-gender marriages were a threat to the "traditional" family and to traditional "family values." DOMA also made same-gender couples ineligible for federal benefits programs reserved for legally married couples.

Significance

Throughout the 1990's, same-gender couples had begun seeking domestic partnership benefits from

> **FROM *BAEHR V. LEWIN* (1999)**
>
> *Majority opinion by Chief Justice Ronald Moon:* Applying the foregoing standards to the present case, we do not believe that a right to same-sex marriage is so rooted in the traditions and collective conscience of our people that failure to recognize it would violate the fundamental principles of liberty and justice that lie at the base of all our civil and political institutions. Neither do we believe that a right to same-sex marriage is implicit in the concept of ordered liberty, such that neither liberty nor justice would exist if it were sacrificed. Accordingly, we hold that the applicant couples do not have a fundamental constitutional right to same-sex marriage arising out of the right to privacy or otherwise.
>
> Our holding, however, does not leave the applicant couples without a potential remedy in this case. As we will discuss below, the applicant couples are free to press their equal protection claim. If they are successful, the State of Hawaii will no longer be permitted to refuse marriage licenses to couples merely on the basis that they are of the same sex. But there is no fundamental right to marriage for same-sex couples under article I, section 6 of the Hawaii Constitution.
>
> *Dissenting opinion by Judge Walter Heen:* In my view, the statute's classification is clearly designed to promote the legislative purpose of fostering and protecting the propagation of the human race through heterosexual marriages and bears a reasonable relationship to that purpose. I find nothing unconstitutional in that. . . .
>
> Appellants complain that because they are not allowed to legalize their relationships, they are denied a multitude of statutory benefits conferred upon spouses in a legal marriage. However, redress for those deprivations is a matter for the legislature, which can express the will of the populace in deciding whether such benefits should be extended to persons in Appellants' circumstances. Those benefits can be conferred without rooting out the very essence of a legal marriage. This court should not manufacture a civil right which is unsupported by any precedent, and whose legal incidents—the entitlement to those statutory benefits—will reach beyond the right to enter into a legal marriage and overturn long standing public policy encompassing other areas of public concern. This decision will have far-reaching and grave repercussions on the finances and policies of the governments and industry of this state and all the other states in the country.

The case in Hawaii brought the issue of same-gender marriage into the national spotlight, and it helped change public attitudes and opinions on same-gender marriage. Around the nation, same-gender couples began challenging laws opposed to gay and lesbian marriage, and state officials around the country began taking positions on the issue.

In 1998, an Alaska court ruled that it was unconstitutional to ban same-gender marriage, but the legislature quickly enacted a constitutional amendment to do just that. In 1999, Vermont's Supreme Court ruled that same-gender and opposite-gender couples were entitled to the same protections under that state's constitution. In 2000, Vermont's governor issued a civil-union bill, and Vermont officially became the first state to recognize same-gender civil unions. In 2004, Massachusetts became the first state to recognize same-gender marriages, and the state's supreme court announced that civil unions would not grant couples the same protections as marriages. In the same year, New Jersey legalized civil unions for gay and lesbian couples and the state's Supreme Court, on October 25, 2006, ruled that same-gender couples are entitled to the same legal rights as heterosexual married couples. Also in 2004, San Francisco's mayor announced that the California statutes limiting marriage to one man and one woman were in violation of the state constitution, and he issued more than two thousand marriage licenses to gay and lesbian couples, though the state later invalidated his action and the licenses were revoked.

employers, forcing corporate America to reexamine its position on gay and lesbian rights, and the couples gained successes for the entire decade. In 1996, the Southern Baptist Convention threatened to boycott The Walt Disney Company because the company extended equal benefits to same-gender domestic partners, but the boycott had no financial impact on the company; indeed, it increased corporate support for domestic partner benefits.

In 2003, in *Lawrence v. Texas*, the U.S. Supreme Court overturned its 1986 *Bowers v. Hardwick* decision and threw out the laws in thirteen states that made consensual sodomy illegal. Though the justices specifically stated in their decision that the ruling was not intended to affect the legality of same-gender marriage, it has opened the door for challenges to the U.S. Constitution. Around the world, the Netherlands, in 2001, became the first country to recognize same-gender marriages, followed by Belgium in 2003 and Spain and Canada in 2005. South Africa is expected to determine same-gender marriage rights by the end of 2006.

In 2004, U.S. president George W. Bush called for a constitutional amendment banning gay and lesbian marriage, arguing that DOMA might well be overturned on constitutional grounds and that traditional family values and the traditional view of marriage were in danger of being completely redefined. However, the attempt failed in the Senate. Amendment proponents would have needed at least sixty votes to bring the issue to the Senate floor for formal discussion, and proponents were able to muster just forty-eight votes. (The vote was 48-50, and to actually advance a proposed constitutional amendment through the process of amending the constitution, either sixty-six or sixty-seven senators would have had to vote in favor of the bill, depending on the number of senators actually voting.) The proposed amendment's failure was a success for GLBT rights activists under a conservative administration and a strong indication that the change in public attitudes is slowly bringing a change in legislative behavior as well.

—*Jessie Bishop Powell*

FURTHER READING

Coolidge, David Orgon. "Same-Sex Marriage, as Hawaii Goes." *First Things: The Journal of Religion, Culture, and Public Life* 72 (April, 1997): 33-37. http://www.firstthings.com/ftissues/ft9704/articles/coolidge.html.

Hull, Kathleen E. "The Political Limits of the Rights Frame: The Case of Same-Sex Marriage in Hawaii." *Sociological Perspectives* 44, no. 2 (2001): 207-232.

Kotulski, Davina. *Why You Should Give a Damn About Gay Marriage*. Los Angeles: Advocate Books, 2004.

Mello, Michael. *Legalizing Gay Marriage*. Philadelphia: Temple University Press, 2004.

Moats, David. *Civil Wars: A Battle for Gay Marriage*. Orlando, Fla.: Harcourt, 2004.

National Gay and Lesbian Task Force. "Differences Between Marriage, Civil Union, and Domestic Partnerships" (August 18, 2004). http://thetaskforce.org/.

Rauch, Jonathan. *Gay Marriage: Why It Is Good for Gays, Good for Straights, and Good for America*. New York: Times Books/Henry Holt, 2004.

"Same-Sex Marriage: A Selective Bibliography of the Legal Literature." Law Library, Rutgers School of Law. http://law-library.rutgers.edu/SSM.html.

SEE ALSO: 1981: Gay and Lesbian Palimony Suits Emerge; 1986: *Bowers v. Hardwick* Upholds State Sodomy Laws; Aug. 6, 1994: Japanese American Citizens League Supports Same-Gender Marriage; Sept. 21, 1996: U.S. President Clinton Signs Defense of Marriage Act; Dec. 20, 1999: *Baker v. Vermont* Leads to Recognition of Same-Gender Civil Unions; Feb. 21, 2003: Australian Court Validates Transsexual Marriage; Apr., 2003: Buenos Aires Recognizes Same-Gender Civil Unions; June 17, 2003, and July 19, 2005: Canada Legalizes Same-Gender Marriage; June 26, 2003: U.S. Supreme Court Overturns Texas Sodomy Law; Nov. 18, 2003: Massachusetts Court Rules for Same-Gender Marriage; Nov. 18, 2004: United Kingdom Legalizes Same-Gender Civil Partnerships; Apr. 4, 2005: United Kingdom's Gender Recognition Act Legalizes Transsexual Marriage.

March-April, 1993
BATTELLE SEX STUDY PROMPTS CONSERVATIVE BACKLASH

A 1993 survey, countering the well-known Kinsey Reports on human sexuality, showed a lower prevalence of gay men in the U.S. population. Conservatives continue to use the survey as "proof" that gays and lesbians should be discounted as significant constituents by politicians.

LOCALE: United States
CATEGORIES: Publications; government and politics; organizations and institutions; civil rights

KEY FIGURES
John O. G. Billy,
Koray Tanfer,
William R. Grady, and
Daniel H. Klepinger, research scientists and authors of the report
Alfred Kinsey (1894-1956), sex researcher, whose 1948 survey report on male sexuality was compared to the Battelle sex study

SUMMARY OF EVENT
In 1993, the results of a survey by the Battelle Human Affairs Research Centers, based in Seattle, Washington, countered common knowledge. Most gays and lesbians had accepted Alfred Kinsey's 1948 research that gay men made up 10 percent of the U.S. population. The new report, published in the March-April issue of *Family Planning Perspectives*, challenged Kinsey's numbers, stating that 2.3 percent of men in the United States had reported any homosexual activity in a ten-year period.

Whereas the Christian Right rejoiced in the new report, gay and lesbian leaders worried that the lower numbers would translate into less political clout. The chair of the anti-gay Traditional Values Coalition, Lou Sheldon, weighed in with the words "Tremendous political impact!" Conservatives stressed that the numbers meant that the needs of gays and lesbians could be discounted by politicians and policymakers. Conservative Phyllis Schlafly said, "It shows politicians they don't need to be worried about 1 percent of the population." AIDS activist Larry Kramer predicted political fallout, saying, "This will give [U.S. president] Bill Clinton a chance to welch [*sic*] on promises. Democracy is all about proving you have the numbers. The more numbers you can prove you have, the more likely you'll get your due."

Roger MacFarlane, a founder of New York's Gay Men's Health Crisis, countered, "I don't care if there are only 10 of us in the whole country. Do we have equal rights or not?" His point underscored the need for health care, AIDS research dollars, and protection from hate crimes.

Reportedly, the Battelle Center's aim in completing the study was not to jeopardize the needs of gays and lesbians but to look at the sexual behavior of men twenty to thirty-nine years of age. In 1991, the center surveyed 3,321 men and finalized its report, which was authored by John O. G. Billy, Koray Tanfer, William R. Grady, and Daniel H. Klepinger (all research scientists at the Battelle Center). Subjects were asked about their sexual history, initiation, partners, risk-taking activities, attitudes, knowledge of contraception, and condom use.

Data indicated that in the ten years previous to the study's end date, only 2.3 percent of the interviewed men had gay sex. Gay sex, exclusively, was practiced by 1.1 percent of the men surveyed. Because the Battelle survey was not conducted exactly like the Kinsey study, however, comparing the two is somewhat like comparing apples with oranges. For instance, Kinsey studied a larger group, and he used a rating scale. Kinsey rated orientation from zero (exclusively heterosexual) to six (exclusively homosexual), and he found that 10 percent of the men surveyed thought that they were about a 5 to 6 on the scale; 8 percent rated themselves a 6.

Also, the Kinsey and Battelle studies differ in the length of time that had been under survey: For

> **FROM THE BATTELLE STUDY**
>
> The percentages of same-gender sexual activity in our results appear slightly lower than those from some other recent surveys, but none is close to the 10% figure that persists from Kinsey's study. The 1989 General Social Survey (GSS) found that 98% of sexually active men aged 18 and older were exclusively heterosexual during the 12-month period prior to interview. Using GSS data on the number of male and female sex partners that respondents (men and women) had had since age 18, Smith estimated that "three percent have not been sexually active as adults, 91-93 percent have been exclusively heterosexual, 5-6 percent have been bisexual and less than 1 percent have been exclusively homosexual."
>
> *Source:* John O. G. Billy et al. "The Sexual Behavior of Men in the U.S." *Family Planning Perspectives* 25, no. 2 (March/April, 1993).

Kinsey, the time in question was the previous three years; for Battelle, the previous ten years. Of the 5,000 men in the Kinsey group, 10 percent said that they had had sex with men in the previous three years. Of the 3,321 Battelle men, 1 percent said that they had had sex with men in the previous ten years. Men in the Battelle study, who had not come out completely as gay for ten years, may not have been "counted" as gay. Also, the Battelle categories do not recognize bisexual men or men older than age forty (more of whom are out).

Some limitations existed in the Battelle study. The interviewers were exclusively female, with no prior training in sex research. The women talked to the men in the men's homes, face-to-face, as strangers (but not anonymously). The men in the study may have been reluctant to tell the truth to the surveyors because of religious or social taboos against homosexuality, or because of legal implications. Sexologist Samuel S. Janus, who has conducted many sex surveys, notes that face-to-face interviews often have faulty results.

The women did not ask the men about being gay, only about men having sex with men, so closeted or celibate men would not have been counted. Each subject was asked (reportedly at the end of the survey) for his social security number, place of employment, and two references. If they suspected that these questions would be asked, they might not have answered truthfully for fear of losing jobs, housing, reputations, or family. Of the men who were approached for an interview, 30 percent had declined to take part in the survey. One possible reason for there being few gays in the survey is that gays tend to cluster in urban areas, and that surveying a particular region would not account for these clusters.

There have been other studies about the prevalence of homosexuality, the first being the survey of sexologist Magnus Hirschfeld in 1903-1904. This report found 2.3 percent of surveyed men to be exclusively gay; bisexuals accounted for 3.4 percent. In 1953, Kinsey surveyed 5,940 women, finding 2 to 6 percent exclusively lesbian. A 1973 study by John Gagnon and William Simon, and one in 1974 by M. Hunt, were similar to those of Kinsey. Data collected in 1970 and 1980, later released in 1988-1991 by the National Opinion Research Center, showed that 6 percent of those surveyed had at least one gay or lesbian sexual experience. The wide survey by Samuel and Cynthia Janus in 1993 reported that same-gender sex occurred more than just occasionally for 9 percent of men and 5 percent of women. In that same year, the Yankelovich Monitor Survey found 5.7 percent of the population regarded itself as gay or lesbian. In the next year, Robe T. Mitchell and research partners noted that 2.8 percent of men identified as gay or bisexual, and 2.8 percent of women as lesbian or bisexual.

SIGNIFICANCE

Curiously, the Battelle study never intended to scrutinize the size of the gay population. Instead, the Battelle Center wanted to find out whether or not men (of all sexual orientations) were practicing safer sex. The survey provided much data about male sexual behavior in addition to the figures about the frequency of gay sex. In particular, data showed that men were still having a lot of unprotected sex, which could lead to HIV transmission, but this critical finding was forgotten by the public in the controversy over the survey's numbers.

As for the lasting impact of the 1993 Battelle study, the report is still being used by conservatives to discount the needs of gays and lesbians. In Ontario, Canada, for example, the report was being used in 2004 by religious groups trying to get schools to "convert" gay and lesbian children to heterosexuality.

—Jan Hall

FURTHER READING

Adler, Jerry. "Sex in the Snoring 90's." *Newsweek*, April 26, 1993, 54-57.

Billy, John O. G., Koray Tanfer, William R. Grady, and Daniel H. Klepinger. "The Sexual Behavior of Men in the U.S." *Family Planning Perspectives* 25, no. 2 (March/April, 1993): 52-60.

Kinsey, Alfred C., Wardell B. Pomeroy, and Clyde E. Martin. *Sexual Behavior in the Human Male*. Oxford, England: Saunders, 1948.

Kinsey, Alfred C., Wardell B. Pomeroy, Clyde E. Martin, and Paul H. Gebhard. *Sexual Behavior in the Human Female*. Oxford, England: Saunders, 1953.

Minton, Henry L. *Departing from Deviance: A History of Homosexual Rights and Emancipatory Science in America*. Chicago: University of Chicago Press, 2002.

Painton, Priscilla. "The Shrinking Ten Percent." *Time*, April 26, 1993, 27-29.

Tanfer, Koray, and Battelle Human Affairs Research Center. "National Survey of Men: Design and Execution." *Family Planning Perspectives* 25, no. 2 (March/April, 1993): 83-86.

SEE ALSO: 1948: Kinsey Publishes *Sexual Behavior in the Human Male*; Mar. 5, 1974: Antigay and Antilesbian Organizations Begin to Form; 1977: Anita Bryant Campaigns Against Gay and Lesbian Rights; Nov. 7, 1978: Antigay and Antilesbian Briggs Initiative Is Defeated; 1979: Moral Majority Is Founded; Spring, 1984: AIDS Virus Is Discovered; Nov., 1986: Californians Reject LaRouche's Quarantine Initiative; June 27, 1988: Report of the Presidential AIDS Commission; Nov. 3, 1992: Oregon and Colorado Attempt Antigay Initiatives; Sept. 21, 1996: U.S. President Clinton Signs Defense of Marriage Act.

April 24, 1993
FIRST DYKE MARCH IS HELD IN WASHINGTON, D.C.

The first Dyke March, held in conjunction with the 1993 March on Washington for Lesbian, Gay, and Bi Equal Rights and Liberation, called for the celebration of lesbian sexuality and the promotion of lesbian activism and visibility in the middle of an apathetic cogender activist environment.

LOCALE: Washington, D.C.
CATEGORIES: Marches, protests, and riots; feminism; organizations and institutions

KEY FIGURES

Sarah Schulman, cofounder of the Lesbian Avengers

Judy Sisneros, member of the national ACT UP Women's Committee

SUMMARY OF EVENT

Lesbian invisibility in cogender activist movements has been an issue since lesbians and gays in the United States began organizing in the 1950's. In the 1970's, "gay liberation" was an umbrella term that was supposed to mean gays *and* lesbians. With the advent of second-wave feminism and critiques of sexism, lesbians who felt that their agenda was being subsumed under a male agenda left to form their own movement and to demand that the term "lesbian" be used to distinguish female from male homosexuals.

Marchers lead the third annual New York City Dyke March in 1995. (Hulton Archive/Getty Images)

"Lesbian" now is used to refer to female homosexuals and "gay" to male homosexuals, in most cases but not all; some lesbian women prefer the term "gay woman" or, simply, "gay." One can see the effects of the distinction between lesbians and gays in the name changes of cogender organizations founded in the early 1970's. In the 1980's, to take a few examples, the National Gay Task Force, the Gay Community Services Center in Los Angeles, and Gay Latinos Unidos added "lesbian" to their official names.

One direct response to the problem of lesbian invisibility was the founding of the group Lesbian Avengers, formed in 1992 by six New York lesbian activists interested in forming a lesbian direct-action group. The Lesbian Avengers soon gained a reputation for engaging in guerrilla-type "zaps," street theater, and other political actions. According to Sarah Schulman, a cofounder, the group planned a lesbian march in Washington, D.C., as part of the 1993 March on Washington weekend.

Great ideas sometimes manifest simultaneously. Judy Sisneros, a member of the national-level ACT UP Women's Committee, recalls that in late 1992, her group also began networking to organize a lesbian march; they later collaborated with the Lesbian Avengers and other Washington, D.C., groups. The first Dyke March, April 24, 1993, drew twenty thousand women. Organizers did not obtain a "parade" permit, keeping with the groups' oppositional political ideology. According to Schulman, it was "the largest lesbian event in the history of the world." When marchers had reached the front of the White House on their way to the Washington Monument, the Lesbian Avengers stopped and demonstrated their prowess as fire-eaters, an activity that is now a Lesbian Avengers trademark.

Significance

Sarah Schulman noted that by the summer of 1993, "the Dyke March had caught on around the country." The first San Francisco Dyke March drew ten thousand women, while the march in New York City drew three thousand. Chicago held its first march in 1996 with one thousand women. Although the first Los Angeles Dyke March, in 1994, drew only three hundred fifty women, fifteen hundred women showed up for the march in 1997. Lesbian rights veterans from the 1970's who have attended the dyke marches have noted that unlike the marches of the 1970's, these later events generally have been more multicultural and multigenerational.

Attempts to create a lesbian presence during gay and lesbian pride has often generated controversy, including accusations of lesbian separatism. Some gays and lesbians have disapproved of a "separate" or "radical" lesbian event diverting attention from the "main" pride event. Even lesbians involved in organizing dyke marches sometimes disagree vehemently with one another about ideology. For example, in 1998, longtime lesbian activist and singer Alix Dobkin was invited to sing and speak at the Philadelphia Dyke March. However, after Dobkin wrote an article for Chicago's *Frontlines*, discussing her belief in the importance of lesbian-only space and in her hope that the march not include MTF (male-to-female) women, she was "disinvited" by march organizers. In the end, and after much debate and acrimony, Dobkin was reinvited.

Internationally, the idea of lesbian-focused pride marches began to spread. The first Dyke March in Vancouver, British Columbia, Canada, was held in June, 1995. Ireland held its first march in 1998. In the same year, Toronto, Canada, held its third march. As in many dyke marches, participants included dykes on bikes, leatherwomen, bare breasts, waving flags, drumming, cheering, singing, dancing, and whistleblowing.

In Japan, according to the *Daily Yomiuri*, "[m]ore than 200 people" participated in Dyke March, Tokyo '97, in which "women, many with buzz cuts and wearing karate uniforms or black suits, paraded along a six-kilometer route . . . [with] loud music blaring from portable stereos" and "colorful costumes" garnering "the most attention."

Like lesbians in many other countries, lesbians in Mexico grew weary of the campiness, phallocentrism, and commercialism of the male-dominated gay pride parades and decided to affirm their lesbian identity by organizing their own dyke march. They met with resistance from some gay pride organizers, who thought the lesbian-only march would detract from the "main" parade. In spite of the opposition, the first Mexico Dyke March took to the streets of Mexico City in 2003. Participating groups included Les Voz, Telemanita, Lesbianas en Colectiva, Archivo Historico Lésbico, Lesbianas Independientes, Grupo Lésbico Club 84, and Lesbianas de San Luis Potosí.

The 2003 march in Mexico City was the first lesbian-only march in Latin America. One of the organizers explained the march's importance as an expression of visibility that aimed to dispel stereotypes and prejudice and allowed participants to be publicly proud of their lesbian identity.

Dyke marches signify an attempt to celebrate and promote lesbian activism and visibility in a cogender, sometimes politically apathetic environment, where many agendas compete. Lisa Kung, a founding member of Atlanta Avengers, noted that the dyke march in general "is about empowerment [for lesbians]." Dyke marches are symbols of lesbian pride, independence, and resistance.

—*Yolanda Retter*

FURTHER READING

Pope, Lisa, et al. *One Million Strong: The 1993 March on Washington for Lesbian, Gay, and Bi Equal Rights*. New York: Alyson, 1993.

Retter, Yolanda. "Dyke Marches: A Brief Herstory." *Lesbian News*, June, 1999.

Schulman, Sarah. *My American History: Lesbian and Gay Life During the Reagan Years*. New York: Routledge, 1994.

SEE ALSO: July 2-Aug. 28, 1963: Rustin Organizes the March on Washington; Aug., 1966: Queer Youth Fight Police Harassment at Compton's Cafeteria in San Francisco; June 27-July 2, 1969: Stonewall Rebellion Ignites Modern Gay and Lesbian Rights Movement; July 31, 1969: Gay Liberation Front Is Formed; May 1, 1970: Lavender Menace Protests Homophobia in Women's Movement; June 28, 1970: First Lesbian and Gay Pride March in the United States; Oct. 12-15, 1979: First March on Washington for Lesbian and Gay Rights; Mar., 1987: Radical AIDS Activist Group ACT UP Is Founded; Oct. 11, 1987: Second March on Washington for Lesbian and Gay Rights; Dec. 10, 1989: ACT UP Protests at St. Patrick's Cathedral; Mar. 20, 1990: Queer Nation Is Founded; Apr. 25, 1993: March on Washington for Gay, Lesbian, and Bi Equal Rights and Liberation; June, 1994: Stonewall 25 March and Rallies Are Held in New York City; June 19, 2002: Gays and Lesbians March for Equal Rights in Mexico City.

April 25, 1993
MARCH ON WASHINGTON FOR GAY, LESBIAN, AND BI EQUAL RIGHTS AND LIBERATION

LGBT people and their supporters gathered in Washington, D.C., for marches, demonstrations, vigils, conferences, and other events. The march marked the start of a new era for the LGBT movement, as it recognized more explicitly the need to embrace transgender people as well as people of all races and backgrounds. Also, the issue of GLBT persons in the military became a major part of the movement's platform.

LOCALE: Washington, D.C.
CATEGORIES: Marches, protests, and riots; civil rights; government and politics; transgender/transsexuality; religion; organizations and institutions

SUMMARY OF EVENT

The lesbian, gay, bisexual, and transgender rights movement (also known as the LGBT movement) has been based upon equality since its conception. Organizers, however, had more than equality on their minds when they planned the 1993 March on Washington for Gay, Lesbian, and Bi Equal Rights and Liberation. Organizers also wanted to have a balanced and inclusive decision-making group for the march, one that would include people from many races and which represented all genders. Backed by the NAACP (National Association for the Advancement of Colored People), march organizers also were able to meld their concerns about fairness and inclusion into the march agenda.

The march platform included issues pertaining to GLBT rights as well as civil rights in general, and to issues of discrimination, education, family rights, and others. HIV-AIDS concerns, too, were high on the list of demands and priorities, as was the demand to end the ban that kept gays and lesbians out of the military and that discharged those found to be gay, lesbian, or bisexual while in the service.

The preamble to the march's platform stated,

> The Lesbian, Gay, Bisexual, and Transgender movement recognizes that our quest for social justice fundamentally links us to the struggles against racism and sexism, class bias, economic injustice, and religious intolerance. We must realize if one of us is oppressed we all are oppressed. The diversity of our movement requires and compels us to stand in opposition to all forms of oppression that diminish the quality of life for all people. We will be vigilant in our determination to rid our movement and our society of all forms of oppression and exploitation, so that all of us can develop to our full human potential without regard to race, religion, sexual orientation/identification, identity, gender and gender expression, ability, age, or class.

The week of the march included more than 150 political and cultural events. The AIDS Memorial Quilt, a stark reminder of the HIV-AIDS epidemic, was on display on the Washington Mall. Visitors to

Activists lead the third March on Washington, April, 1993. (Hulton Archive/Getty Images)

D.C. could take part in conferences and workshops, congressional lobbying, and religious ceremonies. Couples had the chance to join in a symbolic wedding ceremony held in front of the IRS (Internal Revenue Service) building. A candlelight vigil was held at the U.S. Holocaust Memorial Museum, and there was a gathering at Arlington National Cemetery to honor lesbian, gay, and bisexual veterans.

Protesters demonstrated in front of the U.S. Supreme Court the Monday after the march. Organizers had planned for groups of people to cross police lines and sit on the plaza in front of the Court building. That morning, protester Herb Donaldson and a group of his friends from San Francisco had decided to join the demonstration, even if it meant their arrest. At the end of the day, standing in the courtroom after being arrested, protesters reported that the feeling of pride and camaraderie was tremendous.

A major goal of the march was to reach Congress members and bring the GLBT message directly to them. Many lawmakers, however, avoided activists throughout the weekend. The LGBT community felt they had been supported politically by President Bill Clinton and his positive position on lesbian and gay rights. Regrettably to activists, Clinton seemed to have become somewhat embarrassed by his own support. Although he submitted a statement that was read to the crowd assembled after the march, some protesters felt his support had diminished. David Mixner, a gay rights leader who had worked on Clinton's campaign in 1991, criticized Clinton for being absent from Washington the day of the march. Mixner pointed out that the stronger the march had become, the greater the evacuation of Washington by politicians.

Although march organizers said the 1993 march was the largest demonstration in U.S. history, officials have not been able to agree on a definite number. U.S. Park Police estimated the crowd to have numbered about 300,000 individuals, whereas organizers argued that there were more than 1 million protesters and marchers. Regardless of the numbers, it is clear that the event received unprecedented media coverage. Major television networks covered the event, many with live broadcasts. The following day, 156 newspapers nationwide carried front page stories of the landmark gathering.

SIGNIFICANCE

Years after the 1993 march, the United States has seen some change regarding the rights of LGBT individuals, especially regarding same-gender civil unions, employment discrimination, and domestic partnership benefits. Also, the unity of the event was unprecedented; for the first time in history, the LGBT movement connected with the NAACP.

Although organizers of the march chose not to use the term "transgender" in the march's name, they still were able to bridge gaps within the LGBT community by making sure to include a wider range of individuals under the lesbian, gay, and bisexual rights umbrella. It was not too long after the march that the acronym "LGBT," and its variations, began to be used by the movement as an all-inclusive acronym.

—Lisa Dalton

FURTHER READING

Clendinen, D., and A. Nagourney. *Out for Good.* New York: Simon & Schuster, 1999.

Coxe, Cece, Lisa Means, and Lisa Pope. *One Million Strong: The 1993 March on Washington for Lesbian, Gay, and Bi Equal Rights*. Boston: Alyson, 1993.

Marcus, Eric. *Making Gay History: The Half Century Fight for Lesbian and Gay Equal Rights.* New York: HarperCollins, 2002.

Vaid, Urvashi. *Virtual Equality: The Mainstreaming of Gay and Lesbian Liberation*. New York: Anchor/Doubleday, 1995.

Witt, L., S. Thomas, and Eric Marcus, eds. *Out in All Directions: A Treasury of Gay and Lesbian America*. New York: Warner Books, 1995.

SEE ALSO: July 2-Aug. 28, 1963: Rustin Organizes the March on Washington; Aug., 1966: Queer Youth Fight Police Harassment at Compton's Cafeteria in San Francisco; June 27-July 2, 1969: Stonewall Rebellion Ignites Modern Gay and Lesbian Rights Movement; July 31, 1969: Gay Liberation Front Is Formed; May 1, 1970: Lavender Menace Protests Homophobia in Women's Movement; June 28, 1970: First Lesbian and Gay Pride March in the United States; Oct. 12-15, 1979: First March on Washington for Lesbian and Gay Rights; Mar., 1987: Radical AIDS Activist Group ACT UP Is Founded; Oct. 11, 1987: Second March on Washington for Lesbian and Gay Rights; Dec. 10, 1989: ACT UP Protests at St. Patrick's Cathedral; Mar. 20, 1990: Queer Nation Is Founded; Apr. 24, 1993: First Dyke March Is Held in Washington, D.C.; June, 1994: Stonewall 25 March and Rallies Are Held in New York City; June 19, 2002: Gays and Lesbians March for Equal Rights in Mexico City.

May 24, 1993
ACHTENBERG BECOMES ASSISTANT HOUSING SECRETARY

After a bitter debate and public mudslinging that included conservative U.S. senator Jesse Helms calling Roberta Achtenberg a "damn lesbian," Achtenberg was approved by the Senate as assistant housing secretary, becoming the highest-ranking out lesbian or gay individual in the U.S. government.

LOCALE: Washington, D.C.
CATEGORY: Government and politics

KEY FIGURES
Roberta Achtenberg (b. 1950), civil rights attorney, law professor, and San Francisco city and county supervisor
Bill Clinton (b. 1946), U.S. president, 1993-2001, who nominated Achtenberg
Jesse Helms (b. 1921), U.S. Republican senator from North Carolina, who opposed Achtenberg's nomination

SUMMARY OF EVENT
On May 24, 1993, in a historic 58-31 vote in the U.S. Senate, Roberta Achtenberg was confirmed as assistant secretary for Fair Housing and Equal Opportunity for the U.S. Department of Housing and Urban Development (HUD), thereby becoming, according to the *Congressional Quarterly Weekly Report*, "the first avowed lesbian appointed to such a high federal office." The acrimony surrounding Achtenberg's confirmation made history as well because conservative senators excoriated Achtenberg as a public servant and "militant activist" lesbian. Achtenberg's nomination, however, was one of many threatened nominations and policies put forth by the fledgling Clinton administration.

President Bill Clinton's nomination of Achtenberg was logical because she was respected within the legal field, the lesbian and gay community, and the Democratic Party. Her work as a civil rights attorney, who advocated the equal treatment of gays and lesbians in housing, parenting, child care, and HIV-AIDS-related care, was well known. Equally important was that Achtenberg was a prominent player in bringing lesbian and gay concerns to the Clinton camp during the California primary; even then Clinton had promised her a post in Washington. After Clinton's election, William Waybourn, of the National Gay and Lesbian Victory Fund, persuaded Clinton's transition team that Achtenberg might obtain that promise. For these reasons Achtenberg received the offer to be HUD assistant secretary—along with the promise of a grueling confirmation process.

To prepare for the difficult hearings held by the Senate's Banking, Housing, and Urban Affairs Committee, Achtenberg became familiar with an inclusive document on all fair housing law, which had been collated by concerned Washington, D.C., lawyers. For her testimony, Achtenberg introduced her life partner, Mary Morgan (a former San Francisco municipal court judge), her family, and staff, then proceeded to deliver, according to authors David Mixner and David Bailey, a "thoroughgoing assessment of public policy, fortified by statistics and case studies."

After her testimony, several committee members orchestrated a barrage of questions impugning Achtenberg's ability to deal fairly with those who did not have a "gay rights" agenda—the same argument that senators Trent Lott, Orin Hatch, Bob Dole, and the notorious Jesse Helms reiterated during Senate proceedings. Their critique focused on Achtenberg's vote as a board member of the United Way to cut off funding to the Boy Scouts of America because of its policy against having gay or bisexual scouts or scout leaders, and on her urging the city of San Francisco to discontinue doing business with Bank of America for its support of the Boy Scouts. Even Achtenberg's relationship with Morgan was grist for the conservatives' mill. Achtenberg dealt with these mischaracterizations with determination, and she documented her actions, placing them in context. Supportive senators fought for confirmation.

> ### From the Senate Hearings on the Nomination of Roberta Achtenberg
>
> *[Sen. Jesse] Helms:* Who would have thought, even 5 years ago, that the President of the United States would nominate a homosexual person [Roberta Achtenberg] for a high-ranking Federal job, a person who helped orchestrate an action against the Boy Scouts because the Scouts refused to lower their moral and spiritual standards.
>
> Some are trying to say she did not do it. The heck she did not. I understand why they do not want to talk about it. I understand why they do not want it a matter of record. But the facts are the facts. That is precisely what happened.
>
> Just for the [Congressional] Record, perhaps we ought to review just a little bit of the facts. On February 20, 1991, several radical homosexual groups, such as the one called Queer Nation, launched a national boycott of the United Way demanding funding be withdrawn from the Boy Scouts because the Scouts forbade homosexuals from becoming Scoutmasters.
>
> The next day—and it was reported in all of the media—the local board of the United Way of the Bay Area in San Francisco, on which Ms. Achtenberg was serving as a member, voted unanimously to deliver an ultimatum to the Boy Scouts of America that the national office of the Boy Scouts must allow homosexuals and atheists to become Scoutmasters; otherwise, the United Way chapter in San Francisco must withdraw almost $1 million in funding which had previously been allocated each year to the San Francisco area Scout Council. . . .
>
> I want Senators to see a little piece of film that was taken about a year ago in San Francisco when the Gay Pride Week Parade rolled through the streets of San Francisco. That is what this issue is. It is not about all this stuff—she is a law professor or has been a law dean or whatever—but how has she acted in public.
>
> *[Sen. Barbara] Boxer:* Mr. President, the Senator from North Carolina held up a newspaper and read a couple of the headlines. But I would say, what does that have to do with the qualifications of Roberta Achtenberg for this position?
>
> The Senator has invited people to see a film. I asked some of my colleagues who saw that film, did the film have anything to do with Roberta Achtenberg and her qualifications for this position? And they said "no."
>
> So you can hold up a newspaper. You can invite people to see a film. But tell us why you believe this woman is not qualified.
>
> And when you cut through it, there appears to me to be only one reason. There are Senators who do not approve of her private life, and that is the issue here. . . .

A highly influential factor, however, in Achtenberg's confirmation is that supportive senators were well briefed and lobbied by savvy lesbian and gay politicos. Sensing that Achtenberg's nomination was in trouble during committee hearings, these leaders turned out support for Achtenberg and lobbied swing-vote senators. Despite opposition, Achtenberg would become the first out lesbian or gay individual to be confirmed to such a high-level position in the federal government.

Significance

Roberta Achtenberg's 1993 confirmation is a landmark for a number of reasons. First, it is historic that Achtenberg was the first out lesbian to take office via presidential appointment and Senate approval. Second, according to journalist Larry Leibert, her "nomination produced a bi-partisan consensus in Congress that no one should be barred from a government position solely because of their sexual orientation." Third, strong and influential lesbian and gay activists worked for Achtenberg's nomination and confirmation. Thus, Democratic presidential candidates and U.S. politicians who were enlightened enough to incorporate the GLBT community into the political landscape, saw a community, which included Achtenberg, prepared for party politics and leadership.

—Mary L. Cutler

Further Reading

Achtenberg, Roberta, ed. *Sexual Orientation and the Law*. Deerfield, Ill.: Clark Bordman Callaghan, 1985.

"Achtenberg Confirmed for HUD Post." *Congressional Quarterly Weekly Report* 51, no. 22 (1993).

Borlund, John. "Profile: Roberta Achtenberg." *CJ Weekly* 24 (April, 1995): 4.

Katz, Jeffrey L. "HUD Nominee's Lesbianism Sets off Senate Debate." *Congressional Quarterly Weekly Report* 51, no. 21 (1993).

Leibert, Larry. "Washington Perspective: The Achtenberg Nomination." *California Journal* 24, no. 7 (July, 1993).

Miller, Diane Helene. *Freedom to Differ: The Shaping of the Gay and Lesbian Struggle for Human Rights*. New York: New York University Press, 1998.

Mixner, David, and Dennis Bailey. *Brave Journeys*. New York: Bantam Books, 2000.

Rayside, David. *On the Fringe: Gays and Lesbians in Politics*. Ithaca, N.Y.: Cornell University Press, 1998.

SEE ALSO: 1961: Sarria Is First Out Gay or Lesbian Candidate for Public Office; 1971: Kameny Is First Out Candidate for U.S. Congress; Mar. 5, 1974: Antigay and Antilesbian Organizations Begin to Form; Nov. 5, 1974: Noble Is First Out Lesbian or Gay Person to Win State-Level Election; Nov. 27, 1978: White Murders Politicians Moscone and Milk; 1979: Moral Majority Is Founded; July 14, 1983: Studds Is First Out Gay Man in the U.S. Congress; Nov. 6, 1984: West Hollywood Incorporates with Majority Gay and Lesbian City Council; May 30, 1987: U.S. Congressman Frank Comes Out as Gay; June 28, 2000: *Boy Scouts of America v. Dale*; Jan., 2006: Jiménez Flores Elected to the Mexican Senate.

June 25, 1993
CLINTON APPOINTS FIRST AIDS CZAR

In an effort to control the HIV-AIDS epidemic and its debilitating health and socioeconomic effects, U.S. president Bill Clinton appointed Kristine Gebbie as the first National AIDS Policy coordinator, or AIDS czar. Gebbie's mandate was to implement policies and programs that would offer viable solutions to the epidemic.

LOCALE: Washington, D.C.
CATEGORIES: HIV-AIDS; health and medicine; government and politics

KEY FIGURES
Kristine Gebbie (b. 1943), nurse, health science educator, and health official
Bill Clinton (b. 1946), president of the United States, 1993-2001

SUMMARY OF EVENT

When Bill Clinton ran for the U.S. presidency in 1992, he promised to address HIV-AIDS concerns. Part of his campaign platform included increased funding for AIDS research; a concentrated effort to prevent the spread of HIV, the virus that causes AIDS; and the appointment of a national AIDS czar.

Once in office, however, Clinton was frequently criticized for not acting on his campaign promise to launch a decisive attack on AIDS. In response to the accusations, Clinton announced at a press conference held at the White House on June 25, 1993, that Kristine Gebbie would be the first National AIDS Policy coordinator, or AIDS czar.

Having served as a state public health administrator, a member of the first presidential commission on AIDS, and a member of various national AIDS committees, as well having served in many other health-related positions, Gebbie was well qualified to direct government programs to promote and centralize the funding, research, treatment, and prevention of HIV-AIDS. During her first four months in office, Gebbie spent most of her time meeting with AIDS policy experts and lawmakers, particularly Donna Shalala, secretary of Health and Human Services, and Joycelyn Elders, the U.S. surgeon general. Gebbie interviewed many adolescents who were HIV-positive, then advocated distributing condoms to sexually active high school students. Gebbie and Shalala worked with health experts and legislators to promote the development of a microbicide vaginal foam that would protect women against HIV and sexually transmitted diseases. Regardless of her efforts, many AIDS activists were highly disappointed that she was not doing more.

While addressing the Association of Reproductive Health Professionals about teenage pregnancy and the prevention of AIDS in October, 1993, Gebbie publicly stated her perceptions about traditional morality, suggesting that Americans should alter their views about sex and should no longer repress frank discussions about sex and sexuality, including homosexuality. Her statements stirred significant controversy, and she immediately came under the scrutiny of Christian and pro-family coalitions, including the American Family Association and the Family Research Council. Under pressure, Gebbie clarified her position by pointing out that abstinence from sex was the best way to prevent the spread of HIV, but otherwise it was necessary to use condoms. AIDS activists criticized her for backing down and being weak.

In February, 1994, Gebbie pointed out that about 30 percent of all AIDS cases originated from drug abuse through the use of HIV-contaminated needles. She advocated distributing clean needles to drug addicts and joined President Clinton and the director of the Office of National Drug Control Policy, Lee Brown, in supporting a strategy to stop the illegal use of drugs. Carrying out her duties with a rather low profile, Gebbie received continued criticism from AIDS activists. By June, 1994, many activists were clamoring for her resignation. On July 8, 1994, she announced her resignation, effective August 2. Shortly thereafter, Clinton appointed Patsy S. Fleming, a declared AIDS activist and an assistant to Secretary Shalala, as the interim AIDS czar. On November 10, 1994, Clinton announced that Fleming had accepted the appointment to serve as the second AIDS czar.

SIGNIFICANCE

Because of the dramatic increase in AIDS cases during the 1980's and 1990's, Clinton appointed Kristine Gebbie to the position of AIDS czar to address and find solutions to the raging epidemic. Gebbie's goals had included increasing public awareness and understanding of the disease and obtaining substantial funding for research efforts and preventive measures to control its spread. During her tenure of a little more than one year, Gebbie had some success: She opened lines of effective communication about the AIDS epidemic through discussions with key government and public personnel. She emphasized that AIDS is a nondiscriminatory disease, affecting not only homosexuals and drug addicts but also heterosexuals.

Gebbie successfully identified and helped implement some reasonable AIDS policies and programs. Through her guidance and the leadership of Clinton, the budget for HIV-AIDS research and prevention was increased by more than 30 percent, HIV-AIDS education was provided for federal employees and the public, new HIV-AIDS drugs were researched and developed, and funding was boosted for the Ryan White Comprehensive AIDS Resources Emergency (CARE) Act, which was passed in 1990. The appointment of a national AIDS czar was a critical step in centralizing HIV-AIDS care.

Although some positive steps were taken by Gebbie in addressing HIV-AIDS and some of the associated issues, a majority of AIDS activists felt that she was too inexperienced, relied mostly on rhetoric, and kept too low of a profile. Even as the controversy and criticism increased, and Gebbie resigned, a very important pattern had been established in the fight against HIV-AIDS—the selection of an individual who was mandated with federal government power to focus on ways to control and eventually defeat the insidious disease.

—*Alvin K. Benson*

FURTHER READING

Andriote, John-Manuel. *Victory Deferred: How AIDS Changed Gay Life in America*. Chicago: University of Chicago Press, 1999.

D'Emilio, John, William B. Turner, and Urvashi Vaid. *Creating Change: Sexuality, Public Policy, and Civil Rights*. New York: St. Martin's Press, 2000.

Gebbie, Kristine M., Linda Rosenstock, and Lyla M. Hernandez, eds. *Who Will Keep the Public Healthy?* Washington, D.C.: National Academy of Sciences Press, 2003.

Gostin, Lawrence O., and Michael Kirby. *The AIDS Pandemic: Complacency, Injustice, and Unfulfilled Expectations.* Chapel Hill: University of North Carolina Press, 2004.

Rimmerman, Craig A., Kenneth D. Wald, and Clyde Wilcox, eds. *The Politics of Gay Rights.* Chicago: University of Chicago Press, 2000.

Smith, Raymond A., ed. *Encyclopedia of AIDS: A Social, Political, Cultural, and Scientific Record of the HIV Epidemic.* New York: Penguin Books, 2001.

SEE ALSO: June 5 and July 3, 1981: Reports of Rare Diseases Mark Beginning of AIDS Epidemic; July, 1982: Gay-Related Immunodeficiency Is Renamed AIDS; Spring, 1984: AIDS Virus Is Discovered; July 25, 1985: Actor Hudson Announces He Has AIDS; Sept., 1986: AZT Treats People with AIDS; Mar., 1987: Radical AIDS Activist Group ACT UP Is Founded; June 27, 1988: Report of the Presidential AIDS Commission; Dec. 1, 1988: First World AIDS Day.

September 21, 1993-April 21, 1995
Lesbian Mother Loses Custody of Her Child

In Bottoms v. Bottoms, *the Virginia Court of Appeals expanded the rights of a lesbian mother to retain custody of her birth child, but the ruling was overturned in 1995 by the state's high court, which awarded custody to the woman's mother.*

ALSO KNOWN AS: *Bottoms v. Bottoms* (1995)
LOCALE: Virginia
CATEGORIES: Laws, acts, and legal history; civil rights

KEY FIGURES
Sharon Bottoms (b. 1970), who sought custody of her birth son
April Wade, Sharon Bottoms's partner
Tyler Doustou (b. 1991), son of Sharon Bottoms
Pamela Kay Bottoms, mother of Sharon Bottoms, who sought custody of her grandson Tyler Doustou
Buford M. Parsons, Jr., trial judge of the Henrico County Circuit Court, who ruled in favor of custody
A. Christian Compton, senior justice of the Virginia Supreme Court, who overturned the earlier custody decision

SUMMARY OF EVENT
After Pamela Kay Bottoms learned in 1993 that her daughter, Sharon Bottoms, had a lesbian partner who was living with her, she went to court to try to obtain custody of her two-year-old grandson, Tyler Doustou. Pamela Kay Bottoms alleged that it would be mentally and physically harmful for the boy to grow up with and be raised by two women in a lesbian relationship. In view of "social condemnation," she asserted that remaining in that environment would be harmful to the boy's associations with "his peers and with the community at large." On September 21, 1994, Judge Buford Parsons, Jr., of the Henrico County Circuit Court, ruled in favor of the grandmother and transferred the custody of young child to her.

Judge Parsons based his ruling on the belief that a person who engages in homosexual conduct, which was illegal in Virginia, was "an unfit parent." In addition to this ruling, he also issued a visitation order, prohibiting Sharon Bottoms from having Tyler in her home, which she shared with her partner, April Wade. The order further stipulated that Sharon was not to visit her son in the presence of Wade. Sharon appealed the custody ruling. The case emphasized the precedent of *Doe v. Doe* (1981), in which the state's Supreme Court had earlier held that a parent's homosexual orientation did not necessarily disqualify that parent from obtaining custody of his or her child.

On June 21, 1994, the Virginia Court of Appeals agreed to review the decision. During the hearing before a three-judge panel, Sharon testified that she and her partner had a lifetime commitment to each other. She presented substantial evidence refuting the claim that she was an unfit parent. Charlotte Patterson, a psychologist at the University of Virginia, testified that scientific studies had shown that a child raised by a gay or lesbian parent was at no disadvantage relative to a child raised by a heterosexual parent.

On June 21, 1994, the three judges of the court of appeals unanimously reversed the ruling and remanded the case to the county court to restore custody to Sharon. The three judges found no evidence that lesbians were necessarily unfit parents, and they noted that the custody law of the state presumes that it is normally in the best interest of a child to live with a birth parent. In the court's judgment, "the evidence showed that Sharon Bottoms is and has been a fit and nurturing parent who has adequately provided and cared for her son." Pamela Kay Bottoms appealed the decision to the Virginia Supreme Court.

From *Bottoms v. Bottoms* (1995)

Majority opinion by Justice A Christian Compton: This is a child custody dispute between a child's mother and maternal grandmother. The sole issue is whether the Court of Appeals erred in deciding that the child's best interests would be served by awarding custody to the mother. We conclude that the Court of Appeals erred, and reverse its decision.

[W]e shall not overlook the mother's relationship with Wade, and the environment in which the child would be raised if custody is awarded the mother. We have previously said that living daily under conditions stemming from active lesbianism practiced in the home may impose a burden upon a child by reason of the "social condemnation" attached to such an arrangement, which will inevitably afflict the child's relationships with its "peers and with the community at large." . . . We do not retreat from that statement; such a result is likely under these facts. . . .

Accordingly, we hold that the trial court, based on all the facts and circumstances, correctly ruled on the custody question. And, the study of the grandmother's home by the Chesterfield-Colonial Heights Department of Social Services determined there was "no reason" why she should not be awarded custody should the trial court make such a ruling.

Thus, the judgment of the Court of Appeals will be reversed and the case will be remanded, . . . awarding custody of the child to Pamela Kay Bottoms.

Keenan, Justice, with whom Whiting and Lacy, Justices, join, dissenting:

This Court has held, as the majority states, that a lesbian mother is not *per se* an unfit parent. . . . Nevertheless, the majority ignores the trial court's refusal to follow this established law of the Commonwealth.

The record plainly shows that the trial court made a *per se* finding of unfitness based on the mother's homosexual conduct. The trial court stated: "I will tell you first that the mother's conduct is illegal. It is a Class 6 felony in the Commonwealth of Virginia. I will tell you that it is the opinion of this Court that her conduct is immoral. And it is the opinion of this Court that the conduct of Sharon Bottoms renders her an unfit parent." The trial court added to this statement only by citing two other factors to support its custody award. These factors were the "social condemnation" that would "inevitably" affect the child, and "other evidence of the child being affected or afflicted with the evidence [*sic*] which is unrebutted of the cursing, the evidence of the child standing in the corner."

As the Court of Appeals properly recognized, "adverse effects of a parent's homosexuality on a child cannot be assumed without specific proof." . . . Although there is no evidence in this record showing that the mother's homosexual conduct is harmful to the child, the majority improperly presumes that its own perception of societal opinion and the mother's homosexual conduct are germane to the issue whether the mother is an unfit parent. Thus, the majority commits the same error as the trial court by attaching importance to factors not shown by the evidence to have an adverse effect on the child.

Because of its important legal implications, *Bottoms v. Bottoms* elicited a number of well-researched *amici curaie* briefs, or documents giving arguments and legal precedents for the Court to consider. Several respected organizations, including the American Psychological Association and the National Association of Social Workers, joined forces in producing a single brief, which argued that a parent-child bond should be disrupted only for compelling reasons. According to the brief, "social science research shows that an individual's sexual orientation does not correlate with the person's fitness as a parent."

On April 21, 1995, the Virginia Supreme Court, voting four-to-three, reinstated the circuit court's custody decision. Writing for the majority, Justice A. Christian Compton insisted that lesbian conduct, because it was a felony in Virginia, must be an "important consideration in determining custody." Compton claimed to find evidence in the record that Sharon had not been a good mother. In the ruling, however, Compton rejected the key element of Judge Parson's legal rationale. Reaffirming *Doe v. Doe*, he wrote that it was well established that "a lesbian mother is not *per se* an unfit parent."

Although Pamela Kay Bottoms retained custody, Compton's ruling overturned Parson's visitation order, which had prohibited contact between the child and his mother's partner. The three dissenters wanted to affirm the holding of the court of appeals. They argued that because Parson's ruling was based on the wrong rule of law, the case should have been remanded to the trial court for entirely new proceedings.

The 1995 ruling did not end the dispute between Sharon and her mother. On several occasions the two women were back in Parsons's court disputing visitation rights. In 1997, the case again went to the court of appeals. As late as 1998, Parsons continued to ignore rulings by higher courts, and he disallowed any contact between Tyler and his mother while April Wade was present.

SIGNIFICANCE

The 1995 ruling in *Bottoms v. Bottoms* represented little more than a reaffirmation of the ruling in *Doe v. Doe*. Thus, the court of appeals' liberal ruling of 1994, which had not penalized Sharon Bottoms for her sexual orientation, did not become a judicial precedent. The 1995 ruling by Virginia's Supreme Court meant that lesbian sexual activity, which was a crime at that time, would be a negative consideration in custody decisions. It is important to note, nevertheless, that the court explicitly reaffirmed that in some cases, awarding custody to a gay or lesbian individual would be in the child's best interest.

Bottoms v. Bottoms, however, stopped being a binding precedent when the U.S. Supreme Court, in the landmark case *Lawrence v. Texas* (2003), disallowed criminalization of gay and lesbian sex among consenting adults in private. Since Justice Compton's opinion was based primarily on the fact that such conduct was illegal at that time, the logical inference is that sexual orientation should no longer be an "important consideration" in determining custody in the state of Virginia.

—*Thomas Tandy Lewis*

FURTHER READING

Abrams, Nancy. *The Other Mother: A Lesbian's Fight for Her Daughter.* Madison: University of Wisconsin Press, 1999.

Bozett, Frederick. *Gay and Lesbian Parents.* Westport, Conn.: Greenwood Press, 1994.

Curry, Hayden, and Frederick Hertz. *Legal Guide for Lesbian and Gay Couples.* Santa Cruz, Calif.: Nolo Press, 2004.

Howey, Noelle, and Ellen Samuels, eds. *Out of the Ordinary: Essays on Growing Up with Gay, Lesbian, and Transgender Parents.* New York: St. Martin's Press, 2000.

Patterson, Charlotte J. "The Family Lives of Children Born to Lesbian Mothers." In *Lesbian, Gay, and Bisexual Identities in Families: Psychological Perspectives*, edited by Charlotte J. Patterson and Anthony R. D'Augelli. New York: Oxford University Press, 1998.

Senak, Mark. *Every Trick in the Book: The Essential Lesbian and Gay Legal Guide.* New York: M. Evans, 2003.

Wells, Jess, ed. *Lesbians Raising Sons: An Anthology.* Los Angeles: Alyson, 1997.

SEE ALSO: Jan. 12, 1939: *Thompson v. Aldredge* Dismisses Sodomy Charges Against Lesbians; 1952-1990: U.S. Law Prohibits Gay and Lesbian Immigration; May 22, 1967: U.S. Supreme Court Upholds Law Preventing Immigration of Gays and Lesbians; Jan. 22, 1973: *Roe v. Wade* Legalizes Abortion and Extends Privacy Rights; June 21, 1973: U.S. Supreme Court Supports Local Obscenity Laws; Aug., 1973: American Bar Association Calls for Repeal of Laws Against Consensual Sex; Nov. 17, 1975: U.S. Supreme Court Rules in "Crimes Against Nature" Case; 1981: Gay and Lesbian Palimony Suits Emerge; 1982-1991: Lesbian Academic and Activist Sues University of California for Discrimination; 1986: *Bowers v. Hardwick* Upholds State Sodomy Laws; May 1, 1989: U.S. Supreme Court Rules Gender-Role Stereotyping Is Discriminatory; Dec. 17, 1991: Minnesota Court Awards Guardianship to Lesbian Partner; 1992-2006: Indians Struggle to Abolish Sodomy Law; 1993-1996: Hawaii Opens Door to Same-Gender Marriages; Dec. 20, 1999: *Baker v. Vermont* Leads to Recognition of Same-Gender Civil Unions; June 28, 2000: *Boy Scouts of America v. Dale*; June 26, 2003: U.S. Supreme Court Overturns Texas Sodomy Law.

November 30, 1993
DON'T ASK, DON'T TELL POLICY IS IMPLEMENTED

U.S. president Bill Clinton's Don't Ask, Don't Tell policy was designed to end the practice of asking U.S. servicemembers and potential recruits their sexual orientation and then discharging them, or denying them entry into the services, if they were homosexual or bisexual or if they had engaged in homosexual acts. However, the policy has led to a significant increase in the number of military personnel discharged for being gay, lesbian, or bisexual.

ALSO KNOWN AS: Don't Ask, Don't Tell, Don't Pursue, Don't Harass
LOCALE: Washington, D.C.
CATEGORIES: Military; civil rights

KEY FIGURES
Bill Clinton (b. 1946), U.S. president, 1993-2001
Leslie Aspin (1938-1995), secretary of defense
Colin Powell (b. 1937), chair of the Joint Chiefs of Staff and former secretary of state
Allen R. Schindler, Jr. (1969-1992), Navy petty officer
Samuel Nunn (b. 1938), Democratic senator from Georgia
Barney Frank (b. 1940), Democratic congressmember from Massachusetts

SUMMARY OF EVENT
The U.S. Congress passed an official ban on gays and lesbians in the military in 1950, when it enacted the Uniform Code of Military Justice (UCMJ), which also banned homosexual sex among servicemembers. Three decades later, the Defense Department issued Directive 1332.14 (Enlisted Administrative Separations, December 21, 1993), a policy change that made it more restrictive for enlisted homosexuals and bisexuals to serve in the military. The directive states that "homosexuality is incompatible with military service." Between 1980 and 1990, the U.S. military expelled approximately fifteen hundred lesbian, gay, and bisexual soldiers, and those believed to be lesbian, gay, or bisexual because of a past sexual experience or experiences.

On October 27, 1991, Seaman Terry Helvey of the USS *Belleau Wood* beat to death fellow shipmate Petty Officer Allen Schindler, in a park in Sasebo, Japan. Schindler's wounds were so severe that military police officers had difficulty identifying the body as that of Schindler. Schindler had informed the *Belleau Wood*'s captain one month before his murder that he was gay. He was awaiting discharge when word of his sexual orientation spread among the crew. Helvey later admitted to investigators that he hated homosexuals and that he did not regret his actions: "Schindler was gay and deserved it," Helvey said. He pled guilty to "murder with intent to inflict great bodily harm" and was sentenced to life in a military prison.

GLBT rights groups described the murder as a classic example of gay bashing in the military. On May 29, 1992, during a campaign speech in California, presidential hopeful Bill Clinton promised, "If I'm the president of the United States, I think my job, rather than to inquire into the private lives of those who might serve, is to get the best people I can to serve this country." On November 19, president-elect Clinton told reporters that he would come up with a policy that would consider that many lesbians, gays, and bisexuals, who had not been discharged, have served the U.S. military with distinction.

In late December, Clinton directed his nominee for secretary of defense, Leslie Aspin, to consider how the administration would lift the ban. Clinton's efforts came under fire from members of Congress and the Joint Chiefs of Staff. Senate Armed Services Committee chairman Sam Nunn, a Democrat, vehemently opposed changing the policy. On January 29, 1993, General Colin Powell, chair of the Joint Chiefs, along with the other five members of the Joint Chiefs staff, strongly voiced their concerns to the president during a two-hour Cabinet meeting, a meeting that came as callers opposed to changing the military's policy flooded the White House and Pentagon switchboards.

Aspin argued that there was support neither in the military nor in Congress to lift the ban. On January 30, in response to growing opposition, Clinton announced a two-step compromise on the matter: Between February 1 and July 15, 2003, the military would stop asking recruits their sexual orientation, and on July 15, the Department of Defense would submit a draft executive order that would officially stop the exclusion of homosexuals and bisexuals from serving in the armed forces, if that exclusion were based solely on the servicemember's sexual orientation. Additionally, both the Pentagon and Congress would study the matter to ascertain how best to implement the policy change.

The Pentagon was slow to develop a study, and tense hearings by the House of Representatives and the Senate Armed Services Committee skewed heavily toward opponents of the change. Congres-

---

May 10, 1993:

Statement of Petty Officer Second Class Al Portes, U.S. Navy

(90) When you, if you do this [a communal shower situation) with a man who professes that kind of orientation, I find it morally and personally unacceptable.... I find it morally, morally incorrect. This is an act of rebellion. This is an act of rebelling against the God I believe in. I am sorry, I am 32 years old, and I cannot divorce myself of who I am as of this day, or what I believe.... Now, I came into this service because yes, I was not lied to, and I knew that there were no gays, openly, allowed in the military. 524

(91) But I will testify in front of this committee today and say that I hope, if Mr. Clinton decides to lift the ban and allow gays through, then also with that measure he gives us our outright release from active duty.
Because Al Portes will refuse... to serve with gays in the military; 525

Statement of Master Chief Harry Schafer, U.S. Navy

(92) Some people in the private sector may accept these sexually oriented homosexuals, or tolerate them, for at the end of the workday they go their separate ways....
It would be totally disruptive to good order and discipline if our American family of volunteers, our sons and daughters, were forced to work around people whom they feel have a sexual preference that is not consistent with what they believe is right....
... in my view sensitivity training will not work. How do you break with traditional family, religious value training that our society at large, and our parents, have ingrained into us?
Many excellent soldiers are seriously concerned about

Statements by two U.S. Navy personnel at hearings held in May, 1993, by the Senate Armed Services Committee on the issue of lesbians and gays in the military. (Robert Crown Law Library, Stanford Law School)

> **A CONDUCT-BASED POLICY FOR GAYS AND LESBIANS IN THE MILITARY: FROM RAND'S STUDY**
>
> In light of this research [by RAND], the team examined a range of potential policy options. Most of the options were judged to be inconsistent with the President's memorandum, internally contradictory, or both. Only one policy option was judged consistent with the findings of this research and the criteria of the Presidential memorandum, and to be logically and internally consistent. That policy would consider sexual orientation, by itself, as not germane to determining who may serve in the military.
>
> The policy would establish clear standards of conduct for all military personnel, to be equally and strictly enforced, in order to maintain the military discipline necessary for effective operations. The option requires no major changes in other military personnel policies and no change in current law. The "not germane" option could be implemented without any changes to the administrative guidelines for prosecutions under the Uniform Code of Military Justice (UCMJ).
>
> However, several considerations lead us to conclude that the policy would be more legally defensible and less costly and cumbersome to implement if the guidelines were revised to exclude private sexual behavior between consenting adults.
>
> *Source: Sexual Orientation and U.S. Military Personnel Policy* (Santa Monica, Calif.: RAND Corporation, 2003).

sional and military leaders ignored a 1993 report (*Sexual Orientation and U.S. Military Personnel Policy*) by the private think tank, RAND Corporation, which found no justification to continue the exclusionary policy.

The emotional testimony of Col. Fred Peck, who revealed that his son is gay (Peck had learned this one week prior to his testimony), weighed heavily in the considerations of congressional and military leaders. Peck argued that there was no place in the military for his gay son. He further claimed that the service would not only be too dangerous for his son but also that the cohesive bond among troops would be undermined with the presence of out gay servicemembers.

Aspin, however, soon threw his support behind the policy that would soon be called Don't Ask, Don't Tell, Don't Pursue, better known as Don't Ask, Don't Tell, which was a compromise measure proposed by Congressmember Barney Frank, an out gay Democrat from Massachusetts. The compromise would allow homosexuals and bisexuals to serve in the military as long as they keep their sexual orientation private. That is, the policy would theoretically end the practice of discharging lesbians, gays, and bisexuals solely on the basis of their "revealed" sexual orientation. The policy also was designed to end the practice of asking servicemembers their sexual orientation or aggressively investigating allegations that a servicemember is homosexual or bisexual, and it would end the policy of asking about the sexual orientation of potential recruits. Recruits who convey that they are homosexual or bisexual, or that they have had same-gender sexual experiences, would be barred from serving.

On November 30, 1993, Clinton signed Don't Ask, Don't Tell into law. On December 23, 1993, he issued rules on how the military would handle the new policy, rules that left wide latitude to commanding officers. In February, 2000, "Don't Harass" was added to the policy's title by Pentagon officials.

SIGNIFICANCE

Don't Ask, Don't Tell has proven to be a failure. The most significant difference between the 1993 policy and the earlier policy of exclusion is that the new rules bar the military from asking directly if a person is gay, lesbian, or bisexual, and it allows servicemembers to refuse to answer questions about their sexuality. However, the new policy explicitly states that commanders can infer homosexual conduct from homosexual status. That is, actions that raise the possibility that a servicemember is homosexual, from making progay or prolesbian statements to effeminate gestures, allow commanding officers to recommend discharge if a servicemember cannot disprove the allegations. Discharging a person because they are thought to be lesbian, gay,

> ### CLINTON'S "REMARKS ANNOUNCING THE NEW POLICY ON GAYS AND LESBIANS IN THE MILITARY"
>
> [O]n grounds of both principle and practicality, this is a major step forward. It is, in my judgment, consistent with my responsibilities as President and Commander in Chief to meet the need to change current policy. It is an honorable compromise that advances the cause of people who are called to serve our country by their patriotism, the cause of our national security, and our national interest in resolving an issue that has divided our military and our Nation and diverted our attention from other matters for too long.
>
> The time has come for us to move forward. As your Commander in Chief, I charge all of you to carry out this policy with fairness, with balance, and with due regard for the privacy of individuals. We must and will protect unit cohesion and troop morale. We must and will continue to have the best fighting force in the world. But this is an end to witch hunts that spend millions of taxpayer dollars to ferret out individuals who have served their country well.
>
> Improper conduct, on or off base, should remain grounds for discharge. But we will proceed with an even hand against everyone, regardless of sexual orientation.
>
> Such controversies as this have divided us before. But our Nation and our military have always risen to the challenge before. That was true of racial integration of the military and changes in the role of women in the military.
>
> Each of these was an issue, because it was an issue for society as well as for the military. And in each case our military was a leader in figuring out how to respond most effectively.
>
> *Source:* "Fort McNair Speech," *Weekly Compilation of Presidential Documents* 29 (July 19, 1993). Don't Ask, Don't Tell, Don't Pursue Digital Database, Stanford University Law School. http://dont.stanford.edu.

or bisexual (or for displaying a "propensity" to engage in same-gender sexual acts) is not new but is considered a change in policy because it now is part of a statute and not just a regulation.

The policy has led to the discharge of more than ten thousand servicemembers and has cost more than $200 million dollars to manage. In 1994, the court case *Hensala v. U.S. Air Force* opened gay and lesbian servicemembers to significant financial liability for revealing their sexual orientation. A July, 2002, audit of the Air Force discovered forms that specifically asked recruits about their sexual orientation, despite a 1997 order from Secretary of Defense William Cohen reinforcing the Don't Ask, Don't Tell policy.

Furthermore, in 2002, although facing a significant shortage of Arabic language translators who were needed to process a backlog of communication intercepts from operatives of the terrorist group Al Qaeda, the Pentagon moved to discharge several translators suspected of being gay, lesbian, or bisexual.

—*Jamie Patrick Chandler*

FURTHER READING

Anderson, Clinton, and C. Dixon Osburn. "Ending Discrimination in the U.S. Military." In *Everyday Activism*, edited by Michael R. Stevenson and Jeanine C. Cogan. New York: Routledge, 2003.

Defense Force Management: DoD's Policy on Homosexuals in the Military, edited by the Government Accounting Office. (GAO Code 381137/ OSD Case 8983. March 9, 1992)

Don't Ask, Don't Tell, Don't Pursue Digital Database, Stanford University Law School. http://dont.stanford.edu.

Halley, Janet E. *Don't: A Reader's Guide to the Military's Anti-Gay Policy*. Durham, N.C.: Duke University Press, 1999.

Herek, Gregory, and Aaron Belkin. "Sexual Orientation and Military Service: Prospects for Organizational and Individual Change in the United States." In *Military Life: The Psychology of Serving in Peace and Combat*, edited by Thomas W. Britt, Amy B. Adler, and Carl Andrew Castro. Westport, Conn.: Greenwood Press, 2006.

Human Rights Watch. *Uniform Discrimination: The "Don't Ask, Don't Tell" Policy of the U.S.

Military. New York: Author, 2003.
Lehring, Gary. *Officially Gay: The Political Construction of Sexuality in the U.S. Military*. Philadelphia: Temple University Press, 2003.
Rostker, Bernard D., et al. *Sexual Orientation and U.S. Military Personnel Policy*. National Defense Research Institute, RAND Corporation, 1993. http://www.rand.org/pubs/.
Scott, Wilbur J., and Sandra Carson Stanley, eds. *Gays and Lesbians in the Military: Issues, Concerns, and Contrasts*. New York: Aldine De Gruyter, 1994.
Servicemembers' Legal Defense Network. *Conduct Unbecoming: The Tenth Annual Report on "Don't Ask, Don't Tell"* (2004). http://www .sldn.org.
_____. *Survival Guide: A Comprehensive Guide to "Don't Ask, Don't Tell, Don't Pursue, Don't Harass," and Related Military Policies*. 4th ed. Washington, D.C.: Author, 2003.
Wolinsky, Marc, and Kenneth Sherrill, eds. *Gays and the Military: Joseph Steffan Versus the United States*. Princeton, N.J.: Princeton University Press, 1993.

SEE ALSO: Mar. 15, 1919-1921: U.S. Navy Launches Sting Operation Against "Sexual Perverts"; July 3, 1975: U.S. Civil Service Commission Prohibits Discrimination Against Federal Employees; 1976-1990: Army Reservist Ben-Shalom Sues for Reinstatement; May-Aug., 1980: U.S. Navy Investigates the USS *Norton Sound* in Antilesbian Witch Hunt; May 3, 1989: *Watkins v. United States Army* Reinstates Gay Soldier; 1990, 1994: *Coming Out Under Fire* Documents Gay and Lesbian Military Veterans; Aug. 27, 1991: *The Advocate* Outs Pentagon Spokesman Pete Williams; Oct., 1992: Canadian Military Lifts Its Ban on Gays and Lesbians; Jan. 12, 2000: United Kingdom Lifts Ban on Gays and Lesbians in the Military.

December 24, 1993-December 31, 1993
TRANSGENDER MAN BRANDON TEENA RAPED AND MURDERED

Brandon Teena was raped and murdered by two acquaintances after they found him to have female genitalia. The crime increased public awareness about gender-based violence and the right of transgender and gender-ambiguous persons to equal protection under the law. The case also sparked a focused transgender activism and was memorialized in the film Boys Don't Cry.

LOCALE: Humboldt and Falls City, Nebraska
CATEGORIES: Transgender/transsexuality; crime; civil rights; laws, acts, and legal history

KEY FIGURES
Brandon Teena (1972-1993), a gender-ambiguous man who was raped and murdered
JoAnn Brandon, Brandon Teena's mother
Lana Tisdel, Brandon Teena's girlfriend
Thomas Nissen, convicted murderer
John Lotter, convicted murderer

SUMMARY OF EVENT
Brandon Teena was named Teena Renae Brandon at birth on December 12, 1972, in Lincoln, Nebraska. Brandon, who dressed at an early age in what were considered boys' clothes, referred to herself after high school as a man and used masculine names such as Tena Ray, Billy, and Brandon. Brandon dated women exclusively, had several girlfriends, and was twice engaged to be married. Later, he would tell others that he was a hermaphrodite and needed surgery in order to fully become a man and that he was undergoing, or would soon be undergoing, gender reassignment surgery.

Brandon left Lincoln in November, 1993, for several reasons: A number of people knew that he had been born female, his fiancé had recently broken up with him, and he had gotten into legal trouble over check forgery. Moving to Humboldt, Nebraska, where he would be a newcomer to town, was an opportunity for him to live as a man.

Brandon first stayed in Humboldt with his friend, Lisa Lambert, but shortly after the move, Brandon began dating Lana Tisdel and then lived with her at her mother's home in nearby Falls City. He also began hanging out with Lana's friends, including John Lotter and Thomas Nissen, the two who would rape and murder Brandon before the end of the year.

Brandon passed easily as a man, but in mid-December he was arrested for check forgery and was booked as a woman into jail. Law enforcement released information about the arrest, and the local newspaper, the *Falls City Journal*, published a crime report that identified Brandon as female.

Tisdel convinced Nissen to post bail for Brandon on December 22, 1993, and two days later the couple went to a Christmas Eve party at Nissen's. At the party, Nissen and Lotter, who by this time suspected that Brandon was female, restrained Brandon and pulled down his pants to show Tisdel that he was female. Soon after, Tisdel was apparently called home by her mother; she left Brandon at the party and vowed to return. After she left, Nissen and Lotter physically assaulted Brandon at the party, then carried him out to a car. The men drove to a secluded area where they repeatedly raped and beat Brandon.

Brandon reported the assault and rapes to the Richardson County Sheriff's Department, but it made no arrests. Sheriff Charles Laux, during his interview of Brandon, seemed more interested in Brandon's self-identification as a man than in the rape and assault, often getting off track during questioning to discuss Brandon's personal life and gender identity. (Although activists and scholars, as well as the media, have identified Brandon as transgender, it is not clear if Brandon self-identified as transgender or transsexual. The taped interview with the sheriff's department, however, does reveal Brandon using the words "gender identity disorder" to describe what he "has.")

On December 28, 1993, Nissen and Lotter were questioned by deputies, but, again, no arrests were made. A deputy said later that Laux advised against making an arrest even though the deputy believed there was enough evidence to arrest Nissen and Lotter.

On December 31, sometime after midnight, Nissen and Lotter arrived at the Lambert farmhouse, where Brandon was once again staying with his friend, Lisa Lambert. Nissen and Lotter entered the home and then shot and killed Brandon, Lambert, and a houseguest, Philip DeVine, who was visiting from out of town; only Lisa's infant son survived.

Nissen and Lotter were arrested later that day and eventually convicted of the murders. Nissen was sentenced to life imprisonment, without the possibil-

Brandon Teena and his girlfriend Lana Tisdel in an undated photograph. (AP/Wide World Photos)

ity of parole, and Lotter was sentenced to death. Lotter appealed his death sentence, but his appeal had been denied in 2003.

SIGNIFICANCE

Transgender individuals have been the victims of hate-crimes violence, including murder, long before the murder of Brandon Teena. However, Brandon's rape and murder stands out because it received national press coverage and brought the realities of transgender experience to the public. American society came to be drawn to Brandon—both out of curiosity and out of anger. People were curious because Brandon was able to pass as a man (some argue it was deception) and some were outraged because of the absolute failure of law enforcement to protect him. Many believe that Sheriff Laux signed Brandon's death warrant by his failure to arrest Nissen and Lotter. Transgender activists argue that this kind of indifference by law enforcement is widespread.

At Lotter's trial, transgender activists from around the United States held a vigil outside the courtroom. Vigil participants included noted authors and activists Leslie Feinberg, Minnie Bruce Pratt, and Kate Bornstein.

Brandon's mother, JoAnn Brandon, filed a wrongful death lawsuit against Laux and Richardson County, Nebraska. A judge initially awarded Brandon Teena's mother a mere $17,360, but the state Supreme Court ordered the judge to reconsider that amount; in April, 2001, the judge awarded JoAnn Brandon $98,223. She appealed the new award as well, but the state Supreme Court in March, 2003, ruled the award reasonable.

Because of the publicity regarding Nissen and Lotter's rape and murder of Brandon Teena, mainstream America has become aware of transgender people and attitudes toward them. In the more than a decade following the case, there has been a great demand for civil rights protection for transgender people. There are now numerous cities, a few states, and large corporations, such as Hewlett-Packard and Nike, which have instituted nondiscrimination legislation, including hate crime laws, and policies to protect transgender individuals.

Riki Wilchins, executive director of the Washington-based Gender Public Advocacy Coalition (or GenderPAC), summed up this increased social awareness in an interview.

> How many times do you get to see a giant sea change like this in people's perceptions? But you look at Congress, corporate America, and cities and states, and you see this enormous change in how people are looking at gender as a civil rights issue.
>
> —*Kim Hackford-Peer*

FURTHER READING

"'Boys Don't Cry' Sheriff Found Negligent." *Contemporary Sexuality* 35, no. 5 (May, 2001).

Gilbert, Michael, ed. *International Journal of Transgenderism* 4, no. 3 (July/September, 2000). Special issue, "What Is Transgender?" http://www.symposion.com/ijt/index.htm.

Halberstam, Judith. *In a Queer Time and Place: Transgender Bodies, Subcultural Lives*. New York: New York University Press, 2005.

Huegel, Kelly. *GLBTQ: The Survival Guide for Queer and Questioning Teens*. Minneapolis, Minn.: Free Spirit, 2003.

Jones, Aphrodite. *All She Wanted*. New York: Pocket Books, 1996.

Lambda Legal and National Youth Advocacy Coalition. *Bending the Mold: An Action Kit for Transgender Youth*. 2004. http://www.lambdalegal.org.

Sánchez, María Carla, and Linda Schlossberg, eds. *Passing: Identity and Interpretation in Sexuality, Race, and Religion*. New York: New York University Press, 2001.

Swigonski, Mary E., Robin S. Mama, and Kelly Ward. *From Hate Crimes to Human Rights: A Tribute to Matthew Shepard*. New York: Harrington Park Press and Haworth Social Work Practice Press, 2001.

Wilchins, Riki. *Queer Theory, Gender Theory: An Instant Primer*. Los Angeles: Alyson, 2004.

Willox, Annabelle. "Branding Teena: (Mis)Representations in the Media." *Sexualities* 6, nos. 3-4 (August/November, 2003).

See also: Nov. 27, 1978: White Murders Politicians Moscone and Milk; Jan. 21, 1989: Death of Transgender Jazz Musician Billy Tipton; Dec. 4, 1995: Lesbian Couple Murdered in Oregon; 1996: Hart Recognized as a Transgender Man; Apr. 2, 1998: Canadian Supreme Court Reverses Gay Academic's Firing; Oct. 6-7, 1998: Gay College Student Shepard Is Beaten and Murdered; Mar. 21, 2000: Hollywood Awards Transgender Portrayals in Film; Oct. 4, 2002: Transgender Teen Gwen Araujo Is Murdered in California.

1994
Employment Non-Discrimination Act Is Proposed to U.S. Congress

The Employment Non-Discrimination Act, still pending, would add the category of "sexual orientation" to antidiscrimination employment regulations of the U.S. government. Whereas early attempts to pass the act focused on amending the 1964 Civil Rights Act, later efforts targeted employment guidelines in a stand-alone measure. President Bill Clinton, in a partial victory for GLBT rights, issued an executive order in 1998 prohibiting discrimination based on sexual orientation in federal civilian employment.

Locale: United States
Categories: Civil rights; government and politics; laws, acts, and legal history

Key Figures
Edward M. Kennedy (b. 1932), U.S. senator
Bill Clinton (b. 1946), U.S. president, 1993-2001

Summary of Event

The proposed Employment Non-Discrimination Act (ENDA) would extend federal protection to gays and lesbians under a legal framework similar to Title VII of the Civil Rights Act of 1964. As of 2006, sixteen states and the District of Columbia have passed antidiscrimination measures based on sexual orientation in employment. Additionally, as of 2004, eighteen states have executive orders and eighty-seven counties or cities prohibit discrimination based on sexual orientation. There is no federal law, however, that protects lesbians and gays.

The earliest versions of ENDA date from between 1975 and 1993. These legislative proposals would have amended Title VII of the Civil Rights Act, adding sexual orientation to classes of prohibited discrimination. The attempts met with political rancor and failure. In 1994, a new approach had been taken, proposing a stand-alone regulation against discrimination in employment. The revised version was on the surface similar to the original versions of the bill forbidding discrimination based on sexual orientation regarding hiring, firing, employment, and workplace practices.

The stripped-down version of ENDA introduced to Congress in 1994 made a dramatic shift in achieving lesbian and gay rights. Previous attempts by activists and supporters to win civil rights protection under Title VII had failed. The bill would prohibit discrimination only in workplaces with more than fifteen employees, and it would exempt certain workplaces or organizations, such as religious organizations.

The chief sponsor of ENDA in 1994 had been Senator Edward M. Kennedy (D-MA), who chaired the Senate Committee on Labor and Human Resources. He was joined by 146 congressional cosponsors: 30 senators and 116 representatives. Democrats accounted for 116 of the sponsors.

Kennedy stated the bill was narrowly proscribed and crafted to avoid unneeded controversy. The issue was not the granting of special rights; instead, it

> **CLINTON'S ORDER AGAINST DISCRIMINATION IN FEDERAL GOVERNMENT EMPLOYMENT (1998)**
>
> By the authority vested in me as President by the Constitution and the laws of the United States, and in order to provide for a uniform policy for the Federal Government to prohibit discrimination based on sexual orientation, it is hereby ordered that Executive Order 11478, as amended, is further amended as follows:
> Section 1. The first sentence of section 1 is amended by substituting "age, or sexual orientation" for "or age."
> Section 2. The second sentence of section 1 is amended by striking the period and adding at the end of the sentence ", to the extent permitted by law."
>
> *William J. Clinton*
> The White House
>
> *Source:* Executive Order 13087. Federal GLOBE: Gay, Lesbian, Bi, and Transgender Employees of the Federal Government. http://www.fedglobe.org/actions/eo13087.htm.

was about righting senseless wrongs. Kennedy declared, "Federal law rightly prohibits job discrimination because of race, gender, religion, and national origin, age, and disability." He continued, "We now seek to take the next step on this journey of justice by banning discrimination based on sexual orientation."

ENDA would prohibit employers with more than fifteen workers from using an employee's sexual orientation as a deciding factor in employment decisions, maintaining that sexual orientation has no relevancy in terms of contributions to the economic demands of society. Therefore, a person's sexual orientation would not affect the economic success of business. The bill carried provisions for meaningful and effective remedies for proven discrimination, including rehiring and punitive damages.

Under proposed ENDA guidelines, employers also could not implement affirmative action programs, or utilize quota or goal systems, based on sexual orientation. Religious organizations have been exempted from ENDA regulations, but not church-operated businesses. The antidiscrimination measure would not apply to gays and lesbians in the military, however.

The new language helped bring the bill to a vote in Congress in 1996. The bill was nearly successful because it came to a vote at the same time as the highly controversial Defense of Marriage Act (1996), or DOMA, which banned federal recognition of same-gender marriages. Kennedy and lesbian and gay lobbyists agreed to bring both bills to a vote at the same time. They had hoped that doing this would make ENDA appear more palatable.

The approach nearly worked. While DOMA was approved by the Senate 85-14, ENDA lost 50-49. Senator David Pryor (D-AR) was absent from voting, attending to his son, who was undergoing surgery for cancer. Had Pryor been present to cast his intended vote for support, Vice President Al Gore would have returned from the campaign trail to cast the tie-breaking vote in favor of passage.

Because the act was just one vote shy of passing, gay and lesbian lobbyists declared that no longer was it the case of will sexual-orientation discrimination in employment be illegal, but when. Ensuing sessions of Congress with Republican-led majorities, however, were less likely to approve the act.

Support for ENDA comes from a diverse array of civil rights, political, business, and labor organizations. It has received endorsements from corporations such as Xerox, Harley-Davidson, AT&T, RJR Nabisco, and many others. It has received broad acceptance from organized labor groups and support from some religious groups.

Congress members opposed to the measure believe that the act would provide special legal status to lesbians and gays, and they believe the issue to be a moral one. Conservative groups such as the Family Research Council state that ENDA cannot be compared to civil rights legislation because the act would protect a sexual *behavior* rather than a nonbehavioral characteristic such as race or gender. Furthermore, they have argued that gays and lesbians have higher annual incomes and occupy greater percentages of professional and managerial positions. Because of this, they argue, lesbians and gays are not being "held back" by employment discrimination.

SIGNIFICANCE

Since 1996, modified versions of ENDA have been introduced into successive sessions of Congress. The bill has languished in committee because of a lack of support from Republican and conservative members of Congress. Republican leadership did not want to bring the legislation to floor vote. President Bill Clinton expressed support for the passage of ENDA, and he issued Executive Order 13087 on May 28, 1998, which banned discrimination against lesbians and gays (specifically, it now includes "sexual orientation" as a protected status) in federal civilian employment. President George W. Bush has not rescinded Clinton's executive order, but prospects for the passage of ENDA have diminished.

In June, 2005, Representatives Henry Waxman (D-CA), Chris Shays (R-CT), and others introduced the Clarification of Federal Employment Protections Act to Congress, legislation that simply asks for affirmation "that Federal employees are protected from discrimination on the basis of sexual orientation and to repudiate any assertion to the contrary." The House Government Reform Committee passed the act in September; a Senate committee hearing was pending as of early 2006.

Aside from the discriminatory aspect of firing lesbians and gays from their jobs, or keeping them from being employed in the first place, there are economic reasons why the act should be passed. According to research done by the National Commission on Employment Policy, an estimated 42,000 gay and lesbian workers are dismissed every year in the United States. This, in turn, equals a loss of more than $47 million annually in training expenditures and unemployment payments. Meanwhile, discrimination in the American workplace against gays and lesbians is not uncommon. Also, a survey conducted in 2000 found that 83 percent of Americans believe lesbians and gays should be protected against discrimination in employment. ENDA would provide a comprehensive, uniform, federal standard for protections against sexual-orientation discrimination.

—*Michael A. Lutes*

FURTHER READING

Bull, Christopher. "No ENDA in Sight." *The Advocate*, May 13, 1997, 40.

Human Rights Campaign Foundation. *The State of the Workplace for Gay, Lesbian, Bisexual, and Transgender Americans, 2005-2006.* http://www.hrc.org.

Jasiunas, J. Banning. "Is ENDA the Answer? Can a 'Separate but Equal' Federal Statute Adequately Protect Gays and Lesbians from Employment Discrimination?" *Ohio State Law Journal* 61 (2000): 1529.

Kovach, Kenneth. "Non-Discrimination ENDA Gains Support." *HR Focus* 72, no. 7 (July, 1995): 15.

_____. "Proposal Would Expand Civil Rights Legislation." *Employment Relations Today* 22, no. 3 (Autumn, 1995): 9.

Rimmerman, Craig. *From Identity to Politics: The Lesbian and Gay Movements in the United States.* Philadelphia: Temple University Press, 2002.

SEE ALSO: Apr. 27, 1953: U.S. President Eisenhower Prohibits Federal Employment of Lesbians and Gays; 1972-1973: Local Governments Pass Antidiscrimination Laws; June 27, 1974: Abzug and Koch Attempt to Amend the Civil Rights Act of 1964; July 3, 1975: U.S. Civil Service Commission Prohibits Discrimination Against Federal Employees; 1978: Lesbian and Gay Workplace Movement Is Founded; June 2, 1980: Canadian Gay Postal Workers Secure Union Protections; Dec. 4, 1984: Berkeley Extends Benefits to Domestic Partners of City Employees; Nov. 8, 1988: Oregon Repeals Ban on Antigay Job Discrimination; May 1, 1989: U.S. Supreme Court Rules Gender-Role Stereotyping Is Discriminatory; July 26, 1990: Americans with Disabilities Act Becomes Law; Sept. 29, 1991: California Governor Wilson Vetoes Antidiscrimination Bill; Sept. 23, 1992: Massachusetts Grants Family Rights to Gay and Lesbian State Workers; Apr. 2, 1998: Canadian Supreme Court Reverses Gay Academic's Firing; July, 2003: Singapore Lifts Ban on Hiring Lesbian and Gay Employees; July, 2003: Wal-Mart Adds Lesbians and Gays to Its Antidiscrimination Policy.

1994
NATIONAL ASSOCIATION OF LESBIAN AND GAY COMMUNITY CENTERS IS FOUNDED

A nationwide coalition of lesbian and gay community service centers assists lesbian, gay, bisexual, and transgender persons at the local level with various programs, resources, and training, and through increased visibility and political support.

LOCALE: New York, New York
CATEGORY: Organizations and institutions

SUMMARY OF EVENT

In 1994, representatives of more than thirty lesbian and gay centers from around the United States, a group that had been meeting informally since 1987, met at the Lesbian & Gay Community Services Center of New York during the celebrations for the twenty-fifth anniversary of the Stonewall Rebellion. The National Association of Lesbian and Gay Community Centers was launched at this meeting, led by the centers in New York, Minneapolis, Minnesota; Denver, Colorado; and Los Angeles. In 2000, the association included "bisexual" and "transgender" as part of its name, incorporated, received Internal Revenue Service (IRS) tax-exempt status, created by-laws, and compiled job descriptions to prepare for hiring a national staff; offices are staffed in Washington, D.C., and Garden Grove, California.

The national association acts as the national voice for the centers and, especially, for the LGBT clients they serve. Also, the national office organizes national and regional conferences, publishes a quarterly newsletter, and hosts an e-mail Listserv that provides an ongoing support and discussion network. The association assists in the development

---

NATIONAL ASSOCIATION OF LESBIAN AND GAY COMMUNITY CENTERS: MISSION STATEMENT

To assist community centers in building a movement that honors and promotes full human rights and dignity for LGBT people and meets the health, social, cultural, and political advocacy needs of LGBT people. The NALGBTCC will build capacity, strengthen linkages, and advocate empowerment, self-reliance, inclusion, and diversity among every community center in our national coalition. The NALGBTCC also acts as a voice for community centers in national grass roots organizing and coalition building.

Goals

1. Codify and articulate the NALGBTCC and its member centers belief that community centers are primary social change agents in a national movement working toward the liberation and empowerment of LGBT people.

2. Identify democratic and progressive mechanisms to empower individuals to create progressive social change.

3. Support and honor other communities whose civil right struggles paved the way for our movement.

4. Prioritize, value and work for full human rights, dignity, health, and self-determination for all people.

5. Maintain a national LGBT community-based association, governed by an inclusive process with open and honest communication, that is independent of, but collaborating with, other national LGBT organizations.

6. Facilitate a sense of organizational self-esteem and self-direction for each NALGBTCC constituent LGBT Community Center.

7. Facilitate perceptions of value for all NALGBTCC constituent LGBT Community Centers regardless of agency size, services or programs. We value the worth and dignity of all people—clients, volunteers, and staff—and strive to create community institutions that make this value a reality in the workplace.

8. Celebrate our queer identity and value our cultural and political heritage.

of newly formed community centers through peer-based technical assistance, leadership training, and financial resources. It also undertakes national projects, which are implemented locally. The New York affiliate publishes a directory of the centers and contact information for all members of the association.

As of 2006, there were 150 centers associated with the national office, all of them vital because they are often the first points of contact for persons coming out as lesbian, gay, bisexual, or transgender or for those seeking referrals or information about the local GLBT community; the centers are often the only community resource for GLBT persons in many locations, especially outside major cities.

The New York affiliate, Lesbian, Gay, Bisexual, and Transgender Community Center, founded in 1983, is the most active center. It is the largest LGBT multiservice organization on the East Coast and is the second largest LGBT community center in the world, second only to the Gay and Lesbian Center in Los Angeles, which formed in 1971. Steven Powsner was the lead negotiator in the purchase in 1983 of the former Food and Maritime Trades High School on 13th Street in Greenwich Village. This building would come to house the New York City center. Powsner served two terms on the center's board of directors and as board president. Sheila Healy was the center's first executive director.

The New York center, with a large amount of available meeting space, saw sixty groups meeting there regularly in its first year. Groups that have used the space include the Harvey Milk High School for LGBT students, a program of the Hetrick-Martin Institute, and Dignity, a Catholic lesbian and gay religious organization. Dignity had been prohibited from meeting in Roman Catholic churches. As of 2006, more than three hundred groups meet at the center and more than six thousand persons each week use its services. The center provides social services, works on public policy, and offers educational, cultural, and recreational programs. It has served as the meeting location for grassroots groups such as ACT UP New York and for national organization such as the Gay and Lesbian Alliance Against Defamation (GLAAD).

The New York center's programs include the following:

- *Promote the Vote*, a nonpartisan voter registration and mobilization project, founded in 1992 and one of the largest LGBT voter registration programs in the United States.
- *Center Kids* promotes the legitimacy and visibility of LGBT families.
- *Youth Enrichment Services* (YES) focuses on ending isolation experienced by many LGBT youths. YES offers professional development training for youth workers, child welfare workers, teachers, guidance counselors, and school administrators. YES also has a leadership training and networking project for students working to end heterosexism in their schools.
- *Gender Identity Project* offers transgender persons opportunities to build their community (www.gaycenter.org/gip/).
- *National Archive of Lesbian, Gay, Bisexual & Transgender History* at the Center preserves the LGBT community's heritage. The archive is a national leader because of its large size and the scope of its collection (www.gaycenter.org/resources/).
- *The Pat Parker/Vito Russo Center Library*, the largest LGBT lending library in New York City (www.gaycenter.org/resources/).

SIGNIFICANCE

Lesbian and gay community centers emerged after the Stonewall Rebellion of June, 1969, during a fledgling but strong and vocal lesbian and gay rights movement. The main goal of the centers at that time was to connect isolated persons to an organized community.

Center programs, as strong as ever, were at the forefront of the HIV-AIDS pandemic, especially in the 1980's. Their focus on health and wellness continues, and community service in general remains a priority for many. The centers also provide a political voice for LGBT communities, working with local governments to ensure that the LGBT communities' needs are adequately met. The national association of LGBT centers works to foster the growth of the centers around the country and to share ideas and program models.

—Ski Hunter

FURTHER READING

Hellman, R., and J. Dreschner. *Handbook of LGBT Issues in Community Mental Health*. Binghamton, N.Y.: Haworth Press, 2004.

Kenley, D. L., M. R. Stevenson, and J. Cogan. *Everyday Activism: A Handbook for Lesbian, Gay, and Bisexual People and Their Allies*. New York: Routledge, 2003.

National Association of Lesbian, Gay, Bisexual, and Transgender Community Centers. http://www.lgbtcenters.org.

SEE ALSO: Mar., 1971: Los Angeles Gay and Lesbian Center Is Founded; 1982: Lesbian and Gay Youth Protection Institute Is Founded; May, 1988: Lavender Youth Recreation and Information Center Opens.

1994
NAVRATILOVA HONORED FOR HER CAREER IN TENNIS

Martina Navratilova was the first woman tennis player and the first out athlete of any gender to be honored with a banner in Madison Square Garden in New York. In 1982, she became the first woman athlete to earn more than $1 million in a single season, and with her earnings, victories, and style of play came a new interest in women's tennis.

LOCALE: New York, New York
CATEGORIES: Sports; civil rights; organizations and institutions

KEY FIGURES

Martina Navratilova (b. 1956), Czech-born American tennis player
Billie Jean King (b. 1943), American tennis player
Gladys Heldman (1922-2003), editor of *World Tennis Magazine*
Joseph Cullman (1912-2004), CEO of Philip Morris Company

SUMMARY OF EVENT

A great career in women's tennis ended at the 1994 Virginia Slims Championship Tournament in New York City—or so it seemed. In the first round of play, thirty-eight-year-old Martina Navratilova, America's reigning tennis champion, lost to twenty-four-year-old Gabriela Sabatini. Navratilova announced her retirement after the match. To honor her career accomplishments, tournament organizers hung a large banner emblazoned with her name in Madison Square Garden in New York City. She was the first woman tennis player, and the first out athlete, to be so honored. Navratilova, and the Virginia Slims Tournament itself, had revolutionized women's tennis.

Before 1968, sport was still ruled by the amateur principle. Tennis players had to compete for love of the game only, and they lost their amateur status if they derived any income from sport. The men's professional tour was small, the women's tour was nonexistent, and public interest in the sport was dwindling. In 1968, as a desperate measure, the four Grand Slams (the U.S., British, French, and Australian) declared themselves open to male and female pros. In 1972, in the midst of a growing women's rights movement, Title IX of the Education Amendments was passed, requiring all educational programs or activities that receive federal funding to offer equal opportunity to girls and women in all activities, including sports. While Title IX did not affect professional sports directly, it galvanized many pro women athletes. The U.S. Lawn Tennis Association (USLTA) seemed to not hear, or not care,

Martina Navratilova announces her retirement from professional tennis. (Hulton Archive/Getty Images)

about women's complaints regarding the conditions they faced, including lower media visibility and smaller tournament purses.

In 1970, Billie Jean King and several other leading players were outraged at the financial inequities of an upcoming tournament: $12,500 was to be given to the male champion and a measly $1,500 to the female champion. The group took a gamble and broke ranks with the tennis establishment, hoping to form a pro tour.

Help came from the editor of *World Tennis Magazine*, Gladys Heldman, who put the women in touch with Joseph Cullman, chief executive officer of Philip Morris Company. The tobacco giant had just introduced the Virginia Slims brand in hopes of tapping the growing market that included young women. The company's ads featured models who looked fashionably lean and active and had the line "you've come a long way, baby." Cullman, a tennis lover, already sponsored the U.S. Open. He did not need much persuading to sponsor a high-profile women's tour. In fall of 1970, the first Virginia Slims Tournament was launched in Houston with $7,500 in prize money. The USLTA retaliated against the women who protested earlier by suspending them, but the tour was such a hit that the USLTA finally backed down.

By 1971 the Virginia Slims tour had exploded—nineteen cities and a purse of $309,100. King became the first woman athlete to earn a six-digit income in a single season. In 1973, the Women's International Tennis Association (now the Women's Tennis Association), founded by King, established the Virginia Slims Championship as the climax event of each season.

Meanwhile, Navratilova had come a long way herself. Born in Prague, Czechoslovakia, in 1956, she already had been a powerful left-handed talent at age twelve and was coached by her father, a former tennis player. She came out of the communist world's farm system, which aimed to produce athletes that would dominate in international competition. Typically, the women athletes who came out of this system were not discouraged or afraid to be strong and aggressive, and they often had contempt for the "femininity" that female athletes of Democratic nations felt compelled to display. Gender expression was such a hot issue that many Westerners actually convinced themselves that some Eastern-bloc women athletes were really men in disguise, prompting the International Olympic Committee to start its gender-testing policy in 1968.

In 1972, at age sixteen, Navratilova won the Czech women's singles title. She then came to international attention when she led the Czech team to victory in the Federation Cup, the top team competition in women's tennis, sponsored by the International Tennis Federation. The following year the Czech government sent her to the U.S. Open. The seventeen-year-old fell in love with the United States. Navratilova looked at the Virginia Slims tour and realized she could make a life for herself in the United States. In 1975, overcoming the Czech officials nervous about her loyalty, she wangled another visa to the U.S. Open. Once there, she contacted U.S. officials and asked for political asylum. Navratilova boldly told them that she was bisexual, taking the risk that her application would be denied. It was not, and she got her green card.

Settling into American life, Navratilova increased her strength and speed by cross-training in other sports—notably with women's basketball pioneer Nancy Lieberman. Rumors circulated about a sexual relationship between the two, but Navratilova ignored the rumors and kept training. She was the best woman tennis player in the world by the early 1980's. Her aggressive serve-and-volley game was more typical of male players, and it proved devastating to her female opponents, who were accustomed to making strategic shots off the baseline. Her blunt, outspoken manner and her more masculine look—tousled hair, shorts, well-defined muscles—stood in stark contrast to the girl-next-door appeal of many women she faced on the court.

Indeed, her toughest competitor, Chris Evert, was the embodiment of the old-style American tennis game and of traditional femininity. *Sports Illustrated* noted,

> Just as the NBA had [Larry] Bird and Magic [Johnson], as boxing had [Muhammad] Ali and [Joe] Frazier, and as golf had [Jack] Nicklaus and [Arnold] Palmer, so did women's tennis once boast an epic rivalry. For upwards of 15 years, Chris Evert and Martina Navratilova matched each other shot for shot, fighting over the sport's most coveted titles and playing an ongoing game of leapfrog for the No. 1 ranking.... Evert was the picture of consistency, keeping her foes at bay with classic, impeccably positioned strokes and a will of iron. Navratilova was a relentlessly aggressive athlete who attacked at every opportunity and forced the action.

Evert's fans saw Martina as a "bad guy," and they reviled her openly, but this rivalry packed the stands and pushed TV ratings—it ended up being good for women's tennis, and women's sports.

By this time hundreds of women were playing the Virginia Slims tour, which offered forty-seven events and $10 million in prize money. In 1982, Navratilova became the first woman to earn more than $1 million in a single season. In 1984, she received a $1-million bonus from the International Tennis Federation for winning all four Grand Slam singles in the same year. Indeed, by this time the women were earning more than the men—when Navratilova broke the $2 million barrier for one season, she earned more than John McEnroe, the leading male player at the time. By 1986, Navratilova, thirty years old and seemingly unstoppable, handily winning games against younger players, passed $10 million in career earnings.

Times were changing, however. The movement against tobacco kicked in, and growing numbers of women rejected the idea that smoking could make women attractive, as the Virginia Slims cigarette ads implied. In 1990, another Philip Morris company, Kraft General Foods, took over the tour's permanent sponsorship, though the Virginia Slims name was still associated with the event through 1994. The season's purse soared to $23 million.

By the mid-1990's, Navratilova's grit and her power game had finally won a huge following, including thousands of lesbians and bisexual women. Asked about the fierce partisan applause, Navratilova said, "For years I felt I was unappreciated and now I'm over-appreciated. I hit an average shot and get a standing ovation and I hit a great shot and they go, like, well, nice. It's like—I'm the home team everywhere I go."

Tennis insiders had known about Navratilova's sexual orientation. In 1981, after she became a U.S. citizen, she stated publicly that she was bisexual. She once told Barbara Walters that she enjoyed sleeping with both women and men but preferred waking up with women. By 1991, palimony litigation by former life-partner Judy Nelson put Navratilova's name in the tabloids. However, coming out cost her heavily in commercial endorsements. Not until 2000 did a major corporation, Subaru, sign her for an advertising contract.

SIGNIFICANCE

Coming out in U.S. sports has been more challenging to GLBT people than coming out in the arts or even politics. While most sports require male athletes to live up to a strict heterosexual and hypermasculine image, female athletes are held to an equally strict standard of heterosexual femininity. Inevitably, the 1969 Stonewall Rebellion in New York City led to the first wave of athletes who came out: pro-football player David Kopay, decathlete Tom Waddell, baseball umpire Dave Pallone, tennis player Billie Jean King, and others. In 1995, gay diver Greg Louganis came out not only as gay but also HIV-positive, the first out gay athlete to announce his HIV status.

In the early twenty-first century, more than one hundred prominent GLBT athletes and coaches are listed as "out athletes" by Outsports.com. However, the old biases still hold painful leverage on the lives of athletes. While lesbians and bisexual women are more visible in some individual sports, such as tennis, golf, fencing, boxing, and equestrian, the "L" issue is still a taboo one in team sports, such as soccer and basketball.

As the 1990's arrived, Navratilova kept winning and was seemingly indestructible. However, her direct style had forced a paradigm shift in the game of other players. Younger players were now attacking with the same cannonball serves and blistering volleys. Plus, the thirty-eight-year-old veteran was slowing down just a little. After Sabatini beat her at the 1994 Virginia Slims Tournament, Navratilova announced her retirement from singles competition, but she said she would continue in doubles and exhibitions. As the historic banner went up, she told a reporter, "Emotionally, I've been doing well, I've been ready for this."

Overall, Navratilova has set a hard-to-beat record with 9 victories at Wimbledon, 167 singles titles, 173 doubles titles, 18 singles and 40 doubles wins in Grand Slams, and more than $21 million in career earnings. When *Sports Illustrated* put together its 100 Greatest Women Athletes list, it gave her the edge over Chris Evert, placing her at number 5 and Evert at number 6.

A moving tribute came from Evert herself, who told *Women's Sport & Fitness* magazine, "I always admired her maturity, her wisdom and her ability to transcend the sport. You could ask her about her forehand or about world peace and she always had an answer. She really is a world figure, not just a sports figure."

With the new millennium, Navratilova returned to limited doubles competition. In 2001, when she played the Open Day España tournament in Madrid, Kathleen Wilkinson wrote in the *Lesbian News*, "Navratilova became the oldest woman to win a tour event—singles or doubles.... Most of the players on the women's tennis circuit today are less than half Navratilova's age. Her current Grand Slam doubles partner, Iroda Tulyaganova, is just 20." Navratilova liked to joke that she was called "grandma" behind her back.

In 2004, Navratilova's doubles comeback was capped—at age forty-eight—by being selected for the 2004 U.S. Olympic team. She and tennis partner Lisa Raymond made it to the Athens quarterfinals, defeating younger players such as France's Amelie Mauresmo. Along with two other tennis figures—Mauresmo and Spain's Conchita Martinez—Navratilova was one of eleven out athletes in the 2004 Summer Olympic Games.

—*Patricia Nell Warren*

FURTHER READING

Cahn, Susan K. *Coming on Strong: Gender and Sexuality in Twentieth-Century Women's Sport*. New York: Free Press, 1994.

International Tennis Hall of Fame. "Martina Navratilova." http://www.tennisfame.org.

Navratilova, Martina. *Shape Your Self*. Emmaus, Pa.: Rodale Books, 2006.

Navratilova, Martina, with George Vecsey. *Martina*. New York: Knopf, 1985.

Phillips, Caryl, ed. *The Right Set: A Tennis Anthology*. New York: Vintage Books, 1999.

Women's Tennis Association. http://www.wtatour.com.

Zwerman, Gilda. *Martina Navratilova*. New York: Chelsea House, 1995.

SEE ALSO: Aug. 28, 1982: First Gay Games Are Held in San Francisco; 1995: Athlete Louganis Announces He Is HIV-Positive; May 17, 2004: Transsexual Athletes Allowed to Compete in Olympic Games.

June, 1994
STONEWALL 25 MARCH AND RALLIES ARE HELD IN NEW YORK CITY

The twenty-fifth anniversary of the Stonewall Rebellion saw a march on the United Nations and rally at Central Park, a Spirit of Stonewall march from Greenwich Village to Central Park, and other social and political actions and events in New York City.

LOCALE: New York, New York
CATEGORIES: Marches, protests, and riots; civil rights; government and politics

SUMMARY OF EVENT
Although there were many events associated with Stonewall 25, the march on the United Nations (U.N.) was the focal point. On Sunday, June 26, 1994, lesbians, gays, bisexuals, drag queens and kings, and transgender individuals marched to the United Nations. The six-hour march included a mile-long rainbow flag, members of the Stonewall Veterans' Association (those involved in the original Stonewall Rebellion), and participation by many other groups of supporters. The march culminated in a Central Park rally with various speakers, including AIDS activists, transgender activists, and international politicians. Performers at the rally included Liza Minelli, which was especially appropriate, given that Minelli is the daughter of Judy Garland, whose death, it is thought by some, was one of the events that triggered the original Stonewall uprising.

The rally also included a moment of silence to remember those who had died of AIDS-related complications and from hate-crime violence. There was also a moment for expression of anger and rage at the injustices experienced by gays, lesbians, transgender, and bisexual people.

On Monday, June 27, events continued with a focus on global human rights. Individuals from more than forty countries met with their U.N. representatives to raise awareness about human rights violations affecting the gay, lesbian, bisexual and transgender communities.

March documents included the following set of demands:

That the promises of the Universal Declaration of Human Rights not be denied to gay, lesbian, bisexual, drag, and transgender people, or to those with HIV or AIDS.

That the global effort to combat HIV-AIDS be intensified.

That the U.N. proclaim an "international year" of lesbian and gay people.

That funding for U.N. activities be increased to implement these issues of concern.

That the U.N. and its affiliates denounce and seek the elimination of travel, immigration, and other cross-border restrictions based on HIV-AIDS status.

That the U.N. and people of the world join in affirming the dignity and legitimacy of lesbian, gay, bisexual, and drag/transgender people.

SIGNIFICANCE
The significance of the march may be best summarized by a statement by one of the Stonewall 25 cochairs, Pat Norman. Norman said that "Stonewall 25 brought more of our grass-roots organizers from around the globe to one city at one time with the purpose of planning our future than ever before. We gathered to fight the [Christian] right, to fight for AIDS services, to fight for a cure and to fight for our freedom of expression."

Many younger gays and lesbians were unaware, at the time, of the history of gay and lesbian activism, much of which stemmed from the original Stonewall Rebellion. Stonewall 25 did several things, including bringing attention to the historic event, showing how diverse groups could work together for a national and international goal, and setting forth measurable goals for the U.N. and its affiliates.

Stonewall 25 included a mile-long rainbow flag carried by marchers through the streets of New York City. (AP/Wide World Photos)

ety; Gay Male S/M Activists; International Gay/Lesbian Archives; International Gay/Lesbian Human Rights Commission; International Lesbian/Gay/Bisexual Appointed & Elected Officials; Lesbian & Gay Bands of America; Log Cabin Clubs of America; National Black Gay & Lesbian Leadership Forum; National Gay & Lesbian Task Force; National Gay Officers Action League; Parents, Family, and Friends of Lesbians & Gays; U.S. Student Association; Universal Fellowship of the Metropolitan Community Church; War Resisters League; and the World Congress of Gay/Lesbian Jewish Organizations.

Stonewall 25 was a historic set of events, much more than just a march. It was a concerted focus upon human rights issues that used a variety of approaches (for example, forums, conferences, hearings with the United Nations, and the march and rally) to make sure its messages were heard. In terms of lasting impact, the groups who had collaborated on Stonewall 25 continue to seek support for the demands that were presented at the march. GLBT pride weeks (held annually, beginning mostly in June) continue to draw more and more people in many cities across the United States and the world. Segments of the mile-long-rainbow flag have appeared in many rallies and events in the years after Stonewall 25.

The effort to produce and organize the march and other activities was not without controversy. Documents produced during the planning meetings show evidence of racial strife, concerns about representation, and dismay with the organizing committee by the original Stonewall Veterans' Association.

Still, the march involved also a massive effort on the part of many diverse groups: Amnesty International, Members for Lesbian/Gay Concerns; BiNet USA; Forgotten Scouts; Gay/Lesbian Arab Soci-

The question, Has the march inspired lasting political change at the global level? remains unanswered, but for those who participated in Stonewall 25, and for those who planned it, there certainly has been a personal impact. Additionally, the consciousness-raising, as well as the strife, that was generated through the working together of so many different and divergent groups and organizations has made LGBT communities stronger and more aware and sensitive to the differences, and similarities, among communities.

—Mary Ware

FURTHER READING

Adam, Barry. *The Rise of a Gay and Lesbian Movement*. New York: Twayne, 1995.

Miller, Diane. *Freedom to Differ: The Shaping of the Gay and Lesbian Struggle for Civil Rights*. New York: New York University Press, 1996.

Miller, Neil. *Out of the Past: Gay and Lesbian History from 1869 to the Present*. New York: Vintage Books, 1995.

Nelson, Lisa. "Marches and Parades." In *Gay Histories and Cultures*, edited by George E. Haggerty. New York: Garland, 2000.

Scott, Janny. "Gay Marchers Celebrate History in 2 Parades." *The New York Times*, June 27, 1994, p. A1.

Stewart, Chuck. *Gay and Lesbian Issues: A Reference Handbook*. Santa Barbara, Calif.: ABC-CLIO, 2003.

Williams, Walter, and Yolanda Retter. *Gay and Lesbian Rights in the United States: A Documentary History*. Westport, Conn.: Greenwood Press, 2003.

SEE ALSO: July 2-Aug. 28, 1963: Rustin Organizes the March on Washington; Aug., 1966: Queer Youth Fight Police Harassment at Compton's Cafeteria in San Francisco; June 27-July 2, 1969: Stonewall Rebellion Ignites Modern Gay and Lesbian Rights Movement; June 28, 1970: First Lesbian and Gay Pride March in the United States; Oct. 12-15, 1979: First March on Washington for Lesbian and Gay Rights; Oct. 11, 1987: Second March on Washington for Lesbian and Gay Rights; 1990: International Gay and Lesbian Human Rights Commission Is Founded; Apr. 24, 1993: First Dyke March Is Held in Washington, D.C.; Apr. 25, 1993: March on Washington for Gay, Lesbian, and Bi Equal Rights and Liberation; Sept. 16, 1994: U.N. Revokes Consultative Status of International Lesbian and Gay Association; June 19, 2002: Gays and Lesbians March for Equal Rights in Mexico City.

August 6, 1994
JAPANESE AMERICAN CITIZENS LEAGUE SUPPORTS SAME-GENDER MARRIAGE

The Japanese American Citizens League was the first Asian American civil rights organization that was not focused on gay and lesbian issues exclusively, to support same-gender marriage. The organization's support inspired early same-gender marriage activism in Hawaii and Alaska.

LOCALE: Salt Lake City, Utah
CATEGORIES: Civil rights; laws, acts, and legal history; organizations and institutions

KEY FIGURES
Lia Shigemura, former JACL program director
Carole Hayashino, associate director of JACL in San Francisco
Norman Y. Mineta, California Democratic congressman and former president of JACL

SUMMARY OF EVENT

The Japanese American Citizens League (JACL), founded in 1930, is one of the oldest Asian American civil rights groups. Group members were instrumental in contributing leadership during the internment of Japanese Americans during World War II. In 1994, the year JACL showed its support for same-gender marriage, JACL had twenty-six thousand members and 114 chapters.

The movement to support same-gender marriage started with discussion on the issue at the JACL Pacific Southwest district council meeting in Hawaii on February 28, 1994. Hawaii had earlier banned same-gender marriage. Ruth Mizobe, president of the chapter, said, "The government should not deny gays and lesbians equal benefits and privileges and sanctions that are accorded to all married couples." The chapter agreed, and then voted to support same-gender marriage.

Then, in May of 1994, six district representatives and seven officers of the JACL national board took up the issue. Someone at the meeting had reminded the others that the first Japanese immigrants were not allowed to marry whites because interracial marriage was considered morally repugnant and unnatural. Some Japanese people were harassed and sometimes attacked for marrying whites. In the end, the board voted 10-3 in support of same-gender marriage. The JACL's "marriage resolution" affirmed marriage as a basic human right that should not be denied to same-gender couples.

The JACL then held its national convention on August 6, 1994 in Salt Lake City, Utah. This national convention became an important event for both JACL members and LGBT Asian Americans. Several former JACL leaders, including Lia Shigemura, a former JACL program director, came out of the closet at the convention. Shigemura had come to the national convention after talking with her former colleague, Carole Hayashino, who mentioned that even though the JACL national board had passed a resolution in support of same-gender marriages, homophobic JACL members would try to reject that resolution at the convention.

At the convention, the Mt. Olympus chapter asked JACL members to oppose same-gender marriage. There was a motion on the floor (resolution six) that would have made opposition to same-gender marriage the official national JACL position. However, there were many more members in support of same-gender marriage than those opposed, who spoke to the issue. The debate over the resolution was extended many times so that all the delegates and members who wanted to indeed could speak on the issue. Shigemura announced her support for same-gender marriage and then courageously came out as lesbian in front of her Japanese American colleagues. It was the first time she had come out in public.

Also, there was a speech made by California con-

ABOUT THE JAPANESE AMERICAN CITIZENS LEAGUE

The Japanese American Citizens League (JACL), one of the oldest and largest Asian American civil rights organizations in the United States, was formed by Japanese Americans in San Francisco who identified themselves as *nisei*, or second-generation Japanese Americans. Thomas Yatabe, Tom Okawara, Tokutato Hayashi, Hideki Hayashi, and Kay Tsukamoto formed several discussion sessions to talk about their life experiences as second-generation Americans. Those discussion groups transformed into an organization for *nisei* who were eager to advocate their civil rights as Japanese Americans.

The organization was first named the American Loyalty Club, but group members soon changed the name to the American Loyalty League (ALL). Cofounder Yatabe left San Francisco for Fresno, California, in 1922, and ALL became inactive. In 1929, Jimmie Sakamoto envisioned a coastwide alliance of Japanese Americans that could respond to discrimination and prejudice directed toward citizens of Japanese descent. He officially established the Japanese American Citizens League in 1930 as an educational and socially active group.

The JACL mission soon turned to protecting and upholding the human rights of all American racial groups and promoting and preserving the cultural heritage and values of Japanese Americans. JACL has worked on immigration rights in the United States for first-generation Japanese Americans (*issei*) since its establishment. The most recent and progressive action that JACL took was passing a resolution in 1994 that affirmed its commitment to and support of the basic human right of marriage, including the right of same-gender couples to marry. JACL was the first national civil rights membership organization to publicly and actively adopt this position, and the group continues to be in the forefront of advocating human rights in the United States.

gressman Norman Mineta, a former president of the JACL. He stated that marriage was a civil rights issue and asked members to support same-gender marriage. He also talked about appreciation for gay U.S. congressman Barney Frank from Massachusetts, who had given his unconditional support to the JACL. At last, a vote was taken on resolution six.

There was silence during the vote count. By a count of fifty against, thirty-eight for, eleven abstentions, and four split votes, resolution six failed. With the rejection of this resolution, the JACL had announced its national support of same-gender marriage. By rejecting the resolution, the national JACL had upheld the national board's marriage resolution.

SIGNIFICANCE

The JACL's denial of the resolution inspired same-gender couples across the nation, especially Asian Americans, to continue advocating for their rights and continue celebrating their commitments. The vote also had an impact on national politics. It led to premature same-gender marriage movements in the late 1990's in both Hawaii and Alaska, where the Alaskan and Hawaiian courts found that denying same-gender marriage violated their state's constitution. However, those court opinions were subsequently reversed by state constitutional amendments in 1998.

The vote also emboldened the JACL: It later officially opposed the Knight Initiative, a proposed marriage law in California sponsored by Republican state senator Pete Knight of Palmdale, whose son is gay. The initiative was passed by ballot on March 7, 2000. The Knight Initiative, in turn, influenced antigay and antilesbian extremists in other states. They crafted similar marriage laws to challenge or deny all equal rights and protections to LGBT people, rights such as hospital visitation, domestic-partner benefits, and even local nondiscrimination laws.

Yet, after they announced their support, the JACL has been joined by other supportive Asian and Pacific Islander organizations, such as the Asian American Legal Defense and Education Fund, the Gay Asian Pacific Alliance, the Gay Asian Pacific Support Network, and the Japanese American Bar Association. Asian Americans have supported same-gender marriage in greater numbers, as a group, than any other ethnic or racial group in the United States.

—*Mitsunori Misawa*

FURTHER READING

Berlet, Chip. *Eyes Right! Challenging the Right Wing Backlash*. Somerville, Mass.: Political Research Associates, 1995.

"Same-Sex Marriage: A Selective Bibliography of the Legal Literature." Law Library, Rutgers School of Law. http://law-library.rutgers.edu/SSM.html.

Sullivan, Andrew. *Same-Sex Marriage, Pro and Con: A Reader*. New York: Vintage Books, 1997.

Watt, Eric C. *The Making of a Gay Asian Community: An Oral History of Pre-AIDS Los Angeles*. New York: Rowman & Littlefield, 2002.

Zia, Helen. *Asian American Dreams: The Emergence of an American People*. New York: Farrar, Straus and Giroux, 2000.

SEE ALSO: Oct. 12-15, 1979: Lesbian and Gay Asian Collective Is Founded; 1981: Gay and Lesbian Palimony Suits Emerge; 1982-1991: Lesbian Academic and Activist Sues University of California for Discrimination; 1987: Asian Pacific Lesbian Network Is Founded; 1993-1996: Hawaii Opens Door to Same-Gender Marriages; Sept. 21, 1996: U.S. President Clinton Signs Defense of Marriage Act; Dec. 20, 1999: *Baker v. Vermont* Leads to Recognition of Same-Gender Civil Unions; May 25, 2001: Japanese Human Rights Council Recommends Lesbian and Gay Rights; Apr., 2003: Buenos Aires Recognizes Same-Gender Civil Unions; June 17, 2003, and July 19, 2005: Canada Legalizes Same-Gender Marriage; Nov. 18, 2003: Massachusetts Court Rules for Same-Gender Marriage; Nov. 18, 2004: United Kingdom Legalizes Same-Gender Civil Partnerships.

September 16, 1994
U.N. Revokes Consultative Status of International Lesbian and Gay Association

The United Nations Economic and Social Council revoked the consultative status granted the International Lesbian and Gay Association on grounds that some of its members were affiliated with pedophile groups. The association has yet to be reinstated.

Locale: Worldwide

Categories: Government and politics; organizations and institutions; civil rights

Key Figure

Jesse Helms (b. 1921), Republican U.S. senator from North Carolina and chair of the Senate Foreign Relations Committee

Summary of Event

The Economic and Social Council (ECOSOC) is the main United Nations body responsible for human rights. ECOSOC initiates studies, makes recommendations, and organizes international conferences. As part of its mandate, ECOSOC may grant consultative status to nongovernmental organizations (NGOs). This status gives NGOs the ability to participate as observers in ECOSOC meetings on human rights as well as the opportunity to submit written statements to the council on various issues.

The International Lesbian and Gay Association (ILGA) was founded in 1978 as a worldwide federation of gay and lesbian groups dedicated to fighting discrimination against sexual minorities. Since its foundation, ILGA, with administrative offices in Brussels, Belgium, has led successful campaigns to convince Amnesty International to include lesbians and gays in its mandate and to persuade the World Health Organization to eliminate "homosexuality" from its list of diseases and disorders.

Given the importance of the human rights work conducted by ECOSOC, ILGA attempted to gain consultative status with the United Nations body in 1991. The application was deferred for two years in the face of opposition from several nations. In July, 1993, the NGO committee of ECOSOC approved ILGA's application, but the decision still had to go to the full ECOSOC council. On July 30, 1993, ILGA finally won accreditation to ECOSOC. Only four countries voted against ILGA's application: Syria, Malaysia, Swaziland, and Togo.

In October, 1993, *Lambda Report*, an antigay publication in the United States, alerted the U.S. media that the North American Man/Boy Love Association (NAMBLA) was an ILGA member. The United States threatened to seek the revocation of ILGA's consultative status unless ILGA expelled NAMBLA and any other pedophile group. Concerned about losing its consultative status, ILGA decided to comply with U.S. demands. At its Annual World Conference held in New York City in June, 1994, ILGA expelled three pedophile groups: NAMBLA, Project Truth/Free Will, and Vereniging Martijn.

Despite ILGA's attempts to distance itself from pedophilia, the United States pushed ECOSOC to suspend ILGA's status, claiming that the organization's purge did not go far enough. Citing one member organization, the Munich-based Verein für Sexuelle Gleichberechtigung (VSG), as supporting pedophilia, conservative Republican U.S. senator Jesse Helms amended a congressional bill making U.S. funding of the United Nations contingent on the United Nations refusing to grant status to any organization that condones pedophilia. In applying the congressional prohibition, the United States threatened to cut off $118 million a year in U.N. funding unless VSG, or ILGA, got the boot. ILGA announced that the U.S. request that it prove that there were no ILGA members with ties to pedophilia was no longer acceptable. ECOSOC suspended ILGA on September 16, 1994.

> **FROM THE U.N. CONVENTION ON THE RIGHTS OF THE CHILD (1990)**
>
> *Article 34*
> States Parties undertake to protect the child from all forms of sexual exploitation and sexual abuse. For these purposes, States Parties shall in particular take all appropriate national, bilateral and multilateral measures to prevent:
> (a) The inducement or coercion of a child to engage in any unlawful sexual activity;
> (b) The exploitative use of children in prostitution or other unlawful sexual practices;
> (c) The exploitative use of children in pornographic performances and materials.
>
> *Source:* Office of the United Nations High Commissioner for Human Rights. http://www.ohchr.org/english/law/crc.htm.

SIGNIFICANCE

In 1993, significant gains had been made in many Western industrialized countries, but those gains benefited only a small fraction of lesbians and gays worldwide. In many countries, homosexuality was still diagnosed as a mental disease, penalized as a crime, and condemned as a sin. Some states continued to imprison and execute individuals for their homosexuality. Even when not criminalized, gays and lesbians were provided with little protection from harassment and persecution. Sexual minorities were also severely restricted in exercising freedom of expression and freedom of assembly.

The U.N. record on the protection of gay and lesbian people was poor. ECOSOC had taken only one initiative related to sexual minorities: a 1988 study on the legal and social problems of sexual minorities that was denounced by gay and lesbian groups as a grossly inadequate representation of homosexual men and women. In June, 1993, three lesbian and gay organizations were accredited for the U.N. World Conference on Human Rights in Vienna, Austria, but the recognition was only for the two-week conference.

Given that no government fully respected and protected human rights related to sexual orientation, the accreditation of ILGA at the United Nations was a significant breakthrough in the recognition of lesbian and gay rights at the international level. Its suspension months later was likewise a major setback. Consultative status would have given ILGA the ability to attend ECOSOC meetings and other annual human rights meetings at the United Nations, and to submit written statements on issues of concern to gays and lesbians. With the suspension of ILGA, sexual minorities around the world lost a chance to educate the world about human rights violations against lesbians and gays.

Following its suspension, ILGA in 1995 broadened its mission statement to adhere to international human rights standards, including the United Nations Convention on the Rights of the Child. ILGA's new policy recognized the right of every individual, regardless of age, to explore his or her own sexuality; at the same time ILGA supported the right of every child to protection from sexual exploitation and abuse.

ILGA has reapplied for consultative status, but ECOSOC voted on April 30, 2002, and again on January 23, 2006, to reject the organization's bid to regain admission. In May, 2006, ILGA-Europe and a German GLBT group were denied NGO status, and on June 1, the Dutch LGBT organization Cultuur en Ontspannings-Centrum, or COC, had applied for NGO consultative status, with a decision pending as of mid-June.

Despite ILGA's continued suspension from the world body, important progress has been made. Other NGOs, such as Amnesty International and Human Rights Watch, have begun to advocate on behalf of sexual minorities. On March 31, 1994, the United Nations Human Rights Committee found that gays and lesbians are covered by the privacy and equality provisions of the Covenant of Civil and Political Rights. The 1995 United Nations World Conference on Women, held in Beijing, saw U.N. member states debate human rights issues related to sexual orientation. Finally, the first resolution to deal specifically with human rights and sexual orientation was introduced at the United Nations Commission on Human Rights in 2003.

—*Nicole LaViolette*

Further Reading

Adam, Barry D., Willem Jan Duyvendak, and André Krouwel, eds. *The Global Emergence of Gay and Lesbian Politics: National Imprints of a Worldwide Movement*. Philadelphia: Temple University Press, 1999.

LaViolette Nicole, and Sandra Whitworth. "No Safe Haven: Sexuality as a Universal Human Right and Gay and Lesbian Activism in International Politics." *Millennium: Journal of International Studies* 23, no. 3 (1994): 563.

Ogilvie, Dayne. "NAMBLA Expelled from Rights Group." *Capital Xtra!*, July 15, 1994, p. 17.

Osborne, Duncan. "The Trouble with NAMBLA." *The Advocate*, December 14, 1993.

Walker, Kristen. "New Uses of the Refugees Convention: Sexuality and Refugee Status." In *The Refugees Convention Fifty Years On: Globalisation and International Law*, edited by Susan Kneebone. Burlington, Vt.: Ashgate, 2003.

See also: Aug. 8, 1978: International Lesbian and Gay Association Is Founded; Dec. 1, 1988: First World AIDS Day; 1990: International Gay and Lesbian Human Rights Commission Is Founded; June 17, 1995: International Bill of Gender Rights Is First Circulated; Oct. 9-12, 1998: First International Retreat for Lesbian and Gay Muslims Is Held.

1995
The Advocate Outs Oscar Nominee Nigel Hawthorne

British actor Nigel Hawthorne was recognized as the first openly gay best-actor nominee in the history of the Academy Awards after he was outed by The Advocate *magazine.*

Locale: Los Angeles, California
Categories: Cultural and intellectual history; publications; organizations and institutions; arts

Key Figures

Sir Nigel Hawthorne (1929-2001), British actor
Trevor Bentham (b. 1943), British writer and Hawthorne's partner
Ian McKellen (b. 1939), British actor

Summary of Event

Nigel Hawthorne was born in Coventry, England, in 1929. When he was three years old, his family moved to Cape Town, South Africa, where he later attended college at the University of Cape Town. It was there he turned to acting, despite strong opposition from his family.

Hawthorne moved to London in 1951 to be among the best actors, but London proved to be difficult. By 1957 he gave up trying to break into British theater and returned to Cape Town. Through the next five years, he was cast in leading roles at major theaters, which helped his confidence. In 1962, he returned to London, and three years later he was accepted into Joan Littlewood's Theatre Workshop. It was at this workshop that he was noticed by the prestigious Royal Court Theatre, and he was invited to act in the company.

By the 1970's, Hawthorne was working steadily, playing roles both classic and contemporary. In 1973, he played Major Flack in Peter Nichols's *Privates on Parade*, which led to his being cast in a leading role in a British sitcom called *Yes, Minister*. The program was hugely successful and finally allowed Hawthorne to pick and choose future projects. He returned to the stage during the 1980's, appearing in numerous high-profile productions, including *Shadowlands*, performed both in London and on Broadway, winning him the 1991 best actor Tony Award.

> ### HAWTHORNE "ACTING OUT"
>
> "I'm not somebody who sets himself up as an icon of sexual orientation," says veteran English actor Nigel Hawthorne. "But my private life has never been a secret. I've never been a closet queen." In fact, the 65-year-old Hawthorne is being introduced to most Americans not as a queen but as king—in the film *The Madness of King George*. With this bravura performance the unassuming actor, who defines himself as a "quiet man," is making history as the first openly gay Best Actor nominee in the history of the Academy Awards. . . .
>
> For better or worse, however, the Oscar nomination plucks Hawthorne out of the ensemble, and exposes him, basically for the first time, to the white-hot light of American publicity. And unlike his longstanding fans in Britain, his new American fans will know from the outset that Hawthorne is gay. Will this change in the actor's image carry with it the potential for negative typecasting? "Oh, I hope not!" laughs [English theater director Nicholas] Hytner. "I'm not entirely sure how Hollywood casting works. But I think only that very small group of men whose careers depend on making $10 million a movie for, to be frank, arousing teenage girls would be worried. And even then, teenage girls love all that!"
>
> As for the March 27 Oscar ceremonies, Hawthorne will be attending, accompanied by Trevor [his long-time partner]. "My friends have said, 'What about those Oscar's—with banks of photographers all clicking away and interviews all the time?'" Hawthorne says with a laugh. "And I said 'I dread it,' because I'm quite a quiet person. Trevor and I are both very quiet people, and we just want to live and keep the peace."
>
> Doubts aside, however, both partners wouldn't think of missing it. Says Hawthorne: "My idea is to have a good evening and do a bit of star spotting."
>
> *Source:* Michelle Clarkin, "Acting Out," *The Advocate*, April 4, 1995.

In part because of his success in *Shadowlands*, Hawthorne was cast in *The Madness of King George*, where he played a king descending into madness. He won an Olivier Award for his role and transferred with the production to Broadway. He was then asked to reprise his role in the film version of the play, which led to his Oscar nomination in 1995.

Hawthorne led a very happy life for many decades with his partner, writer Trevor Bentham. When his Oscar nomination was announced, he was interviewed by the American GLBT newsmagazine *The Advocate*. The magazine article (April, 1995) outed Hawthorne, declaring that he was "making history as the first openly gay best actor nominee in the history of the Academy Awards." Hawthorne claimed, however, that the magazine assured him it would not print personal information about him, such as his sexual orientation.

Hawthorne's outing seemed to have little negative impact on his career, and he continued working successfully in film, television, and on stage. In 1999, he was awarded knighthood. Shortly thereafter, he was diagnosed with pancreatic cancer, and, after having battled it for eighteen months, died from a heart attack on December 26, 2001. He finished his memoirs, *Straight Face*, two days before his death, and his autobiography was published posthumously in 2002.

SIGNIFICANCE

There are two primary issues surrounding Nigel Hawthorne's Oscar nomination. The first deals with the manner in which his sexual orientation was made public. Upon completing his interview with *The Advocate*, Hawthorne requested the newsmagazine keep his private life private, but it did not. Hawthorne felt violated after the article hit newsstands. *The Advocate* considered the article an accurate record of an open interview. The idea of outing celebrities was a hot-button issue during the early and mid-1990's, and there was tremendous backlash against the gay press for what were considered cruel and unfair practices.

The British press, especially known for its biting and cutting headlines and exposes, made much of Hawthorne's admission, with headlines such as "The Madness of Queen Nigel" and "Yes, Minister, I'm Gay!" The paparazzi became so fierce in their desire to photograph Hawthorne and partner Bentham that bodyguards were hired to protect the private couple.

The harshness of the media, along with Hawthorne's frustrations over the outing, created a backlash, as cautiousness became a part of life in Hollywood. Rather than opening the door for other closeted celebrities, Hawthorne's experience frightened them. Many celebrities refused to be interviewed by the gay press.

The second issue surrounding Hawthorne's outing was the impact an openly gay actor had on future Oscar nominations. Since his outing, there have been few openly gay Oscar nominees in acting categories, except for fellow Brit Ian McKellen, nominated in the best-actor category in 1998. In fact, most out, gay actors in the 1990's and into the twenty-first century have been British or from the United Kingdom: Rupert Everett, Alan Cumming, Simon Callow, and Steven Fry. Many others who are gay or assumed to be gay remain closeted for fear audiences will question their ability to play heterosexual characters convincingly. The early years of the twenty-first century saw lawsuits from celebrities such as Tom Cruise, suits brought against men claiming to have had sexual relationships with certain celebrities.

Although there is much to be said about the manner in which Hawthorne's orientation was discovered, there was little negative impact on his career. In fact, following his nomination, he became appreciated as one of the foremost actors of his generation. He continued to work in film, television, and theater, and even accepted gay roles, such as in the film *The Object of My Affection*.

Sir Nigel Hawthorne believed that living a positive life with his partner was as political as he should be. Though GLBT activists pleaded with him to take a vocal stand for GLBT rights, Hawthorne remained a quiet man, refusing to become politically involved.

Hawthorne's experience has shown that, despite being outed, one's career can thrive, but also that, even if one's career is not adversely affected by being outed, GLBT celebrities, too, have a right to privacy.

—*Tom Smith*

FURTHER READING

Barber, Lynn. "The King and I." *Observer Magazine*, September 5, 1999, 14-18.

Clarkin, Michelle. "Acting Out." *The Advocate*, April 4, 1995.

Gross, Larry. "Contested Closets: The Politics and Ethics of Outing." In *The Columbia Reader on Lesbians and Gay Men in Media, Society, and Politics*, edited by Larry Gross and James D. Woods. New York: Columbia University Press, 1999.

Hawthorne, Nigel. *Straight Face*. London: Sceptre, 2003.

Koenig, Rhoda. "Mad About the Boy." *The Independent: The Weekend Review*, October 16, 1999, p. 5.

Landesman, Cosmo. "The Saint and the Civil Serpent." *Sunday Times News Review*, January 3, 1999, p. 3.

Lister, David. "Old Singing Stars Set a Sixties Note." *The Independent*, December 31, 1998, p. 12.

SEE ALSO: 1930's-1960's: Hollywood Bans "Sexual Perversion" in Films; 1967: *Los Angeles Advocate* Begins Publication; 1979-1981: First Gay British Television Series Airs; July 25, 1985: Actor Hudson Announces He Has AIDS; Mar., 1987: Radical AIDS Activist Group ACT UP Is Founded; Aug. 27, 1991: *The Advocate* Outs Pentagon Spokesman Pete Williams; 1992-2002: Celebrity Lesbians Come Out; 1993: *The Wedding Banquet* Is First Acclaimed Taiwanese Gay-Themed Film; Dec. 3, 1998-Feb. 25, 1999: Screening of *Fire* Ignites Violent Protests in India; Mar. 21, 2000: Hollywood Awards Transgender Portrayals in Film; Sept. 7, 2001: First Gay and Lesbian Television Network Is Launched in Canada; Mar. 5, 2006: *Brokeback Mountain, Capote,* and *Transamerica* Receive Oscars.

1995
ATHLETE LOUGANIS ANNOUNCES HE IS HIV-POSITIVE

Diver and Olympic gold medalist Greg Louganis came out as gay to the public in his autobiography Breaking the Surface, *announcing that he was HIV-positive as well. Louganis was the first out gay athlete to come out as HIV-positive.*

LOCALE: United States
CATEGORIES: Sports; HIV-AIDS; publications

KEY FIGURE
Greg Louganis (b. 1960), diver and Olympic gold medalist

SUMMARY OF EVENT
In his youth, Greg Louganis was ridiculed for both his ethnicity (Samoan and Swedish) and his dyslexia. His interest in dance and gymnastics fueled his classmates' taunts, so at age nine his adoptive father enrolled him in diving classes. Louganis found great success there, and at age eleven he amazed crowds at the 1971 Junior Olympics when he scored a perfect 10 in competition.

Four years later, Louganis moved into the home of his coach, Sammy Lee, an Olympic diving gold medalist. Louganis began a disciplined training regime that helped him win an Olympic silver medal in 1976 for platform diving and a sixth-place finish in springboard.

In 1978, Louganis won the world platform title and accepted a diving scholarship from the University of Miami. A year later at the Pan-American Games, Louganis won both the springboard and platform and was the favorite to win the gold medal the following year at the Moscow Olympics. However, a U.S. boycott of the Games prevented him from competing.

In 1981, Louganis, who was majoring in theater, transferred to the University of California, Irvine, to train with coach Ron O'Brien. There he met Kevin, a fellow theater student, with whom he began a passionate relationship. However, the difficulty of keeping their relationship closeted from the public became too stressful, and they eventually ended their relationship.

The following year Louganis began a long winning streak, including milestones such as winning a perfect 10 from all seven judges in an international competition; he was the first man to win both springboard and platform in more than fifty years at the 1984 Olympics in Los Angeles, and the first to pass 700 points in both events at the Olympics.

Although his professional life was exceptional, Louganis's personal life was riddled with extreme highs and lows. He met and fell in love with Tom

Greg Louganis. (LAOOC, Department of Special Collections, University Research Library, UCLA)

> **LOUGANIS: "WHAT IF I'M BLEEDING?"**
>
> As I [Greg Louganis] swam toward the side of the pool, all kinds of thoughts raced through my head: What if I cut my scalp? What if I'm bleeding? Is there blood in the pool? What happens if I get blood on someone? In normal circumstances that wouldn't have been such a bug deal, but these were anything but normal circumstances. I was in a total panic that I might cause someone else harm. It was sheer terror. I didn't even pause to think that I might be badly injured. But whatever was going through my mind, I had to get out of the pool.
>
> *Source:* Greg Louganis, *Breaking the Surface* (New York: Random House, 1995), p. 5.

Barrett, and the two quickly moved in together. Barrett soon took over Louganis's personal and business affairs, and the relationship eventually turned abusive. Years later, Barrett became ill with AIDS; six months before the 1988 Summer Olympics in Seoul, Korea, Louganis was tested and discovered he was HIV-positive. He decided to keep quiet about his status, and he continued to train and compete.

In 1988 at the Seoul Olympics, leading as he went into the ninth round of the preliminaries, Louganis hit his head on the springboard, breaking the skin and causing his head to bleed. He returned thirty-five minutes later with sutures, finished the competition, then went to the hospital for stitches. He returned the next day, hitting all eleven dives and easily winning the competition.

"I was in a total panic that I might cause someone else harm," Louganis wrote in his 1995 autobiography *Breaking the Surface*. "I wanted to warn Puffer [who treated his head injury in 1988 without wearing gloves] but I was paralyzed. Everything was all so mixed up at that point: the HIV, the shock and embarrassment of hitting my head and an awful feeling that it was all over."

Louganis retired from competition in 1989 and turned to acting, in which he had majored in college. He most notably appeared as a chorus boy who dies of AIDS in the 1993 Off-Broadway production of *Jeffrey*.

Louganis eventually broke off his relationship with Barrett, who threatened to go public with Louganis's HIV status. Barrett eventually rescinded his threat, but only after Louganis had agreed to pay all his expenses until he died. Barrett died a short time later, and Louganis decided it was time to come out as an HIV-positive and gay athlete.

In 1994, Louganis publicly declared that he was gay during a videotaped message to athletes competing at Gay Games IV in New York. His memoir, *Breaking the Surface*, was ultimately adapted as a television movie, in which he came out as HIV-positive. The release of his book was met with a media blitz, including an interview on the television show *20/20* in which Louganis confirmed his HIV status publicly to interviewer Barbara Walters.

Louganis has since worked for organizations supporting dyslexia and drug and alcohol awareness. He lives in Southern California.

SIGNIFICANCE

Greg Louganis was not the first major athlete to come out as HIV-positive; tennis player Arthur Ashe and basketball star Magic Johnson had done so before him. However, Louganis was the first out *gay* athlete to do so. In that respect, he opened a door in professional sports.

Although many were shocked by Louganis's disclosure, it gave a new and famous face to the AIDS epidemic and renewed lagging vigilance to raise funds for AIDS research. Also, it is important to remember that Louganis achieved many of his career goals after the development of seroconverting; thus, he gave the world a positive view of living with HIV. When he made public his status in 1995, he had already been living with the virus for many years, and people benefited from being able to attach a healthy and successful image to an HIV-positive person.

Upon revealing his status, much was made in the press about his 1988 diving accident and the possibility he infected other divers. Many questioned whether or not Louganis had an obligation to notify Olympic officials of his HIV status. Ultimately, this debate brought AIDS education to the national airwaves as health care professionals discussed the unlikelihood of transmission of HIV in a heavily chlorinated pool.

This scandal only helped Louganis's autobiography, *Breaking the Surface*, to the top of *The New York Times* best-seller list. The further admissions in his book about gay spousal abuse, addictions to drugs and alcohol, a tortured childhood, and his ultimate climb to the top of the diving world helped Americans, who had been consumed with the O. J. Simpson trial, renew their faith in an athlete who overcame great obstacles to become an American hero.

—*Tom Smith*

FURTHER READING

Anderson, Eric. *In the Game: Gay Athletes and the Cult of Masculinity*. Albany: State University of New York Press, 2005.

Bronski, Michael, ed. *Outstanding Lives: Profiles of Lesbians and Gay Men*. New York: Visible Ink Press, 1997.

International Olympic Committee. "Policy on HIV/AIDS." http://www.multimedia.olympic.org/pdf/en_report_1053.pdf.

Louganis, Greg, and Eric Marcus. *Breaking the Surface*. New York: Plume Books, 1995.

Lutes, Michael A. "Greg Louganis." In *Gay and Lesbian Biography*, edited by Michael J. Tyrkus. Detroit, Mich.: St. James Press, 1997.

Mackay, Duncan. "Gay Greg Dives into New Script." *The Observer Sport*, January, 2000, 16.

"U.S. Olympic Gold Medalist Has AIDS." *Gay Times*, April, 1995, p. 33.

SEE ALSO: Aug. 28, 1982: First Gay Games Are Held in San Francisco; Spring, 1984: AIDS Virus Is Discovered; July 25, 1985: Actor Hudson Announces He Has AIDS; 1992-2002: Celebrity Lesbians Come Out; 1994: Navratilova Honored for Her Career in Tennis; May 17, 2004: Transsexual Athletes Allowed to Compete in Olympic Games.

June 17, 1995
INTERNATIONAL BILL OF GENDER RIGHTS IS FIRST CIRCULATED

The International Bill of Gender Rights, a statement created to address and outline the rights of transgender people but applicable to all, regardless of gender expression or sexuality, is the first circulated document of its kind. The bill has yet to be adopted by any official governmental body, but it has been used as a guide for a number of governmental agencies around the world that have adopted similar civil rights bills.

LOCALE: Houston, Texas
CATEGORIES: Transgender/transsexuality; civil rights; government and politics; organizations and institutions

KEY FIGURES

JoAnn Roberts, scholar, who wrote an early draft of a gender rights bill
Sharon Stuart (b. 1940), attorney, who wrote an early draft of a gender rights bill and is now the principal drafter and compiler for the IBGR
Phyllis Randolph Frye, attorney, who convened the conference that adopted the bill

SUMMARY OF EVENT

The International Bill of Gender Rights (IBGR) was adopted by the International Conference on Transgender Law and Employment Policy (ICTLEP) on June 17, 1995, in Houston, Texas. The bill has no authoritative or legal effect as it has yet to be adopted by any legislative body such as the United Nations or by any country. The bill contains ten rights for all people, regardless of their claimed gender identity.

The text of the bill was written and edited by several people. A bill of gender rights was first written by JoAnn Roberts in 1991 and then circulated for community input. This first draft is considered the basis for the current IBGR that was developed and maintained by the ICTLEP. Roberts is a cofounder of the Renaissance Transgender Association, Inc., the largest open-membership support organization for transgender people in the United States.

In 1991, attorney Sharon Stuart proposed a gender bill of rights in the newsletter of the International Foundation for Gender Education (IFGE). While Roberts and Stuart approached the text of the bill differently, the underlying premises were sufficiently similar. Thus, Stuart was able to incorporate the ideas from both documents into the first draft of the existing bill, the International Bill of Gender Rights. Stuart's draft was presented at the second annual meeting of the ICTLEP in 1993. Those who worked extensively on the draft at that time include Susan Stryker, Jan Eaton, Martine Rothblatt, and Phyllis Randolph Frye.

The ICTLEP was formed in 1992 by transgender activists and attorneys Stuart and Frye to convene law conferences for transgender lawyers and laypersons. The conferences provide a forum for the discussion of strategies for changing existing policy and creating new laws at community and national levels. Stuart has served as ICTLEP's gender rights director and is a law librarian. Frye has been a trial attorney in private practice since 1981 and was an adjunct professor at the Thurgood Marshall Law School at Texas Southern University in Houston. Frye was awarded the Creating Change Community Services Award, along with "the transgender community," from the National Gay and Lesbian Task Force in 1995, and the Virginia Prince Lifetime Contribution Award from the International Foundation for Gender Education in 1999.

SIGNIFICANCE

The International Bill of Gender Rights has not been adopted in its totality by any country or any lo-

---

INTERNATIONAL BILL OF GENDER RIGHTS

- The right to define gender identity.
- The right to free expression of gender identity.
- The right to secure and retain employment and to receive just compensation.
- The right of access to gendered space and participation in gendered activity.
- The right to control and change one's own body.
- The right to competent medical and professional care.
- The right to freedom from psychiatric diagnosis or treatment.
- The right to sexual expression.
- The right to form committed, loving relationships and enter into marital contracts.
- The right to conceive, bear, or adopt children; the right to nurture and have custody of children and to exercise parental capacity.

Source: Phyllis Randolph Frye. http://www.transgenderlegal.com/ibgr.htm.

---

cal government, and there is no federal U.S. law that protects transgender people from discrimination. However, several of the principles expressed in the document have been included in antidiscrimination laws in at least four states and fifty cities and counties in the United States. California, Minnesota, New Mexico, and Rhode Island protect transgender people from discrimination through state laws. Among the cities that have passed this legislation are Atlanta, Boston, Chicago, Dallas, Houston, New York, Philadelphia, San Diego, and San Francisco, as well as the smaller municipalities of Covington, Kentucky; Huntington Woods, Michigan; Iowa City, Iowa; New Hope, Pennsylvania; and Peoria, Illinois.

In 2002, the New York city council adopted a law that protects the rights of transgender people in housing, employment, and public accommodations, but discrimination against transgender people has not ended in the city. Charges had been brought against the city's Equal Employment Practices Commission, claiming that the commission failed to investigate a number of complaints of discrimination in housing and employment. Internationally, countries that have worked on legislation recognizing and protecting the rights of transgender people include Canada, South Africa, Australia, the United Kingdom, and other countries of western Europe.

—Shelley Bannister

FURTHER READING

Frye, Phyllis Randolph. "The International Bill of Gender Rights vs. the Cider House Rules: Transgenders Struggle with the Courts over What Clothing They Are Allowed to Wear on the Job, Which Restroom They Are Allowed to Use on the Job, Their Right to Marry, and the Very Definition of Their Sex." *William & Mary Journal of Women and the Law* 7, no. 3 (2000).

Gilbert, Michael, ed. *International Journal of Transgenderism* 4, no. 3 (July/September, 2000). Special issue, "What Is Transgender?" http://www.symposion.com/ijt/index.htm.

Hunter, Nan D., Courtney G. Joslin, and Sharon M. McGowan. *The Rights of Lesbians, Gay Men, Bisexuals, and Transgender People*. 4th ed. Carbondale: Southern Illinois University Press, 2004.

Sharpe, Andrew N. *Transgender Jurisprudence: Dysphoric Bodies of Law*. London: Cavendish, 2002.

Swan, Wallace K., ed. *Gay/Lesbian/Bisexual/Transgender Public Policy Issues: A Citizen's and Administrator's Guide to the New Cultural Struggle*. New York: Haworth Press, 1997.

"When Is a Man a Man, and When Is a Woman a Woman?" *Florida Law Review* 52 (2000).

Whittle, Stephen. *Respect and Equality: Transsexual and Transgender Rights*. Portland, Oreg.: Cavendish, 2002.

SEE ALSO: Aug. 8, 1978: International Lesbian and Gay Association Is Founded; Dec. 1, 1988: First World AIDS Day; 1990: International Gay and Lesbian Human Rights Commission Is Founded; 1992: Transgender Nation Holds Its First Protest; Sept. 16, 1994: U.N. Revokes Consultative Status of International Lesbian and Gay Association; Nov. 20, 2003: Transgender Day of Remembrance and Remembering Our Dead Project; May 17, 2004: Transsexual Athletes Allowed to Compete in Olympic Games.

December 4, 1995
LESBIAN COUPLE MURDERED IN OREGON

Roxanne Ellis and Michelle Abdill, lesbian activists and property managers, were brutally murdered in what most consider a hate crime. GLBT rights organizations subsequently demanded a U.S. Justice Department inquiry into the link between hate crimes and antigay ballot initiatives, which had been proliferating in the state of Oregon, where the murders occurred. Furthermore, there was a national push to have sexual orientation covered by federal hate-crime legislation.

LOCALE: Medford, Oregon
CATEGORIES: Crime; laws, acts, and legal history; civil rights

KEY FIGURES
Roxanne Ellis (1941-1995), co-owner of a property management company, lesbian rights activist, and Abdill's domestic partner
Michelle Abdill (1953-1995), co-owner of a property management company, lesbian rights activist, and Ellis's domestic partner
Robert Acremant (b. 1968), convicted murderer

SUMMARY OF EVENT
Roxanne Ellis and Michelle Abdill, along with Ellis's daughter and granddaughter, had left Colorado Springs, Colorado, in 1990 to relocate to Medford, Oregon. The women, who in 1995 (the year of their deaths) had been partners for twelve years,

Roxanne Ellis and Michelle Abdill are remembered at a candlelight vigil in West Hollywood, California, twenty-five days after they were murdered in Medford, Oregon. (AP/Wide World Photos)

were very active in their new community. They set up a property management company, worked rigorously to defeat the 1992 and 1994 antigay ballot initiatives in Oregon, spoke at schools and churches about their experiences as lesbians, appeared on television to talk about local GLBT rights causes, and served on the board of their local church.

At 11:00 A.M. on December 4, 1995, Ellis had been showing a rental property to a prospective client. As the day progressed, Ellis failed to respond to several calls from her daughter, Lori Ellis. At 4:00 P.M., Lori received what she called a "strange" phone call from her mother saying she was going shopping. Roxanne Ellis then called her partner, Michelle Abdill, saying that her car battery had died. At around 5:00 P.M., Abdill left the office to help Ellis with her car. Later in the day, Lori drove to the apartment where her mother had the morning appointment and saw her mother's pickup truck. As Lori pulled into the complex, the pickup drove off, but Lori could not catch up. The truck was discovered in the parking lot of an apartment complex across town by a cable television installer on December 7. Police found the bodies of Ellis and Abdill in the bed of the truck. Both women were bound, gagged, and blindfolded with duct tape, and each had been fatally shot twice in the head.

The mother of Robert Acremant, the convicted killer of Ellis and Abdill, had contacted police after hearing about the case, saying she believed her son was involved in the murders. Police tracked Acremant and found him in Stockton, California, and arrested him there on December 13, 1995. Acremant had worked as a trucking company efficiency expert and in computer software development, and had served in the U.S. Air Force for four years.

Acremant told police first that he had intended to rob Ellis and Abdill and win back his estranged former girlfriend with the money. Acremant claimed that when the women refused to write him a $50,000 check, he tied them up, put them in the truck, and shot them. In this first account, Acremant said that since he knew the two women were lesbians, it was easier to kill them.

While awaiting trial, Acremant sent a letter to the *Stockton Record*, his hometown newspaper, claiming he killed Ellis and Abdill because he hated homosexuals. He admitted to making up the robbery story because he was afraid he would be mistreated by fellow inmates if he were sent to prison. Despite this admission, much of the news media maintained the robbery story, mostly neglecting to mention Acremant's reaction to Ellis's and Abdill's sexual orientation. The women's purses, wallets, jewelry, cell phones, and money were all found with their bodies in the truck.

On October 27, 1997, Robert Acremant was sentenced to death for the murders of Roxanne Ellis and Michelle Abdill. Acremant then stood trial in California for the murder of his twenty-three-year-old friend, Scott George. On October 4, 2002, Acremant was given a second death sentence. He is on death row at Oregon State Penitentiary in Salem. He has appealed his death sentence for Ellis's and Abdill's murders and is awaiting trial.

SIGNIFICANCE

Nationally, the women's murders came at a time when hate crimes against lesbians and gays—and those perceived to be lesbian or gay—were on the rise. According to the National Gay and Lesbian Task Force, there were 151 murders between 1992 and 1994 of persons assumed to be lesbian or gay. The same time period saw antigay ballot initiatives surfacing in Oregon, Colorado, Idaho, and Maine. Lesbian and gay rights organizations asserted that the push to limit legal protections for lesbians and gays had caused a surge in antigay violence.

The murder of Ellis and Abdill impelled GLBT rights organizations to demand a U.S. Justice Department inquiry into the link between the rise in hate crimes and antigay ballot initiatives. There also was a national push to have sexuality covered by federal hate-crime legislation. In 1999, the Hate Crimes Prevention Act was introduced into Congress with the support of President Bill Clinton. The bill passed in the Senate but was defeated by the House of Representatives. The administration of President George W. Bush has not supported the Hate Crimes Prevention Act, arguing that all murders are hateful, so therefore women, homosexuals, and the disabled (those excluded from existing federal hate crime legislation) do not need "special status."

Locally, Oregon's lesbian and gay community and its supporters were outraged and terrified by the murders of Ellis and Abdill. In both 1992 and 1994, the community narrowly defeated two statewide ballot measures prohibiting legal protections for lesbian, gay, and bisexual residents of the state. Ellis and Abdill were very active in helping to defeat these statewide measures, and their murders came as a blow to the entire community.

Additionally, Medford is home to several ultraconservative hate groups, including the Aryan Nations, Christian Identity, and the Ku Klux Klan, as well as two citizens' militias. Two years before the murders, Medford and surrounding counties approved local antigay rights ordinances. The murders sparked a split and debate within the local community. Some voiced their concerns about what they saw as growing violence directed toward lesbian and gay people, while others insisted that the murders were not in any way motivated by the women's sexual orientation.

In 1996, community members opened the Abdill-Ellis Lambda Community Center, which offers programs that range from support groups to HIV education to a hotline. The center, always seeking funds and other support, remains a vital local resource, and it serves as a memorial to Abdill and Ellis. Their deaths—and their lives—have left an everlasting impression, both locally and nationally.

—Jenn Rosen

FURTHER READING

Abdill-Ellis Lambda Community Center. http://www.abdellis.org.

Bright, Susie. *Susie Bright's Sexual State of the Union*. New York: Simon & Schuster, 1997.

Murphy, Kim. "No Place to Rest." *Los Angeles Times*, December 20, 1995, p. E1.

Neff, Lisa. "When Lesbians Are Targets." *The Advocate*, September 12, 2000, 36-37.

"Suspect Says He Killed Couple Because They Were Homosexual." Associated Press, August 21, 1996.

Tuller, David. "An End to Innocence: Killing of Lesbians Rattles Oregon Town." *San Francisco Chronicle*, December 11, 1995, p. A1.

SEE ALSO: Nov. 27, 1978: White Murders Politicians Moscone and Milk; 1981: Parents, Families, and Friends of Lesbians and Gays Is Founded; Nov. 8, 1988: Oregon Repeals Ban on Antigay Job Discrimination; Nov. 3, 1992: Oregon and Colorado Attempt Antigay Initiatives; Dec. 24, 1993-Dec. 31, 1993: Transgender Man Brandon Teena Raped and Murdered; Oct. 6-7, 1998: Gay College Student Shepard Is Beaten and Murdered; Oct. 4, 2002: Transgender Teen Gwen Araujo Is Murdered in California.

1996
HART RECOGNIZED AS A TRANSGENDER MAN

Physician and novelist Alan Hart, who was named Lucille at birth but lived his life as a man, was one of the first individuals to reassign his gender through surgical means, inspiring transsexual and transgender activists beginning in the late twentieth century. In 1995, Oregon activists demanded that a local political action committee stop using "Lucille" Hart as part of the name of its annual awards event and to recognize Hart's chosen and preferred gender identity.

LOCALE: Portland, Oregon
CATEGORIES: Transgender/transsexuality; health and medicine; organizations and institutions

KEY FIGURES
Alan Lucill Hart (1890-1962), physician, novelist, and female-to-male transgender
Joshua Allen Gilbert (1867-1948), psychiatrist who treated and wrote about Hart

SUMMARY OF EVENT

Alan Hart's story became known to the GLBT community with the publication of gay historian Jonathan Ned Katz's seminal work *Gay American History: Lesbians and Gay Men in the U.S.A.* In this 1976 book, Katz described Hart as a "passing woman," one of several in the late nineteenth and early twentieth centuries who donned male apparel and worked in traditionally male jobs. While some of these passing women were lesbians, others were what are now called transgender men.

Hart, originally named Alberta Lucille, was born in Hall's Summit, Kansas, on October 4, 1890. As a child, he enjoyed boys' chores and disliked girls' housework and amusements. Hart later recalled that he always regarded himself as a boy and believed he could live as a boy if his family let him cut his hair and wear trousers. From his teen years onward, he preferred tailored men's clothing and had a succession of emotionally and physically intimate relationships with women, in which he always took on a role defined as masculine.

After attending Albany College and Stanford University, Hart—the only female-born person in the class—obtained a medical degree from the University of Oregon in 1917. That same year, feeling conflicted about his identity and having contemplated suicide, Hart consulted psychiatrist Joshua Allen Gilbert. After attempting various forms of therapy without success, Hart asked Gilbert to help him obtain a hysterectomy and to adopt a male role permanently. In 1917, Hart underwent the surgery, changed his name, and married a schoolteacher, Inez Stark, who knew that Hart had been born female.

Hart started a medical practice in Oregon, but before long he was recognized by a former associate, forcing him to embark on a life of attempts to outrun his past by frequently relocating. Nevertheless, he built a successful medical career, obtained master's degrees from the University of Pennsylvania and Yale University, and published a medical text on radiology as well as four novels. After Stark left Hart in 1925, he soon married Edna Ruddick, with whom he remained until his death from heart disease on July 1, 1962.

In the October, 1920, issue of the *Journal of Nervous and Mental Disease*, Gilbert wrote a case report about Hart (referred to as "H") entitled "Homosexuality and Its Treatment." Historian Katz discovered Gilbert's report while researching his pioneering book on gay and lesbian history. Katz surmised that, "[D]espite the confusion of Dr. Gilbert and 'H' herself about her sexual nature, 'H' is clearly a Lesbian, a woman-loving woman." As Katz saw it, Hart wanted to live a man's life—not possess a male body—and had a hysterectomy only to "legitimize for herself her socially unsanctioned relations."

However, in the early 1990's, the burgeoning transgender movement began to reclaim historical figures believed to have been wrongly considered gay or lesbian; one of these figures was Hart. In Portland, Oregon, a debate ensued between the transgender community and a gay and lesbian political action committee called Right to Privacy (RTP), which had named its long-running fund-raising awards dinner after "Lucille" Hart. Candace Hellen Brown, a male-to-female transsexual, wrote in a letter to the editor published in the October 7, 1994, issue of *Just Out* that "Alan Hart is one of our heroes. Please don't let him be taken away from us." The following spring, transgender activists organized the Ad Hoc Committee of Transsexuals to Recognize Alan Hart. On October 14, 1995, the committee and the activist group Lesbian Avengers—wearing buttons proclaiming "His Name Was Alan"—protested at the Portland convention center during the annual RTP awards dinner. "Rather than a lesbian unable to bear life as a woman, Hart should be recognized for what he was, a transsexual man who had the courage to be true to himself," read the ad hoc group's flier.

In January, 1996, RTP leaders met with transgender activists to discuss the matter. Later that year, RTP dropped Hart's name from its event. After RTP dissolved in 1999, some former members joined another gay and lesbian group called Basic Rights Oregon (BRO). In September, 2000, BRO revived the tradition of hosting a fund-raising dinner named after Hart, but they called it the Hart Dinner—with no first name—and referred to Hart as "her/him."

Significance

Alan Hart's story illustrates the changing understanding of queer identities over time. Neither Hart nor Gilbert used the term "transsexual," which was not coined until 1949. Yet at a time when hormone therapy was not readily available, Hart took all the measures available to him—including one of the first-ever gender reassignment surgeries—to live the gender of his choice. The steps he took to reconcile the gender assigned to him at birth with his own gender identity place Hart him firmly on the transgender spectrum. Ascribing modern identities to individuals from the past remains problematic, however.

Historian Susan Stryker (a transgender woman) wrote that she had reservations about using the contemporary word "transsexual" to describe people who lived or flourished before the mid-twentieth century, and in a 1998 article, scholar and transgender activist C. Jacob Hale (a transgender man) described Hart as a key figure in the "butch/FTM border wars" in which different groups each seek to claim revered historical figures as their own.

Although the "border wars" continue, the transgender community has made great strides in the past decade or so in organizing as a distinct movement, and also in educating the lesbian and gay community and society at large about gender and sexual identity, and the blurred and fluid boundaries of gender, sex, and sexuality.

—*Liz Highleyman*

Further Reading

Gilbert, J. Allen. "Homosexuality and Its Treatment." *Journal of Nervous and Mental Disease*

52, no. 4 (October, 1920): 297-332.

Hansen, Bert. "Public Careers and Private Sexuality: Some Gay and Lesbian Lives in the History of Medicine and Public Health." *American Journal of Public Health* 92, no. 1 (January, 2002).

Katz, Jonathan Ned. *Gay American History: Lesbians and Gay Men in the U.S.A., a Documentary History*. 1976. Reprint. New York: Meridian, 1992.

Lauderdale, Thomas, and Tom Cook. "The Incredible Life and Loves of the Legendary Lucille Hart." *Alternative Connection* 2, nos. 12-13 (September/October, 1993).

O'Hartigan, Margaret Deirdre. "Alan Hart." In *The Phallus Palace: Female to Male Transsexuals*, edited by Dean Kotula and William Parker. Los Angeles: Alyson, 2002.

SEE ALSO: Nov. 11, 1865: Mary Edwards Walker Is Awarded the Medal of Honor; Jan.-June, 1886: Two-Spirit American Indian Visits Washington, D.C.; 1912-1924: Robles Fights in the Mexican Revolution; Sept. 24, 1951: George Jorgensen Becomes Christine Jorgensen; 1976: Katz Publishes First Lesbian and Gay History Anthology; Jan. 21, 1989: Death of Transgender Jazz Musician Billy Tipton; 1992: Transgender Nation Holds Its First Protest; 1998: Transgender Scholarship Proliferates; Mar. 21, 2000: Hollywood Awards Transgender Portrayals in Film; Mar., 2003-Dec., 2004: Transsexuals Protest Academic Exploitation; Nov. 20, 2003: Transgender Day of Remembrance and Remembering Our Dead Project; May 17, 2004: Transsexual Athletes Allowed to Compete in Olympic Games.

September 21, 1996
U.S. PRESIDENT CLINTON SIGNS DEFENSE OF MARRIAGE ACT

U.S. president Bill Clinton signed into law an act that defines marriage as "the legal union between one man and one woman" and that denies federal benefits to same-gender married couples. The law asserts that although no state is required to recognize same-gender marriages conducted in other states, the law does not keep states from recognizing those same marriages if they choose to do so.

LOCALE: Washington, D.C.
CATEGORIES: Civil rights; government and politics; laws, acts, and legal history; religion

KEY FIGURES
Robert Barr (b. 1948), Republican U.S. representative, Georgia
Lou Sheldon (b. 1934), reverend, Traditional Values Coalition
Bill Clinton (b. 1946), U.S. president, 1993-2001

SUMMARY OF EVENT
Motivated by concerns over same-gender marriage litigation in Hawaii, the 104th Congress passed the Defense of Marriage Act (DOMA) during the summer and fall of 1996. The law defines "marriage" as the union between a man and a woman, prevents same-gender couples legally married in a given state from receiving federal benefits, and allows states to refuse to recognize same-gender marriages from other states. Although the necessity and constitutionality of DOMA have been questioned, the bill may be the most important piece of national legislation to date affecting the lives of gays and lesbians.

The salience of same-gender marriage has increased considerably since the Hawaii Supreme Court opened the door to its legal recognition in 1993, but as a political issue, same-gender marriage is nothing new. For lesbian and gay civil rights advocates in particular, the issue has been part of the

> **FROM THE DEFENSE OF MARRIAGE ACT**
>
> *An Act*
> *To define and protect the institution of marriage.*
> Be it enacted by the Senate and House of Representatives of the United States of America in Congress assembled,
> Sec. 1. Short Title. This Act may be cited as the "Defense of Marriage Act."
> Sec. 2. Powers Reserved to the States.
> (a) In General—Chapter 115 of Title 28, United States Code, is amended by adding after Section 1738B the following:
> "Sec. 1738C. *Certain acts, records, and proceedings and the effect thereof*
> 'No State, territory, or possession of the United States, or Indian tribe, shall be required to give effect to any public act, record, or judicial proceeding of any other State, territory, possession, or tribe, respecting a relationship between persons of the same sex that is treated as a marriage under the laws of such other State, territory, possession, or tribe, or a right or claim arising from such relationship.'" . . .
> Sec. 3. *Definition of Marriage.*
> (a) In General—Chapter 1 of Title 1, United States Code, is amended by adding at the end the following:
> "Sec. 7. Definition of 'marriage' and 'spouse'
> 'In determining the meaning of any Act of Congress, or of any ruling, regulation, or interpretation of the various administrative bureaus and agencies of the United States, the word "marriage" means only a legal union between one man and one woman as husband and wife, and the word "spouse" refers only to a person of the opposite sex who is a husband or a wife.'" . . .

political agenda since the early 1970's. In 1993, however, the Hawaii Supreme Court ruled in *Baehr v. Lewin* (renamed *Baehr v. Miike*) that the state's denial of marriage licenses to same-gender couples amounted to gender discrimination and was unconstitutional under the Hawaii constitution. The ruling ignited both hope and fear that same-gender marriages might become legal in Hawaii and that other states might be forced to recognize these marriages.

By late 1995 and early 1996, a broad coalition of national conservative Christian groups, including the American Family Association, the Christian Coalition, Concerned Women of America, the Eagle Forum, the Family Research Council, Focus on the Family, and the Traditional Values Coalition, began a nationwide legislative campaign to ban the recognition of same-gender marriages. In January, 1996, the main arm of the coalition, the National Campaign to Protect Marriage (NCPM) formed during meetings of Christian Right groups in Memphis, Tennessee. The NCPM helped to distribute a video called *The Ultimate Target of the Gay Agenda: Same Sex Marriages* to national and state legislators. The NCPM officially kicked-off its campaign at a February 10, 1996, rally in Des Moines, Iowa, with a display of a "marriage protection resolution," endorsed by all of the 1996 Republican presidential candidates. The campaign was so successful that by March, 1998, all but two states had considered legislation banning the recognition of same-gender marriages, twenty-eight had adopted such bans, and the federal government had adopted DOMA.

DOMA (H.R. 3396) outlines the denial of federal benefits to same-gender married couples and allows individual states to deny the recognition of such marriages conducted in other states. H.R. 3396 had 105 Republican and 12 Democratic cosponsors. The U.S. Senate companion bill was S.R. 1740, sponsored by Republican senator Don Nickles of Oklahoma and twenty-four cosponsors. H.R. 3396 was drafted by Representative Robert Barr, a Republican from Georgia, with the help of Reverend Lou Sheldon of the Traditional Values Coalition, as part of a Republican package of "family values" legislation. Barr argued that proponents of same-gender marriage wanted "to throw open the doors of the U.S. Treasury . . . to be raided by the homosexual movement." Out gay representative Barney Frank, a Democrat from Massachusetts, failed in his attempt to amend the bill—after a vote of 103-311—and therefore limit its scope. With the support of out gay representative Steve Gunderson, a Republican from

Wisconsin, a California Democrat tried to amend the bill with language that would have required the General Accounting Office to study the differences and the benefits, rights, and privileges available to persons in a marriage versus those persons in a domestic partnership. This amendment failed as well, and the bill passed 342-67, with some Democrats (65), one independent (Bernard Sanders of Vermont), and one Republican (Gunderson) opposing the measure.

House hearings on DOMA contained arguments on morality, civil rights, and gay and lesbian families. For example, Republican representative James Sensenbrenner of Wisconsin argued that "one of the problems our society faces today is the erosion of the family and the erosion of the marriage because the marriage is the bond that keeps the family together, and that's why I strongly support this legislation." Meanwhile, gay activist and writer Andrew Sullivan argued against DOMA, countering that allowing same-gender marriage would "promote stability, responsibility, the disciplines of family life among people."

DOMA hearings in the Senate also revolved around the notion of a "normal" family and deciding if that definition could be expanded. The hearings included testimony from religious conservatives and gay and lesbian activists, including the president of Parents, Families, and Friends of Lesbians and Gays (PFLAG).

House and Senate floor debate on DOMA mirrored the committee testimony. In referring to DOMA, Representative Steve Largent, a Republican from Oklahoma, argued that there "is absolutely nothing that we can do that is more important than protecting our families and protecting the institution of marriage." House Democrats who opposed the bill chose not to argue their point in terms of the legitimacy of gay and lesbian families, but argued instead that DOMA was unconstitutional and was a political maneuver designed to coincide with a presidential election year. However, Gunderson did argue that Congress should consider adopting a national domestic-partnership law for gay and lesbian couples. Finally, perhaps the most dramatic episode of the Senate debate was when Senator Robert Byrd, a Democrat from West Virginia, held up his family Bible to support the legislation and his definition of the American family.

Although President Clinton has been called the most GLBT-friendly U.S. president ever, he chose to sign DOMA late on a Saturday night (September 21, 1996), making the legislation law (Public Law No: 104-199). The oldest national GLBT rights group in the United States, the National Gay and Lesbian Task Force, responded harshly.

SIGNIFICANCE

Although Congress grew more conservative following the passage of DOMA, GLBT activists have gained some legislative victories. For example, efforts by conservatives to overturn Clinton's 1998 ban on sexual-orientation discrimination for federal civilian employees were defeated, and Republican efforts to pass legislation prohibiting unmarried couples from jointly adopting children in the District of Columbia were blocked in 1998. Although GLBT activists were deeply upset and even confused by Clinton's signing of DOMA, he still is viewed in a positive light by many in the GLBT community.

With or without the passage of DOMA, the debate over same-gender marriage grew far more intense in 2003 and 2004. As the U.S. Supreme Court overturned state sodomy laws and Canadian provinces upheld same-gender marriages in the summer of 2003, calls increased for a constitutional amendment to ban same-gender marriage. Barr, however, said he was opposed to the federal-level amendment because it would be unnecessary, that the issue of same-gender marriage is an issue the states should handle.

In November, 2003, the Massachusetts Supreme Judicial Court legalized same-gender marriage in that state, setting off a new round of federal and state activity on the issue, including a failed attempt in the U.S. Senate in July, 2004, to pass a constitutional ban. The Senate was scheduled to debate and vote again in June, 2006, on a constitutional amendment defining marriage as a union between a woman and a man.

In August of 2004, DOMA was upheld as constitutional for the first time by a federal court. At the same time, the House of Representatives had been considering the Marriage Protection Act (or Amendment), which would invoke a provision of DOMA to strip federal courts of their jurisdiction to rule on challenges to state bans on same-gender marriages. On November 29, 2004, however, the Supreme Court refused to overturn same-gender marriage rights in Massachusetts. Clearly, the passage of DOMA did not settle the same-gender marriage debate.

—Donald P. Haider-Markel

FURTHER READING

Gross, Larry, and James D. Woods. *The Columbia Reader on Lesbians & Gay Men in Media, Society, and Politics*. New York: Columbia University Press, 1999.

Haider-Markel, Donald P. "Defense, Morality, Civil Rights, and Family: The Evolution of Lesbian and Gay Issues in the U.S. Congress." In *Queer Families, Queer Politics: Challenging Culture and the State*, edited by Mary Bernstein and Renate Reimann. New York: Columbia University Press, 2001.

_____. "Policy Diffusion as a Geographical Expansion of the Scope of Political Conflict: Same-Sex Marriage Bans in the 1990's." *State Politics and Policy Quarterly* 1, no. 1 (2001): 5-26.

Kotulski, Davina. *Why You Should Give a Damn About Gay Marriage*. Los Angeles: Alyson, 2004.

Rayside, David Morton. *On the Fringe: Gays and Lesbians in Politics*. Ithaca, N.Y.: Cornell University Press, 1998.

Rimmerman, Craig A., Kenneth D. Wald, and Clyde Wilcox, eds. *The Politics of Gay Rights*. Chicago: University of Chicago Press, 2000.

"Same-Sex Marriage: A Selective Bibliography of the Legal Literature." Law Library, Rutgers School of Law. http://law-library.rutgers.edu/SSM.html.

SEE ALSO: 1981: Gay and Lesbian Palimony Suits Emerge; 1993-1996: Hawaii Opens Door to Same-Gender Marriages; Aug. 6, 1994: Japanese American Citizens League Supports Same-Gender Marriage; Dec. 20, 1999: *Baker v. Vermont* Leads to Recognition of Same-Gender Civil Unions; Feb. 21, 2003: Australian Court Validates Transsexual Marriage; Apr., 2003: Buenos Aires Recognizes Same-Gender Civil Unions; June 17, 2003, and July 19, 2005: Canada Legalizes Same-Gender Marriage; Nov. 18, 2003: Massachusetts Court Rules for Same-Gender Marriage; Nov. 18, 2004: United Kingdom Legalizes Same-Gender Civil Partnerships; Apr. 4, 2005: United Kingdom's Gender Recognition Act Legalizes Transsexual Marriage.

1998
Transgender Scholarship Proliferates

The late 1990's saw a rise in the number of scholarly texts exploring gender, transgender, and transsexuality, reflecting an increase in academic interest in transgender issues and the beginning of transgender studies in higher education.

Locale: New York, New York
Categories: Transgender/transsexuality; publications; cultural and intellectual history

Key Figures
Jay Prosser, female-to-male transgender scholar
Judith Halberstam (b. 1961), transgender scholar
Dallas Denny (b. 1949), male-to-female transgender author

Summary of Event
Women's studies and gay and lesbian studies paved the way for the emergence of the more expansive fields of queer studies and queer theory as areas of academic inquiry in universities and colleges in the 1990's, but not all scholars or activists were satisfied with how queer studies often neglected to examine transgenderism and transsexuality. Many scholars felt that transgender and transsexual issues and concerns were either enveloped, and subsequently erased, under the umbrella of homosexuality, were labeled complicit in maintaining the male/female binary system for classifying sexed identities, or both. In response, the late 1990's saw a proliferation of texts centered on transgender and transsexual concerns and the emergence of a new and distinct field of academic investigation called transgender studies.

Jay Prosser's *Second Skins: The Body Narratives of Transsexuality* (1998), was the first in-depth study of transsexual autobiography, detailing how narrative and body interact to illuminate transsexual identity. Prosser's work examines the body and its borders, critiques poststructuralist theories about the body and its relationship to language, and then presents his own theories of the body as transsexual. He explores and discusses a number of transsexual autobiographies and two well-known works of fiction featuring transgender characters: Radclyffe Hall's *The Well of Loneliness* (1928) and Leslie Feinberg's *Stone Butch Blues* (1993). Prosser's work also contains more than thirty photographs of transsexuals.

A variety of other scholarly works that helped to illuminate the numerous and varied facets of transgender studies were published in 1998. Judith "Jack" Halberstam's book *Female Masculinity* was the first full-length study of its kind. In the book, Halberstam argues that, rather than merely imitating masculine characteristics, female masculinity constitutes its own unique configuration of various gender identity markers. The book presents a historical analysis of the development of female masculinity, starting with nineteenth century behaviors and progressing to the drag king performances of the late twentieth and early twenty-first centuries. It also includes numerous photos, including portraits, movie stills, and shots from drag king competitions.

Also published in 1998 was the fifth version of the Harry Benjamin International Gender Dysphoria Association's (HBIGDA) *Standards of Care for Gender Identity Disorders*, first published in 1979 (a sixth version was published in 2001). The manual, a guide for mental and medical health professionals who diagnose and treat individuals seeking gender reassignment, explores assessment and treatment for adolescents, psychotherapy, hormone therapy, breast and genital surgery, and post-transition follow up. In a significant development that improved the relationship between transsexuals and medical and other health professionals, the HBIGDA elected transgender and transsexual individuals to its board of directors in 1997.

Dallas Denny, a male-to-female transsexual, edited a collection of essays titled *Current Concepts in Transgender Identity* (1998), which explore developments in cultural and social theories about transgender experiences and examine advance-

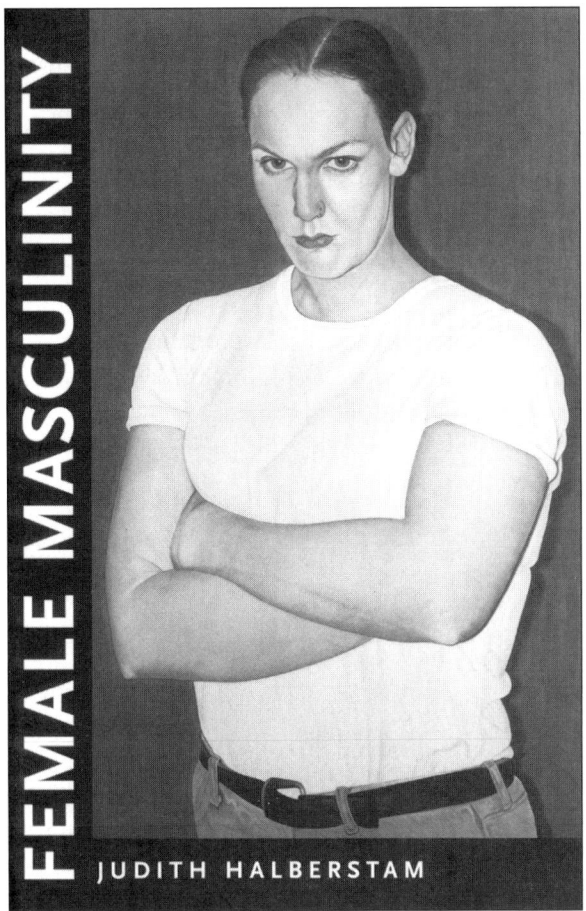

The cover of Halberstam's Female Masculinity *(1998).* (Duke University Press)

ments in medical treatment and technology. Essays address topics such as mythology, cross-cultural connections, free expression, cross-dressing, sexual orientation, family therapy, and hormone treatment. In 1994, Denny published *Gender Dysphoria: A Guide to Research*, an extensive bibliography that lists works of fiction and nonfiction, including book chapters, journal articles, and legal cases on what was called "gender dysphoria."

Also, new academic journals emerged in the late 1990's, adding to a group of already established academic journals that were beginning to address transgender studies and transgender theories. In 1997, *The International Journal of Transgenderism* made its debut, focusing on transgender issues and the social sciences. The academic journal *GLQ: A Journal of Lesbian and Gay Studies*, published a special edition of its journal on transgenderism, edited and introduced by Susan Stryker. Contributors to this issue include Halberstam, C. Jacob Hale, Cheryl Chase, and Katrina Roen. Topics ranged from the role of phenomenology in transgender studies, to questions of embodiment and politics, to mass-media dissemination of information about gender-change technology, to the "border wars" between butch lesbians and female-to-male transsexuals. At least four other academic journals addressed transgenderism in the late 1990's: *Social Text*, *Journal of Gender Studies*, *Velvet Light Trap*, and *Sexualities*.

SIGNIFICANCE

Transgender studies is still developing as a field of critical inquiry in universities and colleges, and its impact is still evolving, even beyond the academy. The increase in transgender scholarship has opened the door not only to more academic studies of gender and sex identity but also to the inclusion of transgender issues in social and political commentary and to transgender civil rights.

—*Jennifer A. Smith*

FURTHER READING

Denny, Dallas, ed. *Current Concepts in Transgender Identity*. New York: Garland, 1998.

_____. *Gender Dysphoria: A Guide to Research*. New York: Garland, 1994.

Feinberg, Leslie. *Stone Butch Blues: A Novel*. Ithaca, N.Y.: Firebrand Books, 1993.

Halberstam, Judith. *Female Masculinity*. Durham, N.C.: Duke University Press, 1998.

Hale, C. Jacob. "Consuming the Living, Dis-(re)membering the Dead in the Butch/FTM Borderlands." *GLQ: A Journal of Lesbian and Gay Studies* 4, no. 2 (April, 1998): 311-328.

Harry Benjamin International Gender Dysphoria Association. *Standards of Care for Gender Identity Disorders*. 6th version. http://www.hbigda.org/soc.htm.

Namaste, Viviane K. *Invisible Lives: The Erasure of Transsexual and Transgendered People*. Chicago: University of Chicago Press, 2000.

Prosser, Jay. *Second Skins: The Body Narratives of Transsexuality*. New York: Columbia University Press, 1998.

_____. "Skin Memories." In *Thinking Through the Skin*, edited by Sara Ahmed and Jackie Stacey. New York: Routledge, 2001.

Stryker, Susan. *The Transgender Issue. GLQ: A Journal of Lesbian and Gay Studies* 4, no. 2 (1998).

_____, ed. "Transgender Studies: Queer Theory's Evil Twin." *GLQ: A Journal of Lesbian and Gay Studies* 10, no. 2 (2004).

Wilson, Robin. "Transgendered Scholars Defy Convention, Seeking to be Heard and Seen in Academe." *Chronicle of Higher Education*, February 6, 1998.

SEE ALSO: Mar. 20, 1990: Queer Nation Is Founded; 1992: Transgender Nation Holds Its First Protest; Mar., 2003-Dec., 2004: Transsexuals Protest Academic Exploitation; Nov. 20, 2003: transgender Day of Remembrance and Remembering Our Dead Project.

April 2, 1998
CANADIAN SUPREME COURT REVERSES GAY ACADEMIC'S FIRING

Instructor Delwin Vriend, who was fired from an ecumenical college in Alberta because of his sexual orientation, won his appeal to Canada's Supreme Court, which found that the provincial human rights code was deficient in not aligning with section 15 of the federal Charter of Rights and Freedoms.

ALSO KNOWN AS: Vriend v. Alberta
LOCALE: Edmonton, Alberta, Canada
CATEGORIES: Civil rights; laws, acts, and legal history

KEY FIGURES
Delwin Vriend, instructor at King's University College
Ralph Klein (b. 1942), premier of the province of Alberta
John Wesley McClung, court of appeal judge

SUMMARY OF EVENT
Since 1988, Delwin Vriend had been a full-time lab instructor at King's University College, a liberal arts college in Edmonton, Alberta, with about five hundred students run by the Christian Reformed Church, a conservative Christian denomination. Vriend's work record was unblemished and he gained merit accordingly. However, his 1990 disclosure that he was gay prompted the school's board of governors to adopt a position on homosexuality, enacted in the following year, and Vriend was fired for not complying with the new policy, which barred gays and lesbians from its staff.

Vriend was denied reinstatement after he appealed. Asserting that his employer had discriminated against him because of his sexual orientation, Vriend tried to file a complaint with the Alberta Human Rights Commission. The commission found, however, that the complaint had no merit under the province's Individual Rights Protection Act (IRPA) because sexual orientation was not a protected ground. Vriend sued the commission in a lower court, where, in 1994, the trial judge ruled in his favor. The Alberta government appealed the decision and won its appeal in February, 1996.

In agreeing with the government's petition, the court of appeal, in the 2-1 ruling, said that the omission of sexual orientation from the Individual Rights Protection Act was not a violation of Section 15 of the federal Charter of Rights and Freedoms because the constitutional nature of Alberta's civil rights act and laws need not reflect the federal charter perfectly. One of the judges, John Wesley McClung, went so far as to assert that sexual orientation could not be "read into" the IRPA by federal courts, which might be presumably motivated by contrary ideology. This was seen to be a preemptive action in the event that the Supreme Court of Canada, at some point in the future, should decide to hear an appeal from Vriend. When the Alberta government amended the IRPA in May of that year, it conspicuously left out sexual orientation.

Vriend indeed did appeal the case to the Supreme Court, which agreed to hear it, in November, 1997. The Alberta government argued that legislatures and not courts should decide on equality provisions. Nevertheless, on April 2, 1998, the court, in *Vriend v. Alberta*, agreed with Vriend, stating that the best remedy was to read sexual orientation as one of the protections covered by the IRPA.

SIGNIFICANCE

The Vriend decision is significant as much for its favorable outcome—most other Canadian provinces already had similar laws in place—as for the almost visceral hatred it unleashed. Alberta, long known as the most deeply conservative province, has often cried of "judicial activism" against Canadian Supreme Court decisions that have run contrary to the province's socially conservative values. In newspaper advertisements and columns and in calls from the pulpit, Alberta premier Ralph Klein was urged to invoke the override provision of the federal charter, in section 33, which is more popularly known as the "notwithstanding clause." This clause allows any province to opt out, for a period of five years, of freedom provisions in federal legislation the province may deem contrary to its wishes. Klein, likely fearing the legislative and social mess that would result, declined.

Significant, too, is that the decision did not reinstate Vriend in his old job; rather, the court gave him the right to appeal. Since his former employer was a religious institution, it was exempt from certain legislation and would assert that its constitution allowed it to discriminate. Yet the Supreme Court's decision, which is still used as a touchstone by those fighting against the federal government's consideration of GLBT marriage, reveals that vigilance in gaining and maintaining protection under the law is always needed.

A subsequent Ontario case, *M. v. H.*, illustrates the Vriend case's legal impact: A lesbian couple separated; M. moved out of their common home and sued H. for spousal support pursuant to the Ontario Family Law Act. Section 29 of that act, however, stipulated that the support provisions in the law applied only to married and common-law spouses. M. went on to argue that this restrictive definition of "spouse" violated the rights of lesbians to equality under the federal charter. In 1999, the Supreme Court again agreed, giving the Ontario government six months to rewrite its provincial laws in relation to the case. It did, as did other provinces, including Alberta.

—Andrew Lesk

FURTHER READING

Laghi, Brian. "Rage Finds Its Voice in Alberta." *Globe and Mail*, April 11, 1998.

Warner, Tom. *Never Going Back: A History of Queer Activism in Canada*. Buffalo, N.Y.: University of Toronto Press, 2002.

SEE ALSO: Aug. 26, 1969: Canada Decriminalizes Homosexual Acts; Dec. 19, 1977: Quebec Includes Lesbians and Gays in Its Charter of Human Rights and Freedoms; June 2, 1980: Canadian Gay Postal Workers Secure Union Protections; 1982-1991: Lesbian Academic and Activist Sues University of California for Discrimination; Jan. 1, 1988: Canada Decriminalizes Sex Practices Between Consenting Adults; Dec. 30, 1991-Feb. 22, 1993: Canada Grants Asylum Based on Sexual Orientation; 1992: Canadian YMCA Extends Family Discounts to Gays and Lesbians; Apr. 27, 1992: Canadian Government Antigay Campaign Is Revealed; June 28, 2002: Irish American Lesbian Gains Canadian Immigrant Status; June 17, 2003, and July 19, 2005: Canada Legalizes Same-Gender Marriage.

October 6-7, 1998
GAY COLLEGE STUDENT SHEPARD IS BEATEN AND MURDERED

The shocking beating and murder of Matthew Shepard in Wyoming led to the gay college student becoming an icon of sorts in the movement for GLBT equality and awareness. In addition to the brutality of his murder, the hate crime had significant religious, legal, political, cultural, and academic ramifications.

LOCALE: Laramie, Wyoming
CATEGORIES: Crime; civil rights; government and politics; laws, acts, and legal history; marches, protests, and riots; religion

KEY FIGURES
Matthew Shepard (1976-1998), University of Wyoming student, who was beaten and murdered by Aaron McKinney and Russell Henderson
Aaron McKinney and
Russell Henderson, convicted of murdering Shepard
Fred Phelps (b. 1929), radical conservative pastor who preaches against gays and lesbians
Judy Shepard and
Dennis Shepard, Matthew's parents and campaigners for GLBT causes

SUMMARY OF EVENT
On the night of October 6, 1998, around the time of Gay Awareness Week at the University of Wyoming, Matthew Shepard met two young men at the Fireside Bar, a gay-friendly hangout in downtown Laramie, Wyoming. Aaron McKinney (age twenty-two), Russell Henderson (age twenty-one), and Shepard stepped out of the bar and into a pick-up truck driven by one of the two men. They then drove off with Shepard to another part of town, where McKinney and Henderson brutally beat Shepard with the butt of a .357 magnum pistol, stole his wallet (including his credit card, which provided a first clue to the police), took away his shoes (so that he could not walk away), and tied him to a wooden fence in a remote area, leaving him to die.

In freezing temperatures, Shepard soon became comatose. About eighteen hours later, a mountain biker found Shepard, brutalized and near death. (At first glance from a distance, the cyclist thought he had seen a scarecrow.) Shepard was rushed to a hospital in Fort Collins, Colorado, and put on life support. He was so badly injured—with severe trauma to his brain stem and massive head fractures—and

Thousands held candlelight vigils across the United States after the beating and murder of Matthew Shepard. (Hulton Archive/Getty Images)

A memorial at the site where Matthew Shepard was beaten and left to die. (Hulton Archive/Getty Images)

had such severe hypothermia that doctors were unable to perform surgery. In the early hours of October 12, without regaining consciousness, Shepard died with his parents by his side.

Justice was served swiftly, but under intense media scrutiny and immense political pressure that at times imperiled a fair trial for the defendants. McKinney and Henderson had argued in court that Shepard had propositioned them at the bar, so McKinney's lawyers tried to advance the "gay panic defense" for their client, but the judge dismissed the attempt because that particular defense was not recognized by Wyoming law. For McKinney, the jury returned a verdict of guilty on two counts of felony murder (he was acquitted of first-degree murder). At the request of Shepard's parents, McKinney was spared capital punishment and received two consecutive life sentences, without the possibility of appeal or parole, plus a lifelong gag order about the crime, preventing him from profiting by selling his story. Henderson, to avoid the death penalty, plea bargained and was sentenced to life imprisonment.

Significance

The cyclist's image of the scarecrow became a symbolic and vivid reminder that gays and lesbians often are outcasts and objects of derision. That image, coupled with the biblical symbol of a crucifixion evoked by Shepard being tied, beaten and bloody, to a wooden fence, caused a global outcry. Certainly the most enduring detail about Shepard tied to the fence was his completely disfigured face, humanized only by the rivulets of tears from his eyes that had washed away the blood, an image evoked in countless poems, paintings, portraits, and other media. Shepard also made the cover of *Time* magazine and the front page of *The New York Times*. Thousands of candlelight vigils were held across the nation; within weeks, Shepard's parents had received ten thousand letters and seventy thousand e-mails.

Hate-monger reverend Fred Phelps from Topeka, Kansas, whose mantra is "God Hates Fags," stood outside Shepard's funeral with his followers and proclaimed "No Tears for Queers." Mourners, however, in heavy snow, shielded Shepard's grieving family and friends with their umbrellas and sang "Amazing Grace." Phelps returned to Wyoming for McKinney's murder trial, but once again there were counter-protesters, dressed as white angels with enormous wings.

Phelps later caused more controversy with his plan to erect a monument in Casper, Wyoming (Shepard's burial site), to celebrate Shepard's "damnation." A constitutional battle over free speech ensued. Since a privately sponsored monument to the Ten Commandments sits in the same park, Phelps argued that the site must be opened to his monument, too. In response, the Casper City Council chose to exclude all private displays in the park.

To counter the Christian Right, Shepard's parents have become vocal activists for GLBT rights and have lobbied in support of hate crimes legislation. Such laws were adopted in several jurisdictions, including Laramie, but failed to pass in many states and at the federal level. In 1999, the Shepards established the Matthew Shepard Foundation (www.matthewshepard.org); they also maintain a personal Web-based tribute called Matthew's Place (www.matthewsplace.com), with many links to online resources, including the Matthew Shepard Memorial Quilt.

Matthew Shepard also has become a cultural icon. His recognition stretches throughout American culture, from politics and academics to television, film, music, and theater. Ellen DeGeneres and Barbra Streisand attended a rally on Capitol Hill just days after the incident. Inspired by Shepard's death, Melissa Etheridge wrote "Scarecrow" on her album *Breakdown* and dedicated it in Shepard's memory. At a concert in Laramie, Elton John sang "Don't Let the Sun Go Down on Me" for Shepard. In 2000, MTV aired the drama *Anatomy of a Hate Crime*, directed by Tim Hunter. Also in 2000, Moisés Kaufman and the Tectonic Theater Project performed the play *The Laramie Project* across the country. Made into a film that was first shown on HBO in 2002, *The Laramie Project* has since become a staple of university and community theater. Also in 2002, NBC broadcast a made-for-television movie called *The Matthew Shepard Story*, starring Stockard Channing and Sam Waterston.

Academia also has addressed the Shepard case, with studies of topics including hate crimes and violence, sexuality, and public mourning, and by supporting students through scholarships and other funding sources. Every year, three out gay and lesbian seniors from Iowa high schools are eligible for free tuition at Iowa's public universities. Weber State University set up a Matthew Shepard scholarship to "promote awareness." Monmouth University has a fund, supported through the royalties from the book *From Hate Crimes to Human Rights* (2001), for students who plan to work for "human rights advocacy."

—*Nikolai Endres*

FURTHER READING

American Behavioral Scientist. Special issues, "Matthew Shepard." Vols. 45, no. 4, and 46, no. 1 (2002).

Connolly, Catherine. "Matthew's Murderers' Defense." *Gay and Lesbian Review Worldwide* 8, no. 1 (2001): 22-26.

Delahaye, Alfred N. "The Case of Matthew Shepard (1999)." In *Illusive Shadows: Justice, Media, and Socially Significant American Trials*, edited by Lloyd Chiasson, Jr. Westport, Conn.: Praeger, 2003.

Ingebretsen, Edward J. "Jesus and Matthew: Monsters, Si[g]ns, and Wonders." *International Journal of Sexuality and Gender Studies* 6, no. 4 (October, 2001): 235-249.

Loffreda, Beth. *Losing Matt Shepard: Life and Politics in the Aftermath of Anti-Gay Murder*. New York: Columbia University Press, 2000.

Normand, Sasha. "The Parable of Matthew: Identity Politics, Politics of Desire, and the Politics of Performance." *Journal of Gay, Lesbian, and Bisexual Identity* 4, no. 4 (1999): 315-326.

Ott, Brian L., and Eric Aoki. "The Politics of Negotiating Public Tragedy: Media Framing of the Matthew Shepard Murder." *Rhetoric & Public Affairs* 5, no. 3 (Fall, 2002): 483-505.

Patterson, Romaine, and Patrick Hinds. *The Whole World Was Watching: Living in the Light of Matthew Shepard*. New York: Advocate Books, 2005.

Swigonski, Mary E., Robin S. Mama, and Kelly Ward, eds. *From Hate Crimes to Human Rights: A Tribute to Matthew Shepard*. New York: Harrington Park Press/Haworth Social Work Practice Press, 2001. Published simultaneously as a special issue of the *Journal of Gay & Lesbian Social Services* 13, nos. 1-2 (2001).

Tigner, Amy. "*The Laramie Project:* Western Pastoral." *Modern Drama* 45, no. 1 (Spring, 2002): 138-156.

SEE ALSO: June 30-July 1, 1934: Hitler's Night of the Long Knives; Nov. 27, 1978: White Murders Politicians Moscone and Milk; Nov. 3, 1992: Oregon and Colorado Attempt Antigay Initiatives; Dec. 24, 1993-Dec. 31, 1993: Transgender Man Brandon Teena Raped and Murdered; Dec. 4, 1995: Lesbian Couple Murdered in Oregon; Oct. 4, 2002: Transgender Teen Gwen Araujo Is Murdered in California.

October 9-12, 1998
FIRST INTERNATIONAL RETREAT FOR LESBIAN AND GAY MUSLIMS IS HELD

GLBT Muslims, who founded the Al-Fatiha Foundation in 1997 as an online community, held its first international retreat to reconcile sexual orientation or gender identity with religion, namely Islam. The group has held annual conferences, mostly in the United States, since its founding retreat. Al-Fatiha's existence has been met with both positive reinforcement and encouragement and with fierce opposition and controversy.

LOCALE: Boston, Massachusetts
CATEGORIES: Religion; organizations and institutions

KEY FIGURES
Faisal Alam (b. 1977), Pakistani American student at Northeastern University and director of Al-Fatiha, 1999-2004
Surina Khan (b. 1967), Pakistani American researcher and executive director of the International Gay and Lesbian Human Rights Commission, 2000-2002
Omar Nahas, Syrian director of the Yoesuf Foundation in the Netherlands for research on Islam and homosexuality

SUMMARY OF EVENT
Until the late 1990's, many gay, lesbian, bisexual, and transgender Muslims thought they were alone. Some of them struggled to suppress their sexual orientation or gender identity, as they thought their faith and sexuality could not coexist. Others thought that being both Muslim and gay, lesbian, bisexual, or transgender was irreconcilable and thus felt compelled to abandon Islam. There were also those who lived as Muslims during the day and lived as a GLBT person at night. Faisal Alam belonged to the last category.

Born in 1977 to Pakistani parents, Alam immigrated with his family at the age of eleven to the United States. After he had come out as gay at college in Boston, he was asked to resign from his position as secretary of the national Muslim Students Association. Alam turned to the Internet in 1997 and started a Listserv for GLBT Muslims, thus founding the Al-Fatiha Foundation. After months of online discussions, Alam organized the first international retreat for GLBT Muslims, which took place October 9 to 12, 1998, in Boston, Massachusetts. Forty-five individuals—Americans, Canadians, Indians, Lebanese, Maldivians, Pakistanis, Saudis, South Africans, Swiss, Syrians, and Turks—flew from all over the world to attend the retreat.

> ### AL-FATIHA: MISSION STATEMENT
>
> The Al-Fatiha Foundation is an international organization dedicated to Muslims who are lesbian, gay, bisexual, and transgendered, those questioning their sexual orientation or gender identity, and their friends. Al-Fatiha's goal is to provide a safe space and a forum for LGBTQ Muslims to address issues of common concern, share individual experiences, and institutional resources. The Al-Fatiha Foundation aims to support LGBTQ Muslims in reconciling their sexual orientation or gender identity with Islam. Al-Fatiha promotes the Islamic notions of social justice, peace, and tolerance through its work, to bring all closer to a world that is free from injustice, prejudice, and discrimination.
>
> *Goals and Objectives*
> 1. Support Muslims who self-identify as lesbian, gay, bisexual, transgender, and those who are questioning their sexual orientation or gender identity.
> 2. Provide a supportive and understanding environment for LGBTQ Muslims who are trying to reconcile their sexuality or gender identity with Islam.
> 3. Empower LGBTQ Muslims by creating safe spaces to share individual experiences, advocating on their behalf in national and international forums, and providing information about institutional resources.
> 4. Foster spirituality among LGBTQ Muslims.
> 5. Encourage dialogue with the larger Muslim community around issues of sexuality and gender.
>
> The Al-Fatiha Foundation aims to accomplish its mission, goals, and objectives by:
> 1. Establishing local support and discussion groups for LGBTQ Muslims in the U.S. and abroad.
> 2. Holding regional, North American, and international meetings.
> 3. Outreach on the Internet.
>
> *Source:* http://www.tegenwicht.org/16_imams/al_fatiha_en.htm.

The workshops addressed topics of faith and sexuality, historical perspectives on GLBT behavior in Muslim societies, and the current oppression of GLBT persons in some Muslim countries. Furthermore, retreat participants, including Omar Nahas, examined the different interpretations of Prophet Lot's story in the Qurʾān. The story refers to the punishment of the people of Lot for their lewd acts: Married men raped male travelers to dishonor them, did not treat their guests honorably, and attempted to molest Prophet Lot's guests, who were angels disguised as handsome young men. Lot's story is traditionally referenced to condemn homosexuality, but the story does not address consensual homosexual relationships between adults.

A key player at the retreat was Surina Khan, a Pakistani American who was, at the time, a researcher who monitored the "exgay" movement and the Christian Right in the United States while working at a progressive Boston think tank. She was executive director of the International Gay and Lesbian Human Rights Commission, becoming the first Muslim-raised lesbian to lead a major GLBT organization. She held that position from 2000 to 2002. At the first Al-Fatiha retreat, Khan was instrumental in placing women's issues at the top of the agenda of the newly born GLBT Muslim movement.

SIGNIFICANCE

The highlight of Al-Fatiha's retreat was the collective decision to establish an international organization for GLBT Muslims. "Al-Fatiha," which means "the beginning" in Arabic, happens to be the title of the opening chapter of the Qurʾān. The name caused some controversy.

Although progressive organizations and the media hailed the efforts of GLBT Muslims to organize, conservative imams in countries of all faiths were opposed to GLBT Muslims reclaiming their faith. For example, a conservative magazine broke the silence on homosexuality and published a cover article in Arabic. The article, translated into English as "The Latest Catastrophes for Arabs in the Twentieth Century: Islamic Conference and Arab Organizations for Sexual Deviations" (*Al-Majalla: The International Magazine of the Arabs*, October 24-30, 1999), detailed the work of Alam and of Al-Fatiha, work the journalist considered a threat to Muslim youth.

The reporter interviewed Sheik Abdel-Azim El-Motaeny, a professor at Al-Azhar University in Egypt, who affirmed the death sentence for homosexuals who do not repent. In the same article, however, Ramzi Zakharia, the head of the Gay and Lesbian Arab Society (GLAS) in New York, affirmed the basic rights of GLBT people. *Al-Majalla*'s coverage of the GLBT Muslim movement, while scornful, fueled awareness in Arab countries, where many GLBT people came to discover they were not alone, and they flooded Al-Fatiha and GLAS with requests to join the two organizations.

Anissa Hélie, a French-Algerian feminist working for the international solidarity network Women Living Under Muslim Laws, wrote,

> Why is sexuality and sexual conformity the focus of so much attention by fundamentalist forces? A possible answer is that, when people exercise individual choice, it appears as a challenge: autonomy—especially for women—is seen as a threat. It is interesting to note that, in past centuries, Arabs attributed homosexual behaviour to the bad influence of Persians. Today, it's much the same story, . . . homosexuality is currently denounced as a "Western disease."

The GLBT Muslim movement developed rapidly. Chapters of Al-Fatiha were founded in major U.S. cities, and affiliate organizations were established in Canada, the United Kingdom, and South Africa. Muslim scholars who joined Al-Fatiha include Ghazala Anwar, a renowned South Asian Muslim feminist and lecturer in religious studies at the University of Canterbury, New Zealand, and Imam Daayiee Abdullah, an African American Muslim scholar who joined Al-Fatiha's board of directors and became the first out gay imam.

Alam has coordinated the yearly conferences, the first of which was held in New York in May of 1999. Annual conferences have been held in London in 2000; San Francisco in 2001; Washington, D.C., in 2002; Toronto, Canada, in 2003; New York in 2003; and Los Angeles in 2004. Al-Fatiha's conferences provide not only a space to discuss sexual orientation and gender identity within Islam but also a chance for breakthrough reform toward a progressive Islam. During the conferences, women have prayed alongside men (a traditionally prohibited practice), and women and transgender people have led prayers. Al-Fatiha's chapters in Toronto and Philadelphia started their own GLBT mosques.

Addressing homosexuality as a human rights issue, Khalid Duran (in *Homosexuality and World Religions*, 1993) suggests that GLBT Muslims' only hope is to find a "theological accommodation" with Islam by developing a "new *shari'a* [Muslim law] comparatively detached from the social climate of seventh-century Arabia," a law that emphasizes "the ethical principles of freedom and justice enunciated by the Prophet Muhammad in Mecca."

—*Bassam Kassab*

FURTHER READING

Duran, Khalid. "Homosexuality and Islam." In *Homosexuality and World Religions*, edited by Arlene Swidler. Valley Forge, Pa.: Trinity Press International, 1993.

Hari, Johann. "Outcast Heroes: The Story of Gay Muslims." Available at JohannHari.com.

Khan, Badruddin. *Sex, Longing, and Not Belonging: A Gay Muslim's Quest for Love and Meaning*. Bangkok, Thailand: Floating Lotus Books, 1997.

Murray, Stephen O., and Will Roscoe. *Islamic Homosexualities: Culture, History, and Literature*. New York: New York University Press, 1997.

Schmitt, Arno, and Jehoeda Safer. *Sexuality and Eroticism Among Males in Moslem Societies*. New York: Haworth Press, 1991.

SEE ALSO: Aug. 8, 1978: International Lesbian and Gay Association Is Founded; Dec. 1, 1988: First World AIDS Day; 1990: International Gay and Lesbian Human Rights Commission Is Founded; Sept. 16, 1994: U.N. Revokes Consultative Status of International Lesbian and Gay Association; June 17, 1995: International Bill of Gender Rights Is First Circulated; Nov., 1999: First Middle Eastern Gay and Lesbian Organization Is Founded.

December 3, 1998-February 25, 1999
SCREENING OF *FIRE* IGNITES VIOLENT PROTESTS IN INDIA

Indian-Canadian filmmaker Deepa Mehta's film Fire, *the story of two married Hindu women who fall in love with each other, sparked violent attacks on theaters in India in 1998 and ignited debates about lesbian sexuality in India.*

LOCALE: India; Canada
CATEGORIES: Arts; cultural and intellectual history

KEY FIGURES
Deepa Mehta (b. 1950), Indian-born Canadian film director and screenwriter
Nandita Das (b. 1969), Indian actor
Shabana Azmi (b. 1950), Indian actor

SUMMARY OF EVENT
After its premiere at the Toronto Film Festival in September, 1996, Indian-Canadian director Deepa Mehta's film *Fire* won several awards for its portrayal of a lesbian relationship between two Indian women. The film was not shown in India until November 13, 1998, when India's Censor Board of Film Certification released the film uncut.

Fire opens with the arranged marriage of beautiful young Sita (Nandita Das) to Jatin, the younger brother of Ashok, who is married to Radha (Shabana Azmi), a woman who has long accepted the duties imposed on her by her traditional role as wife. Jatin and Ashok run a video store and restaurant, and when Sita moves into their joint-family life, she quickly learns that her marriage is not going to be the romantic fantasy portrayed in the Bollywood films she loves. Her new husband Jatin carries in his wallet a photograph of his Chinese mistress, and Ashok has devoted himself to a swami who teaches that "desire is the root of all evil." Consequently, Ashok and Radha have been in a celibate marriage for thirteen years.

As Sita becomes a part of the household, her life comes to match the rhythms of Radha's life, filled with work in the restaurant, caring for the elderly family matriarch, Biji, and cooking for their household. The two women become friends, and Sita soon finds that she is falling in love with Radha. When she initiates a sexual relationship with her late at night while their husbands are gone, Radha—who is at first startled—soon reciprocates. The awakening relationship between Radha and Sita encourages both of them gradually to change the way they behave at home and to resist the traditional bonds of marriage that have restricted them both. After their household servant discovers that they are lovers and tells their husbands, Sita decides to leave and urges Radha to come with her. Radha follows after an argument with her husband, during which she is nearly burned in a kitchen fire. The film ends with the two women reunited and apparently about to continue their lives together.

Although *Fire* played for two weeks in India without incident, on December 3, 1998, two hundred men and women from the conservative Shiv Sena political party stormed the New Empire and Cinemax theaters in Bombay. Burning posters of *Fire* and damaging the theaters' display cases and a ticket counter, they claimed the film was "against Indian tradition." Twenty-nine people were arrested in connection with the vandalism, and Bombay theaters stopped showing the film. In Delhi, members of Shiv Sena invaded movie theaters showing the film, causing theater owners to shut down their screenings.

On December 5, six people brought a writ to the Indian Supreme court demanding the right to show *Fire* and asking for protection at the screenings under the authority of several articles of the Indian constitution. While the Supreme Court debated whether *Fire* should be screened in India, violent protests led by Shiv Sena continued throughout India. Simultaneously, the Campaign for Lesbian Rights (CALERI), a coalition of several lesbian organizations, organized counter-protests and held a candlelight vigil in front of one of the vandalized theaters in Delhi. On February 12, 1999, the Censor Board once again released an uncut version of *Fire*,

> ## DEEPA MEHTA
>
> Deepa Mehta tackles controversial subjects in her work. Born in Amritsar, India, in 1950, the themes of her films often relate to her native country and have included topics that deal with religious fundamentalism, homosexuality, and relations between India and Pakistan. Despite protest and opposition to her films, Mehta continues to confront difficult issues and to challenge the traditional patriarchal perspectives of Indian society in relation to the role of women in India.
>
> Mehta earned a degree in philosophy from the University of New Delhi, and then worked for a documentary film company in the same city. In 1973, she emigrated to Canada and cofounded a documentary film company with her then-husband Paul Saltzman and her brother, photojournalist Dilip Mehta. She also directed film and television documentaries, for which she won a number of awards, including an award for her first major film, *At 99: A Portrait of Louise Tandy Murch* (1975).
>
> Mehta then turned her attention to the fictional films for which she is best known. She often depicts women, how they communicate, and how they try to transcend gender roles; she also shows relationships between people of different ages, religions and cultures. Her best known films are *Fire* (1996) and *Earth* (1998), which have been criticized and found offensive in her native India. *Earth* portrays the bloody division of India and Pakistan and the clashes of religion that tore apart friendships and families. *Fire* explores the sexual relationship of two women in unfulfilling marriages. Turning to each other for friendship and love, the female characters in this film challenge women's traditional roles in Indian society. *Water* (2005) focuses on the plight of a young widow forced into poverty who wants to escape the social constraints imposed on her; Mehta tells the story of the woman's relationship with a man from a lower caste who also is a follower of Gandhi.

and by February 25 both Hindi and English versions of the film reopened in India without additional violence.

Western audiences primarily viewed *Fire* as a lesbian film, but within India and the Indian diaspora *Fire* was clearly embedded in historical debates about Hinduism, Western colonialism, obscenity standards, and the role of women in India. Much of the debate surrounding *Fire* focused on what constituted Indian tradition and whether or not lesbian sexuality had existed in India before British colonialism imposed Victorian moral standards on Indian culture in the nineteenth century. Indeed, one of the main problems raised by the debates about *Fire* was the difficulty of separating out the issue of lesbian rights from the broader discourse on tradition and culture, which many right-wing protesters felt were attacked by the film.

SIGNIFICANCE

Fire was undeniably the first widely distributed film depicting lesbian sexuality in India, and its significance lies in the debate that it prompted about lesbian sexuality. Before the release of *Fire*, Indian lesbians were tolerated if their relationships remained hidden. Although *Fire* did not result in the freedom to be lesbian, or gay, it nonetheless opened the door to discourse about lesbian sexuality and gave Indian lesbians their first positive representations on the big screen. Newspaper reports of the protests following the release of *Fire* show that the film had a profound impact on lesbians in India, resulting in never-before-seen large-scale organizing and demonstrations.

Fire did not, however, result in additional film representations of lesbian sexuality until 2004, when the Bollywood film *Girlfriend*, directed by Karan Razdan, was released. *Girlfriend* tells the story of Tanya, who becomes obsessed with her roommate Sapna after Sapna falls in love with a man; the film underscores the stereotype of the psychotic lesbian stalker.

Once again, members of Shiv Sena vandalized movie theaters showing the film in the name of defending Indian tradition. In this case, however, *Girlfriend* was also protested by Indian lesbian groups, who objected to lesbian sexuality being coupled in the film with psychosis and stalking. While progress in positive representations of lesbian sexuality has not been obvious in India, it is clear that the debate that was ignited by *Fire* has had a noticeable political effect, as lesbian rights groups were well prepared to respond to *Girlfriend*.

—*Malinda Lo*

Further Reading

Bachmann, Monica. "After the Fire." In *Queering India: Same-Sex Love and Eroticism in Indian Culture and Society*, edited by Ruth Vanita. New York: Routledge, 2002.

Ghosh, Shohini. "From the Frying Pan to the Fire: Dismantled Myths and Deviant Behaviour." In *Re-searching Indian Women*, edited by Vijaya Ramaswamy. Delhi, India: Manohar, 2003.

Gopinath, Gayatri. "Local Sites, Global Contexts: The Transnational Trajectories of Deepa Mehta's *Fire*." In *Queer Globalizations: Citizenship and the Afterlife of Colonialism*, edited by Arnoldo Cruz-Malave and Martin F. Manalansan IV. New York: New York University Press, 2002.

Parameswaran, Uma. "Contextualizing Diasporic Locations In Deepa Mehta's *Fire* and Srinivas Krishna's *Masala*." In *In Diaspora: Theories, Histories, Texts*, edited by Makarand Paranjape. New Delhi, India: Indialog, 2001.

Patel, Geeta. "On Fire: Sexuality and Its Incitements." In *Queering India: Same-Sex Love and Eroticism in Indian Culture and Society*, edited by Ruth Vanita. New York: Routledge, 2002.

Puri, Jyoti. *Woman, Body, Desire in Post-Colonial India: Narratives of Gender and Sexuality*. New York: Routledge, 1999.

Ramaswamy, Vijaya. "Deepa Mehta's Images of Fire: An Interview." In *Re-searching Indian Women*, edited by Vijaya Ramaswamy. Delhi, India: Manohar, 2003.

Vanita, Ruth, and Saleem Kidwai, eds. *Same-Sex Love in India: Readings from Literature and History*. New York: Palgrave, 2001.

See also: Feb., 1927: Wales Padlock Law Censors Risque Theater; 1929: *Pandora's Box* Opens; 1930's-1960's: Hollywood Bans "Sexual Perversion" in Films; 1988: *Macho Dancer* Is Released in the Philippines; Mar. 20, 1988: *M. Butterfly* Opens on Broadway; 1992-2002: Celebrity Lesbians Come Out; 1992-2006: Indians Struggle to Abolish Sodomy Law; 1993: *The Wedding Banquet* Is First Acclaimed Taiwanese Gay-Themed Film; 1995: *The Advocate* Outs Oscar Nominee Nigel Hawthorne; Mar. 21, 2000: Hollywood Awards Transgender Portrayals in Film; Mar. 5, 2006: *Brokeback Mountain*, *Capote*, and *Transamerica* Receive Oscars.

October 27, 1999
Littleton v. Prange Withholds Survivor Rights from Transsexual Spouses

Male-to-female transsexual Christie Lee Littleton was determined by the courts to be legally male based on her genetic sex and therefore not eligible to file a medical malpractice suit as a surviving spouse.

Locale: San Antonio, Texas
Categories: Laws, acts, and legal history; transgender/transsexuality; civil rights

Key Figures

Phil Hardberger, chief justice, Texas Court of Appeals
Christie Lee Littleton (b. 1952), appellant and petitioner in *Littleton v. Prange*
Jonathan Mark Littleton (1961-1996), husband of Christie Lee Littleton
Mark A. Prange, medical doctor, appellee, and respondent in *Littleton v. Prange*

Summary of Event

On October 27, 1999, a Texas Court of Appeals denied an appeal by male-to-female transsexual Christie Lee Littleton, who had sued the doctor of her deceased husband. Littleton filed the appeal in response to a medical malpractice suit she filed in her capacity as the surviving spouse of Jonathan Mark Littleton. She appealed the summary judgment that was made in favor of Mark Prange, M.D. Christie's husband had been one of Prange's patients, but Jonathan died in 1996 after developing blood clots in his lungs. Christie filed suit against Prange. The Court of Appeals, however, found that because Christie had been born "a physically healthy male" in San Antonio, Texas, in 1952, and that "at the time of birth, Christie was a male, both anatomically and genetically," she, therefore, "cannot be [legally] married to another male." Because her marriage to Jonathan was deemed by the court to be invalid on that basis, the court upheld the summary judgment that dismissed her cause of action as the surviving spouse in the malpractice suit.

Born Lee Cavazos, Jr., Christie legally changed her name to Christie Lee Cavazos in 1977 and underwent a series of gender reassignment surgeries between November, 1979, and February, 1980. She married Jonathan in Kentucky in 1989 and lived with him until his death in 1996 at the age of thirty-five. After her appeal of the summary judgment was denied by the Fourth Court of Appeals, she was denied discretionary review by the Texas Supreme Court, and she ultimately filed a petition for writ of certiorari to the Supreme Court of Texas with the U.S. Supreme Court. On October 2, 2000, her petition was denied.

Significance

In the decision for *Littleton v. Prange*, Texas Court of Appeals chief justice Phil Hardberger stated that the case involved the following deep philosophical and legal question: "Can a physician change the gender of a person with a scalpel, drugs and counseling, or is a person's gender immutably fixed by our Creator at birth?" The issue of the legality of sex and gender had been applied in this specific case to the question of transsexual marriage. Hardberger found that Littleton's assigned (male) sex/gender at birth is her legal sex/gender because "the male chromosomes do not change with either hormonal treatment or sex reassignment surgery"; so, he reasoned, "biologically a post-operative female transsexual is still a male."

At issue in the appeal and the subsequent petition for writ of certiorari was how the legality of sex/gender is determined, and whether the inconsistency of the determination on a state-by-state basis leads to a violation of a transsexual person's right and ability to marry. As pointed out in the 2000 petition, there had been three central questions: First, should a legal marriage entered into in one state be recognized by other states? Second, should the legal sex/gender of a transsexual be defined by medical professionals post-operatively or as stated on an original birth certificate? Third, does the constitutionally protected right to marry extend to transsexuals?

By holding that the legal sex/gender of a transsexual born in Texas is genetically determined and may not be changed, the court invalidated Christie Littleton's marriage and denied her the rights afforded to a legal spouse. The Littleton case, however, has since led to several legal marriages between lesbians, in which one partner was a male-to-female transsexual with XY chromosomes (determined to be male at birth), who was partnered with a woman and therefore in a lesbian relationship. The case also informed a decision in 2002 in Kansas involving J'Noel Gardiner, a transsexual woman whose marriage was similarly challenged in an inheritance case. The Kansas court ruled that a "man," determined to be male at birth, cannot marry another man.

—K. Surkan

Further Reading

Coombs, Mary. "Sexual Dis-Orientation: Transgendered People and Same-Sex Marriage." *UCLA Women's Law Journal* 8 (Spring/Summer, 1998): 219.

Flynn, Taylor. "Protecting Transgender Families: Strategies for Advocates." *Human Rights Magazine* (American Bar Association), Summer, 2003. http://www.abanet.org/irr/hr/summer03/transgender.html.

Greenberg, Julie A. "When Is a Man a Man, and When Is a Woman a Woman?" 52 *Florida Law Review* 745 (September, 2000).

Littleton v. Prange. No. 04-99-00010-CV. Court of Appeals of Texas, San Antonio. October 27, 1999.

Littleton v. Prange. No. 00-25. On Petition for Writ of Certiorari to the Supreme Court of Texas. Supreme Court of the United States. July 3, 2000.

Minter, Shannon. "Transgender Persons and Marriage: The Importance of Legal Planning." National Center for Lesbian Rights. January, 2004. http://www.nclrights.org/publications/tgmarriage.htm.

Morgan, Laura. "Boys Will Be Boys: *Littleton v. Prange* and *In re Estate of Gardiner*." *Family Law Reader*, April, 2002. http://www.famlawconsult.com/archive/reader200204.html.

Tallant, Kevin. "My 'Dude Looks Like a Lady': The Constitutional Void of Transsexual Marriage." 36 *Georgia Law Review* 635 (Winter, 2002).

Texas Gender Advocacy Information Network. "The Christie Lee Littleton Story." http://christielee.net.

SEE ALSO: Sept. 24, 1951: George Jorgensen Becomes Christine Jorgensen; Nov. 21, 1966: First Gender Identity Clinic Opens and Provides Gender Reassignment Surgery; 1978: Harry Benjamin International Gender Dysphoria Association Is Founded; Jan. 21, 1989: Death of Transgender Jazz Musician Billy Tipton; 1992: Transgender Nation Holds Its First Protest; June 17, 1995: International Bill of Gender Rights Is First Circulated; 1996: Hart Recognized as a Transgender Man; 1998: Transgender Scholarship Proliferates; 2002: Sylvia Rivera Law Project Is Founded; Apr. 30, 2002: Transgender Rights Added to New York City Law; Feb. 21, 2003: Australian Court Validates Transsexual Marriage; Mar., 2003-Dec., 2004: Transsexuals Protest Academic Exploitation; Nov. 20, 2003: Transgender Day of Remembrance and Remembering Our Dead Project; May 17, 2004: Transsexual Athletes Allowed to Compete in Olympic Games; Apr. 4, 2005: United Kingdom's Gender Recognition Act Legalizes Transsexual Marriage.

November, 1999
FIRST MIDDLE EASTERN GAY AND LESBIAN ORGANIZATION IS FOUNDED

Helem, the first lesbian, gay, bisexual, and transgender organization in the Middle East, formed in Lebanon in defiance of religious, social, legal, and governmental norms, and in a region of the world where homosexuality remains illegal.

LOCALE: Beirut, Lebanon
CATEGORIES: Organizations and institutions; civil rights

KEY FIGURES
Mazen Khaled (b. 1967), Lebanese human rights activist, who founded Helem
Ralph Shayne (b. 1974), Lebanese journalist, key in restructuring Helem

SUMMARY OF EVENT
Until the late 1990's, there was no safe place in Lebanon, or in the Middle East in general, for gays and lesbians to come together other than an "underground" dominated by risky sex, drugs, and alcohol. The lack of existing structures to address LGBT concerns was replaced by police brutality, conversion therapy, public humiliation, and banishment. Without support, the majority of LGBT individuals led double lives, or, for those who could afford it, fled the country for more accepting societies in Europe and in North America.

Helem's major goal is the annulment of an ancient clause in the Lebanese penal code, article 534, which criminalizes "unnatural sexual intercourse."

With the rise and popularity of the World Wide Web came the formation of an e-mail group called

GayLebanon. Through this virtual group, Lebanese LGBT individuals were able, for the first time, to hold online discussions and organize social gatherings. Serious social and political issues were rarely, if ever, brought up for discussion. Taking note of the need to address such issues, Mazen Khaled, a Lebanese human rights activist, formed a group called Club Free (which would later be called Helem) that would dedicate itself to LGBT concerns.

In the summer of 1999, with the help of a few friends, Khaled gathered every LGBT person he knew for a secret meeting in his apartment. Club Free, the first group dealing solely with LGBT issues in the Middle East, was formed at this meeting. While the first few years of Club Free were slowed by the internalized homophobia, fear, and self-acceptance issues of some of its members, the group still organized numerous events and received significant press coverage. Most notably, Club Free organized a successful art exhibition called EXIST, which tackled issues of personal freedom, the first such exhibition in the region.

Ralph Shayne, a Lebanese journalist, first heard of Club Free while attending the exhibition, and he became a key club member. He was instrumental in restructuring Club Free, renaming it "Helem" (from the Arabic acronym of "Lebanese Protection for Lesbians, Gays, Bisexuals and Transgenders") and giving the group a major push toward the public sphere, allowing it to work more effectively.

Significance

Helem has given Middle Eastern LGBT persons an identity, a positive role model, and hope. Helem's resource center, the first of its kind in the Middle East, was opened to anyone in the community (regardless of their sexuality). The center is an educational resource that counters the foreign statistics and negative images and viewpoints imposed by government, religious, and social leaders. As a result of the pioneering steps of Helem, other local non-LGBT organizations, most notably Hurriyyat Khassa, which now lobbies the government to decriminalize homosexuality, took up queer issues as part of their agendas.

Also, Helem members have participated in a number of public events, most important, the antiwar demonstrations of March 15, 2003. The day marked the first time that a group of queers marched down the streets of Beirut, and they did so under one rainbow flag, alongside other groups. Having many members publicly affirm their sexualities and thereby attack preconceived notions about homosexuality, Helem has had a positive impact on society at large. Lebanese society is slowly realizing that there are LGBT individuals in Lebanon and that homosexuality is not a Western phenomenon, as is commonly assumed.

Also, Helem has had an impact on the media, which has slowly introduced nonpejorative Arabic words to refer to LGBT individuals, positive words that had never been used before. In addition, Helem has secured a significant amount of press coverage, raising awareness for a group that, for the most part, society still pretends does not exist. This press coverage has been positive on the whole, but smaller publications, such as *Al Muhayed*, have attempted to raise their sales figures by publishing photographs of LGBT individuals, accompanied by insults and derogatory words. Led by Helem, a group of nongovernmental organizations (NGOs), journalists, and individuals have counterattacked, setting the stage for positive press coverage. Helem also has become actively involved in the national HIV peer-awareness program, a program that ignored the gay community prior to Helem's involvement.

Helem's reach extends throughout the Middle East, bringing together those wanting to fight for LGBT rights in their country. Helem branches have been formed throughout the world, in countries with important Lebanese or Arab diasporas, namely Sydney, Paris, Montreal, and San Francisco.

—*Raja Farah*

Further Reading

"Armenian Lesbian Fights Invisibility." *Off Our Backs* 21, no. 9 (October 31, 1991): 9.

Halwani, Raja. "Gay Lebanon." *Gay & Lesbian Review Worldwide* 8, no. 6 (January/February, 2002): 18.

I Exist: Voices from the Lesbian and Gay Middle Eastern Community in the United States. Peter

Barbosa and Garrett Lenoir, producers. San Francisco, Calif.: EyeBite Productions, 2003. Video recording. Synopsis: http://eyebite.com/iexist_presskit/IExist.Info.pdf.

Likosky, Stephan, ed. *Coming Out: An Anthology of International Gay and Lesbian Writings*. New York: Pantheon Books, 1992. Includes the article "Iran, The Middle East, and North Africa: Homosexuality in the Arab and Moslem World."

Massad, Joseph. "Re-orienting Desire: The Gay International and the Arab World." *Public Culture* 14, no. 2 (2002): 361-385.

Safi, Omid, ed. *Progressive Muslims: On Justice, Gender and Pluralism*. Oxford, England: Oneworld, 2003.

SEE ALSO: Aug. 8, 1978: International Lesbian and Gay Association Is Founded; Dec. 1, 1988: First World AIDS Day; 1990: International Gay and Lesbian Human Rights Commission Is Founded; Sept. 16, 1994: U.N. Revokes Consultative Status of International Lesbian and Gay Association; June 17, 1995: International Bill of Gender Rights Is First Circulated; Oct. 9-12, 1998: First International Retreat for Lesbian and Gay Muslims Is Held.

December 20, 1999
BAKER V. VERMONT LEADS TO RECOGNITION OF SAME-GENDER CIVIL UNIONS

The Vermont Supreme Court held that the state constitution prohibited exclusion of same-gender couples from the benefits of marriage. In response, the state legislature enacted the first civil union law in the United States.

LOCALE: Vermont
CATEGORIES: Laws, acts, and legal history; civil rights; government and politics

KEY FIGURES
Beth Robinson (b. 1965),
Susan M. Murray, and
Mary Bonauto (b. 1961), attorneys for plaintiffs
Stan Baker,
Peter Harrigan,
Nina Beck,
Stacy Jolles,
Holly Puterbaugh, and
Lois Farnham, plaintiffs
Jeffrey L. Amestoy (b. 1946), Vermont Supreme Court chief justice
Denise Johnson, Vermont Supreme Court justice
Bill Lippert (b. 1950), Vermont house member

SUMMARY OF EVENT
On July 22, 1997, attorneys Beth Robinson, Susan M. Murray, and Mary Bonauto announced that they had filed suit on behalf of three same-gender couples, including Stan Baker, whose name became shorthand for the case itself. The other plaintiffs in the case were Peter Harrigan, Nina Beck, Stacy Jolles, Holly Puterbaugh, and Lois Farnham. Each of the couples had presented themselves to their local clerk's office to request a marriage license, only to be turned away. As a result, they challenged the denial of their right to marry under Vermont law.

The case was initially dismissed by the Superior Court in December, 1997. The plaintiffs appealed and presented their arguments before the Vermont Supreme Court on November 18, 1998.

In its decision of December 20, 1999, written by Chief Justice Jeffrey L. Amestoy, the Vermont Supreme Court held that under the common benefits clause of the state constitution, "the State is constitutionally required to extend to same-gender couples the common benefits and protections that flow from marriage under Vermont law." The court,

Protesters gather in front of the statehouse in Vermont on July 1, 2000, the day the state's same-gender civil union law went into effect. (Hulton Archive/Getty Images)

however, rejected the argument that the plaintiffs were entitled to a marriage license under current law; the constitution guaranteed benefits of marriage only, not marriage itself.

While courts should defer to legislative ends, Amestoy required that the means to achieve those ends "bear a just and reasonable relation to the governmental objective." This is a more stringent standard than required under the federal Fourteenth Amendment, which is often satisfied with means that are rational, with no requirement that they also be just.

State analysis also emphasized the "core value" of the constitutional provision—in contrast to interpretation of the federal constitution, which more specifically focuses on the legislative intent. Thus, while the framers of the state constitution could not have intended to protect same-gender couples, the values they expressed, most notably "the principle of inclusion," embraced all persons, homosexuals included.

Against that background, the state's professed interest in excluding same-gender marriages—to "further . . . the link between procreation and child rearing"—was deemed fatally over- and under-inclusive in that it extends the privileges of marriage "to many persons with no logical connection to the stated governmental goal" but also denies those privileges to many couples with children.

Finding "a constitutional obligation to extend to plaintiffs the common benefit, protection, and security that Vermont law provides opposite-gender married couples," the court declined to order the state to issue the withheld marriage licenses, a timidity that prompted Justice Denise Johnson to dissent from this part of the decision. Instead, the court ordered the legislature "to craft an appropriate means of addressing this constitutional mandate." Jurisdiction of the court was retained, however, so that the court would be free to impose a remedy if the legislature failed to respond adequately.

The legislative debate that followed proved divisive and rancorous. Of the many town meetings held across the state in 2000, none voted to support same-gender marriage. Domestic partnerships received stronger support, but still a minority. On March 16, 2000, in large part because of the personal commitment of Vermont house members such as Bill Lippert, the bill passed its final reading by a 76-69 vote.

After the senate passed the bill, and the house accepted the amendments, Governor Howard Dean signed the nation's first civil union law on April 26, 2000. Codified as Title XV, chapter 23 of the Vermont Statutes, the law reads in part,

> Parties to a civil union shall have all the same benefits, protections and responsibilities under law, whether they derive from statute, administrative or court rule, policy, common law or any other source of civil law, as are granted to spouses in a marriage.

> **FROM *BAKER V. VERMONT***
>
> *Jeffrey L. Amestoy, Vermont Supreme Court chief justice:* May the State of Vermont exclude same-sex couples from the benefits and protections that its laws provide to opposite-sex married couples? That is the fundamental question we address in this appeal, a question that the Court well knows arouses deeply-felt religious, moral, and political beliefs. Our constitutional responsibility to consider the legal merits of issues properly before us provides no exception for the controversial case. The issue before the Court, moreover, does not turn on the religious or moral debate over intimate same-sex relationships, but rather on the statutory and constitutional basis for the exclusion of same-sex couples from the secular benefits and protections offered married couples. We conclude that under the Common Benefits Clause of the Vermont Constitution, which, in pertinent part, reads, "That government is, or ought to be, instituted for the common benefit, protection, and security of the people, nation, or community, and not for the particular emolument or advantage of any single person, family, or set of persons, who are a part only of that community," Vt. Const., ch. I, art 7., plaintiffs may not be deprived of the statutory benefits and protections afforded persons of the opposite sex who choose to marry. We hold that the State is constitutionally required to extend to same-sex couples the common benefits and protections that flow from marriage under Vermont law. Whether this ultimately takes the form of inclusion within the marriage laws themselves or a parallel "domestic partnership" system or some equivalent statutory alternative, rests with the Legislature. Whatever system is chosen, however, must conform with the constitutional imperative to afford all Vermonters the common benefit, protection, and security of the law.

By the beginning of 2004 the number of reported civil unions in the state of Vermont had reached 6,613.

SIGNIFICANCE

The Vermont debate markedly shifted the terms of the discussion about gay and lesbian relationships. While in 2000 civil unions had been the progressive compromise position, the idea had become so familiar that by the 2004 Massachusetts debates over the issue, civil unions had been positioned as a conservative alternative to same-gender marriage.

The advent of civil unions in Vermont immediately created a rift in the gay and lesbian community. Some, represented by William Eskridge, had viewed civil unions as a reasonable, perhaps temporary intermediate step on the way to the full marriage equality that wider society is not ready to accept. Others, such as Evan Wolfson, had argued that marriage should always be the goal and that civil rights activists should never set out to get a legal institution that is "separate but equal."

At the practical level, civil unions have proven too limited to offer a permanent solution to the debate over gay and lesbian domestic relationships. Participants in civil unions do not enjoy the "same benefits" of a Vermont marriage after the couples leave Vermont, not least because the union provides no federal benefits. No state has a regular policy of recognizing this form of relationship, causing difficulties for those who wish either to terminate the union without returning to Vermont or to invoke the union as a basis for exercising some power ordinarily associated with a spouse, such as making medical decisions.

—*James M. Donovan*

FURTHER READING

Baker v. Vermont. 744 Atlantic Reporter (2d ser.), 864-912 (1999).

Eskridge, William N. *Equality Practice: Civil Unions and the Future of Gay Rights.* New York: Routledge, 2002.

Mello, Michael. *Legalizing Gay Marriage.* Philadelphia: Temple University Press, 2004.

Moats, David. *Civil Wars: A Battle for Gay Marriage.* New York: Harcourt, 2004.

"Same-Sex Marriage: A Selective Bibliography of the Legal Literature." Law Library, Rutgers School of Law. http://law-library.rutgers.edu/SSM.html.

Starr, Justin W. "Law Review Articles Citing *Baker*

v. Vermont." Brigham Young University Journal of Public Law 18 (2004): 353-370.

Wolfson, Evan. *Why Marriage Matters: America, Equality, and Gay People's Right to Marry*. New York: Simon & Schuster, 2004.

SEE ALSO: 1981: Gay and Lesbian Palimony Suits Emerge; 1993-1996: Hawaii Opens Door to Same-Gender Marriages; Aug. 6, 1994: Japanese American Citizens League Supports Same-Gender Marriage; Sept. 21, 1996: U.S. President Clinton Signs Defense of Marriage Act; Feb. 21, 2003: Australian Court Validates Transsexual Marriage; Apr., 2003: Buenos Aires Recognizes Same-Gender Civil Unions; June 17, 2003, and July 19, 2005: Canada Legalizes Same-Gender Marriage; Nov. 18, 2003: Massachusetts Court Rules for Same-Gender Marriage; Nov. 18, 2004: United Kingdom Legalizes Same-Gender Civil Partnerships; Apr. 4, 2005: United Kingdom's Gender Recognition Act Legalizes Transsexual Marriage.

January 12, 2000
UNITED KINGDOM LIFTS BAN ON GAYS AND LESBIANS IN THE MILITARY

The British government followed a 1999 ruling by the European Court of Human Rights and ended its ban on gays and lesbians in the military. Great Britain joined other European nations that have changed their policies against gay and lesbian service personnel, leaving the United States and Turkey as the only members of NATO with the ban intact.

LOCALE: United Kingdom
CATEGORIES: Military; civil rights; government and politics; laws, acts, and legal history

KEY FIGURES

John Beckett, weapons engineering mechanic in the Royal Navy
Graeme Grady, personnel administrator in the Royal Air Force
Duncan Lustig-Prean, lieutenant commander in the Royal Navy
Jeanette Smith, nurse in the Royal Air Force

SUMMARY OF EVENT

Until the year 2000, the United Kingdom had a longstanding policy of subjecting gays and lesbians in its military branches to intrusive investigations and dishonorable discharges. The policy had continued after the 1967 repeal of the Labouchere Amendment, which had criminalized all sexual contact among civilian men in Britain. Homosexual acts by servicemen remained criminal acts in civil law until 1994, when the acts were covered as offenses under military law punishable by immediate dismissal.

While other Western European nations abandoned bans on gays and lesbians in their armed forces, Britain continued to expel homosexual military personnel. Between 1989 and 1998, Britain discharged thirty-three officers and more than five hundred enlisted service members for homosexuality. Many of those discharged had good service records and had caused no disruption to their colleagues. The Ministry of Defence defended these discharges on the grounds that the presence of out gay troops would hurt morale and discipline—an argument used by the U.S. armed forces as well—among the 210,000 British uniformed personnel. Defence argued that surveys indicated that 95 percent of the troops were reluctant to serve with gays and lesbians. Opponents of the ban pointed out that because military policy was typically not decided on democratic grounds, the opinion of the troops should not hold any weight on the matter. Additionally, since most other North Atlantic Treaty Organization (NATO) countries had a lenient attitude toward gay and lesbian service personnel, British soldiers on multinational peacekeeping operations worked without problems alongside gays (and, sometimes, lesbians) in such places as Kosovo.

On June 7, 1995, Britain's High Court found that the no-gays rule was unjustified and inhumane but stopped short of changing it. On September 27, 1999, the European Court of Human Rights in Strasbourg, France, ruled in favor of four gay military personnel who had been dismissed from the British military in the mid-1990's because of their homosexuality. The plaintiffs were John Beckett and Duncan Lustig-Prean, formerly of the Royal Navy; and Jeanette Smith and Graeme Grady, formerly of the Royal Air Force. After unsuccessful judicial review proceedings in British courts, in which they invoked English administrative law and European Union gender-discrimination law, the four applicants took their cases to the court of human rights. The court held that the dismissals violated European human rights treaties, specifically the right of the plaintiffs to privacy as stated by Article 8 of the Convention on Human Rights. With its decision, the court became the first final appellate court in the world to invalidate a ban on lesbian, gay, and bisexual military personnel under a human rights treaty or constitution.

The verdict could not force Britain to change its laws. However, Britain was a signatory to the 1950 Convention for the Protection of Human Rights and Fundamental Freedoms. As such, it obliged itself to abide by the rulings of the European Court of Human Rights. Accordingly, the Ministry of Defence immediately suspended discharges of homosexuals despite protests from senior officers.

On January 12, 2000, the British government announced that sexual orientation would no longer be relevant in military recruitment, assignment, promotion, and disciplinary decisions. The Ministry of Defence replaced the ban on gays and lesbians with a code of conduct that applies to all service members, whether homosexual or heterosexual. Military personnel experts had decided that it would be impractical to try to write specific rules on various types of sexual conduct. Instead, the military implemented a more general service test that makes no reference to sexuality. The new guidelines permitted commanders to respond to inappropriate conduct such as sexual relations between commanders and subordinates or overt displays of affection that might offend others. The code gives commanders

---

"HOMOSEXUALITY AND THE ARMED FORCES"

Details of the Policy on Sexual Conduct in the Armed Forces and the Armed Forces Code of Social Conduct.

. . . The Code of Social Conduct firmly recognises the right to privacy, including sexual orientation. Accordingly the new policy lifting the ban on homosexuals, and firmly underpinned by the Code of Social Conduct, was considered the most appropriate solution for the UK Armed Forces.

The "Armed Forces Code of Social Conduct" sets out a policy based on behaviour and whether an individual's conduct may impact adversely on the cohesion, efficiency or operational effectiveness of the Service. In setting out this policy, no account or distinction is made on the basis of the individual's gender or sexual orientation, which is taken to be a private matter for the individual. The Code of Social Conduct is based on an assessment of the potential or actual impact of social conduct on operational effectiveness and, as a start point, operates on the principle that the Services will only interfere in an individual's private life where the actions or behaviour of an individual have adversely impacted, or are they likely to impact, on the efficiency or operational effectiveness of the Service. It therefore recognises an individuals right to a private life in line with the intent of Article 8 of the HRA [Human Rights Act].

To summarise, the policy to bar homosexuals from the Armed Forces was not legally sustainable and has now been replaced with a new policy which recognises sexual orientation as a private matter. It was formulated with the full consultation and support of the three Service Chiefs and is firmly underpinned by a code of social conduct that applies to all regardless of their sexual orientation.

Source: U.K. Ministry of Defence.

the right and the obligation to intervene in the personal lives of subordinates if there is an overriding operational need to do so to sustain team cohesion and maintain trust. Also, military authorities reinstated personnel discharged under the previous policy barring gays and lesbians.

Most observers regarded the end of the ban as inevitable. The Labour Party government of Prime Minister Tony Blair had fostered a socially progressive climate conducive to change. Blair had scheduled a vote in Parliament on the question of gays and lesbians in the military as part of the review of the Armed Services Bill. In a nation increasingly tolerant of homosexuality, it was no longer deemed socially or politically acceptable to denigrate or dismiss gays and lesbians. Many of the conservative military officials who had backed the ban had retired. The new leaders were unwilling to copy the U.S. government's Don't Ask, Don't Tell policy because they believed that it had failed. The government, the public, and the military were ready for a change in policy.

When the British government ended the ban, the announcement attracted relatively little news coverage. Many citizens appeared indifferent. Most of the attention came from organizations such as Rank Outsiders, a group for gays and lesbians who were serving or had served in the British military. Gay organizations expected that gays would now be able to serve with dignity and respect, but gay and lesbian service members were concerned a backlash could result if gays and lesbians came out of the closet. In subsequent years, no backlash has been evident.

Significance

The change in British policy leaves the U.S. military nearly alone among Western nations in its official policy of discrimination against lesbians and gays. The United States and Turkey are the only members of the NATO defense coalition that ban gays and lesbians from military service. The Netherlands became the first nation to end its ban on gays in the military in 1972, and nearly every other Western nation followed the lead of the Dutch.

The continued resistance of the U.S. military to ending its discriminatory policy is based on the argument that out gays and lesbians negatively affect unit cohesion and discipline, and the British continue to debate the effect of the change in policy on attitudes among soldiers. Some commanders still fear that heterosexual soldiers will have difficulty existing in close proximity with people who are gay and that violence will result. However, there have been no publically reported episodes of antigay violence within the British military since the policy change in 2000.

—*Caryn E. Neumann*

Further Reading

Belkin, Aaron, and R. L. Evans. "The Effects of Including Gay and Lesbian Soldiers in the British Armed Forces: Appraising the Evidence." November, 2000. Center for the Study of Sexual Minorities in the Military, University of California, Santa Barbara. http://www.gaymilitary.ucsb.edu/.

Center for the Study of Sexual Minorities in the Military, University of California, Santa Barbara. http://www.gaymilitary.ucsb.edu/.

Elwood, Nick. *All the Queen's Men*. London: Gay Men's Press, 1999.

McGhee, Derek. *Homosexuality, Law, and Resistance*. New York: Routledge, 2001.

Reid, T. R. "Britain Ends Its Curbs on Gays in Military." *Washington Post*, January 13, 2000, p. A13.

Robertson, A. H. *Human Rights in Europe*. Manchester, England: Manchester University Press, 1977.

Segal, David R., et al. "Gender and Sexual Orientation Diversity in Modern Military Forces: Cross-National Patterns." In *Beyond Zero Tolerance: Discrimination in Military Culture*, edited by Mary Fainsod Katzenstein and Judith Reppy. Lanham, Md.: Rowman & Littlefield, 1999.

Tatchell, Peter. *Europe in the Pink: Lesbian and Gay Equality in the New Europe*. London: Gay Men's Press, 1992.

_____. *We Don't Want to March Straight: Masculinity, Queers, and the Military*. New York: Cassell, 1995.

Wintemute, Robert. "European Court of Human Rights Strikes Down British Ban on Lesbians, Gays, and Bisexuals in the Armed Forces." *Lesbian/Gay Law Notes*, October, 1999, 1-5.

SEE ALSO: Mar. 15, 1919-1921: U.S. Navy Launches Sting Operation Against "Sexual Perverts"; July 3, 1975: U.S. Civil Service Commission Prohibits Discrimination Against Federal Employees; 1976-1990: Army Reservist Ben-Shalom Sues for Reinstatement; May-Aug., 1980: U.S. Navy Investigates the USS *Norton Sound* in Antilesbian Witch Hunt; May 3, 1989: *Watkins v. United States Army* Reinstates Gay Soldier; 1990, 1994: *Coming Out Under Fire* Documents Gay and Lesbian Military Veterans; Aug. 27, 1991: *The Advocate* Outs Pentagon Spokesman Pete Williams; Oct., 1992: Canadian Military Lifts Its Ban on Gays and Lesbians; Nov. 30, 1993: Don't Ask, Don't Tell Policy Is Implemented.

March 21, 2000
HOLLYWOOD AWARDS TRANSGENDER PORTRAYALS IN FILM

Actor Hilary Swank won the Academy Award for Best Actress for her portrayal of transgender Brandon Teena in the film Boys Don't Cry, *and Pedro Almodóvar's film* All About My Mother, *in which several complex transgender characters are featured, won the Oscar for Best Foreign Language Film. The awards mark the first formal, mainstream recognition of the significance and import of transgender and gender-ambiguous characters in film.*

LOCALE: Los Angeles, California
CATEGORIES: Transgender/transsexuality; arts; cultural and intellectual history; organizations and institutions

KEY FIGURES
Hilary Swank (b. 1974), American actor
Pedro Almodóvar (b. 1949), Spanish film maker

SUMMARY OF EVENT
While the use of gender impersonation or ambiguity as a plot device has been used in film since the inception of motion pictures, the inclusion of fully developed characters who are lesbian, gay, bisexual, and (especially) transgender is a late twentieth century phenomenon. A watershed year for depictions of transgender characters and themes was 2000, when the Academy of Motion Picture Arts and Sciences awarded (on March 21) Oscars to Hilary Swank for her portrayal of Brandon Teena in *Boys Don't Cry* (1999) and to film maker Pedro Almodóvar for his *Todo sobre mi madre* (1999; *All About My Mother*) as Best Foreign Language Film.

As the rise of hate crimes against transgender individuals can attest, however, these awards were not necessarily a sign of widespread public support toward people who choose to define gender on their own terms. Rather, the recognition indicated the increasing amount of discourse surrounding the collective fears, desires, and questions about gender and sexuality.

SIGNIFICANCE
According to film scholar Rebecca Bell-Metereau, more than two hundred films employ gender "illusion" as a key plot element or a focus of a critical scene. Decades before Dustin Hoffman took on the role of *Tootsie* (1982), Charlie Chaplin played an out of work actor who disguises himself as a woman in *The Masquerader* (1914) to get work as an actress. A number of early actors used humor as the context for men dressing as women: Chaplin, who cross-dressed again in *A Woman* (1915); Fatty

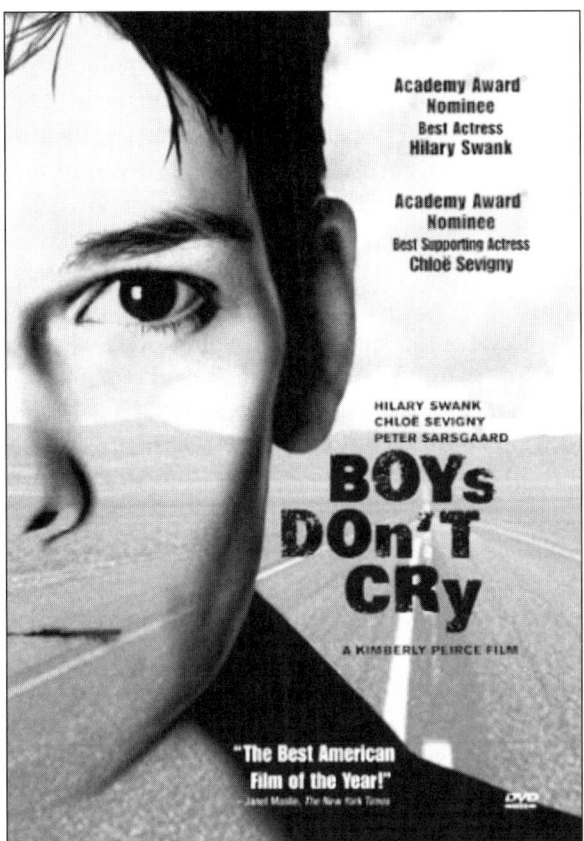

Poster for Boys Don't Cry *(1999).*

Arbuckle (*The Minstrel Man*, 1915; *Miss Fatty's Seaside Lovers*, 1915; *Miss Fatty in Coney Island*, 1917); Wallace Beery in the successful "Sweedie" series (1914-1916); and the numerous creators of the matron character (*Charley's Aunt* and Old Mother Riley). Most early filmic depictions of women dressing as men, however, more often than not show the female character punished for her audacity in claiming male privilege.

While film continued the stage convention of having adult women play boys and young male characters—Hamlet, Peter Pan, *The Prince and Pauper*, Oliver Twist, Little Lord Faunteroy—male impersonators on the screen usually don pants to get out of a scrape (Mary Pickford in *Poor Little Peppina*, 1915; Louise Brooks in *The Beggars of Life*, 1928; Gertrude Michael in *The Return of Sophie Lang*, 1936) or to commit a crime (Mae Murray in *Danger, Go Slow*, 1918; Gloria Swanson in *The Humming Bird*, 1924; Signe Hasso in *The House on 92nd Street*, 1945).

The Florida Enchantment (1914) and *The Amazons* (1917) brought the British Music Hall tradition of women in male tailored tuxedos to the screen, which found its apex in *Morocco* (1930) with Marlene Dietrich and *Zouzou* with Josephine Baker (1934). Greta Garbo in *Queen Christina* (1933) and Katharine Hepburn in *Sylvia Scarlett* (1935) contributed to the national dialogue concerning the culturally restrictive role placed on women, but self-censorship motivated by the Motion Picture Production Code in the 1930's meant that the screen depiction of gays, lesbians, bisexuals, and transgender characters for the next thirty years resorted to shop-worn stereotypes, innuendo, and the demonization of those who challenged heteronormativity and gender binaries.

With the women's movement and the so-called sexual revolution, male impersonation virtually disappeared from film, as "women in pants" were no longer novelties. The gradual societal shift in the status of women also suggested that to be upwardly mobile, women no longer had to be men (or look like men), even though they still needed "masculine" attributes, such as aggressiveness and assertiveness, power, and boldness. Since the 1970's, most films featuring male impersonators have been period pieces: *Victor/Victoria* (1982), *Yentl* (1983), and *Orlando* (1993). Nia Vardalos added a twist to the genre with *Connie and Carla* (2004), where two women hide out from mobsters by pretending to be gay men who perform as drag queens.

The 1960's ushered in a wide range of female impersonation, including portraits of cross-dressing as part of gay and lesbian culture (*Outrageous*, 1977; *Torch Song Trilogy*, 1988; *Paris Is Burning*, 1991) and films featuring transsexual characters (*The Christine Jorgensen Story*, 1970; *I Want What I Want*, 1972; *The World According to Garp*, 1982). High camp found its way to the silver screen with *Myra Breckinridge* (1970), *The Adventures of Priscilla, Queen of the Desert* (1994), *To Wong Foo, Thanks for Everything, Julie Newmar* (1995), with "Divine" in numerous John Waters films, and the "gender-bending" of Tim Curry in *The Rocky*

Horror Picture Show (1975). Several films have explored the "Tiresias effect," where one person has the experience of living in both a male and female body (*Goodbye, Charlie*, 1964; *All of Me*, 1984; *Switch*, 1991; *The Hot Chick*, 2002).

The use of cross-dressing as low farce has continued into the twenty-first century, with films including *The Nutty Professor* (1996), *Juwanna Mann* (2002), *Sorority Boys* (2002), and *She's the Man* (2006). Keenen Ivory Wayans and Shawn Wayans complicated the discussion of the use of drag in film with race when they played two African American FBI agents who impersonate two Caucasian women in *White Chicks* (2004). The many accusations of racism over the film's use of whiteface seemingly were not of concern twenty years earlier when Linda Hunt won an Oscar for Best Supporting Actress for her portrayal of photographer Billy Kwan in *The Year of Living Dangerously* (1982).

Despite the proliferation of explorations of gender illusion in film in the later part of the century, most depictions tend to be negative: The cross-dresser is often killed or commits suicide—*Frebbie and the Bean* (1974); *In a Year of 14 Moons* (1979); *Boys Don't Cry*—or is a psychotic killer: Alfred Hitchcock's *Psycho* (1960); *Dressed to Kill* (1980); *Silence of the Lambs* (1991). Even in those films that present the transgender individual in a more sympathetic light–*Come Back to the Five and Dime Jimmy Dean, Jimmy Dean* (1982); *Kiss of the Spider Woman* (1985); *The Adventures of Sebastian Cole* (1998); *Flawless* (1999)—the cinematic narrative is more concerned with the main (gender-conforming heterosexual) character's journey. With the exception of *La Cage aux Folles* (1979)— which spawned two sequels, including a stage musical and an American remake (*The Birdcage*, 1996)—and *Transamerica* (2005), which garnered for Felicity Huffman a Golden Globe Award for Best Actress as well as a best actress Oscar nomination, most commercially successful drag movies preserve the heterosexuality of their cross-dressing characters: *Some Like It Hot* (1959), *Tootsie* (1982), and *Mrs. Doubtfire* (1993).

Ever since *Glen or Glenda?* (1954), Hollywood's depiction of transgender lives rarely has moved beyond cheap comedy, surface titillation, or melodramatic shock. Neil Jordan's *The Crying Game* (1992) is a notable exception, as the character "Dil" challenges other characters (and the audience's) ability to categorize her sexuality, gender, race, and nationality. Similarly, most of the films of Pedro Almodóvar contain characters who have crafted integrated lives that confound conventional expectations of gender and sexuality. Indeed, the most nuanced films about alternate-gendered lives come not from Hollywood but from world cinema: *Ma Vie en Rose* (Spain, 1997); *Madame Satá* (Brazil, 2003); *Lola and Billy the Kid* (Germany, 1999); *Beautiful Boxer* (Thailand, 2004); and *Osama* (Afghanistan, 2004). Also of note, the First International Transgender Film and Video Festival was held in London in 1997.

In many ways the voyeurism of watching film is the perfect medium to explore presentations and re-presentations of gender. Through camera angles, lighting, costume, and makeup, film is able to control the physical body to a certain degree, collaborating with the character to present their self to the world.

—*Bud Coleman*

FURTHER READING

Baker, Roger. *Drag: A History of Female Impersonation in the Performing Arts.* New York: New York University Press, 1994.

Bell-Metereau, Rebecca. *Hollywood Androgyny.* 2d ed. New York: Columbia University Press, 1993.

Bruzzi, Stella. *Undressing Cinema: Clothing and Identity in the Movies.* New York: Routledge, 1997.

Dickens, Homer. *What a Drag: Men as Women and Women as Men in the Movies.* New York: Quill, 1984.

Hadleigh, Boze. *The Lavender Screen: The Gay and Lesbian Films, Their Stars, Makers, Characters, and Critics.* Secaucus, N.J.: Carol, 1993.

McLellan, Diana. *The Girls: Sappho Goes to Hollywood.* New York: LA Weekly Books, 2000.

Russo, Vitto. *The Celluloid Closet: Homosexuality in the Movies.* Rev. ed. New York: Harper & Row, 1987.

Sánchez, María Carla, and Linda Schlossberg, eds. *Passing: Identity and Interpretation in Sexuality, Race, and Religion.* New York: New York University Press, 2001.

Straayer, Chris. *Deviant Eyes, Deviant Bodies: Sexual Re-Orientation in Film and Video.* New York: Columbia University Press, 1996.

SEE ALSO: 1929: *Pandora's Box* Opens; 1930's-1960's: Hollywood Bans "Sexual Perversion" in Films; 1985: Lesbian Film *Desert Hearts* Is Released; 1988: *Macho Dancer* Is Released in the Philippines; 1990, 1994: *Coming Out Under Fire* Documents Gay and Lesbian Military Veterans; 1992-2002: Celebrity Lesbians Come Out; 1993: *The Wedding Banquet* Is First Acclaimed Taiwanese Gay-Themed Film; Dec. 24, 1993-Dec. 31, 1993: Transgender Man Brandon Teena Raped and Murdered; Dec. 3, 1998-Feb. 25, 1999: Screening of *Fire* Ignites Violent Protests in India; Mar. 5, 2006: *Brokeback Mountain, Capote,* and *Transamerica* Receive Oscars.

June 28, 2000
BOY SCOUTS OF AMERICA V. DALE

The U.S. Supreme Court ruled that the Boy Scouts of America has the right to exclude gays from its membership and leadership. The Court agreed with the Scouts' contention that the presence of gays communicates a message contrary to the organization's professed values.

LOCALE: Monmouth County, New Jersey
CATEGORIES: Laws, acts, and legal history; organizations and institutions; civil rights

KEY FIGURES
James Dale (b. 1970), assistant scoutmaster expelled from the Boy Scouts
James W. Kay, Boy Scout council executive in Monmouth, New Jersey

SUMMARY OF EVENT
James Dale joined the Boy Scouts of America (B.S.A.) in 1978 at the age of eight. He excelled in the goals of the organization, earned the rank of Eagle Scout in 1988, and subsequently attained the position of assistant scoutmaster. While attending Rutgers University, Dale acknowledged that he was gay, and he eventually led the campus's lesbian and gay alliance. In July of 1990, he was interviewed by the *Star-Ledger* of Newark, New Jersey, which published an article on July 8, 1990, that identified Dale as a gay student.

On August 5, Dale was notified by James W. Kay, Monmouth scout council executive, that his membership in the Boy Scouts was revoked, stating, according to trial records, that "the Boy Scouts of America . . . specifically forbid membership to homosexuals." The basis for this position was the scout oath promise to be "morally straight" and the scout "law" requirement to be "clean," both construed to mean "heterosexual." Denied an opportunity to appeal his case, Dale filed a six-count complaint against the B.S.A. on July 29, 1992.

While the trial court sided with the B.S.A., the appellate court, and ultimately a unanimous state supreme court, ruled in favor of Dale. The courts found that the scouts constituted a public accommodation and thus was subject to New Jersey's Law Against Discrimination, which had been amended in 1991 to prohibit discrimination because of a person's "affectional or sexual orientation."

The U.S. Supreme Court, in a 5-4 decision, reversed the ruling of the New Jersey appellate court, holding that to apply New Jersey's public accommodations law to the scouts violated the organization's First Amendment right of expressive association. Claiming to not take a position on the

A Christian Right protester outside the U.S. Supreme Court in April, 2000. The Court was hearing arguments in the case of Boy Scouts of America v. Dale. *(Hulton Archive/Getty Images)*

soundness of the scout's exclusion of gays, the majority opinion, written by Chief Justice William Rehnquist, explained,

> The forced inclusion of an unwanted person in a group infringes the group's freedom of expressive association if the presence of that person affects in a significant way the group's ability to advocate public or private viewpoints.

The Court relied significantly upon its earlier decision to exclude a gay and lesbian group from Boston's St. Patrick's Day parade (*Hurley v. Irish-American Gay, Lesbian and Bisexual Group of Boston, Inc.*, 1995). Dale's mere presence, according to the Court, was sufficiently communicative to send a message equal to the sign-carrying gay and lesbian parade participants in the *Hurley* case. On the principle that speakers should be allowed to control the message they send, the Court permitted the scouts to exclude Dale from its membership.

SIGNIFICANCE

Dale arguably represents the nadir of American judicial activism against lesbians and gays. Unlike cases that addressed the actions of homosexuals, such as *Bowers v. Hardwick* (1986), which had upheld the criminalization of state sodomy laws, and *Hurley*, which barred a gay and lesbian group from carrying its own sign in a parade, *Dale* held that the mere *presence* of a gay man had toxic effects upon an organization's constitutional guarantees. James Dale was found to have "done" nothing more than exist without shame; at no time was he accused of seeking to use his B.S.A. position to speak about homosexuality, or to influence others to adopt his views or his sexual identity.

Conceivably, under this new lax standard, no "known" homosexual can be protected by antidiscrimination laws: Paradoxically, antidiscrimination laws will only protect those who stay in the closet, removing a person's *expressed* sexual orientation and gender identity from antidiscrimination protections.

Contrary to this negative outcome, some scholars, including Nancy Knauer, have argued that *Dale* highlights "the uniquely expressive character of the openly gay individual." Both sides of the culture war, she argues, "agree [that] an openly gay individual sends a message of gay pride, encourages others to embrace homosexuality, and puts an ordinary face on homosexuality for the non-gay majority." Because society assumes a standard of "heteronormativity," that is, "the largely unstated assumption that heterosexuality is the essential and elemental ordering [principle] of society," the majority in *Dale* rightly concluded that the unapologetic presence of an "openly gay" individual communicates a message that raises First Amendment issues. This "presence," in effect, can be interpreted as a form of expressive power as well. That is, being gay or lesbian in the presence of those who are not, or in the presence of those who are "uncomfortable" with lesbians and gays, sends a message of its own.

No subsequent decisions have applied the more draconian implications of the *Dale* decision. On the contrary, the opinion that was viewed by some as a sword against gay and lesbian equality has more frequently become a shield. For example, in an opinion rendered by the U.S. Court of Appeals for the Third Circuit (*Forum for Academic and Institutional Rights v. Rumsfeld*, 2004), the court granted an injunction against enforcement of the Solomon Amendment, which penalized colleges and universities that restricted military recruiters from their campuses, in this case because of the military's exclusion of lesbians, gays, and bisexuals from service. The opinion cites *Dale* for the point that forcing colleges and universities to accept recruiters on their campuses would force the campuses to express the military's message of discriminatory hiring (just as the scouts would have been forced to communicate the message that homosexuality was

---

FROM *BOY SCOUTS OF AMERICA V. DALE*

Chief Justice Rehnquist delivered the opinion of the Court: . . . The Boy Scouts is a private, not-for-profit organization engaged in instilling its system of values in young people. The Boy Scouts asserts that homosexual conduct is inconsistent with the values it seeks to instill. Respondent is James Dale, a former Eagle Scout whose adult membership in the Boy Scouts was revoked when the Boy Scouts learned that he is an avowed homosexual and gay rights activist. The New Jersey Supreme Court held that New Jersey's public accommodations law requires that the Boy Scouts admit Dale. This case presents the question whether applying New Jersey's public accommodations law in this way violates the Boy Scouts' right of expressive association. We hold that it does. . . .

In *Roberts v. United States Jaycees* (1984), we observed that "implicit in the right to engage in activities protected by the First Amendment" is "a corresponding right to associate with others in pursuit of a wide variety of political, social, economic, educational, religious, and cultural ends." This right is crucial in preventing the majority from imposing its views on groups that would rather express other, perhaps unpopular, ideas. . . . Government actions that may unconstitutionally burden this freedom may take many forms, one of which is "intrusion into the internal structure or affairs of an association" like a "regulation that forces the group to accept members it does not desire." Forcing a group to accept certain members may impair the ability of the group to express those views, and only those views, that it intends to express. Thus, "[f]reedom of association . . . plainly presupposes a freedom not to associate."

The forced inclusion of an unwanted person in a group infringes the group's freedom of expressive association if the presence of that person affects in a significant way the group's ability to advocate public or private viewpoints. . . . But the freedom of expressive association, like many freedoms, is not absolute. We have held that the freedom could be overridden "by regulations adopted to serve compelling state interests, unrelated to the suppression of ideas, that cannot be achieved through means significantly less restrictive of associational freedoms." . . .

Because this is a First Amendment case where the ultimate conclusions of law are virtually inseparable from findings of fact, we are obligated to independently review the factual record to ensure that the state court's judgment does not unlawfully intrude on free expression. . . . The record reveals the following. The Boy Scouts is a private, nonprofit organization. . . . We are not, as we must not be, guided by our views of whether the Boy Scouts' teachings with respect to homosexual conduct are right or wrong; public or judicial disapproval of a tenet of an organization's expression does not justify the State's effort to compel the organization to accept members where such acceptance would derogate from the organization's expressive message. "While the law is free to promote all sorts of conduct in place of harmful behavior, it is not free to interfere with speech for no better reason than promoting an approved message or discouraging a disfavored one, however enlightened either purpose may strike the government." . . .

The judgment of the New Jersey Supreme Court is reversed, and the cause remanded for further proceedings not inconsistent with this opinion.

It is so ordered.

acceptable had they been forced to accept Dale as a scoutmaster). The appellate court found that being forced to accept recruiters on campus would violate the campuses' First Amendment rights against communicating another's message (that of the military and its discriminatory hiring practices).

Although it won its case, the scouts did not emerge unscathed. After the B.S.A. won the right to openly discriminate (it should be noted that Girl Scouts of the United States of America does not discriminate against lesbians), many funding organizations withheld their support. United Way chapters across the country withdrew their funding, and local governments, such as the cities of Los Angeles and San Diego, in California, reduced their dealings with the organization. Connecticut excluded the scouts from its state employee charitable campaign.

Dale currently works as the vice president of a health-care publishing company. His story became the subject of a documentary titled *Heroes*.

—*James M. Donovan*

FURTHER READING

Boy Scouts of America v. Dale, 530 U.S. 640 (2000).

Brower, Todd. "Of Courts and Closets: A Doctrinal and Empirical Analysis of Lesbian and Gay Identity in the Courts." *San Diego Law Review* 38, no. 565 (2001).

Knauer, Nancy J. "'Simply So Different': The Uniquely Expressive Character of the Openly Gay Individual After *Boy Scouts of America v. Dale*." *Kentucky Law Journal* 89, no. 997 (2001).

Mechling, Jay. *On My Honor: Boy Scouts and the Making of American Youth*. Chicago: University of Chicago Press, 2001.

Shepard, Tom, director. *Scout's Honor*. Hohokus, N.J.: New Day Films, 2001. Video recording.

Walzer, Lee, ed. *Gay Rights on Trial: A Reference Handbook*. Santa Barbara, Calif.: ABC-CLIO, 2002. Includes discussion of *Dale*.

SEE ALSO: Jan. 12, 1939: *Thompson v. Aldredge* Dismisses Sodomy Charges Against Lesbians; 1952-1990: U.S. Law Prohibits Gay and Lesbian Immigration; May 22, 1967: U.S. Supreme Court Upholds Law Preventing Immigration of Gays and Lesbians; Jan. 22, 1973: *Roe v. Wade* Legalizes Abortion and Extends Privacy Rights; June 21, 1973: U.S. Supreme Court Supports Local Obscenity Laws; Aug., 1973: American Bar Association Calls for Repeal of Laws Against Consensual Sex; Nov. 17, 1975: U.S. Supreme Court Rules in "Crimes Against Nature" Case; 1981: Gay and Lesbian Palimony Suits Emerge; 1982-1991: Lesbian Academic and Activist Sues University of California for Discrimination; 1986: *Bowers v. Hardwick* Upholds State Sodomy Laws; May 1, 1989: U.S. Supreme Court Rules Gender-Role Stereotyping Is Discriminatory; Dec. 17, 1991: Minnesota Court Awards Guardianship to Lesbian Partner; 1992-2006: Indians Struggle to Abolish Sodomy Law; 1993-1996: Hawaii Opens Door to Same-Gender Marriages; Sept. 21, 1993-Apr. 21, 1995: Lesbian Mother Loses Custody of Her Child; Nov. 30, 1993: Don't Ask, Don't Tell Policy Is Implemented; Dec. 20, 1999: *Baker v. Vermont* Leads to Recognition of Same-Gender Civil Unions; June 26, 2003: U.S. Supreme Court Overturns Texas Sodomy Law.

April 20, 2001
CHINESE PSYCHIATRIC ASSOCIATION REMOVES HOMOSEXUALITY FROM LIST OF MENTAL DISORDERS

The Chinese Psychiatric Association removed "homosexuality" from the third revision of the Chinese Classification and Diagnostic Criteria of Mental Disorders. *Critics, however, called for the association to remove "ego-dystonic homosexuality" as a diagnostic category for individuals who remain dissatisfied with their same-gender sexual orientation.*

LOCALE: China
CATEGORIES: Health and medicine; science; organizations and institutions; publications

KEY FIGURES
Douglas Kimmel, American psychologist
Jia Yicheng, Chinese psychiatrist and professor

SUMMARY OF EVENT
On April 20, 2001, the Chinese Psychiatric Association (CPA) published the third revision of its *Chinese Classification and Diagnostic Criteria of Mental Disorders* (commonly known as the "Chinese Classification of Mental Disorders," or CCMD), its official list. In this revision, "homosexuality" was removed from the list.

This change came as the culmination of both internal and international pressure to bring this Chinese classification schema into line with the World Health Organization's guidelines and with other mental health organizations around the world. Like the 1973 revision of the American Psychiatric Association's (APA) *Diagnostic and Statistical Manual of Mental Disorders* (DSM), this revision, however, retained the diagnostic category "ego-dystonic homosexuality" for individuals who remain dissatisfied with their same-gender sexual orientation. This particular diagnosis was later removed from the APA's DSM.

Even with the 1994 revision of the CCMD (CCMD-2R), the CPA's manual contained statements regarding its opposition to the World Health Organization's guidelines that depathologize homosexuality. Since that time, however, social pressure had been building both within and outside China. In 1997 a new penal code was implemented that included the removal of criminal penalties for sodomy (termed "hooliganism"). Also, Chinese nationals in other countries began to marshal their resources and organize for the 2001 revision process.

The debate on such a revision was triggered when the Chinese translation of a paper by noted American psychologist Douglas Kimmel was distributed at a medical conference in China in the spring of 1997. The paper presents a historical perspective on homosexuality as a diagnostic entity. Jia Yicheng, a well-respected Chinese psychiatrist and professor, denounced Kimmel's assertion in the paper that homosexuality is normal and requested that the Zhejiang Province Mental Health Institute launch an open debate on the matter.

Twelve articles were published in *Mental Health Information*, the official publication of Zhejiang Province Mental Health Institute which had been made available to the Chinese public from August through December, 1997. Although more articles were included that opposed depathologizing homosexuality, Chinese mental health professionals for the first time voiced arguments in favor of depathologizing homosexuality; more significantly, their opinions were heard and read by the general public directly. Some professionals had been speaking and writing on the topic for several years, but their voices were heard only at professional conferences and their opinions were seldom reported by the media.

On September 1, 1997, the Chinese Society for the Study of Sexual Minorities (CSSSM) was established in Los Angeles, California. The group was to coordinate the efforts of Chinese living outside China who wished to see the CCMD changed. Because information regarding lesbian, gay, and bisexual issues was quite limited in China and its dissemination still largely restricted by government policy, CSSSM developed a biweekly Web journal, *Tao Hong Man Tian Xia* (www.csssm.org), which is published in both Chinese and English. The first issue appeared on September 5, 1997, and it has been published continuously since. Featured in the journal are articles written by CSSSM members or free-lance articles commissioned by CSSSM.

Significance

The Chinese Psychiatric Association had stressed that its decision to take "homosexuality" off its list of mental disorders was based on its own empirical findings as well as those from their counterparts in other countries. In 1996, the CPA had established a special task force to assess the mental status of lesbians and gays in China. That task force developed a sample of fifty-four homosexually oriented persons, six of whom had approached psychiatrists to change their sexual orientation, and found that some of the subjects in this sample showed signs of psychological problems. The researchers did not address whether those problems were caused by the individuals' sexual orientations or resulted from living in a negative and oppressive environment.

Statements of support for the revision of the CCMD came also from psychiatric, psychological, counseling, and other professional mental health associations around the world. The governing bodies of such organizations as the American Psychiatric Association, the American Psychological Association, the American Counseling Association, and others passed strongly worded resolutions urging the removal of "homosexuality" as a mental disorder. Presidents of these associations wrote strongly worded letters to the CPA.

The CPA then sent members to the annual conference of the APA in 2000, soliciting both pro and con suggestions from attendees. The tenth revision of the *International Statistical Classification of Diseases and Related Health Problems* (ICD-10), issued by the World Health Organization, also had an influence on CPA's decision. The standing committee of the CPA elected to pass the resolution, thus depathologizing homosexuality for CCMD-3 at the end of 2000. The decision has been warmly welcomed by the gay, lesbian, and bisexual community in China. Some, however, believe the delisting did not go far enough and are urging the removal of "ego-dystonic homosexuality" from the CCMD.

—*Mark Pope*

Further Reading

Choong, Tet Sieu. "Revolution by Stages: Things Are Gradually Getting Better for Asia's Homosexuals, but Acceptance Is Still a Long Way Off." *Asiaweek.com*. August 7, 1998. http://www.asiaweek.com/asiaweek/98/0807.

CSSSM News Digest, October 26, 2000. Special issue, "Update of CSSSM Work, 1997-2000." http://www.csssm.org/English/e6.htm.

Fann, Rodge Q. "Growing Up Gay in China." In *Gay, Lesbian, and Transgender Issues in Education: Programs, Policies, and Practices*, edited by James T. Sears. New York: Harrington Park Press, 2005.

Immigration and Naturalization Service. *China: Information on Treatment of Homosexuals*. Washington, D.C.: United States INS Resource Information Center, March 1, 2001. http://uscis.gov/graphics/services/asylum/ric/documentation/CHN01001.htm.

Wu, Jin. "Open Debate on Homosexuality in China and CSSSM in 1997." Chinese Society for the Study of Sexual Minorities, 1998. http://www.csssm.org/English/e3.htm.

Zhou, Huashan. "Individual Strategies of Tongshi Empowerment." In *Different Rainbows*, edited by Peter Drucker. Chicago: InBook/LPC Group, 2000.

_____. *Tongzhi: Politics of Same-sex Eroticism in Chinese Societies*. New York: Haworth Press, 2000.

See also: May 6, 1868: Kertbeny Coins the Terms "Homosexual" and "Heterosexual"; 1869: Westphal Advocates Medical Treatment for Sexual Inversion; 1897: Ellis Publishes *Sexual Inversion*; May 14, 1897: Hirschfeld Founds the Scientific-Humanitarian Committee; 1905: Freud Rejects

Third-Sex Theory; 1929: Davis's Research Identifies Lesbian Sexuality as Common and Normal; 1948: Kinsey Publishes *Sexual Behavior in the Human Male*; 1952: APA Classifies Homosexuality as a Mental Disorder; 1953: Kinsey Publishes *Sexual Behavior in the Human Female*; 1953-1957: Evelyn Hooker Debunks Beliefs That Homosexuality Is a "Sickness"; Dec. 15, 1973: Homosexuality Is Delisted by APA.

May 25, 2001
JAPANESE HUMAN RIGHTS COUNCIL RECOMMENDS LESBIAN AND GAY RIGHTS

The Japanese Ministry of Justice's Council for Human Rights Promotion recommended the addition of "sexual orientation" to Japan's human rights laws. The council's decision marks the first time that lesbian and gay rights had been acknowledged by the Japanese government. The proposal, sent to the Japanese house of representatives in March, 2003, was rejected, however.

LOCALE: Tokyo, Japan
CATEGORIES: Laws, acts, and legal history; civil rights

KEY FIGURES
Masashi Nagata, president of the Japan Association for the Lesbian and Gay Movement, or OCCUR
Masaki Inaba, OCCUR's program director for advocacy

SUMMARY OF EVENT
Following the direction of the United Nations in 1998, Japan's Ministry of Justice planned to renew Japan's outdated human rights protections. The ministry created the Council for Human Rights Promotion (CHRP), under the Law of Promotion of Measures for Human Rights Protection, to determine the changes that needed to be made to the civil rights code.

The interim report of the council, released in November of 2000, indicated that the council needed to investigate further the issue of discrimination based on sexual orientation to determine if it indeed was a national human rights issue. The council then held five public hearings in five big cities. Three representatives from OCCUR (Japan Association for the Lesbian and Gay Movement) were invited to the council hearings in Osaka, Fukuoka, and Sapporo.

OCCUR also sent out appeals to LGBT individuals and organizations around the world, asking them to urge the CHRP to include LGBT rights in its final proposal. OCCUR gained strong support from the International Gay and Lesbian Human Rights Commission (IGLHRC). Acting together, OCCUR and IGLHRC persuaded the Tokyo municipal government to add to its human rights guidelines a section prohibiting discrimination against LGBT people in the same month the interim report was released by the CHRP. Tokyo, then, became the first city in Asia to have sexual-orientation legislation.

The CHRP released its final report on May 25, 2001. It recommended creating an independent National Human Rights Commission (NHRC), and clearly specified that the commission would solve the problems of human rights violations and discrimination based on sexual orientation through positive actions. There already were many countries that publicly prohibited discrimination based on sexual orientation, but for Japan, this was the first public recognition of LGBT rights.

Including LGBT rights in the final report resulted from the actions and efforts of lesbians and gays. In the report, lesbians and gays are described as entitled to full human rights. The final report stated that there had been cases of discrimination in employment and also harassment and public defamation against homosexuals, and it proposed that discriminatory treatment based on sexual orientation would be targeted by positive actions of the NHRC to make society more fair.

Masaki Inaba, OCCUR's program director for advocacy, said that he was glad the final report touched on discrimination based on sexual orientation. He emphasized that it was a historical moment for LGBT people in Japan because the human rights of sexual minorities would finally be recognized at the state level. Inaba said, "We are delighted to share good news from Japan: the Council for HRP, the Japanese Justice Ministry's special council for founding a new national human rights commission, included LGBT rights as one of the categories of human rights which should be protected by the new commission. There are no antidiscrimination laws in Japan, but if the commission is legally established, it will be a good substitute for antidiscrimination laws as a measure to protect Japanese LGBT human rights."

Significance

The proposal of the Council for Human Rights Promotion was drafted into a bill and sent to the Japanese house of representatives (Shugiin) in March of 2002. A backlash ensued, particularly over language in the bill that indicated the NHRC would have the power to reduce invasive media action toward minorities and children. There were many abusive expressions about homosexuals being used in Japan's media at the time, especially on television. The final report stressed promoting positive, or good, images of LGBT people to the Japanese people, and major media companies argued that the report's recommendations would violate their right to free speech.

OCCUR soon gained attention not only from the Japanese people but also foreign organizations pursuing LGBT rights. Since this was the first time in Japan that LGBT rights had been acknowledged, OCCUR's strategy became a model on how to pursue civil rights throughout the world.

On October 10, 2003, the human rights protection bill had been thrown out along with all the other pending bills when the house of representatives was dissolved by Prime Minister Junichiro Koizumi. It appears that unless the bill is amended to make the NHRC more independent from the ministry, and more protective of free speech for the media, it will stall. However, many LGBT rights organizations in Japan have become active because of CHRP's proposal.

—*Mitsunori Misawa*

Further Reading

Broadbent, Jeffrey. *Environmental Politics in Japan: Networks of Power and Protest.* New York: Cambridge University Press, 1998.

Brody, Betsy. *Opening the Door: Immigration, Ethnicity, and Globalization in Japan.* New York: Routledge, 2001.

Chan-Tiberghien, Jennifer. *Gender and Human Rights Politics in Japan: Global Norms and Domestic Network.* Stanford, Calif.: Stanford University Press, 2004.

McLelland, Mark. *Queer Japan from the Pacific War to the Internet Age.* Lanham, Md.: Rowman & Littlefield, 2005.

Narita, Norihiko. *About Japan Series: Political Changes in the 1990's.* Tokyo: Foreign Press Center, 1999.

Sattler, Cheryl L. *Teaching to Transcend.* Albany: State University of New York Press, 2000.

Summerhawk, Barbara, Cheiron McMahill, and Darren McDonald, eds. and trans. *Queer Japan: Personal Stories of Japanese Lesbians, Gays, Transsexuals, and Bisexuals.* Norwich, Vt.: New Victoria, 1998.

Wendt, Alexander. *Social Theory of International Politics.* New York: Cambridge University Press, 1999.

See also: Oct. 12-15, 1979: Lesbian and Gay Asian Collective Is Founded; 1987: Asian Pacific Lesbian Network Is Founded; Aug. 6, 1994: Japanese American Citizens League Supports Same-Gender Marriage; Apr. 20, 2001: Chinese Psychiatric Association Removes Homosexuality from List of Mental Disorders; July, 2003: Singapore Lifts Ban on Hiring Lesbian and Gay Employees.

September 7, 2001
First Gay and Lesbian Television Network Is Launched in Canada

In September of 2001, Canada's PrideVision TV, the world's first GLBT television network to broadcast around the clock, began broadcasting to subscribers on digital cable.

Locale: Toronto, Ontario, Canada
Categories: Cultural and intellectual history; arts; economics

Summary of Event

The social, political, and media climate of the late 1990's made the beginning of the twenty-first century a perfect time to explore the chance to launch a queer television network. The idea had been raised by major networks as well as independent players in the United States for years, but had never matured into a viable media option. Because of decreased arts funding and the election of a conservative Republican president (George W. Bush) in 2000, the social and political landscape in the United States did not seem poised to embrace such a new and controversial media presence. In Canada, however, the moment seemed to have arrived. After receiving its license to operate from the Canadian Radio-Television Telecommunications Commission (CRTC) in November of 2000, PrideVision TV ran its first broadcast on September 7, 2001.

Policymakers in Canada around this time had been fully engaged in the debate on same-gender marriage, with more than half of the Canadian population supporting the legalization of marriage for lesbians and gays. Ontario began issuing marriage licenses to same-gender couples. Winnipeg had elected an out gay mayor. The leader of the national Progressive Conservative Party, Joe Clark, served as grand marshal of the Gay Pride Parade in Calgary, the city widely identified as Canada's most conservative. In the midst of all this change, Canada was quickly becoming an international leader in equal rights for sexual minorities.

Public interest in issues concerning sexuality helped make the case for the launch of a GLBT network in the new digital television roll out. With the success of various television shows featuring gay and lesbian hosts and characters, it seemed timely and appropriate to pursue a larger, more sustained presence on television, and with the proliferation of specialty channels offered by digital television, the idea of creating a niche-market TV station that would attract the subscription dollars of a sizeable queer population in Canada seemed more plausible than ever.

The producers of PrideVision TV capitalized on the GLBT market, dedicating itself to airing programs that would represent all facets of the Canadian queer community and the global community as well. PrideVision's programming schedule included drama, comedy, cooking, gardening, fitness, travel, erotica, and dating shows. They also had proposed a full slate of documentaries, reality shows, and news programs. In keeping with this ambitious agenda, PrideVision guaranteed that the programming on the network would provide, more than ever before, positive coverage of gay and lesbian issues, from a documentary line of "PrideVisionairies" featuring biographies of influential GLBT figures throughout history, to weekly news programming from the country's various queer communities. The word "celebration" featured heavily in much of PrideVision's promotional materials. Indeed, the bulk of the programming seems to have been directly and explicitly committed to celebrating all aspects of gay and lesbian life—the social, the sexual, the political, the historical, and the entertaining.

Significance

The impact of PrideVision TV was felt in both the media and political landscapes in Canada and internationally. Although many expected the network to falter early, citing its high price tag for digital sub-

On the set of "Fairy Tale," a match-making show for GLBT persons that aired on PrideVision television in Canada beginning in November, 2003. (AP/Wide World Photos)

scribers and perceived limited audience, the network continued programming as PrideVision until March, 2005, when it was renamed OUTtv. OUTtv continues PrideVision's legacy as the first twenty-four-hour GLBT network in the world. PrideVision now operates, with a new name, as a premium-pay gay erotica channel on digital cable.

The introduction of PrideVision had an obvious impact upon the Canadian queer community, who, for the first time, had a television station dedicated exclusively to queer experience. However, the general population was impacted as well. The launch of the network received a great deal of mainstream media attention, culminating in a widely publicized lawsuit against western Canada's major cable company, Shaw Communications. During the free preview period for PrideVision, Shaw implemented a small but significant roadblock, which forced viewers to incur a one-cent charge and "approve" their access to the network at every single program change. Shaw attempted to defend itself with the claim that they were protecting the sensitivities of their subscribers, but the CRTC ultimately ruled in favor of PrideVision, indicating that the "additional steps required to sample PrideVision will act as a strong disincentive for subscribers to view the service," a disincentive that contravened the commission's regulations against giving undue preference to any person or network.

The CRTC ruling was integral to gay and lesbian activist groups across Canada, but it also drew a great deal of attention from mainstream Canadian news media, the kind of publicity that a small network just cannot buy. PrideVision—a stand-alone, specialty, niche-market, premium-pay digital network—had been featured on the cover of major publications around the country. The network's name was heard and spoken by people who would likely never have regarded the station in the first place, let alone subscribed to it.

Suddenly, though, PrideVision and its success or failure became a major issue for every liberal in the country concerned about media censorship. In many ways, Shaw's assumptions about the tolerance levels of their paying customers exposed attitudes that many Canadians were unwilling to accept as representative of their own views. The public attention to the battle between PrideVision and Shaw Communications ceased to be, in public perception, a gay and lesbian rights issue only; rather, it became a human rights issue.

—*Dawn Elizabeth B. Johnston*

FURTHER READING

Capsuto, Steven. *Alternate Channels: The Uncensored Story of Gay and Lesbian Images on Radio and Television, 1930's to the Present*. New York: Ballantine Books, 2000.

Johnson, Phylis, and Michael C. Keith. *Queer Airwaves: The Story of Gay and Lesbian Broadcasting*. Armonk, N.Y.: M.E. Sharpe, 2001.

Keller, James R., and Leslie Stratyner, eds. *The New Queer Aesthetic on Television: Essays on Recent Programming*. Jefferson, N.C.: McFarland, 2006.

Kryhul, Angela. "Pridevision's Tough Sell." *Marketing Magazine* 106, no. 41 (October 15, 2001): 21.

Tropiano, Stephen. *The Prime Time Closet: A History of Gays and Lesbians on TV*. New York: Applause Theatre & Cinema Books, 2002.

Vilanch, Bruce. "A Channel of Our Own." *The Advocate*, April 29, 2003, 52.

Wockner, Rex. "Lack of Vision Cited for Pridevision's Troubles." *Gay Life* 25, no. 13 (March 7, 2003): 21.

SEE ALSO: 1930's-1960's: Hollywood Bans "Sexual Perversion" in Films; Mar. 7, 1967: CBS Airs *CBS Reports: The Homosexuals*; Oct. 31, 1969: *Time* Magazine Issues "The Homosexual in America"; 1979-1981: First Gay British Television Series Airs; June 5 and July 3, 1981: Reports of Rare Diseases Mark Beginning of AIDS Epidemic; 1985: GLAAD Begins Monitoring Media Coverage of Gays and Lesbians; 1985: Lesbian Film *Desert Hearts* Is Released; July 25, 1985: Actor Hudson Announces He Has AIDS; 1988: *Macho Dancer* Is Released in the Philippines; 1992-2002: Celebrity Lesbians Come Out; Mar. 21, 2000: Hollywood Awards Transgender Portrayals in Film; Mar. 5, 2006: *Brokeback Mountain, Capote,* and *Transamerica* Receive Oscars.

2002
Sylvia Rivera Law Project Is Founded

The Sylvia Rivera Law Project, named for transgender rights activist and advocate Sylvia Rivera, was formed to provide free legal services to transgender, transsexual, intersex, and other gender-nonconforming persons. The project has a special focus on persons of color and those with low incomes.

Locale: New York, New York
Categories: Organizations and institutions; transgender/transsexuality; laws, acts, and legal history; economics; race and ethnicity

Key Figures
Dean Spade (b. 1978), lawyer, activist, and founder of the Sylvia Rivera Law Project
Sylvia Rivera (1951-2002), activist and cofounder of Gay Liberation Front and Street Transvestite Action Revolutionaries

Summary of Event
The Sylvia Rivera Law Project (SRLP), founded by transgender lawyer and activist Dean Spade, provides free legal services to transgender, intersex, and gender-nonconforming individuals, especially people of color, those with a low income, and the homeless in New York City. The nonprofit organization is named in honor of Sylvia Rivera, a transgender and civil rights advocate and activist whose political efforts date back to the Stonewall Rebellion of 1969. The SRLP has since grown and is now collectively run by a group of more than twenty people.

In addition to providing direct services to fight discrimination on the basis of gender identity, gender expression, or intersex status, the law project is engaged in efforts to change policies that create obstacles to full inclusion and equal access to all who are disempowered by discrimination and violence. It also provides training materials and services to organizations seeking information about transgender/transsexual rights and the law. The SRLP also provides information on making work environments welcoming and accessible to transgender, intersex, and gender nonconforming people. Legal cases, policy formation, and training have focused on housing and homeless services, adult and juvenile justice, health care provision and insurance, police practices, employment, and education.

Significance
Several pivotal cases have been argued and won by the Sylvia Rivera Law Project on behalf of transgender clients in New York. These include the case *Jean Doe v. Bell* (2002), in which it was determined that "youth in foster care have the right to dress in clothing appropriate to their gender identity," and *Matter of Guido* (2003), which established that "transgender name change applicants cannot be held to a higher evidentiary standard than non-transgender applicants." In 2003, the SRLP also won a ruling enabling a transgender woman to visit her children when she expressed her gender as a woman.

In collaboration with transgender videographer Tara Mateik, the SRLP produced the 2003 documentary film *Toilet Training*, which explores the implications—including harassment and violence—of being gender variant and accessing not only public restrooms but also private restrooms in schools and workplaces. The production of this video was prompted by Spade's arrest in February, 2002, for entering the men's restroom in Grand Central Station in New York. Although he and several friends were detained by police for more than twenty-four hours, they ultimately were released from custody and charges against them were dropped. Furthermore, the SRLP's transgender awareness and sensitivity training comes with a history of legal battles against discrimination faced by transgender and transsexual people in housing, employment, foster care, homeless shelters, and prisons.

—*K. Surkan*

FURTHER READING

Crane, Kate. "Trannie Legal Aid, Part One." *New York Press*, January 20, 2004. http://www.nypress.com/17/3/news&columns/louder.cfm.

———. "Trannie Legal Aid, Part Two." *New York Press*, February 3, 2004. http://www.nypress.com/17/5/news&columns/louder.cfm.

Mottet, L., and J. Ohle. *Transitioning Our Shelters: A Guide to Making Homeless Shelters Safe for Transgender People*. New York: National Coalition for the Homeless and the National Gay and Lesbian Task Force Policy Institute, 2003. http://www.thetaskforce.org/downloads/TransHomeless.pdf.

Osborne, Duncan. "A Collective Effort at Change." *Gay City News*, May 12-18, 2005. http://www.gaycitynews.com/gcn_419/acollectiveeffortat.html.

Sylvia Rivera Law Project. http://www.srlp.org.

SEE ALSO: Nov. 21, 1966: First Gender Identity Clinic Opens and Provides Gender Reassignment Surgery; June 27-July 2, 1969: Stonewall Rebellion Ignites Modern Gay and Lesbian Rights Movement; 1978: Harry Benjamin International Gender Dysphoria Association Is Founded; 1992: Transgender Nation Holds Its First Protest; 1993: Intersex Society of North America Is Founded; June 17, 1995: International Bill of Gender Rights Is First Circulated; 1998: Transgender Scholarship Proliferates; Oct. 27, 1999: *Littleton v. Prange* Withholds Survivor Rights from Transsexual Spouses; Apr. 30, 2002: Transgender Rights Added to New York City Law; Mar., 2003-Dec., 2004: Transsexuals Protest Academic Exploitation; Nov. 20, 2003: Transgender Day of Remembrance and Remembering Our Dead Project; May 17, 2004: Transsexual Athletes Allowed to Compete in Olympic Games.

April 30, 2002
TRANSGENDER RIGHTS ADDED TO NEW YORK CITY LAW

Transgender rights were officially recognized in New York City with the passage of a bill that amended the city's human rights ordinance. The law protects against discrimination based on a person's gender identity or gender expression. Also, the bill's passage raised awareness of transgender concerns in the city's public and political arenas.

ALSO KNOWN AS: Local Law 3
LOCALE: New York, New York
CATEGORIES: Civil rights; transgender/transsexuality; government and politics; laws, acts, and legal history; organizations and institutions

KEY FIGURES

Tim Sweeney, key strategist of the bill
Bill Perkins, council member and lead sponsor of the bill
Margarita Lopez, council member and key proponent of the bill
Pauline Park, coordinator of the bill's working group
Rudolph Giuliani (b. 1944), New York City mayor and key opponent of the bill
Peter Vallone, council speaker and key opponent of the bill
Michael Bloomberg (b. 1942), New York City mayor who signed the bill into law

SUMMARY OF EVENT

The history of New York City's landmark transgender rights law begins on June 30, 1998, with the founding of the New York Association for Gender Rights Advocacy (NYAGRA). Created to combat the pervasive discrimination and violence faced by transgender and gender-variant people, NYAGRA was the first statewide transgender advocacy organization in New York.

On November 24, 1998, NYAGRA members met with the Empire State Pride Agenda (ESPA)—the state's largest and most influential lesbian and gay political organization—to seek its support for inclusion of "gender identity" and "gender expression" in the Sexual Orientation Non-Discrimination Act (SONDA), which was then pending in the New York state legislature. ESPA's deputy director, Tim Sweeney, proposed instead that ESPA and NYAGRA work at the local level first. NYAGRA members agreed, with the understanding that the two organizations would revisit the question of transgender inclusion in SONDA at a future date after assessing the progress of the New York City transgender rights bill.

On October 8, 1999, NYAGRA convened the first meeting of the working group on gender-based discrimination, which chose Pauline Park to serve as its coordinator. The working group included ESPA (represented by ESPA executive director Matt Foreman after Sweeney's departure in November, 2000), the Gender Identity Project (represented by Carrie Davis) of the Lesbian & Gay Community Services Center (later renamed the LGBT Community Center) and the six original sponsors of the bill—New York city council members Bill Perkins, Margarita Lopez, Christine Quinn, Ronnie Eldridge, Philip Reed, and Steven DiBrienza, all Democrats.

The core members (including Perkins, Lopez, Sweeney, and Park) crafted a strategy for enlisting the support of a majority of council members and building a broad coalition of LGBT and non-LGBT organizations. On February 29, 2000, the coalition launched the public phase of the campaign with a press conference on the steps of City Hall. Council members announced they were submitting a formal request for legislation.

> **FROM NEW YORK CITY'S LOCAL LAW 3**
>
> A local law to amend the administrative code of the city of New York, in relation to gender-based discrimination.
>
> *Section 1.* Legislative findings and intent. The City Council finds and declares that it is in the interest of the City of New York to protect its citizens from discrimination. Discrimination, prejudice, intolerance and bigotry directly and profoundly threaten the rights and freedom of New Yorkers. The City Council established the Human Rights Law to protect its inhabitants from these dangers. Included in the City's Human Rights Law is a prohibition of discrimination against individuals based on gender. The scope of this gender-based protection, however, requires clarification. This local law is intended to make clear that all gender-based discrimination—including, but not limited to, discrimination based on an individual's actual or perceived sex, and discrimination based on an individual's gender identity, self-image, appearance, behavior, or expression—constitutes a violation of the City's Human Rights Law.
>
> Gender-based discrimination effects a broad range of individuals. But the impact of gender-based discrimination is especially debilitating for those whose gender self-image and presentation do not fully accord with the legal sex assigned to them at birth. For those individuals, gender-based discrimination often leads to pariah status including the loss of a job, the loss of an apartment, and the refusal of service in public accommodations such as restaurants or stores. The impact of such discrimination can be especially devastating for those who endure other prejudices due to their race, ethnicity, national origin, or citizenship status, in addition to gender-based discrimination. In adopting this legislation, the City Council declares that the ability of all New Yorkers to work and to live free from invidious discrimination based on gender is the guiding principle of public policy and law.

When the bill was introduced on June 5, a majority of council members signed on as cosponsors. The working group was able to generate sustained coverage in the LGBT press and even occasional major media coverage for the campaign, culminating in a *New York Times* editorial (August 29) in favor of the bill, the newspaper's first editorial on transgender issues. With that editorial and an opinion article in *Newsday* magazine by former mayor Ed Koch, it became clear that the city's political establishment was now behind the bill. What had been a marginal issue in 1998, not even seriously discussed by LGBT activists, became central to the LGBT community's political agenda, with ESPA and the LGBT political clubs insisting that candidates seeking their support in the 2001 elections for council and citywide office (mayor, public advocate, comptroller) endorse the bill. In fact, leading Democratic candidates for those offices rushed to endorse the bill and to show their support for transgender rights.

The one exception among candidates for the Democratic mayoral nomination was Speaker Peter Vallone, who, though refusing to state his opposition to the bill publicly, blocked it until he was forced out of office in December, 2001, because of term limits. Mayor Rudolph Giuliani (also term-limited by December, 2001) sent human rights commissioner Marta Varela to the general welfare committee hearing on the bill on May 4, 2001, to testify that the administration considered the legislation unnecessary, arguing that existing case law already protected those who are transgender from discrimination. Park insisted, however, that the legislation was necessary and rejected suggestions even from Sweeney, Perkins, and Lopez (and from Joe Grabarz, who succeeded Sweeney as ESPAs deputy director) that the bill be scrapped and that transgender rights be pursued through litigation.

Incoming council speaker Gifford Miller made the bill's passage a priority, and it was reintroduced in January, 2002. On April 24, the new council passed the bill with a vote of 45-5, with one abstention, and on April 30 the new mayor, Michael Bloomberg, a Republican, signed it into law.

SIGNIFICANCE

Enactment of Local Law 3 of 2002 amended New York City human rights law to add a definition of "gender" that included "gender identity" and "gender expression," thereby protecting transgender and gender-variant people throughout the five boroughs from discrimination in employment, housing, and public accommodations. The passage of the bill represents the greatest achievement to date for the city's transgender and gender-variant communities. Not only did the bill win transgender rights under law; the campaign for the bill transformed the political context in which transgender issues were understood.

—*Pauline Park*

FURTHER READING

Hunter, Nan D., Courtney G. Joslin, and Sharon M. McGowan. *The Rights of Lesbians, Gay Men, Bisexuals, and Transgender People*. 4th ed. Carbondale: Southern Illinois University Press, 2004.

The New York Times. "Transgender Rights." Editorial, August 29, 2000.

Park, Pauline. "The Making of a Movement: The Story of the Successful Campaign for a Transgender Rights Law in New York City." Paper presented at the eighth annual Mark E. Ouderkirk Lecture, the Museum of the City of New York, June 27, 2002.

Schindler, Paul. "Bloomberg Set to Sign Transgender Rights Law." *Lesbian and Gay New York*, May 9, 2002, p. 4.

———. "Transgender Activists Push Human Rights Amendment." *Lesbian and Gay New York*, March 23, 2000, p. 17.

Sharpe, Andrew N. *Transgender Jurisprudence: Dysphoric Bodies of Law*. London: Cavendish, 2002.

SEE ALSO: 1992: Transgender Nation Holds Its First Protest; June 17, 1995: International Bill of Gender Rights Is First Circulated; 1998: Transgender Scholarship Proliferates; Oct. 27, 1999: *Littleton v. Prange* Withholds Survivor Rights from Transsexual Spouses; 2002: Sylvia Rivera Law Project Is Founded; Feb. 21, 2003: Australian Court Validates Transsexual Marriage; Mar., 2003-Dec., 2004: Transsexuals Protest Academic Exploitation; Mar. 21, 2003: New Mexico Amends Its Human Rights Act; Nov. 20, 2003: Transgender Day of Remembrance and Remembering Our Dead Project; May 17, 2004: Transsexual Athletes Allowed to Compete in Olympic Games.

June 19, 2002
Gays and Lesbians March for Equal Rights in Mexico City

Mexico City's 2002 gay and lesbian pride parade saw thirty thousand marchers of all sexual orientations promoting even greater visibility for sexual minorities and calling for political, social, and cultural changes to combat homophobia and heterosexism and to gain basic civil rights.

Locale: Mexico City, Mexico
Categories: Marches, protests, and riots; civil rights; organizations and institutions; race and ethnicity

Summary of Event

In 1978, a small contingent of lesbians and gays joined a major demonstration against political repression, but the contingent faced an uneasy group of fellow demonstrators. Left-wing groups at the demonstration were endorsing a culture of masculinity and manliness and a life of procreation and domesticity for women. Even in the face of this less-than-warm, even hostile, environment, lesbians and gays continued to march, holding the first annual lesbian and gay march in 1982.

In 2002, Mexico's gay and lesbian community celebrated the twentieth anniversary of the annual pride parade by marching through the heart of Mexico City, down the famous Avenida Reforma from Chapultepec Park to the Zocalo. While the parade once drew only about one thousand onlookers, the 2002 parade attracted a crowd of gays, lesbians, bisexuals, and transgender persons estimated at thirty thousand by the organizers. The parade also included hundreds of heterosexual participants, who joined in to show their support. The parade was held in June in commemoration of the Stonewall Rebellion of June, 1969.

The parade traditionally has been a major social event for Mexicans who have endured discrimination because of their sexual orientation or gender expression. Between five million and ten million Mexicans in a total population of 105 million define themselves as homosexual. In a survey conducted in May, 2005, by the Mexican Secretariat of Social Development and the National Council to Prevent Discrimination, 94.7 percent of members of the queer community said that they suffered from discrimination and 45 percent reported that their families had tried to force them to change their sexual orientation.

The parade has been the ideal venue for voicing political demands. According to one organizer, Tito Vasconselos, pride marches give visibility to queers and opens a space where gays and lesbians can exercise their rights as citizens. Participants even have shouted from the parade that they took to the streets to demand respect for their civil rights. Slogans on posters have included "Equality Begins When We Recognize That We All Have the Right to Be Different" and "For An Influential, Tolerant, and Pluralistic Mexico." At parade's end, near the presidential palace, marchers have chanted "Equal rights for lesbians and gays!" and "Fight, fight for the freedom to love." Importantly, in 2002, demonstrators demanded respect for all sexual orientations, recognition of same-gender marriages, greater efforts investigating crimes committed against homosexuals, and public health-care support for gender reassignment surgery. A representative of the Committee for Sexual Diversity said that the 2002 demonstration aimed to hold people accountable at all levels of government. Representatives of the Roman Catholic Church and conservative groups, not surprisingly, have bitterly opposed the march, arguing that the messages on placards and chants served to promote homosexuality.

Most of the marchers have been young men, with the largest group hailing from the National Autonomous University. Among the other forty groups that were represented were HIV-AIDS awareness groups, human rights leagues, and nongovernmental organizations (NGOs). Visually, the parade was marked by transparent black suits, naked bodies covered in red and pink paint, vividly colored balloons, and many rainbow flags. Some couples held symbolic weddings, with men in suits wearing wedding veils over their heads and joining the throngs of people. There was also a condom mobile from which condoms were tossed into the crowd.

SIGNIFICANCE

Although Mexican law does not prohibit homosexuality or outlaw sodomy, homosexuality is not tolerated culturally or socially. A series of public-morality civil laws enable police to arrest gays and lesbians or, more commonly, to extort them, not for sodomy or homosexuality but for "morals violations." Police abuse of gays and lesbians in Mexico is well documented. The belief that gays are failures at masculinity and are, therefore, *maricónes* (sissies), makes them culturally, if not legally sanctioned targets.

Because of these proscriptions, homosexual activity has a long history of repression and secrecy. Mexico City had gay bars and baths since the 1930's, as well as traditional cruising areas, but there were no organizations for gays and lesbians. In the 1950's, many of the bars were shut down by a crusading mayor. In the early 1970's, influenced by the American gay and lesbian rights movement, short-lived gay liberation groups appeared in Mexico City. Generally, sexual liberation in the late 1970's in Mexico was mistaken as support for those who wanted to engage in "peculiar" sexual activities. Many of the gay liberation groups, especially lesbian groups, disappeared during the economic crisis of the 1980's, a decade during which people had limited time and money to engage in politics. In the 1990's, lesbians and gays gained greater visibility in Mexico; along with this greater visibility came a growing body of literature by and about lesbians and gays.

By the millennium, gays and lesbians continue to face many of the same problems and dilemmas. Violence continues to be a major concern. Gay organizations have claimed that death squads in the Chiapas region targeted gay men, particularly transvestites and cross-dressers. Also, it has been estimated that, at minimum, three men are killed each month in Mexico simply for being gay. According to a report by the Mexico City Catholic Diocese, the Mexican army was rumored to be collaborating with the police to kill gay men. For the most part, the deaths, if indeed true, have been hushed up, as even the families of the deceased refuse to speak of their dead family members. The attackers usually remain at large.

Protests like the 2002 march for gay and lesbian equal rights emphasize that Mexican gays and lesbians have no intention of returning to a shadowy or secret existence. In the twenty-first century, the Mexican GLBT population is refusing to be placed back in the closet, whether by the government or by the people.

—*Caryn E. Neumann*

FURTHER READING

Carrier, Joseph M. *De Los Otros: Intimacy and Homosexuality Among Mexican Men.* New York: Columbia University Press, 1995.

Prieur, Annick. *Mama's House, Mexico City: On Transvestites, Queens, and Machos.* Chicago: University of Chicago Press, 1998.

Schaefer, Claudia. *Danger Zones: Homosexuality, National Identity, and Mexican Culture.* Tucson: University of Arizona Press, 1996.

SEE ALSO: Nov. 17, 1901: Police Arrest "Los 41" in Mexico City; 1912-1924: Robles Fights in the Mexican Revolution; Nov., 1965: Revolutionary Cuba Imprisons Gays; Oct. 12-15, 1979: First March on Washington for Lesbian and Gay Rights; Oct. 14-17, 1987: Latin American and Caribbean Lesbian Feminist Network Is Formed; Apr., 2003: Buenos Aires Recognizes Same-Gender Civil Unions; Jan., 2006: Jiménez Flores Elected to the Mexican Senate.

June 28, 2002
Irish American Lesbian Gains Canadian Immigrant Status

A woman launched a legal challenge to Canadian immigration laws that excluded gays and lesbians from family sponsorship rules, thereby sparking reforms that would eventually allow same-gender partners some of the same immigration rights as heterosexual couples.

Locale: Canada

Categories: Civil rights; laws, acts, and legal history; government and politics

Key Figures

Bridget Coll, Irish and U.S. citizen, partner of Christine Morrissey

Christine Morrissey, Canadian citizen, partner of Coll, and founder of the Lesbian and Gay Immigration Task Force of Canada

Summary of Event

In 1991, Canadian immigration laws allowed only heterosexual Canadians to sponsor their spouses as immigrants. Definitions of conjugal relationships, such as "spouse," "fiancee" or "marriage," referred only to opposite-gender couples. Binational same-gender partners were left with few options. In order to stay together with their Canadian partners, lesbians and gays were forced to rely on student visas, marriages of convenience, or no legal status at all.

Christine Morrissey, a Canadian citizen, and Bridget Coll, an Irish and American citizen, had been in a committed relationship for more than fourteen years despite being separated by international borders. When Morrissey filed an application to sponsor Coll for permanent residency as her life companion in 1991, immigration authorities refused to process the application because the women did not fit the definition of "family" under Canadian immigration law.

On January 14, 1992, Morrissey filed a court challenge in the Federal Court of Canada, arguing that the government's refusal constituted discrimination on the basis of sexual orientation. Morrissey was a founder of a newly formed national lobby group, the Lesbian and Gay Immigration Task Force. She argued that the Canadian Charter of Rights and Freedoms, which guarantees citizens equal treatment before the law, prohibits the Canadian government from discriminating against gays and lesbians.

The exclusion of gays and lesbians from the family class of immigration laws was also brought to the attention of the Canadian public in another highly publicized case that same year. For more than one year, Canadian citizen Andrea Underwood had been seeking to sponsor her British partner Anna Carrott. When immigration officials refused to consider Underwood's application, she also launched legal action, in March, 1992. Underwood claimed that she was being discriminated against on the basis of her sexual orientation, in violation of the charter.

Soon after the Morrissey lawsuit was filed, immigration officials asked Coll to fill out an application under the independent immigrant class, ostensibly for the purposes of the lawsuit. However, that form was then quickly processed to grant her residency status in October, 1992, not as a sponsored family class member but as an independent immigrant. Morrissey and Coll were the first to benefit from a new policy adopted by the Canadian government to respond to gay and lesbian sponsorship applications. Although Coll was granted the right to stay in Canada, the couple was denied the opportunity to challenge the law.

All subsequent challenges to the immigration laws were processed quickly before the courts had an opportunity to decide. Carrott was allowed to stay as a permanent resident as of October, 1994. The government was thus able to avoid successive legal challenges that could have required a formal rewriting of the family reunification provisions.

SIGNIFICANCE

The Morrissey case, along with the other legal challenges, forced the Canadian government to admit that it was unlikely to win a constitutional challenge to immigration laws that excluded gays and lesbians from family class sponsorship provisions. Thus, in June, 1994, the minister of employment and immigration devised a plan that would unite binational same-gender couples without formally enshrining equality in the immigration laws. The policy officially recognized that the separation of binational same-gender couples may cause "undue hardship," and the minister delegated the authority to grant same-gender partner applications to program officers in visa offices abroad.

The new policy directed immigration officers to process all lesbian and gay sponsorships as independent applications. If the same-gender partner did not meet the requirement for landing as a member of the independent class, officials were to then determine whether separation created undue hardship and was grounds for exercising humanitarian and compassionate discretion. In June, 1995, it was reported that more than sixty couples had successfully used these criteria to obtain residency for a gay or lesbian partner.

However, the adoption of a discretionary mechanism to deal with gay and lesbian family sponsorship was viewed as a half measure by lesbian and gay rights activists, immigration advocates, and lawyers. There was concern about the absence of clear and transparent rules, the unavailability of appeals, and the lack of consistency of decision making by visa officers in various embassies and consulates.

In response, the immigration minister announced in January, 1999, proposed changes to the immigration law and regulations to include lesbian and gay partners in the family class provisions. On June 28, 2002, the Immigration and Refugee Protection Act and Immigration and Refugee Protection Regulations came into effect. The new law and regulations expanded the family class to include gay and lesbian couples. For the first time in Canadian immigration history, lesbians and gays were now able to sponsor their partners formally.

In changing its immigration policy toward same-gender couples, Canada joined several other countries in extending rights to prospective gay and lesbian immigrants. In addition to Canada, many other countries recognize same-gender couples for immigration purposes, including Australia, Belgium, Denmark, Finland, France, Iceland, the Netherlands, New Zealand, Norway, South Africa, Sweden, and the United Kingdom. A decade after Christine Morrissey launched her constitutional challenge, same-gender partners were officially recognized as family under Canadian immigration laws.

—*Nicole LaViolette*

FURTHER READING

Dhir, Aaron A. "Same-Sex Family Class Immigration: Is the Definition of 'Spouse' in Canada's *Immigration Regulations, 1978* Unconstitutional?" *University of New Brunswick Law Journal* 49 (2000): 183.

Duenas, Christopher. "Coming to America: The Immigration Obstacle Facing Binational Same-Sex Couples." *Southern California Law Review* 73 (2000): 811.

Epps, Brad, Keja Valens, and Bill Johnson Gonzalez, eds. *Passing Lines: Sexuality and Immigration.* Cambridge, Mass.: Harvard University Press, 2005.

Green, Richard. "'Give Me Your Tired, Your Poor, Your Huddled Masses' (Of Heterosexuals): An Analysis of American and Canadian Immigration Policy." *Anglo-American Law Review* 16 (1987): 139.

Hart, John. *Stories of Gay and Lesbian Immigration: Together Forever.* New York: Harrington Park Press, 2002.

LaViolette, Nicole. "Coming Out in Canada: The Immigration of Same-Sex Couples Under the Immigration and Refugee Protection Act." *McGill Law Journal/Revue de droit de McGill* 49 (2004): 3.

McGloin, Brian. "Diverse Families with Parallel Needs: A Proposal for Same-Sex Immigration Benefits." *California Western International Law Journal* 30 (1999): 159.

Walker, Kristen. "New Uses of the Refugees Convention: Sexuality and Refugee Status." In *The Refugees Convention Fifty Years On: Globalisation and International Law*, edited by Susan Kneebone. Burlington, Vt.: Ashgate, 2003.

SEE ALSO: 1972-1973: Local Governments Pass Antidiscrimination Laws; Dec. 19, 1977: Quebec Includes Lesbians and Gays in Its Charter of Human Rights and Freedoms; June 2, 1980: Canadian Gay Postal Workers Secure Union Protections; Jan. 1, 1988: Canada Decriminalizes Sex Practices Between Consenting Adults; Dec. 30, 1991-Feb. 22, 1993: Canada Grants Asylum Based on Sexual Orientation; Apr. 27, 1992: Canadian Government Antigay Campaign Is Revealed; Oct., 1992: Canadian Military Lifts Its Ban on Gays and Lesbians; Apr. 2, 1998: Canadian Supreme Court Reverses Gay Academic's Firing; June 17, 2003, and July 19, 2005: Canada Legalizes Same-Gender Marriage.

October 4, 2002
TRANSGENDER TEEN GWEN ARAUJO IS MURDERED IN CALIFORNIA

Gwen Araujo, a transgender teen, was beaten unconscious, strangled to death, and buried in a shallow grave by a group of young men who had "discovered" she was anatomically male. The case, in which the killers were found guilty in the second of two trials, has captured the hearts and minds not only of the GLBT community and its supporters but also the general public and state lawmakers, who have introduced legislation regarding the use of the "panic defense" in criminal trials.

LOCALE: Newark, California
CATEGORIES: Transgender/transsexuality; crime; civil rights; laws, acts, and legal history

KEY FIGURES
Gwen Araujo (1985-2002), transgender teen who was beaten and murdered
Jaron Chase Nabors,
Michael Magidson,
Jose Merel, and
Jason Cazares, accused murderers of Araujo

SUMMARY OF EVENT
Gwen Araujo disappeared from Newark, California, on October 3, 2002. Two weeks later, in a suburb less than 30 miles from the famously progressive city of San Francisco, nineteen-year-old Jaron Chase Nabors confessed to knowing about Araujo's murder, and led authorities to a shallow grave 150 miles away, near Placerville, in the central valley of California. Araujo's body was found there in the blouse, skirt, and jewelry she had worn to a party on the evening of October 3. Her hands and feet had been bound, she had sustained blunt force injuries to the head, and had been strangled with a rope. Her body was wrapped in a comforter.

Four young men were arrested in conjunction with the brutal killing. Along with Nabors, those charged with Araujo's murder were Michael Magidson of Fremont, Jose Merel of Newark, and Jason Cazares of Fremont (all three were twenty-two years old). The murder charge included an enhanced charge for hate crimes (thus making the crime punishable by death). Details of the killing slowly came to light as the trial opened. Araujo had been excited about going to a party that night. She had never before worn a skirt and had borrowed one from a friend; she also wore her mother's blouse. The people at the party were new friends who did not know the history of her gender identity and the harassment she faced at school. Araujo had come out to her parents at age fourteen as transgender. At that time, she began to grow her hair long and to dress in women's clothing.

She told her new friends that her name was Lida and that she had become sexually involved with two young men. Speculation swirled among the friends, however, that she was not born female. That evening, partygoers began to harass Araujo about her gender identity, asking if she were a man or a woman. Somehow it was confirmed that she was "anatomically male," whether by accident or by "forcible inspection" in a bathroom.

Nabors testified that he and the other three men took Araujo to the garage of the home where the party was held and, for up to 3.5 hours, punched her and beat her in the head with metal objects—including a soup can and a 10-inch skillet—before kneeing her in the face so hard that her head broke through the wall. Two of her assailants went home to get shovels. The men then bound her hands and feet and strangled her with rope until she appeared dead. They struck her head twice with the shovels to make sure she was dead. Her body was wrapped in a comforter and loaded in the back of Magidson's truck.

All of the defendants initially pleaded not guilty to first degree manslaughter during the trial. Nabors, however, changed his plea to guilty (but on a lesser charge of voluntary manslaughter, receiving an eleven-year sentence) and testified that the remaining three men, after learning she was biologically male, had conspired days before the murder to kill her. Cazares, Magidson, and Merel then mounted a "gay panic" defense, claiming that Araujo had deceived them into thinking she was female, thus justifying, in their eyes, their actions. Furthermore, Nabors testified that while Magidson repeatedly tried to choke Araujo, it was Merel who appeared more and more agitated by the idea that he had anal

Family and friends remembered transgender teenager Gwen Araujo at a wake at the Fremont Memorial Chapel in Fremont, California. Araujo had been murdered three weeks earlier. (AP/Wide World Photos)

> ### Araujo's Mother: "Life After Gwen"
>
> I am not sure how I expected to feel at this point. When my daughter Gwen, a transgender teenager, was brutally murdered on Oct. 4, 2002, I was sure that I would never feel whole again. Looking back, I didn't yet know exactly what "transgender" meant or how to fully embrace my child's identity. But I knew one thing: I wanted justice for my child....
>
> No amount of justice can return the part of me that these men took when they killed Gwen....
>
> I'm angry. Angry that Gwen's brothers and her nieces and nephews won't get to grow up knowing her the way her aunts, uncles, older sister and I did. Angry that instead of celebrating her birthday, we get together each year to commemorate her death. Angry that, in both trials, the defendants tried to blame Gwen for her own murder. Angry that other young lesbian, gay, bisexual or transgender kids continue to face the discrimination she did in our public schools and our workforce.
>
> I'm also grateful. Grateful that my family and our friends rose to the challenge and sat through two gruesome and explicit criminal trials to make sure that everyone knew that Gwen was loved for who she was. I'm grateful for the support we've all received from perfect strangers who have told us in-person and through e-mail that we are in their thoughts and prayers. I'm grateful for the remorse that two of the defendants and some of their family members have expressed to me and my family.
>
> And I'm sad. Sad that I'll never get to see Gwen grow into the beautiful woman she would have become. Sad that four men chose to end my daughter's life, and throw away their own simply because they thought they were acting like "real men." And sad that other transgender women have been killed since Gwen's murder and that we don't have a realistic end in sight to that violence.
>
> Within this mix of emotions, though, the one that I hold onto most dearly is hope. Since that tragic night, my own family has grown by two beautiful grandchildren. More and more parents are supporting their transgender children. California has become the country's most protective state for transgender people. And just this month, a new law has been proposed in Sacramento, the Gwen Araujo Justice for Victims Act, authored by Assemblywoman Sally Lieber, D-Mountain View, and sponsored by Equality California, an LGBT civil-rights lobbying group, to protect people from being blamed for their own murder.
>
> Maybe the reason I don't have closure around Gwen's death is that there is still work to do. If I've learned anything since Gwen's murder, it is that hope alone is not enough. Each of us who hopes to live in a state where our families are protected needs to work toward making California that place. For instance, boys and girls in schools throughout the Bay Area need to hear, firsthand, how important it is to be themselves and to respect each other's differences.
>
> None of us can change the way the world was on Oct. 4, 2002. But each of us now has an important role to play in creating a state where we can celebrate more birthdays and commemorate fewer murders.
>
> *Source:* Sylvia Guerrero, SF Gate.com. January 26, 2006.

sex with a boy, crying to his younger brother that he could not be gay. The defendants had reported that they felt "shame, humiliation, shock, and revulsion."

On June 22, 2004, the court declared a mistrial because of a hung jury. Although jurors later said that they had not accepted the "gay panic" defense, they were, however, divided over the question of premeditation, which would mean the difference between a first- or a second-degree manslaughter conviction. The jury's verdict hinged on the issue of public disclosure: When did Gwen's male anatomy become so much of a problem to the men that they would kill to cover their attraction to her?

The men were retried in 2005, and two—Magidson and Merel—were convicted of second-degree murder (minus the hate-crime enhancement), on September 13, 2005. Cazares pleaded "no contest" to voluntary manslaughter and received a six-year sentence. Magidson and Merel received the maximum sentence for second-degree murder: fifteen years to life. Nabors pleaded guilty to voluntary manslaughter before the start of the first trial.

SIGNIFICANCE

Gwen Araujo was named Edward Araujo at birth on February 4, 1985, and she was aware of her feminine gender identity from an early age. According to her mother, Sylvia Guerrero, Gwen never identified with the name "Eddie." After Araujo's death, her name was legally changed to Gwen Amber Rose Araujo, partially in response to the media's insistence on identifying her as male, on using her birth name, or on using some combination of male and female names. Araujo's family was exceptionally supportive of her. Since her death, her mother has become a public spokesperson for transgender acceptance.

The four men convicted of killing Araujo, much like the men who killed young transgender man Brandon Teena in 1993, not only were ignorant about the ways gender can be expressed "differently"; they also expressed a deep hatred and rage based on that ignorance, a "panic" as they called it. Araujo's death has made it clear that legal protection is needed for those who are transgender or gender ambiguous, and it has led to a rethinking in legal circles about the "gay panic" defense.

—*Leah Sheppard*

FURTHER READING

Gender Public Advocacy Coalition. "Hate Crime Portraits." http://www.gpac.org/violence/hatecrimes.html.

Gwen Araujo Memorial Web Site. http://www.jaimesite.homestead.com/ gwenaraujo.html. An excellent resource that includes links to media coverage of the trials.

Lambda Legal and The National Youth Advocacy Coalition. "Bending the Mold: An Action Kit for Transgender Youth." http://www.lambdalegal.org.

Letellier, Patrick. "2003 Exceeds Others in Transgender Killings." http://www.planetout.com/news/article.html?2003/11/26/4.

Namaste, Viviane K. *Invisible Lives: The Erasure of Transsexual and Transgendered People*. Chicago: University of Chicago Press, 2000.

National Transgender Advocacy Coalition. http://www.ntac.org.

Sharpe, Andrew N. *Transgender Jurisprudence: Dysphoric Bodies of Law*. London: Cavendish, 2002.

Steinberg, Victoria L. "A Heat of Passion Offense: Emotions and Bias in 'Trans Panic' Mitigation Claims." *Boston College Third World Law Journal* 25, no. 2 (2005). Available at http://www.bc.edu/schools/law/lawreviews/thirdworld/.

SEE ALSO: Sept. 24, 1951: George Jorgensen Becomes Christine Jorgensen; Nov. 21, 1966: First Gender Identity Clinic Opens and Provides Gender Reassignment Surgery; 1978: Harry Benjamin International Gender Dysphoria Association Is Founded; Jan. 21, 1989: Death of Transgender Jazz Musician Billy Tipton; 1992: Transgender Nation Holds Its First Protest; Dec. 24, 1993-Dec. 31, 1993: Transgender Man Brandon Teena Raped and Murdered; June 17, 1995: International Bill of Gender Rights Is First Circulated; 1996: Hart Recognized as a Transgender Man; 1998: Transgender Scholarship Proliferates; Mar. 21, 2000: Hollywood Awards Transgender Portrayals in Film; 2002: Sylvia Rivera Law Project Is Founded; Apr. 30, 2002: Transgender Rights Added to New York City Law; Nov. 20, 2003: Transgender Day of Remembrance and Remembering Our Dead Project.

February 21, 2003
Australian Court Validates Transsexual Marriage

The Full Bench of the Family Court of Australia validated a transsexual marriage after it was challenged on appeal by the federal government of Australia. The court decision effectively legalized transsexual marriage.

Locale: Sydney, Australia
Categories: Transgender/transsexuality; government and politics; laws, acts, and legal history

Key Figures
Daryl Williams, Australian federal attorney-general
"Kevin," female-to-male transsexual whose 1999 marriage was challenged by the Australian government
Gina Mather, president of the Australian Transsexual Support Association
Darren Tudehope, spokesperson for the Australian Family Association
Rachel Wallbank, transsexual lawyer who represented "Kevin"

Summary of Event

On February 21, 2003, the federal government of Australia lost its bid to invalidate the marriage of a Sydney transsexual and his wife when the Full Bench of the Family Court threw out an appeal of a 2001 decision declaring the marriage legal. The appeal was brought by Australian attorney-general Daryl Williams, who argued that the marriage was invalid because a transsexual could not be a "man" under the Marriage Act of 1961. The Full Bench disagreed, upholding the ruling by Justice Richard Chisholm in 2001 that validated the marriage.

The case involved "Kevin" and "Jennifer," from Sydney, who had married on August 21, 1999, after Kevin had gender reassignment surgery to become a man. Kevin's birth certificate and passport both state that he is male, and he had begun hormone therapy in 1995. Although he had chest surgery in 1997 and a hysterectomy in 1998, Kevin opted not to undergo genital surgery to construct a penis. Kevin and Jennifer's case, with their attorney Rachel Wallbank, was therefore the first in the world in which a transsexual marriage was deemed valid without the transsexual person having had genital-reconstructive surgery.

The Full Bench of the Family Court held that on the question of marriage, the determination of a person's legal sex/gender depends on whether the person is a man or woman at the time of marriage rather than of birth. In addition, the court judgment said, "we reject the argument that one of the principal purposes of marriage is procreation . . . similarly it is inappropriate and incorrect to suggest that consummation is in any way a requirement to the creation of a valid marriage."

In opposition, Australian Family Association spokesperson Darren Tudehope told the Australian Associated Press that "if he (Kevin) has had a sex change that means he no longer wants to be in a relationship that has the purpose of producing children." At the time of the hearing, Kevin and Jennifer had two children, conceived using donor sperm through in-vitro fertilization. According to Gina Mather, president of the Australian Transsexual Support Association, the court decision on marriage will enable other couples with one or more transsexual partners to legally adopt children, which had been prohibited under Australian law before the Kevin and Jennifer case.

Significance

The Australian court's decision to affirm transsexual marriage was groundbreaking for transsexual rights around the world, particularly because the decision defines "legal" sex/gender to be based on the date of marriage rather than the assigned sex/gender at birth, and because it carries no requirement of genital surgery, which is often a barrier to low-income transsexuals, female-to-male transsexuals, and those not wanting the surgery.

This case had an immediate impact on an estimated fifteen hundred transsexual Australians, who could legally marry in their new gender if they so desired. While most transsexual advocates interpreted the decision as progressive, some cautioned that in the absence of a surgery requirement, the court may rely on the judgment of family members and peers to determine "legal" gender at time of a proposed marriage. If a transsexual does not pass well as their "chosen" gender or is estranged from his or her family, the individual may have difficulty gaining legal recognition of his or her gender.

Opponents of the decision cite the ruling as a blow to traditional marriage and the family, a view that relies heavily on the notion that marriage is an institution defined as procreative and that marriage ensures procreation. However, married heterosexual couples often choose not to have children. Furthermore, married transsexuals are redefining "family" in new ways, and many have or want children. Significantly, the Australian court finding that marriage is not just for ensuring procreation enables transsexuals and all married people to make a conscious choice about whether or not to have children and under what circumstances they might wish to do so.

—*K. Surkan*

FURTHER READING

"Attorney-General for the Commonwealth and 'Kevin and Jennifer' and Human Rights and Equal Opportunity Commission" (February 21, 2003). Decision of the Family Law Court of Australia. http://www.austlii.edu.au/au/cases/cth/family_ct/2003/94.html.

Council for Civil Liberties, University of New South Wales. "Transsexual Marriage in Australia." http://www.nswccl.org.au/unswccl/issues/transexual.php.

Griffith, Chris. "Family Court Ruling Changes Meaning, Intent of Marriage." *Queensland Courier Mail*, February 22, 2003, p. 11.

Knowles, Lorna. "Transsexual Marriage Valid." *Daily Telegraph*, February 22, 2003, p. 15.

Sharpe, Andrew N. *Transgender Jurisprudence: Dysphoric Bodies of Law*. London: Cavendish, 2002.

Webber, Graeme. "Transsexual Case Will Help Drive Equality Reforms." *Australian Associated Press*, February 21, 2003.

Webber, Graeme, Sheree Went, and Kylie Williams. "Transsexual Marriage Stands, but Commonwealth May Appeal." *Australian Associated Press*, February 21, 2003.

Williams, Kylie. "Family Court Transsexual Decision a World First." *Australian Associated Press*, February 21, 2003.

SEE ALSO: 1981: Gay and Lesbian Palimony Suits Emerge; 1992: Transgender Nation Holds Its First Protest; June, 1992: Feinberg Publishes *Transgender Liberation*; 1993-1996: Hawaii Opens Door to Same-Gender Marriages; Aug. 6, 1994: Japanese American Citizens League Supports Same-Gender Marriage; Sept. 21, 1996: U.S. President Clinton Signs Defense of Marriage Act; Oct. 27, 1999: *Littleton v. Prange* Withholds Survivor Rights from Transsexual Spouses; Dec. 20, 1999: *Baker v. Vermont* Leads to Recognition of Same-Gender Civil Unions; Apr., 2003: Buenos Aires Recognizes Same-Gender Civil Unions; June 17, 2003, and July 19, 2005: Canada Legalizes Same-Gender Marriage; Nov. 18, 2003: Massachusetts Court Rules for Same-Gender Marriage; Nov. 18, 2004: United Kingdom Legalizes Same-Gender Civil Partnerships; Apr. 4, 2005: United Kingdom's Gender Recognition Act Legalizes Transsexual Marriage; June 30, 2005: Spain Legalizes Same-Gender Marriage.

March, 2003-December, 2004
TRANSSEXUALS PROTEST ACADEMIC EXPLOITATION

Transsexual women accused a Northwestern University psychology professor of using them as research subjects without their consent for his controversial 2003 book on transsexuality, The Man Who Would Be Queen. *For the first time, transsexual activists succeeded in speaking out publicly against academic exploitation.*

LOCALE: Evanston, Illinois
CATEGORIES: Publications; transgender/transsexuality; marches, protests, and riots

KEY FIGURES
Lynn Conway (b. 1938), professor emerita, University of Michigan
Becky Allison (b. 1946), medical doctor
Andrea James, transsexual activist and writer
Joan Roughgarden (b. 1946), biology and geophysics professor
Charlotte Angelica Kieltyka (b. 1951), artist, photographer, and research subject known as "Cher Mondovi" in *The Man Who Would Be Queen*
J. Michael Bailey (b. 1957), professor and author of *The Man Who Would Be Queen*

SUMMARY OF EVENT
In March, 2003, J. Michael Bailey published *The Man Who Would Be Queen: The Science of Gender-Bending and Transsexualism*, a book that immediately became the center of a debate over the origins of male-to-female transsexualism and its relationship to sexuality. Employing a theory first advanced in the 1980's by Ray Blanchard, a researcher and head of the clinical sexology program at the Clarke Institute of Psychiatry in Toronto, Canada, Bailey stated that there are two types of male-to-female transsexuals: homosexual transsexuals and nonhomosexual transsexuals. The former group, he wrote, are "extremely feminine gay men," whereas the latter "suffer" from a condition called "autogynephilia." Bailey argued that transsexuals with autogynephilia are "men erotically obsessed with the image of themselves as women."

By describing transsexualism as a phenomenon best understood in terms of deviant sexual desire rather than as an issue of gender identity, Bailey angered many male-to-female transsexuals, and others, who felt that such a characterization ran counter to their own experiences and was not supported by valid, scientific research data. In response, former computer science professor Lynn Conway created a Web site dedicated to the investigation of Bailey's research methodology and the implications of his conclusions. Activists Andrea James and Becky Allison also began posting criticisms of Bailey's work on their online transsexual resource sites in April, 2003, stating that they, too, profoundly disagreed with his findings.

In late April, 2003, Stanford University biology and geophysics professor Joan Roughgarden attended a psychology lecture given by Bailey and wrote a scathing critique in the university's newspaper, *The Stanford Daily*, of what she viewed as a "vulgar performance" of unfounded assertions about transsexuals based on stereotypes. Dismissing *The Man Who Would Be Queen* as "junk science," she then wrote an open letter to two presidents of divisions of the National Academy of Sciences in which she called for the academy to discredit the book as a scholarly publication. (Joseph Henry Press, which published the book, is an imprint of National Academies Press.) Roughgarden warned that Bailey's conclusions are not based on empirical data and have worrisome implications for gay and lesbian people as well as transsexuals, "setting the stage for others to advocate the persecution of gays from a scientific perspective."

In early May of 2003, Charlotte Angelica Kieltyka discovered that aspects of her personal life and sexual history had been published in Bailey's book, under the pseudonym "Cher Mondovi," without her knowledge or consent. Kieltyka contacted Conway, who posted a series of e-mails and interviews online on her behalf. On July 3, 2003, Kieltyka filed a formal complaint with Northwestern University, stating that she had never been aware that Bailey considered her a research subject, and that he had not obtained her informed consent to participate as a human subject in his study. By the end of July, three more individuals used in Bailey's research had filed formal complaints against him. On November 12, 2003, Northwestern University launched a formal investigation in response to the allegations that Bailey did not obtain the consent of his research subjects.

On December 12, 2003, the weekly academic newsmagazine *Chronicle of Higher Education* reported that Bailey had been accused by a transsexual woman of "having sex with her while she was a subject of his research." In January, 2004, an article by the Southern Poverty Law Center (SPLC) linked support of Bailey's research to the Human Biodiversity Institute, which the SPLC terms a "neo-eugenics outfit" that also promotes racist scientific research.

One month later, *The Man Who Would Be Queen* was nominated for a Lambda Literary Award in the "Transgender/Genderqueer" category, spurring a massive protest and petition drive to have the title removed from the nomination list. On March 12, 2004, the nomination was rescinded after the panel of judges found that "the book was not appropriate for the category."

In April of 2004, further complaints were filed with the Illinois Department of Professional Regulation against Bailey for practicing clinical psychology without a license and for publishing clinical case histories without permission. Bailey denied the allegations, saying he had "done nothing wrong." On December 1, 2004, the *Chronicle of Higher Education* reported that Bailey had resigned his position as chairman of the psychology department at Northwestern in October, in a move that a university spokesman said "had nothing to do with the investigation." In letters to the transsexual women who had filed complaints against Bailey, Northwestern provost Lawrence Dumas wrote that the investigation had been concluded and he had "taken action that" he thought to be "appropriate in this situation."

Significance

The series of protests stemming from Bailey's publication of *The Man Who Would Be Queen* represented one of the most organized and unified examples of transgender activism seen to date. Linking issues of exploitation of human subjects to the politics of scientific research on homosexuality and transsexualism, the efforts of Lynn Conway, Andrea James, Charlotte Angelica Kieltyka, Joan Roughgarden, and other transsexual women marked a new moment in transgender history.

—K. Surkan

Further Reading

Bailey, J. Michael. *The Man Who Would Be Queen: The Science of Gender-Bending and Transsexualism.* Washington, D.C.: Joseph Henry Press, 2003. Available at http://fermat.nap.edu/books/0309084180/html.

Beirich, Heidi, and Bob Moser. "Queer Science: An 'Elite' Cadre of Scientists and Journalists Tries to Turn Back the Clock on Sex, Gender, and Race." *Intelligence Report.* Southern Poverty Law Center (January 1, 2004). http://www.splcenter.org/intel/intelreport/article.jsp?sid = 96.

Bockting, Donald O. "Biological Reductionism Meets Gender Diversity in Human Sexuality." Review of Bailey, *The Man Who Would Be Queen* (2003). *Journal of Sex Research* 42, no. 3 (August, 2005): 267-270. Available at http://ai.eecs.umich.edu/people/conway/.

Conway, Lynn. An Investigation into the Publication of J. Michael Bailey's Book on Transsexualism by the National Academies. http://ai.eecs.umich.edu/people/conway/.

Ehrenstein, David. "Kinder, Gentler Homophobia." *Advocate.com*, April 6, 2006. http://www.advocate.com.

James, Andrea. "Categorically Wrong? A Bailey-Blanchard-Lawrence Clearinghouse." http://www.tsroadmap.com/info/bailey-blanchard-lawrence.html.

Roughgarden, Joan. "Open Letter to the National Academies." J. Michael Bailey Investigation. http://ai.eecs.umich.edu/people/conway/.

———. "Psychology Lecture Lacks Sensitivity to

Sexual Orientation." *Stanford Daily Online*. April 25, 2003. http://daily.stanford.edu.

Wilson, Robin. "Dr. Sex." *Chronicle of Higher Education*, June 20, 2003.

_____. "Northwestern U. Concludes Investigation of Sex Researcher but Keeps Results Secret." *Chronicle of Higher Education*, December 1, 2004.

_____. "Northwestern U. Psychologist is Accused of Having Sex with Research Subject." *Chronicle of Higher Education*, December 12, 2003.

SEE ALSO: Nov. 21, 1966: First Gender Identity Clinic Opens and Provides Gender Reassignment Surgery; 1978: Harry Benjamin International Gender Dysphoria Association Is Founded; June 2, 1989: Lambda Literary Award Is Created; 1992: Transgender Nation Holds Its First Protest; June, 1992: Feinberg Publishes *Transgender Liberation*; 1993: Intersex Society of North America Is Founded; 1996: Hart Recognized as a Transgender Man; 1998: Transgender Scholarship Proliferates.

March 21, 2003
NEW MEXICO AMENDS ITS HUMAN RIGHTS ACT

The New Mexico state senate added not only "sexual orientation" but also "gender identity" to its nondiscrimination clause of its Human Rights Act. California and other states soon followed suit in adding protection for those who are transgender, transsexual, or who are otherwise gender variant.

LOCALE: Santa Fe, New Mexico
CATEGORIES: Laws, acts, and legal history; transgender/transsexuality; civil rights

KEY FIGURES
Bill Richardson (b. 1947), governor of New Mexico
Gail C. Beam, New Mexico state representative
Cisco McSorley, New Mexico state senator

SUMMARY OF EVENT
On February 24, 2003, the New Mexico House of Representatives voted 39-27 to broaden the state's Human Rights Act by approving House Bill 314 to prohibit bias against people based on sexual orientation and gender identity. The amendment, introduced by Representative Gail C. Beam, prohibits discrimination in employment, housing, credit, public accommodations, and union membership for all governments and businesses in New Mexico.

On March 21, Senator Cisco McSorley then introduced the bill before the New Mexico Senate. After some debate, it was passed 22-18. Governor Bill Richardson signed it a few days later, converting the bill into law. It was a strong victory for GLBT citizens of New Mexico. The bill was first introduced in 1991 and rejected 35-31 by the house in 2001. Much of the credit for the change in votes goes to Governor Richardson, a staunch supporter of the bill. New Mexico became only the third state to cover gender identity explicitly in its antidiscrimination law.

It was a risky venture. While many supported the antidiscrimination clause to include sexual orientation, there was greater debate surrounding the addition of gender identity. Proponents on both sides often wondered if inclusion of gender identity would ultimately defeat the measure. However, activists, including an arm of the National Gay and Lesbian Task Force (NGLTF), the Transgender Civil Rights Project, insisted gender identity be part of the antidiscrimination bill. They sought grassroots support and regularly met with legislators. The Coalition for Equality of New Mexico and New Mexico Gender Advocacy Information Network (NMGAIN) also led lobbying efforts and helped tip the scales.

Many initially saw the decision of New Mexico's senate as one clearly along party lines. Republicans were vocal about excising gender identity from the amendment, often debating that gender discrimination was necessary as a practical matter: For example, segregating company restrooms and changing rooms. However, due in large part to grassroots efforts, these arguments were refuted, and a strongly Democratic senate pushed the bill through.

The amendment established a state hate crime law, providing extra prison time for offenders whose crimes are found to have been motivated by hate caused by actual or perceived race, religion, color, national origin, ancestry, gender, gender identity, or sexual orientation of the victim. More important, the law forbids housing and job discrimination based on those same protected classes.

In 2004, efforts to repeal the bill were unsuccessful. New Mexico's constitution allows citizens to attempt to overturn a law passed by the legislature by putting a repeal question on the ballot in the next general election. Opponents, including Representative Earlene Roberts, submitted a referendum to get the appeal put on the November 2 ballot, but New Mexico's referendum provision does not apply to laws providing for the "preservation of the public peace, health or safety." Attorney General Patricia Madrid said in a legal opinion that the Human Rights Act was protected against referenda because the antidiscrimination protections "represent an exercise of the state's inherent police powers."

> **NEW MEXICO'S HUMAN RIGHTS ACT: AN AMENDMENT**
>
> *Section 1.* . . . Is amended to read:
> *Definitions.*—As used in the Human Rights Act: . . .
> P. "sexual orientation" means heterosexuality, homosexuality or bisexuality, whether actual or perceived; and
> Q. "gender identity" means a person's self-perception, or perception of that person by another, of the person's identity as a male or female based upon the person's appearance, behavior or physical characteristics that are in accord with or opposed to the person's physical anatomy, chromosomal sex or sex at birth.

SIGNIFICANCE

Transgender and gender-variant people have often felt alienated from their own communities. The gay and lesbian community, too, often disassociates itself from those who are transgender and from the fight for transgender rights. New Mexico's inclusion of gender identity with sexual orientation in its Human Rights Act was a significant step forward not only for transgender rights but also for the unification of the GLBT community.

Thanks in large part to New Mexico's efforts, California also explicitly banned discrimination based on gender identity. Minnesota enacted such a ban in 1993, as had Rhode Island in 2001. Kentucky and Pennsylvania prohibit bias against transgender state workers. Eight other states (Connecticut, Florida, Hawaii, Illinois, Massachusetts, New Jersey, New York, and Vermont) interpret their antibias laws as already giving protection to those who are transgender. Pressure in the remaining states is mounting to include gender identity in all antidiscrimination policies.

An important case for transgender rights occurred on June 1, 2004, in Ohio. A transgender employment discrimination decision was made in favor of Jimmie Smith, a male firefighter transitioning to female who encountered hostility on the job. The ruling also applies to employers in Kentucky, Michigan, Ohio, and Tennessee who have fifteen workers or more. Similar cases are being heard in courts around the country.

Many consider New Mexico, generally thought to be a somewhat conservative state, a new leader in transgender-rights legislation. Countless cities and businesses, including a large percentage of *Fortune* 500 companies, have since included gender identity in their own antidiscrimination policies. Businesses that operate in multiple cities, those of which have gender identity antidiscrimination laws, have largely adopted the policy for all locations in which their company does business.

States have been somewhat slower than the private sector to adopt amended policies. Some claim that gender identity is already covered in their policies under the category of "gender" and therefore further legislation is not needed. Still others maintain a policy for state workers but do not extend that to private businesses. Overall, however, transgender and human rights activists have challenged policies in almost all states and will continue to do so.

What is clear from New Mexico's amendment to include gender identity in its antidiscrimination and hate crimes policy is that transgender rights have become the next step in the evolution of equitable rights for all people and that individual companies and organizations have, by and large, been more open to adopt inclusive antidiscrimination policies than have state and federal government agencies.

—*Tom Smith*

FURTHER READING

Best Companies to Work For. http://www.tgender.net/taw/goodcomp.html.

Currah, Paisley, and Shannon Minter. "Unprincipled Exclusions: The Struggle to Achieve Judicial and Legislative Equality for Transgender People." *William & Mary Journal of Women and the Law* 7 (Fall, 2000): 37-66.

Human Rights Campaign. http://www.hrc.org.

Leonard, Arthur S. "New Mexico Legislative/Executive Trifecta: Simultaneous Measures on Discrimination, Hate Crimes, and Partner Benefits—State High Court Recognizes Consortium Claim." *Lesbian and Gay Law Notes* (May, 2003): 65.

New Mexico Legislature. House Bill 314. http://legis.state.nm.us/Sessions/03%20Regular/bills/house/HB0314.html.

Sharpe, Andrew N. *Transgender Jurisprudence: Dysphoric Bodies of Law*. London: Cavendish, 2002.

SEE ALSO: 1992: Transgender Nation Holds Its First Protest; June 17, 1995: International Bill of Gender Rights Is First Circulated; 1998: Transgender Scholarship Proliferates; Oct. 27, 1999: *Littleton v. Prange* Withholds Survivor Rights from Transsexual Spouses; 2002: Sylvia Rivera Law Project Is Founded; Apr. 30, 2002: Transgender Rights Added to New York City Law; Feb. 21, 2003: Australian Court Validates Transsexual Marriage; Mar., 2003-Dec., 2004: Transsexuals Protest Academic Exploitation; Nov. 20, 2003: Transgender Day of Remembrance and Remembering Our Dead Project; May 17, 2004: Transsexual Athletes Allowed to Compete in Olympic Games.

April, 2003
BUENOS AIRES RECOGNIZES SAME-GENDER CIVIL UNIONS

The autonomous city of Buenos Aires, Argentina, included sexual orientation in its antidiscrimination law in 1996. In 2002 the city council had approved civil unions for same-gender couples, which became law in April, 2003. The civil union laws also have helped in the arena of reproductive rights at the city and national level, and a debate continues about a proposed law on sex education that makes discussion of queer identities mandatory while forbidding discriminatory references.

LOCALE: Buenos Aires, Argentina
CATEGORIES: Civil rights; laws, acts, and legal history; government and politics

SUMMARY OF EVENT

Although the first queer organization in Argentina, Nuestro Mundo, was founded in 1969, the dictatorship in power from 1976 through 1983 killed many activists and forced others to leave the country. The young LGBT movement disappeared overnight. Only with the return of democracy in 1984 did a queer group emerge again, Comunidad Homosexual Argentina (Argentine Homosexual Community, or CHA). Despite many efforts to obtain legal benefits for lesbians, gays, bisexuals, transsexuals, and transvestites (a locally acceptable term), the CHA was unable to get any law passed defending homosexual rights. However, in the early 1990's the movement began to see results from its own battles and the influence of the international queer movement. After a history of legal persecution of homosexuals, the Argentine state legally recognized the CHA in 1992.

When President Carlos Menem arrived in the United States in 1992, queer demonstrators denounced his regime for discrimination against LGBT people. As a result, Menem lobbied the Argentine Supreme Court to grant the CHA legal recognition to avoid a negative international image.

With the legal separation of Buenos Aires as an autonomous city, queer people found new opportunities to secure their rights. In 1996, the newly written constitution of Buenos Aires included sexual orientation in an antidiscrimination law, and in December, 2002, the Buenos Aires city council approved civil unions for people of the same gender. The law was passed with strong pressure from the queer movement, whose members remained in the city council chambers during the entire debate in order to pressure legislators on behalf of the queer movement.

The civil union law was passed in a social environment in which the influence of the Roman Catholic Church had been strongly undermined by a child abuse scandal. Julio Cesar Grassi, a priest whose television and media appearances gave him a high public profile, was found guilty of systematically raping children. As the most public figure of the Catholic Church at the time, he had damaged the Church's image profoundly. The Church's refusal to take a strong stance against Grassi worked against the institution itself. In this environment, it was difficult for the Church to raise a moral voice against civil unions, especially at a time when the crisis had mobilized an important sector of the population toward the political left.

The city council's approval of civil unions was also an attempt to appear "modern" and "civilized" at a time that saw a brutal economic and political crisis and the state had lost credibility. The law took effect in April, 2003, with the creation of a Public Register for Civil Unions, and it allowed the union between any two adults to be officially recognized within the city limits. To apply for civil union, both members of the couple have to be legal residents of the city of Buenos Aires, and they have to prove that their relationship has been stable and public for at least two years.

SIGNIFICANCE

The law has been more important in terms of its political consequences in Argentina and Latin America than for the rights it provides. There have been attempts to extend civil unions to the entire province of Buenos Aires, and it has encouraged debate in other countries where similar discussions have been waiting for public expression. This is the case in the Mexico City municipal council and the Brazilian and Colombian congresses. The current law does not deal with inheritance or adoption, two main rights heterosexuals legally enjoy through marriage. The law equally grants to civil unions some welfare rights granted to those in heterosexual marriages, such as joint health coverage. However, this right applies only to city employees. Other benefits include family leave and the legal right to make decisions for a partner in case of illness.

Despite the limitations of the Buenos Aires civil union law, symbolically it means a step forward for the LGBT community. The first union took place in July, 2003, between Cesar Cigliutti (forty-five years old) and Marcelo Suntheim (thirty-five years old), and it received full media coverage. Despite Church opposition, a growing number of people in Buenos Aires support civil unions. As part of the same process, new laws on reproductive rights have been passed both at a city and national level, and now there is a debate about a proposed law on sex education that makes discussion of queer identities mandatory while forbidding discriminatory references.

In August, 2003, the Vatican urged legislatures in predominantly Catholic countries to stop voting for measures that violate "nature" and "Christian values." The Catholic Church, despite numerous scandals in the first few years of the twenty-first century involving priests, consistently argues against lesbian and gay rights, basing its arguments on the support of heterosexual marriage. Priests continue to oppose not only civil unions but also sexual minorities and transgender people in general, especially the most visible, such as artists and actors.

Since the civil union law was passed in Buenos Aires, the Mexican LGBT movement has pushed for the renewal of the discussion of a bill legalizing "domestic partnership" in the municipal legislature. If this bill is passed, it will cover any two people who live together, assuring bank credits and some of the social welfare benefits provided by the Mexican state. Although Chile still has not approved heterosexual divorce, the Homosexual Integration and Liberation Movement lobbied the Chamber of Deputies to pass a bill assuring inheritance and common property for all those who live together. In Colombia, some senators tried to pass a law granting queer couples many of the legal rights enjoyed by heterosexuals. Fifty-five members of Colombia's parliament voted against the bill and only thirty-two supported it, defeating the struggle for equal rights in that country.

—*Pablo Ben*

FURTHER READING

Balderston, Daniel, and Donna Guy. *Sex and Sexuality in Latin America*. New York: New York University Press, 1997.

Bazán, Osvaldo. *Historia de la homosexualidad en la Argentina: De la Conquista de América al siglo XXI*. Buenos Aires, Argentina: Marea, 2004.

Berco, Cristian. "Silencing the Unmentionable: Non-reproductive Sex and the Creation of a Civilized Argentina, 1860-1900." *The Americas* 58, no. 3 (January, 2002): 419-441.

Brown, Stephen. "Democracy and Sexual Difference: The Lesbian and Gay Movement in Argentina." *The Global Emergence of Gay and Lesbian Politics: National Imprints of a Worldwide Movement*, edited by Barry D. Adam, Jan Willem Duyvendak, and André Krouwel. Philadelphia: Temple University Press, 1999.

The Gully.com. "Buenos Aires Approves Gay Civil Unions." http://www.thegully.com/essays/argentina/021214_gay_rights_ar.html.

Grupo Nexo. "Union Civil: Buenos Aires, Primero." http://www.nexo.org/noticias86.htm.

SEE ALSO: 1981: Gay and Lesbian Palimony Suits Emerge; Nov. 6, 1984: West Hollywood Incorporates with Majority Gay and Lesbian City Council; Dec. 4, 1984: Berkeley Extends Benefits to Domestic Partners of City Employees; 1992: Transgender Nation Holds Its First Protest; June, 1992: Feinberg Publishes *Trans-*

gender Liberation; 1993-1996: Hawaii Opens Door to Same-Gender Marriages; Aug. 6, 1994: Japanese American Citizens League Supports Same-Gender Marriage; Sept. 21, 1996: U.S. President Clinton Signs Defense of Marriage Act; Oct. 27, 1999: *Littleton v. Prange* Withholds Survivor Rights from Transsexual Spouses; Dec. 20, 1999: *Baker v. Vermont* Leads to Recognition of Same-Gender Civil Unions; Feb. 21, 2003: Australian Court Validates Transsexual Marriage; June 17, 2003, and July 19, 2005: Canada Legalizes Same-Gender Marriage; Nov. 18, 2003: Massachusetts Court Rules for Same-Gender Marriage; Nov. 18, 2004: United Kingdom Legalizes Same-Gender Civil Partnerships; Apr. 4, 2005: United Kingdom's Gender Recognition Act Legalizes Transsexual Marriage; June 30, 2005: Spain Legalizes Same-Gender Marriage.

June 17, 2003, and July 19, 2005
Canada Legalizes Same-Gender Marriage

Canada became only the fourth country, after Belgium, the Netherlands, and Spain, to legalize same-gender marriage with its passage of the Civil Marriage Act.

Also known as: Bill C-38; Civil Marriage Act
Locale: Ottawa, Canada
Categories: Civil rights; laws, acts, and legal history

Key Figures
Kevin Bourassa (b. 1958) and
Joe Varnell (b. 1969), first gay couple in North America to marry
Anne Vatour and
Elaine Vatour, first lesbian couple in North America to marry
Jean Chrétien (1934-1999), Canadian prime minister
Michael Leshner (b. 1948) and
Michael Stark, Canadian gay couple that played a key role in the Canadian court decision ruling that banning same-gender marriage was unconstitutional

Summary of Event

The battle to win the right for same-gender marriages in Canada formally began in 2001, when a gay couple and a lesbian couple were married in the Metropolitan Community Church of Toronto on January 14. Because the province of Ontario did not recognize same-gender marriages at the time, the couples used an older tradition, the reading of the banns, to formalize their vows. The church read their intent to marry before three regular services prior to the weddings. The couples, Kevin Bourassa and Joe Varnell, and Anne and Elaine Vatour, then asked the governments of Toronto and Ontario to recognize the legality of their unions. The governments refused.

In 2002, the Ontario Superior Court ruled that it was unconstitutional to exclude same-gender couples from marriage, ordering the province to change its laws within twenty-four months to end the discriminatory exclusion. Toronto crown attorney Michael Leshner, who had previously won GLBT rights successes in the Canadian court, and his partner, Michael Stark, applied for a license at that time and were turned down. In the meantime, the government appealed the Superior Court decision. On June 10, 2003, the Ontario Court of Appeals upheld the Superior Court ruling. Ontario retroactively recognized the 2001 weddings, and Leshner and Stark, after the law took effect, became the first couple to marry legally in Canada. (A lesbian couple known by the initials M. M. and J. H. carry the unfortunate distinction of being the first same-gender couple to divorce in Canada, on September 13, 2004.)

Additionally, on June 17, during a parliamentary

meeting, the Liberal Party of Canada, led by Prime Minister Jean Chrétien, introduced legislation to legalize same-gender marriage across the country. The conservative Alliance Party called for legislation that would have limited marriage to a union between a man and a woman; however, on September 16, 2003, their motion was defeated. The motion would have required the Canadian parliament to invoke the country's "notwithstanding" clause, which essentially states that the Canadian government can make legal decisions that go against the Canadian Charter of Rights and Freedoms as long as it admits that its decision goes against that charter.

Only Alberta, Prince Edward Island, Nunavut, and the Northwest Territories had yet to ratify the legislation when, in December, 2004, Canada's Supreme Court ruled it constitutional to enact a national law recognizing same-gender marriages. In 2005, the Canadian Liberal Party, led by Prime Minister Paul Martin, introduced Bill C-38 (the Civil Marriage Act) with just that intent. The bill passed the House of Commons in June, 2005, the Canadian Senate approved it on July 19, and same-gender marriages became a nationwide reality.

SIGNIFICANCE

Canada is only the fourth country to legalize same-gender marriages, following the Netherlands (2001), Belgium (2003), and Spain (2005). Because Canada's 2003 decision required ratification from each individual province, it filtered across the country for two years before Bill C-38 became national law in 2005. Thus, Canada follows Spain in the chronology of legalizing same-gender marriages, even though Canada's legislative process was in progress much longer.

CANADIAN CIVIL MARRIAGE ACT: AN EXCERPT

The preamble to Bill C-38 includes statements of principle and fact, asserting Parliament's commitment to uphold the Constitution and equality rights under section 15 of the Canadian Charter of Rights and Freedoms; noting the scope of judicial rulings across the country to have legalized same-sex marriage on Charter equality grounds, and the reliance of same-sex married couples on those rulings; asserting that only equal access to civil marriage, as distinct from civil union, respects same-sex couples' Charter equality rights; noting that Parliament's constitutional jurisdiction does not extend to creating an institution other than marriage for same-sex couples; affirming the Charter's section 2 freedom of conscience and religion guarantee; asserting that the bill is without effect on that guarantee, with particular reference to the freedom of members of religious groups to hold their beliefs and that of officials to refuse to perform marriages that conflict with their beliefs; stating that the public expression of differing views on marriage is compatible with the public interest; noting that Parliament's commitment to equality precludes use of the Charter's section 33 notwithstanding clause to deny same-sex couples access to civil marriage; affirming Parliament's responsibility to support the fundamental institution of marriage; and asserting that in light of Charter values, access to civil marriage for same-sex couples should be legislated. . . .

B. Civil Marriage (Clause 2)

Bill C-38's key provision defines civil marriage as "the lawful union of two persons to the exclusion of all others." It is worth stressing that Bill C-38 is concerned exclusively with civil marriage, and does not affect gender-neutral survivor or common-law partner entitlements in federal legislation.

Because there is no residency requirement to marry in Canada, same-gender couples from the United States have been marrying across the border since 2003. It remains to be seen which U.S. states will honor same-gender marriages performed in Canada. The experience of Bourassa and Varnell trying to travel to the United States as a couple is an example of the probable obstacles. The two wanted to fill out and submit to U.S. customs the customs form appropriate for a married couple, but their request was denied; so they went home after officials asked them to fill out forms for individuals instead.

Still, the new Canadian law has the potential to impact legal decisions in the United States. As U.S. couples marry in Canada, U.S. businesses and officials are being forced to deal with the implications of legal lesbian and gay unions. U.S. president

George W. Bush's attempt to draft a constitutional amendment banning same-gender marriage was defeated in the U.S. Senate in September of 2004. Massachusetts, in 2004, became the first U.S. state to recognize same-gender marriage. Vermont legalized civil unions for gay and lesbian couples in 2000, and New Jersey did the same in 2004. Also, New Jersey's Supreme Court ruled on October 25, 2006, that same-gender couples are entitled to the same legal rights as heterosexual couples who are married.

Some Canadian opponents of same-gender marriage have used the same antigay and antilesbian arguments used by Anita Bryant in Dade County, Florida, in 1977. They claim the legalization of same-gender marriages will be followed by legal pedophilia and bestiality. Other antagonists claim to be defending traditional marriages. The Canadian government has explicitly stated no church will be forced to marry same-gender couples against its will, but this only pacified a few critics. The Roman Catholic Church also has launched an attack upon same-gender marriage, urging politicians not to condone it. However, Canadian attitudes appear to be changing in favor of same-gender marriages.

—*Jessie Bishop Powell*

Further Reading

Bourassa, Kevin, and Joe Varnell. "Fifth Anniversary of the First Legal Gay Marriage." January 12, 2006. http://www.samesexmarriage.ca.

_____. *Just Married: Gay Marriage and the Expansion of Human Rights*. Madison: University of Wisconsin Press, 2002.

"Canada Lawmakers Approve Gay Marriage Bill." *Advocate.com* (June 30, 2005).

Equal Marriage for Same-Sex Couples. http://www.samesexmarriage.ca.

Kimmel, Michael S., and Amy Aronsen, eds. *The Gendered Society Reader*. New York: Oxford University Press, 2000.

Kotulski, Davina. *Why You Should Give a Damn About Gay Marriage*. Los Angeles: Alyson, 2004.

Robinson, Bruce A. "Homosexual (Same Sex) Marriages In Canada: Ontario Court Case." Part 1. Toronto: Ontario Consultants on Religious Tolerance, 1995. http://www.religioustolerance.org/hom_marb2.htm.

"Same-Sex Marriage: A Selective Bibliography of the Legal Literature." Law Library, Rutgers School of Law. http://law-library.rutgers.edu/SSM.html.

Stychin, Carl, and Didi Herman, eds. *Law and Sexuality: The Global Arena*. Minneapolis: University of Minnesota Press, 2001.

See also: Aug. 26, 1969: Canada Decriminalizes Homosexual Acts; 1981: Gay and Lesbian Palimony Suits Emerge; Jan. 1, 1988: Canada Decriminalizes Sex Practices Between Consenting Adults; Oct., 1992: Canadian Military Lifts Its Ban on Gays and Lesbians; 1993-1996: Hawaii Opens Door to Same-Gender Marriages; Aug. 6, 1994: Japanese American Citizens League Supports Same-Gender Marriage; Sept. 21, 1996: U.S. President Clinton Signs Defense of Marriage Act; Dec. 20, 1999: *Baker v. Vermont* Leads to Recognition of Same-Gender Civil Unions; Feb. 21, 2003: Australian Court Validates Transsexual Marriage; Apr., 2003: Buenos Aires Recognizes Same-Gender Civil Unions; Nov. 18, 2003: Massachusetts Court Rules for Same-Gender Marriage; Nov. 18, 2004: United Kingdom Legalizes Same-Gender Civil Partnerships; Apr. 4, 2005: United Kingdom's Gender Recognition Act Legalizes Transsexual Marriage; June 30, 2005: Spain Legalizes Same-Gender Marriage.

June 26, 2003
U.S. Supreme Court Overturns Texas Sodomy Law

In a 6-3 decision, the U.S. Supreme Court lifted Texas's ban on homosexual sodomy while nullifying all remaining state laws against sodomy, homosexual and heterosexual alike.

Also known as: *Lawrence v. Texas*
Locale: Houston, Texas; Washington, D.C.
Categories: Laws, acts, and legal history; civil rights

Key Figures

Tyron Garner (d. 2006), street-stand barbecue vendor, petitioner in *Lawrence v. Texas*

John Geddes Lawrence, medical technologist and petitioner with Garner in the *Lawrence* case

Anthony M. Kennedy (b. 1936), Supreme Court justice who wrote the majority opinion to overturn Texas's "homosexual conduct" law

Antonin Scalia (b. 1936), chief justice of the United States, who wrote the dissenting opinion in favor of upholding the Texas law

Summary of Event

At the time that Houston police officers responded to the report of a weapons disturbance at the home of John Geddes Lawrence on September 17, 1998, fourteen U.S. states maintained laws against sodomy. Four states—Texas, Missouri, Oklahoma, and Kansas—criminalized specifically same-gender sodomy. When the officers dispatched to the scene found no weapons disturbance but rather Lawrence engaging in anal sex with another man, Tyron Garner, they arrested the two men for violating Texas's "homosexual conduct" law. Lawrence and Garner were held in police custody overnight and posted $200 bail.

On November 20, the two men were charged and convicted by a justice of the peace. They pleaded no contest and requested that the court dismiss the charges on the basis of equal protection, claiming that Texas's law was unconstitutional to the extent that it applied only to homosexual, but not to heterosexual, sodomy. Lawrence and Garner also claimed their right to privacy, protected under the due process clause of the Fourteenth Amendment to the U.S. Constitution. The neighbor who reported the false weapons disturbance was later convicted for filing a false report.

The report of the gun that neither Lawrence nor Garner fired that night nonetheless echoed throughout America, setting into motion the chain of events that would irremediably change both judicial precedent and the ongoing fight for gay and lesbian rights. The ground that *Lawrence v. Texas* (2003) gained for gay and lesbian rights did not, however, simply build upon Lawrence and Garner's violation of the Texas statute in the fall of 1998. The *Lawrence* precedent also had to revisit the U.S. Supreme Court's *Bowers v. Hardwick* (1986) decision from seventeen years earlier.

In writing the majority opinion of the *Lawrence* court, Justice Anthony M. Kennedy challenged the arguments that the *Bowers* court so strongly supported. Where the *Bowers* court asserted that the central issue in laws like the Texas statute was whether individuals have a "fundamental right to commit homosexual sodomy," the *Lawrence* court interpreted the petitioners' challenge to the Texas law as a broader, more inclusive right to privacy

Fourteen U.S. States with Laws Against Sodomy Prior to the 2003 *Lawrence v. Texas* Ruling	
Alabama	Missouri
Florida	North Carolina
Idaho	Oklahoma
Kansas	South Carolina
Louisiana	Texas
Michigan	Utah
Mississippi	Virginia

> ### *LAWRENCE V. TEXAS*: FROM THE MAJORITY OPINION (2003)
>
> *Justice Kennedy delivered the opinion of the Court:* Liberty protects the person from unwarranted government intrusions into a dwelling or other private places. In our tradition the State is not omnipresent in the home. And there are other spheres of our lives and existence, outside the home, where the State should not be a dominant presence. Freedom extends beyond spatial bounds. Liberty presumes an autonomy of self that includes freedom of thought, belief, expression, and certain intimate conduct. The instant case involves liberty of the person both in its spatial and more transcendent dimensions.
>
> I. The question before the Court is the validity of a Texas statute making it a crime for two persons of the same sex to engage in certain intimate sexual conduct. . . .
>
> The rationale of *Bowers [v. Hardwick*, 1986] does not withstand careful analysis. In his dissenting opinion in *Bowers* Justice Stevens came to these conclusions: "Our prior cases make two propositions abundantly clear. First, the fact that the governing majority in a State has traditionally viewed a particular practice as immoral is not a sufficient reason for upholding a law prohibiting the practice; neither history nor tradition could save a law prohibiting miscegenation from constitutional attack. Second, individual decisions by married persons, concerning the intimacies of their physical relationship, even when not intended to produce offspring, are a form of 'liberty' protected by the Due Process Clause of the Fourteenth Amendment. Moreover, this protection extends to intimate choices by unmarried as well as married persons." . . .
>
> Justice Stevens' analysis, in our view, should have been controlling in *Bowers* and should control here.
>
> *Bowers* was not correct when it was decided, and it is not correct today. It ought not to remain binding precedent. *Bowers v. Hardwick* should be and now is overruled.
>
> The present case does not involve minors. It does not involve persons who might be injured or coerced or who are situated in relationships where consent might not easily be refused. It does not involve public conduct or prostitution. It does not involve whether the government must give formal recognition to any relationship that homosexual persons seek to enter. The case does involve two adults who, with full and mutual consent from each other, engaged in sexual practices common to a homosexual lifestyle. The petitioners are entitled to respect for their private lives. The State cannot demean their existence or control their destiny by making their private sexual conduct a crime. Their right to liberty under the Due Process Clause gives them the full right to engage in their conduct without intervention of the government. "It is a promise of the Constitution that there is a realm of personal liberty which the government may not enter." . . . The Texas statute furthers no legitimate state interest which can justify its intrusion into the personal and private life of the individual. . . .
>
> The judgment of the Court of Appeals for the Texas Fourteenth District is reversed, and the case is remanded for further proceedings not inconsistent with this opinion.
>
> It is so ordered.

under the Fourteenth Amendment's due process clause. Where the *Bowers* court asserted that proscriptions against sodomy have "ancient roots," the *Lawrence* court demonstrated that this was not necessarily obvious. *Lawrence v. Texas* not only broadened the definition of "personal liberty" but also, in the context of the Court's history of legislating sexual freedoms, called into question the notion of "history" itself.

Even from within the Court's majority opinion, one heard a voice of dissent. Justice Sandra Day O'Connor filed an opinion independent of Justice Kennedy's, which supported the *Lawrence* decision not on the basis of due process but rather under the auspices of equal protection: that a law cannot discriminate against one class of people in favor of another. While Justice O'Connor ultimately agreed with the Court's decision to overturn the Texas statute, she did not support the Court's overruling *Bowers v. Hardwick*. Her position was that the Georgia law against sodomy at issue in *Bowers* applied both to heterosexual and to homosexual sodomy, whereas the Texas "homosexual conduct" law did not.

The grounds for Justice Antonin Scalia's sharply written dissenting opinion challenged the limits this decision imposed upon the states' ability to legislate morality. Justice Scalia's rejoinder to Justices Kennedy and O'Connor argued that this case could result in much more than the legalization of sodomy. Scalia predicted that *Lawrence v. Texas* not only would legalize sodomy but also would eventually restrict the states' ability to prohibit "bigamy, same-gender marriage, adult incest, prostitution, masturbation, adultery, fornication, bestiality, and obscenity."

SIGNIFICANCE

Lawrence v. Texas might not have inaugurated an era of sexual and moral anarchy, as Scalia's description predicted, but without a doubt the case had implications that reached far beyond the lives of John Geddes Lawrence and Tyron Garner—and far beyond overturning the remaining sodomy laws of Texas and other states. Above and beyond broadening the scope of what rights and individuals the due process clause protects, in the following year the *Lawrence v. Texas* decision initiated a series of legal landmarks in addition to a swell of conservative backlash.

On July 30, 2003, President George W. Bush announced his support of a constitutional amendment against same-gender marriage, undoubtedly motivated by Scalia's ominous predictions. On July 31, 2003, the Vatican issued a treatise on the virtues of heterosexual marriage, recommending not only that same-gender marriage should be forbidden but also that same-gender partners should not be parents. Though the Vatican's document was in progress for two years prior to *Lawrence*, its release only a month afterward seemed more than coincidental.

Refusing to heed Scalia's warnings or to follow President Bush's lead or to give credence to the Vatican's doctrines, on May 17, 2004, the state of Massachusetts legalized same-gender marriage, a decision that was undoubtedly encouraged by the federal Court's ruling less than one year before. Though no other states followed suit—California and Missouri actively rejected appeals to legalize gay and lesbian marriage—after *Lawrence* it became increasingly clear that gay and lesbian marriage, and not simply the "right to commit homosexual sodomy," was at issue in the case. Scalia realized this in his dissenting opinion, as did Justice Kennedy in his Opinion of the Court, and it is this end to which *Lawrence v. Texas* brought the United States that much closer in July of 2003.

—Ashley T. Shelden

FURTHER READING

Cain, Patricia A. *Rainbow Rights: The Role of Lawyers and Courts in the Lesbian and Gay Civil Rights Movement*. Cambridge, Mass.: Westview Press, 2000.

Curry, Lynne. *The Human Body on Trial: A Handbook with Cases, Laws, and Documents*. Santa Barbara, Calif.: ABC-CLIO, 2002.

Goldberg, Jonathan. *Reclaiming Sodom*. New York: Routledge, 1994.

Hickey, Adam. "Between Two Spheres: Comparing State and Federal Approaches to the Right to Privacy and Prohibitions Against Sodomy." *Yale Law Review* 111, no. 4 (January, 2002): 993-1030.

Lawrence v. Texas. 539 U.S. 558, 123 S.Ct. 2472, 156 L.Ed.2d 508. Summary: http://www.supremecourtus.gov/opinions/02pdf/02-102.pdf.

Murdoch, Joyce, and Deb Price. *Courting Justice: Gay Men and Lesbians v. the Supreme Court*. New York: Basic Books, 2001.

Richards, David A. J. *The Case for Gay Rights: From Bowers to Lawrence and Beyond*. Lawrence: University Press of Kansas, 2005.

Rubenstein, William B. *Cases and Materials on Sexual Orientation and the Law*. St. Paul, Minn.: West, 1997.

Tribe, Lawrence H. "*Lawrence v. Texas:* The 'Fundamental Right' That Dare Not Speak Its Name." *Harvard Law Review* 117, no. 6 (April, 2004): 1893-1955.

Warner, Michael. *The Trouble with Normal: Sex, Politics, and the Ethics of Queer Life*. Cambridge, Mass.: Harvard University Press, 2000.

SEE ALSO: 1885: United Kingdom Criminalizes "Gross Indecency"; Jan. 12, 1939: *Thompson v. Aldredge* Dismisses Sodomy Charges Against Lesbians; 1961: Illinois Legalizes Consensual Homosexual Sex; Jan. 22, 1973: *Roe v. Wade* Legalizes Abortion and Extends Privacy Rights; June 21, 1973: U.S. Supreme Court Supports Local Obscenity Laws; Aug., 1973: American Bar

Association Calls for Repeal of Laws Against Consensual Sex; Oct. 18, 1973: Lambda Legal Authorized to Practice Law; Nov. 17, 1975: U.S. Supreme Court Rules in "Crimes Against Nature" Case; 1981: Gay and Lesbian Palimony Suits Emerge; 1986: *Bowers v. Hardwick* Upholds State Sodomy Laws; Jan. 1, 1988: Canada Decriminalizes Sex Practices Between Consenting Adults; 1992-2006: Indians Struggle to Abolish Sodomy Law.

July, 2003
SINGAPORE LIFTS BAN ON HIRING LESBIAN AND GAY EMPLOYEES

To foster a more progressive economic image, Singapore lifted a government ban on hiring lesbian and gay civil servants. However, homosexual acts remain illegal in the socially conservative and tightly controlled republic.

LOCALE: Singapore, Republic of Singapore
CATEGORIES: Civil rights; economics; government and politics

KEY FIGURE
Goh Chok Tong (b. 1941), People's Action Party prime minister of Singapore, 1990-2004

SUMMARY OF EVENT
Singapore is a small island city-state in Southeast Asia. Around three-fourths of the population of approximately four million are Chinese; Muslim Malays make up the largest minority group. A British colony until 1959 and independent since 1963, Singapore inherited much of its political and legal framework from the British, including proscriptions against homosexual conduct. These laws include Section 377 of the penal code, which prohibits "carnal intercourse against the order of nature with any man, woman or animals"; Section 377A, which applies only to acts by a man "of gross indecency with another male person"; and sections on outrage of modesty, soliciting, and obscene gestures.

Given both the illegality of homosexual acts and the social stigma attached to nonnormative gender identity and sexual behavior, it has long been assumed that gay or lesbian civil servants (ranging from diplomats to local bureaucrats to teachers) would be at risk of blackmail. Therefore, they were—usually quietly—kept from at least high-level or sensitive positions. While some private sector firms, especially multinational ones, do have policies of nondiscrimination on grounds of sexuality, such provisions are rare in Singapore. Few Singaporeans are "out" as gay, lesbian, bisexual, or transgender, despite the availability of gay bars and other venues since the 1960's. Nevertheless, especially since the late 1980's, an increasingly vibrant GLBT community, a lively Internet scene, and a GLBT organization known as People Like Us (PLU), which formed in 1993, have made Singapore more friendly to GLBT persons, if only incrementally.

In July, 2003, Singapore's prime minister Goh Chok Tong announced in an interview with Simon Elegant of *Time* magazine that gays and lesbians would henceforth be allowed to serve openly in the civil service, even in sensitive positions. The policy change was not formally codified, and in fact Goh and the Public Service Department (PSD) suggested that administrators had already been quietly turning a blind eye to sexual orientation. In a speech delivered at the National Day Rally on August 17, 2003, he explained that "gays too need to make a living" and suggested that the private sector would likely follow the lead of the public sector.

The motive for the change was economic. Goh and others cited in particular a study by economics and urban planning specialist Richard Florida (*The Rise of the Creative Class*, 2002), which argues that creativity is key to competitive advantage in the contemporary global economy. A city's tolerance for gays and lesbians proves a good indicator of the sort of openness and diversity that attract the high-tech workers and other talented people who comprise the "creative class" and spur economic dynamism.

At the time, Singapore was in the midst of an ongoing economic recession and rising unemployment. For Singapore to "move up the value chain into higher-skilled jobs" thus required fostering creativity and taking innovative steps to lure foreign talent and investment. Goh elaborated the following month that his government would "have to cut loose the apron strings" so Singapore could "become a vibrant society with a strong entrepreneurial streak . . . less strait-laced and Victorian [and more] self-reliant and robust." At the same time, Goh and other government officials wished both to avoid endorsing homosexuality and to deter vocal gay rights activism in socially conservative Singapore.

SIGNIFICANCE

The change in civil service policy seemed to indicate a loosening of Singapore's "nanny state" mentality (the government's reputation for meddling) and accelerated a shift toward openness and activism. Goh's remarks were followed by a spate of positive media attention to GLBT issues and the power of the "pink dollar," stepped-up relaxation of censorship controls on arts and media, and a newly optimistic effort by PLU to press for official recognition of the group and decriminalization of homosexual activity.

Such trends and initiatives had begun much earlier, but Goh's imprimatur both forced the issue out into the open and helped legitimate gays' and lesbians' claims to equal rights. Within a matter of months, however, the media had retreated from its prolific favorable coverage of GLBT issues, the government had reasserted its determination to sustain the ban on same-gender sexuality, and PLU was officially declared an illegal organization and ordered to cease all public activities.

It is impossible to say what impact, if any, the new civil service policy has had, but many GLBT activists remain pessimistic. The Public Service Department claims not to have received any reports of "blackmail or discrimination against any civil servant due to his or her sexual orientation," and coming out will not be grounds for prosecution. However, the PSD "does not track the statistics on the sexual orientation of civil servants."

Anecdotal evidence suggests that there has been some greater openness toward lesbian and gay employees. All the same, as PLU asserts that "It is a glaring contradiction to ask civil servants to declare openly that they are gay and then still to say that it is a crime."

—*Meredith L. Weiss*

FURTHER READING

Au Waipang. "Gay Civil Servants, and What Next?" July, 2003. http://www.yawningbread.org/index2.htm.

Elegant, Simon. "The Lion in Winter." *Time*, July 7, 2003.

Florida, Richard. *The Rise of the Creative Class: And How It's Transforming Work, Leisure, Community, and Everyday Life*. New York: Basic Books, 2002.

Heng, Russell Hiang Khng. "Tiptoe Out of the Closet: The Before and After of the Increasingly Visible Gay Community in Singapore." *Journal of Homosexuality* 40, nos. 3/4 (2001): 81-97.

Lo, Joseph, and Huang Guoqin. *People Like Us: Sexual Minorities in Singapore*. Singapore: Select Books, 2003.

Lo, Leona. *My Sisters, Their Stories*. Singapore: Select Books, 2003.

People Like Us. "Frequently Asked Questions About People Like Us." http://www.geocities.com/plusg1/faq_01.htm.

Singapore Penal Code. http://statutes.agc.gov.sg.

Weiss, Meredith L. "Who Sets Social Policy in Metropolis? Economic Positioning and Social Reform in Singapore." Paper presented at the annual meeting of American Political Science Association, Chicago, September 2-5, 2004.

SEE ALSO: Apr. 27, 1953: U.S. President Eisenhower Prohibits Federal Employment of Lesbians and Gays; 1972-1973: Local Governments Pass Antidiscrimination Laws; June 27, 1974: Abzug and Koch Attempt to Amend the Civil Rights Act of 1964; July 3, 1975: U.S. Civil Service Commission Prohibits Discrimination Against Federal Employees; 1978: Lesbian and Gay Workplace Movement Is Founded; June 2, 1980: Canadian Gay Postal Workers Secure Union Protections; Dec. 4, 1984: Berkeley Extends Benefits to Domestic Partners of City Employees; Nov. 8, 1988: Oregon Repeals Ban on Antigay Job Discrimination; May 1, 1989: U.S. Supreme Court Rules Gender-Role Stereotyping Is Discriminatory; Sept. 29, 1991: California Governor Wilson Vetoes Antidiscrimination Bill; Sept. 23, 1992: Massachusetts Grants Family Rights to Gay and Lesbian State Workers; 1994: Employment Non-Discrimination Act Is Proposed to U.S. Congress; Apr. 2, 1998: Canadian Supreme Court Reverses Gay Academic's Firing; July, 2003: Wal-Mart Adds Lesbians and Gays to Its Antidiscrimination Policy.

July, 2003
WAL-MART ADDS LESBIANS AND GAYS TO ITS ANTIDISCRIMINATION POLICY

Wal-Mart Stores, the world's largest private employer and largest corporation, added gay and lesbian employees to its antidiscrimination policy, thereby prohibiting discrimination against any employee because of his or her sexual orientation.

LOCALE: Bentonville, Arkansas
CATEGORIES: Economics; organizations and institutions; civil rights

SUMMARY OF EVENT

Wal-Mart Stores, which opened its first store in Rogers, Arkansas, in 1962, has become the world's largest corporation. With its annual sales of more than $316 billion for fiscal year ending January 31, 2006, and its more than 100 million customers per week, the company's total revenue accounted for 15 percent of the entire U.S. retail market in 2002, excluding automobiles, and it is the largest employer in twenty-one states. Wal-Mart has also been the largest private employer in the United States since 1997 and in the world since 1999. This represents more than 1.3 million jobs worldwide working in more than 3,200 facilities in the United States and more than 1,100 internationally. It is the largest retailer in Mexico and Canada and has locations in Argentina, Brazil, China, Puerto Rico, Korea, Germany, and the United Kingdom.

In July, 2003, Wal-Mart expanded its antidiscrimination policy to protect its lesbian and gay employees. As of 2004, more than four hundred of the *Fortune* 500 companies included sexual orientation in their nondiscrimination policies. The most notable exception was Exxon Mobil, the world's second largest corporation. When Exxon bought Mobil Oil in 1999, it rescinded the sexual orientation portion of Mobil Oil's antidiscrimination policy and overturned that company's policy of offering medical benefits to same-gender partners. Exxon Mobil is the last of the *Fortune* 500 top forty companies to lack such protections for their LGBT employees.

In addition to its antidiscrimination policy, Wal-Mart also revised its policy on harassment and inappropriate conduct to include sexual orientation. This step is intended to encourage employees to report discriminatory actions to management.

Wal-Mart prides itself on its commitment to diversity. It currently employs more than 160,000 African Americans, 105,000 Hispanics, and 164,000 associates age fifty-five or older. It is recognized as one of the leading employers of disabled Americans as well. In 2001 and 2002, it also won the Billion-Dollar Roundtable Award, given for spending in excess of $1 billion with women and minority-owned suppliers. Also in 2002, it was honored with the Ron Brown Award, the highest presidential award given to a company in recognition of outstanding achievement in employee relations and community initiatives. In 2003, Wal-Mart was named by *Fortune* magazine as the most admired company in America.

Nevertheless, it took several years of lobbying to convince the company to extend protection to its LGBT employees. The decision was no doubt influenced by the consistent efforts of the Pride Foundation, a Seattle-based gay rights organization with investments in Wal-Mart, which had been pressuring the company for two years prior to the decision. Pride Foundation had previously been successful in similar attempts at both General Electric and McDonald's. Representatives of Pride Foundation originally met with Wal-Mart in August, 2001, at Wal-Mart's Bentonville, Arkansas, headquarters. Wal-Mart has generally acknowledged the role such shareholders had in their decision but claims that it was a letter from several gay and lesbian company employees, indicating a feeling of exclusion, that was the most important factor.

SIGNIFICANCE

In addition to corporate entities, as of 2004 more than 400 colleges and universities, 1,900 private sector companies, 38 federal agencies or departments, 250 city and county governments, and 25 state governments had nondiscrimination policies that included sexual orientation. However, without a federal law prohibiting such discrimination, antidiscrimination policies remain at the discretion of other companies, agencies, academic institutions, and state and local governments.

The inclusion of sexual orientation in the antidiscrimination policy of the world's largest corporation, retailer, and employer was clearly an important step not only for the many LGBT employees of Wal-Mart but also for the GLBT rights movement in general. Many have noted that if a company like Wal-Mart—which has been labeled conservative due to company policies such as not selling CDs with explicit lyrics and banning a number of books and recording artists—can extend protection to its gay and lesbian employees, then surely the battle for workplace equality is moving in the right direction.

However, although Wal-Mart's gay and lesbian employees are now under policy protection against discrimination, as of 2004 the company had no plans of extending medical benefits to same-gender partners. In January of 2005, Wal-Mart did, however, as part of its conflict-of-interest policy, include in its definition of "immediate family" same-gender partners recognized by state law: in effect, an extension of responsibilities but not benefits. It also did not cover gender identity or gender expression in its policy. LGBT employees also lacked an official company group. Thus, although Wal-Mart's extension of its antidiscrimination policy was both a practical and a symbolic step in the right direction, there is still a long way to go before LGBT employees of Wal-Mart, and many other corporations, attain true equality with their heterosexual coworkers.

—*Michael Ryan*

FURTHER READING

Human Rights Campaign WorkNet. http://www.hrc.org/worknet.

Norman, Al. *The Case Against Wal-Mart*. St. Johnsbury, Vt.: Raphel Marketing, 2004.

Ortega, Bob. *In Sam We Trust: The Untold Story of Sam Walton and How Wal-Mart Is Devouring America*. New York: Times Business, 1998.

Vance, Sandra S., and Roy V. Scott. *Wal-Mart: A History of Sam Walton's Retail Phenomenon*. New York: Twayne, 1994.

Walton, Sam, with John Huey. *Sam Walton: Made in America: My Story*. New York: Doubleday, 1992.

SEE ALSO: Apr. 27, 1953: U.S. President Eisenhower Prohibits Federal Employment of Lesbians and Gays; 1972-1973: Local Governments Pass Antidiscrimination Laws; June 27, 1974: Abzug and Koch Attempt to Amend the Civil Rights Act of 1964; July 3, 1975: U.S. Civil Service Commission Prohibits Discrimination Against Federal Employees; 1978: Lesbian and Gay Workplace Movement Is Founded; June 2, 1980: Canadian Gay Postal Workers Secure Union Protections; Dec. 4, 1984: Berkeley Extends Benefits to Domestic Partners of City Employees; Nov. 8, 1988: Oregon Repeals Ban on Antigay Job Discrimination; May 1, 1989: U.S. Supreme Court Rules Gender-Role Stereotyping Is Discriminatory; Sept. 29, 1991: California Governor Wilson Vetoes Antidiscrimination Bill; Sept. 23, 1992: Massachusetts Grants Family Rights to Gay and Lesbian State Workers; 1994: Employment Non-Discrimination Act Is Proposed to U.S. Congress; Apr. 2, 1998: Canadian Supreme Court Reverses Gay Academic's Firing; July, 2003: Singapore Lifts Ban on Hiring Lesbian and Gay Employees.

November 18, 2003
MASSACHUSETTS COURT RULES FOR SAME-GENDER MARRIAGE

The highest court in Massachusetts heard the case of seven same-gender couples who sued the state for the right to wed. The court ruled that the state had not proven why same-gender couples should not marry. The decision initiated an ongoing wave of lawsuits and legislation from proponents as well as opponents to same-gender marriage and same-gender civil unions.

ALSO KNOWN AS: *Goodridge v. Department of Public Health*
LOCALE: Boston, Massachusetts
CATEGORIES: Civil rights; government and politics; laws, acts, and legal history

KEY FIGURES
Hillary Goodridge and
Julie Goodridge, lead plaintiffs
Mary Bonauto (b. 1961), lead attorney
Margaret H. Marshall, chief justice, Massachusetts Supreme Judicial Court
Mitt Romney (b. 1947), Republican governor of Massachusetts

SUMMARY OF EVENT
On November 18, 2003, the Massachusetts Supreme Judicial Court (SJC) ruled, in *Goodridge v. Department of Public Health*, that the Massachusetts state constitution required the issuance of marriage licenses to same-gender couples. That decision, though surprising to many, represented the endpoint of a series of events that serve as background and context for the SJC ruling. It is important to acknowledge this background as foundational to the issue of same-gender marriage.

Even prior to this case, Massachusetts was regarded as a liberal state with respect to GLBT rights. It was the second state to have passed (in 1989) antidiscrimination protection based on a person's sexual orientation. The state already had granted a degree of legal recognition to same-gender families by legalizing second-parent adoption.

An important context was building outside Massachusetts as well. Same-gender marriage had been a topic of public debate for more than a decade prior to the SJC ruling. In 1991, three same-gender couples in Hawaii sued for the right to marry. When their initial suit was denied, they appealed to the Hawaii Supreme Court. That court ruled in 1993 that the state must demonstrate a compelling state interest for refusing marriage to same-gender couples; in 1996, the court ruled that the state had not met that standard. In 1998, however, the citizens of Hawaii passed an amendment to their state constitution that allowed the state to circumvent its own equal protection clause in the case of same-gender couples wanting to marry.

The backlash that began with Hawaii's constitutional amendment spread, as a number of states soon passed laws blocking same-gender couples from marriage. At the federal level, largely in reaction to the Hawaii case and the possibility that other states might move in similar directions, Congress passed the Defense of Marriage Act (DOMA) in 1996, and it was signed by President Bill Clinton. DOMA excludes same-gender couples from any federal benefits attached to marriage, and it allows individual states to refuse, if it so choose, to recognize legal same-gender marriages performed in any other state.

Proponents of same-gender marriage were also busy in the wake of events in Hawaii. In 1997, attorneys Mary Bonauto, Beth Robinson, and Susan Murray filed a lawsuit on behalf of six plaintiffs challenging the exclusion of same-gender couples from marriage in Vermont. When they lost this case, the legal team appealed to the Vermont Supreme Court. The Supreme Court's ruling, announced on December 20, 1999, concluded that the refusal of marriage to same-gender couples violated Vermont's constitution, and then instructed the state legislature to fashion a remedy.

Vermont's legislature, amid much acrimony, settled on the creation of civil unions—an arrangement that gave same-gender couples access to the privileges and responsibilities granted by the state to married couples, but without the social and psychological benefit inherent in the name and status of marriage. The first civil unions in Vermont took place on July 1, 2000. In the aftermath, legislators who had supported the creation of civil unions, as well as Vermont governor Howard Dean, who had signed the civil union bill into law, were targeted in the next election. The governor and some of the legislators who supported civil unions won their elections; others did not.

Another event that forms a significant backdrop for the Massachusetts ruling on same-gender marriage was the U.S. Supreme Court's decision in the case of *Lawrence v. Texas*, issued on June 26, 2003. That decision held that GLB people have a constitu-

> **FROM *GOODRIDGE V. DEPARTMENT OF PUBLIC HEALTH***
>
> Whether the Commonwealth may use its formidable regulatory authority to bar same-sex couples from civil marriage is a question not previously addressed by a Massachusetts appellate court. It is a question the United States Supreme Court left open as a matter of Federal law in *Lawrence*, . . . where it was not an issue. There, the Court affirmed that the core concept of common human dignity protected by the Fourteenth Amendment to the United States Constitution precludes government intrusion into the deeply personal realms of consensual adult expressions of intimacy and one's choice of an intimate partner. The Court also reaffirmed the central role that decisions whether to marry or have children bear in shaping one's identity. . . . The Massachusetts Constitution is, if anything, more protective of individual liberty and equality than the Federal Constitution; it may demand broader protection for fundamental rights; and it is less tolerant of government intrusion into the protected spheres of private life.
>
> Barred access to the protections, benefits, and obligations of civil marriage, a person who enters into an intimate, exclusive union with another of the same sex is arbitrarily deprived of membership in one of our community's most rewarding and cherished institutions. That exclusion is incompatible with the constitutional principles of respect for individual autonomy and equality under law. . . .
>
> We construe civil marriage to mean the voluntary union of two persons as spouses, to the exclusion of all others. This reformulation redresses the plaintiffs' constitutional injury and furthers the aim of marriage to promote stable, exclusive relationships. It advances the two legitimate State interests the department has identified: providing a stable setting for child rearing and conserving State resources. It leaves intact the Legislature's broad discretion to regulate marriage. . . .
>
> In their complaint the plaintiffs request only a declaration that their exclusion and the exclusion of other qualified same-sex couples from access to civil marriage violates Massachusetts law. We declare that barring an individual from the protections, benefits, and obligations of civil marriage solely because that person would marry a person of the same sex violates the Massachusetts Constitution. We vacate the summary judgment for the department. We remand this case to the Superior Court for entry of judgment consistent with this opinion. . . .
>
> So ordered.

tional right to form intimate relationships, including sexual relationships; the court ruled that sodomy laws were unconstitutional not just in Texas where the suit originated but also throughout the country.

In the *Goodridge* case, originally filed in April, 2001, two years before the *Lawrence* decision, seven same-gender couples, including lead plaintiffs Julie and Hillary Goodridge, complained that the state of Massachusetts violated its constitutional provision of equality for all citizens by blocking their access to marriage. After a trial court rejected this argument, the plaintiffs' attorney, Bonauto, filed an appeal to the Massachusetts SJC. During her appearance before the SJC, Bonauto explicitly spoke against the creation of civil unions as a remedy for discrimination against same-gender couples. The very word "marriage," she argued, has significant, positive meaning, and thus it plays a major part in making marriage, and the protections it affords, so meaningful to society.

The Massachusetts SJC had already heard arguments in the *Goodridge* case but had not yet issued their ruling by the time the *Lawrence* ruling was handed down. Perhaps because of the implications of this decision, the SJC justices delayed their ruling beyond their own internally imposed deadline for rendering the decision. On November 18, 2003, the SJC announced its decision: By a 4-3 vote, the Massachusetts high court ruled that the state could no longer deny marriage to same-gender couples. The court's opinion, with Massachusetts chief justice Margaret H. Marshall writing for the majority, explicitly acknowledged the impact of the earlier U.S. Supreme Court ruling in the *Lawrence* case. The court stayed its ruling for 180 days in order to give the state legislature time to make necessary changes to laws and practices.

The decision generated strong reaction both among supporters as well as opponents of same-gender marriage. Conservatives immediately initiated efforts to undermine the ruling. Massachusetts governor Mitt Romney made clear his intention to do what he could to ensure the ruling never took effect. Opponents of same-gender marriage seized on the 180-day stay as an opportunity to interrupt the progression toward full marriage rights. Members of the legislature made a formal request to the SJC for an opinion on creating civil unions rather than granting marriage to same-gender couples. The SJC response was unequivocal: Civil unions were not acceptable; same-gender couples would have access not only to the rights, privileges, and responsibilities of marriage but also to the name and status of marriage as well.

Members of the legislature who opposed same-gender marriage moved to take legislative control over the situation. In February, 2004, they convened a constitutional convention, a gathering of both houses of the Massachusetts legislature, to consider the issue. While the legislature met in session, legislators and lobbyists for both sides were engaged in political maneuvers and behind-the-scenes strategizing. Some opponents of same-gender marriage worked to fashion an amendment to the state constitution that would ban legal recognition for any same-gender relationships. Others preferred a constitutional amendment that would ban marriage but would create civil unions for same-gender couples. Proponents of same-gender marriage lobbied against any constitutional amendment. The constitutional convention closed without having agreed on an amendment; another meeting of the convention had been scheduled for March.

Political maneuvering continued between sessions, and just before the March convention, leaders of both chambers sent a joint letter to legislators, urging them to agree to a compromise amendment. During the convention, some legislators and lobbyists again engaged in legal wrangling, even as other legislators took to the podium to express their views on same-gender marriage. Throughout both meetings of the constitutional convention, hundreds of GLB citizens and their allies held watch outside the legislative chamber, and some legislators spoke of having been won over by their presence.

The second convention ended with the passage of a proposed amendment, one that would ban marriage and create civil unions for same-gender couples. This amendment reflected a compromise among three groups of legislators: those who wanted no state recognition of same-gender relationships, those who wanted full marriage rights for same-gender couples, and those who promoted civil unions at the expense of marriage for same-gender couples. According to Massachusetts law, the legislative passage of an amendment is only the first step in a multistage process. Before an amendment can become law, it must be approved by a second constitutional convention that would meet in a new legislative session, in this case, in 2005. The amendment then would have to be ratified by a majority of Massachusetts voters in 2006.

This extended time line for passing a constitutional amendment kept the legislature's block of the SJC decision from going into effect: On May 17, 2004, same-gender marriage became legal in Massachusetts. Just after midnight on that date, Marsha Hams and Susan Shepherd applied for their marriage license in Cambridge, becoming the first same-gender couple to be granted a fully legal and uncontested license to marry in the United States. Later that same day, having received a waiver of the usual three-day delay between license and marriage, Hillary and Julie Goodridge became the first same-gender couple to marry. By the end of that day, at least nine hundred same-gender couples had been granted marriage licenses in the Commonwealth of Massachusetts.

Even as this milestone event occurred, efforts were underway to delimit access to marriage. Governor Romney invoked a 1913 state statute that prohibited issuing marriage licenses to out-of-state couples whose marriage would not be legal in their home states. The statute, originally designed to prevent out-of-state interracial couples from marrying in Massachusetts, had not been applied for decades. A number of city clerks defied the long-dormant statute and issued licenses to couples without proof of residency.

Significance

The long-term impact of the same-gender marriage decision in Massachusetts has yet to be felt. A brief review of the decision's short-term impact might reflect what it could mean for the future, however.

Same-gender couples from other states have had a difficult time having their relationships recognized outside Massachusetts. Some who were able to slip past the 1913 statute have encountered resistance from agencies within their home states. Many whose licenses were voided by their home states filed a suit, with Mary Bonauto acting as their attorney. They lost the suit in court, but Bonauto appealed the ruling.

In Massachusetts, a familiar comment in the face of so many newly married same-gender couples is the simple declaration: The sky has not fallen. Nonetheless, a very significant backlash is evident in the state and throughout the country. Efforts to roll back the freedom to marry continue in Massachusetts. Some of these efforts have been spearheaded by national organizations. The Roman Catholic Church has publicly opposed and condemned the decision and its implementation. A cadre of African American ministers in Boston

A woman in support of same-gender marriage protests outside the Massachusetts statehouse in February, 2004. The legislature was debating a proposed amendment to the state constitution that would ban same-gender marriage. (AP/Wide World Photos)

have been vocal in their rejection of same-gender marriage as well. Members of the Massachusetts legislature who worked to keep same-gender marriages legal were targeted during election campaigns by conservative organizations working to have them ousted.

Elsewhere, the backlash has been dramatic as well. Beginning even before the marriages of same-gender couples in Massachusetts, and often explicitly in response to the Massachusetts decision, many states had considered legislation and citizen referenda to institute new or to strengthen existing prohibitions against same-gender marriage. Eleven states voted on such referenda in the November, 2004, election, passing legislation banning same-gender marriage.

The backlash also occurred at the federal level. President George W. Bush signaled his opposition to same-gender marriage during his January 20, 2004, state of the union address, and the following month, he called for an amendment to the U.S. Constitution that would outlaw same-gender marriage. Congress considered this amendment in the summer of 2004. The U.S. Senate voted to close debate on the matter, but the U.S. House of Representatives passed the Marriage Protection Act (MPA), a bill designed to divest all federal courts—including lower courts and the Supreme Court—of the power to hear cases involving either DOMA or the MPA. On November 29, 2004, however, the Supreme Court refused to overturn same-gender marriage rights in Massachusetts.

The backlash has been significant, but so, too, have efforts in support of same-gender marriages. In February, 2004, San Francisco's mayor Gavin Newsom, a Republican, authorized clerks in that city to issue licenses to same-gender couples. More than four thousand couples—including longtime partners and lesbian activists Del Martin and Phyllis Lyon—received licenses before judges in the state stopped the mayor's mandate. The city has since sued the state of California, challenging the state's ban on same-gender marriages.

Also in February, 2004, Mayor Jason West of New Paltz, New York, performed same-gender marriages, stopping only after an injunction and criminal charges were filed against him. Some ministers in New Paltz picked up where West had to stop and began performing the marriages as well. In Oregon, the Multnomah city commission authorized the issuance of licenses to same-gender couples until a court intervened. Similarly, a county clerk in New Mexico began issuing licenses to same-gender couples until she was enjoined to stop.

Lawsuits challenging prohibitions on same-gender marriage made their way through the courts in a number of states, and the new laws against same-gender marriage passed in eleven states in the November, 2004, elections, despite the Supreme Court's refusal to overturn the Massachusetts case that same month, will make the challenge against these prohibitions more difficult and complex.

—*Glenda M. Russell*

FURTHER READING

Bonauto, Mary L. "Civil Marriage as a Locus of Civil Rights Struggles." *Human Rights* 30, no. 3 (Summer, 2003): 3-7.

Cahill, Sean. *Same-Sex Marriage in the United States: Focus on the Facts*. Lanham, Md.: Lexington Books, 2004.

Curry, Hayden, Denis Clifford, and Frederick Hertz. *A Legal Guide for Lesbian and Gay Couples*. Berkeley, Calif.: Nolo Press, 2004.

Goldberg, Suzanne B. "A Historical Guide to the Future of Marriage for Same-Sex Couples." *Columbia Journal of Gender & Law* 15 (2006): 249-272.

Graff, E. J. *What Is Marriage For? The Strange Social History of Our Most Intimate Institution*. Boston: Beacon Press, 1999.

Jordan, Mark D. *Blessing Same-sex Unions: The Perils of Queer Romance and the Confusions of Christian Marriage*. Chicago: University of Chicago Press, 2005.

Kotulski, Davina. *Why You Should Give a Damn About Gay Marriage*. Los Angeles: Alyson, 2004.

Massachusetts Trial Court Law Libraries. "Mass. Law About Same-Sex Marriage." http://www.lawlib.state.ma.us/gaymarriage.html.

Moats, David. *Civil Wars: A Battle for Gay Marriage*. Orlando, Fla.: Harcourt, 2004.

Samar, Vincent J. "Privacy and the Debate over Same-Sex Marriage Versus Unions" *DePaul Law Review* 54 (2005): 783-804.

"Same-Sex Marriage: A Selective Bibliography of the Legal Literature." Law Library, Rutgers School of Law. http://law-library.rutgers.edu/SSM.html.

Wolfson, Evan. *Why Marriage Matters: America, Equality, and Gay People's Right to Marry*. New York: Simon & Schuster, 2004.

SEE ALSO: 1981: Gay and Lesbian Palimony Suits Emerge; 1993-1996: Hawaii Opens Door to Same-Gender Marriages; Aug. 6, 1994: Japanese American Citizens League Supports Same-Gender Marriage; Sept. 21, 1996: U.S. President Clinton Signs Defense of Marriage Act; Dec. 20, 1999: *Baker v. Vermont* Leads to Recognition of Same-Gender Civil Unions; Feb. 21, 2003: Australian Court Validates Transsexual Marriage; Apr., 2003: Buenos Aires Recognizes Same-Gender Civil Unions; June 17, 2003, and July 19, 2005: Canada Legalizes Same-Gender Marriage; Nov. 18, 2004: United Kingdom Legalizes Same-Gender Civil Partnerships; Apr. 4, 2005: United Kingdom's Gender Recognition Act Legalizes Transsexual Marriage; June 30, 2005: Spain Legalizes Same-Gender Marriage.

November 20, 2003
TRANSGENDER DAY OF REMEMBRANCE AND REMEMBERING OUR DEAD PROJECT

Supporters gathered in more than one hundred locations worldwide to observe the fifth annual Transgender Day of Remembrance, a memorial for those who were killed because of hatred and fear of individuals who are transgender or who otherwise are gender ambiguous.

LOCALE: Worldwide
CATEGORIES: Transgender/transsexuality; civil rights; marches, protests, and riots; organizations and institutions; crime

KEY FIGURES
Gwendolyn Ann Smith, founder of the Day of Remembrance and the Remembering Our Dead project
Ethan St. Pierre, organizer of the Day of Remembrance and the Remembering Our Dead project
Rita Hester (d. 1998), transgender woman whose murder led to the founding of the Day of Remembrance
Brandon Teena (1972-1993), transgender man whose 1993 murder inspired a new wave of transgender activism
Gwen Araujo (1985-2002), transgender teen whose 2002 murder received extensive national media coverage

SUMMARY OF EVENT
The Transgender Day of Remembrance was founded by Gwendolyn Ann Smith to memorialize, honor, and mourn transgender individuals who are killed each year in hate crimes. The original memorial took place in San Francisco in 1999, when one hundred people gathered in a candlelight vigil to honor male-to-female transsexual Rita Hester, who was stabbed to death in her home on November 28, 1998, in Allston, Massachusetts. By 2003, the Day of Remembrance had become an annual event, observed each November in more than one hundred locations in eight different countries. The seventh annual event was held in November of 2005.

The unsolved murder of Hester prompted Smith to found both the Day of Remembrance and to launch the Web site Remembering Our Dead (www

.rememberingourdead.org), an online memorial for victims of transphobic hate crimes. Smith based the design of the project's Web site—launched in February, 1999—on the Vietnam War Memorial after discovering through an online transgender community forum that even among those who are transgender, few are aware of how many transgender people are slain each year in transphobic hate crimes.

Remembering Our Dead was launched with a list of eighty-eight names. By 2003, there were more than three hundred names posted on the site, with thirty-eight new murders reported between November 20, 2002, and November 20, 2003. The memorial day and Web site are projects of Gender Education and Advocacy (www.gender.org).

Transgender activist Ethan St. Pierre is another organizer involved with the two projects. His aunt Debra Forte was stabbed to death in a transphobic hate crime on May 15, 1995, in the greater Boston area; her name is listed on the site. St. Pierre is also a host of TransFM Internet Radio (www.transfm.com). He has been active in mobilizing other family members of victims to lobby Congress to include transphobic violence in hate crimes and employment rights legislation.

The two projects memorialize members of a vast cross-section of the transgender community. As Smith notes on the Remembering Our Dead site,

> There is no "safe way" to be transgendered: as you look at the many names collected here, note that some of these people may have identified as drag queens, some as heterosexual cross-dressers, and some as transsexuals. Some were living very out lives, and some were living fully "stealth" lives. Some were identifying as male, and some, as female. Some lived in small towns, and some in major metropolitan areas.

What all had in common was that each was killed because they were transgender. By including the names of the dead on the Web site, Smith has ensured that their stories will not be forgotten.

The murders of transgender individuals are exceedingly violent, often involving multiple stab or gunshot wounds, strangling, burning, or mutilation of the victim. Misreporting a victim's gender identity has been a common media blunder, particularly in cases involving transgender youth. In one case, Brandon Teena, who had been raped and murdered in 1993 at the age of twenty-one, personally identified as a man and used a man's name. Yet the media referred to him by his birth name, *Teena* Brandon. (Brandon was the subject of the documentary film *The Brandon Teena Story*, 1998, and the feature film *Boys Don't Cry*, 1999.) In another case, Gwen Araujo, who was seventeen years old at the time she was beaten, raped, and murdered in 2002, was most often identified in the media with male pronouns and her male birth name, despite her preferred identity and self-naming as female.

Male-to-female transsexuals are often mistaken for gay men, adding to the invisibility of transphobic hate crimes. In the initial coverage of Rita Hester's murder, even *Bay Windows*—New England's largest gay and lesbian newspaper—used male pronouns and wrongly referred to her as a "gay transgender person." The *Boston Globe* used Hester's male birth name and described her as a "cross-dresser."

SIGNIFICANCE

The vigils held during the Transgender Day of Remembrance honor the chosen gender identity of each murder victim; their names are read each year in cities all over the world in late November. The

---

GUIDING PRINCIPLES OF THE TRANSGENDER DAY OF REMEMBRANCE

- "Those who cannot remember the past are doomed to repeat it" (George Santayana).
- All who die due to anti-transgendered violence are to be remembered.
- It is up to us to remember these people, as their killers, law enforcement, and the media often seek to erase their existence.
- Transgendered lives are affirmed to have value.
- We can make a difference: by being visible and speaking out about anti-transgender violence, we can effect change.

Source: Gender Education and Advocacy, Day of Remembrance. http://www.gender.org/remember/day.

event raises awareness of hate crimes against transgender people, and it enables survivors of antitransgender violence to speak out. Together, the Remembering Our Dead project Web site and the Day of Remembrance function to document transgender history and the reality of hate crimes on the basis of gender identity.

Increased participation in the Day of Remembrance shows a growing international transgender community. The documentation of transgender hate crimes has been instrumental in political efforts to lobby for more stringent penalties for perpetrators of these murders in the United States, and for increased civil rights for transgender people. Most important, it has resulted in increased visibility and an increase in the political strength of the transgender community.

—*K. Surkan*

FURTHER READING

Califia, Patrick. *Sex Changes: The Politics of Transgenderism*. 2d ed. San Francisco, Calif.: Cleis Press, 2003.

Feinberg, Leslie. *Transgender Liberation: A Movement Whose Time Has Come*. New York: World View Forum, 1992.

Halberstam, Judith. *Female Masculinity*. Durham, N.C.: Duke University Press, 1998.

Lambda Legal and The National Youth Advocacy Coalition. "Bending the Mold: An Action Kit for Transgender Youth." http://www.lambdalegal.org/cgi-bin/iowa/documents/record?record=1504.

Namaste, Viviane K. *Invisible Lives: The Erasure of Transsexual and Transgendered People*. Chicago: University of Chicago Press, 2000.

Nangeroni, Nancy, and Gordene O. MacKenzie. "National Transgender Day of Remembrance: Grace Stowell, Kathleen and Diana Hester, and Ethan St. Pierre." GenderTalk Web Radio. November 26, 2001. http://www.gendertalk.com/real/300/gt338.shtml.

SEE ALSO: Sept. 24, 1951: George Jorgensen Becomes Christine Jorgensen; Aug., 1966: Queer Youth Fight Police Harassment at Compton's Cafeteria in San Francisco; Nov. 21, 1966: First Gender Identity Clinic Opens and Provides Gender Reassignment Surgery; June 27-July 2, 1969: Stonewall Rebellion Ignites Modern Gay and Lesbian Rights Movement; July 31, 1969: Gay Liberation Front Is Formed; 1978: Harry Benjamin International Gender Dysphoria Association Is Founded; 1992: Transgender Nation Holds Its First Protest; June, 1992: Feinberg Publishes *Transgender Liberation*; 1993: Intersex Society of North America Is Founded; Dec. 24, 1993-Dec. 31, 1993: Transgender Man Brandon Teena Raped and Murdered; June 17, 1995: International Bill of Gender Rights Is First Circulated; 1996: Hart Recognized as a Transgender Man; 1998: Transgender Scholarship Proliferates; Apr. 30, 2002: Transgender Rights Added to New York City Law; Oct. 4, 2002: Transgender Teen Gwen Araujo Is Murdered in California; Mar., 2003-Dec., 2004: Transsexuals Protest Academic Exploitation; Mar. 5, 2006: *Brokeback Mountain, Capote,* and *Transamerica* Receive Oscars.

March 7, 2004
ROBINSON BECOMES FIRST OUT GAY BISHOP IN CHRISTIAN HISTORY

V. Gene Robinson was selected by New Hampshire clergy and parishioners and confirmed as the state's ninth Anglican bishop. His consecration and investment created a historic schism among conservatives in the worldwide Anglican communion, especially in Africa. The controversy led also to the establishment of a commission, called for by the archbishop of Canterbury, to address the schism.

LOCALE: New Hampshire
CATEGORIES: Religion; organizations and institutions; civil rights

KEY FIGURES

V. Gene Robinson (b. 1947), Anglican bishop of New Hampshire
Peter Akinola (b. 1944), Nigerian Anglican archbishop
Rowan Williams (b. 1950), archbishop of Canterbury

SUMMARY OF EVENT

Historically, the Anglican Church and its representative Episcopal Church in the United States have been more liberal than Roman Catholicism, Methodism, Presbyterianism, and most other Christian denominations. Unlike evangelicals and biblical literalists, Episcopalians found their theology on a "three-legged stool" of faith, tradition, and, perhaps most significantly, reason.

The unusual emphasis on reason has fostered pragmatic, progressive debates on homosexuality, abortion, women's rights, and other social issues. In 1976, Episcopalians officially began ordaining female priests, and liberal Episcopal clergy (such as Bishop John Shelby Spong) argue that ancient passages traditionally considered to be proscriptions against homosexuality—embedded in Leviticus and elsewhere in Scripture—have little modern relevance and should be interpreted only in a historical context.

The liberalism of many Episcopalians, however, has not gone uncontested, nor is it shared with many in the Anglican communion's conservative African and Asian territories. Out gay clergyman V. Gene Robinson was ordained as the bishop of New Hampshire in November, 2003, and invested on March 7, 2004, to become Christianity's first serving bishop who is gay and out. (A former bishop, Otis Charles of Utah, came out as gay but did so after retirement.) Episcopalian and Anglican traditionalists soon believed their theology was under assault from a growing liberal majority.

Conservative bishops resented that Robinson's sexuality was being framed as a civil rights issue,

V. Gene Robinson. (AP/Wide World Photos)

not a theological one. Many of Robinson's fellow Anglicans still refused to accept women priests, sex education, birth control, or gay and lesbian parishioners. They were concerned that Robinson was not only gay but also divorced from a heterosexual marriage, was noncelibate, and was living with his male partner of many years. Though conservatives framed Robinson as a symbol of family disintegration, the dissolution of Robinson's 1972 marriage to Isabella Martin was mutual, with Robinson and Martin pledging to raise their two daughters jointly. Moreover, before their marriage, Robinson confided to Martin that he had undergone two years of counseling, while still a seminarian, about his sexual identity. Apart from the "impropriety" of being gay, Robinson is, in his words, "orthodox" in faithfully interpreting all relevant areas of Anglican ritual and doctrine.

Although Episcopalians have a presiding bishop and Anglicans accept a spiritual leader in the archbishop of Canterbury, the controversies surrounding Robinson have been exacerbated because Anglicans recognize no centralized authority (such as a pope) who can decree final judgments on policy issues. Instead, Anglicans distribute authority across regional, autonomous bishoprics; periodically, bishops worldwide congregate around the archbishop of Canterbury at the Lambeth Conference to draw resolutions and air grievances; often, little is accomplished. Anglicans pride themselves on their civility, but excessive diplomatic politesse can lead to ambiguity and contradiction. For example, in 1998, the conference issued a statement promising inclusion of gay and lesbian voices but took no firm stand supporting gay and lesbian rights, and while the presiding bishop and the archbishop privately support church liberalization, they are obliged to project a noncommittal centrism for the sake of Anglican unity.

In 2003, however, a Lambeth commission was established at the request of the archbishop of Canterbury, Rowan Williams, to address the concerns raised by Robinson's consecration and investiture. The commission's mandate was to explore tensions within the communion but *not* to address the ethics of homosexuality or same-gender unions. The commission issued the Windsor Report in 2004, concluding, in part, that on the matter of human sexuality, there should be ongoing, open, and frank study and discussion among and within the church's provinces.

SIGNIFICANCE

Since the time of Bishop V. Gene Robinson's investment, conservatives had warned of a cataclysmic schism in the Anglican communion and have threatened that an angry diocese would split from the church. The schism arrived, and the Windsor Report addressed it.

Robinson's most hostile opponents have been African archbishops, most notably Nigeria's Peter Akinola but also Uganda's Henry Luke Orombi and Kenya's Benjamin Nzimbi. Their rhetoric is reminiscent of Zimbabwean president Robert Mugabe, infamous for calling homosexuals "lower than dogs." African conservatives have been engaged in a kind of economic blackmail, threatening either to withhold contributions to or to reject outright donations from any diocese supporting Robinson's investment. Unfortunately, impoverished Africans needing Western aid have suffered from an ideological conflict they probably knew little about.

African Anglicans have considered the acceptance of gay clergy as a modern, colonialist imposition upon their faith, without realizing that their own biases originate from the influence of nineteenth century missionaries. While Africans see the Robinson affair as another example of the West's intrusive, unilateral foreign policies, liberals argue that Episcopalian support for Robinson benefits a disenfranchised minority only, not the powers-that-be, and is thus in keeping with Christian teaching. Episcopalian liberals also have chided African conservatives for obsessing about homosexuality while condoning the rape and stoning of women, polygamy, and other un-Christian practices routinely tolerated on the African continent. Furthermore, in a November, 2005, speech, retired Anglican archbishop and Nobel Peace Prize recipient Desmond Tutu called on Anglicans around the world to support Bishop Robinson and to oppose all forms of discrimination.

> **THE DEFROCKING OF ELIZABETH STROUD**
>
> Seven years before V. Gene Robinson was consecrated bishop of the Episcopal Church in New Hampshire, Irene Elizabeth (Beth) Stroud was ordained a minister in the United Methodist Church. Two years later, she was appointed associate pastor of the First United Methodist Church of Germantown, Pennsylvania. Stroud served with distinction, as she had in a previous assignment in West Chester.
>
> As she grew comfortable in her position and became convinced of her congregation's support, she made little effort to mask the monogamous lesbian relationship she had with her partner, Chris Paige, with whom she lived. On April 27, 2003, she preached a sermon in which she told of her relationship with Paige to her congregation, which responded with a standing ovation.
>
> Despite the virtually unanimous support of her parishoners and of her colleagues in Germantown, Stroud, on December 1, 2004, was brought before a jury composed of thirteen Methodist ministers on charges that she had violated church policy by actively engaging in a lesbian relationship. The jury was recommended on July 23 and again on October 11 by an investigatory committee of the church. She was found "guilty" by a vote of twelve to one.
>
> The Northeast Jurisdictional Committee on Appeals negated this ruling on April 29, 2005, causing Bishop Marcus Matthews to restore Stroud's credentials. Matthews appealed her case to the church's judicial council, which, on October 31, again defrocked her. A further appeal caused the judicial council to restore Stroud's credentials because of legal errors made in her previous trial. The church's judicial body has yet to decide whether to file another appeal that could again result in Stroud's being defrocked.

To bolster their ranks, Episcopal conservatives have joined forces with African bishops, whose voices were heretofore considered marginal; meanwhile, the archbishop of Uganda has taken under his oversight at least three conservative Episcopalian parishes in Los Angeles that support the African dissension. Anglican leaders in Kenya, Nigeria, and Uganda have claimed a state of "impaired" communion with American Episcopalians, and a small but growing number of conservative Episcopal dioceses, including the Church of the Redeemer and St. Mark's Church in Robinson's home state of New Hampshire, have demanded a visiting bishop attend to their needs in lieu of Robinson. As of the fall of 2004, the Episcopal Church had lost only an estimated 7 percent of its operating budget as a result of boycotts by conservatives.

For centuries, it has been known that a disproportionate number of clergymen, which some estimates place at 25 percent or more, are gay. Clerical celibacy had often been the only socially acceptable vehicle to mask homosexual desire, and gradually it became a convenient cultural answer to a dominant theological problem. Bishop Robinson's investment not only has delivered homosexuality from the clerical closet but also has forever raised the stakes by elevating the discussion of gay clergy from alarmist, reactionary stories about pedophilic priests to the story of a devout, monogamous gay man risen to an unprecedented position of hierarchical authority.

—*Andrew Grossman*

FURTHER READING

Boyd, Malcolm. *Take off the Masks: The Classic Spiritual Autobiography*. 1978. Rev. ed. San Francisco, Calif.: HarperSanFrancisco, 1993.

Clatworthy, Jonathan, and David Bruce Taylor, eds. *The Windsor Report: A Liberal Response*. Winchester, England: O Books, 2005.

Episcopal Church, Diocese of New Hampshire: Bishop V. Gene Robinson. Web site includes a biography, interview, and personal statements. http://www.nhepiscopal.org.

Linzey, Andrew, and Richard Kirker, eds. *Gays and the Future of Anglicanism: Responses to the Windsor Report*. New York: O Books, 2005.

Righter, Walter. *A Pilgrim's Way*. New York: Random House, 1998.

Spong, Shelby S. *Why Christianity Must Change or Die: A Bishop Speaks to Believers in Exile*. San Francisco, Calif.: HarperCollins, 1998.

Temple, Gray, et al. *Gospel Opportunity or Gospel Threat? The Church's Debate on Sexuality.* New York: Church, 1998.

The Unofficial Anglican Pages of Louie Crew. A comprehensive online database maintained by Louie Crew, member of the Executive Council, Episcopal Church. http://newark.rutgers.edu/~lcrew/rel.html.

See also: Oct. 6, 1968: Metropolitan Community Church Is Founded; Mar., 1972-Mar., 1973: First Gay and Lesbian Synagogue in the United States Is Formed; June 25, 1972: First Out Gay Minister Is Ordained; Oct. 9-12, 1998: First International Retreat for Lesbian and Gay Muslims Is Held; Nov. 29, 2005: Roman Catholic Church Bans Gay Seminarians.

May 17, 2004
Transsexual Athletes Allowed to Compete in Olympic Games

Through a change in policy, the International Olympic Committee permitted transsexual athletes to compete in the Olympic Games. The athletes can compete only if they have had gender reassignment surgery and at least two years of hormone therapy.

Locale: Athens, Greece
Categories: Transgender/transsexuality; sports; organizations and institutions

Key Figures

Mianne Bagger (b. 1966), transsexual professional golfer who competed at the Women's Australian Open in 2004

Michelle Dumaresq (b. 1970), transsexual professional mountain biker and national champion on the Canadian women's circuit in 2003

Ewa Klobukowska (b. 1946), Polish sprinter and first woman to fail the Olympic "gender verification test" before the 1968 Olympic Games

Alyn Libman (b. 1985), transsexual figure skater and college student who was permitted by the U.S. Figure Skating Association to compete as a man in 2004

Renee Richards (b. 1934), transsexual professional tennis player who won a court battle enabling her to compete in the U.S. Women's Open in 1977

Stella Walsh (1911-1980), Polish-born sprinter and 100-meter gold medalist in the 1932 Olympic Games, found, after her death, to have been born male

Summary of Event

On May 17, 2004, the International Olympic Committee (IOC) convened in Athens and voted to allow transsexual athletes to compete in the Olympic Games, and to do so as transsexuals. The new policy took effect immediately, enabling eligible male-to-female (MTF) and female-to-male (FTM) transsexuals to compete in the 2004 Summer Olympic Games; however, none were reported to have done so.

The IOC decision came after lengthy consideration of the issue in consultation with medical experts. The new ruling stipulated that to be able to compete as a member of one's reassigned gender, the athlete must have undergone legally recognized gender reassignment (usually involving genital reconstructive surgery), and also must have had at least two years of hormone therapy after surgery.

The IOC ruling followed an attempt to settle a long history of controversy surrounding gender requirements for athletic competition. Gold medalist Stella Walsh, a Polish-born sprinter who competed

> **IOC STATEMENT ON SEX REASSIGNMENT IN SPORTS**
>
> The Executive Board of the International Olympic Committee (IOC) today [May 17, 2004] approved the consensus proposed by the IOC Medical Commission stating the conditions to be respected for a person who has changed sex to compete in sports competitions. These conditions will be applied as of the Games of the XXVIII Olympiad in 2004 in Athens. The consensus reads as follows:
>
> *Statement of the Stockholm consensus on sex reassignment in sports*
>
> On 28 October 2003, an ad-hoc committee convened by the IOC Medical Commission met in Stockholm to discuss and issue recommendations on the participation of individuals who have undergone sex reassignment (male to female and vice versa) in sport. . . .
>
> The group confirms the previous recommendation that any "individuals undergoing sex reassignment of male to female before puberty should be regarded as girls and women" (female). This also applies to individuals undergoing female to male reassignment, who should be regarded as boys and men (male).
>
> The group recommends that individuals undergoing sex reassignment from male to female after puberty (and vice versa) be eligible for participation in female or male competitions, respectively, under the following conditions:
>
> Surgical anatomical changes have been completed, including external genitalia changes and gonadectomy.
>
> Legal recognition of their assigned sex has been conferred by the appropriate official authorities.
>
> Hormonal therapy appropriate for the assigned sex has been administered in a verifiable manner and for a sufficient length of time to minimise gender-related advantages in sport competitions.
>
> In the opinion of the group, eligibility should begin no sooner than two years after gonadectomy.
>
> It is understood that a confidential case-by-case evaluation will occur.
>
> In the event that the gender of a competing athlete is questioned, the medical delegate (or equivalent) of the relevant sporting body shall have the authority to take all appropriate measures for the determination of the gender of a competitor.
>
> *Explanatory note to the recommendation on sex reassignment and sports*
>
> In the past there have been rare cases of athletes who have competed under one gender and later in life undergone sex reassignment. Occasionally, such an athlete has gone on competing under the new gender. Such cases seem to have been dealt with individually by the responsible sports federations without any clear rules. They have, however, been extremely rare and do not seem to have created a significant problem for sport in general.
>
> With the arrival of improved methods for the identification of transsexual individuals, and improved possibilities to rectify any sexual ambiguity, the number of individuals undergoing sex reassignment has increased. The increase has become particularly significant after the introduction of legislation with respect to sex reassignment in many countries.
>
> *Source:* International Olympic Committee press release, May 18, 2004. http://www.olympic.org/uk/news/media_centre/.

in the 1932 Olympic Games in Los Angeles, was discovered, after her accidental shooting death in 1980, to have been born anatomically male. Through the years, other athletes were suspected of fooling officials by participating as women in order to gain an unfair advantage. In 1964, the IOC began conducting gender verification tests designed to eliminate men from women's competitions. However, chromosome tests resulted in the unfair disqualification of some female athletes who were born without standard sex chromosomes. Ewa Klobukowska, also a Polish sprinter, was the first woman-born-female to fail the gender verification test. She was disqualified from competing in the 1968 Games in Mexico City, Mexico. Thirteen more female athletes had been disqualified between 1972 and 1984, before the test was discontinued in 1999, and prior to the start of the 2000 Games in Sydney, Australia.

Transsexual athletes worldwide applauded the IOC decision, including Australian golfer Mianne Bagger, Canadian mountain biker Michelle Dumaresq, and American figure skater Alyn Libman. One surprising voice of dissent came from Renee Richards, who made headlines in 1977 by winning a court battle against the United States Tennis Association in order to play in the Women's Open after her gender was reassigned in 1975 from being a man to being a woman. Richards, also an ophthalmologist, argued that hormone therapy for transsexual athletes is similar to the steroid use banned for nontranssexual Olympians. The IOC decision "defies fairness," she said, because it works against previous attempts to keep a level playing field in athletic competition.

Significance

The IOC ruling was a landmark decision for transgender civil rights, given the difficulty faced by transgender people in gender-segregated environments such as athletic competitions. The question of fairness in athletic competition is central to the controversy over transsexual athletes, whose bodies are inevitably shaped to some degree by their original exposure to the hormones associated with their birth sex. Critics of the IOC policy maintain that to allow transsexuals to compete after hormone therapy contradicts the strict antidoping rules for Olympic athletes. The IOC has maintained that the new gender policy does not interfere with the ban on illegal drugs because transsexual athletes will be tested for normal hormone levels, as will all other athletes.

Most of the discussion about transsexual athletes has been focused on MTF competitors and whether having been male would give unfair advantage to a transsexual woman competing against a nontranssexual woman. There has been no comparable argument made about FTM athletes competing as men. For example, the stipulation calling for both gender reassignment surgery and two subsequent years of hormone therapy as a prerequisite for transsexuals to enter Olympic competition is designed to ensure that a sufficient period of time has elapsed to neutralize the prior effects of testosterone on the MTF transsexual body. Until their testes are removed, transsexual women may have elevated levels of testosterone, even if they are taking estrogen as hormone therapy. IOC officials argue that an elevated testosterone level could provide them with an unfair advantage against nontranssexual women.

However, transgender advocates have argued that the IOC requirement of genital surgery is not fair to FTM transsexuals because sex hormones are not involved in the construction of a penis and such surgeries are costly and often ineffective. FTMs argue that regulating gender requirements in sport cannot level the playing field in any case, because body types vary considerably, even within the categories "man" and "woman."

The debate surrounding transsexuals in sport, and the biological effects of gender reassignment for athletes, will continue until there is systematic research on the effects of gender reassignment and hormone therapy on athletic performance. The IOC ruling will likely have an effect on other professional sports organizations and their policies regarding transsexual athletes.

—*K. Surkan*

Further Reading

"IOC to Allow Transsexual Athletes in Olympics." *Sports Illustrated.com*. http://sportsillustrated.cnn.com/2003/more/11/13/bc.eu.spt.oly.transsexual.ap/.

Letellier, Patrick. "Olympics to Let Transsexuals Compete." *PlanetOut Network*. http://www.planetout.com/news/article.html?2004/05/18/3.

Mackay, Duncan. "Transsexual Fears After New Olympic Ruling." *Guardian Unlimited*. http://sport.guardian.co.uk/athletics/story/0,,1222411,00.html.

Marech, Rona. "Olympics' Transgender Quandary: Debate Rages on the Fairness of New Inclusion Rule." *San Francisco Chronicle*, June 14, 2004, p. A1.

Richards, Renee, with John Ames. *Second Serve: The Renee Richards Story*. New York: Stein & Day, 1983.

Teetzel, Sarah. "On Transgendered Athletes, Fairness, and Doping: An International Challenge." *Sport in Society* 9, no. 2 (2006): 227-251.

Wilson, J. D. "Sex Testing in International Athletics." *Journal of the American Medical Association* 267, no. 6 (1992).

See also: Aug. 28, 1982: First Gay Games Are Held in San Francisco; 1994: Navratilova Honored for Her Career in Tennis; 1995: Athlete Louganis Announces He Is HIV-Positive.

November 18, 2004
UNITED KINGDOM LEGALIZES SAME-GENDER CIVIL PARTNERSHIPS

The United Kingdom's recognition of same-gender civil partnerships gives gay and lesbian couples the same inheritance, financial, and next-of-kin rights as those of heterosexual married couples. Some, however, believe "partnership" is not legally or symbolically comparable to "marriage."

ALSO KNOWN AS: Civil Partnership Act 2004
LOCALE: United Kingdom
CATEGORIES: Laws, acts, and legal history; civil rights; government and politics

KEY FIGURE
Tony Blair (b. 1953), prime minister of the United Kingdom, 1997-

SUMMARY OF EVENT
Rituals that solemnize same-gender relationships have been part of world history, including ancient Greece. In the late twentieth century, especially, these ceremonies became increasingly visible in Western countries along with a growing demand by lesbians and gays that they be allowed to marry legally. On November 18, 2004, the United Kingdom, by royal assent, legalized civil partnerships, providing lesbians and gays with most of the benefits of marriage. The Civil Partnership Act took effect just over one year later, on December 5, 2005.

The process of extending marriage rights to gays and lesbians began in June, 2003, when the Labour Party government of Prime Minister Tony Blair issued a white paper proposing civil partnerships for same-gender couples. Part of Blair's plan to modernize Great Britain, the partnership legislation was promoted by his administration as an act of fairness. Labour leaders argued that it was only fair that gay and lesbian couples should enjoy the same social security, tax, pension, and inheritance rights as do married couples. The government estimated that up to 7 percent of the British population is gay or lesbian and it projected that one-third of this population would enter civil partnerships.

The bill to establish same-gender civil partnership was introduced in Parliament in March, 2004. A few conservatives in the unelected House of Lords objected to the bill, but it eventually passed the House of Commons. The government aided passage by dropping the word "marriage" from the legislation rather than run afoul of lawmakers who believed that the word has religious connotations. Opposition to the legislation remained fairly muted. Officials in the Church of England had long preached tolerance of homosexuality and the major political parties in Britain vie to have gay politicians prominent in their ranks. The few objections came mostly from religious traditionalists. The Roman Catholic archbishop of Cardiff, Peter Smith, accused the government of attempting to undermine marriage.

In answer to objections from religious groups, civil partnerships in the United Kingdom cannot be registered in churches. The range of places where lesbians and gays can register a civil partnership are broadly similar to those available for civil marriages,

---

FROM THE CIVIL PARTNERSHIP ACT

Be it enacted by the Queen's most Excellent Majesty, by and with the advice and consent of the Lords Spiritual and Temporal, and Commons, in this present Parliament assembled, and by the authority of the same, as follows: . . .
Civil partnership
(1) A civil partnership is a relationship between two people of the same sex ("civil partners")— (a) which is formed when they register as civil partners of each other . . .
(3) A civil partnership ends only on death, dissolution or annulment.

including registry offices and country hotels. Every local authority is required to provide a venue for registration. The legislation does not require local councils to offer same-gender ceremonies. Two councils, including Bromley in London, refused to allow ceremonies because council members view same-gender marriages as immoral acts that undermine family values. In some Calvinist districts on islands off Scotland, registrars declined to perform ceremonies when registering couples. In contrast, officials in Liverpool expressed eagerness to attract the "pink pound" and produced a glossy brochure featuring same-gender couples to lure business into the city.

The Civil Partnership Act was signed into law November 18, 2004, and went into effect one year later. Same-gender couples age sixteen and older gained the chance to give legal notice of their intention to form a partnership. Ceremonies were held after a waiting period that ranged from fourteen days in Northern Ireland to fifteen days in Scotland and sixteen days in England and Wales. The first same-gender partners to register in full accordance with the law were Grainne Close and Shannon Sickles in Belfast on December 19. However, the first registrants were Matthew Roche and Christopher Cramp, who were given special permission to register in Brighton on December 5 because of Roche's imminent death from lung cancer. On December 21, 687 same-gender marriages took place across England and Wales, including the well-publicized union of singer Sir Elton John and filmmaker David Furnish. The government had expected 22,000 couples to follow suit within five years, including many older couples who have so far preferred to keep their relationship private.

Civil partnership is a step toward legal equality, but *marriage* rights for gays and lesbians had been sought in particular because of the protection that marriage provides. Gay and lesbian partners gain next-of-kin rights (visiting a loved one in the hospital) and protection from domestic violence as well as the ability to apply for parental responsibility for a civil partner's child and access to compensation if a partner dies in an accident. Civil partners enjoy the same tax advantages as married couples, ending inheritance-tax discrimination that forced some surviving partners to sell their homes. Gay and lesbian couples can now pass assets to each other without having to pay inheritance tax, in the same way transfers of assets between husband and wife are already exempt. A survivor will be recognized if his or her partner dies without leaving a will, giving the surviving partner the opportunity to assume an apartment lease instead of being evicted as well as the chance to inherit a home and possessions.

Differences between a civil union and a marriage chiefly involve details at the beginning and end of relationships. For civil unions, prenuptial agreements are known as preregistration agreements. The end of a civil union is known as a dissolution instead of a divorce. Adultery cannot be cited as a cause for a dissolution because a civil union is, by legal definition, a nonsexual relationship with no "need" to consummate the union.

Significance

While most British gays and lesbians consider the Civil Partnership Act long overdue, a few activists believe that the new statute does not go far enough. Many have denounced the differing treatment of heterosexual and homosexual couples before the law. While heterosexuals cannot obtain civil partnerships, homosexuals cannot obtain marriages.

The legislation, still, remains a significant step for lesbian and gay rights. The Civil Partnership Act made Britain the fifteenth country to recognize same-gender unions in Europe. The countries that recognize gay civil unions are Denmark (1989), Norway (1993), Sweden (1995), Luxembourg (1996), Iceland (1996), Hungary (1996), France (1999), Spain (some regions only, 2000), Germany (2001), Portugal (2001), Switzerland (some regions only, 2001), Finland (2002), Croatia (2003), Poland (2004), and Scotland (2004). The Netherlands became the first country to legalize same-gender *marriage* in 2001, Belgium followed in 2003, and Spain followed suit in 2005. Roman Catholic pope Benedict XVI has condemned such partnerships as inauthentic and as an expression of anarchic personal freedom that threatens the future of the family.

Despite opposition from some Christian groups, the issue is far less contentious in Europe than in the United States. Europe's experience with same-gender marriage and civil partnerships has influenced the debate in the United States on the same issues. U.S. lawmakers have highlighted declining marriage trends in Europe to argue that same-gender marriage and civil unions would lead to a weakening of the tradition of marriage.

—Caryn E. Neumann

FURTHER READING

Eskridge, William, Jr. *Equality Practice: Civil Unions and the Future of Gay Rights.* New York: Routledge, 2001.

Gray, Nichole, and Dominic Brazil. *Blackstone's Guide to the Civil Partnership Act 2004.* New York: Oxford University Press, 2005.

Merin, Yuval. *Equality for Same-Sex Couples: The Legal Recognition of Gay Partnerships in Europe and the United States.* Chicago: University of Chicago Press, 2002.

Rozenberg, Joshua. "All-embracing Partnership Act." *Telegraph.co.uk.* October 6, 2005. http://www.telegraph.co.uk/news/main.jhtml?xml = /news/2005/10/06/nlaw06.xml.

"Same-Sex Marriage: A Selective Bibliography of the Legal Literature." Law Library, Rutgers School of Law. http://law-library.rutgers.edu/SSM.html.

Snyder, R. Claire. *Gay Marriage and Democracy: Equality for All.* Lanham, Md.: Rowman & Littlefield, 2006.

Sullivan, Andrew, ed. *Same-Sex Marriage, Pro and Con: A Reader.* Rev. and updated. New York: Vintage Books, 2004.

Wolfson, Evan. *Why Marriage Matters: America, Equality, and Gay People's Right to Marry.* New York: Simon & Schuster, 2004.

SEE ALSO: July 27, 1967: United Kingdom Decriminalizes Homosexual Sex; 1981: Gay and Lesbian Palimony Suits Emerge; 1993-1996: Hawaii Opens Door to Same-Gender Marriages; Aug. 6, 1994: Japanese American Citizens League Supports Same-Gender Marriage; Sept. 21, 1996: U.S. President Clinton Signs Defense of Marriage Act; Dec. 20, 1999: *Baker v. Vermont* Leads to Recognition of Same-Gender Civil Unions; Feb. 21, 2003: Australian Court Validates Transsexual Marriage; Apr., 2003: Buenos Aires Recognizes Same-Gender Civil Unions; Nov. 18, 2003: Massachusetts Court Rules for Same-Gender Marriage; Apr. 4, 2005: United Kingdom's Gender Recognition Act Legalizes Transsexual Marriage; June 30, 2005: Spain Legalizes Same-Gender Marriage.

April 4, 2005
United Kingdom's Gender Recognition Act Legalizes Transsexual Marriage

The United Kingdom passed legislation enabling changes to sex/gender designations on birth certificates, allowing transsexuals to legally marry in their "acquired" gender. The act has been heralded especially because it does not require that a person undergo gender reassignment surgery for the change on his or her birth certificate to be valid.

Locale: United Kingdom
Categories: Transgender/transsexuality; civil rights; laws, acts, and legal history; government and politics

Key Figures
April Ashley, male-to-female transsexual whose marriage to English aristocrat Arthur Corbett was annulled in 1970
Elizabeth Bellinger, male-to-female transsexual whose marriage was ruled illegal in 2003
Lord Irvine, Lord Chancellor, forced by superiors to pay half of Bellinger's legal costs
Michael Scott-Joynt, bishop of Winchester, who opposed the act

Summary of Event
After more than thirty years of struggle, transsexuals in the United Kingdom gained the right to marry in their "acquired" gender after the country's Gender Recognition Bill received royal assent on July 1, 2004, becoming the Gender Recognition Act. The act went into force on April 4, 2005. The new legislation made it possible for transsexuals to change the sex/gender designation on their birth certificates, a designation that is required in order for transsexual marriages to be legally recognized as "heterosexual."

Until the passage of the law, the United Kingdom was one of only four European countries that refused to recognize gender reassignment legally. The others are Ireland, Albania, and Andorra. Gender recognition under the new law does not require applicants to have undergone gender reassignment surgery, and it prohibits disclosure of the applicant's change-in-gender status.

Since the high court first annulled the marriage of April Ashley and aristocrat Arthur Corbett in 1970, the British had refused to allow transsexual marriage. However, the European Court of Human Rights, beginning with two rulings in July, 2002, had found that British law violated the human rights of transsexuals. That finding was reiterated on January 7, 2004, when the European Court of Justice ruled that British law, which denied transsexuals the right to marry, was in violation of European law because it would make couples in question ineligible for a survivor's pension.

One of the highest-profile cases was that of Elizabeth Bellinger, a male-to-female transsexual who had gender reassignment surgery in 1981. Before the surgery, Bellinger had lived as a woman for ten years. She married Michael Bellinger in 1981 in Lincolnshire, at which time she was not asked to produce legal proof of her gender. After twenty-two years of living together as husband and wife, the couple was unable to get British courts to recognize their marriage, losing appeals in the high court, the appeal court, and, ultimately, in the House of Lords on April 10, 2003. Although rejecting Bellinger's claim to a legal marriage, the law lords found that her human rights had been violated and so directed Lord Irvine, the Lord Chancellor, to pay half the legal costs of Bellinger's appeal.

Opposition to the gender recognition bill came from the bishop of Winchester, Michael Scott-Joynt, and several Tories in the House of Lords, who argued that the bill would undermine marriage and that it ran counter to logic and the beliefs of more than one religion. The Press Association News quoted Lord Filkin in rebuttal; he explained that

> ## From the Gender Recognition Act
>
> An act to make provision for and in connection with change of gender.
> Be it enacted by the Queen's most Excellent Majesty, by and with the advice and consent of the Lords Spiritual and Temporal, and Commons, in this present Parliament assembled, and by the authority of the same, as follows:
>
> *Applications for gender recognition certificate.*
> *Applications*
> (1) a person of either gender who is aged at least 18 may make an application for a gender recognition certificate on the basis of:
> (a) living in the other gender, or
> (b) having changed gender under the law of a country or territory outside the United Kingdom.
> (2) in this Act "the acquired gender," in relation to a person by whom an application under subsection (1) is or has been made, means:
> (a) in the case of an application under paragraph (a) of that subsection, the gender in which the person is living, or
> (b) in the case of an application under paragraph (b) of that subsection, the gender to which the person has changed under the law of the country or territory concerned.
> (3) an application under subsection (1) is to be determined by a Gender Recognition Panel.
> (4) schedule 1 (Gender Recognition Panels) has effect.
>
> *Determination of applications*
> (1) in the case of an application under section 1(1)(a), the panel must grant the application if satisfied that the applicant:
> (a) has or has had gender dysphoria,
> (b) has lived in the acquired gender throughout the period of two years ending with the date on which the application is made,
> (c) intends to continue to live in the acquired gender until death, and
> (d) complies with the requirements imposed by and under section 3.

"the law is not seeking to change the sex of an individual, it is seeking to recognize that a change has happened." The new legislation is administered by the Gender Recognition Panel.

Significance

The Gender Recognition Act has changed the lives of thousands of transsexuals in the United Kingdom. In addition to legalizing transsexual marriage and enabling transsexuals to claim pensions with their acquired gender, the law also ensures that male-to-female transsexuals are not sent to male prisons in the event that they are convicted of a crime by British courts. The passage of this law also brings the United Kingdom into compliance with the human rights conventions of the European Union.

The British law has been heralded as progressive by transgender activists especially because it does not require that a person undergo gender reassignment surgery before receiving a new birth certificate. Some transsexuals are unable or unwilling to have the surgery.

—K. Surkan

Further Reading

"Britain's Bar on Transsexual Marriages Contrary to EU Law." *Agence France Presse*, Brussels, January 7, 2004.

Brown, Amanda, and Anthony Looch. "Bishop Condemns Transsexual Marriage Plans." *Press Association News*, December 18, 2003.

Evans, Andrew. "Transsexuals Marriage Bill Clears Lords." *Press Association News*, February 10, 2004.

"Gender Recognition Act 2004." Gender Recognition Panel. Tribunal Services, Department for Constitutional Affairs. http://www.grp.gov.uk/.

Goodchild, Sophie. "Ministers to Change Law on

Transsexual Marriages." *The Independent*, July 6, 2003.

International Commission on Civil Status. *Transsexualism in Europe*. Strasbourg, France: Council of Europe, distributed by Croton-on-Hudson, N.Y.: Manhattan, 2000.

Rozenberg, Joshua. "Lords Reject Appeal over Transsexual Marriage." *The Daily Telegraph*, April 11, 2003, p. 13.

Sharpe, Andrew N. *Transgender Jurisprudence: Dysphoric Bodies of Law*. London: Cavendish, 2002.

SEE ALSO: 1981: Gay and Lesbian Palimony Suits Emerge; 1992: Transgender Nation Holds Its First Protest; June, 1992: Feinberg Publishes *Transgender Liberation*; 1993-1996: Hawaii Opens Door to Same-Gender Marriages; Aug. 6, 1994: Japanese American Citizens League Supports Same-Gender Marriage; Sept. 21, 1996: U.S. President Clinton Signs Defense of Marriage Act; Oct. 27, 1999: *Littleton v. Prange* Withholds Survivor Rights from Transsexual Spouses; Dec. 20, 1999: *Baker v. Vermont* Leads to Recognition of Same-Gender Civil Unions; Feb. 21, 2003: Australian Court Validates Transsexual Marriage; Apr., 2003: Buenos Aires Recognizes Same-Gender Civil Unions; June 17, 2003, and July 19, 2005: Canada Legalizes Same-Gender Marriage; Nov. 18, 2003: Massachusetts Court Rules for Same-Gender Marriage; Nov. 18, 2004: United Kingdom Legalizes Same-Gender Civil Partnerships; June 30, 2005: Spain Legalizes Same-Gender Marriage.

June 30, 2005
SPAIN LEGALIZES SAME-GENDER MARRIAGE

Spain became only the third country, after the Netherlands and Belgium, to legalize same-gender marriages, granting the same rights enjoyed by heterosexual couples, including adoption and inheritance, to same-gender couples.

LOCALE: Madrid, Spain
CATEGORIES: Civil rights; laws, acts, and legal history

KEY FIGURES

Emilio Menéndez, Spanish store-window decorator, married Carlos Baturin

Carlos Baturin, American-born psychiatrist, married Emilio Menéndez

José Luis Rodríguez Zapatero (b. 1960), prime minister of Spain, 2004-   , legalized same-gender marriage in Spain

Francisco Franco (1892-1975), dictator of Spain, ruled homosexuality illegal in 1954

SUMMARY OF EVENT

Historically, Spain has been a country with strong ties to the Roman Catholic Church and in strong agreement with the Church's position against homosexuality. Indeed, under the rule of Spanish dictator, General Francisco Franco, homosexuality was outlawed in 1954. The 1950's and 1960's in Spain saw large numbers of gays imprisoned. However, some cities were more tolerant than others, and homosexual communities formed secretly in Barcelona, Ibiza, and Sitges. After Franco's death in 1975, Prince Juan Carlos, who was far more liberal than his predecessor, moved to make the country more democratic, bringing a nationwide attitude shift that encouraged a much more socially open and tolerant atmosphere. Though Spain has retained strong connections to the Catholic Church, it has begun to distinguish between civil and religious life, and between public law and private conviction.

To that end, by the 1990's, same-gender couples were commonly accepted in enough communities that some city councils allowed civil unions, granting local recognition to both homosexual and heterosexual couples. Although gay and lesbian couples still could not adopt children jointly, single people were allowed to adopt in Spain, which meant one partner could adopt a child who would then be raised by the couple together. As recently as 2001, though, the Spanish parliament was controlled by the conservative People's Party, which had rejected a bill that would have created some equality for heterosexual and homosexual civil unions. National legal recognition was not possible for same-gender couples until the election of the liberal-socialist prime minister José Luis Rodríguez Zapatero in March of 2004. One of Zapatero's election promises included the legalization of same-gender marriages.

On June 30, 2004, nearly a year before the final law passed Parliament, the Spanish Congress of Deputies (Parliament's lower house) provisionally approved marriage rights for same-gender couples. However, this legislation did not become law without some intense controversy. In addition to heavy criticism and opposition from the Church, the legislation also faced disfavor from some politicians and from conservatives in the general populace. Nonetheless, a formal bill legitimizing same-gender marriage passed the Spanish cabinet on October 1, 2004, and was subsequently submitted to the Congress of Deputies on December 31 of that year. The bill added one sentence to existing Spanish marriage law: It states explicitly that a couple, of any gender make up, married in Spain has the same rights and responsibilities. The bill passed the Congress of Deputies on April 21, 2005, but then it ran into more heavy opposition in Spain's senate (the upper house of Spanish parliament). Indeed, the senate rejected the bill on June 22, which in many situations means the death of a bill. However, once a bill is rejected by the Spanish senate, it goes back to the Congress of Deputies, which can override the upper house. The congress did just that, approving the controversial law by a vote of 187 to 147 on June 30. The bill's final approval, on July 2, included royal assent and publication in Spain's *Boletin Oficial De Estato* (official bulletin of the state); the new law took effect on July 3.

SIGNIFICANCE

The first same-gender Spanish couple to marry under the new law was Spanish store-window decorator Emilio Menéndez and American-born psychiatrist Carlos Baturin. They held a small civil ceremony in the Madrid suburb of Tres Cantos on July 11, 2005. The couple stated they had not intended to be the first same-gender couple to marry in Spain, but that the marriage docket and timing of their paperwork had placed them first in line. On July 27, the Spanish government added that same-gender couples of which one member was a foreign national who married in Spain could expect to have their marriages considered valid under Spanish law, although the country of origin of the foreign national might not respect the union. The Spanish government, however, maintained the same residency requirement for all marriages, regardless of gender, stating that one member of the couple must be a Spanish citizen.

In May, 2006, the European Union (EU), of which Spain is a part, approved the cross-border rights of same-gender couples in the EU. The new requirements grant same-gender couples, who are legally married in a country that permits same-gender marriage, the same rights as heterosexual married couples in all EU member countries, regardless of the legality of same-gender marriage in those other countries.

The Spanish law's opponents, including the Catholic Church, consider same-gender marriage an attack on the traditional family and believe the new law weakens the institution of marriage. The Spanish Conference of Catholic Bishops considers the legislation unfair but has placed the burden upon individual Catholics to defend traditional marriage and families. Politically, the conservative People's Party has voiced a constitutional challenge to the law, and conservative newspapers have insisted that few gay and lesbian couples have married. However, the government estimates that the law will benefit 5 to 10 percent of the population.

Polls suggest that roughly 60 percent of the country, which is 80 percent Catholic, supports same-gender marriage, and roughly 50 percent of the population supports same-gender adoption.

Throughout the process, Prime Minister Zapatero has balanced a respect for the Catholic Church while rejecting the use of Church doctrine to shape or otherwise influence Spanish law. He has stated repeatedly that the legislation allows individuals to make their own choices without imposing religious morality upon secular and civil issues.

—*Jessie Bishop Powell*

FURTHER READING

Castresana, Carlos. "Gay Marriage in Spain." *Peace Review* 17, nos. 2/3 (2005): 131-136.

Eskridge, William N. *The Case for Same-Sex Marriage: From Sexual Liberty to Civilized Commitment.* New York: Free Press, 1996.

Mello, Michael. "Legalizing Gay Marriage." *Journal of Marriage and Family* 67, no. 5 (2005): 1348-1349.

Moats, David. *Civil Wars: A Battle for Gay Marriage.* Orlando, Fla.: Harcourt, 2004.

Roca, Encarna. "Same-Sex Partnerships in Spain: Family, Marriage, or Contract?" *European Journal of Law Reform* 3, no. 3 (2001): 365-382.

"Same-Sex Marriage: A Selective Bibliography of the Legal Literature." Law Library, Rutgers School of Law. http://law-library.rutgers.edu/SSM.html.

"Spanish Lawmakers Green-Light Same-Sex Marriage." *The Advocate*, July 1, 2005.

SEE ALSO: 1981: Gay and Lesbian Palimony Suits Emerge; 1993-1996: Hawaii Opens Door to Same-Gender Marriages; Aug. 6, 1994: Japanese American Citizens League Supports Same-Gender Marriage; Sept. 21, 1996: U.S. President Clinton Signs Defense of Marriage Act; Dec. 20, 1999: *Baker v. Vermont* Leads to Recognition of Same-Gender Civil Unions; Feb. 21, 2003: Australian Court Validates Transsexual Marriage; Apr., 2003: Buenos Aires Recognizes Same-Gender Civil Unions; June 17, 2003, and July 19, 2005: Canada Legalizes Same-Gender Marriage; Nov. 18, 2003: Massachusetts Court Rules for Same-Gender Marriage; Nov. 18, 2004: United Kingdom Legalizes Same-Gender Civil Partnerships; Apr. 4, 2005: United Kingdom's Gender Recognition Act Legalizes Transsexual Marriage.

November 29, 2005
ROMAN CATHOLIC CHURCH BANS GAY SEMINARIANS

The Roman Catholic Church publicly issued an official "instruction" that banned gays from admission to seminaries for training for the priesthood. The new document came at the end of several years of controversy over the sexual abuse of children by priests and subsequent cover-ups by the Church.

LOCALE: Vatican City, Rome, Italy
CATEGORIES: Religion; organizations and institutions

KEY FIGURE
Benedict XVI (Joseph Ratzinger; b. 1927), Roman Catholic pope, 2005-

SUMMARY OF EVENT

Rumors of a ban on gay priests and seminarians first rose in the late 1990's and early twenty-first century and were especially widespread in the weeks leading up to the Roman Catholic Church's ban on gay seminarians issued on November 4, 2005 (announced November 29). Contrary to some fears, the ban did not affect men who had already been ordained as priests. Rather, the ban was aimed at applicants to seminary training.

The document, Instruction Concerning the Criteria for the Discernment of Vocations with Regard to Persons with Homosexual Tendencies In View of Their Admission to the Seminary and to Holy Orders, offered twenty-one paragraphs of guidance to

> **ROMAN CATHOLIC CHURCH: INSTRUCTION ON GAYS AND THE PRIESTHOOD**
>
> *1. Introduction*
> ... [T]he present Instruction does not intend to dwell on all questions in the area of affectivity and sexuality that require an attentive discernment during the entire period of formation. Rather, it contains norms concerning a specific question, made more urgent by the current situation, and that is: whether to admit to the seminary and to holy orders candidates who have deep-seated homosexual tendencies. ...
>
> *2. Homosexuality and the Ordained Ministry*
> From the time of the Second Vatican Council until today, various Documents of the Magisterium, and especially the *Catechism of the Catholic Church*, have confirmed the teaching of the Church on homosexuality. The Catechism distinguishes between homosexual acts and homosexual tendencies.
>
> Regarding *acts*, it teaches that Sacred Scripture presents them as grave sins. The Tradition has constantly considered them as intrinsically immoral and contrary to the natural law. Consequently, under no circumstance can they be approved.
>
> Deep-seated homosexual *tendencies*, which are found in a number of men and women, are also objectively disordered and, for those same people, often constitute a trial. Such persons must be accepted with respect and sensitivity. Every sign of unjust discrimination in their regard should be avoided. They are called to fulfil God's will in their lives and to unite to the sacrifice of the Lord's Cross the difficulties they may encounter.
>
> In the light of such teaching, this Dicastery, in accord with the Congregation for Divine Worship and the Discipline of the Sacraments, believes it necessary to state clearly that the Church, while profoundly respecting the persons in question, cannot admit to the seminary or to holy orders those who practise homosexuality, present deep-seated homosexual tendencies or support the so-called "gay culture."
>
> Such persons, in fact, find themselves in a situation that gravely hinders them from relating correctly to men and women. One must in no way overlook the negative consequences that can derive from the ordination of persons with deep-seated homosexual tendencies.
>
> Different, however, would be the case in which one were dealing with homosexual tendencies that were only the expression of a transitory problem—for example, that of an adolescence not yet superseded. Nevertheless, such tendencies must be clearly overcome at least three years before ordination to the diaconate.
>
> *Source:* Congress for Catholic Education, Instruction Concerning the Criteria for the Discernment of Vocations with Regard to Persons with Homosexual Tendencies in View of Their Admission to the Seminary and to Holy Orders (November 4, 2005). http://www.vatican.va/roman_curia/congregations/ccatheduc/.

bishops and seminary rectors on the proper response to gay applicants for the priesthood. Issued by the Church's Congregation for Catholic Education, the instruction banned from the seminary men who "practice homosexuality," exhibit "deep-seated homosexual tendencies," or "support the so-called 'gay culture.'" At the same time, the instruction suggested that men who had overcome transitory homosexual impulses for at least three years could be considered for admission to seminary. The instruction further suggested that its prohibition against gay seminarians was issued in the context of deep respect for the persons affected by the ban.

Work on the 2005 instruction had begun years before—by some estimates, as long as a decade before. Since at least 1961, the Vatican had actively discouraged the admission of gay men to the priesthood. At that time, the Vatican issued the Instruction on the Careful Selection and Training of Candidates for the States of Perfection and Sacred Orders. That document not only banned gays from the priesthood but also implicitly linked homosexuality and pederasty.

In 1986, the Congregation for the Doctrine of the Faith, the Church unit empowered to ensure orthodoxy among adherents, issued a denunciation of gay priests. At that time, the Congregation for the Doctrine of the Faith was headed by Joseph Ratzinger, widely regarded as a highly conservative member of the Church hierarchy. Ratzinger became Pope Benedict XVI in 2005.

In 2002, the Congregation for Divine Worship and the Discipline of the Sacraments also advised against admitting gays into the priesthood. Despite this and earlier Vatican pronouncements discouraging gay priests, most of the 229 seminaries in the United States had not uniformly rejected candidates who were gay.

The issue of gays in the priesthood took on new currency with the start, in the late twentieth century, of a sexual abuse scandal involving priests, which roiled the Archdiocese of Boston and eventually much of the Church in the United States and beyond. Social science research disavows any link between sexual orientation and child sexual abuse. Nevertheless, when the scandal of priests' sexual abuse of children and the Church's cover-up of the abuse came to light, the disproved link emerged in both media and popular discourse. During the height of the sexual abuse scandal, the Congregation for Catholic Education had been reportedly developing guidelines addressing admission to the priesthood. It was widely expected that these guidelines would specifically address whether gays should become priests.

The stage for the eventual ban was set in April, 2005, when Ratzinger became pope, succeeding John Paul II as patriarch of the Church. Benedict indicated a need to "purify" the Church in the aftermath of the child sexual abuse scandal. Like many people both inside and outside the Church, Benedict continued to perpetuate the myth of a relationship between homosexuality and the sexual abuse of children. Under the sway of that myth, however ill-advised, Benedict's next step was to approve the instruction, which he did on August 31, 2005. The instruction was announced to the public by the Congregation for Catholic Education in late November.

SIGNIFICANCE

The 2005 Roman Catholic instruction has been widely regarded as having perpetuated the myth of a link between homosexuality child sexual abuse. At the same time, the instruction did not address the presence of gay priests who had already been ordained and who were serving the Church. This distinction was a relief to some who had feared the potential for a purge of gay priests. Nonetheless, the ban against admitting gays to seminaries was publicly described by some ordained priests as a witch hunt. This description took on a new intensity when the Vatican announced visits to seminaries to make sure the seminaries were complying with the ban.

The ban was met by strong reactions both in favor and in opposition. Some conservative groups—for example, the American Family Association—welcomed the ban. In statements of support, these groups often explicitly repeated the disproved connection between sexual orientation and child sexual abuse. Some gay priests reacted to the ban by announcing they were gay. Some stayed in the priesthood; others chose to leave. Critics of the ban suggested that it would carry several dangerous effects, including the creation of an unhealthy, sexually repressed environment in the Church and the establishment of a barrier to clear communication between seminarians and their spiritual advisers. Ultimately, the ban suggested that the Church was resolving its sexual abuse scandal by insisting that gay priests were the cause of the scandal—in spite of contradictory social science research as well as a wealth of evidence implicating institutional self-protection and secrecy as significant in the development of the sexual abuse crisis.

—*Glenda M. Russell*

FURTHER READING

Congress for Catholic Education. Instruction Concerning the Criteria for the Discernment of Vocations with Regard to Persons with Homosexual Tendencies In View of Their Admission to the Seminary and to Holy Orders (November 4, 2005). http://www.vatican.va/roman_curia/congregations/ccatheduc/.

Lieblich, J. "'An Appalling Sin,' Pope Says: Vatican Session with Cardinals on Sex Abuse Also Opens Debate on Homosexuality in Priesthood." *Chicago Tribune*, April 24, 2002, p. 1.

Ripley, A. "Inside The Church's Closet: Gay Priests Talk About Their Hidden Lives, Love of the Church and Fear of Being Scapegoated in the Sex Scandals." *Time*, May 20, 2002.

Russell, Glenda M., and Nancy Kelly. *Subtle Stereotyping: The Media, Homosexuality, and the Priest Sexual Abuse Scandal*. Amherst, Mass.: Institute for Gay and Lesbian Strategic Studies, 2003. http://iglss.org.

Stevenson, Michael R. "Understanding Child Sexual Abuse and the Catholic Church: Gay Priests Are Not the Problem." *Angles: The Policy Journal of the Institute for Gay and Lesbian Strategic Studies* 6, no. 2 (September, 2002). http://iglss.org.

See also: Oct. 6, 1968: Metropolitan Community Church Is Founded; Mar., 1972-Mar., 1973: First Gay and Lesbian Synagogue in the United States Is Formed; June 25, 1972: First Out Gay Minister Is Ordained; Dec. 10, 1989: ACT UP Protests at St. Patrick's Cathedral; Oct. 9-12, 1998: First International Retreat for Lesbian and Gay Muslims Is Held; Mar. 7, 2004: Robinson Becomes First Out Gay Bishop in Christian History.

January, 2006
Jiménez Flores Elected to the Mexican Senate

After serving as an appointed deputy in the Mexican assembly and becoming the first out lesbian or gay individual in Mexico's legislature, Patria Jiménez Flores was elected to the Mexican senate in 2006, the first out lesbian or gay individual elected to the lawmaking body.

Locale: Mexico
Categories: Government and politics; civil rights

Key Figure
Patria Jiménez Flores (b. 1957), lesbian and gay rights activist, socialist, and politician

Summary of Event
Although Mexican women have played active roles during key moments in the country's history (for example, the War of Independence, the Mexican Revolution), they could not vote until 1947 and could not run for office until 1953. Women who loved women were often closeted and circumspect. One example is the famed poet, nun, and scholar Sor Juana Inéz de la Cruz, who wrote love poems dedicated to several female viceregal mentors. Some women who might in the past be thought of as lesbian might today be thought of as transgender, like the notable Amelia (Amelio) Robles, who fought in the Mexican Revolution. Amelio, as she preferred to be called, dressed in male clothing and was a fierce combatant.

Gay Mexicans also have been generally closeted. Some remembered the 1901 scandal of "Los 41," forty-one being the number of gay men arrested at a private ball hosted by a politician. Most lesbians and gays had been closeted until the 1970's. In 1971, Frente de Liberación Homosexual, the first cogender LGBTI (lesbian, gay, bisexual, transgender, intersex) group in Mexico, was formed in Mexico City. While some lesbians preferred to work in cogender groups, many who objected to the sexism in those groups and those who had been influenced by feminism, chose to form women-only groups.

Over the decades, lesbians created groups to meet a variety of interests and needs, groups such as Ácratas, who were separatists; Lesbos (1977); Oikabeth (a leftist progressive group that had several incarnations); Oasis (a separatist group); La Comuna de las Lesbianas Morelenses (a living collective formed in the 1980's); MULA (Mujeres Urgidas de un Lesbianismo Auténtico) in 1984; and a lesbian mothers group called GRUMALE (1986). Patlatonalli (1986) is still active as is El Closet de Sor Juana (1992), a lesbian-feminist activist group named after Sor Juana Inéz de la Cruz. Groups from the 1990's include Telemanita (1991), Musas de Metal (1995), and Lesbianas Zapatistas (1997).

At the International Women's Year Conference held in Mexico in 1975, lesbians were present but not on the program. A workshop had been hastily arranged, however, after an Australian woman demanded that the subject be part of the conference. Mexican lesbian activist Nancy Cárdenas wrote a brief statement that was read at the meeting. In 1978, the first Mexican lesbian conference was held at Cárdenas's home. Four years later, the first Gay Pride March in Mexico took place in Mexico City.

Almost twenty years later, in April of 2003, the Mexican parliament passed legislation to prevent and eliminate discrimination based on sexual orientation and declared that sexual preference was a protected class. A government office was also created to investigate cases of discrimination perpetrated by public officers. As of 2006, Mexico and Ecuador are the only Latin American countries that provide national protection on the basis of sexual orientation. Some of the credit for the landmark Mexican law goes to Patria Jiménez Flores, the first out lesbian or gay person elected to the Mexican Federal Congress (1997).

Elsa Patria Jiménez Flores, the ninth of ten children, was born in 1957 in San Luis Potosi, México. She came out publicly when she was sixteen, and in the late 1970's she joined the cogender lesbian and gay movement. During the years in which Flores struggled with her family's negative reaction to her sexuality, the famed singer and lesbian, Chavela Vargas, became her surrogate parent.

In 1982, Claudia Hinojosa, a woman named Guadalupe, and two gay men ran for seats in the Mexican congress. Knowing they would not win, they nevertheless ran as out lesbian and gay candidates because they knew that their mere presence as out candidates would generate discussion and raise awareness. (American José Sarria had run for a seat on the San Francisco board of supervisors in 1961 as well, also knowing his presence would have some political effect.)

For the next fifteen years, Flores networked with both lesbian and cogender groups. The first Encuentro de Lesbianas took place in Cuernavaca, Morelos, in October of 1987, with more than two hundred women in attendance from Latin American countries and the United States. Prior to that conference, a national lesbian coordinating meeting took place with twelve Mexican lesbian and feminist organizations. In 1991, Flores stood as a candidate for the Revolutionary Workers Party along with Claudia Colimoro, a sex worker. Again, although knowing they would not win, they knew that their candidacy would raise awareness and energize sectors of the LGBTI movement in Mexico.

In 1997, Flores ran for a seat in the Mexican congress as a candidate for the Democratic Revolutionary Party. When her party won a certain percentage of the votes in Mexico City, they won the right to appoint a number of candidates to the congress, and Flores was selected. During her time as a *diputada* (deputy), Flores helped change the term "homosexuality" to "sexual practices" in regulations related to the corruption of minors in Article 201 of Mexico's penal code. She sponsored legislation to prohibit the media from revealing the names of victims of sexual crimes. She worked against hate crimes, violations of civil and human rights, and domestic violence. She worked on behalf of sexuality education and HIV-AIDS awareness and supported peace negotiations with the Zapatista rebels in Chiapas, Mexico. Lesbians and gays were invited to participate in the first Zapatista Conference (1994), where they presented various proposals.

In 2000, Enoé Uranga was elected to the legislative assembly of the capital city of Mexico and was appointed president of the human rights commission. She sponsored a *convivencia* (domestic partnership) law, which, although endorsed by diverse groups, was not acted upon by the Mexican congress.

In 2003, México Posible (M.P.), a new political party, sponsored four gay and lesbian candidates, including drag queen Glenda in Monterrey and transgender Amaranta (formerly Jorge) Gómez in Juchitán. Gómez, who helped to found México Posible, is also the recipient of a MacArthur Fellowship. Although M.P. candidates did not win, their candidacy raised awareness, especially in the provinces.

During her tenure in the assembly, Flores received criticism from lesbians who perceived her as being expedient, allying with gays or lesbians depending on what the situation required. The lesbian organization she helped to found, El Closet de Sor Juana, was criticized by some for not participating in the annual dyke marches. Yet the personable politician gathered enough support from a variety of sectors to be elected in 2006 as the first out lesbian or gay individual in the Mexican senate.

SIGNIFICANCE

Even in the face of opposition from the Roman Catholic Church, fundamentalists, and deep cultural prejudice, out LGBTI people in Mexico and other Latin American countries are beginning to run for political office. In 2001 in Argentina, Lohana Berkins (a male-to-female [MTF] transsexual), ran for a seat in congress. Two year later, Flavio Raspisari, Maria Rachid, and MTF transsexual Diana Sacavan also ran for office. In 2006, Susel Paredes, an out lesbian and a lawyer, and Belissa Andía, an MTF transsexual and a leader in the transgender movement in Peru, both ran for seats in the Peruvian congress.

—*Yolanda Retter*

FURTHER READING

Cimacnoticias. "Con Patria Jiménez la Diversidad Sexual Llega al Senado." http://www.cimacnoticias.com/ noticias/06feb/06020105.html.

Cuomo, Kerry Kennedy. Interview with Patria Jimenéz Flores. Speak Truth to Power. http://www.speak truth.org.

Díaz-Cotto, Juanita. Interview with Patria Jiménez. In *Compañeras: Latina Lesbians*, edited by Juanita Ramos. 3d ed. New York: Latina Lesbian History Project, 2004.

Walker, S. Lynn. "Transgender Candidate Roils México." June 29, 2003. http://www.signonsandiego.com/ news/mexico/20030629-9999_1n29mexelect.html.

SEE ALSO: Nov. 17, 1901: Police Arrest "Los 41" in Mexico City; 1912-1924: Robles Fights in the Mexican Revolution; Nov., 1965: Revolutionary Cuba Imprisons Gays; 1969: Nuestro Mundo Forms as First Queer Organization in Argentina; Oct. 14-17, 1987: Latin American and Caribbean Lesbian Feminist Network Is Formed; June 19, 2002: Gays and Lesbians March for Equal Rights in Mexico City; Apr., 2003: Buenos Aires Recognizes Same-Gender Civil Unions.

March 5, 2006
BROKEBACK MOUNTAIN, *CAPOTE*, AND *TRANSAMERICA* RECEIVE OSCARS

Pre-Oscar buzz dubbed 2005 the year of the queer, with LGBT-themed films screening in more mainstream venues than ever before. Movies such as Brokeback Mountain, Capote, *and* Transamerica *garnered multiple Oscar nominations and awards and also awards from other media and entertainment organizations.*

LOCALE: Los Angeles, California
CATEGORIES: Arts; cultural and intellectual history; organizations and institutions

KEY FIGURES
Philip Seymour Hoffman (b. 1967), American actor
Felicity Huffman (b. 1962), American actor
Ang Lee (b. 1954), Taiwanese director
Heath Ledger (b. 1979), Australian actor
Jake Gyllenhaal (b. 1980), American actor

SUMMARY OF EVENT
The year 2005 was heralded as a turning point for films featuring lesbian, gay, transgender, and bisexual stories. Sources that track box-office information, such as Box Office Mojo show that films with LGBT-related content played consistently at theaters throughout the year, and were major draws. Many of these films made the transition from art houses to suburban multiplexes, and several were nominated for various industry awards, such as the Golden Globes, Independent Spirit Awards, and, most notably, the Academy Awards, or Oscars.

As the Oscars approached, *Brokeback Mountain*, the most honored film of 2005—and definitely the most talked about—had already won several awards, including best picture from BAFTA (British Academy of Film and Television Arts), the Golden Globes (Hollywood Foreign Press Association), the New York Film Critics Circle, and the Satellite Awards (International Press Academy).

With eight Oscar nominations, *Brokeback Mountain* was considered a frontrunner for the Academy Award for Best Picture. The film, which centers on the long-term and, ultimately, tragic relationship between two Wyoming cowboys—played by Heath Ledger and Jake Gyllenhaal—spurred much controversy and discussion over its subject matter. Conservatives disapproved of the gay relationship between the two main characters, while LGBT groups criticized the film's marketing, which omitted gay references, and its lack of LGBT people in production and performing roles. However, many

Poster for TransAmerica (2005).

Brokeback Mountain, Capote, and Transamerica Receive Oscars

Taiwanese director Ang Lee (center), who won the Academy Award for directing Brokeback Mountain, *visits Tainen, Taiwan, in April, 2006. Lee is the first Asian to win the Oscar best-director award.* (AP/Wide World Photos)

other filmgoers commented on the universality of the motion picture. The uproar over the film, plus its many nominations and awards, generated widespread interest, which went from a modest opening in only five theaters to its wider release in more than two thousand theaters. To the surprise and chagrin of many, *Brokeback Mountain* lost the Best Picture Oscar to *Crash* but won in three other categories: Best Director (Ang Lee); Best Adapted Screenplay (Larry McMurtry and Diana Ossana); and Best Original Score (Gustavo Santaolalla).

Another critically acclaimed film, *Capote*, was nominated for five Academy Awards, including Best Picture. A biographical film (biopic) about gay American journalist and writer Truman Capote, played by Philip Seymour Hoffman, the story focuses on Capote's research for his "nonfiction novel" *In Cold Blood: A True Account of a Multiple Murder and Its Consequences* (1965). Hoffman had been recognized for his work as Capote by BAFTA, the Golden Globes, the Independent Spirit Awards, and the Screen Actors Guild among others, and he continued his winning spree by receiving the best actor Oscar for his amazing performance. Hoffman's award was the only Oscar that *Capote* received. Many noticed, however, that Hoffman did not acknowledge Capote in his acceptance speech.

Transamerica, starring Felicity Huffman, who also has a lead role in the popular television series *Desperate Housewives*, earned two Academy Award nominations. Huffman, as a male-to-female (MTF) preoperative transsexual, earned critical praise and many best actress awards, including a Golden Globe, an Independent Spirit, an award from the National Board of Review, and an award from the International Press Academy; the Oscar, however, went to Reese Witherspoon, who one the award for *Walk the Line*.

Other Oscar-nominated films with LGBT characters included *The Constant Gardener* and *Mrs. Henderson Presents*, bringing the total number of Academy Award nominations for LGBT-related films to twenty-one. Other motion pictures released in the United States in 2005 with LGBT-related themes or characters include (from the United States) *D.E.B.S., Dorian Blues, The Dying Gaul, Eating Out, The Family Stone, Happy Endings, Heights, Loggerheads, Mysterious Skin, Rent, Saving Face,* and *Kiss Kiss, Bang Bang*; from the United Kingdom came *Breakfast on Pluto, Imagine Me and You,* and *My Summer of Love.* France offered the films *Crustacés et coquillages* (*Cote d'Azur*, U.S. title) and *Le Clan* (*Three Dancing Slaves*, U.S. title), India produced *My Brother Nikhil*, Israel offered *Lalehet al hamayim* (*Walk on Water*), and Thailand had *Sud Pralad*

(*Tropical Malady*, U.S. title) and *Beautiful Boxer*.

Although LGBT-themed films became more mainstream, starring roles continued to go to straight actors, or to actors believed to be straight. Neither of the Academy Award-nominated actors or actresses of the films discussed above was an out LGBT person during the productions or screenings of the films. No major Hollywood actors have come out at the height of their fame; rather, many LGBT actors chose to remain in the closet for fear of compromising their careers, a situation that scholar Larry Gross characterizes as "an unmistakable tinge of minstrelsy . . . when gay actors are locked into the closet by their own ambitions and the paranoia of the industry, and audiences must be firmly assured of the heterosexual credentials of those playing gay for pay."

Significance

Films with a lesbian, gay, bisexual, and transgender or transsexual focus and characters have had wider distribution and have received more critical accolades and awards. While many of these films were, and will be, independently produced, their success will likely encourage more major studios to produce and finance similar projects.

—*Ellen Greenblatt*

Further Reading

Academy of Motion Picture Arts and Sciences. http://www.oscars.org.

Gay and Lesbian Alliance Against Defamation. "And the Award Goes to. . . ." http://www.glaad.org/eye/nominees.php.

_____. *"Brokeback Mountain" Resource Guide*. http://www.glaad.org/eye/brokeback_mountain.php.

_____. *CineQueer: GLAAD's 2005 Guide to What's LGBT in Film*. http://www.glaad.org/eye/cinequeer.php.

Gross, Larry. "Year of the Queer: Hollywood and Homosexuality." http://www.truthdig.com/dig/.

Holleran, Andrew. "The Magic Mountain." *Gay and Lesbian Review Worldwide*, March/April, 2006. A review of *Brokeback Mountain*.

Scott, A. O. "A Complex Metamorphosis of the Most Fundamental Sort." *The New York Times*, December 2, 2005. A review of *Transamerica*.

Taylor, Ella. "Chameleon." *LA Weekly*, September 29, 2005. A review of Capote.

See also: 1930's-1960's: Hollywood Bans "Sexual Perversion" in Films; Mar. 7, 1967: CBS Airs *CBS Reports: The Homosexuals*; 1979-1981: First Gay British Television Series Airs; 1985: GLAAD Begins Monitoring Media Coverage of Gays and Lesbians; 1985: Lesbian Film *Desert Hearts* Is Released; July 25, 1985: Actor Hudson Announces He Has AIDS; 1988: *Macho Dancer* Is Released in the Philippines; 1992-2002: Celebrity Lesbians Come Out; Mar. 21, 2000: Hollywood Awards Transgender Portrayals in Film; Sept. 7, 2001: First Gay and Lesbian Television Network Is Launched in Canada.

BIBLIOGRAPHY

GENERAL REFERENCE

Adam, Barry. *The Rise of the Gay and Lesbian Movement.* 1987. Reprint. New York: Twayne, 1995. Detailed overview of how gays and lesbians organized in the last half of the twentieth century to press for their civil rights.

Bagemihl, Bruce. *Biological Exuberance: Animal Homosexuality and Natural Diversity.* New York: St. Martin's Press, 1998. Examination of many species in which homosexual behavior is apparent.

Chauncey, George. *Gay New York: Gender, Urban Culture, and the Makings of the Gay Male World, 1890-1940.* New York: Basic Books, 1994. Sociological survey of the gay subculture in New York City over a half century.

Clendinen, Dudley, and Adam Nagourney. *Out for Good: The Struggle to Build a Gay Rights Movement in America.* New York: Simon & Schuster, 1999. Account of demands for lesbian and gay rights in protests such as the Stonewall Rebellion of 1969.

D'Emilio, John. *The World Turned: Essays on Gay History, Politics, and Culture.* Durham, N.C.: Duke University Press, 2002. Exploration of the social, political, and cultural contributions of gays and lesbians.

Dynes, Wayne R., ed. *Encyclopedia of Homosexuality.* New York: Garland, 1990. This two-volume encyclopedia, now out-of-print and somewhat dated, is available in many library collections.

Ericksen, Julia A., and Sally A. Steffen. *Kiss and Tell: Surveying Sex in the Twentieth Century.* Cambridge, Mass.: Harvard University Press, 1999. Brilliant overview of sexual mores in the twentieth century.

Herman, Didi. *The Antigay Agenda.* Chicago: University of Chicago Press, 1997. Survey of the arguments leveled against homosexuality by various groups, including politicians and clergymen, many of whom consider homosexuality pathological.

Katz, Jonathan Ned. *Gay American History: Lesbians and Gay Men in the U.S.A., a Documentary History.* Rev. ed. New York: Plume, 1992. Publication of these primary documents established gays and lesbians within the country's history and stimulated the growth of gay and lesbian historical research and the growth of gay and lesbian archives.

Marcus, Eric. *Making Gay History: The Half Century Fight for Gay and Lesbian Equal Rights.* New York: HarperCollins, 2002. Overview of the growth of the gay and lesbian movement during the second half of the twentieth century.

Roughgarden, Joan. *Evolution's Rainbow: Diversity, Gender, and Sexuality in Nature and People.* Berkeley: University of California Press, 2004. Demonstrates the universality of homosexuality in nature.

Stein, Marc, ed. *Encyclopedia of Lesbian, Gay, Bisexual, and Transgender History in America.* New York: Charles Scribner's Sons, 2004. Three-volume encyclopedia covering LGBT lives, issues, and experiences in the United States.

AGING

Adelman, Jeanne, et al., eds. *Lambda Gray: A Practical, Emotional, and Spiritual Guide for Gays and Lesbians Who Are Growing Older.* North Hollywood, Calif.: Newcastle, 1993. Helpful handbook for gays and lesbians approaching old age.

Berger, Raymond M. *Gay and Gray: The Older Homosexual Man.* Urbana: University of Illinois Press, 1982. Considers older gay men from a broad range of socioeconomic backgrounds. Presents detailed case studies.

Clunis, D. Merilee, et al. *Lives of Lesbian Elders: Looking Back, Looking Forward.* New York: Haworth Press, 2005. Oral history of sixty-two lesbian women in the Western United States between the ages of fifty-five and ninety-five.

MacDonald, Barbara. *Look Me in the Eye: Old Women, Aging, and Ageism.* San Francisco, Calif.: Spinsters Ink, 1983. Sensitive consideration of the status of women, many of them lesbians, as they age in American society. Focuses especially on those who face old age without conventional family ties.

ARTS

Clum, John. *Acting Gay: Male Homosexuality in Modern Drama*. New York: Columbia University Press, 1992. Valuable resource on gay sexuality depicted in drama during the last decades of the twentieth century.

Laufe, Abe. *The Wicked Stage: A History of Theater Censorship and Harassment in the United States*. New York: F. Ungar, 1978. Considers many aspects of censorship, including the repression of gay and lesbian themes and allusions by regulators of the entertainment industry.

Wallis, Brian, Marianne Weems, and Philip Yenawine, eds. *Art Matters: How the Culture Wars Changed America*. New York: New York University Press, 1999. Section two deals specifically with HIV-AIDS. In section four, "Homophobia at the N.E.A." is of special interest.

Wolverton, Terry. *Insurgent Muse: Life and Art at the Woman's Building*. San Francisco, Calif.: City Lights, 2002. History of the feminist artists and lesbian artists, and their work, at the Woman's Building, a now-defunct community of artists in Los Angeles.

CITIZENSHIP AND IMMIGRATION

Luibheid, Eithne. *Entry Denied: Controlling Sexuality at the Border*. Minneapolis: University of Minnesota Press, 2002. Emphasizes attempts to "control" sexuality by stopping gays and lesbians along national borders.

Phelan, Shane. *Sexual Strangers: Gays, Lesbians, and the Dilemmas of Citizenship*. Philadelphia: Temple University Press, 2001. Consideration of inhospitable immigration regulations aimed at discouraging gay and lesbian immigration.

ECONOMICS

Bernbach, Jeffrey M. *Job Discrimination II: How to Fight, How to Win*. Englewood Cliffs, N.J.: Voir Dire Press, 1998. Outlines how gays and lesbians can ensure and protect their rights in the workplace.

Friedman, Mack. *Strapped for Cash: A History of American Hustler Culture*. Los Angeles: Alyson, 2003. Deals forthrightly with the motivations, largely economic, that lead young men, many of them heterosexual, into offering sex for money.

Gluckman, Amy, and Betsy Reed, eds. *Homo Economics: Capitalism, Community, and Lesbian and Gay Life*. New York: Routledge, 1997. Detailed study of lesbians and gays as consumers and a look at how GLBT culture is used as a model for marketing.

McNaught, Brian. *Gay Issues in the Workplace*. New York: St. Martin's Press, 1993. Assesses difficulties facing gays and lesbians in the workplace.

Penelope, Julia, ed. *Out of the Class Closet: Lesbians Speak*. Freedom, Calif.: Crossing Press, 1994. A collection of writings examining the personal effects of lesbian sexuality, class, and economics.

Raeburn, Nicole C. *Changing Corporate America from Inside Out: Lesbian and Gay Workplace Rights*. Minneapolis: University of Minnesota Press, 2004. Considers how American corporations have become more accepting of gays and lesbians and of what rights lesbians and gays have won in corporate America.

FAMILY

Drucker, Jane. *Lesbian and Gay Families Speak Out: Understanding the Joys and Challenges of Diverse Family Life*. Oxford, England: Perseus, 2001. Suggests ways to overcome the pitfalls society often imposes on lesbian and gay families.

Fairchild, Betty. *Now That You Know: A Parents' Guide to Understanding Their Gay and Lesbian Children*. New York: Harcourt Brace Jovanovich, 1979. Suggests how parents of gay and lesbian children can address their own feelings and prejudices regarding sexual orientation.

Griffin, Carolyn W., and Marian J. Wirth. *Beyond Acceptance: Parents of Lesbians and Gays Talk About Their Experiences*. New York: St. Martin's Press, 1997. Largely an account from parents of gays and lesbians who reveal how they have faced their children's sexuality.

FEMINISM

Berry, Mary Frances. *Why ERA Failed: Politics, Women's Rights, and the Amending Process of the Constitution*. Bloomington: Indiana University Press, 1986. Survey of the dynamics of attempting to pass the Equal Rights Amendment.

Crow, Barbara A., ed. *Radical Feminism: A Documentary Reader*. New York: New York University Press, 2000. Comprehensive collection of classic primary source documents examining the history of radical feminism.

Edwards, Tim. *Erotics and Politics: Gay Male Sexuality, Masculinity, and Feminism*. New York: Routledge, 1994. A study of the collaborative but also antagonistic relationship between feminism and gay male sexuality and masculinity.

Faderman, Lillian. *Surpassing the Love of Men: Romantic Friendship Between Women from the Renaissance to the Present*. New York: William Morrow, 1981. History of "romantic friendships" between women during a four hundred year period.

―――. *To Believe in Women: What Lesbians Have Done for America—A History*. Boston: Houghton Mifflin, 1999. Considers the suffrage movement and how lesbians helped women win the vote, make gains in education, and helped women enter the professions. Includes a fine chapter on how Emily Blackwell became the first female physician.

Jay, Karla. *Tales of the Lavender Menace: A Memoir of Liberation*. New York: Basic Books, 1999. Personal exploration of the critical import of lesbians—the "lavender menace"—to the women's movement of the late 1960's and the 1970's.

Reinfelder, Monika, ed. *Amazon to Zami: Towards a Global Lesbian Feminism*. New York: Cassell, 1996. Examines lesbian feminism from a global perspective.

Thompson, Becky. "Multiracial Feminism: Recasting the Chronology of Second Wave Feminism." *Feminist Studies* 28, no. 2 (2002). Oft-cited journal article on the contributions of "multiracial feminism" within the feminist movement in general.

GOVERNMENT AND POLITICS

Heger, Heinz. *The Men with the Pink Triangle: The True, Life-and-Death Story of Homosexuals in the Nazi Death Camps*. Translated by David Fernbach. Rev. ed. Boston: Alyson, 1994. Chilling account of the internment of gays in Nazi Germany from 1933 until the end of World War II in 1945.

Hertzog, Mark. *The Lavender Vote: Lesbians, Gay Men, and Bisexuals in American Electoral Politics*. New York: New York University Press, 1996. Argues that America's gay and lesbian population is a potent political force that can, when organized, tilt the electoral balance in close political races.

Johnson, David K. *The Lavender Scare: The Cold War Persecution of Gays and Lesbians in the Federal Government*. Chicago: University of Chicago Press, 2004. Thorough assessment of the witch-hunts of the Cold War period, a time when many gays and lesbians were dismissed from their jobs and blacklisted in part because they were considered subject to blackmail and because many people mistakenly associated being gay or lesbian with being communist.

Rayside, David Morton. *On the Fringe: Gays and Lesbians in Politics*. Ithaca, N.Y.: Cornell University Press, 1998. Assessment of the potential for lesbians and gays to exercise considerable political clout.

HIV-AIDS

Andriote, John-Manuel. *Victory Deferred: How AIDS Changed Gay Life in America*. Chicago: University of Chicago Press, 1999. Sociological consideration of the effects of the HIV-AIDS epidemic on the gay community.

Crimp, Douglas, ed. *Melancholia and Moralism: Essays on AIDS and Queer Politics*. Cambridge, Mass.: MIT Press, 2002. Valuable account of how questions of morality and religious prohibitions against gay sex affect how society has addressed HIV-AIDS.

Gostin, Lawrence O., and Michael Kirby. *The AIDS Pandemic: Complacency, Injustice, and Unfulfilled Expectations*. Chapel Hill: University of

North Carolina Press, 2004. Overall assessment of the treatment of HIV-AIDS in the United States and of a discouraging public indifference to the disease.

Shilts, Randy. *And the Band Played On: Politics, People, and the AIDS Epidemic.* New York: St. Martin's Press, 1987. Excellent account of the AIDS epidemic in the 1980's.

Laws, Acts, and Legal History

Ball, Howard. *The Supreme Court in the Intimate Lives of Americans: Birth, Sex, Marriage, Childbearing, and Death.* New York: New York University Press, 2002. Review of U.S. Supreme Court cases concerning issues of sexuality.

D'Emilio, John, William B. Turner, and Urvashi Vaid, eds. *Creating Change: Sexuality, Public Policy, and Civil Rights.* New York: St. Martin's Press, 2002. Discusses public policy regarding matters of sexuality in the last half of the twentieth century.

Koppleman, Andrew. *The Gay Rights Question in Contemporary American Law.* Chicago: University of Chicago Press, 2002. Thorough investigation of the legal rights of gays and lesbians and how constitutional provisions guarantee their civil liberties.

Murdoch, Joyce, and Deb Price. *Courting Justice: Gay Men and Lesbians v. the Supreme Court.* New York: Basic Books, 2001. Examines the history of the U.S. Supreme Court on issues concerning lesbians and gays.

Pinello, Daniel R. *Gay Rights and American Law.* New York: Cambridge University Press, 2003. Extensive overview of the legal status of lesbians and gays in U.S. society.

Literature

Faderman, Lillian, ed. and comp. *Chloe Plus Olivia: An Anthology of Lesbian Literature from the Seventeenth Century to the Present.* New York: Penguin Books, 1995. Huge collection on all aspects of lesbian literature, including romantic friendships, coded works, lesbian feminism, gender, and more.

Levin, James. *The Gay Novel in America.* New York: Garland, 1991. Considers gay novels in the United States from the mid-1950's until the late 1970's.

Miller, Meredith. *Historical Dictionary of Lesbian Literature.* Lanham, Md.: Scarecrow Press, 2006. Includes several hundred cross-referenced articles on lesbian and woman-identified writers, with entries on literary movements, styles, themes, and more.

Pernal, Mary. *Explorations in Contemporary Feminist Literature: The Battle Against Oppression for Writers of Color, Lesbian, and Transgender Communities.* New York: P. Lang, 2002. Examines the state of lesbian, transgender, and racial and ethnic minority writers within feminist literature.

Robinson, Paul. *Gay Lives: Homosexual Autobiography from John Addington Symonds to Paul Monette.* Chicago: University of Chicago Press, 1999. Survey of notable gay literary figures writing about their own sexual orientation.

Summers, Claude J., ed. *Gay Fictions, Wilde to Stonewall: Studies in a Male Homosexual Literary Tradition.* New York: Continuum, 1990. Overview of gay literature that addresses homosexuality over nearly a century.

Marches, Protests, and Riots

Carter, David. *Stonewall: The Riots That Sparked the Gay Revolution.* New York: St. Martin's Press, 2004. Detailed presentation of how the 1969 Stonewall Rebellion marked a turning point in GLBT activism.

Duberman, Martin. *Stonewall.* New York: Dutton, 1991. Thorough study of the 1969 Stonewall Rebellion and its social, cultural, and political implications.

Pope, Lisa, et al. *One Million Strong: The 1993 March on Washington for Lesbian, Gay, and Bi Equal Rights.* New York: Alyson, 1993. Most-detailed account of the 1993 March on Washington.

Shepard, Benjamin, and Ronald Hayduk, eds. *From ACT UP to the WTO: Urban Protest and Community Building in the Era of Globalization.* New York: Verso, 2002. Anthology on the history of

ACT UP, exploring the group's "innovative use of civil rights era non-violent disobedience, media work and race and community building."

MARRIAGE

Baird, Robert M., and Stuart E. Rosenbaum, eds. *Same-sex Marriage: The Moral and Legal Debate.* 2d ed. Amherst, N.Y.: Prometheus Books, 2004. Comprehensive collection examining same-gender marriage from the perspectives of morality, law, legislation, and ethics. Includes personal stories, legal excerpts and analysis, and the U.S. government's position on the issue.

Bourassa, Kevin, and Joe Varnell. *Just Married: Gay Marriage and the Expansion of Human Rights.* Madison: University of Wisconsin Press, 2002. Written from a Canadian point of view, this study focuses on human rights and gays and lesbians.

Graff, E. J. *What Is Marriage For? The Strange Social History of Our Most Intimate Institution.* Boston: Beacon Press, 1999. Deals with all aspects of marriage and considers such matters as money, procreation, kinship, babies, and sex.

Hull, Kathleen E. *Same-sex Marriage: The Cultural Politics of Love and Law.* New York: Cambridge University Press, 2006. Examines same-gender marriage rights from the perspective of cultural politics.

Mello, Michael. *Legalizing Gay Marriage.* Philadelphia: Temple University Press, 2004. Assesses arguments in favor of and in opposition to same-gender marriage.

Moats, David. *Civil Wars: A Battle for Gay Marriage.* Orlando, Fla.: Harcourt, 2004. Examines recent developments in the move toward same-gender marriage.

Rauch, Jonathan. *Gay Marriage: Why It Is Good for Gays, Good for Straights, and Good for America.* New York: Times Books, 2004. Argues persuasively for same-gender marriage.

"Same-Sex Marriage: A Selective Bibliography of the Legal Literature." Law Library, Rutgers School of Law. http://law-library.rutgers.edu/system.html. A comprehensive collection on the issue of same-gender marriage around the world.

Wolfson, Evan. *Why Marriage Matters: America, Equality, and Gay People's Right to Marry.* New York: Simon & Schuster, 2004. Presents the argument for same-gender marriage under the equal protection clause of the U.S. Constitution.

MEDIA

Barrios, Richard. *Screened Out: Playing Gay in Hollywood, From Edison to Stonewall.* New York: Routledge, 2002. History of how overt gay elements were excluded from Hollywood films for the first six decades of the twentieth century.

Russo, Vito. *The Celluloid Closet: Homosexuality in the Movies.* Rev. ed. New York: Harper & Row, 1987. Classic account of how subtle homosexual allusions were smuggled into Hollywood films.

Tropiano, Stephen. *The Prime Time Closet: A History of Gays and Lesbians on TV.* New York: Applause Theatre & Cinema Books, 2002. Comprehensive account of the exclusion of lesbian and gay topics from television.

MILITARY

Bérubé, Allan. *Coming Out Under Fire: The History of Gay Men and Women in World War Two.* New York: Free Press, 1990. Explores the lives of gays and lesbians who served in the U.S. military during World War II.

Halley, Janet E. *Don't: A Reader's Guide to the Military's Anti-Gay Policy.* Durham, N.C.: Duke University Press, 1999. Discusses the roles President Bill Clinton and Congress played in dealing with the Don't Ask, Don't Tell legislation of the 1990's.

Shilts, Randy. *Conduct Unbecoming: Gays and Lesbians in the U.S. Military.* New York: Fawcett Columbine, 1994. Thorough account of the hazards gays and lesbians faced, and still face, in the military. Gays and lesbians, even long-term military personnel, often receive dishonorable discharges.

PSYCHOLOGY

Bayer, Ronald. *Homosexuality and American Psychiatry: The Politics of Diagnosis.* New York:

Basic Books, 1981. Classic on the politics of homosexuality and psychiatric practice and diagnosis in the United States.

Ellis, Havelock. *Sexual Inversion*. London: Wilson, 1897. A landmark study of homosexuality that considers it pathological. Important work for the discussion and further investigation that it sparked, most of which proved Ellis misguided in his conclusions.

Hegarty, Peter, and Cheryl Chase. "Intersex Activism, Feminism, and Psychology." In *Queer Theory*, edited by Iain Morland and Annabelle Willox. New York: Palgrave Macmillan, 2005. Study of the political partnership between intersex activists and feminists, and their social influence on the field of psychology.

Kinsey, Alfred C., Wardell B. Pomeroy, and Clyde E. Martin. *Sexual Behavior in the Human Female*. Oxford, England: Saunders, 1953. Monumental study of sex practices among a broad and representative range of women.

———. *Sexual Behavior in the Human Male*. Oxford, England: Saunders, 1948. Landmark study that helped spark the sexual revolution of future decades. Based on thousands of interviews with men from all walks of life. Chapter 21, "The Homosexual Outlet," is especially relevant.

RACE AND ETHNICITY

Eng, David L., and Alice Y. Hom, eds. *Q & A: Queer in Asian America*. Philadelphia: Temple University Press, 1998. Assessment of the generational and familial issues faced by queer Asian Americans.

Fenno, Richard F. *Going Home: Black Representatives and Their Constituents*. Chicago: University of Chicago Press, 2003. Examines the responsibilities of African American legislators in dealing with questions that are often at odds with their constituents' beliefs.

Lorde, Audre. *I Am Your Sister: Black Women Organizing Across Sexualities*. Freedom Organizing Pamphlet Series 3. New York: Kitchen Table: Women of Color Press, 1985. Examines lesbian sexuality and political movement in the black community.

Moraga, Cherríe L., and Gloria E. Anzaldúa, eds. *This Bridge Called My Back: Writings By Radical Women of Color*. 3d rev. and expanded ed. Berkeley, Calif.: Third Woman Press, 2002. Classic anthology of work by women and lesbians of color. Oft-used text in literature, women's studies, American studies, lesbian and gay studies, and in courses on race and ethnicity.

Wat, Eric C. *The Making of a Gay Asian Community: An Oral History of Pre-AIDS Los Angeles*. New York: Rowman & Littlefield, 2002. Sociological examination of the development of a gay Asian community in Los Angeles.

RELIGION

Bull, Chris, and John Gallagher. *Perfect Enemies: The Religious Right, the Gay Movement, and Militant Homosexuality*. New York: Crown, 1996. An assessment of the prejudices the Religious Right harbors against homosexuality and of the clash of values.

Harding, Susan Friend. *The Book of Jerry Falwell: Fundamentalist Language and Politics*. Princeton, N.J.: Princeton University Press, 2000. Of special interest is chapter 6, "The Moral Majority Jeremiad."

McNeill, John J. *The Church and the Homosexual*. Boston: Beacon Press, 1993. Considers how mainstream religion often shunned homosexuality, leading to the formation of such gay- and lesbian-friendly churches as the Metropolitan Community Church.

Perry, Troy D. *Don't Be Afraid Anymore: The Story of the Rev. Troy Perry and the Metropolitan Community Churches*. New York: St. Martin's Press, 1990. First-person account of how MCC founder, the Reverend Troy Perry, dealt with his own homosexuality, how he ministered to other gays and lesbians, and how he established gay-friendly churches throughout the United States.

Richards, David A. J. *Identity and the Case for Gay Rights: Race, Gender, Religion as Analogies*. Chicago: University of Chicago Press, 1999. Examines sexual orientation as an aspect of human existence that, like race and gender, is protected as a civil right.

Righter, Walter C. *A Pilgrim's Way: The Personal Story of the Episcopal Bishop Charged with Heresy for Ordaining a Gay Man Who Was in a Committed Relationship.* New York: Random House, 1998. An account of the fallout caused by Righter's decision to ordain a gay man.

Schmitt, Arno, and Johoeda Safer. *Sexuality and Eroticism Among Males in Moslem Societies.* New York: Haworth Press, 1991. Despite the sexual restrictions in Islamic societies—and in many cases because of them—homosexuality, while condemned in the Islamic world, is not absent from it.

Shneer, David, and Caryn Aviv, eds. *Queer Jews.* New York: Routledge, 2002. Collection of accounts of how practicing Jews deal with their own homosexuality.

Spong, Shelby S. *Why Christianity Must Change or Die: A Bishop Speaks to Believers in Exile.* San Francisco, Calif.: HarperCollins, 1998. A rational argument for the church's need to accept gays and lesbians both as members and as clergy.

SPORTS

Griffin, Pat. *Strong Women, Deep Closets: Lesbians and Homophobia in Sport.* Champaign, Ill.: Human Kinetics, 1998. Comprehensive analysis—with oral interviews of lesbian athletes, coaches, and sports administrators—of lesbians, sports, and the prevailing issue of homophobia and stereotyping.

Kopay, David, and Perry Deane Young. *The David Kopay Story: An Extraordinary Self-Revelation.* New York: Arbor House, 1977. After a ten-year NFL career, Kopay became the first prominent male professional athlete to come out publically.

Louganis, Greg, and Eric Marcus. *Breaking the Surface.* New York: Random House, 1995. Self-portrait of the Olympic gold-medal-winning diver who achieved happiness after coming out as HIV-positive and gay.

Navratilova, Martina, with George Vecsey. *Martina.* New York: Knopf, 1985. Account of how tennis champion Martina Navratilova came out as a lesbian and a lesbian athlete.

Richards, Renee, with John Ames. *Second Serve: The Renee Richards Story.* New York: Stein & Day, 1983. Biography of Renee Richards, who continued to play championship tennis and practice medicine following gender-reassignment surgery in 1975.

Tuaola, Esera, and John Rosengren. *Alone in the Trenches: My Life as a Gay Man in the NFL.* Naperville, Ill.: Sourcebooks, 2006. First-person account of Tuaola's nine-year NFL career and his fear of being outed as gay.

Young, Perry Deane, and Martin Duberman, general ed. *Lesbians and Gays and Sports.* New York: Chelsea House, 1995. Concise study of gays and lesbians in the world of sports, including tennis, football, baseball, and the Olympics.

TRANSGENDER/TRANSSEXUALITY

Benjamin, Harry. *The Transsexual Phenomenon.* New York: Julian Press, 1966. Also available online at http://www.symposion.com/ijt/benjamin/. A groundbreaking and now-classic work in the field of transgender and transsexual studies.

Califia, Patrick. *Sex Changes: The Politics of Transgenderism.* 2d ed. San Francisco, Calif.: Cleis Press, 2003. A politically radical perspective on transgender life, written by a female-to-male transgender activist.

Devor, Holly. *FTM: Female to Male Transsexuals in Society.* Bloomington: Indiana University Press, 1997. Particularly useful are chapter 4, "Family Scenes," chapter 10, "Crisis at Puberty," and chapter 20, for its coming-out stories.

Ekins, Richard, and David King, eds. *Blending Genders: Social Aspects of Cross-Dressing and Sex-Changing.* New York: Routledge, 1996. Fifteen selections by thirteen contributors on cross-dressing and transsexuality. Of particular interest is chapter 15, a controversial work called "The Politics of Transgenderism," by Janice Raymond.

Feinberg, Leslie. *Transgender Warriors: Making History from Joan of Arc to RuPaul.* Boston: Beacon Press, 1996. Two especially interesting chapters examine the "holy war" against trans people and the transgender movement "From Germany to Stonewall."

Halberstam, Judith. *Female Masculinity*. Durham, N.C.: Duke University Press, 1998. Readable and imaginative academic account of female masculinity, with chapters on "Looking Butch," "Drag Kings," and "Raging Bull (Dykes)."

Meyerwitz, Joanne. *How Sex Changed: A History of Transsexuality in the United States*. Cambridge, Mass.: Harvard University Press, 2002. Chapter 2 explores Christine Jorgensen's gender-reassignment. Chapter 5, on the sexual revolution, is especially relevant.

—*R. Baird Shuman*

Electronic Resources

Web Sites

The Web sites listed below were visited by the editors of Salem Press in Spring, 2006. Because URL's frequently change, the accuracy of these addresses and sites cannot be guaranteed. However, long-standing sites—such as those of university departments, national organizations, and government agencies—generally maintain links when sites move or upgrade.

General

365Gay
http://www.365gay.com

Colorful and packed with information, *365Gay* is a gay- and lesbian-focused daily, online newspaper. It offers news, entertainment stories, lifestyle and travel sections, and an opinion section with letters to the editor. The site's "Fun Zone" includes standard newspaper staples such as comic strips, horoscopes, and crossword puzzles. Like many sites, *365Gay* also offers a discussion forum.

Bisexual Resource Center
http://www.biresource.org

While the parent organization of this site is physically based in Boston, Massachusetts, its Web site is meant to be a global presence. Offers links that direct visitors to articles on bisexuality, conferences and events calendars, and resources from books and newsletters to merchandise and mail order.

GayCanada
http://www.gaycanada.com

This Canadian Gay, Lesbian & Bisexual Resource Directory is a comprehensive source for GLBT information across Canada. In addition to offering directory information for GLBT travel, community, and professional services, the site posts links to *yahoo.ca* articles on GLBT topics and offers discussion groups and message boards.

Gayscape
http://www.gayscape.com

A search engine that limits its listings to sites of gay, lesbian, and bisexual interests. There is a quick search feature where visitors can enter their own word or choose a search by location in the United States, browse by country, or browse by a lengthy list of topics and subcategories.

glbtq: An Encyclopedia of Gay, Lesbian, Bisexual, Transgender, and Queer Culture
http://www.glbtq.com

A Web site in an encyclopedia format with essays on various GLBT subjects, including arts and entertainment, history, literature, and social issues. Discussion boards are also provided but require membership, which is free, in order to post.

Pridenet
http://www.pridenet.com

This site serves as a virtual yellow pages to GLBT communities around the world. Visitors can search the site geographically or by subject. Advertisers include both GLBT owned and operated as well as gay-friendly establishments and services. This is a no-frills site with category links that lead to advertising and also to specific sites.

Arts

GALA Choruses: The Gay and Lesbian Association of Choruses
http://www.galachoruses.org

Provides information and support to the one hundred-plus choruses in the organization. Also includes listings of GLBT choruses worldwide and of upcoming GALA and individual chorus events.

Lambda Literary Foundation
http://www.lambdaliterary.org

The Lambda Literary Foundation celebrates LGBT literature through its annual Lambda Literary Awards, highlighted on the foundation's Web site. This site includes a "guidelines" page for nominations and lists past winners.

CIVIL RIGHTS

Human Rights Campaign
http://www.hrc.org

This site contains numerous pages for LGBT advocacy in areas such as marriage, the workplace, religion, and state and federal politics. It offers articles on current news stories and links to local and national Human Rights Campaign events.

International Gay and Lesbian Human Rights Commission
http://www.iglhrc.org

The IGLHRC was established to respond to human rights violations around the world. This site offers a clear, concise summary of the mission of the IGLHRC. Well organized and designed, the home page lists the most recent press releases of the organization and also provides links to areas such as the history and mission statement of the commission, information on political asylum, and regional action alerts and news stories, which visitors may select by country.

International Lesbian and Gay Association
http://www.ilga.org

The International Lesbian and Gay Association works to achieve equal rights worldwide for lesbian, gay, bisexual, and transgender persons. The Web site contains links to press releases, information on GLBT-related world events, and a small library of past articles on many subjects. The site can be viewed in several languages, including English, French, and Spanish.

National Gay and Lesbian Task Force
http://www.thetaskforce.org

This site of the first national LGBT civil rights and advocacy organization—the National Gay and Lesbian Task Force—offers an extensive history of the organization. There are also links to information on various political activities such as state ballot measures, fund-raising, and facts on political candidates.

CULTURAL AND INTELLECTUAL HISTORY

Canadian Lesbian & Gay Archives
http://www.clga.ca

This Web site is extremely organized and uncluttered by fancy images and flashy special effects. The home page gives a clear listing of site contents, the most informative of which is the link about the organization itself. It is further divided into the history of the archives, more than six years worth of press releases, and instructions on how to donate material. Halfway down the listing of site contents there is a link to archive materials available online through this and other sites. This section also provides links to essays, news articles, biographies, and publication reviews.

GLBT Historical Society
http://www.glbthistory.org

This site provides information about the GLBT Historical Society (GLBTHS), its history, its physical location in San Francisco and its hours of operation, and its plans to build a museum dedicated to GLBT history and culture. An informative link is included to *CatalogQ*, a comprehensive source on GLBT periodicals that is searchable by multiple criteria and contains information about the holdings of the GLBTHS; the ONE Institute and Archives in Los Angeles; the San Francisco Public Library; the June L. Mazer Lesbian Archives in West Hollywood; the Lavender Library, Archives and Cultural Exchange in Sacramento; and the Transgender Periodicals Collection at California State University, Northridge.

GOVERNMENT AND POLITICS

Log Cabin Republicans
http://online.logcabin.org

The home page of the Log Cabin Republicans features major news, links to additional news releases, and a "reading room" for other news sources. The site includes a history of the organization, contact information for its various chapters across the country, a nationwide calendar of events, and a video library where visitors may download and view a variety of political speeches.

National Stonewall Democrats
http://www.stonewalldemocrats.org

The home page of the National Stonewall Democrats has a simple yet colorful format. Visitors must click on the one featured news story on the front page or click on an unassuming link to the side of the page to reach an additional link to the previous years' news releases. Also includes links to speeches, opinion pieces, and chapters around the country.

LAWS, ACTS, AND LEGAL HISTORY

Lambda Legal
http://www.lambdalegal.org

Achieving GLBT civil rights through litigation, education, and public policy, Lambda Legal's Web site offers links to current as well as historic court cases that have impacted the LGBT community. There is also a "Help Desk" feature, which provides legal information regarding discrimination based on sexual orientation, gender identity, or HIV-AIDS status.

MARCHES, PROTESTS, AND RIOTS

International Association of Lesbian, Gay, Bisexual and Transgender Pride Coordinators
http://www.interpride.org

This site provides links to the organization's mission statement and history, the benefits of having a city's local pride organization become a member of this coordinating organization, and a calendar of pride events throughout the world.

Stonewall Veterans Association
http://www.stonewallvets.org

Stonewall Veterans was formed as an educational organization concerned with the history of the Stonewall Rebellion in New York City in June, 1969. In addition to its archiving goals, the group also provides more immediate resources for veterans of the rebellion who need food, clothing, or shelter. The Web site includes an enormous collection of images of ephemera and photographs from the Stonewall era and later.

ORGANIZATIONS AND INSTITUTIONS

Gay and Lesbian Alliance Against Defamation
http://www.glaad.org

This site offers a history of the organization as well as links to various campaigns, past and present, that have focused and continue to focus attention on the fair and accurate media representation of LGBT persons.

Parents, Families and Friends of Lesbians and Gays
http://www.pflag.org

PFLAG is a support network for the families and friends of gays and lesbians. The Web site includes a Frequently Asked Questions link for those who need information about what to do when family members or friends come out. There is also an extensive page on the structure of PFLAG, including finding a chapter at the national or international level.

Servicemembers Legal Defense Network
http://www.sldn.org

SLDN offers legal services and is a watchdog and policy group focusing on discrimination against lesbians and gays in the military. Its Web site includes an extensive "law library," a blog called "Frontlines," a Don't Ask, Don't Tell "Survival Guide," and an online petition to government representatives.

PUBLICATIONS

Advocate.com
http://www.advocate.com

This award-winning news site is packed with news stories, pop-culture features, arts and entertainment reviews, and a lengthy nationwide events calendar of interest to the LGBT community. Separate from its newsstand counterpart, *The Advocate*, *Advocate.com* offers exclusive online articles and commentaries not found in the print version. There is, however, a separate page where visitors can locate print issues from the past three years and view the full text of the cover stories of past issues.

Sports

Federation of Gay Games
http://www.gaygames.com

The Federation of Gay Games is "Built upon the principles of Participation, Inclusion and Personal Best." The organization's Web site offers extensive information about the 2006 Gay Games in Chicago, Illinois, as well as articles on individual athletes and the history of the games.

Gay and Lesbian International Sport Association
http://www.glisa.org

The home page for this multisport governing body is pleasant but primarily consists of a list of press releases. A separate page discusses the first World Outgames, held in Montreal, Canada in the summer of 2006. The site has an extensive list of participating members of GLISA, organized by continental regions, with brief descriptions and links to the members' own Web sites.

Gaysports
http://www.gaysports.com

Designed as the "preferred destination online for gay and lesbian sports enthusiasts worldwide," this Web site is all inclusive. It includes feature articles on a variety of sports, indoor and outdoor activities, fitness, and recreation. Registering as a member, which is free, allows visitors to browse the profiles of other members, participate in discussion forums, and post classified advertisements.

International Gay and Lesbian Aquatics
http://www.igla.org

IGLA promotes the participation of gays and lesbians in aquatic sports. Its Web site offers a calendar of aquatic sporting events from around the world, a listing of water sports teams, such as swim teams and water polo teams, and subscription lists of offsite discussion groups.

Outsports
http://www.outsports.com

This is an informative site filled with sports articles, both contemporary and historical, dealing with GLBT issues and personalities. The site also includes photo galleries, fitness tips, and discussion boards. A separate feature contains a variety of information on specific sports and sporting events such as baseball, tennis, and the 2002 and 2006 Gay Games.

Transgender/Transsexuality

Gender Public Advocacy Coalition
http://www.gpac.org

The Gender Public Advocacy Coalition, or GenderPAC, works to end workplace, classroom, and community-based discrimination and violence directed at people with alternative or nonconforming gender expressions. GenderPAC's Web site includes pages on "Workplace Fairness," "Violence Prevention," gender and youth, hate crimes, national news, and myths and facts.

GenderTalk
http://www.gendertalk.com

This site is the online home of Web radio broadcast GenderTalk, a weekly program for and about transgender persons. The site offers a link to the live Saturday evening broadcasts as well as an archive of past broadcasts available for download. There is also an extensive listing of resource links to other GLBT topics.

Susan's Place Transgender Resources
http://www.susans.org

A no-frills site, the home page is a directory of links to a variety of articles on transsexuality and lists the Web sites of transgender support groups, personal home pages, and businesses that are trans-friendly. The site also includes downloadable, free chat software.

—*Mark Miller*

Chronological List of Entries

1800's

July 19-20, 1848: Seneca Falls Women's Rights Convention
July 4, 1855: Whitman Publishes *Leaves of Grass*
Nov. 11, 1865: Mary Edwards Walker Is Awarded the Medal of Honor
Aug. 29, 1867: Karl Heinrich Ulrichs Speaks Publicly for Gay and Lesbian Rights
May 6, 1868: Kertbeny Coins the Terms "Homosexual" and "Heterosexual"
1869: Westphal Advocates Medical Treatment for Sexual Inversion
1885: United Kingdom Criminalizes "Gross Indecency"
Jan.-June, 1886: Two-Spirit American Indian Visits Washington, D.C.
Jan., 1892-July, 1892: Alice Mitchell Found Guilty of Murdering Her Lover
May 25, 1895: Oscar Wilde Is Convicted of Gross Indecency
1896: *Der Eigene* Is Published as First Journal on Homosexuality
1896: Raffalovich Publishes *Uranisme et Unisexualité*
1897: Ellis Publishes *Sexual Inversion*
May 14, 1897: Hirschfeld Founds the Scientific-Humanitarian Committee
c. 1899: Transgender Reporter Covers Spanish-American War Revolts

1900's, 1910's, 1920's

Nov. 17, 1901: Police Arrest "Los 41" in Mexico City
1903: Stein Writes *Q.E.D.*
1905: Freud Rejects Third-Sex Theory
1906: Friedlaender Breaks with the Scientific-Humanitarian Committee
1907-1909: The Eulenburg Affair Scandalizes Germany's Leadership
1908: Carpenter Publishes *The Intermediate Sex*
Oct., 1909: Barney Opens Her Paris Salon
1912-1924: Robles Fights in the Mexican Revolution
Mar. 15, 1919-1921: U.S. Navy Launches Sting Operation Against "Sexual Perverts"
Feb. 19, 1923: *The God of Vengeance* Opens on Broadway
1924: Gide Publishes the Signed Edition of *Corydon*
Dec. 10, 1924: Gerber Founds the Society for Human Rights
Feb., 1927: Wales Padlock Law Censors Risque Theater
1928: Hall Publishes *The Well of Loneliness*
1929: Davis's Research Identifies Lesbian Sexuality as Common and Normal
1929: *Pandora's Box* Opens

1930's

1930's-1960's: Hollywood Bans "Sexual Perversion" in Films

1933-1945: Nazis Persecute Homosexuals

June 30-July 1, 1934: Hitler's Night of the Long Knives

1939: Isherwood Publishes *Goodbye to Berlin*

Jan. 12, 1939: *Thompson v. Aldredge* Dismisses Sodomy Charges Against Lesbians

1940's

1947-1948: Golden Age of American Gay Literature

June, 1947-February, 1948: *Vice Versa* Is Published as First Lesbian Periodical

1948: Kinsey Publishes *Sexual Behavior in the Human Male*

1950's

1950: Mattachine Society Is Founded

Sept. 24, 1951: George Jorgensen Becomes Christine Jorgensen

1952: APA Classifies Homosexuality as a Mental Disorder

1952: ONE, Inc., Is Founded

1952-1990: U.S. Law Prohibits Gay and Lesbian Immigration

1953: Kinsey Publishes *Sexual Behavior in the Human Female*

1953: *ONE* Magazine Begins Publication

1953-1957: Evelyn Hooker Debunks Homosexuality as a "Sickness"

Apr. 27, 1953: U.S. President Eisenhower Prohibits Federal Employment of Lesbians and Gays

1955: Daughters of Bilitis Founded as First National Lesbian Group in United States

1956: Baldwin Publishes *Giovanni's Room*

1956: Foster Publishes *Sex Variant Women in Literature*

Jan. 1, 1957: United Kingdom's Sexual Offences Act Becomes Law

Sept. 4, 1957: The *Wolfenden Report* Calls for Decriminalizing Private Consensual Sex

Chronological List of Entries

1960's

May, 1960: First National Lesbian Conference Convenes
1961: Illinois Legalizes Consensual Homosexual Sex
1961: Sarria Is First Out Gay or Lesbian Candidate for Public Office
1963: Rechy Publishes *City of Night*
July 2-Aug. 28, 1963: Rustin Organizes the March on Washington
Nov., 1965: Revolutionary Cuba Imprisons Gays
Feb. 19-20, 1966: First North American Conference of Homophile Organizations Convenes
Aug., 1966: Queer Youth Fight Police Harassment at Compton's Cafeteria in San Francisco
Nov. 21, 1966: First Gender Identity Clinic Opens and Provides Gender Reassignment Surgery
1967: *Los Angeles Advocate* Begins Publication
Mar. 7, 1967: CBS Airs *CBS Reports: The Homosexuals*
Apr. 19, 1967: First Student Homophile League Is Formed
May 22, 1967: U.S. Supreme Court Upholds Law Preventing Immigration of Gays and Lesbians
July 27, 1967: United Kingdom Decriminalizes Homosexual Sex
Fall, 1967: Oscar Wilde Memorial Bookshop Opens as First Gay Bookstore
Aug. 11-18, 1968: NACHO Formally Becomes the First Gay Political Coalition
Oct. 6, 1968: Metropolitan Community Church Is Founded
1969: Nuestro Mundo Forms as First Queer Organization in Argentina
1969-1973: Gay Catholics Find Dignity
June 27-July 2, 1969: Stonewall Rebellion Ignites Modern Gay and Lesbian Rights Movement
July 31, 1969: Gay Liberation Front Is Formed
Aug. 26, 1969: Canada Decriminalizes Homosexual Acts
Oct. 31, 1969: *Time* Magazine Issues "The Homosexual in America"

1970's

1970: Amazon Bookstore Opens as First Feminist-Lesbian Book Shop
May 1, 1970: Lavender Menace Protests Homophobia in Women's Movement
May 1, 1970: Radicalesbians Issues "The Woman Identified Woman" Manifesto
June 28, 1970: First Lesbian and Gay Pride March in the United States
Nov. 28, 1970: Del Martin Quits Gay Liberation Movement
1971: Kameny Is First Out Candidate for U.S. Congress
1971: *Lesbian Tide* Publishes Its First Issue
Mar., 1971: Los Angeles Gay and Lesbian Center Is Founded
June, 1971: The Gay Book Award Debuts
Nov., 1971: *The Body Politic* Begins Publication
1972-1973: Local Governments Pass Antidiscrimination Laws
Mar., 1972-Mar., 1973: First Gay and Lesbian Synagogue in the United States Is Formed
Mar. 22, 1972-June 30, 1982: Equal Rights Amendment Fails State Ratification
June 25, 1972: First Out Gay Minister Is Ordained
Nov. 7, 1972: Jordan Becomes First Black Congresswoman from the South
1973: Brown Publishes *Rubyfruit Jungle*
1973: Naiad Press Is Founded
1973: National Gay Task Force Is Formed
1973: Olivia Records Is Founded

Jan. 22, 1973: *Roe v. Wade* Legalizes Abortion and Extends Privacy Rights
June 21, 1973: U.S. Supreme Court Supports Local Obscenity Laws
Aug., 1973: American Bar Association Calls for Repeal of Laws Against Consensual Sex
Fall, 1973: Lesbian Herstory Archives Is Founded
Oct. 18, 1973: Lambda Legal Authorized to Practice Law
Dec. 15, 1973: Homosexuality Is Delisted by APA
1974: Bisexual Forum Is Founded
1974: *The Front Runner* Makes *The New York Times* Best-Seller List
Mar. 5, 1974: Antigay and Antilesbian Organizations Begin to Form
June 27, 1974: Abzug and Koch Attempt to Amend the Civil Rights Act of 1964
Oct., 1974: *Lesbian Connection* Begins Publication
Nov. 5, 1974: Noble Is First Out Lesbian or Gay Person to Win State-Level Election
1975: First Gay and Lesbian Archives Is Founded
1975: First Novel About Coming Out to Parents Is Published
1975: Gay American Indians Is Founded
1975: Rule Publishes *Lesbian Images*
1975-1983: Gay Latino Alliance Is Formed
July 3, 1975: U.S. Civil Service Commission Prohibits Discrimination Against Federal Employees
Sept., 1975: Anna Crusis Women's Choir Is Formed
Nov. 17, 1975: U.S. Supreme Court Rules in "Crimes Against Nature" Case
1976: Katz Publishes First Lesbian and Gay History Anthology
1976-1990: Army Reservist Ben-Shalom Sues for Reinstatement
Aug. 20-22, 1976: Michigan Womyn's Music Festival Holds Its First Gathering
1977: Anita Bryant Campaigns Against Gay and Lesbian Rights
Apr., 1977: Combahee River Collective Issues "A Black Feminist Statement"
Nov. 18-21, 1977: National Women's Conference Convenes
Dec. 19, 1977: Quebec Includes Lesbians and Gays in Its Charter of Human Rights and Freedoms
Dec. 31, 1977: Toronto Police Raid Offices of *The Body Politic*
1978: Harry Benjamin International Gender Dysphoria Association Is Founded
1978: Lesbian and Gay Workplace Movement Is Founded
July 3, 1978: U.S. Supreme Court Distinguishes Between "Indecent" and "Obscene"
Aug. 8, 1978: International Lesbian and Gay Association Is Founded
Nov. 7, 1978: Antigay and Antilesbian Briggs Initiative Is Defeated
Nov. 27, 1978: White Murders Politicians Moscone and Milk
1979: Moral Majority Is Founded
1979-1981: First Gay British Television Series Airs
Oct. 12-15, 1979: First March on Washington for Lesbian and Gay Rights
Oct. 12-15, 1979: First National Third World Lesbian and Gay Conference Convenes
Oct. 12-15, 1979: Lesbian and Gay Asian Collective Is Founded

Chronological List of Entries

1980's

1980: Alyson Begins Publishing Gay and Lesbian Books
1980-1981: Gay Writers Form the Violet Quill
Apr. 22, 1980: Human Rights Campaign Fund Is Founded
May-Aug., 1980: U.S. Navy Investigates the USS *Norton Sound* in Antilesbian Witch-hunt
June 2, 1980: Canadian Gay Postal Workers Secure Union Protections
1981: Faderman Publishes *Surpassing the Love of Men*
1981: Gay and Lesbian Palimony Suits Emerge
1981: Parents, Families, and Friends of Lesbians and Gays Is Founded
1981: *This Bridge Called My Back* Is Published
1981-1982: GALA Choruses Is Formed
Feb. 5, 1981: Toronto Police Raid Gay Bathhouses
June 5 and July 3, 1981: Reports of Rare Diseases Mark Beginning of AIDS Epidemic
June 6-June 20, 1981: San Francisco Gay Men's Chorus Concert Tour
Oct., 1981: Kitchen Table: Women of Color Press Is Founded
Dec. 8, 1981: New York City Gay Men's Chorus Performs at Carnegie Hall
1982: Lesbian and Gay Youth Protection Institute Is Founded
1982: Lorde's Autobiography *Zami* Is Published
1982-1991: Lesbian Academic and Activist Sues University of California for Discrimination
Feb. 25, 1982: Wisconsin Enacts First Statewide Gay and Lesbian Civil Rights Law
July, 1982: Gay-Related Immunodeficiency Is Renamed AIDS
Aug. 28, 1982: First Gay Games Are Held in San Francisco
July 14, 1983: Studds Is First Out Gay Man in the U.S. Congress
Sept., 1983: First National Lesbians of Color Conference Convenes
Spring, 1984: AIDS Virus Is Discovered
Oct. 9, 1984: San Francisco Closes Gay Bathhouses and Other Businesses
Nov. 6, 1984: West Hollywood Incorporates with Majority Gay and Lesbian City Council
Dec. 4, 1984: Berkeley Extends Benefits to Domestic Partners of City Employees
1985: GLAAD Begins Monitoring Media Coverage of Gays and Lesbians
1985: Lesbian Film *Desert Hearts* Is Released
July 25, 1985: Actor Hudson Announces He Has AIDS
1986: *Bowers v. Hardwick* Upholds State Sodomy Laws
1986: Paula Gunn Allen Publishes *The Sacred Hoop*
Jan., 1986: South Asian Newsletter *Trikone* Begins Publication
Sept., 1986: AZT Treats People with AIDS
Nov., 1986: Californians Reject LaRouche's Quarantine Initiative
1987: Anzaldúa Publishes *Borderlands/La Frontera*
1987: Asian Pacific Lesbian Network Is Founded
1987: *Compañeras: Latina Lesbians* Is Published
1987: Shilts Publishes *And the Band Played On*
1987: VIVA Is Founded to Promote Latina and Latino Artists
Mar., 1987: Radical AIDS Activist Group ACT UP Is Founded
Apr., 1987: Old Lesbians Organize for Change
May, 1987: *Lambda Rising Book Report* Begins Publication
May 30, 1987: U.S. Congressman Frank Comes Out as Gay
Oct. 11, 1987: Second March on Washington for Lesbian and Gay Rights
Oct. 14-17, 1987: Latin American and Caribbean Lesbian Feminist Network Is Formed
1988: *Macho Dancer* Is Released in the Philippines
Jan. 1, 1988: Canada Decriminalizes Sex Practices Between Consenting Adults
Mar. 20, 1988: *M. Butterfly* Opens on Broadway
May, 1988: Lavender Youth Recreation and Information Center Opens

June 27, 1988: Report of the Presidential AIDS Commission
Oct. 11, 1988: First National Coming Out Day Is Celebrated
Nov. 8, 1988: Oregon Repeals Ban on Antigay Job Discrimination
Dec. 1, 1988: First World AIDS Day
1989: Act Up Paris Is Founded
1989: Vaid Becomes Executive Director of the National Gay and Lesbian Task Force
1989-1990: Helms Claims Mapplethorpe's Photographs Are Indecent
Jan. 21, 1989: Death of Transgender Jazz Musician Billy Tipton
May 1, 1989: U.S. Supreme Court Rules Gender-Role Stereotyping Is Discriminatory
May 3, 1989: *Watkins v. United States Army* Reinstates Gay Soldier
June 2, 1989: Lambda Literary Award Is Created
Dec. 10, 1989: ACT UP Protests at St. Patrick's Cathedral

1990's

1990: International Gay and Lesbian Human Rights Commission Is Founded
1990: United Lesbians of African Heritage Is Founded
1990-1993: Artists Sue the National Endowment for the Arts
1990, 1994: *Coming Out Under Fire* Documents Gay and Lesbian Military Veterans
Mar. 20, 1990: Queer Nation Is Founded
June, 1990: BiNet USA Is Formed
July 26, 1990: Americans with Disabilities Act Becomes Law
Dec., 1990: Asian Lesbian Network Holds Its First Conference
1991: LeVay Postulates the "Gay Brain"
1991: Revisionist Criticism Recasts Sor Juana Inés de la Cruz
1991: Stone Publishes "The Posttranssexual Manifesto"
Apr. 6, 1991: Asian Lesbians and Gays Protest Lambda Fund-Raiser
Aug., 1991: Leather Archives and Museum Is Founded
Aug. 27, 1991: *The Advocate* Outs Pentagon Spokesman Pete Williams
Sept. 29, 1991: California Governor Wilson Vetoes Antidiscrimination Bill
Dec. 17, 1991: Minnesota Court Awards Guardianship to Lesbian Partner
Dec. 30, 1991-Feb. 22, 1993: Canada Grants Asylum Based on Sexual Orientation
1992: Canadian YMCA Extends Family Discounts to Gays and Lesbians
1992: Transgender Nation Holds Its First Protest
1992-2002: Celebrity Lesbians Come Out
1992-2006: Indians Struggle to Abolish Sodomy Law
Apr. 27, 1992: Canadian Government Antigay Campaign Is Revealed
June, 1992: Feinberg Publishes *Transgender Liberation*
Sept. 23, 1992: Massachusetts Grants Family Rights to Gay and Lesbian State Workers
Oct., 1992: Canadian Military Lifts Its Ban on Gays and Lesbians
Nov. 3, 1992: Oregon and Colorado Attempt Antigay Initiatives
1993: Intersex Society of North America Is Founded
1993: Monette Wins the National Book Award for *Becoming a Man*
1993: *The Wedding Banquet* Is First Acclaimed Taiwanese Gay-Themed Film
1993-1996: Hawaii Opens Door to Same-Gender Marriages
Mar.-Apr., 1993: Battelle Sex Study Prompts Conservative Backlash
Apr. 24, 1993: First Dyke March Is Held in Washington, D.C.

Chronological List of Entries

Apr. 25, 1993: March on Washington for Gay, Lesbian, and Bi Equal Rights and Liberation
May 24, 1993: Achtenberg Becomes Assistant Housing Secretary
June 25, 1993: Clinton Appoints First AIDS Czar
Sept. 21, 1993-Apr. 21, 1995: Lesbian Mother Loses Custody of Her Child
Nov. 30, 1993: Don't Ask, Don't Tell Policy Is Implemented
Dec. 24, 1993-Dec. 31, 1993: Transgender Man Brandon Teena Raped and Murdered
1994: Employment Non-Discrimination Act Is Proposed to U.S. Congress
1994: National Association of Lesbian and Gay Community Centers Is Founded
1994: Navratilova Honored for Her Career in Tennis
June, 1994: Stonewall 25 March and Rallies Are Held in New York City
Aug. 6, 1994: Japanese American Citizens League Supports Same-Gender Marriage
Sept. 16, 1994: U.N. Revokes Consultative Status of International Lesbian and Gay Association
1995: *The Advocate* Outs Oscar Nominee Nigel Hawthorne
1995: Athlete Louganis Announces He Is HIV-Positive
June 17, 1995: International Bill of Gender Rights Is First Circulated
Dec. 4, 1995: Lesbian Couple Murdered in Oregon
1996: Hart Recognized as a Transgender Man
Sept. 21, 1996: U.S. President Clinton Signs Defense of Marriage Act
1998: Transgender Scholarship Proliferates
Apr. 2, 1998: Canadian Supreme Court Reverses Gay Academic's Firing
Oct. 6-7, 1998: Gay College Student Shepard Is Beaten and Murdered
Oct. 9-12, 1998: First International Retreat for Lesbian and Gay Muslims Is Held
Dec. 3, 1998-Feb. 25, 1999: Screening of *Fire* Ignites Violent Protests in India
Oct. 27, 1999: *Littleton v. Prange* Withholds Survivor Rights from Transsexual Spouses
Nov., 1999: First Middle Eastern Gay and Lesbian Organization Is Founded
Dec. 20, 1999: *Baker v. Vermont* Leads to Recognition of Same-Gender Civil Unions

2000's

Jan. 12, 2000: United Kingdom Lifts Ban on Gays and Lesbians in the Military
Mar. 21, 2000: Hollywood Awards Transgender Portrayals in Film
June 28, 2000: *Boy Scouts of America v. Dale*
Apr. 20, 2001: Chinese Psychiatric Association Removes Homosexuality from List of Mental Disorders
May 25, 2001: Japanese Human Rights Council Recommends Lesbian and Gay Rights
Sept. 7, 2001: First Gay and Lesbian Television Network Is Launched in Canada
2002: Sylvia Rivera Law Project Is Founded
Apr. 30, 2002: Transgender Rights Added to New York City Law
June 19, 2002: Gays and Lesbians March for Equal Rights in Mexico City
June 28, 2002: Irish American Lesbian Gains Canadian Immigrant Status
Oct. 4, 2002: Transgender Teen Gwen Araujo Is Murdered in California
Feb. 21, 2003: Australian Court Validates Transsexual Marriage
Mar., 2003-Dec., 2004: Transsexuals Protest Academic Exploitation
Mar. 21, 2003: New Mexico Amends Its Human Rights Act
Apr., 2003: Buenos Aires Recognizes Same-Gender Civil Unions

June 17, 2003, and July 19, 2005: Canada Legalizes Same-Gender Marriage

June 26, 2003: U.S. Supreme Court Overturns Texas Sodomy Law

July, 2003: Singapore Lifts Ban on Hiring Lesbian and Gay Employees

July, 2003: Wal-Mart Adds Lesbians and Gays to Its Antidiscrimination Policy

Nov. 18, 2003: Massachusetts Court Rules for Same-Gender Marriage

Nov. 20, 2003: Transgender Day of Remembrance and Remembering Our Dead Project

Mar. 7, 2004: Robinson Becomes First Out Gay Bishop in Christian History

May 17, 2004: Transgender Athletes Allowed to Compete in Olympic Games

Nov. 18, 2004: United Kingdom Legalizes Same-Gender Civil Partnerships

Apr. 4, 2005: United Kingdom's Gender Recognition Act Legalizes Transsexual Marriage

June 30, 2005: Spain Legalizes Same-Gender Marriage

Nov. 29, 2005: Roman Catholic Church Bans Gay Seminarians

Jan., 2006: Jiménez Flores Elected to the Mexican Senate

Mar. 5, 2006: *Brokeback Mountain, Capote,* and *Transamerica* Receive Oscars

Category Index

List of Categories

Arts 767	Literature 777
Civil rights 768	Marches, protests, and riots 778
Crime 770	Military 779
Cultural and intellectual history 771	Organizations and institutions 779
Economics 771	Publications 782
Feminism 772	Race and ethnicity 783
Government and politics 772	Religion 784
Health and medicine 774	Science 784
HIV-AIDS 775	Sports 784
Laws, acts, and legal history 775	Transgender/transsexuality 784

ARTS

Feb. 19, 1923: *The God of Vengeance* Opens on Broadway, 66

Feb., 1927: Wales Padlock Law Censors Risque Theater, 74

1929: *Pandora's Box* Opens, 81

1930's-1960's: Hollywood Bans "Sexual Perversion" in Films, 84

1973: Olivia Records Is Founded, 249

Sept., 1975: Anna Crusis Women's Choir Is Formed, 295

Aug. 20-22, 1976: Michigan Womyn's Music Festival Holds Its First Gathering, 304

July 3, 1978: U.S. Supreme Court Distinguishes Between "Indecent" and "Obscene," 327

1979-1981: First Gay British Television Series Airs, 342

1981-1982: GALA Choruses Is Formed, 373

June 6-June 20, 1981: San Francisco Gay Men's Chorus Concert Tour, 380

Dec. 8, 1981: New York City Gay Men's Chorus Performs at Carnegie Hall, 385

1985: Lesbian Film *Desert Hearts* Is Released, 426

July 25, 1985: Actor Hudson Announces He Has AIDS, 429

1987: VIVA Is Founded to Promote Latina and Latino Artists, 455

1988: *Macho Dancer* Is Released in the Philippines, 474

Mar. 20, 1988: *M. Butterfly* Opens on Broadway, 479

1989-1990: Helms Claims Photographs Are Indecent, 500

Jan. 21, 1989: Death of Transgender Jazz Musician Billy Tipton, 505

1990-1993: Artists Sue the National Endowment for the Arts, 520

1990, 1994: *Coming Out Under Fire* Documents Gay and Lesbian Military Veterans, 522

Apr. 6, 1991: Asian Lesbians and Gays Protest Lambda Fund-Raiser, 542

Aug., 1991: Leather Archives and Museum Is Founded, 545

1992-2002: Celebrity Lesbians Come Out, 565

1993: *The Wedding Banquet* Is First Acclaimed Taiwanese Gay-Themed Film, 591

1995: *The Advocate* Outs Oscar Nominee Nigel Hawthorne, 634

Dec. 3, 1998-Feb. 25, 1999: Screening of *Fire* Ignites Violent Protests in India, 660

Mar. 21, 2000: Hollywood Awards Transgender Portrayals in Film, 672

Sept. 7, 2001: First Gay and Lesbian Television Network Is Launched in Canada, 683

Mar. 5, 2006: *Brokeback Mountain, Capote,* and *Transamerica* Receive Oscars, 744

Civil rights

Aug. 29, 1867: Karl Heinrich Ulrichs Speaks Publicly for Gay and Lesbian Rights, 9

Nov. 17, 1901: Police Arrest "Los 41" in Mexico City, 41

1906: Friedlaender Breaks with the Scientific-Humanitarian Committee, 49

Dec. 10, 1924: Gerber Founds the Society for Human Rights, 72

1950: Mattachine Society Is Founded, 106

1952: ONE, Inc., Is Founded, 114

1952-1990: U.S. Law Prohibits Gay and Lesbian Immigration, 117

1953: *ONE* Magazine Begins Publication, 124

Apr. 27, 1953: U.S. President Eisenhower Prohibits Federal Employment of Lesbians and Gays, 129

Jan. 1, 1957: United Kingdom's Sexual Offences Act Becomes Law, 140

Sept. 4, 1957: The *Wolfenden Report* Calls for Decriminalizing Private Consensual Sex, 142

May, 1960: First National Lesbian Conference Convenes, 144

1961: Illinois Legalizes Consensual Homosexual Sex, 147

1961: Sarria Is First Out Gay or Lesbian Candidate for Public Office, 149

July 2-Aug. 28, 1963: Rustin Organizes the March on Washington, 154

Nov., 1965: Revolutionary Cuba Imprisons Gays, 157

Feb. 19-20, 1966: First North American Conference of Homophile Organizations Convenes, 160

Aug., 1966: Queer Youth Fight Police Harassment at Compton's Cafeteria in San Francisco, 163

Apr. 19, 1967: First Student Homophile League Is Formed, 172

May 22, 1967: U.S. Supreme Court Upholds Law Preventing Immigration of Gays and Lesbians, 176

July 27, 1967: United Kingdom Decriminalizes Homosexual Sex, 178

Aug. 11-18, 1968: NACHO Formally Becomes the First Gay Political Coalition, 182

1969: Nuestro Mundo Forms as First Queer Organization in Argentina, 187

June 27-July 2, 1969: Stonewall Rebellion Ignites Modern Gay and Lesbian Rights Movement, 192

July 31, 1969: Gay Liberation Front Is Formed, 195

Aug. 26, 1969: Canada Decriminalizes Homosexual Acts, 199

June 28, 1970: First Lesbian and Gay Pride March in the United States, 212

Nov., 1971: *The Body Politic* Begins Publication, 226

1972-1973: Local Governments Pass Antidiscrimination Laws, 228

Mar. 22, 1972-June 30, 1982: Equal Rights Amendment Fails State Ratification, 233

Nov. 7, 1972: Jordan Becomes First Black Congresswoman from the South, 239

1973: National Gay Task Force Is Formed, 246

Jan. 22, 1973: *Roe v. Wade* Legalizes Abortion and Extends Privacy Rights, 252

Aug., 1973: American Bar Association Calls for Repeal of Laws Against Consensual Sex, 258

Oct. 18, 1973: Lambda Legal Authorized to Practice Law, 263

Mar. 5, 1974: Antigay and Antilesbian Organizations Begin to Form, 271

June 27, 1974: Abzug and Koch Attempt to Amend the Civil Rights Act of 1964, 273

1975: First Gay and Lesbian Archives Is Founded, 280

1975: Gay American Indians Is Founded, 285

1975-1983: Gay Latino Alliance Is Formed, 290

July 3, 1975: U.S. Civil Service Commission Prohibits Discrimination Against Federal Employees, 292

Nov. 17, 1975: U.S. Supreme Court Rules in "Crimes Against Nature" Case, 297

1976-1990: Army Reservist Ben-Shalom Sues for Reinstatement, 302

1977: Anita Bryant Campaigns Against Gay and Lesbian Rights, 307

Dec. 19, 1977: Quebec Includes Lesbians and Gays in Its Charter of Human Rights and Freedoms, 315

Category Index

Dec. 31, 1977: Toronto Police Raid Offices of *The Body Politic*, 318

July 3, 1978: U.S. Supreme Court Distinguishes Between "Indecent" and "Obscene," 327

Nov. 7, 1978: Antigay and Antilesbian Briggs Initiative Is Defeated, 333

Nov. 27, 1978: White Murders Politicians Moscone and Milk, 337

Oct. 12-15, 1979: First March on Washington for Lesbian and Gay Rights, 344

Oct. 12-15, 1979: First National Third World Lesbian and Gay Conference Convenes, 347

May-Aug., 1980: U.S. Navy Investigates the USS *Norton Sound* in Antilesbian Witch Hunt, 357

June 2, 1980: Canadian Gay Postal Workers Secure Union Protections, 360

1981: Gay and Lesbian Palimony Suits Emerge, 365

1981: Parents, Families, and Friends of Lesbians and Gays Is Founded, 367

1981: *This Bridge Called My Back* Is Published, 370

Feb. 5, 1981: Toronto Police Raid Gay Bathhouses, 376

1982: Lorde's Autobiography *Zami* Is Published, 392

1982-1991: Lesbian Academic and Activist Sues University of California for Discrimination, 395

Feb. 25, 1982: Wisconsin Enacts First Statewide Gay and Lesbian Civil Rights Law, 397

Oct. 9, 1984: San Francisco Closes Gay Bathhouses and Other Businesses, 417

Dec. 4, 1984: Berkeley Extends Benefits to Domestic Partners of City Employees, 422

1986: *Bowers v. Hardwick* Upholds State Sodomy Laws, 432

Nov., 1986: Californians Reject LaRouche's Quarantine Initiative, 442

Mar., 1987: Radical AIDS Activist Group ACT UP Is Founded, 458

Oct. 11, 1987: Second March on Washington for Lesbian and Gay Rights, 469

1988: *Macho Dancer* Is Released in the Philippines, 474

Jan. 1, 1988: Canada Decriminalizes Sex Practices Between Consenting Adults, 477

Nov. 8, 1988: Oregon Repeals Ban on Antigay Job Discrimination, 491

May 1, 1989: U.S. Supreme Court Rules Gender-Role Stereotyping Is Discriminatory, 508

May 3, 1989: *Watkins v. United States Army* Reinstates Gay Soldier, 510

Dec. 10, 1989: ACT UP Protests at St. Patrick's Cathedral, 514

1990: International Gay and Lesbian Human Rights Commission Is Founded, 517

1990, 1994: *Coming Out Under Fire* Documents Gay and Lesbian Military Veterans, 522

Mar. 20, 1990: Queer Nation Is Founded, 524

July 26, 1990: Americans with Disabilities Act Becomes Law, 530

Sept. 29, 1991: California Governor Wilson Vetoes Antidiscrimination Bill, 550

Dec. 17, 1991: Minnesota Court Awards Guardianship to Lesbian Partner, 552

Dec. 30, 1991-Feb. 22, 1993: Canada Grants Asylum Based on Sexual Orientation, 555

1992: Canadian YMCA Extends Family Discounts to Gays and Lesbians, 559

1992: Transgender Nation Holds Its First Protest, 562

1992-2006: Indians Struggle to Abolish Sodomy Law, 568

Apr. 27, 1992: Canadian Government Antigay Campaign Is Revealed, 570

June, 1992: Feinberg Publishes *Transgender Liberation*, 573

Sept. 23, 1992: Massachusetts Grants Family Rights to Gay and Lesbian State Workers, 576

Oct., 1992: Canadian Military Lifts Its Ban on Gays and Lesbians, 579

1993-1996: Hawaii Opens Door to Same-Gender Marriages, 593

Mar.-Apr., 1993: Battelle Sex Study Prompts Conservative Backlash, 596

Apr. 25, 1993: March on Washington for Gay, Lesbian, and Bi Equal Rights and Liberation, 601

Sept. 21, 1993-Apr. 21, 1995: Lesbian Mother Loses Custody of Her Child, 608

Nov. 30, 1993: Don't Ask, Don't Tell Policy Is Implemented, 611

Dec. 24, 1993-Dec. 31, 1993: Transgender Man Brandon Teena Raped and Murdered, 615

1994: Employment Non-Discrimination Act Is Proposed to U.S. Congress, 618

June, 1994: Stonewall 25 March and Rallies Are Held in New York City, 627

Aug. 6, 1994: Japanese American Citizens League Supports Same-Gender Marriage, 629

Sept. 16, 1994: U.N. Revokes Consultative Status of International Lesbian and Gay Association, 632

June 17, 1995: International Bill of Gender Rights Is First Circulated, 639

Sept. 21, 1996: U.S. President Clinton Signs Defense of Marriage Act, 646

Apr. 2, 1998: Canadian Supreme Court Reverses Gay Academic's Firing, 652

Oct. 6-7, 1998: Gay College Student Shepard Is Beaten and Murdered, 654

Oct. 27, 1999: *Littleton v. Prange* Withholds Survivor Rights from Transsexual Spouses, 662

Nov., 1999: First Middle Eastern Gay and Lesbian Organization Is Founded, 664

Dec. 20, 1999: *Baker v. Vermont* Leads to Recognition of Same-Gender Civil Unions, 666

Jan. 12, 2000: United Kingdom Lifts Ban on Gays and Lesbians in the Military, 669

June 28, 2000: *Boy Scouts of America v. Dale*, 675

May 25, 2001: Japanese Human Rights Council Recommends Lesbian and Gay Rights, 681

Apr. 30, 2002: Transgender Rights Added to New York City Law, 687

June 19, 2002: Gays and Lesbians March for Equal Rights in Mexico City, 690

June 28, 2002: Irish American Lesbian Gains Canadian Immigrant Status, 692

Oct. 4, 2002: Transgender Teen Gwen Araujo Is Murdered in California, 694

Mar. 21, 2003: New Mexico Amends Its Human Rights Act, 702

Apr., 2003: Buenos Aires Recognizes Same-Gender Civil Unions, 705

June 17, 2003, and July 19, 2005: Canada Legalizes Same-Gender Marriage, 707

June 26, 2003: U.S. Supreme Court Overturns Texas Sodomy Law, 710

July, 2003: Singapore Lifts Ban on Hiring Lesbian and Gay Employees, 713

July, 2003: Wal-Mart Adds Lesbians and Gays to Its Antidiscrimination Policy, 715

Nov. 18, 2003: Massachusetts Court Rules for Same-Gender Marriage, 717

Nov. 20, 2003: Transgender Day of Remembrance and Remembering Our Dead Project, 722

Mar. 7, 2004: Robinson Becomes First Out Gay Bishop in Christian History, 725

Nov. 18, 2004: United Kingdom Legalizes Same-Gender Civil Partnerships, 731

Apr. 4, 2005: United Kingdom's Gender Recognition Act Legalizes Transsexual Marriage, 734

June 30, 2005: Spain Legalizes Same-Gender Marriage, 736

CRIME

1885: United Kingdom Criminalizes "Gross Indecency," 18

Jan., 1892-July, 1892: Alice Mitchell Found Guilty of Murdering Her Lover, 23

May 25, 1895: Oscar Wilde Is Convicted of Gross Indecency, 26

Nov. 17, 1901: Police Arrest "Los 41" in Mexico City, 41

Feb. 19, 1923: *The God of Vengeance* Opens on Broadway, 66

Jan. 1, 1957: United Kingdom's Sexual Offences Act Becomes Law, 140

Sept. 4, 1957: The *Wolfenden Report* Calls for Decriminalizing Private Consensual Sex, 142

July 27, 1967: United Kingdom Decriminalizes Homosexual Sex, 178

Aug. 26, 1969: Canada Decriminalizes Homosexual Acts, 199

Aug., 1973: American Bar Association Calls for Repeal of Laws Against Consensual Sex, 258

Category Index

Nov. 27, 1978: White Murders Politicians Moscone and Milk, 337

1986: *Bowers v. Hardwick* Upholds State Sodomy Laws, 432

Dec. 24, 1993-Dec. 31, 1993: Transgender Man Brandon Teena Raped and Murdered, 615

Dec. 4, 1995: Lesbian Couple Murdered in Oregon, 641

Oct. 6-7, 1998: Gay College Student Shepard Is Beaten and Murdered, 654

Oct. 4, 2002: Transgender Teen Gwen Araujo Is Murdered in California, 694

Nov. 20, 2003: Transgender Day of Remembrance and Remembering Our Dead Project, 722

CULTURAL AND INTELLECTUAL HISTORY

July 19-20, 1848: Seneca Falls Women's Rights Convention, 1

May 6, 1868: Kertbeny Coins the Terms "Homosexual" and "Heterosexual," 12

Jan.-June, 1886: Two-Spirit American Indian Visits Washington, D.C., 21

1905: Freud Rejects Third-Sex Theory, 46

1906: Friedlaender Breaks with the Scientific-Humanitarian Committee, 49

Oct., 1909: Barney Opens Her Paris Salon, 58

Feb. 19, 1923: *The God of Vengeance* Opens on Broadway, 66

1929: Davis's Research Identifies Lesbian Sexuality as Common and Normal, 79

1929: *Pandora's Box* Opens, 81

1930's-1960's: Hollywood Bans "Sexual Perversion" in Films, 84

1952: ONE, Inc., Is Founded, 114

1953: *ONE* Magazine Begins Publication, 124

Mar. 7, 1967: CBS Airs *CBS Reports: The Homosexuals*, 169

1970: Amazon Bookstore Opens as First Feminist-Lesbian Book Shop, 203

May 1, 1970: Radicalesbians Issues "The Woman Identified Woman" Manifesto, 209

Fall, 1973: Lesbian Herstory Archives Is Founded, 260

1975: First Gay and Lesbian Archives Is Founded, 280

1976: Katz Publishes First Lesbian and Gay History Anthology, 300

Aug. 20-22, 1976: Michigan Womyn's Music Festival Holds Its First Gathering, 304

1979-1981: First Gay British Television Series Airs, 342

1980: Alyson Begins Publishing Gay and Lesbian Books, 351

1981: Faderman Publishes *Surpassing the Love of Men*, 362

1981: *This Bridge Called My Back* Is Published, 370

June 6-June 20, 1981: San Francisco Gay Men's Chorus Concert Tour, 380

Dec. 8, 1981: New York City Gay Men's Chorus Performs at Carnegie Hall, 385

1985: Lesbian Film *Desert Hearts* Is Released, 426

Oct. 14-17, 1987: Latin American and Caribbean Lesbian Feminist Network Is Formed, 472

1991: Revisionist Criticism Recasts Sor Juana Inés de la Cruz, 537

1991: Stone Publishes "The Posttranssexual Manifesto," 540

Apr. 6, 1991: Asian Lesbians and Gays Protest Lambda Fund-Raiser, 542

1992-2002: Celebrity Lesbians Come Out, 565

1993: *The Wedding Banquet* Is First Acclaimed Taiwanese Gay-Themed Film, 591

1995: *The Advocate* Outs Oscar Nominee Nigel Hawthorne, 634

1998: Transgender Scholarship Proliferates, 650

Dec. 3, 1998-Feb. 25, 1999: Screening of *Fire* Ignites Violent Protests in India, 660

Mar. 21, 2000: Hollywood Awards Transgender Portrayals in Film, 672

Sept. 7, 2001: First Gay and Lesbian Television Network Is Launched in Canada, 683

Mar. 5, 2006: *Brokeback Mountain, Capote,* and *Transamerica* Receive Oscars, 744

ECONOMICS

Fall, 1967: Oscar Wilde Memorial Bookshop Opens as First Gay Bookstore, 180

1970: Amazon Bookstore Opens as First Feminist-Lesbian Book Shop, 203

1973: Olivia Records Is Founded, 249
1978: Lesbian and Gay Workplace Movement Is Founded, 323
1980: Alyson Begins Publishing Gay and Lesbian Books, 351
1988: *Macho Dancer* Is Released in the Philippines, 474
Sept. 7, 2001: First Gay and Lesbian Television Network Is Launched in Canada, 683
2002: Sylvia Rivera Law Project Is Founded, 686
July, 2003: Singapore Lifts Ban on Hiring Lesbian and Gay Employees, 713
July, 2003: Wal-Mart Adds Lesbians and Gays to Its Antidiscrimination Policy, 715

FEMINISM

July 19-20, 1848: Seneca Falls Women's Rights Convention, 1
Nov. 11, 1865: Mary Edwards Walker Is Awarded the Medal of Honor, 7
Oct., 1909: Barney Opens Her Paris Salon, 58
1955: Daughters of Bilitis Founded as First National Lesbian Group in United States, 132
May, 1960: First National Lesbian Conference Convenes, 144
1970: Amazon Bookstore Opens as First Feminist-Lesbian Book Shop, 203
May 1, 1970: Lavender Menace Protests Homophobia in Women's Movement, 206
May 1, 1970: Radicalesbians Issues "The Woman Identified Woman" Manifesto, 209
Nov. 28, 1970: Del Martin Quits Gay Liberation Movement, 214
1971: *Lesbian Tide* Publishes Its First Issue, 219
Mar. 22, 1972-June 30, 1982: Equal Rights Amendment Fails State Ratification, 233
1973: Olivia Records Is Founded, 249
Jan. 22, 1973: *Roe v. Wade* Legalizes Abortion and Extends Privacy Rights, 252
Fall, 1973: Lesbian Herstory Archives Is Founded, 260
Oct., 1974: *Lesbian Connection* Begins Publication, 275
Sept., 1975: Anna Crusis Women's Choir Is Formed, 295

Aug. 20-22, 1976: Michigan Womyn's Music Festival Holds Its First Gathering, 304
Apr., 1977: Combahee River Collective Issues "A Black Feminist Statement," 309
Nov. 18-21, 1977: National Women's Conference Convenes, 311
Oct. 12-15, 1979: First National Third World Lesbian and Gay Conference Convenes, 347
1981: Faderman Publishes *Surpassing the Love of Men*, 362
1981: *This Bridge Called My Back* Is Published, 370
Oct., 1981: Kitchen Table: Women of Color Press Is Founded, 383
1982: Lorde's Autobiography *Zami* Is Published, 392
1982-1991: Lesbian Academic and Activist Sues University of California for Discrimination, 395
Sept., 1983: First National Lesbians of Color Conference Convenes, 411
1986: Paula Gunn Allen Publishes *The Sacred Hoop*, 435
1987: Anzaldúa Publishes *Borderlands/ La Frontera*, 446
Apr., 1987: Old Lesbians Organize for Change, 462
Oct. 14-17, 1987: Latin American and Caribbean Lesbian Feminist Network Is Formed, 472
1990-1993: Artists Sue the National Endowment for the Arts, 520
June, 1990: BiNet USA Is Formed, 527
1991: Revisionist Criticism Recasts Sor Juana Inés de la Cruz, 537
Apr. 24, 1993: First Dyke March Is Held in Washington, D.C., 598

GOVERNMENT AND POLITICS

May 14, 1897: Hirschfeld Founds the Scientific-Humanitarian Committee, 36
Nov. 17, 1901: Police Arrest "Los 41" in Mexico City, 41
1906: Friedlaender Breaks with the Scientific-Humanitarian Committee, 49
1907-1909: The Eulenburg Affair Scandalizes Germany's Leadership, 52

Category Index

Mar. 15, 1919-1921: U.S. Navy Launches Sting Operation Against "Sexual Perverts," 63

Dec. 10, 1924: Gerber Founds the Society for Human Rights, 72

1933-1945: Nazis Persecute Homosexuals, 86

June 30-July 1, 1934: Hitler's Night of the Long Knives, 89

Apr. 27, 1953: U.S. President Eisenhower Prohibits Federal Employment of Lesbians and Gays, 129

1961: Sarria Is First Out Gay or Lesbian Candidate for Public Office, 149

Nov., 1965: Revolutionary Cuba Imprisons Gays, 157

Feb. 19-20, 1966: First North American Conference of Homophile Organizations Convenes, 160

May 22, 1967: U.S. Supreme Court Upholds Law Preventing Immigration of Gays and Lesbians, 176

1971: Kameny Is First Out Candidate for U.S. Congress, 217

Nov., 1971: *The Body Politic* Begins Publication, 226

1972-1973: Local Governments Pass Antidiscrimination Laws, 228

Mar. 22, 1972-June 30, 1982: Equal Rights Amendment Fails State Ratification, 233

Nov. 7, 1972: Jordan Becomes First Black Congresswoman from the South, 239

Oct. 18, 1973: Lambda Legal Authorized to Practice Law, 263

Mar. 5, 1974: Antigay and Antilesbian Organizations Begin to Form, 271

June 27, 1974: Abzug and Koch Attempt to Amend the Civil Rights Act of 1964, 273

Nov. 5, 1974: Noble Is First Out Lesbian or Gay Person to Win State-Level Election, 277

1975-1983: Gay Latino Alliance Is Formed, 290

July 3, 1975: U.S. Civil Service Commission Prohibits Discrimination Against Federal Employees, 292

Nov. 17, 1975: U.S. Supreme Court Rules in "Crimes Against Nature" Case, 297

Aug. 8, 1978: International Lesbian and Gay Association Is Founded, 330

Nov. 7, 1978: Antigay and Antilesbian Briggs Initiative Is Defeated, 333

1979: Moral Majority Is Founded, 339

Apr. 22, 1980: Human Rights Campaign Fund Is Founded, 355

May-Aug., 1980: U.S. Navy Investigates the USS *Norton Sound* in Antilesbian Witch Hunt, 357

June 2, 1980: Canadian Gay Postal Workers Secure Union Protections, 360

Feb. 25, 1982: Wisconsin Enacts First Statewide Gay and Lesbian Civil Rights Law, 397

July, 1982: Gay-Related Immunodeficiency Is Renamed AIDS, 401

July 14, 1983: Studds Is First Out Gay Man in the U.S. Congress, 407

Spring, 1984: AIDS Virus Is Discovered, 413

Nov. 6, 1984: West Hollywood Incorporates with Majority Gay and Lesbian City Council, 419

Dec. 4, 1984: Berkeley Extends Benefits to Domestic Partners of City Employees, 422

Mar., 1987: Radical AIDS Activist Group ACT UP Is Founded, 458

May 30, 1987: U.S. Congressman Frank Comes Out as Gay, 466

1988: *Macho Dancer* Is Released in the Philippines, 474

Jan. 1, 1988: Canada Decriminalizes Sex Practices Between Consenting Adults, 477

June 27, 1988: Report of the Presidential AIDS Commission, 485

1989: Vaid Becomes Executive Director of the National Gay and Lesbian Task Force, 498

1989-1990: Helms Claims Photographs Are Indecent, 500

Dec. 10, 1989: ACT UP Protests at St. Patrick's Cathedral, 514

1990-1993: Artists Sue the National Endowment for the Arts, 520

Mar. 20, 1990: Queer Nation Is Founded, 524

Aug. 27, 1991: *The Advocate* Outs Pentagon Spokesman Pete Williams, 547

Dec. 30, 1991-Feb. 22, 1993: Canada Grants Asylum Based on Sexual Orientation, 555

1992-2006: Indians Struggle to Abolish Sodomy Law, 568

Apr. 27, 1992: Canadian Government Antigay Campaign Is Revealed, 570

Sept. 23, 1992: Massachusetts Grants Family Rights to Gay and Lesbian State Workers, 576

Oct., 1992: Canadian Military Lifts Its Ban on Gays and Lesbians, 579

Nov. 3, 1992: Oregon and Colorado Attempt Antigay Initiatives, 582

1993-1996: Hawaii Opens Door to Same-Gender Marriages, 593

Mar.-Apr., 1993: Battelle Sex Study Prompts Conservative Backlash, 596

Apr. 25, 1993: March on Washington for Gay, Lesbian, and Bi Equal Rights and Liberation, 601

May 24, 1993: Achtenberg Becomes Assistant Housing Secretary, 604

June 25, 1993: Clinton Appoints First AIDS Czar, 606

1994: Employment Non-Discrimination Act Is Proposed to U.S. Congress, 618

June, 1994: Stonewall 25 March and Rallies Are Held in New York City, 627

Sept. 16, 1994: U.N. Revokes Consultative Status of International Lesbian and Gay Association, 632

June 17, 1995: International Bill of Gender Rights Is First Circulated, 639

Sept. 21, 1996: U.S. President Clinton Signs Defense of Marriage Act, 646

Oct. 6-7, 1998: Gay College Student Shepard Is Beaten and Murdered, 654

Dec. 20, 1999: *Baker v. Vermont* Leads to Recognition of Same-Gender Civil Unions, 666

Jan. 12, 2000: United Kingdom Lifts Ban on Gays and Lesbians in the Military, 669

Apr. 30, 2002: Transgender Rights Added to New York City Law, 687

June 28, 2002: Irish American Lesbian Gains Canadian Immigrant Status, 692

Feb. 21, 2003: Australian Court Validates Transsexual Marriage, 698

Apr., 2003: Buenos Aires Recognizes Same-Gender Civil Unions, 705

July, 2003: Singapore Lifts Ban on Hiring Lesbian and Gay Employees, 713

Nov. 18, 2003: Massachusetts Court Rules for Same-Gender Marriage, 717

Nov. 18, 2004: United Kingdom Legalizes Same-Gender Civil Partnerships, 731

Apr. 4, 2005: United Kingdom's Gender Recognition Act Legalizes Transsexual Marriage, 734

Jan., 2006: Jiménez Flores Elected to the Mexican Senate, 741

HEALTH AND MEDICINE

Nov. 11, 1865: Mary Edwards Walker Is Awarded the Medal of Honor, 7

1869: Westphal Advocates Medical Treatment for Sexual Inversion, 16

1905: Freud Rejects Third-Sex Theory, 46

Sept. 24, 1951: George Jorgensen Becomes Christine Jorgensen, 108

1952: APA Classifies Homosexuality as a Mental Disorder, 111

1953-1957: Evelyn Hooker Debunks Beliefs that Homosexuality Is a "Sickness," 126

Nov. 21, 1966: First Gender Identity Clinic Opens and Provides Gender Reassignment Surgery, 165

Mar., 1971: Los Angeles Gay and Lesbian Center Is Founded, 221

Dec. 15, 1973: Homosexuality Is Delisted by APA, 265

1978: Harry Benjamin International Gender Dysphoria Association Is Founded, 320

June 5 and July 3, 1981: Reports of Rare Diseases Mark Beginning of AIDS Epidemic, 378

July, 1982: Gay-Related Immunodeficiency Is Renamed AIDS, 401

Spring, 1984: AIDS Virus Is Discovered, 413

Oct. 9, 1984: San Francisco Closes Gay Bathhouses and Other Businesses, 417

July 25, 1985: Actor Hudson Announces He Has AIDS, 429

Sept., 1986: AZT Treats People with AIDS, 440

1987: Shilts Publishes *And the Band Played On*, 453

Category Index

Mar., 1987: Radical AIDS Activist Group ACT UP Is Founded, 458
June 27, 1988: Report of the Presidential AIDS Commission, 485
Dec. 1, 1988: First World AIDS Day, 494
1989: Act Up Paris Is Founded, 496
Dec. 10, 1989: ACT UP Protests at St. Patrick's Cathedral, 514
1991: LeVay Postulates the "Gay Brain," 535
1993: Intersex Society of North America Is Founded, 586
June 25, 1993: Clinton Appoints First AIDS Czar, 606
1996: Hart Recognized as a Transgender Man, 644
Apr. 20, 2001: Chinese Psychiatric Association Removes Homosexuality from List of Mental Disorders, 679

HIV-AIDS

Mar., 1971: Los Angeles Gay and Lesbian Center Is Founded, 221
1975: Gay American Indians Is Founded, 285
June 5 and July 3, 1981: Reports of Rare Diseases Mark Beginning of AIDS Epidemic, 378
June 6-June 20, 1981: San Francisco Gay Men's Chorus Concert Tour, 380
July, 1982: Gay-Related Immunodeficiency Is Renamed AIDS, 401
Spring, 1984: AIDS Virus Is Discovered, 413
Oct. 9, 1984: San Francisco Closes Gay Bathhouses and Other Businesses, 417
July 25, 1985: Actor Hudson Announces He Has AIDS, 429
Sept., 1986: AZT Treats People with AIDS, 440
Nov., 1986: Californians Reject LaRouche's Quarantine Initiative, 442
1987: Shilts Publishes *And the Band Played On*, 453
Mar., 1987: Radical AIDS Activist Group ACT UP Is Founded, 458
June 27, 1988: Report of the Presidential AIDS Commission, 485
Dec. 1, 1988: First World AIDS Day, 494
1989: Act Up Paris Is Founded, 496

Dec. 10, 1989: ACT UP Protests at St. Patrick's Cathedral, 514
July 26, 1990: Americans with Disabilities Act Becomes Law, 530
1993: Monette Wins the National Book Award for *Becoming a Man*, 588
June 25, 1993: Clinton Appoints First AIDS Czar, 606
1995: Athlete Louganis Announces He Is HIV-Positive, 637

LAWS, ACTS, AND LEGAL HISTORY

Aug. 29, 1867: Karl Heinrich Ulrichs Speaks Publicly for Gay and Lesbian Rights, 9
May 6, 1868: Kertbeny Coins the Terms "Homosexual" and "Heterosexual," 12
1869: Westphal Advocates Medical Treatment for Sexual Inversion, 16
1885: United Kingdom Criminalizes "Gross Indecency," 18
May 25, 1895: Oscar Wilde Is Convicted of Gross Indecency, 26
May 14, 1897: Hirschfeld Founds the Scientific-Humanitarian Committee, 36
1906: Friedlaender Breaks with the Scientific-Humanitarian Committee, 49
1907-1909: The Eulenburg Affair Scandalizes Germany's Leadership, 52
Mar. 15, 1919-1921: U.S. Navy Launches Sting Operation Against "Sexual Perverts," 63
Feb., 1927: Wales Padlock Law Censors Risque Theater, 74
1928: Hall Publishes *The Well of Loneliness*, 76
1933-1945: Nazis Persecute Homosexuals, 86
June 30-July 1, 1934: Hitler's Night of the Long Knives, 89
Jan. 12, 1939: *Thompson v. Aldredge* Dismisses Sodomy Charges Against Lesbians, 95
1952: APA Classifies Homosexuality as a Mental Disorder, 111
1952-1990: U.S. Law Prohibits Gay and Lesbian Immigration, 117
1953: *ONE* Magazine Begins Publication, 124
Apr. 27, 1953: U.S. President Eisenhower Prohibits Federal Employment of Lesbians and Gays, 129

Jan. 1, 1957: United Kingdom's Sexual Offences Act Becomes Law, 140

Sept. 4, 1957: The *Wolfenden Report* Calls for Decriminalizing Private Consensual Sex, 142

1961: Illinois Legalizes Consensual Homosexual Sex, 147

Nov., 1965: Revolutionary Cuba Imprisons Gays, 157

May 22, 1967: U.S. Supreme Court Upholds Law Preventing Immigration of Gays and Lesbians, 176

July 27, 1967: United Kingdom Decriminalizes Homosexual Sex, 178

Aug. 26, 1969: Canada Decriminalizes Homosexual Acts, 199

1972-1973: Local Governments Pass Antidiscrimination Laws, 228

Mar. 22, 1972-June 30, 1982: Equal Rights Amendment Fails State Ratification, 233

Jan. 22, 1973: *Roe v. Wade* Legalizes Abortion and Extends Privacy Rights, 252

June 21, 1973: U.S. Supreme Court Supports Local Obscenity Laws, 255

Aug., 1973: American Bar Association Calls for Repeal of Laws Against Consensual Sex, 258

Oct. 18, 1973: Lambda Legal Authorized to Practice Law, 263

June 27, 1974: Abzug and Koch Attempt to Amend the Civil Rights Act of 1964, 273

July 3, 1975: U.S. Civil Service Commission Prohibits Discrimination Against Federal Employees, 292

Nov. 17, 1975: U.S. Supreme Court Rules in "Crimes Against Nature" Case, 297

1976-1990: Army Reservist Ben-Shalom Sues for Reinstatement, 302

1977: Anita Bryant Campaigns Against Gay and Lesbian Rights, 307

Dec. 19, 1977: Quebec Includes Lesbians and Gays in Its Charter of Human Rights and Freedoms, 315

Dec. 31, 1977: Toronto Police Raid Offices of *The Body Politic*, 318

July 3, 1978: U.S. Supreme Court Distinguishes Between "Indecent" and "Obscene," 327

Nov. 7, 1978: Antigay and Antilesbian Briggs Initiative Is Defeated, 333

May-Aug., 1980: U.S. Navy Investigates the USS *Norton Sound* in Antilesbian Witch Hunt, 357

1981: Gay and Lesbian Palimony Suits Emerge, 365

1982-1991: Lesbian Academic and Activist Sues University of California for Discrimination, 395

Feb. 25, 1982: Wisconsin Enacts First Statewide Gay and Lesbian Civil Rights Law, 397

Nov. 6, 1984: West Hollywood Incorporates with Majority Gay and Lesbian City Council, 419

1986: *Bowers v. Hardwick* Upholds State Sodomy Laws, 432

Nov., 1986: Californians Reject LaRouche's Quarantine Initiative, 442

Jan. 1, 1988: Canada Decriminalizes Sex Practices Between Consenting Adults, 477

June 27, 1988: Report of the Presidential AIDS Commission, 485

Nov. 8, 1988: Oregon Repeals Ban on Antigay Job Discrimination, 491

1989-1990: Helms Claims Photographs Are Indecent, 500

May 1, 1989: U.S. Supreme Court Rules Gender-Role Stereotyping Is Discriminatory, 508

May 3, 1989: *Watkins v. United States Army* Reinstates Gay Soldier, 510

1990: International Gay and Lesbian Human Rights Commission Is Founded, 517

1990-1993: Artists Sue the National Endowment for the Arts, 520

1990, 1994: *Coming Out Under Fire* Documents Gay and Lesbian Military Veterans, 522

July 26, 1990: Americans with Disabilities Act Becomes Law, 530

Sept. 29, 1991: California Governor Wilson Vetoes Antidiscrimination Bill, 550

Dec. 17, 1991: Minnesota Court Awards Guardianship to Lesbian Partner, 552

Dec. 30, 1991-Feb. 22, 1993: Canada Grants Asylum Based on Sexual Orientation, 555

1992: Canadian YMCA Extends Family Discounts to Gays and Lesbians, 559

Category Index

1992-2006: Indians Struggle to Abolish Sodomy Law, 568

Apr. 27, 1992: Canadian Government Antigay Campaign Is Revealed, 570

Sept. 23, 1992: Massachusetts Grants Family Rights to Gay and Lesbian State Workers, 576

Oct., 1992: Canadian Military Lifts Its Ban on Gays and Lesbians, 579

Nov. 3, 1992: Oregon and Colorado Attempt Antigay Initiatives, 582

1993-1996: Hawaii Opens Door to Same-Gender Marriages, 593

Sept. 21, 1993-Apr. 21, 1995: Lesbian Mother Loses Custody of Her Child, 608

Dec. 24, 1993-Dec. 31, 1993: Transgender Man Brandon Teena Raped and Murdered, 615

1994: Employment Non-Discrimination Act Is Proposed to U.S. Congress, 618

Aug. 6, 1994: Japanese American Citizens League Supports Same-Gender Marriage, 629

Dec. 4, 1995: Lesbian Couple Murdered in Oregon, 641

Sept. 21, 1996: U.S. President Clinton Signs Defense of Marriage Act, 646

Apr. 2, 1998: Canadian Supreme Court Reverses Gay Academic's Firing, 652

Oct. 6-7, 1998: Gay College Student Shepard Is Beaten and Murdered, 654

Oct. 27, 1999: *Littleton v. Prange* Withholds Survivor Rights from Transsexual Spouses, 662

Dec. 20, 1999: *Baker v. Vermont* Leads to Recognition of Same-Gender Civil Unions, 666

Jan. 12, 2000: United Kingdom Lifts Ban on Gays and Lesbians in the Military, 669

June 28, 2000: *Boy Scouts of America v. Dale*, 675

May 25, 2001: Japanese Human Rights Council Recommends Lesbian and Gay Rights, 681

2002: Sylvia Rivera Law Project Is Founded, 686

Apr. 30, 2002: Transgender Rights Added to New York City Law, 687

June 28, 2002: Irish American Lesbian Gains Canadian Immigrant Status, 692

Oct. 4, 2002: Transgender Teen Gwen Araujo Is Murdered in California, 694

Feb. 21, 2003: Australian Court Validates Transsexual Marriage, 698

Mar. 21, 2003: New Mexico Amends Its Human Rights Act, 702

Apr., 2003: Buenos Aires Recognizes Same-Gender Civil Unions, 705

June 17, 2003, and July 19, 2005: Canada Legalizes Same-Gender Marriage, 707

June 26, 2003: U.S. Supreme Court Overturns Texas Sodomy Law, 710

Nov. 18, 2003: Massachusetts Court Rules for Same-Gender Marriage, 717

Nov. 18, 2004: United Kingdom Legalizes Same-Gender Civil Partnerships, 731

Apr. 4, 2005: United Kingdom's Gender Recognition Act Legalizes Transsexual Marriage, 734

June 30, 2005: Spain Legalizes Same-Gender Marriage, 736

LITERATURE

July 4, 1855: Whitman Publishes *Leaves of Grass*, 3

Aug. 29, 1867: Karl Heinrich Ulrichs Speaks Publicly for Gay and Lesbian Rights, 9

May 25, 1895: Oscar Wilde Is Convicted of Gross Indecency, 26

1896: *Der Eigene* Is Published as First Journal on Homosexuality, 29

1896: Raffalovich Publishes *Uranisme et Unisexualité*, 31

1903: Stein Writes *Q.E.D.*, 43

1908: Carpenter Publishes *The Intermediate Sex*, 55

Oct., 1909: Barney Opens Her Paris Salon, 58

1924: Gide Publishes the Signed Edition of *Corydon*, 69

1928: Hall Publishes *The Well of Loneliness*, 76

1939: Isherwood Publishes *Goodbye to Berlin*, 92

1947-1948: Golden Age of American Gay Literature, 97

1953: *ONE* Magazine Begins Publication, 124

1956: Baldwin Publishes *Giovanni's Room*, 135

1956: Foster Publishes *Sex Variant Women in Literature*, 138
1963: Rechy Publishes *City of Night*, 151
Fall, 1967: Oscar Wilde Memorial Bookshop Opens as First Gay Bookstore, 180
1970: Amazon Bookstore Opens as First Feminist-Lesbian Book Shop, 203
June, 1971: The Gay Book Award Debuts, 223
1973: Brown Publishes *Rubyfruit Jungle*, 241
1973: Naiad Press Is Founded, 244
1974: *The Front Runner* Makes *The New York Times* Best-Seller List, 269
1975: First Novel About Coming Out to Parents Is Published, 283
1975: Rule Publishes *Lesbian Images*, 287
1976: Katz Publishes First Lesbian and Gay History Anthology, 300
1980: Alyson Begins Publishing Gay and Lesbian Books, 351
1980-1981: Gay Writers Form the Violet Quill, 353
1981: Faderman Publishes *Surpassing the Love of Men*, 362
1981: *This Bridge Called My Back* Is Published, 370
June 5 and July 3, 1981: Reports of Rare Diseases Mark Beginning of AIDS Epidemic, 378
Oct., 1981: Kitchen Table: Women of Color Press Is Founded, 383
1982: Lorde's Autobiography *Zami* Is Published, 392
1985: Lesbian Film *Desert Hearts* Is Released, 426
1986: Paula Gunn Allen Publishes *The Sacred Hoop*, 435
1987: Anzaldúa Publishes *Borderlands/La Frontera*, 446
1987: *Compañeras: Latina Lesbians* Is Published, 450
1987: Shilts Publishes *And the Band Played On*, 453
May, 1987: *Lambda Rising Book Report* Begins Publication, 464
Mar. 20, 1988: *M. Butterfly* Opens on Broadway, 479

June 2, 1989: Lambda Literary Award Is Created, 512
1991: Revisionist Criticism Recasts Sor Juana Inés de la Cruz, 537
1993: Monette Wins the National Book Award for *Becoming a Man*, 588

Marches, protests, and riots

July 2-Aug. 28, 1963: Rustin Organizes the March on Washington, 154
Aug., 1966: Queer Youth Fight Police Harassment at Compton's Cafeteria in San Francisco, 163
June 27-July 2, 1969: Stonewall Rebellion Ignites Modern Gay and Lesbian Rights Movement, 192
July 31, 1969: Gay Liberation Front Is Formed, 195
May 1, 1970: Lavender Menace Protests Homophobia in Women's Movement, 206
May 1, 1970: Radicalesbians Issues "The Woman Identified Woman" Manifesto, 209
June 28, 1970: First Lesbian and Gay Pride March in the United States, 212
Mar. 5, 1974: Antigay and Antilesbian Organizations Begin to Form, 271
1975-1983: Gay Latino Alliance Is Formed, 290
Dec. 31, 1977: Toronto Police Raid Offices of *The Body Politic*, 318
1978: Lesbian and Gay Workplace Movement Is Founded, 323
Nov. 27, 1978: White Murders Politicians Moscone and Milk, 337
Oct. 12-15, 1979: First March on Washington for Lesbian and Gay Rights, 344
Oct. 12-15, 1979: First National Third World Lesbian and Gay Conference Convenes, 347
Oct. 12-15, 1979: Lesbian and Gay Asian Collective Is Founded, 349
Feb. 5, 1981: Toronto Police Raid Gay Bathhouses, 376
Mar., 1987: Radical AIDS Activist Group ACT UP Is Founded, 458
Oct. 11, 1987: Second March on Washington for Lesbian and Gay Rights, 469

Oct. 11, 1988: First National Coming Out Day Is Celebrated, 489

1989: Act Up Paris Is Founded, 496

Dec. 10, 1989: ACT UP Protests at St. Patrick's Cathedral, 514

Mar. 20, 1990: Queer Nation Is Founded, 524

Apr. 6, 1991: Asian Lesbians and Gays Protest Lambda Fund-Raiser, 542

Sept. 29, 1991: California Governor Wilson Vetoes Antidiscrimination Bill, 550

1992: Transgender Nation Holds Its First Protest, 562

Apr. 24, 1993: First Dyke March Is Held in Washington, D.C., 598

Apr. 25, 1993: March on Washington for Gay, Lesbian, and Bi Equal Rights and Liberation, 601

June, 1994: Stonewall 25 March and Rallies Are Held in New York City, 627

Oct. 6-7, 1998: Gay College Student Shepard Is Beaten and Murdered, 654

June 19, 2002: Gays and Lesbians March for Equal Rights in Mexico City, 690

Mar., 2003-Dec., 2004: Transsexuals Protest Academic Exploitation, 700

Nov. 20, 2003: Transgender Day of Remembrance and Remembering Our Dead Project, 722

MILITARY

Nov. 11, 1865: Mary Edwards Walker Is Awarded the Medal of Honor, 7

c. 1899: Transgender Reporter Covers Spanish-American War Revolts, 39

1912-1924: Robles Fights in the Mexican Revolution, 61

Mar. 15, 1919-1921: U.S. Navy Launches Sting Operation Against "Sexual Perverts," 63

June 30-July 1, 1934: Hitler's Night of the Long Knives, 89

Nov., 1965: Revolutionary Cuba Imprisons Gays, 157

1976-1990: Army Reservist Ben-Shalom Sues for Reinstatement, 302

May-Aug., 1980: U.S. Navy Investigates the USS *Norton Sound* in Antilesbian Witch Hunt, 357

May 3, 1989: *Watkins v. United States Army* Reinstates Gay Soldier, 510

1990, 1994: *Coming Out Under Fire* Documents Gay and Lesbian Military Veterans, 522

Aug. 27, 1991: *The Advocate* Outs Pentagon Spokesman Pete Williams, 547

Oct., 1992: Canadian Military Lifts Its Ban on Gays and Lesbians, 579

Nov. 30, 1993: Don't Ask, Don't Tell Policy Is Implemented, 611

Jan. 12, 2000: United Kingdom Lifts Ban on Gays and Lesbians in the Military, 669

ORGANIZATIONS AND INSTITUTIONS

July 19-20, 1848: Seneca Falls Women's Rights Convention, 1

Aug. 29, 1867: Karl Heinrich Ulrichs Speaks Publicly for Gay and Lesbian Rights, 9

1869: Westphal Advocates Medical Treatment for Sexual Inversion, 16

1896: *Der Eigene* Is Published as First Journal on Homosexuality, 29

May 14, 1897: Hirschfeld Founds the Scientific-Humanitarian Committee, 36

1906: Friedlaender Breaks with the Scientific-Humanitarian Committee, 49

Dec. 10, 1924: Gerber Founds the Society for Human Rights, 72

1930's-1960's: Hollywood Bans "Sexual Perversion" in Films, 84

1948: Kinsey Publishes *Sexual Behavior in the Human Male*, 103

1950: Mattachine Society Is Founded, 106

1952: APA Classifies Homosexuality as a Mental Disorder, 111

1952: ONE, Inc., Is Founded, 114

1953: Kinsey Publishes *Sexual Behavior in the Human Female*, 121

1955: Daughters of Bilitis Founded as First National Lesbian Group in United States, 132

May, 1960: First National Lesbian Conference Convenes, 144

July 2-Aug. 28, 1963: Rustin Organizes the March on Washington, 154

Feb. 19-20, 1966: First North American Conference of Homophile Organizations Convenes, 160

Nov. 21, 1966: First Gender Identity Clinic Opens and Provides Gender Reassignment Surgery, 165

Apr. 19, 1967: First Student Homophile League Is Formed, 172

Aug. 11-18, 1968: NACHO Formally Becomes the First Gay Political Coalition, 182

Oct. 6, 1968: Metropolitan Community Church Is Founded, 184

1969: Nuestro Mundo Forms as First Queer Organization in Argentina, 187

1969-1973: Gay Catholics Find Dignity, 189

July 31, 1969: Gay Liberation Front Is Formed, 195

1970: Amazon Bookstore Opens as First Feminist-Lesbian Book Shop, 203

May 1, 1970: Lavender Menace Protests Homophobia in Women's Movement, 206

May 1, 1970: Radicalesbians Issues "The Woman Identified Woman" Manifesto, 209

June 28, 1970: First Lesbian and Gay Pride March in the United States, 212

Nov. 28, 1970: Del Martin Quits Gay Liberation Movement, 214

Mar., 1971: Los Angeles Gay and Lesbian Center Is Founded, 221

June, 1971: The Gay Book Award Debuts, 223

Nov., 1971: *The Body Politic* Begins Publication, 226

Mar., 1972-Mar., 1973: First Gay and Lesbian Synagogue in the United States Is Formed, 230

Mar. 22, 1972-June 30, 1982: Equal Rights Amendment Fails State Ratification, 233

1973: National Gay Task Force Is Formed, 246

Aug., 1973: American Bar Association Calls for Repeal of Laws Against Consensual Sex, 258

Fall, 1973: Lesbian Herstory Archives Is Founded, 260

Oct. 18, 1973: Lambda Legal Authorized to Practice Law, 263

Dec. 15, 1973: Homosexuality Is Delisted by APA, 265

1974: Bisexual Forum Is Founded, 267

Mar. 5, 1974: Antigay and Antilesbian Organizations Begin to Form, 271

Oct., 1974: *Lesbian Connection* Begins Publication, 275

1975: First Gay and Lesbian Archives Is Founded, 280

1975: Gay American Indians Is Founded, 285

1975-1983: Gay Latino Alliance Is Formed, 290

Sept., 1975: Anna Crusis Women's Choir Is Formed, 295

Aug. 20-22, 1976: Michigan Womyn's Music Festival Holds Its First Gathering, 304

Nov. 18-21, 1977: National Women's Conference Convenes, 311

Dec. 31, 1977: Toronto Police Raid Offices of *The Body Politic*, 318

1978: Harry Benjamin International Gender Dysphoria Association Is Founded, 320

1978: Lesbian and Gay Workplace Movement Is Founded, 323

Aug. 8, 1978: International Lesbian and Gay Association Is Founded, 330

1979: Moral Majority Is Founded, 339

Oct. 12-15, 1979: First March on Washington for Lesbian and Gay Rights, 344

Oct. 12-15, 1979: First National Third World Lesbian and Gay Conference Convenes, 347

Oct. 12-15, 1979: Lesbian and Gay Asian Collective Is Founded, 349

1980-1981: Gay Writers Form the Violet Quill, 353

Apr. 22, 1980: Human Rights Campaign Fund Is Founded, 355

1981: Parents, Families, and Friends of Lesbians and Gays Is Founded, 367

1981-1982: GALA Choruses Is Formed, 373

June 6-June 20, 1981: San Francisco Gay Men's Chorus Concert Tour, 380

Dec. 8, 1981: New York City Gay Men's Chorus Performs at Carnegie Hall, 385

1982: Lesbian and Gay Youth Protection Institute Is Founded, 387

1982-1991: Lesbian Academic and Activist Sues University of California for Discrimination, 395

Category Index

Aug. 28, 1982: First Gay Games Are Held in San Francisco, 405

Sept., 1983: First National Lesbians of Color Conference Convenes, 411

Spring, 1984: AIDS Virus Is Discovered, 413

1985: GLAAD Begins Monitoring Media Coverage of Gays and Lesbians, 424

Jan., 1986: South Asian Newsletter *Trikone* Begins Publication, 438

Sept., 1986: AZT Treats People with AIDS, 440

1987: Asian Pacific Lesbian Network Is Founded, 448

1987: VIVA Is Founded to Promote Latina and Latino Artists, 455

Mar., 1987: Radical AIDS Activist Group ACT UP Is Founded, 458

Apr., 1987: Old Lesbians Organize for Change, 462

Oct. 11, 1987: Second March on Washington for Lesbian and Gay Rights, 469

Oct. 14-17, 1987: Latin American and Caribbean Lesbian Feminist Network Is Formed, 472

May, 1988: Lavender Youth Recreation and Information Center Opens, 482

June 27, 1988: Report of the Presidential AIDS Commission, 485

Oct. 11, 1988: First National Coming Out Day Is Celebrated, 489

Dec. 1, 1988: First World AIDS Day, 494

1989: Act Up Paris Is Founded, 496

1989: Vaid Becomes Executive Director of the National Gay and Lesbian Task Force, 498

June 2, 1989: Lambda Literary Award Is Created, 512

Dec. 10, 1989: ACT UP Protests at St. Patrick's Cathedral, 514

1990: International Gay and Lesbian Human Rights Commission Is Founded, 517

1990: United Lesbians of African Heritage Is Founded, 519

1990-1993: Artists Sue the National Endowment for the Arts, 520

1990, 1994: *Coming Out Under Fire* Documents Gay and Lesbian Military Veterans, 522

Mar. 20, 1990: Queer Nation Is Founded, 524

June, 1990: BiNet USA Is Formed, 527

Dec., 1990: Asian Lesbian Network Holds Its First Conference, 533

Apr. 6, 1991: Asian Lesbians and Gays Protest Lambda Fund-Raiser, 542

Aug., 1991: Leather Archives and Museum Is Founded, 545

1992: Canadian YMCA Extends Family Discounts to Gays and Lesbians, 559

1992: Transgender Nation Holds Its First Protest, 562

1993: Intersex Society of North America Is Founded, 586

Mar.-Apr., 1993: Battelle Sex Study Prompts Conservative Backlash, 596

Apr. 24, 1993: First Dyke March Is Held in Washington, D.C., 598

Apr. 25, 1993: March on Washington for Gay, Lesbian, and Bi Equal Rights and Liberation, 601

1994: National Association of Lesbian and Gay Community Centers Is Founded, 621

Aug. 6, 1994: Japanese American Citizens League Supports Same-Gender Marriage, 629

Sept. 16, 1994: U.N. Revokes Consultative Status of International Lesbian and Gay Association, 632

June 17, 1995: International Bill of Gender Rights Is First Circulated, 639

1996: Hart Recognized as a Transgender Man, 644

Oct. 9-12, 1998: First International Retreat for Lesbian and Gay Muslims Is Held, 657

Nov., 1999: First Middle Eastern Gay and Lesbian Organization Is Founded, 664

Mar. 21, 2000: Hollywood Awards Transgender Portrayals in Film, 672

June 28, 2000: *Boy Scouts of America v. Dale*, 675

Apr. 20, 2001: Chinese Psychiatric Association Removes Homosexuality from List of Mental Disorders, 679

2002: Sylvia Rivera Law Project Is Founded, 686

Apr. 30, 2002: Transgender Rights Added to New York City Law, 687

June 19, 2002: Gays and Lesbians March for Equal Rights in Mexico City, 690

July, 2003: Wal-Mart Adds Lesbians and Gays to Its Antidiscrimination Policy, 715

Nov. 20, 2003: Transgender Day of Remembrance and Remembering Our Dead Project, 722

Mar. 7, 2004: Robinson Becomes First Out Gay Bishop in Christian History, 725

May 17, 2004: Transsexual Athletes Allowed to Compete in Olympic Games, 728

Nov. 29, 2005: Roman Catholic Church Bans Gay Seminarians, 738

Publications

July 19-20, 1848: Seneca Falls Women's Rights Convention, 1

July 4, 1855: Whitman Publishes *Leaves of Grass*, 3

May 6, 1868: Kertbeny Coins the Terms "Homosexual" and "Heterosexual," 12

1896: *Der Eigene* Is Published as First Journal on Homosexuality, 29

1896: Raffalovich Publishes *Uranisme et Unisexualité*, 31

1897: Ellis Publishes *Sexual Inversion*, 33

1903: Stein Writes *Q.E.D.*, 43

1905: Freud Rejects Third-Sex Theory, 46

1908: Carpenter Publishes *The Intermediate Sex*, 55

1924: Gide Publishes the Signed Edition of *Corydon*, 69

Dec. 10, 1924: Gerber Founds the Society for Human Rights, 72

1928: Hall Publishes *The Well of Loneliness*, 76

1939: Isherwood Publishes *Goodbye to Berlin*, 92

1947-1948: Golden Age of American Gay Literature, 97

June, 1947-Feb., 1948: *Vice Versa* Is Published as First Lesbian Periodical, 101

1948: Kinsey Publishes *Sexual Behavior in the Human Male*, 103

1950: Mattachine Society Is Founded, 106

1952: ONE, Inc., Is Founded, 114

1953: Kinsey Publishes *Sexual Behavior in the Human Female*, 121

1953: *ONE* Magazine Begins Publication, 124

1955: Daughters of Bilitis Founded as First National Lesbian Group in United States, 132

1956: Baldwin Publishes *Giovanni's Room*, 135

1956: Foster Publishes *Sex Variant Women in Literature*, 138

Sept. 4, 1957: The *Wolfenden Report* Calls for Decriminalizing Private Consensual Sex, 142

1963: Rechy Publishes *City of Night*, 151

1967: *Los Angeles Advocate* Begins Publication, 167

Fall, 1967: Oscar Wilde Memorial Bookshop Opens as First Gay Bookstore, 180

Oct. 31, 1969: *Time* Magazine Issues "The Homosexual in America," 201

1970: Amazon Bookstore Opens as First Feminist-Lesbian Book Shop, 203

May 1, 1970: Radicalesbians Issues "The Woman Identified Woman" Manifesto, 209

Nov. 28, 1970: Del Martin Quits Gay Liberation Movement, 214

1971: *Lesbian Tide* Publishes Its First Issue, 219

Nov., 1971: *The Body Politic* Begins Publication, 226

1973: Brown Publishes *Rubyfruit Jungle*, 241

1973: Naiad Press Is Founded, 244

June 21, 1973: U.S. Supreme Court Supports Local Obscenity Laws, 255

Dec. 15, 1973: Homosexuality Is Delisted by APA, 265

1974: *The Front Runner* Makes *The New York Times* Best-Seller List, 269

Oct., 1974: *Lesbian Connection* Begins Publication, 275

1975: First Gay and Lesbian Archives Is Founded, 280

1975: First Novel About Coming Out to Parents Is Published, 283

1975: Rule Publishes *Lesbian Images*, 287

1976: Katz Publishes First Lesbian and Gay History Anthology, 300

Apr., 1977: Combahee River Collective Issues "A Black Feminist Statement," 309

Dec. 31, 1977: Toronto Police Raid Offices of *The Body Politic*, 318

1980: Alyson Begins Publishing Gay and Lesbian Books, 351

Category Index

1980-1981: Gay Writers Form the Violet Quill, 353
1981: Faderman Publishes *Surpassing the Love of Men*, 362
1981: *This Bridge Called My Back* Is Published, 370
Oct., 1981: Kitchen Table: Women of Color Press Is Founded, 383
1982: Lorde's Autobiography *Zami* Is Published, 392
1985: GLAAD Begins Monitoring Media Coverage of Gays and Lesbians, 424
1986: Paula Gunn Allen Publishes *The Sacred Hoop*, 435
Jan., 1986: South Asian Newsletter *Trikone* Begins Publication, 438
1987: Anzaldúa Publishes *Borderlands/La Frontera*, 446
1987: *Compañeras: Latina Lesbians* Is Published, 450
1987: Shilts Publishes *And the Band Played On*, 453
May, 1987: *Lambda Rising Book Report* Begins Publication, 464
June 2, 1989: Lambda Literary Award Is Created, 512
1991: Revisionist Criticism Recasts Sor Juana Inés de la Cruz, 537
1991: Stone Publishes "The Posttranssexual Manifesto," 540
Aug. 27, 1991: *The Advocate* Outs Pentagon Spokesman Pete Williams, 547
June, 1992: Feinberg Publishes *Transgender Liberation*, 573
1993: Monette Wins the National Book Award for *Becoming a Man*, 588
Mar.-Apr., 1993: Battelle Sex Study Prompts Conservative Backlash, 596
1995: *The Advocate* Outs Oscar Nominee Nigel Hawthorne, 634
1995: Athlete Louganis Announces He Is HIV-Positive, 637
1998: Transgender Scholarship Proliferates, 650
Apr. 20, 2001: Chinese Psychiatric Association Removes Homosexuality from List of Mental Disorders, 679

Mar., 2003-Dec., 2004: Transsexuals Protest Academic Exploitation, 700

RACE AND ETHNICITY

Jan.-June, 1886: Two-Spirit American Indian Visits Washington, D.C., 21
July 2-Aug. 28, 1963: Rustin Organizes the March on Washington, 154
1975: Gay American Indians Is Founded, 285
1975-1983: Gay Latino Alliance Is Formed, 290
Apr., 1977: Combahee River Collective Issues "A Black Feminist Statement," 309
Oct. 12-15, 1979: First National Third World Lesbian and Gay Conference Convenes, 347
Oct. 12-15, 1979: Lesbian and Gay Asian Collective Is Founded, 349
1981: *This Bridge Called My Back* Is Published, 370
Oct., 1981: Kitchen Table: Women of Color Press Is Founded, 383
1982: Lorde's Autobiography *Zami* Is Published, 392
1982-1991: Lesbian Academic and Activist Sues University of California for Discrimination, 395
Sept., 1983: First National Lesbians of Color Conference Convenes, 411
1986: Paula Gunn Allen Publishes *The Sacred Hoop*, 435
1987: Anzaldúa Publishes *Borderlands/La Frontera*, 446
1987: Asian Pacific Lesbian Network Is Founded, 448
1987: *Compañeras: Latina Lesbians* Is Published, 450
1987: VIVA Is Founded to Promote Latina and Latino Artists, 455
Mar. 20, 1988: *M. Butterfly* Opens on Broadway, 479
1990: United Lesbians of African Heritage Is Founded, 519
Dec., 1990: Asian Lesbian Network Holds Its First Conference, 533
1991: Revisionist Criticism Recasts Sor Juana Inés de la Cruz, 537

1993: *The Wedding Banquet* Is First Acclaimed Taiwanese Gay-Themed Film, 591
2002: Sylvia Rivera Law Project Is Founded, 686
June 19, 2002: Gays and Lesbians March for Equal Rights in Mexico City, 690

RELIGION
1930's-1960's: Hollywood Bans "Sexual Perversion" in Films, 84
Oct. 6, 1968: Metropolitan Community Church Is Founded, 184
1969-1973: Gay Catholics Find Dignity, 189
Mar., 1972-Mar., 1973: First Gay and Lesbian Synagogue in the United States Is Formed, 230
Mar. 22, 1972-June 30, 1982: Equal Rights Amendment Fails State Ratification, 233
June 25, 1972: First Out Gay Minister Is Ordained, 236
Mar. 5, 1974: Antigay and Antilesbian Organizations Begin to Form, 271
1979: Moral Majority Is Founded, 339
1989-1990: Helms Claims Photographs Are Indecent, 500
Dec. 10, 1989: ACT UP Protests at St. Patrick's Cathedral, 514
1991: Revisionist Criticism Recasts Sor Juana Inés de la Cruz, 537
Sept. 21, 1996: U.S. President Clinton Signs Defense of Marriage Act, 646
Oct. 6-7, 1998: Gay College Student Shepard Is Beaten and Murdered, 654
Oct. 9-12, 1998: First International Retreat for Lesbian and Gay Muslims Is Held, 657
Mar. 7, 2004: Robinson Becomes First Out Gay Bishop in Christian History, 725
Nov. 29, 2005: Roman Catholic Church Bans Gay Seminarians, 738

SCIENCE
1869: Westphal Advocates Medical Treatment for Sexual Inversion, 16
1897: Ellis Publishes *Sexual Inversion*, 33
1905: Freud Rejects Third-Sex Theory, 46
1906: Friedlaender Breaks with the Scientific-Humanitarian Committee, 49
1929: Davis's Research Identifies Lesbian Sexuality as Common and Normal, 79
1948: Kinsey Publishes *Sexual Behavior in the Human Male*, 103
Sept. 24, 1951: George Jorgensen Becomes Christine Jorgensen, 108
1952: APA Classifies Homosexuality as a Mental Disorder, 111
1953: Kinsey Publishes *Sexual Behavior in the Human Female*, 121
1953-1957: Evelyn Hooker Debunks Beliefs that Homosexuality Is a "Sickness," 126
Dec. 15, 1973: Homosexuality Is Delisted by APA, 265
1978: Harry Benjamin International Gender Dysphoria Association Is Founded, 320
June 5 and July 3, 1981: Reports of Rare Diseases Mark Beginning of AIDS Epidemic, 378
July, 1982: Gay-Related Immunodeficiency Is Renamed AIDS, 401
Spring, 1984: AIDS Virus Is Discovered, 413
Sept., 1986: AZT Treats People with AIDS, 440
June 27, 1988: Report of the Presidential AIDS Commission, 485
1991: LeVay Postulates the "Gay Brain," 535
1993: Intersex Society of North America Is Founded, 586
Apr. 20, 2001: Chinese Psychiatric Association Removes Homosexuality from List of Mental Disorders, 679

SPORTS
Aug. 28, 1982: First Gay Games Are Held in San Francisco, 405
1994: Navratilova Honored for Her Career in Tennis, 623
1995: Athlete Louganis Announces He Is HIV-Positive, 637
May 17, 2004: Transsexual Athletes Allowed to Compete in Olympic Games, 728

TRANSGENDER/TRANSSEXUALITY
Nov. 11, 1865: Mary Edwards Walker Is Awarded the Medal of Honor, 7
Jan.-June, 1886: Two-Spirit American Indian Visits Washington, D.C., 21

c. 1899: Transgender Reporter Covers Spanish-American War Revolts, 39

1912-1924: Robles Fights in the Mexican Revolution, 61

Sept. 24, 1951: George Jorgensen Becomes Christine Jorgensen, 108

Aug., 1966: Queer Youth Fight Police Harassment at Compton's Cafeteria in San Francisco, 163

Nov. 21, 1966: First Gender Identity Clinic Opens and Provides Gender Reassignment Surgery, 165

1978: Harry Benjamin International Gender Dysphoria Association Is Founded, 320

1986: Paula Gunn Allen Publishes *The Sacred Hoop*, 435

Jan. 21, 1989: Death of Transgender Jazz Musician Billy Tipton, 505

May 1, 1989: U.S. Supreme Court Rules Gender-Role Stereotyping Is Discriminatory, 508

1991: Stone Publishes "The Posttranssexual Manifesto," 540

1992: Transgender Nation Holds Its First Protest, 562

June, 1992: Feinberg Publishes *Transgender Liberation*, 573

Apr. 25, 1993: March on Washington for Gay, Lesbian, and Bi Equal Rights and Liberation, 601

Dec. 24, 1993-Dec. 31, 1993: Transgender Man Brandon Teena Raped and Murdered, 615

June 17, 1995: International Bill of Gender Rights Is First Circulated, 639

1996: Hart Recognized as a Transgender Man, 644

1998: Transgender Scholarship Proliferates, 650

Oct. 27, 1999: *Littleton v. Prange* Withholds Survivor Rights from Transsexual Spouses, 662

Mar. 21, 2000: Hollywood Awards Transgender Portrayals in Film, 672

2002: Sylvia Rivera Law Project Is Founded, 686

Apr. 30, 2002: Transgender Rights Added to New York City Law, 687

Oct. 4, 2002: Transgender Teen Gwen Araujo Is Murdered in California, 694

Feb. 21, 2003: Australian Court Validates Transsexual Marriage, 698

Mar., 2003-Dec., 2004: Transsexuals Protest Academic Exploitation, 700

Mar. 21, 2003: New Mexico Amends Its Human Rights Act, 702

Nov. 20, 2003: Transgender Day of Remembrance and Remembering Our Dead Project, 722

May 17, 2004: Transsexual Athletes Allowed to Compete in Olympic Games, 728

Apr. 4, 2005: United Kingdom's Gender Recognition Act Legalizes Transsexual Marriage, 734

Indexes

Personages Index

Abbitt, Diane, 442
Abbott, Sydney, 209
Abdill, Michelle, 641
Abella, Rosalie Silberman, 477
Abry, Phyllis, 522
Abse, Leo, 142, 178
Abzug, Bella, 273, 311-312
Achtenberg, Roberta, 604
Acremant, Robert, 641
Adam, Margie, 305
Adkins, Warren, 169
Akinola, Peter, 725
Alam, Faisal, 657
Aldredge, J. C., 95
Alfaro, Luis, 455
Allen, Don Merriam, 151
Allen, Paula Gunn, 435
Allison, Becky, 700
Almodóvar, Pedro, 672
Alyson, Sasha, 351
Amestoy, Jeffrey L., 666
Anabitarte, Héctor, 187
Antoinette, Marie, 363
Anzaldúa, Gloria, 370, 446
Apuzzo, Virginia, 246
Aquino, Corazon, 474
Araujo, Gwen, 694, 722
Arenas, Reinaldo, 157
Arnold, Ervin, 63
Arnold, June, 241
Arran, Earl of, 142, 178
Asch, Sholem, 66
Ashe, Arthur, 638
Ashkinazy, Steve, 387
Ashley, April, 734
Aspin, Leslie, 611
Attwell, Michael, 342
Azmi, Shabana, 660

Bachardy, Don, 92
Baehr, Ninia, 593
Bagger, Mianne, 728
Bailey, J. Michael, 700
Baker, Josephine, 673
Baker, Stan, 666
Baldwin, James, 135

Bamburger, Rose, 132
Bannon, Ann, 243
Banton, Joab H., 74
Barbee, Lloyd, 397
Barnett, Marilyn, 365
Barney, Natalie Clifford, 58
Barr, Robert, 646, 647
Barrett, Ellen Marie, 238
Barrie, Dennis, 500
Baturin, Carlos, 736
Bauman, Robert, 466
Beam, Gail C., 702
Bean, Babe, 39
Bean, Joseph, 545
Beck, Nina, 666
Beckett, John, 669
Bédard, Marc-André, 315
Bellinger, Elizabeth, 734
Ben, Lisa, 101
Ben-Shalom, Miriam, 302
Benedict XVI, 515
Benjamin, Harry, 165, 320
Bentham, Trevor, 634
Berger, Jack C., 320
Berson, Ginny, 249
Bérubé, Allan, 522
Beteta, Aura L., 347
Bianco, José "Pepe," 188
Bieber, Irving, 111
Billings, Robert, 339
Billy, John O. G., 596
Birch, Joshua, 579
Biron, Chartres, 76
Blackmun, Harry A., 252, 432
Blair, Tony, 671
Blase, Anthony De, 545
Blewitt, Tom, 524
Block, Martin, 124
Blomberg, Werner von, 90
Bloomberg, Michael, 687
Blumenthal, Marc, 231
Boer, Jo den, 203
Bonauto, Mary, 666, 717
Bookstaver, May, 43
Bornstein, Kate, 540, 541
Bottini, Ivy, 207, 209

Bottoms, Pamela Kay, 608
Bottoms, Sharon, 608
Bouchet, Joëlle, 496
Boulton, Ernest, 18
Bourassa, Kevin, 707
Bourland, Roger, 588
Boutilier, Clive Michael, 176
Bowers, Michael J., 432
Bowman, Parke, 241
Boxer, Barbara, 605
Brand, Adolf, 29, 36, 49
Brandon, JoAnn, 615
Breen, Joseph, 84
Brennan, William J., 256, 297, 327
Briggs, John V., 333
Brock, Carole, 357
Brocka, Lino, 474
Broder, Samuel, 440
Bronstein, Sidney, 281
Brooks, Louise, 81
Brown, Mark, 405
Brown, Rita Mae, 206, 209, 241
Browne, Karen, 203
Brownmiller, Susan, 207, 209
Bryant, Anita, 229, 251, 271, 307, 333, 340, 709
Bueno, Pilo, 489
Burger, Warren E., 432
Burns, Randy, 285
Burton, Dan, 530
Bush, George H. W., 485, 530, 547
Bush, George W., 485, 595, 620, 643, 712, 721
Bussell, Letantia, 429
Butler, Judith, 540
Byrd, Robert, 648

Callow, Simon, 636
Cameron, Barbara, 285
Campbell, Edward H., 63
Campbell, Ken, 271
Campbell, Kim, 579
Capote, Truman, 97
Cárdenas, Nancy, 742
Carlin, George, 327
Carlyle, Thomas, 114

Carpenter, Edward, 3, 55
Carter, Jimmy, 8, 314
Casasola, Agustin Victor, 62
Castro, Fidel, 157
Catzman, Marvin, 477
Cazares, Jason, 694
Celler, Emanuel, 233
Chan, June, 448
Chang, Kevin, 593
Chao, Winston, 591
Chaplin, Charlie, 672
Chapman, Jim, 530
Charbonneau, Patricia, 426
Charcot, Martin, 111
Chase, Cheryl, 586, 651
Cheney, Richard B., 547
Chin, May, 591
Chirac, Jacques, 415
Cho, Milyoung, 542
Chrétien, Jean, 707, 708
Christian, Marc, 429
Christian, Meg, 249, 304
Christian, Paula, 243
Christy, Rosina Richter, 203
Clarenbach, David, 397
Clark, Tom, 429
Cleveland, Grover, 22
Clinton, Bill, 240, 294, 325, 336, 485, 518, 566, 602, 604, 606, 611, 618, 643, 646, 718
Coll, Bridget, 692
Colwell, Clarence, 160
Compton, A. Christian, 608
Conway, Lynn, 700
Corbin, Joan, 124
Cordova, Jeanne, 219
Cox, Christopher, 353
Cranston, Alan, 117
Craven, James Braxton, 169
Crawford, Muriel, 244
Cromey, Robert Warren, 182
Cruz, Sor Juana Inés de la, 537
Cullman, Joseph, 623
Cumming, Alan, 636

Dale, James, 675
Dancel, Genora, 593
Daniels, Josephus, 63
Dannemeyer, William E., 442

Das, Nandita, 660
Das, Suvir, 438
Davidson, Jay, 373, 380
Davis, Katharine Bement, 79
Day, Doris, 430
Dean, Howard, 667, 718
DeGeneres, Ellen, 565
Deitch, Donna, 426
Delanoë, Bertrand, 496
Denny, Dallas, 650
Derrida, Jacques, 540
Dietrich, Marlene, 673
Dirmeyer, Robert, 464
Dlugacz, Judy, 249
Dobkin, Alix, 304
Dodd, Charles H., 74
Dole, Robert, 604
Donaldson, Stephen, 172, 182
Dong, Arthur, 522
Dorf, Julie, 517
Dormont, Dominique, 430
Doucé, Joseph, 330
Douglas, Lord Alfred "Bosie," 26
Douglas, John, 26
Douglas, Michelle, 579
Douglass, Frederick, 1
Doustou, Tyler, 608
Dreyfus, Lee, 397
Dubofsky, Jean, 582
Dudgeon, Jeff, 330
Duesberg, Peter, 441
Dugas, Gaëtan, 401, 453
Dumaresq, Michelle, 728
Duran, John J., 550

Earl, Nancy, 239
Eberhart, John, 126
Edel, Deborah, 260
Edgerton, Milton T., 165
Edwards, Lisa, 231
Eger, Denise, 231
Eichberg, Rob, 489
Eisenhower, Dwight D., 117, 129
Elders, Joycelyn, 495, 606
Elliott, Beth, 540
Ellis, Havelock, 16, 33
Ellis, Roxanne, 641
Endean, Steve, 355

Erickson, Reed, 114, 321
Ernst, Morris, 76
Etheridge, Melissa, 565, 656
Etienne, 545
Eulenburg-Hertefeld, Philipp, prince of, 51, 52
Evans, Linda, 430
Evans, Richard G., 582
Evans, Terence, 302
Everett, Rupert, 636
Evert, Chris, 625

Fabius, Laurent, 496
Faderman, Lillian, 362
Falwell, Jerry, 307, 339
Farnham, Lois, 666
Feinberg, Leslie, 540, 541, 573
Feinstein, Dianne, 337, 417, 442
Feldblum, Chai, 530
Feldman, Maxine, 304
Felix, Diane, 290
Ferro, Robert, 353
Fidus, 29
Fields, Annie, 363
Finley, Karen, 520
Fishman, Israel, 223
Fleck, John, 520
Fleming, Patsy S., 607
Flores, Patria Jiménez, 741
Ford, Gerald, 312
Foreman, Matt, 246
Foster, Jeannette Howard, 138
Foucault, Michel, 540
Fouratt, Jim, 195
Fourier, Charles, 3
Fournier, Bob, 189
Franco, Francisco, 736
Frank, Barney, 117, 466, 611, 647
Freedman, Blanch, 176
Freud, Sigmund, 16, 33, 46, 266
Frey, Noni, 132
Friedan, Betty, 206, 209, 312
Friedlaender, Benedict, 29, 49
Friedland, Lucy, 527
Friedman, Terry B., 550
Frohnmayer, John E., 500, 520
Fry, Steven, 636
Frye, Phyllis Randolph, 639

Personages Index

Fukaya, Michiyo, 347, 349
Fung, Richard, 349
Funk, Cynthia, 209

Gagliostro, Vincent, 514
Gair, Cyndi, 249
Galbreath, Charles, 297
Gallo, Robert, 401, 413
Garbo, Greta, 673
Garner, Tyron, 710
Gaskins, Tangela, 357
Gebbie, Kristine, 606
Gentile, Patrizia, 570
Gerber, Henry, 72, 281
Gernreich, Rudi, 106
Ghandhi, Khushro, 442
Gide, André, 69
Gilbert, Joshua Allen, 644
Gilgamesh, Joe, 189
Gingrich, Newt, 593
Gittings, Barbara, 132, 223, 265
Giuliani, Rudolph, 687
Gladstone, William Ewart, 18
Goebbels, Joseph, 89
Goldman, Albert, 169
Goldschmidt, Neil, 491
Gomez, Jewelle, 424, 512
Goodman, Susanne R., 477
Goodridge, Hillary, 717
Goodridge, Julie, 717
Goodstein, David, 333
Goring, Hermann, 89
Grady, Graeme, 669
Grady, William R., 596
Granville, Lord, 18
Graves, John T., 72
Green, Jamison, 562
Green, Richard, 320
Grice, Warren, 95
Grier, Barbara, 132, 138, 244
Griswold, Rufus W., 3
Gross, Larry, 547
Grumley, Michael, 353
Gua, Ah-Leh, 591
Guerrero, Sylvia, 697
Guevara, Che, 157
Gunderson, Steve, 647
Gyllenhaal, Jake, 744

Haig, Graham, 579
Halberstam, Judith, 650
Hale, C. Jacob, 645, 651
Hall, Radclyffe, 76
Halm, Henry, 477
Hamburger, Christian, 108
Hannon, Gerald, 227, 318
Hannum, Richard, 365
Hansen, Joseph, 124
Hanson, Cindy, 203
Hardberger, Phil, 662
Harden, Maximilian, 49, 51, 52
Harding, William, 84
Hardwick, Michael, 432
Haring, Keith, 489
Harrigan, Peter, 666
Harris, Alicia, 357
Harris, Helaine, 249
Hart, Alan Lucill, 644
Hart, Lois, 209
Hatch, Orin, 604
Hawkes, Brent, 376
Hawkins, John, 269
Hawthorne, Sir Nigel, 634
Hay, Harry, 106
Hayashino, Carole, 629
Hayden, Henry, 236
Haynes, Mable, 43
Hays, Will H., 84
Healey, Shevy, 462
Heckler, Margaret M., 413
Heilman, John, 419
Heldman, Gladys, 623
Helms, Jesse, 155, 331, 500, 520, 530, 604, 632
Helvey, Terry, 611
Henderson, Russell, 654
Henry VIII (king of England), and sodomy laws, 19
Hepburn, Katharine, 673
Herman, Erwin, 231
Hernandez, Aileen, 206
Hester, Rita, 722
Hetrick, Emery, 387
Heydrich, Reinhard, 89
Hickerson, Donald, 292
Hicks, Elias, 3
Hill, Joseph Lister, 129
Hiller, Kurt, 36

Himmler, Heinrich, 86, 89
Hindenburg, Paul von, 89
Hinojosa, Claudia, 742
Hirschfeld, Magnus, 10, 33, 36, 46, 49
Hitler, Adolf, 37, 86, 89
Hobson, Christopher Z., 283
Hobson, Laura Z., 283
Hockney, David, 94
Hoey, Clyde Roark, 129
Hoffman, March, 209
Hoffman, Philip Seymour, 744
Holleran, Andrew, 353
Hooker, Evelyn, 126, 201, 265
Hoopes, John E., 165
Hopkins, Ann B., 508
Horwitz, Roger, 588
Hoy, Claire, 318
Hudson, Erastus Mead, 63
Hudson, Rock, 366, 401, 429
Huffman, Felicity, 744
Hughes, Holly, 520
Hulting, Jane, 295
Hunt, Jane C., 1
Hunter, Joyce, 387
Hwang, David Henry, 479

Inaba, Masaki, 681
Inaudi, Jorge Alberto, 555
Irvine, Lord, 734
Isherwood, Christopher, 30, 92

Jackson, Ed, 318
James, Andrea, 700
Janzen, Wilhelm, 49
Jaques, Emanuel, 319
Jay, Karla, 206, 209
Jennings, Dale, 106, 124
Jewett, Sarah Orne, 363
John, Elton, 656
Johnson, Andrew, 7, 8
Johnson, Denise, 666
Johnson, Ervin "Magic," 638
Johnson, Lillie, 23
Johnson, William R., 236
Jolles, Stacy, 666
Jones, Cleve, 401, 469
Jordan, Barbara, 239, 311, 313
Jorgensen, Christine, 108
Julber, Eric, 124

Kaahumanu, Lani, 527
Kalinin, Roman, 517
Kameny, Franklin, 182, 201, 217, 265, 292
Katz, Jonathan Ned, 300
Kaufman, Liz, 491
Kaufman, Moisés, 656
Kauser, Alice, 68
Kay, James W., 675
Kelley, William, 160
Kennedy, Anthony M., 583, 710
Kennedy, Edward M., 618
Kent, Samuel Neal, 63
Kepner, Jim, 114, 124, 280
Kertbeny, Karl Maria, 12, 33
"Kevin," 698
Khaled, Mazen, 664
Khan, Surina, 657
Kieltyka, Charlotte Angelica, 700
Kight, Morris, 221
Kilhefner, Don, 221
Kimmel, Douglas, 679
King, Billie Jean, 365, 623
King, Martin Luther, Jr., 154
Kinsey, Alfred, 38, 80, 103, 121, 265, 596
Kinsman, Gary, 570
Kirk, Sheila, 320
Kivel, Beth, 482
Klein, Alan, 524
Klein, Fritz, 267
Klein, Ralph, 652
Klepinger, Daniel H., 596
Klippert, Everett George, 199
Klobukowska, Ewa, 728
Koch, Edward, 273
Koop, C. Everett, 404, 445, 485
Kopay, David, 406
Koppelman, Andrew, 509
Kosse, Roberta, 385
Kowalski, Donald, and Della Kowalski, 552
Kowalski, Sharon, 469, 552
Krafft-Ebing, Richard von, 12, 16, 33
Kramer, Dick, 380
Kramer, Larry, 401, 440, 458, 596
Krupp, Alfred, 53
Kuiland-Nazario, Marcus, 455
Kumar, Arvind, 438

Labouchere, Henry Du Pré, 18
Lagon, Pat, 593
Lahusen, Kay Tobin, 132
lang, k. d., 565
Lantz, Brian, 442
Largent, Steve, 648
LaRouche, Lyndon, 442
Larson, Libby, 386
Laub, Donald R., 320
Laux, Charles, 616
Lavrín, Asunción, 537
Lawrence, John Geddes, 710
Lazarus, Harris M., 68
Ledger, Heath, 744
Lee, Ang, 591, 744
Legg, W. Dorr, 114, 124, 280
Leigh, Richard, 63
Leitsch, Dick, 192, 194, 195
Leshner, Michael, 707
Lestrade, Didier, 496
LeVay, Simon, 535
Levi, Jeffrey, 246
Levy, Jay A., 414
Liberace, 365
Libman, Alyn, 728
Lichtenstein, Mitchell, 591
Liebman, Marvin, 522
Lingle, Larry, 180
Lippert, Bill, 666
Lithgow, John, 479
Littleton, Christie Lee, 662
Littleton, Jonathan Mark, 662
Lobel, Kerry, 246
Lopez, Margarita, 687
Lord, Daniel A., 84
Lorde, Audre, 347, 383, 392
Lott, Trent, 604
Lotter, John, 615
Louganis, Greg, 637
Love, Barbara, 209
Loy, Tana, 347, 349
Lung, Sihung, 591
Lustig-Prean, Duncan, 669
Lyon, Phyllis, 132, 144, 206

Mabon, Lon T., 491
McAteer, Ed, 339
McBride, Donna, 244
McCarthy, Joseph, 129

McClatchy, J. D., 588
McClintock, Mary Ann, 1
McClung, John Wesley, 652
McCorvey, Norma Jane, 252
Maccubbin, Deacon, 180, 464, 512
Macdonald, Barbara, 462
MacFarlane, Roger, 596
McFeely, Tim, 530
McGreivy, Susan, 357
McGuire, Jean, 530
McIlvenna, Ted, 163
Mackay, John Henry, 29
McKee, Joseph V., 74
McKellen, Ian, 634, 636
McKinney, Aaron, 654
McKinney, Stewart B., 466, 485
MacLane, Mary, 139
McMurtry, Roy, 318
McNeill, John J., 189
McSorley, Cisco, 702
Magidson, Michael, 694
Manford, Jean, 367
Manford, Morton, 367
Mapplethorpe, Robert, 500
Marchant, Anyda, 244
Marcos, Ferdinand, 474
Marder, Janet, 230
Margulies, Donald, 69
Marino, Joseph A., 327
Marks, Jim, 464
Marshall, Margaret H., 717
Marshall, Thurgood, 297
Mart, Paul, 405
Martet, Christophe, 496
Martin, Damien, 387
Martin, Del, 132, 144, 206, 214, 411
Martin, Paul, 708
Martin, Vera, 462
Mass, Lawrence, 378
Mather, Gina, 698
Matlovich, Leonard, 302
Maupin, Armistead, 512
Mehta, Deepa, 660
Meier, Karl, 29
Meininger, Al, 72
Melilio, Joseph, 593
Mendolia, Victor, 514
Menéndez, Emilio, 736
Merel, Jose, 694

Merrim, Stephanie, 537
Michaels, Dick, 167
Milk, Harvey, 333, 337
Miller, Gary, 373
Miller, Tim, 520
Mineta, Norman Y., 629
Mink, Patsy, 311, 312
Mishaan, Chuck, 267
Mitchell, Alice, 23
Mitsuya, Hiroaki, 440
Mixner, David, 333, 442
Moldenhauer, Jearld, 226
Moll, Albert, 33
Moltke, Kuno von, 51, 52
Monette, Paul, 588
Money, John, 165
Montagnier, Luc, 401, 413
Montagu, Mary Wortley, 363
Moon, Sun Myung, 341
Moraga, Cherríe, 370, 383
Moreno, Mike, 455
Morgan, Mary, 604
Morgan, Robin, 540
Morrissey, Christine, 692
Moscone, George, 337
Mott, Lucretia, 1
Mulroney, Brian, 570
Murray, Susan M., 666

N. (K.U.), 555
Nabors, Jaron Chase, 694
Nagata, Masashi, 681
Nahas, Omar, 657
Nania, Liz, 527
Navratilova, Martina, 623
Near, Holly, 305
Nestle, Joan, 260, 424
Nickles, Don, 647
Nidorf, Patrick X., 189
Niles, Donna, 203
Nissen, Thomas, 615
Nix, Robert, 273
Noble, Elaine, 277
Norris, William, 510
Norton, Clifford, 292
Nunn, Samuel, 611

O'Brien, John, 212
O'Connor, John Cardinal, 514

O'Donnell, Rosie, 565
Ogborn, Anne, 562
O'Leary, Jean, 312, 489
Ordona, Trinity, 448
Orejudos, Dom, 545
Orr-Cahall, Christina, 500
Owles, Jim, 195, 212
Ozawa, Donna, 482

Pabst, Georg Wilhelm, 81
Palencia, Roland, 455
Palmer, A. Mitchell, 63
Paole, Allan, 474
Park, Frederick, 18
Park, Pauline, 687
Parsons, Buford M., Jr., 608
Patton, Jude, 320
Paul, Alice, 233
Paz, Octavio, 537
Peck, Fred, 613
Perkins, Bill, 687
Perón, Juan, 187
Perry, James DeWolf, 63
Perry, Troy, 184, 469
Phelps, Fred, 271, 654
Phelps, Johnnie, 358
Phillips, Howard, 339
Picano, Felice, 353
Pine, Seymour, 192
Plato, 46
Ploen, Richard, 184
Plotkin, Harry M., 327
Pomeroy, Wardell, 201
Popert, Ken, 318
Powell, Adam Clayton, 155
Powell, Colin, 611
Powell, Lewis F., 432
Powell, Lisa, 519
Prange, Mark A., 662
Pregerson, Harry, 510
Pregil, Antoinette, 593
Price, Boo, 304
Prosser, Jay, 650
Puterbaugh, Holly, 666

Quist, Julie Morse, 203

Rado, Sandor, 111
Raffalovich, Marc-André, 31

Ramos, Juanita, 450
Rand, Bill, 167
Randolph, A. Philip, 154
Raymond, Janice, 540
Reagan, Ronald, 333, 401, 415, 453, 485; and immigration law, 120; and Moral Majority, 340
Rechy, John, 151
Reddy, Tom, 522
Rehnquist, William, 327, 677
Reno, Janet, 120
Renslow, Chuck, 545
Reyes, Rodrigo, 290
Reynolds, Charles L., Jr., 320
Richards, Renee, 728
Richardson, Bill, 702
Rideout, Janet, 440
Rivera, Sylvia, 686
Roberts, JoAnn, 639
Robertson, Pat, 582
Robinson, Beth, 666
Robinson, John, 466
Robinson, Marty, 195
Robinson, V. Gene, 725
Robles, Amelio, 61
Rockefeller, John D., Jr., 79
Rodrigues, Tammy, 593
Rodríguez, Aleida, 455
Rodwell, Craig, 180
Roen, Katrina, 651
Rohm, Ernst, 36, 89
Roma, Catherine, 295
Romer, Roy, 582
Romney, Mitt, 717
Roosevelt, Franklin D., 63
Rorem, Ned, 386, 588
Roughgarden, Joan, 700
Routsong, Alma, 223
Rowland, Chuck, 106
Rubin, Marc, 212
Rule, Jane, 287, 426
Rush, Stella, 132
Russell, Stella, 124
Russo, Vito, 424
Rustin, Bayard, 154

St. Pierre, Ethan, 722
Sandoz, Helen, 132
Sarria, José, 149

Scalia, Antonin, 584, 710
Schildkraut, Rudolph, 66
Schindler, Allen R., Jr., 611
Schlafly, John, 235
Schlafly, Phyllis, 233, 312, 596
Schlessinger, Laura, 424
Schons, Dorothy, 537
Schulman, Sarah, 598
Schulte, Steve, 419
Schwarz, Judith, 260
Scott, Bruce, 292
Scott, Peter, 442
Scott-Joynt, Michael, 734
Selwyn, Michael, 66
Sensenbrenner, James, 648
Serrano, Andres, 500
Shalala, Donna, 606
Shapiro, Judith, 540
Sharp, Kathy, 203
Shaver, Helen, 426
Shayne, Ralph, 664
Shays, Chris, 620
Sheldon, Lou, 333, 550, 596, 646, 647
Shelley, Martha, 195, 209
Shepard, Dennis, 654
Shepard, Judy, 654
Shepard, Matthew, 654
Shepodd, Lynn, 489
Shigemura, Lia, 629
Shilts, Randy, 358, 401, 453
Shoemaker, Betty, 462
Shumsky, Ellen, 209
Signorile, Michelangelo, 524, 547
Silverman, Joseph, 66
Silverman, Mervyn, 417
Sims, Jon Reed, 380, 385
Sisneros, Judy, 598
Slater, Don, 114, 124
Smith, Barbara, 383
Smith, Freda, 184
Smith, Gwendolyn Ann, 722
Smith, Howard (reporter), 192, 193
Smith, Howard (U.S. representative), 233
Smith, Jeanette, 669
Smith, Lillian, 154
Smith, Willie, 184
Socarides, Charles, 169

Soehnlein, Karl, 524
Spade, Dean, 686
Spong, John Shelby, 725
Stanton, Elizabeth Cady, 1
Stark, Michael, 707
Starr, Adele, 367
Stead, William Thomas, 18
Stein, Edward, 509
Stein, Gertrude, 43
Stevens, John Paul, 327, 432
Stevenson, Matilda Coxe, 21
Stewart, Potter, 297
Stirner, Max, 29
Stoddard, Tom, 542
Stoll, James, 236
Stone, Allucquére Rosanne, 540
Stone, Ron, 419
Stryker, Susan, 562, 645, 651
Stuart, Sharon, 639
Studds, Gerry, 407, 467
Sullivan, Andrew, 648
Suvarnananda, Anjana Tang, 533
Swank, Hilary, 672
Sweeney, Tim, 687
Symonds, John Addington, 33, 56

Tanfer, Koray, 596
Tayleur, Christine, 562
Tebelak, John-Michael, 365
Teena, Brandon, 615, 722
Tenorio, Marcelo, 555
Terrigno, Valerie, 419
Thompson, Ella, 95
Thompson, Karen, 469, 552
Thompson, Merritt M., 114
Thorson, Scott, 365
Thurmond, Strom, 155
Tignor, Saundra, 519
Tipton, Billy, 505
Tisdel, Lana, 615
Toklas, Alice B., 43
Toledo, Elizabeth, 247
Tomberlin, Karen, 552
Tong, Goh Chok, 713
Traubel, Horace L., 3
Troxell, Jane, 464
Trudeau, Pierre, 199, 477
Truman, Harry, 129

Tudehope, Darren, 698
Tutu, Desmond, 726

Ulrichs, Karl Heinrich, 9, 16, 33, 46, 49
Underwood, Barbara Lee, 357
Uranga, Enoé, 742

Vaid, Urvashi, 246, 498
Vallone, Peter, 687
Vargas, Chavela, 742
Varnell, Joe, 707
Vatour, Anne, 707
Vatour, Elaine, 707
Vidal, Gore, 97, 169
Viguerie, Richard, 339
Voeller, Bruce, 111, 246
Vogel, Kristie, 304

Vogel, Lisa, 304
Vriend, Delwin, 652

Waddell, Tom, 405
Wade, April, 608
Wade, Henry, 252
Wake, Robert, 570
Wales, B. Roger, 74
Walker, James, 74
Walker, Mary Edwards, 7
Walker, Paul A., 320
Wallace, Mike, 169
Wallbank, Rachel, 698
Walsh, Stella, 728
Ward, Freda, 23
Ward, Jo, 23
Warren, Earl, 176
Warren, Patricia Nell, 269
Watkins, James, 485
Watkins, Perry, 510
Waxman, Henry, 620
Weddington, Sarah, 252
Wedekind, Frank, 81
Weinberger, Harry, 66
Weld, William F., 576
West, Jason, 721
West, Mae, 74
Westphal, Karl Friedrich, 16, 111
We'wha, 21
Weyrich, Paul, 339

Personages Index

Wherry, Kenneth Spicer, 129
Whitaker, Bailey, 114
White, Byron, 252, 432
White, Dan, 337
White, Edmund, 353, 512
White, Ryan, 401
Whitman, Walt, 3
Whitmore, George, 353
Whitney, Irene, 203
Whittington, Yolanda, 519
Wieder, Judith, 168
Wieser, Barb, 203
Wilchins, Riki, 541, 617
Wilde, Oscar, 18, 26
Wilde, Winston, 588
Wilder, Billy, 85
Wildmon, Donald, 500
Wiley, Alexander, 125
Wilhelm, Gail, 243
William I (German kaiser), 12, 37
William II (German kaiser), 49, 51, 52
Williams, Cecil, 163
Williams, Daryl, 698
Williams, Pete, 547
Williams, Rowan, 725
Williams, Tennessee, 97
Williams, Wendi, 357
Williamson, Alistair, 352
Williamson, Cris, 249
Wilson, Helen Teresa, 357
Wilson, Pete, 550
Winston, Sam, 167
Winter, Kate, 249
Wolf, Irma "Corky," 124
Wolfenden, Sir John Frederick, 142, 178
Wollman, Leo, 320
Wonder, Roy L., 417
Wong, B. D., 479
Wong, Doreena, 448
Woo, Merle, 395
Wood, Harlington, Jr., 302
Woodhul, Jennifer, 249
Wright, Martha C., 1

Yarchoan, Robert, 440
Yicheng, Jia, 679
Yoshikawa, Yoko, 542

Zapata, Emiliano, 61
Zapatero, José Luis Rodríguez, 736, 737

Subject Index

AB-101, California, 550
AB-2601, California, 551
Abbitt, Diane, 442
Abbott, Sydney, 209
Abdill, Michelle, 641
Abella, Rosalie Silberman, 477
Abortion, legalization of, 252-254
Abortion rights (*primary source*), 253
Abry, Phyllis, 522
Abse, Leo, 142, 178
Abstinence, and HIV-AIDS, 607
Abzug, Bella, 273, 311-312
Académie des Femmes, 59
Académie Française, 60
Academy Awards, 744-746; Pedro Almodóvar, 672; Nigel Hawthorne, 634-636; Hilary Swank, 672
Achtenberg, Roberta, 604
Acquired immunodeficiency syndrome. *See* HIV-AIDS
Acremant, Robert, 641
ACT UP; and Act Up Paris, 496; and AIDS epidemic, 379, 454; and drug companies, 441; founding of, 458-462; National Gay and Lesbian Task Force and, 246; Queer Nation and, 524; radicalism of, 470; St. Patrick's Cathedral protest, 514-516; model for student activism, 173; Transgender Nation, 562; Wall Street protest, 404
Act Up Paris, 496-498
ACT UP Women's Committee, 599
Ad Hoc Taskforce to Challenge Sodomy Laws, 259
Adam, Margie, 305
"Adjustment of the Male Overt Homosexual, The" (Hooker), 127
Adkins, Warren, 169
Advertising; homoeroticism, 504; and mainstream media, 198
Advocate, The, 167-169; outing of Nigel Hawthorne, 634-636; outing of Barbara Jordan, 239; and k. d. lang, 565; and Del Martin, 215; outing of Pete Williams, 547-549
Advocate Books, 352
African American lesbian feminism (*primary source*), 310, 393
African American politicians; Barbara Jordan, 239-241
African Americans; and lesbian feminism, 309-311, 519-520; and political activism, 154-157; and publishing, 383-385, 392-394
African Ancestral Lesbians United for Societal Change, 411
Aging, 462-464
AIDS Action, 246
AIDS activism, 403, 441, 454, 458-462, 494, 514-516, 607
AIDS: An Expanding Tragedy (National Commission on AIDS report), 487
AIDS awareness, 403, 458
AIDS Bhedbhav Virodhi Andolan, India, 568
AIDS Coalition to Unleash Power. *See* ACT UP
AIDS czar, 606-608
AIDS Memorial Quilt, 403; first unveiling, 469; *sidebar*, 471; and World AIDS Day, 494
AIDS Policy, White House Office of National, 487
AIDS Prevention, World Summit of Ministers of Health on Programmes for, 494
AIDS research; early years of, 402, 413-416; politics of, 458
AIDS "rethinker" movement, 441
AIDS virus; and AZT, 440; discovery of, 413-416. *See also* HIV-AIDS
Akinola, Peter, 725
Al-Fatiha Foundation, 657-659

Al-Majalla: The International Magazine of the Arabs, 658
Alam, Faisal, 657
Aldredge, J. C., 95
Alfaro, Luis, 455
Allen, Don Merriam, 151
Allen, Paula Gunn, 435
Allison, Becky, 700
Almodóvar, Pedro, 672
Alternative U, and radical politics, 196
Alyson, Sasha, 351
Alyson Wonderland, 351
Amazon Bookstore, 203-205
Ambitious Amazons, 275
Amendment 2, Colorado, 492, 582-585
American Bar Association; and consensual sex, 258-260; and decriminalization of homosexuality, 143; National Gay and Lesbian Task Force and, 246
American Booksellers Association, 512
American Civil Liberties Union, 176, 293, 358, 521
American Family Association; and AIDS czar, 607; and Defense of Marriage Act, 647; and gay priests, 740; and March on Washington, 470; and Andres Serrano, 501
American Federation of Teachers, 395
American Indians; gay and lesbian, 285-287; and literature, 435-437; and two-spirit persons, 21-23
American Law Institute, 258
American Library Association's Gay and Lesbian Task Force, 138
American Library Association's Stonewall Book Awards, 223

X

Subject Index

American Psychiatric Association; and homosexuality as mental disorder, 48, 111-113, 265-267; and Evelyn Hooker's study, 128; and immigration, 119; National Gay and Lesbian Task Force and, 246; protest by Transgender Nation, 562

American Psychological Association; and Evelyn Hooker's study, 126; and lesbian mothers, 610

Americans with Disabilities Act (1990), 487, 530-532

Amestoy, Jeffrey L., 666

Amnesty International, 330

Anabitarte, Héctor, 187

Anamika (newsletter), 438

Anatomy of a Hate Crime (television movie), 656

And the Band Played On (book), 402, 453-455

And the Band Played On (television movie), 453

Anglican Church; and gay clergy, 725-728; and same-gender marriage, 731

Anglican Church in Africa, and gay clergy, 726

Anjaree, definition of, 533

Anna Crusis Women's Choir, 295-297, 385

Antidiscrimination laws; Canada, 315-317, 652-653; and Civil Rights Amendment Act, 273-275; Japan, 681-682; Massachusetts, 576-578; and municipal governments, 228-230; New Mexico, 702-704; and transgender rights, 687-689; Wisconsin, 397-401; and workplace movement, 323-326

Antigay movement, 271-273, 307-308, 333-336, 339-341, 470, 491-493, 500, 582-585, 596, 655

Antigay violence; Christian Right and, 307; and film protests, 660; Milk and Moscone murders, 337-339; murder of lesbian couple, 641-644; and founding of PFLAG, 367; Queer Nation and, 526; murder of Matthew Shepard, 654-657; in U.S. military, 611; against youth, 388

Anti-Violence Project, 246

Antoinette, Marie, 363

Anzaldúa, Gloria, 370, 446

Apollo Theatre, 68

Apuzzo, Virginia, 246

Aquino, Corazon, 474

Araujo, Gwen, 694, 722

Archives; gay and lesbian, 114-116, 280-282; leather subculture, 545-546; lesbian, 260-262

Arenas, Reinaldo, 157

Army Medical Corps, U.S., 7

Arnold, Ervin, 63

Arnold, June, 241

Arran, Earl of, 142, 178

Arts; and censorship, 520-522; contributions of gays and lesbians, 32; and indecency, 500-504; of leather culture, 545; performing, 295-297, 373-375, 380-382, 385-387, 520-522; photography, 500-504

Asch, Sholem, 66

Ashe, Arthur, 638

Ashkinazy, Steve, 387

Ashley, April, 734

Asian American support of same-gender marriage, 629-631

Asian and Pacific Islander Men of New York, Gay, 542

Asian Collective, Lesbian and Gay, 348-351

Asian Lesbian Network, 533-534

Asian Lesbians of the East Coast, 542

Asian Pacific Lesbian Network, 448-450

Aspin, Leslie, 611

Assimilation; and early gay rights movement, 107, 195; Queer Nation on, 524-527

Association pour les Droits des Gais du Quebec, 316

AT&T, 324

Athletes; Mianne Bagger, 729; Michelle Dumaresq, 729; gay and lesbian, 269; Gay Games, 405-407; Ewa Klobukowska, 729; David Kopay, 406; Alyn Libman, 729; Greg Louganis, 637-639; Martina Navratilova, 623-626; Renee Richards, 729; transsexual, 728-730; Tom Waddell, 405; Stella Walsh, 728. *See also* Gay Games; Sports; *names of specific athletes*

Attwell, Michael, 342

Australia, and transsexual marriage rights, 698-699

Autobiography of Alice B. Toklas, The (Stein), 45

"Autogynephilia," definition of, 700

Avant-garde, and lesbian and gay culture, 58-60

Azidothymidine. *See* AZT

Azmi, Shabana, 660

AZT; and ACT UP, 460; development of, 440-442

Bachardy, Don, 92

Baehr, Ninia, 593

Baehr v. Miike (1991, 1993), 593, 647

Bagger, Mianne, 728

Bailey, J. Michael, 700

Baker, Josephine, 673

Baker, Stan, 666

Baker v. Vermont (1999), 666-669

Baldwin, James, 135

Bamburger, Rose, 132

Bands of America, Lesbian and Gay, 386

Bangkok, Thailand, 533-534

Bannon, Ann, 243

Banton, Joab H., 74

Barbee, Lloyd, 397

Barnett, Marilyn, 365

Barney, Natalie Clifford, 58
Barr, Robert, 646-647
Barrett, Ellen Marie, 238
Barrie, Dennis, 500
Basic Rights Oregon, 493
Bathhouse closures, 417-419
Bathhouse raids, 227, 315, 319, 376-377
Bathhouses, criticism of, 454
Battelle sex study (1993), 596-598
Baturin, Carlos, 736
Bauman, Robert, 466
Beam, Gail C., 702
Bean, Babe, 39
Bean, Joseph, 545
Beck, Nina, 666
Beckett, John, 669
Becoming a Man (Monette), 588-590
Bédard, Marc-André, 315
Before Night Falls (Arenas), 159
Belfast, Northern Ireland, 330
Bella Books, 245
Bellinger, Elizabeth, 734
Ben, Lisa, 101
Ben-Shalom, Miriam, 302
Ben-Shalom v. Marsh (1989), 302
Benedict XVI, 515
Benjamin, Harry, 165, 320
Bentham, Trevor, 634
Berdache, definition of, 21
Berger, Jack C., 320
Berkeley, California, and domestic partner benefits, 422-423
Berkeley, University of California, and discrimination lawsuit against, 395
Berlin, Germany, 92
Berlins drittes Geschlecht (Hirschfeld), 50
Berson, Ginny, 249
Bérubé, Allan, 522
Beteta, Aura L., 347
Beth Ahava (Philadelphia), 231
Beth Mishpaha (Washington, D.C.), 231
Beth Simhat Torah (New York), 231
Bharosa Trust, 568
Bi Any Other Name (Kaahumanu and Hutchins), 529

Bianco, José "Pepe," 188
Bieber, Irving, 111
Billings, Robert, 339
Billy, John O. G., 596
BiNet USA, 527-529
Biology and sexuality, 535-537
Birch, Joshua, 579
Biron, Chartres, 76
Bisexual Forum, 267-268, 528
Bisexual Liberation Group, National, 528
Bisexual Network, National, 527
Bisexual Option, The (Klein), 268, 528
Bisexual Politics (Tucker), 529
Bisexuality; Louise Brooks, 83; Sigmund Freud on, 46-49; U.S. military and, 612
Bisexuals, The (Hurwood), 528
Black Feminist Organization, National, 309
"Black Feminist Statement, A" (Combahee River Collective), 309-311, 372, 383
Black Gay & Lesbian Leadership Forum Conference, National, 519
Black Gays, National Coalition of, 347
Black Power movement, Bayard Rustin and, 155
Blackmun, Harry A., 252, 432
Blair, Tony, 671
Blase, Anthony De, 545
Blewitt, Tom, 524
Block, Martin, 124
Blomberg, Werner von, 90
Blood supply and safety, France, 496
Blood tests, HIV, 415
Bloomberg, Michael, 687
Bluestockings, 363
Blumenthal, Marc, 231
Body, laws against disfiguration of, 166
Body image, transgender/transsexuality, 650
Body Politic, The (periodical), 226-228, 318-320; *sidebar*, 227

Boer, Jo den, 203
Bonauto, Mary, 666, 717
Book Awards, Stonewall, 223-225
Book reviews in *Lambda Rising Book Report*, 464-466
Bookstaver, May, 43
Bookstores; and AIDS epidemic, 352; Amazon, 203-205; A Different Light, 181; Giovanni's Room, 181; Lambda Rising, 181, 464, 512; Oscar Wilde Memorial Bookshop, 180-182; Outwrite Books, 181; Walt Whitman Bookshop, 181; We Think the World of You, 181
Borderlands/La Frontera (Anzaldúa), 446-448
Bornstein, Kate, 540-541
Borrowed Time (Monette), 589
Boston marriages, 363
Boston, Massachusetts, 309
Bottini, Ivy, 207, 209
Bottoms, Pamela Kay, 608
Bottoms, Sharon, 608
Bottoms v. Bottoms (1995), 608
Bouchet, Joëlle, 496
Boulton, Ernest, 18
Bourassa, Kevin, 707
Bourland, Roger, 588
Boutilier, Clive Michael, 176
Boutilier v. INS (1967), 118, 176
Bowers, Michael J., 432
Bowers v. Hardwick (1986), 96, 259, 299, 432-435, 710
Bowman, Parke, 241
Boxer, Barbara, 605
"Boy-love" poetry, 30
Boy Scouts of America v. Dale (2000), 675-678
Bragdon v. Abbott (1998), 532
Brand, Adolf, 29, 36, 49
Brandon, JoAnn, 615
Breaking the Surface (Louganis), 638
Breen, Joseph, 84
Brennan, William J., 256, 297, 327
Briggs, John V., 333

Briggs Initiative, California, 333-336
Britain. *See* United Kingdom
British Academy of Film and Television Arts, 744
Brock, Carole, 357
Brocka, Lino, 474
Broder, Samuel, 440
Brokeback Mountain (film), 744-746
Bronstein, Sidney, 281
Brooks, Louise, 81
Brown, Mark, 405
Brown, Rita Mae, 206, 209, 241
Browne, Karen, 203
Brownmiller, Susan, 207, 209
Bryant, Anita, 229, 251, 271, 307, 333, 340, 709
Büchse der Pandora, Die. *See Pandora's Box*
Bueno, Pilo, 489
Buenos Aires, Argentina; first GLBT organization, 187-189; same-gender civil unions, 705-707
Buggery; and British law, 140, 179; and Canadian law, 477
Buggery Act (1533), 19
Burger, Warren E., 432
Burns, Randy, 285
Burroughs-Wellcome; ACT UP protest against, 460; and AIDS drugs, 440
Burst of Light, A (Lorde), 392
Burton, Dan, 530
Bush, George H. W., 485, 530, 547
Bush, George W., 485, 595, 620, 643, 712, 721
Bussell, Letantia, 429
Butler, Judith, 540
Byrd, Robert, 648
Byton High School, Philadelphia, 390

Cabaret (film), 93
Cabaret (play), 93
Califia Women of Color gathering, 412
California; Briggs Initiative, 333; GLBT discrimination, 550-552
California Defend Our Children, 333
Callow, Simon, 636
Cameron, Barbara, 285
Camp Trans, 305
Campaign for Homosexual Equality, England, 330
Campbell, Edward H., 63
Campbell, Ken, 271
Campbell, Kim, 579
Campos v. Immigration and Naturalization Service (1968), 119
Canada; consensual sex legalized, 477-479; employment rights, 360-362, 652-653; family rights, 559-561; GLBT television in, 683-685; government bias, 570-572; homosexuality legalized, 199-200; immigrant rights, 555-558, 692-694; same-gender marriage, 707-709
"Cancer in the Gay Community" (Mass), 378
Cancer Journals, The (Lorde), 392
Capote, Truman, 97
Capote (film), 744-746
Cárdenas, Nancy, 742
Careful Selection and Training of Candidates for the States of Perfection and Sacred Orders (Roman Catholic Church), 739
Carlin, George, 327
Carlyle, Thomas, 114
Carpenter, Edward, 3, 55
Carrier Pigeon, 351
Carter, Jimmy, 8, 314
Casasola, Agustin Victor, 62
Castro, Fidel, 157
Catholic Church. *See* Roman Catholic Church
Catholic Education, Congregation for, and gay priests, 739
Catzman, Marvin, 477
Cazares, Jason, 694

CBS Reports: The Homosexuals (television program), 169-171
CBS television, 329
Celebrities, and coming out, 565-567
Celler, Emanuel, 233
Celluloid Closet, The (documentary film), 86
Censorship; and American theater, 74-76; of the arts, 500-504, 520-522; of film in India, 660-662; of gay film, 84-86, 474-476; of lesbian literature, 76-78; *primary source*, 85; and radio broadcasting, 327
Censorship and obscenity laws (*primary source*), 256
Centers for Disease Control; and AIDS epidemic, 378; and early AIDS research, 402, 414
Centre du Christ Liberateur, Paris, 331
Chan, June, 448
Chang, Kevin, 593
Changer and the Changed (Williamson), 250
Changing Our Minds: The Story of Dr. Evelyn Hooker (documentary film), 128
Chao, Winston, 591
Chaplin, Charlie, 672
Chapman, Jim, 530
Charbonneau, Patricia, 426
Charcot, Martin, 111
Charter, United Nations, 330
Charter of Human Rights and Freedoms, Quebec, Canada, 315-317, 360
Charter of Rights and Freedoms, Canada, 361, 579, 652, 692
Chase, Cheryl, 586, 651
Cheney, Richard B., 547
Chicana lesbian feminism, 370-373, 446-448
Chicana Lesbians (Trujillo, ed.), 452
Chicks and Salsa (multimedia), 457
Child custody, 608-611
Child sexual abuse, and Roman Catholic Church, 740
Children, California Defend Our, 333

XIII

Children of the Rainbow curriculum, New York City, 390
Children's books, 351
Children's Hour, The (film), 426
Chin, May, 591
Chinese Classification of Mental Disorders (Chinese Psychiatric Association), 679-681
Chinese Psychiatric Association, 265, 679-681
Chinese Society for the Study of Sexual Minorities, 679
Chirac, Jacques, 415
Cho, Milyoung, 542
Choral Festival, first West Coast, 386
Choral Festival, National Gay and Lesbian, 386
Choral movement, 295-297, 373-375, 380-382
Chrétien, Jean, 707-708
Christian, Marc, 429
Christian, Meg, 249, 304
Christian, Paula, 243
Christian church; and gay and lesbian clergy, 236-238, 725-728; GLBT worshippers, 184-186
Christian Church and Daughters of Bilitis (*primary source*), 145
Christian Coalition, 271, 341, 504, 582, 647
Christian faith (*sidebar*), 185
Christian Reformed Church, and firing of gay instructor, 652
Christian Right, 271-273, 307, 333, 339-341, 491, 604; and Battelle sex study, 596; and "ex-gay" movement, 113; and HIV-AIDS, 402, 485; and Oregon Citizens Alliance, 491; and political activism, 470; and same-gender marriage, 647; and Matthew Shepard murder, 654-657; Southern Poverty Law Center and, 271
Christian Voice, 271
Christianity, Social Tolerance, and Homosexuality (Boswell), 223
Christopher and His Kind (Isherwood), 94

Christopher Street Liberation Day, New York City, 212
Christopher Street, New York City, 192
Christy, Rosina Richter, 203
Chronicle of Higher Education (periodical), 701
Church of Christ, United, and first ordained gay minister, 236
Church of England. *See* Anglican Church
City and the Pillar, The (Vidal), 98, 269
City of Night (Rechy), 151-153, 269
Civil Marriage Act (2005), 707
Civil Partnership Act (2004), 731
Civil rights; American Bar Association and, 258-260; and antigay movement, 339-341, 491-493, 582-585; and Boy Scouts of America, 675-678; California, 550-552; Canada, 199-200, 360-362, 707-709; and Canadian government, 570; early organizations for, 72-73; Germany, 36-39; Hawaii, 593-595; and HIV-AIDS, 417; Massachusetts, 576-578; Mexico, 742; municipal governments, 228-230; New Mexico, 702-704; Quebec, Canada, 315-317; Singapore, 713-715; Spain, 736-738; United Kingdom, 669-672; United States, 510-512, 646-649, 710-713; U.S. government employment, 292-295, 618-620; West Hollywood, California, 420; Wisconsin, 397-401; worldwide, 330-332, 517-518
Civil Rights Act (1964), 273-275, 618
Civil Rights Act, Title VII, 233, 508
Civil Rights movement, Bayard Rustin and, 154-157

Civil Service Commission, U.S.; and employment discrimination, 129-132
Civil Service Reform Act (1978), 292
Civil union registry, West Hollywood, California, 420
Civil unions; Argentina, 705-707; Massachusetts, 717-722; New Jersey, 594; United Kingdom, 731-733; Vermont, 594, 666-669
Civil War, U.S., gender bending in, 7-9
Civilized Majority, 272
Clarenbach, David, 397
Clarification of Federal Employment Protections Act (proposed 2005), 620
Clark, Tom, 429
Classism; and African American lesbians, 309; and Latina lesbians, 451; and lesbians of color, 411; in women's movement, 371
Cleveland, Grover, 22
Clinton, Bill, 240, 294, 325, 336, 485, 518, 566, 602, 604, 606, 611, 618, 643, 646, 718
Coalition Against Repression, 316
Coalition for Equality of New Mexico, 702
Colectiva Lesbiana Latinoamericana, 451
Coll, Bridget, 692
Colleges and universities; faculty dismissals, 395-397, 652-653; and human-subject research, 700-702; student groups, 172-175; transgender studies in, 650-652
Colonize This! (Hernández and Rehman, eds.), 372
Colorado antigay intiatives, 582-585
Colorado for Family Values, 582
Colwell, Clarence, 160

Subject Index

Combahee River Collective, 309-311, 383; *primary source*, 310
Come Out! (periodical), 197
Coming Out! (play), 301
Coming Out Day, National, 489-491
Coming-out literature, 283-284
Coming Out Under Fire (Bérubé), 522-524
Commission on Human Rights, United Nations, 331
Committee for Research in Problems of Sex, 80
Committee on Homosexual Offences and Prostitution, 140, 178
Committee on the Rights of Gay People, 259
Communications Act (1934), 327
Community Centers, National Association of Lesbian, Gay, Bisexual & Transgender, 621-623
Community standards, and obscenity laws, 255-257
Compton, A. Christian, 608
Compton's Cafeteria, San Francisco, 163-165
"Comrade lovers," definition of, 56
Comunidad Homosexual Argentina, 705
Concerned Voters of California, 335
Concerned Women of America, 647
Congregation for Divine Worship and the Discipline of the Sacraments (Roman Catholic Church), 740
Congregation for the Doctrine of the Faith (Roman Catholic Church), 739
Congress of Racial Equality, 154
Congress to Unite Women, 207, 209
Conmoción (periodical), 452
Consenting Adult (book), 283-284

Consenting Adult (television movie), 284
Contemporary Arts Center, Cincinnati, 502
"Contrary sexual feeling," definition of, 16, 34
Contrary Sexual Feeling (Moll), 13
Conway, Lynn, 700
Cook and the Carpenter (Arnold), 242
Coors beer family, 340
Copenhagen, Denmark, 109
Coral Ridge, 113
Corbin, Joan, 124
Corcoran Gallery of Art, Washington, D.C., 501
Cordova, Jeanne, 219
Corporations, and domestic partnership benefits, 323-326, 559, 593, 619, 715-717
Corydon (Gide), 69-71
Council for Human Rights Promotion, Japan, 681-682
Council on National Policy, 341
Council on Religion and the Homosexual, 145, 161, 163
Cox, Christopher, 353
Cracker Barrel restaurants, 325
Cranston, Alan, 117
Craven, James Braxton, 169
Crawford, Muriel, 244
Creating Change Conferences, 247, 498
Crime. *See* Antigay violence; Gender-based violence; Hate crime
"Crime against nature," 147, 297-300; *primary source*, 298
Crimes of passion, 23-25
Criminal Law Amendment Act (1885), 27
Cromey, Robert Warren, 182
Cross-dressing; nineteenth century, 7-9; and self-identity, 507; early twentieth century, 39-41. *See also* Gender; Gender ambiguity; Gender-bending; Gender

identity; Transgender; Transsexual; Two-spirit persons
Cruz, Sor Juana Inés de la, 537
Cuba, repression of gays, 157-160
Cuentos: Stories by Latinas (Gómez, Moraga, and Romo-Carmona, eds.), 383
Cullman, Joseph, 623
Cultuur en Ontspannings-Centrum, 633
Cumming, Alan, 636
Cunnilingus, U.S. Supreme Court ruling on, 297-300
"Curing" of homosexuality. *See* Reparative therapy
Current Concepts in Transgender Identity (Denny), 650

Daddy's Roommate (Willhoite), 351
Dade County, Florida, 229, 307
Dale, James, 675
Dancel, Genora, 593
Daniels, Josephus, 63
Dannemeyer, William E., 442
Das, Nandita, 660
Das, Suvir, 438
Daughters, Inc., 241
Daughters of Bilitis, 132-135, 144, 214
David Kopay Story, The (Kopay), 406
Davidson, Jay, 373, 380
Davis, Katharine Bement, 79
Day, Doris, 430
Dean, Howard, 667, 718
Debreta's, Los Angeles, 411
Decency, Legion of, 84
Declaration of Sentiments and Resolutions (1848), 1
Defense of Marriage Act (1996), 593, 619, 646-649, 718
DeGeneres, Ellen, 565
Deitch, Donna, 426
Delanoë, Bertrand, 496
Democratic National Convention; Elizabeth Birch address to, 356; Barbara Jordan address to, 240
Democratic Revolutionary Party, Mexico, 742

Denny, Dallas, 650
Derrida, Jacques, 540
Desert Hearts (film), 287, 426-428
Desert of the Heart, The (Rule), 287, 426
Diagnostic and Statistical Manual of Mental Disorders (American Psychiatric Association), 48, 111, 128, 265, 322; *primary source*, 112
Dietrich, Marlene, 673
"Difference in Hypothalamic Structure Between Heterosexual and Homosexual Men, A" (Levay), 535-537
DignityUSA, 189-192
Dirmeyer, Robert, 464
Disabilities Act, Americans with (1990), 530-532
Disability rights, and guardianship, 552-554
Discovery of the Soul (Jäger), 13
Discrimination; in academia, 395-397; Briggs Initiative, 333-336; California, 550-552; and Christian Right, 339-341, 491-493; Colorado, 582-585; Indian sodomy law, 568-570; Oregon, 582-585; in U.S. government employment, 129-132, 618-620; in U.S. military, 357-359, 510-512, 611-615. *See also* Antidiscrimination laws
Disease Control, Centers for, and AIDS epidemic, 378
"Disease Rumors Largely Unfounded" (Mass), 378
Dlugacz, Judy, 249
Dobkin, Alix, 304
Dr. Laura. See Schlessinger, Laura
Dodd, Charles H., 74
Doe v. Doe (1981), 609
Dole, Robert, 604
DOMA. *See* Defense of Marriage Act
Domestic partnerships. *See* Same-gender
Donaldson, Stephen, 172, 182
Dong, Arthur, 522

Don't Ask, Don't Tell, 179, 218, 511, 522, 549, 580, 611-615, 671. *See also* Military
Dorf, Julie, 517
Dormont, Dominique, 430
Doucé, Joseph, 330
Douglas, Lord Alfred "Bosie," 26
Douglas, John, 26
Douglas, Michelle, 579
Douglas v. Canada (1992), 579-581
Douglass, Frederick, 1
Doustou, Tyler, 608
Drag activism, 562
Drag queens/kings; representations of in film, 673; in gay male culture, 151; and queer youth, 163; and Stonewall Rebellion, 192
Drag shows, in U.S. military, 523
Drama and theater; and AIDS epidemic, 459; censorship of, 74-76; and lesbian sexuality, 66-69; *M. Butterfly*, 479-482
Drei Abhandlungen zur Sexualtheorie. See Three Essays on the Theory of Sexuality
Dreyfus, Lee, 397
Drugs and medications; and ACT UP, 403, 458-462; HIV-AIDS, 440
Drummer magazine, 545
DSM. *See Diagnostic and Statistical Manual of Mental Disorders*
Dubofsky, Jean, 582
Dudgeon, Jeff, 330
Duesberg, Peter, 441
Dugas, Gaëtan, 401, 453
Duke Who Outlawed Jelly Beans, The (Valentine and Schmidt), 351
Dumaresq, Michelle, 728
Duran, John J., 550
Dyke; as a term, 210
Dyke March; Canada, 600; Ireland, 600; Los Angeles, 600; Mexico City, 600;

Philadelphia, 600; Tokyo, 600; Washington, D.C., 598-601

Eagle Forum, 647
Earl, Nancy, 239
Early Modern Women's Writing and Sor Juana Inés de la Cruz (Merrim), 538
East Lansing, Michigan, 228
Eberhart, John, 126
Economics; and GLBT literature, 464-466; women-owned businesses, 203-205, 249-251
Edel, Deborah, 260
Edgerton, Milton T., 165
Education; curriculum debates, 351, 390; and GLBT student groups, 172-175; GLBT youth, 387-391; on HIV-AIDS, 486, 501, 515; transgender studies, 650-652; World AIDS Day, 494-495
Education Amendments, Title IX, 623
Education Network, Gay, Lesbian, and Straight, 390
Edwards, Lisa, 231
Eger, Denise, 231
Ego and His Own, The (Stirner), 29
Eichberg, Rob, 489
Eigene, Der (journal), 29-31
Einzige und sein Eigentum, Der. See Ego and His Own, The
Eisenhower, Dwight D., 117, 129
Elders, Joycelyn, 495, 606
Elliott, Beth, 540
Ellis, Havelock, 16, 33
Ellis, Roxanne, 641
Empire State Pride Agenda, 688
Employment Non-Discrimination Act (proposed 1994), 274, 618-620
"Employment of Homosexuals and Other Sex Perverts in Government" (U.S. government document), 292
Employment rights; California, 550-552; Canada, 360-362;

XVI

Massachusetts, 576-578; municipal governments, 228-230; Singapore, 713-715; United States, 323-326; U.S. government, 129-132, 292-295; Wal-Mart Stores, 715-717. *See also* Civil rights; Corporations; *Fortune* 500
Encuentro, Latina lesbian feminist network, 472-474
ENDA. *See* Employment Non-Discrimination Act
Endean, Steve, 355
England. *See* United Kingdom
England, Church of. *See* Anglican Church
Enlisted Administrative Separations (1993), 611
Entertainment industry, monitoring of, 424-426
Episcopal Church, 145, 725
Equal Rights Amendment, 233-236
ERA. *See* Equal Rights Amendment
Erickson, Reed, 114, 321
Erickson Educational Foundation, 166
Ernst, Morris, 76
Essentialism, 540
Esto no tiene nombre (periodical), 452
Etheridge, Melissa, 565, 656
Etienne, 545
Eugenics, Nazis and, 86
Eulenburg affair, 50, 52-55
Eulenburg-Hertefeld, Philipp, prince of, 51-52
European Court of Human Rights, and military service, 670
European Union; and military service, 670; and same-gender unions, 732, 737
Evans, Linda, 430
Evans, Richard G., 582
Evans, Terence, 302
Everett, Rupert, 636
Evert, Chris, 625

"Ex-gay" movement, Christian Right and, 113
Exodus International, 113

Fabius, Laurent, 496
Factors in the Sex Life of Twenty-Two Hundred Women (Davis), 79
Faderman, Lillian, 362
Faggot; as a term, 210
Faith and Values Coalition, 341
Falls City, Nebraska, 616
Falwell, Jerry, 307, 339
Families Project, 247
Family Planning Perspectives (periodical), 596
Family Research Council, 607, 619, 647
"Family values"; Briggs Initiative and, 333; Colorado, 582; Cuba, 158; and Defense of Marriage Act, 647; and Equal Rights Amendment, 235; Hawaii, 593; Oregon, 491
Farnham, Lois, 666
Federal Bureau of Investigation; "moral" arrests by, 130; and obscenity laws, 125
Federal Communications Commission v. Pacifica Foundation (1978), 327
Feinberg, Leslie, 540-541, 573
Feinstein, Dianne, 337, 417, 442
Feldblum, Chai, 530
Feldman, Maxine, 304
Felix, Diane, 290
Female Masculinity (Halberstam), 650
Femininity; American Indian culture and, 437; gay literature and, 97; gay men and, 29; lesbians and, 427; in women's sports, 624. *See also* Gender; Masculinity; Sex/gender
Feminism; and African American women, 309-311; American Indian cultures and, 435-437; feminist bookstores and, 203-205; and GLBT movement, 214; Latin American and Caribbean, 472-474; and lesbians, 215; and lesbians of color, 370-373, 411-413; and literary salons, 59; National Organization for Women and, 209-211; and National Women's Conference, 311-315; Radicalesbians and, 209-211; in nineteenth century United States, 1-3
Feminist choral music, 295-297
Feminist movement. *See* Feminism
Feminist Perspectives on Sor Juana Inés de la Cruz (Merrim, ed.), 537-539
Ferro, Robert, 353
Festival of Light, 271
Fidus, 29
Fields, Annie, 363
Fight the Right Project, National Gay and Lesbian Task Force, 247
Filipinos, gay, 474-476
Film; and Academy Awards, 744-746; documentary, 522-524; and homosexuality, 84-86, 591-592; and lesbian sex, 81-83, 660-662; Taiwanese, 591-592; transgender characters, 672-675. *See also* Academy Awards; Censorship; *names of specific films*
Film production code (*primary source*), 85
Finley, Karen, 520
Finley v. National Endowment for the Arts (1992), 520
Fire (film), 660-662
Fire from Heaven (Renault), 269
First Amendment; and obscenity, 255; and radio broadcasting, 327; and speech, 675-678
Fishman, Israel, 223
Fleck, John, 520
Fleming, Patsy S., 607
Fleuti v. Rosenberg (1962), 118
Flores, Patria Jiménez, 741
Focus on the Family, 113, 647

Food and Drug Administration; early AIDS research, 402; approval of AZT, 440-442; licensing of HIV antibodies test, 403
Ford, Gerald, 312
Foreman, Matt, 246
Forschungen über das Räthsel der mannmännlichen Liebe. See *Riddle of "Man-Manly" Love, The*
Fortune 500, 323, 559, 715
41, Party of the, 41
Forum for Academic and Institutional Rights v. Rumsfeld (2004), 677
Foster, Jeannette Howard, 138
Foucault, Michel, 540
Fouratt, Jim, 195
Fourier, Charles, 3
Fournier, Bob, 189
Franco, Francisco, 736
Frank, Barney, 117, 466, 611, 647
Freedman, Blanch, 176
Frente de Liberación Homosexual, 188, 741
Freud, Sigmund, 16, 33, 46, 266
Frey, Noni, 132
Friedan, Betty, 206, 209, 312
Friedlaender, Benedict, 29, 49
Friedland, Lucy, 527
Friedman, Terry B., 550
Friendship and Freedom (periodical), 72, 281
Frohnmayer, John E., 500, 520
Front Runner, The (Warren), 269-270
Fry, Steven, 636
Frye, Phyllis Randolph, 639
Fukaya, Michiyo, 347, 349
Funding of the arts, 500-504, 520
Fung, Richard, 349
Funk, Cynthia, 209
Furies, The, 249

Gagliostro, Vincent, 514
Gair, Cyndi, 249
GALA Choruses, 297, 373-375, 380, 386
Galbreath, Charles, 297
"Galimony." See Palimony
Gallo, Robert, 401, 413
Garbo, Greta, 673

Garner, Tyron, 710
Gaskins, Tangela, 357
Gay Academic Union, 174, 260
Gay Activists Alliance, 198, 212
Gay Agenda, The (videotape), 470, 582
Gay American History (Katz), 300-302
Gay American Indians, 285-287, 411
Gay and Lesbian Alliance Against Defamation. See GLAAD
Gay and Lesbian Association of Choruses. See GALA Choruses
Gay and Lesbian Center, Los Angeles, 221-223, 622
Gay and Lesbian Human Rights Commission, International, 517-518
Gay and Lesbian Independent School Teacher's Network, 390
Gay and Lesbian Latinos Unidos, 291, 456
Gay and Lesbian Law Association, National, 259
Gay and lesbian studies. See Queer studies
Gay and Lesbian Task Force, National, 246-249, 498-500
Gay Archives: Natalie Barney/Edward Carpenter Library, 281
Gay Asian and Pacific Islander Men of New York, 542
Gay-bashing. See Antigay violence; Gender-based violence; Hate crime
Gay Book Award, 223-225
"Gay brain," 535-537
"Gay cancer." See Kaposi's sarcoma
Gay Games, 405-407
Gay Insurgent (periodical), 349
"Gay is Good," 150, 217
Gay Latino Alliance, 290-292
Gay/Lesbian Almanac (Katz), 301
Gay, Lesbian, and Straight Education Network, 390

Gay, Lesbian, Bisexual, and Transgendered Round Table, American Library Association, 224
Gay Liberation, Task Force on, American Library Association, 223
Gay Liberation Front, 194-198, 212, 214
Gay Life (television newsmagazine), 342-344
Gay Men's Chorus, San Francisco, 380-382, 385-387
Gay Men's Health Crisis, 402, 458
Gay Olympics. See Athletes; Gay Games; Sports
"Gay-related immunodeficiency." See GRID
Gay Rights, Special Rights (film), 334
Gay-Straight Alliance, 390
Gay "underground" in literature, 151
"Gay" versus "lesbian" as terms, 598
GayLebanon (online group), 665
Gayteens.org, 391
Gaytime TV, 343
Gebbie, Kristine, 606
Gemeinschaft der Eigenen, 29, 49
Gender; American Indian cultures and, 435; and Equal Rights Amendment, 233-236; and film, 672-675; and U.S. Supreme Court rulings, 508-509
Gender Advocacy Information Network, New Mexico, 702
Gender ambiguity; American Indians and, 21-23; terms for, 21
Gender-based violence, 615-618, 672, 694-697, 722-724
Gender-bending; in film, 480, 672; and masculine attire, 673; and patriarchal cultures, 436
Gender-bending women, in U.S. Civil War, 7-9

Subject Index

Gender dysphoria; as a term, 14, 322; transsexuality and, 108. *See also* Gender identity
Gender Dysphoria (Denny), 651
Gender Dysphoria Association, Harry Benjamin International, 320-323
Gender Education, International Foundation for, 640
Gender Education and Advocacy, 723
Gender identity; discrimination and, 686; historical sense of, 645; municipal law and, 689; terms for, 573; early theories of, 50; transsexuality and, 108-111
Gender Identity Clinic, Johns Hopkins University School of Medicine, 165
Gender identity disorder, 562
Gender Identity Disorders, Standards of Care for (Harry Benjamin International Gender Dysphoria Association), 650
Gender Outlaw (Bornstein), 541
Gender pronouns, 574
Gender reassignment; early cases, 108-111, 644-646; and intersexuality, 586-588; first surgical clinic for, 165-167; and transsexuality, 540-542
Gender Recognition Act (2004), 734-736
Gender Rights, International Bill of (1995), 639-641
Gender Rights Advocacy, New York Association for, 687
Gender-role stereotyping, as discriminatory, 508
Gender/sex. *See* Sex/gender
"Genderfuck," definition of, 541
Gentile, Patrizia, 570
Gentleman from Maryland, The (Bauman), 466
Georgia, 95; and *Bowers v. Hardwick*, 432
Georgian society, and women's sexuality, 363

Gerber, Henry, 72, 281
German criminal code, and homosexuality, 36-39
Germany and early gay rights movement, 9-15
Gernreich, Rudi, 106
Gestapo, 87
Ghandhi, Khushro, 442
Gide, André, 69
Gilbert, Joshua Allen, 644
Gilgamesh, Joe, 189
Gingrich, Newt, 593
Giovanni's Room (Baldwin), 135-137
Gittings, Barbara, 132, 223, 265
Giuliani, Rudolph, 687
GLAAD, 424-426, 526
Gladstone, William Ewart, 18
Glide Memorial Methodist Church, 163
Global Programme on AIDS, World Health Organization, 494
Gloria Goes to Gay Pride (Newman and Crocker), 351
GLQ: A Journal of Lesbian and Gay Studies, 651
Go Tell It on the Mountain (Baldwin), 135
"God Hates Fags," 655
God of Vengeance, The (drama), 66-69
Goebbels, Joseph, 89
Golden Globes, 744
Goldman, Albert, 169
Goldschmidt, Neil, 491
Gomez, Jewelle, 424, 512
Goodbye to Berlin (Isherwood), 92-95
Goodman, Susanne R., 477
Goodridge, Hillary, 717
Goodridge, Julie, 717
Goodridge v. Department of Public Health (2003), 717-722
Goodstein, David, 333
Goring, Hermann, 89
Got fun Nekomeh. *See God of Vengeance, The*
Grady, Graeme, 669

Grady, William R., 596
Granville, Lord, 18
Graves, John T., 72
Great Britain. *See* United Kingdom
Greece, ancient; and masculinity, 29, 50, 56; and sexuality, 38
Green, Jamison, 562
Green, Richard, 320
Greenwich Village, 180, 192-195, 212
Grice, Warren, 95
GRID, 378, 401-404
Grier, Barbara, 132, 138, 244
Griswold, Rufus W., 3
Griswold v. Connecticut (1965), 252, 432
Gross, Larry, 547
Gross indecency. *See* Indecency
Grove Press, 152
Grumley, Michael, 353
Gua, Ah-Leh, 591
Guardianship, 552-554
Guerrero, Sylvia, 697
Guevara, Che, 157
Gunderson, Steve, 647
Gyllenhaal, Jake, 744
Gynocentricism; definition of, 436; and lesbian separatism, 372

Haig, Graham, 579
Haig v. Canada (1992), 579
Halberstam, Judith, 650
Hale, C. Jacob, 645, 651
Hall, Radclyffe, 76
Halm, Henry, 477
Halm v. Canada (Minister of Employment and Immigration) (1995), 478
Halton Renaissance Committee, 271
Hamburger, Christian, 108
Hamilton-McMaster Homophile Association, 271
Hannon, Gerald, 227, 318
Hannum, Richard, 365
Hansen, Joseph, 124
Hanson, Cindy, 203
Hardberger, Phil, 662
Harden, Maximilian, 49, 51-52
Harding, William, 84

Hardwick, Michael, 432
Haring, Keith, 489
Harlem, New York, in literature, 392
Harrigan, Peter, 666
Harris, Alicia, 357
Harris, Helaine, 249
Harry Benjamin International Gender Dysphoria Association, 320-323
Hart, Alan Lucill, 644
Hart, Lois, 209
Hart, Michigan, 305
Harvey Milk High School, New York City, 389
Hatch, Orin, 604
Hate crime; antitransgender, 615-618; murder, 641-644, 654-657, 694-697; murders of gay politicians, 337-339; in U.S. military, 611. *See also* Antigay violence; Gender-based violence
Hate Crimes Prevention Act (proposed 1999), 643
Hate speech, in schools, 390
Hawaii, and same-gender marriage, 593-595
Hawkes, Brent, 376
Hawkins, John, 269
Hawthorne, Sir Nigel, 634
Hay, Harry, 106
Hayashino, Carole, 629
Hayden, Henry, 236
Haynes, Mable, 43
Hays, Will H., 84
Hays code. *See* Motion Picture Production Code
Healey, Shevy, 462
Health and medicine; and AIDS quarantine, 442-445; AIDS virus, 637-639; Americans with Disabilities Act, 532; and closure of gay bathhouses, 417-419; and gender identity, 320-323; and gender reassignment, 165-167; HIV-AIDS treatments, 440-442; and intersexuality, 586-588; and transsexuality, 541
Heather Has Two Mommies (Newman and Souza), 351
Heckler, Margaret M., 413

Heilman, John, 419
Heldman, Gladys, 623
Helem, 664
Heller v. Columbia Edgewater Country Club (2002), 509
Helms, Jesse, 155, 331, 500, 520, 530, 604, 632
Helms amendment, and obscenity in the arts, 502, 520
Helvey, Terry, 611
Hemophilia, and AIDS, 402, 496
Henderson, Russell, 654
Henry VIII (king of England), and sodomy laws, 19
Hensala v. U.S. Air Force (1994), 614
Hepburn, Katharine, 673
Herman, Erwin, 231
Hernandez, Aileen, 206
Hesperia, Michigan, and Womyn's Music Festival, 305
Hester, Rita, 722
Heterosexism, Strong Queers United in Stopping, 173
Heterosexism in women's movement, 209-211. *See also* Homophobia
Heterosexual, as a term, 12-15
"Heterosexual and Homosexual Men, A Difference in Hypothalamic Structure Between," (Levay), 535-537
Heterosexualitat, definition of, 13
Hetrick, Emery, 387
Hetrick-Martin Institute, 387
Heydrich, Reinhard, 89
Hickerson, Donald, 292
Hicks, Elias, 3
Hill, Joseph Lister, 129
Hill v. INS (1983), 119
Hiller, Kurt, 36
Himmler, Heinrich, 86, 89
Hindenburg, Paul von, 89
Hinduism, and lesbian sex, 660-662
Hinojosa, Claudia, 742
Hirschfeld, Magnus, 10, 33, 36, 46, 49

Hitler, Adolf, 37, 86, 89. *See also* Nazi Germany
HIV-AIDS; and founding of ACT UP, 458-462; Act Up Paris, 496-498; first AIDS czar, 606-608; and Americans with Disabilities Act, 530-532; and closure of gay bathhouses, 417-419; discovery of HIV, 413-416; early drug treatments, 440-442; first years, 378-380; GLBT community centers and, 222; as a global epidemic, 461; and Rock Hudson, 429-432; Latinos and, 456; critical literature on, 453-455, 588-590; and Greg Louganis, 637-639; naming of AIDS, 401-404; Presidential AIDS Commission and, 485-489; and Proposition 64, 442-445; protests by ACT UP, 514-516; and quarantine, 442-445; U.S. immigration law and, 120; World AIDS Day, 494-495; and youth education, 389
HIV-AIDS, sports and (*primary source*), 638
Hobson, Christopher Z., 283
Hobson, Laura Z., 283
Hockney, David, 94
Hoey, Clyde Roark, 129
Hoffman, March, 209
Hoffman, Philip Seymour, 744
Holleran, Andrew, 353
Holocaust. *See* Hitler, Adolf; Nazi Germany; Pink triangle; World War II
Home Girls (Smith, ed.), 383
Homoeroticism, in publically funded arts, 500-504
"Homogenic love," definition of, 55
Homogenic Love (Carpenter), 56
Homophile, definition of, 13
Homophile Organizations, North American Conference of, 160-163, 182-184
Homophile studies, 116

Homophobia; in Civil Rights movement, 154-157; in women's movement, 134. *See also* Antigay violence; Gender-based violence; Hate crime; Heterosexism; Transphobia

Homosexual, as a term, 12-15, 35, 54, 114

Homosexual Action League, Philadelphia, 214

Homosexual conduct law, Texas, 710

Homosexual Equality, England, Campaign for, 330

"Homosexual in America, The" (*Time* magazine), 201-203

Homosexual Liberation Front. *See* Frente de Liberación Homosexual

"Homosexual Marriage?" (*ONE* magazine), 125

"Homosexual Men, A Difference in Hypothalamic Structure Between Heterosexual and" (Levay), 535-537

Homosexual "nature" (*primary source*), 10

Homosexual Offences and Prostitution, Committee on, 140, 178

Homosexual Tendencies In View of Their Admission to the Seminary and to Holy Orders, Instruction Concerning... (Roman Catholic Church), 738

Homosexualisten, definition of, 13. *See also Uranism; Urning*

"Homosexualities" (Kinsey Institute), 105

Homosexuality; American Psychiatric Association and, 265-267; and British law, 140-144, 178-180; and British military, 669-672; and Canadian law, 199-200; as a crime, 170; Cuban government and, 157-160; early studies of, 33-35, 46-49, 79-81; early theories of, 49-52; early works on, 29-32, 55-58, 69-71; Equal Rights Amendment and, 233-236; in Filipino film, 474-476; and film censorship, 84-86; and the "gay brain," 535-537; government scandals and, 52-55; and Illinois state law, 147-148; Kinsey studies of, 103-105, 121-123; Joseph McCarthy and, 130; as a mental disorder, 111-113, 679-681; and Nazi Germany, 86-91; and laws on parenthood, 608; as pathological, 126-129, 169, 266; psychoanalysis and, 266; Roman Catholic Church on, 738-741; in Singapore, 713. *See also* Bisexuality; Gay; Lesbian; Sexuality

Homosexuality (Bieber), 112

Homosexuality, National Association for Research and Therapy of, 113

"Homosexuals and Other Sex Perverts in Government, Employment of" (U.S. government document), 292

Hooker, Evelyn, 126, 201, 265

Hoopes, John E., 165

Hopkins, Ann B., 508

Horwitz, Roger, 588

Housing Opportunities for Persons with AIDS Act (1991), 488

Houston, Texas, 312

Hoy, Claire, 318

HPA-23, antiviral drug, 430

Hudson, Erastus Mead, 63

Hudson, Rock, 366, 401, 429

Huffman, Felicity, 744

Hughes, Holly, 520

Hulting, Jane, 295

Human immunodeficiency virus. *See* HIV-AIDS

Human Immunodeficiency Virus Epidemic, Presidential Commission on the, 485, 530

Human Rights, Society for, 72-73

Human Rights, United Nations, Commission on, 331

Human Rights Act, Canada (1978), 579

Human Rights Act, New Mexico (2003), 702-704

Human Rights Campaign, 336, 355-357, 490

Human Rights Promotion, Council for, Japan, 681-682

Human T-cell leukemia/lymphotrophic virus type III, 414, 443

Hunt, Jane C., 1

Hunter, Joyce, 387

Hurley v. Irish-American Gay, Lesbian and Bisexual Group of Boston (1995), 676

Hurriyyat Khassa, 665

Hustler, The (Mackay), 30

Hwame, definition of, 436

Hwang, David Henry, 479

Hypothalamus, study of, 535

I Am a Camera (drama), 93

I Am a Camera (film), 93

I Know You Know (Christian), 250

If It Die... (Gide), 70

Immigration Act (1990), 120, 177

Immigration and Naturalization Service, 117, 176

Immigration law; Canada, 555-558, 692-694; lesbians and gays, 176-178; *primary source*, 119; United States, 117-121

In re Thom (1973), 263

In the Interests of the State (Kinsman and Gentile), 572

In the Life (Beam), 351

Inaba, Masaki, 681

Inaudi, Jorge Alberto, 555

Indecency; and the arts, 502, 520; and British law, 18-21, 141, 179; and Canadian law, 199, 477; U.S. Supreme Court on, 327-329; and Oscar Wilde trial, 26-28

Indecency, British law (*primary source*), 19

Independent Spirit Awards, 744

India; film censorship, 660-662; sodomy laws, 568-570
Indian AIDS Project, 286
Individual Rights Protection Act, Canada, 652
Institut für Sexualwissenschaft. *See* Institute for Sexual Science
Institute for Sexual Science, 37
Institute for the Study of Human Resources, 115
Intermediate Sex, The (Carpenter), 55-58
Internal Revenue Service, 263
International Bill of Gender Rights (1995), 639-641
International Conference on Transgender Law and Employment Policy, 639
International Foundation for Gender Education, 640
International Gay and Lesbian Archives, 281
International Gay and Lesbian Human Rights Commission, 517-518
International Gay Association, 330
International Journal of Transgenderism, The, 322, 651
International Lesbian and Gay Association, 330-332, 632-634
International Lesbian Information Service, 473, 533
International Mr. Leather contest, 545
International Olympic Committee. *See* Olympic Committee, International
International Statistical Classification of Diseases and Related Health Problems (World Health Organization), 265, 680
International Women's Year Conference, 311
Intersex persons, discrimination against, 686
Intersex Society of North America, 586-588
Irvine, Lord, 734
Isherwood, Christopher, 30, 92

Islam, and homosexuality, 657-659
It's Time, America, 563

Jackson, Ed, 318
Jacobellis v. Ohio (1964), 255
Jahrbuch für sexuelle Zwischenstufen (journal), 29
James, Andrea, 700
Janzen, Wilhelm, 49
Japan, GLBT rights movement in, 681-682
Japan Association for the Lesbian and Gay Movement, 681
Jaques, Emanuel, 319
Jay, Karla, 206, 209
Jean Doe v. Bell (2002), 686
Jennings, Dale, 106, 124
Jewett, Sarah Orne, 363
John, Elton, 656
Johns Hopkins University School of Medicine, Gender Identity Clinic, 165
Johnson, Andrew, 7-8
Johnson, Denise, 666
Johnson, Ervin "Magic," 638
Johnson, Lillie, 23
Johnson, William R., 236
Jolles, Stacy, 666
Jones, Cleve, 401, 469
Jones v. Daly (1981), 366
Jordan, Barbara, 239, 311, 313
Jorgensen, Christine, 108
Judaism, and gays and lesbians, 230-232, 238
Julber, Eric, 124

Kaahumanu, Lani, 527
Kalinin, Roman, 517
Kameny, Franklin, 182, 201, 217, 265, 292
Kaposi's sarcoma, 378-380, 402, 429
Kathleen and Frank (Isherwood), 94
Katz, Jonathan Ned, 300
Kaufman, Liz, 491
Kaufman, Moisés, 656
Kauser, Alice, 68

Kay, James W., 675
Kelley, William, 160
Kennedy, Anthony M., 583, 710
Kennedy, Edward M., 618
Kent, Samuel Neal, 63
Kepner, Jim, 114, 124, 280
Kertbeny, Karl Maria, 12, 33
Keshet Ga'avah, World Congress of Gay, Lesbian, Bisexual, and Transgender Jews, 231
"Kevin," 698
Khaled, Mazen, 664
Khan, Surina, 657
Kieltyka, Charlotte Angelica, 700
Kight, Morris, 221
Kilhefner, Don, 221
Kimmel, Douglas, 679
King, Billie Jean, 365, 623
King, Martin Luther, Jr., 154
King's University College, Canada, 652
Kinsey, Alfred, 38, 80, 103, 121, 265, 596
Kinsey Institute for Research in Sex, Gender, and Reproduction, 105, 138
Kinsey Reports, 266; counterstudy, 596-598; female sexuality, 121-123; male sexuality, 103-105
Kinsey Scale, 103
Kinsman, Gary, 570
Kirk, Sheila, 320
Kitchen Table: Women of Color Press, 383-385, 392
Kivel, Beth, 482
Klein, Alan, 524
Klein, Fritz, 267
Klein, Ralph, 652
Klein Sexual Orientation Grid, 268
Klepinger, Daniel H., 596
Klippert, Everett George, 199
Klobukowska, Ewa, 728
"Knowledge = Power," 441, 458
Koch, Edward, 273
Koop, C. Everett, 404, 445, 485
Kopay, David, 406
Koppelman, Andrew, 509

Kosse, Roberta, 385
Kowalski, Donald, and Della Kowalski, 552
Kowalski, Sharon, 469, 552
KPFK radio, 329
Krafft-Ebing, Richard von, 12, 16, 33
Kramer, Dick, 380
Kramer, Larry, 401, 440, 458, 596
Kreis, Der (journal), 30
Krupp, Alfred, 53
Kuiland-Nazario, Marcus, 455
Kumar, Arvind, 438

Labouchere, Henry Du Pré, 18
Labouchere Amendment, United Kingdom, 669
Ladder, The (periodical), 132, 210, 244
Ladies of Llangollen, 363
Lagon, Pat, 593
Lahusen, Kay Tobin, 132
Lambda Book Report (periodical), 512
Lambda Legal Defense and Education Fund, 263-264, 542-545
Lambda Literary Award, 512-514, 701
Lambda Rising bookstore, 512
Lambeth Conference, Anglican Church, 726
"Lammy" award, 225, 512
lang, k. d., 565
Lantz, Brian, 442
Laramie Project, The (play), 656
Laramie, Wyoming; and murder of Matthew Shepard, 654-657
Largent, Steve, 648
LaRouche, Lyndon, 442
Larson, Libby, 386
Latecomer, The (Marchant), 244
Latin American Lesbian Collective. *See* Colectiva Lesbiana Latinoamericana
Latina lesbians, and literature, 450-452

Latinas/Latinos; alliance of, 290-292; art and artists, 455-457
Laub, Donald R., 320
Laura Z. (Hobson), 283
Laux, Charles, 616
Lavender Menace, 206-208; and Betty Friedan, 314; and lesbian feminism, 215; protests by, 209
Lavender Youth Recreation and Information Center, 482-484
Lavrín, Asunción, 537
Lawrence, John Geddes, 710
Lawrence v. Texas (2003), 259, 299, 434, 710-713
Lazarus, Harris M., 68
Leather Archives and Museum, 545-546
Leather contest, International Mr., 545
Leather Journal, The, 545
Leaves of Grass (Whitman), 3-6
Lebanon, 664
Ledger, Heath, 744
Lee, Ang, 591, 744
Legal reform; Canada, 707-709; Germany, 50; guardianships, 552-554; Illinois, 147-148; sodomy laws, 95-97; Spain, 736-738; United Kingdom, 140-144, 178-180, 669-672
Legg, W. Dorr, 114, 124, 280
Legion of Decency, 84
Leigh, Richard, 63
Leitsch, Dick, 192, 194-195
Lesbian; definition, 210
Lesbian and Gay Asian Collective, 348-351
Lesbian and Gay Association, International, 330-332, 632-634
Lesbian and Gay Bands of America, 386
Lesbian and gay studies. *See* Queer studies
Lesbian and Gay Youth Protection Institute, 387-391
Lesbian Avengers, 599; and AIDS epidemic, 454
Lesbian celebrities, 565-567

Lesbian Concentrate (Olivia Records), 251
Lesbian Conference, Midwest, 275; West Coast, 411
Lesbian conferences; Asian Lesbian Network, 533-534; Encuentros, 472-474; first in Mexico, 742; first national, 144-146
Lesbian Connection (periodical), 275-277
Lesbian feminism, 206-208, 209-211, 215, 311-315, 598; Chicanas, 446-448; and feminist bookstores, 203-205; Latin American and Caribbean, 472-474; and music, 249-251; and women of color, 370-373. *See also* Feminism
Lesbian Feminist Organization, National, 411
Lesbian Feminists of Los Angeles, 215
Lesbian, Gay, Bisexual, and Transgender Community Center, New York, 622
Lesbian Herstory Archives, 260-262
Lesbian Images (Rule), 287-289
Lesbian Information Service, International, 473, 533
Lesbian separatism, 540
Lesbian sexuality; culture and, 138; in early film, 81-83, 426-428; in Indian film, 660-662; in early novels, 76-78; and sodomy laws, 95-97, 297-300; early studies of, 79-81; and Thai lesbian culture, 534; in early theater, 66-69
Lesbian Tide (periodical), 219-221
"Lesbian" versus "gay" as terms, 598
Lesbian/Woman (Martin and Lyon), 144, 145, 223
Lesbiana Latinoamericana Colectiva, 451
Lesbianas Unidas, Los Angeles, 291, 457
Lesbians; and child custody, 608; military service, 302-304, 357-359, 579-581
Lesbians of Color, Los Angeles, 412
Leshner, Michael, 707

Lestrade, Didier, 496
LeVay, Simon, 535
Levi, Jeffrey, 246
Levy, Jay A., 414
Lhamana, definition of, 21
Liberace, 365
Liberation Publications, 352
Libman, Alyn, 728
Licensed to Kill (documentary film), 523
Lichtenstein, Mitchell, 591
Liebenberg circle, 53
Liebman, Marvin, 522
LIFE Lobby, 444, 551
Life Together (Canadian government report), 316
Lingle, Larry, 180
Lippert, Bill, 666
Literature; American Indian, 435-437; on coming out to parents, 283-284; documentary nonfiction, 522-524; gay, 3-6, 69-71, 92-95, 97-100, 135-137, 151-153, 269-270, 353-355, 588-590; on HIV-AIDS, 453; and Lambda Literary Award, 512-514; lesbian, 43-46, 76-78, 138-140, 241-245, 450-452; lesbian and gay, 223-225; lesbian nonfiction, 287-289, 362-365; Mexican, 537-539
Literature, gay (*primary source*), 99
Literature, lesbian (*primary source*), 139, 288
Lithgow, John, 479
Littleton, Christie Lee, 662
Littleton, Jonathan Mark, 662
Littleton v. Prange (1999), 662-664
Liverpool, England, 732
Living the Spirit (Roscoe et al.), 286
Lobel, Kerry, 246
Local Law 3, New York City, 689
London Declaration on AIDS Prevention (1988), 494
Long Time Passing (Adelman), 351
Look Me in the Eye: Old Women, Aging, and Ageism (MacDonald), 462
Lopez, Margarita, 687

Lord, Daniel A., 84
Lorde, Audre, 347, 383, 392
Los Angeles Advocate. See *Advocate, The*
Los Angeles Gay and Lesbian Center, 221-223, 622
Los Angeles Police Department, 106
Los Angeles Times, early AIDS coverage, 378
"Los 41," 41-43
Lost Weekend, The (film), 85
Lott, Trent, 604
Lotter, John, 615
Louganis, Greg, 637
Love, Barbara, 209
Love, Plato on (*primary source*), 48
"Love that dare not speak its name" (Wilde), 28
Loy, Tana, 347, 349
"Lulu plays," 81
Lung, Sihung, 591
Lustig-Prean, Duncan, 669
Lymphadenopathy-associated virus, 414
Lyon, Phyllis, 132, 144, 206

M. Butterfly (Hwang), 479-482
Mabon, Lon T., 491
McAteer, Ed, 339
McBride, Donna, 244
McCarran-Walter Immigration and Nationality Act (1952), 117, 176; and American Bar Association, 259
McCarthy, Joseph, 129
McCarthyism, 292, 340; and Kinsey Reports, 104, 123
McClatchy, J. D., 588
McClintock, Mary Ann, 1
McClung, John Wesley, 652
McCorvey, Norma Jane, 252
Maccubbin, Deacon, 180, 464, 512
Macdonald, Barbara, 462
MacFarlane, Roger, 596
McFeely, Tim, 530
McGreivy, Susan, 357

McGuire, Jean, 530
Macho Dancer (film), 474-476
McIlvenna, Ted, 163
Mackay, John Henry, 29
McKee, Joseph V., 74
McKellen, Ian, 634, 636
McKinney, Aaron, 654
McKinney, Stewart B., 466, 485
MacLane, Mary, 139
McMurtry, Roy, 318
McNeill, John J., 189
McSorley, Cisco, 702
Madness of King George, The (film), 635
Magidson, Michael, 694
Making Face, Making Soul/Haciendo Caras (Anzaldúa, ed.), 372
Man-boy love, early advocates of, 50
Man/Boy Love Association, North American, 332, 632
Man Who Would Be Queen, The (Bailey), 700-702
Manford, Jean, 367
Manford, Morton, 367
Manila, Philippines, 476
Mapping Gay L.A. (Kenney), 420
Mapplethorpe, Robert, 500
March on Washington (1979), 344-346; *sidebar*, 345
March on Washington (1987), 246, 469-471
March on Washington (1993), 599, 601-603
March on Washington for Jobs and Freedom (1963), 154-157
Marchant, Anyda, 244
Marches and protests. See Protests and marches
Marcos, Ferdinand, 474
Marder, Janet, 230
Margulies, Donald, 69
Maricónes, definition of, 691
Marine Corps Recruit Training Depot, Parris Island, 359
Marino, Joseph A., 327
Marketing; and GLBT books, 269; and lesbian books, 244

Marks, Jim, 464
Marriage, definition of (*primary source*), 647
Marriage, National Campaign to Protect, 647
Marriage; transsexuals, 698-699, 734-736; U.S. legislation on, 646-649. *See also* Civil unions; Same-gender marriage
Marriage Protection Act (2004), 721
Marshall, Margaret H., 717
Marshall, Thurgood, 297
Mart, Paul, 405
Martet, Christophe, 496
Martin, Damien, 387
Martin, Del, 132, 144, 206, 214, 411
Martin, Paul, 708
Martin, Vera, 462
Marvin v. Marvin (1976), 365
Masculine love, Plato on (*primary source*), 48
Masculinity; female, 358, 508, 624, 650; and gay culture, 29; and gay literature, 3-6; gay men and, 50. *See also* Femininity; Gender; Sex/gender
Mass, Lawrence, 378
Mather, Gina, 698
Matlovich, Leonard, 302
Matriarchy, and American Indian cultures, 436
Mattachine Society, 106-107, 114, 194, 214
Matter of Guido (2003), 686
Matthew Shepard Story, The (television movie), 656
Maupin, Armistead, 512
Mayhem statutes, definition of, 166
Measure 8, Oregon, 491
Measure 9, Oregon, 582-585
Medal of Freedom, Barbara Jordan, 240
Medal of Honor, Mary Edwards Walker, 7-9
Media; *The Advocate*, 167-169; and AIDS epidemic, 431; *The Body Politic*, 226-228; documentary film, 522-524; *Lambda Rising Book Report*, 464-466; and lesbian celebrities, 565-567; *Lesbian Connection*, 275-277; and lesbian murder trial, 23-25; *Lesbian Tide*, 219-221; monitoring of, 424-426; *ONE* magazine, 124-126; and outing, 547-549, 634-636; *People* magazine, 566; PrideVision TV, Canada, 683-685; television programs, 169-171; *Time* magazine, 201-203; *Trikone Magazine*, 438-440; *Vanity Fair* magazine, 565; *Vice Versa*, 101-102
Mehta, Deepa, 660
Meier, Karl, 29
Meininger, Al, 72
Melilio, Joseph, 593
Memoirs v. Massachusetts (1966), 255
"Men Loving Boys Loving Men" (Hannon), 227, 318
Men with the Pink Triasngle, The (Heger), 351
Mendolia, Victor, 514
Menéndez, Emilio, 736
Mental Disease, Outlines of Lectures on (Morison), 112
Merel, Jose, 694
Merrim, Stephanie, 537
Metropolitan Community Church, 184-186; and first GLBT synagogue, 231; and pastor's hunger strike, 377
Metropolitan Police Department, Washington, D.C., 130
Metrosexuality (television series), 343
Mexican Federal Congress, 741-743
Mexican history, 537-539
Mexican Revolution, 61
Mexico; and antidiscrimination law, 742; GLBT movement in, 741-743; police abuse and harassment, 41-43; pride marches in, 690-691; and transgender persons, 61-62
México Posible, 742
Michaels, Dick, 167
Michigan Womyn's Music Festival, 304-306
Middle East, and GLBT rights, 664-666
Military, British; and service ban, 669-672
Military, Canadian; and service ban, 579-581
Military, U.S.; antigay witch hunts by, 63-65; and lesbians, 357-359; and service ban, 302-304, 510-512, 522-524, 547-549, 601, 611-615; women in, 7-9
Military Freedom Project, 247
Military Justice, Uniform Code of, 611
Military service, North Atlantic Treaty Organization and, 670
Military Units to Aid Production (Cuban labor camps), 157
Milk, Harvey, 333, 337
Miller, Gary, 373
Miller, Tim, 520
Miller v. California (1973), 255
Mineta, Norman Y., 629
Ministers. *See* Christian church
Mink, Patsy, 311-312
Minneapolis, Minnesota, first feminist-lesbian bookstore, 204
Minnesota Medical Center, University of, 166
Mishaan, Chuck, 267
Miss Saigon (musical), 542
Mitchell, Alice, 23
Mitsuya, Hiroaki, 440
Mittelgeschlecht, Das. See Intermediate Sex, The
Mixner, David, 333, 442
Moldenhauer, Jearld, 226
Moll, Albert, 33
Moltke, Kuno von, 51-52
Monette, Paul, 588
Money, John, 165
Montagnier, Luc, 401, 413

Montagu, Mary Wortley, 363
Moon, Sun Myung, 341
Moraga, Cherríe, 370, 383
Moral Majority, 271, 307, 339-341, 355
Morbidity and Mortality Weekly Report, 378
Moreno, Mike, 455
Morgan, Mary, 604
Morgan, Robin, 540
Morrissey, Christine, 692
Moscone, George, 337
Motion Picture Producers and Distributors Association, 84
Motion Picture Production Code, 84
Mott, Lucretia, 1
Mt. Pleasant, and first Michigan Womyn's Music Festival, 304
Mulroney, Brian, 570
Munich, Germany, 10
Municipal Elections Committee of Los Angeles, 335
Murray, Susan M., 666
Music; choral, 373-375; gay men's choral, 380-382, 385-387; lesbian choral, 295-297; lesbian feminist, 249-251. *See also* Choral movement; Gay Men's Chorus; *names of specific choral groups*
Music Festival, Michigan Womyn's, 304-306
Musicians, Billy Tipton, 505-507

N. (K.U.), 555
Nabors, Jaron Chase, 694
Nagata, Masashi, 681
Nahas, Omar, 657
Naiad Press, 244-245
NAMBLA. *See* North American Man/Boy Love Association
NAMES Project Foundation, 403, 469
Nania, Liz, 527
Narratives: Poems in the Tradition of Black Women (Clarke), 383
NARTH. *See* National Association for Research and Therapy of Homosexuality

National Association for Research and Therapy of Homosexuality, 113
National Association of Lesbian, Gay, Bisexual & Transgender Community Centers, 621-623
National Bisexual Liberation Group, 528
National Bisexual Network, 527
National Black Feminist Organization, 309
National Black Gay & Lesbian Leadership Forum Conference, 519
National Book Award; *And the Band Played On*, 453; *Becoming a Man*, 588-590
National Cancer Institute; and early AIDS funding, 402; and AZT research, 440
National Coalition of Black Gays, 347
National Coming Out Day, 470, 489-491
National Commission on AIDS, 487
National Endowment for the Arts; and homoeroticism, 500-504; and NEA Four lawsuit, 520-522
National Federation of Priests Councils, and gay Catholics, 190
National Gay and Lesbian Law Association, 259
National Gay and Lesbian Task Force, 246-249, 498-500
National Gay Archives, 281
National Institute of Mental Health, 126
National Institutes of Health; and AIDS research, 402, 414; Revitalization Act (1993), 120
National Lesbian Feminist Organization, 411
National Organization for Women, 206-208, 209-211, 215, 234; and Lavender Menace, 206;

and lesbians in military, 358; and Radicalesbians, 209
National Organizations Responding to AIDS, 246
Native Americans. *See* American Indians
Nature versus nurture debate, 49-52
Navratilova, Martina, 623
Navy, U.S.; antigay witch hunts by, 63-65; antilesbian witch hunts by, 357-359
Naz Foundation Trust, India, 568
Nazi Germany; destruction of Institute for Sexual Science, 38; gay literature and, 92; persecution of homosexuals, 86-91
NEA Four, 503, 520-522
NEA v. Finley (1998), 503
Near, Holly, 305
Nerves (Boyd), 242
Nestle, Joan, 260, 424
New Mexico Gender Advocacy Information Network, 702
New York Association for Gender Rights Advocacy, 687
New York City; gay writers in, 353; and transgender rights, 687-689
New York City Gay Men's Chorus, 385-387
New York City Police Department, and Stonewall Rebellion, 192-195
New York Film Critics Circle, 744
New York Lesbian, Gay, Bisexual, and Transgender Community Center, 622
New York Native, early AIDS coverage, 378, 458
New York Stock Exchange, ACT UP protest, 460
New York Times, early AIDS coverage, 378
New York Times best-seller list, and first gay novel on, 269-270
Newark, California, and murder of Gwen Araujo, 694

Newport, Rhode Island, and U.S. Navy sting operation, 63
Nickles, Don, 647
Nicolas v. Azteca Restaurant Enterprises (2001), 509
Nidorf, Patrick X., 189
Night of the Long Knives, Nazi Germany, 89-91
Niles, Donna, 203
Nissen, Thomas, 615
Nix, Robert, 273
No on 6, 334
No on 64—Stop LaRouche, 443
No Special Rights Committee, 492
"No Tears for Queers," 655
Noble, Elaine, 277
Normal Heart, The (Kramer), 459
Norris, William, 510
North American Conference of Homophile Organizations, 160-163, 182-184
North American Man/Boy Love Association, 332, 632
Norton, Clifford, 292
Norton Sound Eight, 357
Norton v. Macy (1969), 131, 293
NOW. *See* National Organization for Women
Nuestro Mundo, Argentina, 187-189
Numbers (Rechy), 153
Nunn, Samuel, 611

O'Brien, John, 212
Obscenity; and the arts, 502; and censorship, 76-78; in American theater, 66-69
Obscenity and indecency, and U.S. Supreme Court ruling on, 327-329
Obscenity laws; and gay publications, 72; *primary source*, 256; and U.S. Supreme Court, 255-257
O'Connor, John Cardinal, 514
Odd Girls and Twilight Lovers (Faderman), 364
O'Donnell, Rosie, 565
Ogborn, Anne, 562

Old Lesbians Organizing for Change, 462-464
Old Time Gospel Hour, The (radio show), 340
O'Leary, Jean, 312, 489
Olivia Records, 249-251, 304; and transsexual staff member, 540
Olympic Committee, International, 405, 728; and Gay Games, 405; and gender-testing policy, 624; and transsexual athletes, 728-730
Olympic Committee, U.S.; and Gay Games, 405
Olympic Games; GLBT athletes, 637-639
Olympics, gay. *See* Gay Games
ONE/IGLA. *See* ONE National Gay & Lesbian Archives
ONE, Inc., 114-116, 214
ONE, Inc. v. Olesen (1958), 125
ONE Institute of Homophile Studies, 114
ONE magazine, 106, 114, 124-126
ONE National Gay & Lesbian Archives, 280-282
One Teenager in 10 (Heron, ed.), 390
"1,112 and Counting" (Kramer), 458
Ordona, Trinity, 448
Oregon; antigay intiatives, 582-585; and antigay politics, 491-493; and murder of lesbian couple, 641
Oregon Citizens Alliance, 491, 582
Oregonians for Fairness, 491
Orejudos, Dom, 545
Organizations. *See* Category Index; *names of specific organizations*
Orr-Cahall, Christina, 500
Oscar Wilde Memorial Bookshop, 180-182
Oscars. *See* Academy Awards
Other Voices, Other Rooms (Capote), 98

Out and Equal in the Workplace, 325
Out of the Closet: Study of Relations Between Homosexual Community and Police (Toronto City Council), 377
Outing; ACT UP and, 460; *The Advocate* and, 239, 547-549, 634-636
Outlines of Lectures on Mental Disease (Morison), 112
Outweek (magazine), 547
Owles, Jim, 195, 212
Ozawa, Donna, 482

Pabst, Georg Wilhelm, 81
Pacifica Foundation, 327
Padlock Law, Wales (1927), 74-76
Palencia, Roland, 455
Palimony, 365-367
Palmer, A. Mitchell, 63
Pandora's Box (film), 81-83
Paole, Allan, 474
Paragraph 143, Prussian antisodomy law, 12
Paragraph 175, German criminal code, 12, 36-39, 50; *primary source*, 36, 88
Parents, Families, and Friends of Lesbians and Gays. *See* PFLAG
Paris Adult Theatre I v. Slaton (1973), 255
Parisian literary salons, 58-60
Park, Frederick, 18
Park, Pauline, 687
Park Slope, Brooklyn, Lesbian Herstory Archives, 261
Parris Island Marine Corps Recruit Training Depot, 359
Parsons, Buford M., Jr., 608
Parti Québécois, 315
Partnerships, civil. *See* Civil unions
Party of the 41, 41
Pasteur Institute, and HIV-AIDS research, 414, 430
Patience and Sarah (Routsong), 223
"Patient zero," and AIDS epidemic, 403, 454
Patriarchy, and American Indian cultures, 436

Patton, Jude, 320
Paul, Alice, 233
Paz, Octavio, 537
Peck, Fred, 613
Pedophilia, 227, 318, 332, 632-634
People magazine, and Melissa Etheridge, 566
People of color. *See* name of specific racial or ethnic group
Perfect Moment, The (Mapplethorpe), 501
Perkins, Bill, 687
Permanent Partners Immigration Act (proposed 2000), 120
Perón, Juan, 187
Perry, James DeWolf, 63
Perry, Troy, 184, 469
Perry Watkins Story, The (documentary film), 511
Persephone Press, 370
Personal Best (film), 426
Personal Rights in Defense and Education, 168
Personality disorder, definition of, 112
Persons with AIDS Act, Housing Opportunities for, 488
PFLAG, 367-370, 648
Phelps, Fred, 271, 654
Phelps, Johnnie, 358
Philadelphia Police Department, 130
Philip Morris company, and women's tennis, 624
Phillips, Howard, 339
Photography, Robert Mapplethorpe controversy, 500-504
Picano, Felice, 353
Picture of Dorian Gray, The (Wilde), 26
Pine, Seymour, 192
Pink Book (International Lesbian and Gay Association), 331
"Pink pound," 732
Pink triangle, Nazi Germany, 12, 88
Piss Christ (Serrano), 501
Place for Us, A (Routsong), 223
Plato, 46
Ploen, Richard, 184
Plotkin, Harry M., 327

Pneumocystis carinii pneumonia; AZT and, 440; first reports of, 378-380
Police abuse and harassment; of gay publishers, 318-320; Los Angeles, 106; Mexico, 41-43; Nazi Germany, 87; New York City, 192-195; Philadelphia, 130; San Francisco, 163-165; Stonewall Rebellion, 192-195; Toronto, Canada, 376-377; U.S. Navy, 63-65; Washington, D.C., 130
Policy Institute, National Gay and Lesbian Task Force, 247
Political activism; ACT UP, 458-462; Act Up Paris, 496-498; and bookstores, 180-182; and Christian Right, 582; conservatives and, 491; early gay rights movement, 9-11; intersexuals and, 586-588; lesbians and, 598-601; marches, 154-157, 212-214, 344-349, 448, 469-471, 598-603, 627-629, 690-691; Mattachine Society, 106-107; political action committees, 182-184; Queer Nation, 524-527; early queer resistance, 163-165; and transgender awareness, 644-646; and transgender/transsexual rights, 562-564, 573-575
Politicians; African American, 239-241; gay, 149-150, 217-219, 337-339, 407-410, 466-468; lesbian, 239-241, 277-280, 604-606, 741-743
Politicians, gay, (*primary source*), 408
Pomeroy, Wardell, 201
Popert, Ken, 318
Postal Service, U.S., 125
Postal workers, Canada, 360-362
"Posttranssexual Manifesto, A" (Stone), 540-542
Powell, Adam Clayton, 155

Powell, Colin, 611
Powell, Lewis F., 432
Powell, Lisa, 519
Prange, Mark A., 662
Pregerson, Harry, 510
Pregil, Antoinette, 593
Presidential AIDS Commission, report of, 485-489
Presidential Commission on the Human Immunodeficiency Virus Epidemic, 485, 530
Presidential Medal of Freedom, Barbara Jordan, 240
Prevent AIDS Now Initiative Committee, 442
Price, Boo, 304
Price Waterhouse v. Hopkins (1989), 508
Pride Institute, 279
Pride Value Fund, 279
PrideVision TV, Canada, 683-685
Priests, Roman Catholic. *See* Roman Catholic Church
Priests Councils, National Federation of, and gay Catholics, 190
Privacy rights, 96, 179, 252-254, 418, 432, 710; *primary source*, 253
"Problem in Greek Ethics, A" (Symonds), 56
Production Code Administration, 84
Profundis, De (Wilde), 28
Project 10, Los Angeles, 390
Project Truth/Free Will, 632
Prometheus (Ulrichs); *primary source*, 10
Promise Keepers, 271
Proposition 6, California, 333
Proposition 64, California, 442
Proposition 69, California, 444
Proposition 96, California, 444
Proposition 102, California, 445
Prosser, Jay, 650
Prostitution, in gay literature, 151
Protests and marches; AB-101, 550-552; ACT UP, 514-516; Compton's Cafeteria, 163-165;

Subject Index

Lavender Menace, 206-208; Mexico City, 690-691; and Milk and Moscone murders, 338; Radicalesbians, 209-211; Stonewall Rebellion, 192-195; Stonewall 25, 627-629; Toronto, Canada, 376; and transgender/transsexual rights, 562-564; first U.S. pride march, 212-214

Psychiatry; and homosexuality, 33-35, 679-681; and transsexuality, 562-564; and "treatment" for sexual inversion, 16-18

Psychoanalysis, 46-49, 266

Psychology, 126-129, 169, 265-267, 700-702

Psychopathia sexualis (Krafft-Ebing), 17

PT&T, 324

Public Health Service, and immigration law, 117

Publications; *The Advocate*, 167-169; Battelle sex study, 596-598; *The Body Politic*, 226-228; *Der Eigene*, 29-31; *Lambda Rising Book Report*, 464-466; Latin American history, 537-539; *Lesbian Connection*, 275-277; *Lesbian Tide*, 219-221; *ONE* magazine, 124-126; *People* magazine, 566; *Time* magazine, 201-203; *Trikone Magazine*, 438-440; *Vanity Fair* magazine, 565; *Vice Versa*, 101-102

Publishing; Alyson Publications, 351-353; and gay books, 269-270; and GLBT books, 512; Kitchen Table: Women of Color Press, 383-385; and lesbian books, 43-46, 76-78, 138-140, 287-289, 362-365; Naiad Press, 244-245

Puppenjunge, Der. See *Hustler, The*

Puterbaugh, Holly, 666

Q.E.D. (Stein), 43-46
Quebec, Canada, and GLBT rights, 315-317
Queer, as a term, 14, 216
Queer as Folk (television series), 343
Queer Latino film festival, 456
Queer Nation; founding of, 524-527; model for student activism, 173; Transgender Nation and, 562
Queer studies, 174, 300-302, 362-365; and transgender studies, 574, 650-652
Queer youth; centers for, 482-484; resistance to police by, 163-165; and student movement, 172-175
Quiroz v. Neelly (1961), 118
Quist, Julie Morse, 203
Qurʾān, 658

Racial Equality, Congress of, 154
Racial purity, Nazis and, 86
Racism; in GLBT movement, 290; in GLBT organizations, 451; and sexuality, 411-413; in women's movement, 309, 383
Racism, White Women Against, 413
Radicalesbians, 207, 210; manifesto, 215
Radicalism; ACT UP, 458-462; Gay Liberation Front, 195-198; Queer Nation, 524-527
Rado, Sandor, 111
Raffalovich, Marc-André, 31
Ramos, Juanita, 450
Rand, Bill, 167
RAND Corporation, report on gays in military, 613
Randolph, A. Philip, 154
Rank Outsiders, 671
Raymond, Janice, 540
Reading Gaol, and Oscar Wilde imprisonment, 27
Reagan, Ronald, 333, 401, 415, 453, 485; and immigration law, 120; and Moral Majority, 340

Rechy, John, 151
Reddy, Tom, 522
Reflections of a Rock Lobster: A Story About Growing Up Gay (Fricke), 390
Refugee rights, Canada, *primary source*, 555
Rehnquist, William, 327, 677
Religion; and film industry, 84-86; gay and lesbian Catholics, 189-192; gay and lesbian Christians, 725-728; gay and lesbian ministers, 236-238; GLBT churches, 184-186; Islam, 657-659; Judaism, 230-232. *See also* Antigay movement; *names of specific religions*
Religion and the Homosexual, Council on, 145, 161, 163
Religious Round Table, 271, 340
Remembering Our Dead Project, 722-724
Renaissance Canada, 271
Renaissance des Eros Uranos (Friedlaender), 29
Renaissance Transgender Association, 640
Rene v. MGM Grand Hotel (2002), 509
Reno, Janet, 120
Renseignements Généraux, France, 331
Renslow, Chuck, 545
Reparative therapy; American Psychiatric Association and, 111-113; and homosexuality, 88
"Report of the Departmental Committee on Homosexual Offences and Prostitution, The" (1957), 142
Republican National Convention, and declarations of "cultural war," 504, 582
Revolutionary Workers Party, 742
Reyes, Rodrigo, 290
Reynolds, Charles L., Jr., 320
Richards, Renee, 728
Richardson, Bill, 702

Richardson County Sheriff's Department, and Brandon Teena rape and murder, 616
Riddle of "Man-Manly" Love, The (Ulrichs), 10
Rideout, Janet, 440
Rights of Gay People, Committee on the, 259
Rivera, Sylvia, 686; Law Project, 686-687
Roberts, JoAnn, 639
Robertson, Pat, 582
Robinson, Beth, 666
Robinson, John, 466
Robinson, Marty, 195
Robinson, V. Gene, 725
Robles, Amelio, 61
Rockefeller, John D., Jr., 79
Rodrigues, Tammy, 593
Rodríguez, Aleida, 455
Rodwell, Craig, 180
Roe v. Wade (1973), 252-254, 433
Roen, Katrina, 651
Rohm, Ernst, 36, 89
Roma, Catherine, 295
Roman Catholic Church; and ACT UP, 514-516; female intellectuals and, 537-539; and film industry, 84; and gay and lesbian Catholics, 189-192; and gay priests, 738-741; and same-gender marriage, 720, 736; same-gender unions and, 705
Roman Catholic Church, and gay priests (*primary source*), 739
Roman Catholics (*sidebar*), 190-191
Romantic friendships, women and, 362
Romer, Roy, 582
Romer v. Evans (1996), 583
Romney, Mitt, 717
Roosevelt, Franklin D., 63
Rorem, Ned, 386, 588
Rose v. Locke (1975), 297
Roth v. United States (1957), 255
Rough News, Daring Views (Kepner), 281
Roughgarden, Joan, 700
Routsong, Alma, 223
Rowland, Chuck, 106

Royal Canadian Mounted Police, antigay campaign of, 570
Rubin, Marc, 212
Rubyfruit Jungle (Brown), 241-244
Rule, Jane, 287, 426
Rush, Stella, 132
Russell, Stella, 124
Russo, Vito, 424
Rustin, Bayard, 154
Ryan White Comprehensive AIDS Resources Emergency Act (1990), 607

St. Patrick's Cathedral, New York; ACT UP protest, 460, 514-516
St. Patrick's Day parade, Boston, 676
St. Pierre, Ethan, 722
Salons, Paris literary, 58-60
Salsa Soul Sisters, 411
Same-gender civil unions; United Kingdom, 731-733
Same-gender marriage, 594; Anglican Church on, 731; Asian Americans and, 629-631; Canada, 707-709; Defense of Marriage Act, 646-649; Hawaii, 593-595; Massachusetts, 717-722; and palimony, 365-367; *primary source*, 647, 668, 718; Roman Catholic Church on, 731; Spain, 736-738
Same-gender relationships; "Boston marriages" as, 363; and domestic partnership benefits, 422-423
Same-gender unions; Vermont, 666-669
Same-sex. *See* Same-gender
San Francisco; board of supervisors, 149, 337; and first Gay Games, 405; and Milk and Moscone murders, 337
San Francisco Gay Men's Chorus, 380-382, 385
San Francisco Police Department, 163-165

Sandoz, Helen, 132
Sarria, José, 149
Satellite Awards, 744
"Save Our Children" campaign, 307-308, 333
Scalia, Antonin, 584, 710
Scandals, 26-28, 52-55
Schildkraut, Rudolph, 66
Schindler, Allen R., Jr., 611
Schlafly, John, 235
Schlafly, Phyllis, 233, 312, 596
Schlegel v. United States (1969), 131
Schlessinger, Laura, 424
Schons, Dorothy, 537
School Teacher's Network, Gay and Lesbian Independent, 390
Schools; and book banning, 351; GLBT teachers, 333; for GLBT youth, 387-391
Schools, antiharassment policies, (*primary source*), 389
Schulman, Sarah, 598
Schulte, Steve, 419
Schutzstaffel, Nazi Germany, 87, 90
Schwarz, Judith, 260
Scientific-Humanitarian Committee, 10, 29, 36-39, 49-52
Scott, Bruce, 292
Scott, Peter, 442
Scott-Joynt, Michael, 734
Scott v. Macy (1965, 1968), 293
Screaming Queens: The Riot at Compton's Cafeteria (documentary film), 164
Second Skins (Prosser), 650
Security Requirements for Government Employment (United States), 129
Selwyn, Michael, 66
Seneca Falls Convention (1848), 1-3
Sensenbrenner, James, 648
Sentiments and Resolutions, Declaration of (1848), 1
September 11, 2001, 341
Serrano, Andres, 500

SUBJECT INDEX

Sex, Committee for Research in Problems of, 80
Sex/gender; and gender-role stereotyping, 508; and transsexual marriage, 663, 734; and transsexuality, 540-542
Sex Life of Twenty-Two Hundred Women, Factors in the (Davis), 79
"Sex police," and AIDS epidemic, 418
"Sex variant," 138
Sex Variant Women in Literature (Foster), 138-140, 223, 288
Sexism; in Civil Rights movement, 309, 383; in GLBT movement, 133, 214-216, 598
Sexology, 33-39, 46-49, 56, 79-81, 103-105, 121-123
Sexual Behavior in the Human Female (Kinsey), 121-123
Sexual Behavior in the Human Male (Kinsey), 103-105
Sexual deviation, definition of, 112; *primary source*, 112
Sexual inversion; definition of, 33; "treatment" for, 16-18
Sexual Inversion (Ellis), 25, 33-35; *primary source*, 24
Sexual Minorities, Chinese Society for the Study of, 679
Sexual Offences Act (1956), 140-142, 179
Sexual Offences Act (1967), 178
Sexual Offences Act (2000), 179
Sexual offenses reform, Canada, 199, 477
Sexual Orientation and U.S. Military Personnel Policy (RAND Corporation), 613; *primary source*, 613
Sexual Orientation Non-Discrimination Act (2002), 688
Sexual perversion; in film, 84-86; government employment and, 129; transgenderism and, 40
"Sexual perverts," and U.S. Navy, 63-65

"Sexual-preference resolution," 313
Sexual Science, Institute for, 37
Sexuality; and American Indians, 435; in American theater, 74-76; Kinsey studies of, 103-105, 121-123; and Latino art, 456; and racism, 411-413; scientific studies of, 535-537
Sexuality in film (*primary source*), 85
Sexuelle Gleichberechtigung, Verein für, 632
Sha'ar Zahav (San Francisco), 231
Shalala, Donna, 606
Shapiro, Judith, 540
Sharp, Kathy, 203
Shaver, Helen, 426
Shayne, Ralph, 664
Shays, Chris, 620
Sheldon, Lou, 333, 550, 596, 646-647
Shelley, Martha, 195, 209
Shepard, Dennis, 654
Shepard, Judy, 654
Shepard, Matthew, 654
Shepodd, Lynn, 489
Shigemura, Lia, 629
Shilts, Randy, 358, 401, 453
Shoemaker, Betty, 462
Shumsky, Ellen, 209
Si le grain ne meurt. See *If It Die . . .*
Signorile, Michelangelo, 524, 547
"Silence = Death," 441, 458
Silkwood (1984), 426
Silverman, Joseph, 66
Silverman, Mervyn, 417
Sims, Jon Reed, 380, 385
Single Man, A (Isherwood), 93
Sisneros, Judy, 598
Sistahfest, 519
Sister Singers Network, 374, 380, 386
Sisters of Perpetual Indulgence, 562
Slater, Don, 114, 124
Smith, Barbara, 383
Smith, Freda, 184

Smith, Gwendolyn Ann, 722
Smith, Howard (reporter), 192, 193
Smith, Howard (U.S. representative), 233
Smith, Jeanette, 669
Smith, Lillian, 154
Smith, Willie, 184
Smithsonian Institution, 22
Socarides, Charles, 169
Social Security, and disability benefits, 488
Society for Human Rights, 72-73
Society for Individual Rights, 149
Society for Individual Rights and Hickerson v. Hampton (1973), 131, 293
Society for the Suppression of Vice, 67
Sodomy; cunnilingus, 297-300; and lesbian sex, 95-97
Sodomy laws; American Bar Association, 258; Canada, 477-479; Germany, 12-15; India, 568-570; *primary source*, 36, 88, 433, 569; Prussia, 12; *table*, 710; United Kingdom, 19, 142-144; United States, 297-300, 432-435, 710-713; worldwide, 517-518
Sodomy Laws, Ad Hoc Taskforce to Challenge, 259
Soehnlein, Karl, 524
Soldaderas, definition of, 61
Sor Juana (Paz), 538
Sor Juana Inés de la Cruz, Early Modern Women's Writing and (Merrim), 538
Sor Juana Inés de la Cruz, Feminist Perspectives on (Merrim, ed.), 537-539
South Asian gays and lesbians, 438-440
Southern Baptist Church, 307
Southern Poverty Law Center, 271
Spade, Dean, 686
Spain, and same-gender marriage, 736-738
"Special rights," 492
Speech, hate, in schools, 390
Spong, John Shelby, 725

Sports; gay athletes, 637-639; Gay Games, 405-407; lesbian athletes, 623-626; transsexual Olympic athletes, 728-730. *See also* Athletes; Gay Games; Olympic Games
SQUISH. *See* Strong Queers United in Stopping Heterosexism
Standards of Care for Gender Identity Disorders (Harry Benjamin International Gender Dysphoria Association), 650
Stanley v. Georgia (1969), 255
Stanton, Elizabeth Cady, 1
Stark, Michael, 707
Starr, Adele, 367
Stead, William Thomas, 18
Stein, Edward, 509
Stein, Gertrude, 43
Stevens, John Paul, 327, 432
Stevenson, Matilda Coxe, 21
Stewart, Potter, 297
Stirner, Max, 29
Stoddard, Tom, 542
Stoll, James, 236
Stone, Allucquére Rosanne, 540
Stone, Ron, 419
Stone Butch Blues (Feinberg), 574
Stonewall (Duberman), 212
Stonewall Book Awards, 223
Stonewall Chorale, 385
Stonewall Rebellion, 164, 180, 192-195, 202, 212
Stonewall riot. *See* Stonewall Rebellion
Stonewall 25 March, 627-629
Stonewall Veterans' Association, 627
Stop AIDS Initiative Committee, 445
Stop ERA, 235
Stop the Church, 514-516
Strawberry and Chocolate (film), 159
Streetcar Named Desire, A (Williams), 98
Strong Queers United in Stopping Heterosexism, 173
Strong Sistahs/Sweet Success, 519
Stryker, Susan, 562, 645, 651
Stuart, Sharon, 639
Studds, Gerry, 407, 467

Student Homophile League, 172-175
Student rights (*primary source*), 388
Studies in the Psychology of Sex (Ellis), 17
Sturmabteilung, Nazi Germany, 89
Sullivan, Andrew, 648
Sunset Strip, 419
Supreme Court, Canadian; discrimination, 579-581, 652-653; homosexual acts, 199; same-gender marriage, 708
Supreme Court, U.S.; abortion, 252-254; arts funding, 521; discrimination, 302, 583, 675-678; gender-role stereotyping, 508-509; immigration, 117-121, 176-178; obscene mailings, 125; obscenity, 255-257; obscenity and indecency, 327-329; privacy, 252-254; sex practices, 297-300, 432-435; sodomy, 432-435, 710-713
Surgeon general, U.S., 119, 352, 404, 445, 485, 495, 606
Surpassing the Love of Men (Faderman), 362-365
Suvarnananda, Anjana Tang, 533
Swank, Hilary, 672
Sweeney, Tim, 687
Sylvia Rivera Law Project, 686-687
Symonds, John Addington, 33, 56
Symposium (Plato), 46
Synagogues, first GLBT, 230-232

Tales of the Lavender Menace (Jay), 210
Tanfer, Koray, 596
Tangents (magazine), 125
Task Force on Gay Liberation, American Library Association, 223
Tayleur, Christine, 562
TBP. See *Body Politic, The*
Teachers, public school, 333

Teatro VIVA—Early Intervention Program, 456
Tebelak, John-Michael, 365
Teena, Brandon, 615, 722
Television; first gay series, 342-344; first GLBT network, 683-685; and early report on homosexuality, 169-171; lesbian celebrities, 565-567; and obscenity, 328; and outing of Pete Williams, 547
Tennis Association, U.S. Lawn, 623
Tenorio, Marcelo, 555
Terrigno, Valerie, 419
Thai lesbians, 533
Theater. *See* Drama and theater
Things as They Are (Stein), 43
Third gender, 21-23
Third sex; as a term, 11, 36; theory of, 46-50
Third wave feminism, emergence of, 384
Third World feminism, 370-373
Third World Lesbian and Gay Conference, 347-349
This Bridge Called My Back (Moraga and Anzaldúa, eds.), 370-373, 383; *primary source*, 371
This Bridge We Call Home (Anzaldúa and Keating, eds.), 372
Thompson, Ella, 95
Thompson, Karen, 469, 552
Thompson, Merritt M., 114
Thompson v. Aldredge (1939), 95-97
Thorson, Scott, 365
Three Essays on the Theory of Sexuality (Freud), 17, 46
Thurmond, Strom, 155
Tignor, Saundra, 519
Time magazine; Ellen DeGeneres cover issue, 566; "The Homosexual in America" (1969), 201-203
Tipton, Billy, 505
Tisdel, Lana, 615

Subject Index

Title VII, Civil Rights Act, 233, 508
Title IX, Education Amendments, 623
Toilet Training (2003), 686
Toklas, Alice B., 43
Toledo, Elizabeth, 247
Tom and *dee* relationships, 533
Tomberlin, Karen, 552
Tong, Goh Chok, 713
Tongues magazine, 457
Toronto Police Service raids, 318-320, 376
Toronto Sun (newspaper), 318
Traditional Values Coalition, 550, 596, 647
Trans Liberation (Feinberg), 574
Transamerica (film), 744-746
Transexual Menace, 563
Transgender; as a term, 322
Transgender advocacy, 639-641
Transgender Civil Rights Project, 702
Transgender Day of Remembrance, 722-724
Transgender Law and Employment Policy, International Conference on, 639
Transgender Liberation (Feinberg), 573-575
Transgender men, 39-41, 61-62, 505-507, 615-618, 644-646
Transgender Nation, 562-564
Transgender people and sexuality, 573
Transgender rights, 164, 687-689, 702-704; *primary source*, 688
Transgender scholarship, 650-652
Transgender/transsexual athletes; and Olympic Games, 728-730; *primary source*, 729
Transgender/transsexual manifesto, 540-542
Transgender/transsexual violence. *See* Gender-based violence
Transgender/transsexuality; academic research on, 700-702; American Indian cultures and, 21-23; court cases and, 662-664; in film, 672-675; and gender reassignment, 108-111; and Michigan Womyn's Music Festival, 305; murder of Gwen Araujo, 694-697; political rights, 573-575; San Francisco, 164; Sylvia Rivera Law Project, 686-687
Transgender Warriors (Feinberg), 574
Transgender women, 640, 645, 694-697
Transgender youth, 163
Transgenderism, The International Journal of, 322, 651
Transition Coalition, 384
Transphobia, 562, 723
Transsexual, as a term, 14, 645
Transsexual Empire, The (Raymond), 540
Transsexual Phenomenon, The (Benjamin), 320
Transsexualism, 562
Transsexualism and Sex Reassignment (Money), 166
Transsexuals; and marriage rights, 698-699, 734-736
Transvestic fetishism, 562
Transvestite, as a term, 14. *See also* Cross-dressing; Gender; Gender ambiguity; Gender-bending; Gender identity; Transgender; Transsexual; Two-spirit persons
Traubel, Horace L., 3
Treatment Action Group, 461
Trikone Magazine, 438-440
Troxell, Jane, 464
Trudeau, Pierre, 199, 477
Truman, Harry, 129
Tudehope, Darren, 698
Tutu, Desmond, 726
20 Rue Jacob, Paris, 58
"Twinkie" defense, 338
Two-spirit persons; definition of, 436; nineteenth century, 21-23

Ulrichs, Karl Heinrich, 9, 16, 33, 46, 49
Ultimate Target of the Gay Agenda: Same Sex Marriages, The (videotape), 647
Underwood, Barbara Lee, 357
Uniform Code of Military Justice, 611
Union of American Hebrew Congregations, and first LGBT synagogue, 231
United Church of Christ, 237; and first ordained gay minister, 236
United Kingdom; decriminalization of "gross indecency," 18-21; and homosexuality, 26-28; and same-gender unions, 731-733; and transsexual marriage rights, 734-736
United Nations; and GLBT organizations, 632-634; and World AIDS Day, 494
United Nations Charter, 330
Universal Fellowship of Metropolitan Community Churches. *See* Metropolitan Community Church
Universities. *See* Colleges and universities
University of California, Berkeley, discrimination lawsuit against, 395
University of Minnesota Medical Center, 166
Uranga, Enoé, 742
Uranism, definition of, 11, 56
Uranisme et Unisexualité (Raffalovich), 31-32
Urban life; and gay literature, 136, 151; youth in San Francisco, 163
Urninds, definition of, 11
Urning, definition of, 11, 13
U.S. Lawn Tennis Association, 623
USS *Belleau Wood*, 611
USS *Norton Sound*, 357-359

Vaid, Urvashi, 246, 498
Vallone, Peter, 687
Vanguard, 163
Vanity Fair magazine, k. d. lang/Cindy Crawford cover, 565
Vargas, Chavela, 742

Varnell, Joe, 707
Vatour, Anne, 707
Vatour, Elaine, 707
Verein für Sexuelle Gleichberechtigung, 632
Vereniging Martijn, 632
Vice, Society for the Suppression of, 67
Vice Versa (periodical), 101-102
Victoria Woodhull All-Women's Marching Band, 385
Victorian society, and women's sexuality, 363
Vidal, Gore, 97, 169
View from Another Closet (Bode), 528
Vigil v. Post Office Department (1969), 131
Viguerie, Richard, 339
Village Voice, The (periodical), 193
Violence. See Antigay violence; Gender-based violence; hate crime
Violet Quill, 353-355
Virginia Slims Tournament, 624
Virtual Equality (Vaid), 498
VIVA Arts Quarterly, 456
Voeller, Bruce, 111, 246
Vogel, Kristie, 304
Vogel, Lisa, 304
Vriend, Delwin, 652
Vriend v. Alberta (1998), 652

Waddell, Tom, 405
Wade, April, 608
Wade, Henry, 252
Wake, Robert, 570
Wal-Mart Stores antidiscrimination policy, 715-717
Wales, B. Roger, 74
Wales Padlock Law (1927), 74-76
Walker, James, 74
Walker, Mary Edwards, 7
Walker, Paul A., 320
Wallace, Mike, 169
Wallbank, Rachel, 698
Walsh, Stella, 728
Ward, Freda, 23
Ward, Jo, 23
Warren, Earl, 176
Warren, Patricia Nell, 269

Washington Project for the Arts, 502
Watkins, James, 485
Watkins, Perry, 510
Watkins Commission, 485
Watkins v. United States Army I (1983), 510
Waxman, Henry, 620
WBAI radio, 327
Wedding Banquet, The (film), 591-592
Weddington, Sarah, 252
Wedekind, Frank, 81
Weinberger, Harry, 66
Weld, William F., 576
Well of Loneliness, The (Hall), 76-78, 242
West, Jason, 721
West, Mae, 74
West Coast Lesbian Conference, 411
West Hollywood, California, as first "gay city," 419-421
Westboro Baptist Church, 271
Western Gay Archives, 281
Westphal, Karl Friedrich, 16, 111
We'wha, 21
Weyrich, Paul, 339
WHAM! protest at St. Patrick's Cathedral, 460, 515
Wherry, Kenneth Spicer, 129
Whitaker, Bailey, 114
White, Byron, 252, 432
White, Dan, 337
White, Edmund, 353, 512
White, Ryan, 401. See also Ryan White Comprehensive AIDS Resources Emergency Act
White House Office of National AIDS Policy, 487
White Women Against Racism, 413
Whitman, Walt, 3
Whitmore, George, 353
Whitney, Irene, 203
Whittington, Yolanda, 519
"Who's the Barbarian?" (Loy), 350
Wieder, Judith, 168
Wieser, Barb, 203

Wilchins, Riki, 541, 617
Wilde, Oscar, 18, 26
Wilde, Winston, 588
Wilder, Billy, 85
Wildmon, Donald, 500
Wiley, Alexander, 125
Wilhelm, Gail, 243
William I (German kaiser), 12, 37
William II (German kaiser), 49, 51-52
Williams, Cecil, 163
Williams, Daryl, 698
Williams, Pete, 547
Williams, Rowan, 725
Williams, Tennessee, 97
Williams, Wendi, 357
Williamson, Alistair, 352
Williamson, Cris, 249
Wilson, Helen Teresa, 357
Wilson, Pete, 550
Windsor Report (Anglican Church), 726
Winston, Sam, 167
Winter, Kate, 249
Wissenschaftlich-humanitäre Komitee. See Scientific-Humanitarian Committee
Wolf, Irma "Corky," 124
Wolfenden, Sir John Frederick, 142, 178
Wolfenden Report (1957), 20, 140, 142-144, 179
Wollman, Leo, 320
"Woman Identified Woman" manifesto (Radicalesbians), 209-211, 215
Women of color; Michigan Womyn's Music Festival, 305
Women of Color gathering, Califia, 412
Women of Color Press, Kitchen Table, 383-385, 392
Women-owned businesses, 203-205, 249-251
Women's Health Action and Mobilization. See WHAM!
Women's movement (*primary source*), 313

Subject Index

Women's rights. *See* Feminism; Lesbian feminism; Women's movement
Women's studies and queer studies, 650
Women's Tennis Association, 624
Women's Year Conference, International, 311
Wonder, Roy L., 417
Wong, B. D., 479
Wong, Doreena, 448
Woo, Merle, 395
Wood, Harlington, Jr., 302
Woodhul, Jennifer, 249
Workplace movement, 323-326
World AIDS Day, 494-495
World Congress of Gay, Lesbian, Bisexual, and Transgender Jews: Keshet Ga'avah, 231
World Health Assembly (1988), 494
World Health Organization; and delisting of homosexuality as illness, 331; and homosexuality, 265, 679
World Summit of Ministers of Health on Programmes for AIDS Prevention, 494
World War II; gay and lesbian servicemembers, 522-524; in gay literature, 92; and Nazi persecution of homosexuals, 86-89
Wright, Martha C., 1

X Portfolio (Mapplethorpe), 501

Yarchoan, Robert, 440
Yicheng, Jia, 679
Yiddish theater, 66
YMCA, Canada, 559-561
Yo, la peor de todas (film), 538
Yoshikawa, Yoko, 542
You Can Do Something About AIDS (Alyson, ed.), 352
Young, Empowered Sistahs, 519
Young, Gay, and Proud! (Alyson, ed.), 351, 390
Young Men's Christian Association. *See* YMCA
Youth centers, 482-484
Youth Pride Chorus, 387
Youth Protection Institute, Lesbian and Gay, 387-391

Zami (Lorde), 392-394
Zapata, Emiliano, 61
Zapatero, José Luis Rodríguez, 736-737